Social Research Methods

Puzzles and Solutions

Rebecca F. Guy *Memphis State University*

Charles E. Edgley *Oklahoma State University*

Ibtihaj Arafat *City University of New York*

Donald E. Allen *Oklahoma State University*

 Allyn and Bacon, Inc.
Boston   London   Sydney   Toronto

Copyright © 1987 by Allyn and Bacon, Inc., 7 Wells Avenue, Newton, Massachusetts 02159. All rights reserved. No part of the material protected by this copyright notice may be reproduced or utilized in any form or by any means, electronic or mechanical, including photocopying, recording, or by any information storage and retrieval system, without written permission from the copyright owner.

Library of Congress Cataloging-in-Publication Data
Main entry under title:

Social research methods.

   Bibliography: p.
   Includes index.
   1. Social sciences—Research—Methodology.   I. Guy,
Rebecca F.
H62.S6739   1987   300'.72   85–30706
ISBN 0-205-08677-2

Series editor: Judy Shaw
Production coordinator: Helyn Pultz
Editorial-production service: Nancy Benjamin
Cover coordinator: Linda K. Dickinson
Cover designer: Susan Hamant

Acknowledgments
Pages 17–18: Excerpts from Ian I. Mitroff, "Norms and Counter-Norms in a Select Group of Apollo Moon Scientists," from *American Sociological Review*, 1974, Vol. 39, pp. 579–595. Reprinted with permission of the American Sociological Association. **Page 44:** Excerpt from *Psychological Abstracts*, Vol. 64, No. 1, July 1980. This citation is reprinted with the permission of the American Psychological Association, publisher of *Psychological Abstracts* and the *PsycINFO* Database (Copyright © 1980 by the American Psychological Association) and may not be reproduced without its prior permission. **Pages 46–47:** Excerpts from *Sociological Abstracts*. Reprinted with permission. **Pages 48–49:** Excerpt from Social Science Citation Index, Vol. 1, 1984. Copied with the permission of the Institute for Scientific Information, © 1985. **Page 56:** Table 2.2, "Percentage of Immigrants' Children Admitted to College," Sage Publications, 1976. **Page 57:** Table 2.3, "Percent of Princeton College Students Assigning Traits to Ethnic Groups." Copyright 1969 by the American Psychological Association. Adapted by permission. **Pages 76–79:** Excerpts from Herbert Gans, "Uses of Poverty — The Poor Pay All," from *Social Policy*, July–August 1971, Vol. 2, No. 2. Used with permission. Copyright 1971 by Social Policy Corporation. **Page 146:** Figure 6.2, Graphic Rating Scale. From *Handbook of Research Design and Social Measurements* by Delbert C. Miller. Copyright © 1977 by Longman Inc. **Pages 150–151:** Figure 6.4, Thurstone Scale. From L. L. Thurstone and E. J. Chane, *The Measurement of Attitude* (Chicago: University of Chicago Press, 1929). Reprinted in Marvin F. Shaw and Jack M. Wright, *Scales for the Measurement of Attitudes* (New York: McGraw-Hill, 1967), pp. 545–546. **Pages 153–154:** Figure 6.5, Likert Scale. From L. A. Kalish, "Scale of Attitudes Toward Death," *Journal of Social Psychology*. **Page 154:** Table 6.1, Assessment of Terms. From G. Rotter, *Journal of Social Psychology*, Vol. 86, 1972, p. 215. **Page 157:** Figure 6.6, Guttman Scale. From *Handbook of Research Design and Social Measurements* by Delbert C. Miller. Copyright © 1977 by Longman Inc. **Pages 389–391:** Excerpts from Rebecca Guy and Donald E. Allen, "Ocular Breaks and Verbal Output" in *Sociometry*, 1977, Vol. 40, No. 1, pp. 90–96. Reprinted with permission from American Sociological Association.

Printed in the United States of America

10 9 8 7 6 5 4 3 2 1   90 89 88 87 86

Contents

Preface vii

I Formulating Research Questions 1

1 What Is Research and Why Do We Do It? 3

The Nature of the Research Process 4
The Scientific Attitude: Myths and Realities 12
The Ethics of Social Research 25

2 Choosing and Formulating a Research Question 33

Defining Terms 34
The Role of Values in Choosing and Formulating Research Questions 35
Factors Influencing the Choice of a Research Question 36
Formulating a Research Question 39
Evaluating a Research Question 58

3 Guiding the Research Process: The Role of Theory 63

The Relationship Between Theory and Method 64
The Nature of a Social Theory 68
Major Theoretical Paradigms in Social Research 74

4 Choosing a Research Design 91

Research Design Defined 92
The Relation of Theory to the Research Design 93
The Importance of the Research Design 94
Factors to Consider in Choosing a Research Design 95
Three Research Designs 106
General Considerations 111
The Research Design and Data Collection 112

5 Hypotheses and Evidence 115

Hypotheses Defined 116
Hypothesis Construction as It Relates to Theory 117
Hypotheses Testing Typology 120

Characteristics of Hypotheses   121
Testing Hypotheses   125
Triangulation   126
Use of Evidence in Hypothesis Testing   127
The Hypothesis Cycle   131

II *Measurement, Data Collection, and Analysis*   135

6 The Process of Measurement   137

The Meaning of Measurement   138
Why Measure?   139
Levels of Measurement   140
Single Indicators as Measures   143
Scales as Measures   145
Comparison of Scaling Techniques   158
Nonreactive Measures   159
The Theory of Measurement   161
Types of Errors   162
Sources of Measurement Error   164
Evaluating the Adequacy of a Measure   167

7 Sampling   173

Some Basic Definitions   174
Why Sample?   174
The Representativeness of a Sample   176
Sampling Theory: How It Works   179
Sampling Plans   184
What Size Sample?   191

8 The Experiment   199

"Deviance in the Dark"   200
Creating Equal Groups   202
Technical Considerations Concerning the Independent Variable   204
Two Experimental Designs   207
Laboratory versus Field Experiment   209
Field Experiment   210
Internal Validity   213
External Validity   216
True Experiment versus Quasi-Experiment   217
Quasi-Experiment   217

9 The Survey 219

The Survey Defined 220
Planning Your Survey Design 224
Constructing a Questionnaire 229
Self-Administered Questionnaires 243
The Mailed Questionnaire 243
Face-to-Face Interviews 244
Telephone Interviews 248
The Interview versus the Self-Administered Questionnaire 249
Strengths and Weaknesses of Survey Research 249
Using Secondary Data to Supplement Interview Data 250

10 Field Research 253

The Nature of Field Research 254
Major Research Strategies in Field Research 259
Recording and Analyzing Field Observations 274
Ethical Issues in Field Research 282

11 Data Reduction and Organization 283

The Meaning of Datum/Data 284
Why We Organize and Reduce Data 285
The Role of the Computer in Data Reduction 287
An Introduction to the Computer 289
Preparing the Data for Computer Input 291
Formatting the Data for Computer Input 295
Keypunching the Data 299
Editing the Data for Errors 302
Storing the Data 304

12 Analyzing Data: Descriptive Statistics 307

The Role of Statistical Methods in the Research Process 309
Discrete and Continuous Data 310
Discrete Frequency Distributions 311
Continuous Frequency Distribution 316
Descriptive Summary Measures 319

13 Analyzing Data: Inferential Statistics 331

The Normal Curve 333
The Standard Normal Curve 334
The Standard Normal Curve as a Probability Distribution 335
The t Test for Two Independent Samples 340
The F Test — Three or More Independent Samples 342
Correlation and Regression 345

III Using Data to Answer Research Questions 365

14 The Interpretation and Consequences of Research Data 367

Back to Paradigms 368
The Consequences of Research 375
Inductive and Deductive Interpretations 378

15 Writing the Research Report 383

Why Write a Research Report? 384
Factors to Consider When Writing 385
Characteristics of Scientific Writing 385
Organization of a Research Report 387

Appendix A Using SPSS: Statistical Package for the Social Sciences 407

What Is an SPSS Program 407
Getting Started 408
Data Definition Commands 408
Task Commands 413
Procedural Commands 414

Appendix B Tables 437

1. Random Numbers 437
2. Areas Under the Normal Curve 439
3. Distribution of t 441
4. Distribution of F 442
5. Distribution of x^2 445

Glossary 447

References 457

Index 465

Preface

This book, if not a radical departure from other choices in the methods field, is different enough to warrant a comment at the outset. What we have tried to accomplish is the integration of theory and methods in ways that show their interrelatedness without destroying the integrity of each. The title of the book, *Social Research Methods: Puzzles and Solutions*, sets the theme. The nature of any methodological solution is linked to the nature of the puzzle, indeed is part of the puzzle. This insight, derived mostly from Thomas Kuhn's influential work in the philosophy of science, is well known by the social sciences, but most methods books do not reflect the enormous potential of his observation. We have tried to do so, asserting an overriding reminder to the student that theory must be given more than lip service, and that method stems from theoretical perspective and not the other way around.

In the course of pursuing methods in this way, we have covered the usual range of topics, techniques, and procedures that represent the technical arsenal of social science. Section I deals with opening questions. Just what is research and why do we do it? How are research questions chosen and formulated? And what role does theory play in guiding and directing the research process? In this section we have not shied away from the difficult questions of ethics, respect for our human subjects, and the politics of findings. Section II deals explicitly with technique with the lessons of Section I in mind. Hypotheses, measurement, and sampling sometimes appear arcane to students just learning about them, but they fall into place if they are hooked to a few relatively simple questions that identify them as tools in a larger, logical plan. Section II also presents some of the major ways of collecting data and in each case ties these models to theoretical paradigms out of which they emerge as logical possibilities. Section III helps the student figure out what research means. The analysis and interpretation of data are really the meat of social science, for there is a larger audience for our studies, and much of it is less interested in the technical concerns of the discipline than in what kind of insights and conclusions are offered to a world hungry for knowledge and understanding of the complex social processes that govern our lives. In addition, Section III provides helpful ideas on writing a research report. Finally, the appendixes offer a guide to the use of one statistical package available for computer-assisted analysis of data—Statistical Package for the Social Sciences (SPSS).

We have tried very hard in this book to be intellectually honest about our craft. The pure world of research is an ideal and an abstraction largely unrelated to reality. Survey researchers need to know that people don't always respond favorably to being interviewed, and that having doors slammed in one's face is not only distressing, but may destroy one's ideal sample. Likewise, field research involves the sometimes dirty work of putting one's hands directly into the social world, where things look very different than they did in a classroom or an office when one formulated the original design. Thus reality checks have been liberally sprinkled through the text, not to confuse students but to remind them that research is a real-world enterprise and not just an idealistic, academic one. If, as Howard Becker suggests, idealism in medical school gives way to cynicism as students discover that things just aren't the way they thought, the same may be said of other educational endeavors too. The way to keep students from becoming disenchanted when things don't work out the way the text indicated is to make the text faithful to the actual contingencies the researcher is likely to find. We have tried to do that without losing our idealism for the liberating potential of good research.

The ability to understand social research has become, in the complex world in which we live, one of the basic literacies. We all consume research whether we know it or not, and many occupations far removed from the formal study of the social sciences wind up having direct links to an understanding of research methods and techniques. Every time we go into a store, market researchers have preceded us; every time we face a political election, researchers have tried to anticipate how we will respond; and even the intimacies of our personal relationships have been pored over by someone trying to know how things work. None of this research need be viewed as sinister, but it does need to be understood so that one can use it instead of being used by it. We hope this book will be of considerable assistance along the road to an understanding of self and society.

Acknowledgments

Even though their work is often solitary, authors are never alone. The authors of a book like this, almost five years in preparation, have so many intellectual, practical, and personal debts to discharge, that writing an acknowledgment hangs them precariously on a cliff between saying too much or acknowledging too little. Nevertheless, it would be the height of arrogance to ignore such a courtesy.

Our colleagues at Memphis State, Oklahoma State, and CUNY were gracious and accommodating during the many conversations we had with them about the topics in this book, as well as the personal affronts that inevitably come from having to barricade oneself in an office and act like a hermit in order to complete a project of this magnitude. Our families are also owed a significant thank-you for the same sense of understanding in the face of affronts that, if anything, were greater than those endured by colleagues.

We also owe a great debt to the many scholars and researchers whose work we used in preparing this book and its examples. Textbooks are the organizational creations of their authors, but their contents depend on the work of literally thousands of researchers whose studies form the basis of a book about the science and art of acquiring social knowledge. We certainly have been standing on the shoulders of giants.

Specifically, Dennis Brissett of the School of Medicine at the University of Minnesota–Duluth taught us how to do research "in the street," and his genius is evident in the sections on field methods. That section also owes a great debt to colleagues who work in the symbolic interactionist tradition through the vehicle of the many excellent journals in the qualitative tradition, and to the Midwest Sociological Association, whose yearly meeting provides a place for those interested in this kind of research to share both findings and methods.

The people at Allyn and Bacon have been, in a word, heavenly. They believed in this project, have seen it through at least two years longer than it should have taken, were patient at the right time, persistent at the right time, and understood, even in the face of the corporate pressures of the publishing world, that books do not come instantly even in this Quick Trip Society, and that quality work takes time. For those individuals, specifically, Al Levitt and Judy Shaw, we will always be grateful. We would also like to thank the reviewers, Shannon Stokes, Ferris Ritchey, Rick Wallace, and Dennis Teitge, for their many hours of hard work and creative criticisms. This book has greatly profited from their input.

Finally, our students at each of our universities had much more to do with this work than they will ever know. In the last analysis, books like this are for them.

Section I

Formulating Research Questions

Chapter 1

What Is Research and Why Do We Do It?

The nature of the research process
  Research as human activity
  Some everyday sources of knowledge
    Common sense
    Tradition
    Authority
  Puzzles and solutions
  What is a paradigm?
  Paradigms as puzzles and solutions
  The ongoing relationship between theory and research
  A definition of methodology
  The need to study methodology
The scientific attitude: myths and realities
  Traditional models of science
    Science is empirical
    Science is logical
    Science is generalizing
    Science is abstract
    Science is public, not private
  The practice of science
    Moon rocks and the scientists
    The real world
    The language and rhetoric of science
      Operational definitions
      Validity and reliability
  The promise and limitations of science
The ethics of social research
  Ethics as an urgent issue
    Deception
    Manipulation
    Project selection
  Toward a resolution

The next best thing to knowing something is knowing how to find it.
—Samuel Johnson

THE NATURE OF THE RESEARCH PROCESS

This book, more than you might believe at the beginning, is about everyday things. For even though we are writing about the seemingly technical, often mysterious, and sometimes feared process of doing social research, the procedures and issues we will be discussing are really a part of everyday activities. You have done the things between the covers of this book many times, even though you may have rarely thought about them in exactly the same way we will be talking about them here. So, in a very real sense, this book is about a topic you already know much about as well as use daily. And since you already know and have done many of the things described here, grasping them in the slightly different vocabulary of social science will not be as difficult as you may think.

One of our objectives in writing this book, then, is to help you think about social science research methods without losing sight of the fact that the research process is basically a systematized version of a set of activities experienced by almost everybody by virtue of the fact that they are curious, thinking, problem-solving creatures who live in the twentieth century, when social research, its problems, and its products abound.

Research as Human Activity

If the purpose of research is to discover answers to questions by applying systematic procedures (Selltiz, 1976), then it can be said that some variety of research is common to all people everywhere. Curiosity has apparently led people for centuries to search for answers to the questions of how and why the world works as it does. Primitive people knew (sometimes far better than modern people do) the relationships among the stars, the tides, the seasons, and the occurrence of weather. Closer to home, the observation of patterns has sometimes led people to quite accurate predictions of weather just by watching the behavior of animals. An instructive test of such weather-predicting ability came a couple of years ago when an Iowa farmer challenged the local weather bureau to a contest. The farmer claimed that he could predict both short- and long-term weather changes more accurately by watching his goats and sheep than the weather bureau could with all of its sophisticated scientific instruments. The arrogant weather bureau took on the challenge, and careful records were kept over the course of a year. It was, as you may have guessed, no contest: the farmer and his goats won hands down.

Now, the Iowa farmer might not have been able to tell you in scientifically accurate terms exactly what his research procedure was, but he had one and it worked. In this sense, both the farmer and his animals were researchers, even though we are hardly recommending their methods as systematic research procedures. We can't do that, for part of good research is to be able to communicate one's procedures to others, and the farmer was not able to do that very well.

Nevertheless, the basic processes of social scientific research are *human processes*. They exist not simply in the world of nature, but in the natural world of human beings. We learn from patterns, and we are curious about the world around us. We recognize that one thing often does follow another, that prediction is possible, at least enough to make it a practical necessity for dealing with life. Not only do we predict, but we want to generalize from our own experiences and from the experiences of others. We hear a story about a man and we conclude, "Men are like that." We know that life is not just a random throw of the dice, that it involves pattern and regularity, and that despite the generally good advice that we treat everyone as individuals, nobody could really deal with anyone else without making inferences and using generalities, and making predictions based on what one has seen and understands about behavior, sex, race, education, money, culture, language, situations—the list is endless.

Some Everyday Sources of Knowledge

People everywhere have a store of knowledge. It is impossible to live in the world without using some kind of knowledge, even if it is sketchy, inaccurate, or even just plain wrong. To examine how people obtain their information, then, is both useful and itself predictive, for if we know the sources of knowledge, we will be in a position to assess how much faith to place in them. There are three common sources of information that deserve mention: common sense, tradition, and authority.

Common Sense. We are told approvingly that a person has a large measure of common sense, or disapprovingly that another has a lot of book learning but no common sense. Common sense is, simply, what "everybody knows." Unfortunately, as a guide to reliable knowledge, common sense leaves much to be desired. Indeed, for years common sense told some people that the world was flat, that blacks were biologically inferior to whites, that if you made a lot of money it was proof that God was smiling on you, and that if you jumped out of an airplane with a parachute on you would suffocate before you touched the ground. Bergen Evans wrote a book entitled *The Natural History of Nonsense* (1958), in which he cataloged a few of the more notorious fictions that for eons (and even to this day among some people in some places) passed themselves off as common sense. For example (p. 19):

1. Thunder sours milk.
2. Lightning never strikes twice in the same place.
3. Undertows and quicksand produce an irresistible suction that drags people down to their deaths.
4. Tornadoes have a dead center in which the law of gravity is inoperative.

As another example of the unreliability of common sense as a guide to knowledge, we might note all the commonsense phrases that are contradicted by other, equally commonsensical phrases. For example:

1. a. Look before you leap.
   b. He who hesitates is lost.
2. a. Repeat a lie often enough and people will believe it.
   b. Truth will prevail.
3. a. Out of sight, out of mind.
   b. Absence makes the heart grow fonder.
4. a. Opposites attract.
   b. Birds of a feather flock together.

Of course, there is at least a grain of truth in each of the preceding statements, and if they were subjected to proper research procedures, we could verify the grain of truth that is in them and also find out how they are *not* true as well as why they were so widely believed.

For example, there *is* a certain empirical truth to the idea that the earth is flat. The human being relying on his or her own senses and, without the perception afforded by advanced instruments and the abstractions of astronomy, concludes experientially that the world is flat. From the standpoint of everyday life, it is difficult to believe that an invisible force called gravity could keep us all from falling off an elliptical ball.

Similarly, the famous sucking force attributed to quicksand is probably a misunderstanding created by the fact that the bog makes a sucking sound when a large object is pulled out of it. But the suction is in the puller, not in the mire. Quicksand is about twice as buoyant as water, and if a person did not struggle and become fatigued, he would sink no higher than his armpits (Evans 1958, 20). On the other hand, careful research would probably also show that people *do* struggle when in quicksand, and as a result sometimes go under. Most people's conception of quicksand probably comes from such reliable sources as old Tarzan movies.

As for lightning, it is far more likely to strike twice in the same place than not. The reason is that lightning passes through conductors, whose total surface constitutes only a very small part of the earth's surface. Evans reports that in the first ten years following its construction, the mast on top of the Empire State Building was struck by lightning some sixty-eight times. And people who have been struck by lightning are more likely to be struck again than people who have never had such a misfortune (Evans 1958, 21).

The notion that thunder sours milk is very simply a confusion between the thunder itself and the humid, stagnant air in which thunderstorms are most likely to occur. Souring is the result of bacterial action, and the bacteria are most likely to multiply in warm, moist air.

So, while common sense is not a very reliable guide to knowledge, the way in which common sense is arrived at is a legitimate concern of sociology, and it has a profound effect on the way people behave. A theoretical point of view in sociology called ethnomethodology makes much of common sense, and we will discuss how it does this a bit later.

These examples all show the validity of Bertrand Russell's assertion that if an idea is part of common sense, there is at least as much chance that it is common nonsense as common sense.

Tradition. Another source of knowledge is tradition, and although it is like common sense in some respects, in other ways it is different. Common sense is always a part of tradition, but what is traditional is not always common sense. People everywhere have a knowledge base simply by virtue of the heritage they have passed along to them by their culture. Previously obtained knowledge (including some gotten from scientific research) becomes the authority for new generations. None of the readers of this book figured out on his or her own that $E = mc^2$ or even exactly why 2 plus 2 equals 4. We come to accept these bits of knowledge along with millions of other bits because they are part of the conventional knowledge of the culture and the groups to which we belong. They "work" in our lives, largely because they *are* conventional. No one could possibly start from scratch and come anywhere close to knowing what modern men and women know. Knowledge is cumulative, and we are constantly building on the taken-for-granted knowledge of past generations. In this sense, the school system teaches not the truth—or even knowledge in the absolute sense of that word—but rather whatever is passing for it at a conventional moment in history. Although none of us could build very much knowledge on our own, the fact that much knowledge is simply traditional is often a stumbling block to further systematic inquiry. What do you do when you discover that you have learned something that completely refutes what has always been regarded as true? How do changes in knowledge occur, especially when the change is radical rather than trivial? The fact is, it *is* difficult to get a new idea across when it conflicts with what has traditionally been known.

Knowledge is not a static thing, but a continual process. Thus, anything held to be the case, no matter how compelling the research on which it is based, must be looked upon as tentative knowledge, based on the best possible research we have at the time. But few responsible researchers would claim that further research could not wash even the most cherished knowledge away.

Authority. Another common source of knowledge is authority. For generations, people have taken things to be true because of the authority of the church, the state, their mother or father, a close friend, or experts. In other words, something is true because of who said it. The last category deserves some special mention, because while many people can accept the notion that an idea is not necessarily so because the pope says it is, these same people sometimes have difficulty applying that principle to those ideas supported by an expert in some particular field. In logic, this is technically known as an *ad hominem* fallacy—an argument that something is true or false because of who said it. And the fallacy is as mistaken when applied to scientists as when applied to popes.

On the other hand, like the previous sources of knowledge we have mentioned, the existence of authority as a source of truth is not without reason. It is usually impossible to track down information fully and to inform ourselves completely on our own when we make decisions. Therefore, part of the process of behaving as human beings in association with others is to rely on those who are presumably "in the know." When the runner Bill Rodgers wins the Boston Marathon, people might be more likely to believe him if he says that eating lots of yogurt is the secret to running twenty-six miles. They are less likely to accept the nutritional advice of even the most intelligent thinker on the subject who has never run farther than the refrigerator to grab another beer. In an age of degrees, certifications, celebrity status, and Nobel prizes, it is hard for us to understand that knowledge really respects none of this and that statements finally stand or fall on their own merits regardless of the authority of those who make them.

Puzzles and Solutions

The student of social research methods might best understand the topic by thinking of it as a series of puzzles. One traditional way of seeing methods is simply as the vehicles in which we travel from a puzzle to its solution. We say *simply* because it has become increasingly apparent in recent years that the relationship between puzzles and solutions, between questions and answers, is much more complicated than we originally thought. Obviously, social scientists do research to find out as much as they can about a given problem. Are Republicans more likely to vote against the Equal Rights Amendment than Democrats? What is the current attitude among Americans toward homosexuality? Are religious conservatives more likely to be authoritarian in their political attitudes than are religious liberals? These are but a few of the thousands of questions that we have sought answers to with social science research over the years. But how is a problem derived? How do social scientists know what to study? How do we know when we have found something important?

Our ways of thinking about these questions have undergone tremendous changes in the last fifteen years or so, especially since the publication of a book by Thomas Kuhn entitled *The Structure of Scientific Revolutions* in 1962. Kuhn is a natural scientist who came to question the traditional scientific explanation of how research develops and how answers are found. Kuhn's work had a profound impact on the way we think about natural science, but if anything, its influence on social science was even greater (Ritzer 1975; Friedrichs 1970).

The essence of Kuhn's book is the way in which changes in knowledge come about in science. According to the traditional view, presented in almost all introductory research methods books, science grows and changes in a progressive manner, with each advance building on those that preceded it. This building-block theory of knowledge conceives of science as a series of blocks, one carefully placed on top of the other, so that we slowly and incrementally move toward greater and greater levels of knowledge. Changes in scientific truths thus come slowly in a step-by-step fashion. Kuhn believes that this view of science is false. He asserts instead that this conception of the history of science is largely an illusion, created by the fact that each generation of scientists rewrites its textbooks to give the impression that the current stage of knowledge is the apex of what has been accumulated. In place of this incremental conception of science Kuhn advances the thesis that revolution marks the important changes in science. Truly major changes come about as a result of revolutions in the basic paradigms, or systems, of science.

What Is a Paradigm?

Kuhn offers, in effect, a sociological theory of science. He says that science takes the particular shape it does from the application of shared paradigms. A paradigm can be defined, in its simplest form, as "the entire constellation of beliefs, values, techniques, and theories shared by the members of a scientific community" (Kuhn 1962, 175). In other words, a paradigm is a fundamental image held by members of the scientific community about the subject matter of science. Ritzer (1975) notes that a paradigm does the following (p. 5):

1. It defines what entities are (and are not) the concern of a particular scientific community.
2. It tells the scientist where to look (and where not to look) in order to find the entities of concern to him.
3. It tells the scientist what he can expect to discover when he finds and examines the entities of concern to his field.

Using these ideas, Ritzer offers a technical definition of a paradigm:

A paradigm is a fundamental image of the subject matter within a science. It serves to define what should be studied, what questions should be asked, how they should be asked, and what rules should be followed in interpreting the answers obtained. The paradigm is the broadest unit of consensus within a science and serves to differentiate one scientific community (or subcommunity) from another. It subsumes, defines, and interrelates the exemplars, theories, and methods and instruments that exist within it. (1975, p. 7)

What these interesting ideas mean is that theory and research blend in what Kuhn calls an "inextricable mixture" (1962, 108). There are, says Kuhn, no such things as independent facts or other factors or standards that are independently true. The idea of what constitutes a fact is, instead, paradigm-dependent, or a judgment rendered by scientists who apply one system or another. The competition that goes on between adherents of one paradigm (what Lewis calls "fist fights in the kitchen") is not the kind of battle that can be resolved by proof, because what constitutes proof is itself dependent on the application of one system or another. Furthermore, says Kuhn, we may have to give up the idea that changes in the prevailing paradigm carry scientists closer to the truth. Instead, we rearrange the criteria for accepting something as the truth.

Paradigms as Puzzles and Solutions

In all of science, paradigms function to set puzzles and, at the same time, set the terms of their solution. When a machine is designed to manufacture jigsaw puzzles, the solution to the puzzle is built in. Once the machine is designed, there can be only one solution to the puzzle. From this point of view, explaining something satisfactorily is dependent on the whole scientific community's understanding of what it means to make a satisfactory explanation (Phillips 1973). The facts to be explained as well as the very idea of an explanation are paradigm-dependent.

Changes in the prevailing paradigms of science come about because no paradigm can handle all of the possible puzzles the human mind is capable of devising. New paradigms arise to handle these problems, and when a scientist gives up an old paradigm and embraces a new one, he or she undergoes a kind of conversion experience, for such a decision can only be made on faith (Phillips 1973). When we speak, then, of the facts, we are speaking about what people in a given social context (science) accept as the facts at any given time.

Scientific activity varies in its use of paradigms. Some sciences use a single paradigm that is dominant and holds a broad consensus among scholars in the field. In other sciences, such as the social sciences, a number of paradigms compete for the same subject matter. When no dominant paradigm exists, practitioners spend a great deal of time defending their own favorite paradigm against attacks (Masterman 1970).

The Ongoing Relationship between Theory and Research

Our discussion of paradigms has underscored the fact that we cannot really separate theory from method, paradigm from procedure, assumptions from conclusions. While scientific research methods are an honest attempt to hold up a camera and not a mirror to the world around us, we never really succeed, for every time we click the shutter, we see part of ourselves in the picture. This is what is meant by Gross's statement "What the sociologist sees when he looks at society is part of his own socialization" (1967, 14) and Russell's remark that "What a physiologist sees when he looks at a brain is part of his own brain."

Does this mean that social science is impossible? Of course not, but it does mean that there is an ongoing relationship between our puzzles and our solutions, and it demonstrates that more than lip service must be given to the role of theory in the research process. One of the most deplorable situations in research methods courses is that they are typically taught separately from theory courses; the two are seen essentially as distant enterprises that have only a peripheral bearing on each other. Although the professors who teach them know better, students often see methods courses as "cooking schools" in which one finds out how to mix up a research project. Ask most students when they finish the project how their solutions related to their puzzles, and what new puzzles were generated by their research, and they look bewildered. Cookbooks don't usually supply that kind of information.

Methods are really part of larger paradigms that include theory, assumptions, goals, and perspectives, as well as techniques. As we proceed with this book, we want you to understand just how all of these things relate to the research process.

A Definition of Methodology

What, then, does the term *methodology* encompass? We have found no better definition than that offered by Bogdan and Taylor:

> The term *methodology* in a broad sense refers to the processes, principles, and procedures by which we approach problems and seek answers. In the social sciences the term applies to how one conducts research. As in everything else we do, our assumptions, interests, and goals greatly influence which methodological procedures we choose. When stripped to their essentials, *most debates over methods are debates over assumptions and goals, over theory and perspective.* (1975, 1)

Note the elements of this definition. Methods are ways in which we (1) approach problems and (2) conduct research; (3) assumptions, interests, theories, and goals are intimately tied to which methods we choose; and (4) debates over methods are really debates over theory and assumptions. Such a definition, without explicitly saying so, underscores Kuhn's notion of the paradigm. In this book, we will try not to study methods without being mindful of the paradigms of which they are a part. We will discuss this matter in greater detail in Chapter 3.

The Need to Study Methodology

We live in a research-saturated environment. Research is used not only to learn things, but to promote, sell, and justify things. The graphs, charts, language, and logic of research can be found in everything from governmental actions to spray deodorants. To sift through this research and find what is consumable is no easy task. Students reading this book will range all the way from budding professional researchers who will not only need to know what is in this text, but will require years of future study as well—to those persons who will never read another book on methodology, but will continue to consume its products (both voluntarily and involuntarily) for the rest of their lives. In short, anyone who buys things, sells things, reads, watches television, votes, tries to persuade others, and is persuaded by others needs to know something about research methods. We can think of no topic that holds more relevance for people in modern society, and we will try to reflect this personal connection you have with the subject as we continue through this book.

THE SCIENTIFIC ATTITUDE: MYTHS AND REALITIES

Traditional Models of Science

The word *science* has become one of the preeminent buzz words of our century. As God and Heaven were to the nineteenth century, science is to the twentieth. In the modern world, to label something as "nonscientific'' has virtually become like saying in past times that something was "of the devil." Nonscience is for many people the same as superstition. The social sciences, being somewhat younger and in more need of justification than the natural sciences, have been particularly wearisome about the use of the term "science." Indeed, the amount of writing produced by social scientists to justify why our work is scientific is so great that Samuel Stouffer once suggested that we "declare a moratorium on the use of the word 'science' in order to avoid all of those acrimonious (and generally profitless) debates over whether a given piece of work is or is not 'scientific'" (1934, 486–487).

Much of this murky passion about science could be cleared away if we think of science as an attitude surrounded by a set of activities designed to make sense out of the world in which we live. From this point of view, we can say that science holds no monopoly on truth, but competes (sometimes fairly and sometimes unfairly) in the marketplace of ideas. None of us, including scientists, act our lives out in a fully scientific way. Scientists, too, have emotions and sentiments, biases and passions. What, then, are the elements that compose the attitude of science? And what are the realities that both facilitate and interfere with this attitude? Traditionally, the attitude of science has been characterized by the following elements.

Science Is Empirical. By *empirical* we mean simply that science rests on sense data. Science is interested (as science) only in what can be seen, touched, tasted, heard, and smelled. The scientific attitude, for better or for worse, excludes from consideration all of those important notions in human affairs that do not have this property. Whether or not God exists is not a scientific question, but what people believe about God can be determined empirically. We can ask people about their concepts of God, and see their actions related to this important belief. This simple idea distinguishes science from many other human pursuits that seek to acquire knowledge. An empirical scientist who wanted to know how many teeth a horse has would not sit at a desk and logically try to figure out the answer to the question. Nor would the scientist waste time on the question of how many teeth a horse ought to have, or what people have traditionally believed about the matter (although that could be an interesting scientific question in its own right), or what the Bible has to say about the subject. The scientist would simply go find a bunch of horses and start counting teeth. In this sense, empirical science is an attitude that places the eyes, ears, nose, and other sensing devices of the human being as the ultimate arbiters of questions. What cannot be determined empirically may still be important, but stands outside the realm of science.

Science Is Logical. Science believes (although it cannot prove) that there is some ultimate link between logical thinking and empirical facts. The attitude of science is that objective reality not only exists, but is essentially in one piece, so that there should be no disparity between what is logical and what is empirical. Thus logic is simply the rules by which inferences are made and constitutes the structure of scientific debate.

Science Is Generalizing. This is one of the characteristics of science that people find frustrating, even though as human beings we use it all the time. Science has no inherent interest in individual cases, for the goal of science is to produce meaningful generalizations. In an age of radical individualism, this seems perverse if not downright anti-American. Nevertheless, science seeks general principles and is not in the business of trying to characterize individual events. One way of understanding this idea is to contrast sociology and history. History is not really a science (although it does at points use scientific techniques) because its main concern is with giving complete and comprehensive descriptions of particular events. There was only one World War II, and a complete description of it would show the differences between it and every other armed conflict that has been waged on this planet. Sociology, on the other hand, is generalizing, and to the extent that it uses scientific techniques, it does so in an effort to reach general principles. World War II, to carry out our example, has no special fascination for sociologists, but is one case in a host of cases that together might lead them to meaningful generalizations about war as a form of organized conflict (Bierstedt 1970, 14).

Looking for meaningful generalizations usually involves two processes well known to both scientists and everyday people. These two processes are known as *induction* and *deduction*. Induction is moving from the specific to the general—from individual cases to general principles. If we study 150 cases of divorce and try to figure out from these individual cases what is common to all of them, the statements we make about divorce in general were produced by the process of induction. We used inductive reasoning because we moved from specific cases to general principles. On the other hand, sometimes we may generalize deductively. In deductive reasoning we move from the general to the specific. To use our previous example, on the bases of whatever general principles of divorce we have arrived at, we might hazard an explanation of why a particular couple split up. Both induction and deduction are used by the scientist. Induction is the essential method of scientists in the effort to create general principles. And the goal of reaching generalizations is that we might better understand and explain the occurrence of particular events.

General principles, whether derived from scientific work or from everyday knowledge, common sense, authority, or some other source, can then be translated into *hypotheses*, which we can check against further experience, thereby verifying or modifying the general principles.

Science is an ongoing, cyclical process of induction, deduction, modification, refinement, further testing, further induction, and further deduction. Scientific knowledge is never fixed; it is always tentative and always subject to further refinements.

Science Is Abstract. Many people want science to be concrete, and social science, especially, to solve the problems of the world. But science is not interested in concrete things, just as it is not interested in particular ones. Instead, the social scientist is interested in making propositional statements that move increasingly up what is called the *ladder of abstraction*. This means that if we want to understand the world around us, it is necessary to abstract, or progressively leave things out of our descriptions in order to move from a low-level, concrete form of understanding to more complex and meaningful ones. Hayakawa (1940, 126) gives us a good example in thinking about a cow (see Figure 1.1).

When we abstract, then, we progressively leave out more and more characteristics for the sake of a more generalized understanding of

**FIGURE 1.1
The Abstraction Ladder of Bessie the Cow***

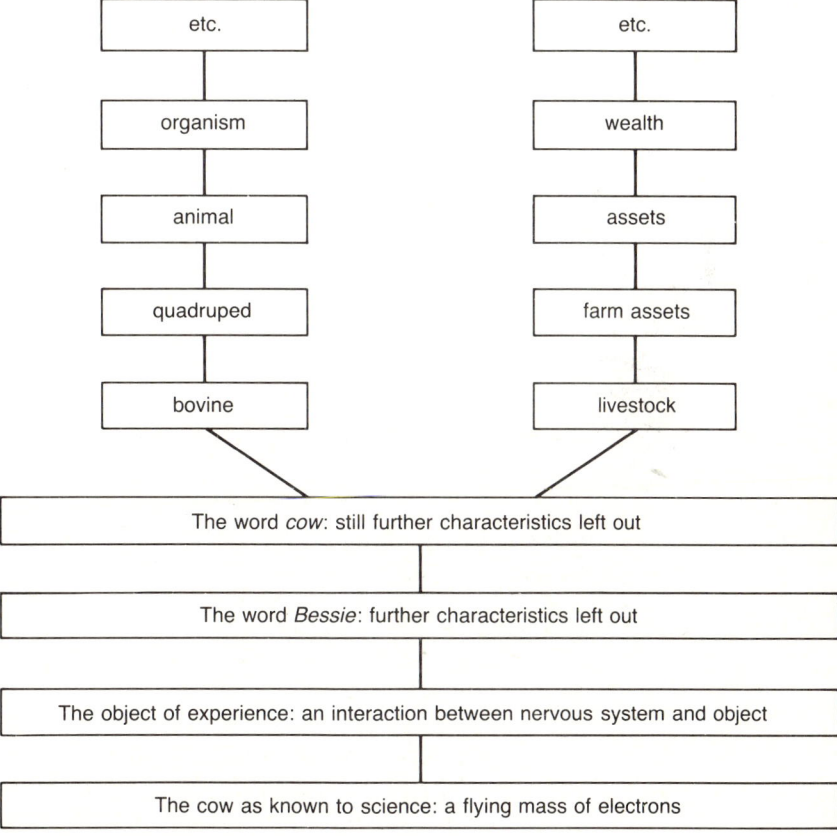

*Read from the bottom up.

something. In the process of research we almost always are looking for ways of combining characteristics of data to seek the most general understanding of a phenomenon that we can.

Science Is Public, Not Private. Science is part of a public universe of discourse, and this is one of the major reasons for studying research methods. By using a common method, scientists are able to communicate their findings to one another in a common language. Methods constitute this language, and presumably, if everything were to work perfectly, the individual scientists' motivations, biases, personal opinions, values, ideologies, and so on, would be excluded from scientific conclusions because the common language of method would distill these contaminating factors out. Scientist A working on a common problem with scientist B and using the same methods ought to achieve the same results. (This almost never happens in the social sciences, but more on that later.)

The Practice of Science

The preceding characteristics of science may be looked at as an ideal, rarely achieved but nevertheless at least partially desirable. To understand and appreciate fully the scientific attitude, we must also investigate how science falls short of its goal, for in so doing we can know the pitfalls as well as the promises of science. Only by understanding both the ideal and the reality of science can we fully understand what we are doing when we try to carry out a research project. An analogy might be what medicine claims to be (see the Hippocratic oath or other such lofty statements) versus how doctors actually practice in the real world of money, power, law, and interpersonal relationships (see Illich 1974). In other words, we might research science itself to see if it is what it claims to be in the same way that social science has investigated other institutions and human activities.

Kuhn's ideal of the paradigm, of course, is a starting point for seeing science as it is and not as we wish it were. A paradigm, by definition, includes a lot of nonrational elements and human frailties. Science, as we indicated at the beginning, is a human enterprise, and none of its methods are really capable of insulating it from this fact. The best single example we have of this, and a perfect case for understanding how scientists actually operate, is the case of moon rocks.

Moon Rocks and the Scientists. When *Apollo II* set down on the surface of the moon in July of 1969, a series of events were set into motion that have come to tell us a great deal about the realities of science. For as long as scientists (and humanity in general) have observed the moon, competing theories have emerged about the origins of the moon, its relationship to

Earth, the beginnings of the solar system, and so forth. All of these hoary problems that led scientists into a number of different theoretical camps were thought to be due to the fact that we had no real physical evidence from the moon itself. *Apollo II* would lead us to a resolution of these scientific problems by providing us with the first sack of moon rocks—real, tangible, physical evidence that could be subjected to close observation, reliable tests, and the like. At last, we would know the answer to these age-old questions. Those scientists who were correct in their theories would be proven so, and those who chased error all these years would be revealed too.

The case led a social scientist named Ian Mitroff to see all of this as a revolutionary chapter in scientific history, one that could tell us far more about the nature of science, perhaps, than even the rocks themselves. The beginnings of his investigation are described as follows:

> The Apollo moon scientists were chosen for study for various reasons. A major initial premise, later confirmed, was that the Apollo program would be an excellent contemporary setting in which to study the nature and function of the commitment of scientists to their pet hypotheses in the face of possibly disconfirming evidence. A review of the scientific and popular literature before the landing of Apollo 11 found that various scientists had strongly committed themselves in print as to what they thought the moon would be like, and in a few cases, what they ardently hoped the moon would be like. (Mitroff 1974, 581)

Mitroff commenced a study of over forty of the most eminent scientists who studied the moon rocks. Each scientist was interviewed four times over a period of three years. The interviews ranged from open-ended discussions in the first round to written questionnaires in subsequent rounds. The results showed that the sack of moon rocks did nothing to resolve competing theories about the nature of the universe. Instead, each camp of scientists, no matter how far they were away from each other in their astronomical theories, interpreted the evidence of the rocks themselves as substantiating their particular theory (p. 11). Furthermore, closer examination of the scientists' attitude toward the traditional view of the scientist as a disinterested, dispassionate, objective observer indicated that they themselves viewed this conception of science as a fairy tale. Most surprising of all, the scientists not only rejected the notion of the disinterested scientist as an accurate descriptive account of the workings of science, but even rejected it as a desired *ideal* or *standard:*

> What was even more surprising was that the scientists rejected the notion of the "emotionally disinterested scientist" as a prescriptive ideal or standard. Strong reasons were evinced why a good scientist *ought* to be highly committed to a point of view. Ideally, they argued, scientists ought not to be

without strong, prior commitments. Even though the general behavior and personality of their more extremely committed colleagues infuriated them, as a rule they still came out in favor of scientists having strong commitments. (Mitroff 1974, 588)

Mitroff concludes his interesting study by claiming that far from the traditional ideas of science, the most creative scientists are intensely aggressive and fiercely passionate about the ideas they hold and the research they conduct.

Now, none of this is to say that these same scientists did not use the traditional methods of science and do their work as honestly as possible. They were also zealous in applying healthy scientific skepticism to the work of their colleagues in competing camps. The real significance of Mitroff's work is that the process of doing scientific research is much more complicated and filled with subjective and even irrational elements than we have usually acknowledged, and certainly more than we have ever studied in much detail.

Apparently, strong commitment and bias on the part of the scientist is one of the strongest sustaining forces in the doing of research. Far from being dispassionate, creative scientists care about the world around them and care about the ideas they themselves are working with. Despite all of this, Mitroff winds up his study with a strong endorsement of scientific methods:

> If scientific knowledge were the product of uncommitted or weakly committed observers, its understanding would be trivial. Given the presumption of untainted, unbiased observers, it is a trivial matter to explain how objectivity results. It is also a trivial matter to justify the concept of objectivity as knowledge independent of the feelings or opinions of the person making them. The problem is how objective knowledge results in science not despite bias and commitment, but because of them. (Mitroff 1974, 591)

The Real World. Just what *does* get in the way of the traditional ideals of the scientific method? First, scientists are human beings. They are motivated by the same emotions, anxieties, personal goals, and sense of value as the rest of us (Maslow 1966). What scientists study, what they deem important, and what they exclude from consideration as a worthy topic of investigation often depend on criteria that may at best be described as whimsical. Given the cost of conducting much research, the needs of the sponsoring agencies are often the determinant of what kinds of research are done, not criteria that are intrinsic to science itself.

Furthermore, what research is published is often the result of the Byzantine politics of the scientific community and its journals. Personality conflicts, jealousies, petty but accepted lines of inquiry, and even the credentials of the researcher or the university he or she works for often become the criteria of publication, and not the intrinsic merits of the research itself. Journal editors have a great deal of power as gatekeepers to let in and keep out what research is reported to other scientists and to the public. The space requirements of the journals are fed not so much by clear-cut scientific demands for quality research, but by the rat race of academia, which makes publication mandatory for faculty and researchers lest they forgo promotion or tenure, or even lose their jobs altogether. Such a circumstance often leads to research being cranked out as if on an assembly line, with additions to the researcher's résumé being the goal and no valid, scientifically sound criteria. Indeed, the idea that science proceeds in carefully selected steps (the building-block theory) is an illusion that can be seen clearly once we understand the ordinary contingencies of money, power, and personalities that circumscribe scientific work.

The matters we have just mentioned might be classified as the social, psychological, economic, and political contexts of science. But scientific work itself is also a compromise between what is and what could have been. The notion that science runs through a clearly defined cycle consisting of the formulation of a question, the development of hypotheses, the operationalization of concepts, the collection and analysis of data, conclusions, and the reformulation of theory is an idea reminiscent of the organizational chart of a corporation: everyone who works there can tell you that the place is not exactly what it says it is on the chart.

Instead of this careful, step-by-step process, in the real world of science, things are much more haphazard. Research questions, as we have mentioned, often reflect scientists' ulterior motives, while the rest of the process is frequently an uncertain and tentative set of activities, filled with unexpected results that sometimes modify original conceptions and sometimes do not. We virtually never *prove* a theory to be correct, especially in the social sciences, nor do we ever fully invalidate existing ideas no matter how wrongheaded they are suspected to be. The idea that science is exciting work with never a dull moment also can be shown to be a myth, probably on a par with people's conceptions of flight attendants leading enchanting lives in the skies. Science, like delivering trays of sandwiches at 40,000 feet, can be dull, boring, onerous work. Sometimes a scientist works for days, weeks, months, or even years on a project, only to see nothing come of it. With contracted and externally funded work, as the deadline for completion approaches, creative fiction often gets produced in an effort to meet the external requirements imposed by the funding agency.

Lest the student doubt that science is as human an enterprise as the portrait painted here, a look at any number of memoirs of research activity will validate the general claim. James Watson's account of the discovery of the DNA molecule has been published in a book entitled *The Double Helix* (1968). The competition between scientists working toward the same goal, the personal animosities, the blind alleys, frustrations, and departures from the traditional scientific norms are well documented in this intensely human portrait of scientists at work. Similarly, Abraham Maslow has done an analysis of the scientist as human being in his book *The Psychology of Science* (1966). In the social sciences, there is still no better "inside" look at the real-work practice of social research than Phillip Hammond's *Sociologists at Work* (1968).

These accounts of scientists at work sometimes give the cynical observer a jaundiced view of the whole enterprise. This is certainly not our intention here, and the student should not conclude that because science and scientists have feet of clay, their work is irrelevant. Instead, the ideals of science should be looked upon as a goal to achieve, a set of norms that guide research but neither should nor always do determine what is done in the name of science. The conclusion to be drawn from this real-world glimpse of science in practice is that science is both a human enterprise and in many ways an art. The art of science is as crucial to understanding research activities as the science of science. This is not to suggest that the beginning student break the rules; in fact, you can't really break them until you know what they are. Being apprised of the actual practice of science in addition to the norms of scientific research can only serve to give you a better appreciation of the complexity of scientific research work. This is our goal.

The Language and Rhetoric of Science. Learning to use the language of research without being used by it is one of the main tasks you will have as a student of methodology. Like all disciplined lines of inquiry, research methods are as much mastering a body of language and symbols as a series of techniques. In this section, we want to mention a few of the major concepts, but in many ways the entire book will be an attempt to introduce you to the rhetoric of scientific method.

OPERATIONAL DEFINITIONS Julian Simon has given us a good example of the need for operational definitions in research:

> A stranger driving a car with California license plates stops you on the street in Urbana, Illinois, and asks "Where is New York?" You, being a lyrical poet with a feeling for the spiritual side of life, tell him, "New York is in the land of the sea, the singers of mercantile songs, and rotten paintings. Why go there?"
>
> The stranger looks annoyed and says, "Come on, fellow, quit the nonsense and tell me where New York is."
>
> "On the East Coast, north of Washington, south of Boston," you answer. He looks bewildered, so you add: "Latitude 40°40' North Longitude 73°48' West."
>
> He looks outraged. "Will you or won't you tell me what road to take?" he says. "How do I get there?"

> What the man really wants is for you to say: "Continue down this street to the first stop sign, about a quarter of a mile. Turn right on Highway 74 . . ." and so on.
>
> Now you have satisfied him. You have provided *instructions* that he can follow. The instructions are unambiguous (you hope) and, if he follows your instructions exactly, he must arrive exactly where you and he agree he is trying to go—New York, in this case. You have told him what he needs to know—nothing around curves, because he needs no instruction to do so. But you have told him which way to turn when he reaches the highway, because you have no reason to assume that he knows whether to go right or left at that point.
>
> Just as with travel instructions, the language of empirical science is made up of instructions that are descriptions of sets of actions or operations (for instance, "turn right at the first street sign") that someone can follow accurately. Such instructions are called an "operational definition." (1978, 12–13)

The language of research is very tuned to operational definitions, that is, definitions that specify the exact procedure for identifying or generating the definition. We can never be confident of the conclusions we reach unless we are confident of the methodological procedures used to arrive at those conclusions. The idea of operationalization was first proposed by Percy Bridgeman in 1927 (Zito 1975). By 1939, George Lundberg had applied it to the social sciences and had made it the cornerstone in his scientific conceptions of social research. The high abstractions of social theory are meaningless, said Lundberg, unless and until these are brought down to the empirical world by the technique of operationalization. If we are going to use theoretical concepts, we should know the exact methodological procedures used to define them. Otherwise, our theories remain pure speculation.

In short, the operational definition of a dish is its recipe (Bachrach 1962, quoted in Simon 1978, 17). If someone were to ask you how much you were worth, your answer would be an operational definition because it would specify assets you could get your hands on. To say that you are worth a million dollars because that is how much you will someday earn is not nearly so precise as saying you are worth a million dollars because that is how much you have in your checking account. The latter is an operational definition of wealth, while the former is pie in the sky.

Now, pie in the sky is also important to science, and the emphasis upon the operationalization of concepts in no way suggests that theory is unimportant. Theory guides our operationalizations, and every good research project begins with a body of good theory. But theory is not enough—we must also know how to translate the language of theory into the language of methods so that we have a way of checking to see if our conceptualizations are correct. This is exactly what operationalization does.

On the other hand, just because we have operationalized a concept does not mean that we have captured all of it. It simply means that we have translated part of it into terms we can measure and employ in a specific context. We could define love in terms of the number of times people kiss, and it would work as an operational definition for certain narrow purposes. But very few people would be satisfied that such a definition really encompassed the concept of love.

Some scientists commit the nothing-but fallacy when they do research. That is, they confuse their own operational definitions with reality. Therefore, some of them become ensnared in the fallacy that reality is nothing but what they are measuring. Love is nothing but a bunch of hormones calling out to themselves. Social class is nothing but income, occupation, education, house type, dwelling area, and whatever else has gone into the operational definition. Behavior is nothing but the interaction of all previous episodes of conditioning. Such a doctrinaire stance is an easy one to fall into when a researcher operationally defines a concept and then starts to believe his or her own definitions. But it is important to know that operationalization is merely a technique, and that for any concept you can think of, there are virtually an infinite number of operationalizations that could be given for it, all of which would lead to a different conclusion about the nature of the reality under investigation. While the language of science is important and we could not get along without it, language never says all there is to say about any given concept. It is not reality itself, merely a procedure with which to assess it. But if there are *no* ways to get at a concept, then operationally the concept must simply collapse insofar as *empirical investigation* of it is concerned.

VALIDITY AND RELIABILITY   These are important words in research, and it will be important to define them now while we are talking about the language of science. In the lexicon of research they are used over and over again. As we have already learned, every research project is an attempt to answer a question. The answer is provided by theory and the research is undertaken in order to test the answer. Validity and reliability are simply ways of determining how good the answer is.

In a general sense, *validity* means that a particular research measure measures what it is supposed to measure. If we can show that a piece of research is really getting at something other than what it says it is getting at, we have poked a large hole in its claim to be valid. More specifically, there are many different types of validity, and there are very few pieces of research that can claim to measure up to all of them. The following are only a few of the many kinds of validity used in social research.

First there is *pragmatic validity*. In essence, this is an answer to the question of whether or not the answer obtained by one's research "works." Are we better off with the answer than we were without it? Does it tell us anything we didn't already know?

There is also *predictive validity*. Does the research enable us to predict cases in the future? Much research in the social sciences is *ex post facto* or *retrospective* research. It tells us a great deal about something that has already come to pass, but very little about what will likely happen in the future. Social scientists, like other scientists, are often quite concerned with the predictive validity of a piece of research.

Another type of validity is *internal validity*. Some types of research are invalid because the procedures used in doing the research were themselves invalid. We can hardly claim that our research as a whole is valid if the elements that make it up are not. For example, when researchers study any particular group in an experimental setting, their research can be shown to be invalid unless they carefully match the results of that group with a *control group*. Otherwise, we have no way of knowing whether the experimental manipulations are really the cause of the outcome of the study.

There is also *construct validity*, sometimes called *external validity*. This applies to the research as a whole. No matter how carefully the internal procedures are performed, no matter how accurate the individual techniques employed can be shown to be, the entire research project might be completely irrelevant to the question under investigation. A study of intellectual achievement, based on the result of IQ tests, no matter how carefully done and error-free, might turn out to be completely invalid when applied to people from different cultural backgrounds. This systematic bias in IQ tests can render all such measures meaningless. In fact, a large amount of research has been done in the last ten years on this very problem (Selltiz et al. 1976). Construct validity deals, then, with the entire project and the theory that underlies it, and not simply with the particular elements of it.

A concept that is often confused with validity is that of reliability. In ordinary discourse, the word *genuineness* (validity, the real thing) is often used synonymously with the term *reliability*, but in social research we mean something quite different. Reliability, in social research, refers to whether a piece of research can be replicated—that is, whether a different investigator can achieve the same results using the same methods. Does a definition or measure of a particular idea always lead to the same result? Does a measure have the property of "same input, same output"? *Consistency* and *repeatability* have about the same meaning as *reliability* (Simon 1978, 21).

When we go to the grocery store, we are concerned with the reliability of the butcher's scale. Does it weigh a pound of meat the same way each time, or are there variations from time to time? Operational definitions need to be reliable. That is, does applying the same definition (methodologically operationalized) produce the same results every time? If not, it is not very reliable. Using our previous examples of IQ testing, a test would be reliable (all other things being equal) if it produced exactly the same score more than once for the same individual.

As you can see, reliability, while earnestly sought, is not very often achieved in the social sciences. Very few pieces of research are replicated. There are good reasons for this, besides the inaccuracy of methods, and we will address ourselves to that question a bit later.

The Promise and Limitations of Science

In the last one hundred years, science, its language, and its promises, both explicit and implicit, have become prominent features of the world in which we live. Products are increasingly sold in the name of science, and political decisions are based on so-called scientific research. A large chemical company promises "better living through chemistry," teams of survey researchers canvass the land to find out everything they can about us from the kinds of shoes we wear to the most intimate details of our sex lives. A portion of this scientific quest is motivated by the pure desire to know, and science has certainly been one of the strongest advocates of knowledge purely for the sake of knowledge. But increasingly we have also wanted science to solve a whole range of human problems, and the natural physical sciences, as well as the social sciences, have been caught up in the demand for the application of scientific research.

Not surprisingly, all of this scientific activity and its applications have generated a good deal of skepticism, for they have created a climate in which promises have been made or implied that science, in reality, cannot deliver. The promise that science might one day solve most, if not all, of our problems has created difficulties not only for the consumers of science, but also for scientists, who often know the impossibility of such a task. Furthermore, as increasing numbers of voices are telling us, science is itself creating certain social problems (Ravetz 1971). Skeptics of science and research now abound, and we may well be approaching the point where the baby will be thrown out with the bathwater.

Actually, the separation between intellectual questions (pure research) and practical questions (applied research) has never been as great as has been the tendency to claim. They are often discussed as though they were somehow opposed or even mutually exclusive (Selltiz et al. 1976, 4), and frequently as if one (usually the one favored by the prejudices of the writer) were better than the other. A close look at the history of science, however, will dispel any such simplistic notions. We have never been satisfied with simply knowing for the sake of knowing, and science has repeatedly and continuously been called upon to demonstrate its responsibility to the larger community by contributing something to the resolution of that community's practical concerns.

Nevertheless, as a practical matter, there is frequently a tension between these two objectives of science. Sometimes the desire to know can be totally subverted by the single-minded concerns of those who want simple, painless, and quick solutions to complex problems. But, by the same token, when scientists are building a body of knowledge, it is easy to lose sight of the problems of the everyday human being as they work in the solitary atmosphere of the laboratory. This tension has never been more eloquently stated than in quotations from two eminent scholars, Morris Cohen and Robert Lynd. Cohen, arguing the case for an unfettered pure science, once observed that purely theoretical contributions to astronomy and mathematics, by increasing the precision of navigation, have saved more lives at sea than any possible improvements in the carpentry of lifeboats. But Lynd, impatient with knowledge for the sake of knowledge, tells us that we are in acute danger of being caught, in the words of one of W. H. Auden's poems, "lecturing on Navigation while the ship is going down."

As in most endeavors, the only reasonable advice that can be given is an appeal to balance and perspective—to strive for keeping research and its products in some proper relationship to the demands of everyday life. Certainly, an understanding of the limitations of science, which we have attempted to point out, should help keep such problems in perspective.

THE ETHICS OF SOCIAL RESEARCH

Ethics as an Urgent Issue

In recent years, the ethics of social research and scientific investigators has become a crucial issue as we have come to see, under the prodding of laypersons as well as sensitive researchers themselves, the moral dilemmas posed by some of our research techniques, uses, and applications. Previously, social researchers did their work without much concern about whether the rights of subjects were being violated, the motives of funding agencies were sullied, the uses to which their findings would ultimately be put were good, and so forth.

Part of this lack of concern for ethical issues in social science research can be traced to the fact that the objects of scientific inquiry are neither moral nor immoral—they are amoral. An atomic reaction is a natural process, and the fact that people may get in the way of such reactions (to say nothing of instigating them) has not been seen as ultimately the responsibility of the investigator. By modeling themselves after natural sciences, the social sciences have often argued for the same kind of immunity from ethical concerns. Indeed, a long-held stance of the scientist has been that of ethical neutrality, the idea that if we are to attain objectivity in our investigations, we must not take an ethical position with regard to our subject matter or the findings of our research.

This strict scientism, as our discussion of moon rocks pointed out, has not stood the test of close scrutiny. If a pure scientific investigation in theoretical physics like the government-sponsored Manhattan Project, which led to the development of the world's first atomic bomb, can produce the deaths of 250,000 people in a second, the project can hardly be exempted from ethical concerns, even though the atomic reaction itself was quite amoral. To control the circumstances of the release of such forces is, of course, to bring ethics into the picture if for no other reason than the fact that we can elect *not* to set such forces into motion. As our capability of controlling more and more of nature has increased, the question of ethics has similarly become more pressing, if only because the option of control leads to the option of no control, and this choice is the basis for all ethical questions. The reason nature itself is not concerned with ethics is that nature has no choice. The reason human beings are always concerned about ethics is that we do.

In the social sciences, because our objects of inquiry are really subjects (human beings and their activities), the concern over ethics is particularly well placed. The phenomena we study may not be of any ethical concern, but the study of them always is. This distinction between phenomena and inquiry into phenomena forms the basis of a consideration of ethics.

Methodology, at its most simplistic level, is about techniques of inquiry. Ethics, at its most simplistic level, is about good and bad. Obviously, a methodological technique may be either good or bad, not only technically, in terms of its effectiveness as a research instrument, but also in terms of its consequences for the people being researched, the society at large, and so on. Inquiry always has consequences: some obvious, some subtle, some long-term, some short-term, some good or bad from someone's point of view. A correlation between two social factors is without moral meaning, but the act of running the correlation, publishing the findings, acting on those findings, and so forth, does have moral consequences, and thus the study can be said to participate in this universe as well as the objective realm of scientific phenomena. In this closing section, it is important to mention some of the more prevalent ethical problems facing social researchers and to show how professionals have tried to systematize basic principles with which to handle them.

Deception. A major issue in social science research is the question of deception. Moral codes for centuries have condemned the practice of lying, and yet social scientists have been doing it for years (Warwick 1975). Strategies range from outright lies, in which experimental subjects are given false information, to the use of confederates as part of the group of subjects. A classic example is a study in social psychology by Rosenthal and Jacobson. In order to find out how much teacher expectations affect student performance, the researchers deceived a number of elementary-school teachers. They told them that certain children in their classes would do well academically and that others probably would not. They said these predictions were based on a test of "intellectual blooming." In fact, there were no significant differences in the children. At the end of the school year, the two researchers found what they had predicted: the children who were expected to achieve did so, and those who were not did not. They called this result the Pygmalion effect, and it has been repeated since in over two hundred separate studies, all of which have used essentially the same deceptive methodology.

Studies based on deception are very difficult to give up. For one thing, they have a dramatic effect and receive widespread publicity when reported. In addition, many researchers do not feel that valid information about various kinds of behavior can be obtained if subjects know the purpose of the experiment. In other words, a Pygmalion effect exists in human affairs. If people know the purpose of an experiment, they are likely to play to it or try to subvert it; in either case, the validity of the research is destroyed.

The ethical dilemmas posed by deceptive research can be obvious or quite subtle. In the case of the Rosenthal and Jacobson study, we can see the problems at a glance. Parents were furious when they discovered that their children had been used as guinea pigs without their knowledge or permission. Moreover, to create the possibilities for such failure and to cost a child a whole year in school for the benefit of proving something seems clearly wrong. On the other hand, the research was unethical to the very extent that it proved to be correct. Had there *not* been a Pygmalion effect, had the research not discovered the predicted relationship, the ethical dilemma posed would not have been nearly so great. The defense given by the researchers in this case is also compelling. They argued that the discovery of the Pygmalion effect has had a profound impact on teaching and that many children who might previously have been impaired by teacher expectations are now more likely to be taught by teachers who are aware of the problem and take steps to do something about it. In other words, we are on balance better for having done the study, even though some might have been hurt in the original doing of it.

Sometimes the deception is more subtle. All Laud Humphreys (1970) did in researching his classic book *Tearoom Trade* was to observe a particular kind of homosexual behavior occurring in public rest rooms, often called *tearooms* in the language of the gay world. In order to obtain information on those who frequented tearooms, Humphreys himself posed as a so-called watch queen. He observed impersonal sex acts between consenting homosexuals while at the same time faithfully signaling the participants if police or "straights" were about to enter the rest room.

Later, Humphreys engaged in a more serious form of deception by following up with a survey of the participants. Having gotten their license-plate numbers while serving as watch queen, he went to their homes doing a "market survey" in order actually to collect social and demographic data about them. He did not tell them that he was doing a study of homosexual behavior, of course, nor did he reveal that he knew they were homosexuals, and he maintained their anonymity by never revealing who they were. By doing his work in a public place, Humphreys minimized the deception to a certain extent. He also was a valid participant as well as an observer in the sense that he performed the role of watch queen competently. However, had his research interests been revealed, his work would have been much more difficult. And, although he was clearly sympathetic to the situation of the homosexuals, he still deceived them.

Humphreys's work set off a hailstorm of criticism and debate, both within the ranks of social scientists and from without. In a celebrated exchange between defenders and opponents, Horowitz and Rainwater defended Humphreys, while newspaper columnist Nicholas Von Hoffman castigated his work as an example of the bad ethics rampant in the field (Horowitz and Rainwater 1970; Von Hoffman 1970).

Horowitz and Rainwater defended Humphreys on two grounds. First, they said, he was sympathetic toward the plight of homosexuals and used his research in an effort to show that their behavior was harmless and did not warrant the police-state tactics being used to stop them. Second, such a strategy provided intimate knowledge of the homosexual world that social scientists did not previously have. Von Hoffman countered by saying that lofty ends do not justify snooping into the private lives of people and deceiving them by social scientists any more than by the CIA or the FBI.

Manipulation. Sometimes subjects are not only deceived but manipulated in ethically questionable ways. This type of methodology is most often employed in laboratory studies. In one of the most famous laboratory studies of our time, *Obedience to Authority,* Milgram (1974) used confederates who faked receiving an electric shock. His aim was to test whether ordinary citizens would engage in behavior that they believed was injuring someone if they were told that some high authority approved it.

A naive experimental subject is told that he or she is taking part in a study of learning with another subject (who is secretly a confederate of the researcher). The two draw to see who is the teacher and who is the subject, but the drawing is rigged so that the experimental subject will be the teacher and the confederate the learner. The subject watches as electrodes are pasted to the confederate's arm. The confederate says he or she is not sure about this procedure because of an earlier heart condition, but the experimenter assures him that everything is all right—the experiment might be painful to him but not harmful. All of this is enacted for the benefit of the experimental subject, who now understands that his supposed partner has a heart condition and will suffer some pain. The subject is then given a series of word pairs such as *nice–day* and *fat–neck* to read to the confederate. The list is then repeated, with the subject reading the first word and the confederate—who is now behind a partition—choosing the second from a list of four multiple-choice options. The learner pushes a button. If his answer is correct, the experimental subject goes on. If he is wrong, the subject pushes a switch that buzzes and supposedly gives him an electric shock.

The experiment begins with what the subject thinks is a 15-volt shock, and the voltage is then increased with every wrong answer. The control board goes from 15 to 450 volts, and also has verbal descriptions of the shock levels, ranging from "slight shock" to "danger: severe shock." If at any point the subject hesitates to push the button, the experimenter calmly tells him to go on. The idea of the study is to find the shock level beyond which the subject will refuse to push the button. A recording coming from behind the partition simulates the resistance from the confederate. The objections start with a grunt at 75 volts and build up to a "Hey, that really hurts" at 125 volts. The voice becomes desperate with "I can't stand the pain, don't do that!" at 180 volts, complains of heart trouble at 195, gives an agonized scream at 285, refuses to answer at 315, and then is silent.

The results were devastating. Believing at first that few people would go all the way through the board to the dangerous levels, Milgram found that virtually all subjects would, especially if they were encouraged by the authority of the experimenter. On the basis of these studies, Milgram concluded a number of important things about obedience to authority. Among them was his idea that, if Nazilike extermination camps were set up around the country, there would be little difficulty in recruiting ordinary citizens to staff them.

This is perhaps the most ingenious scheme of manipulative deception ever devised by a social science researcher, and Milgram has established a high academic reputation on the basis of it. The justification for it is the same: in the name of science, such manipulation is justified because it helps us understand more about human behavior.

Project Selection. In a perceptive section of their book on research methodology, Sjoberg and Nett (1968) point out that every research project holds the potential for changing the subjects under investigation if they know they are being researched either before the project or afterward. If the subject is an organization such as a corporation, business enterprise, or academic institution, a research project can have devastating consequences by pointing up the discrepancies between what the organization claims to be and what it turns out actually to be, given the findings of the research study. The political nature of this dilemma interposes with the ethical one. Conservatives tend to be cautious about upsetting the moral order and might find research to be a threat to what is already established. Political liberals often see themselves as having no vested interest in the prevailing order and wish to carry out research even if the results make it extremely difficult for the organization to continue as before. Both stances pose serious ethical dilemmas, as Sjoberg and Nett point out:

> Because the more conservative social scientist seeks to avoid controversy, and because social research by its very nature involves a degree of exposure, and therefore controversy, the conservative's actions may contravene some of the ideas of science, particularly that calling for freedom of inquiry. Moreover, the mere acceptance of the broader society's definition of what is right may lead one to support and advance policies that are fundamentally at odds with "man's welfare." Thus, many German scientists, who passively accepted the goals and norms of Naziism, were instrumental in aiding and abetting, through their work, the destruction of millions of Jews.
>
> On the other hand, the more liberally inclined may find themselves challenging through their research and analysis their own associational structure—the very system that underwrites and supports the scientific method. The liberal scientist may unwittingly collect data that could be used to question or challenge the democratic political system, some form of which is essential for sustaining social research. (1968, 122–123)

All of this is made even more confusing by the fact that so much of social research is funded by agencies that almost always have a vested interest in what is found out. Governments fund studies of social control; funeral directors fund studies to find out whether funerals are valuable; any number of groups fund evaluation research to find out if their programs are successful. Obviously, money has a way of getting in the way of objectivity, perhaps in subtle ways unrecognized even by the person doing the research.

Toward a Resolution

There can be no easy solution to the ethical dilemmas posed by our research. Several possibilities have been offered, all of which have both benefits and liabilities. Jung (1975) has suggested a time-consuming and expensive procedure in which a representative sample of a group about to be studied would be contacted to review the experimental procedures and advise what they consider to be the major ethical problems associated with them. The American Psychological Association advocates the use of a risk–benefit principle to see whether the potential benefits of a study employing deception or other questionable procedures outweigh its drawbacks. Such a judgment is left to the individual investigator, who, of course, is likely to see the benefits more than the risks, as we have already seen in the examples described.

Babbie (1975) has suggested a number of principles to guide us ethically in our research but concedes that any or all of them may need to be violated in order to obtain valid information in a research project. His principles include voluntary participation of subjects, no harm to the people being studied, respecting either anonymity or confidentiality of sources, and honesty in the analysis and reporting of research data findings. These principles are not always easily realized. For example, do we always know just how voluntary the participation of our subjects was? Even when a subject says that, yes, he or she will participate in a research project, we don't always know what kind of hidden agenda has gone into that decision. Perhaps the subject harbors a secret fear of harm if he or she doesn't cooperate. But whatever the reasons for volunteering, we cannot always be sure that it was a fully uncoerced act.

The idea that harm should not be done to the people studied is obvious, but it, too, may be difficult to carry out in practice. First, we can never know positively that people will not be hurt as a result of our research, because very few researchers fully control the uses to which their data are put. Furthermore, if we add to that the fact that subjects may be psychologically affected in a negative way by their participation in a research project, we can see that it becomes almost impossible to say that our research harmed no one. We can only guess what kind of psychological harm might have come to the subjects in Stanley Milgram's study.

Protecting the confidentiality of respondents is relatively easy to do, although it may require some extra work. If a researcher were studying deviant behavior, for example, he might have to hide identified interview schedules or questionnaires and even be prepared to go to jail were the police to subpoena such records in an effort to enforce existing laws against the people he was studying. One way around the problem is to ensure the anonymity of a respondent by designing the project so that even the researcher does not know the identity of subjects. For some types of projects that require only statistical information, this is reasonable. But for others, where the respondent is to be interviewed, it is obviously impossible.

In the analysis and reporting of the data from social research, there are so many ways to be dishonest that we could write a whole book about this topic alone. After having waded around in data and been party to the many difficulties that confront a researcher in the course of doing a project, the author of the report often knows full well the inadequacies of the research, and the moral dilemma often posed is, "Shall I relay the inadequacies to the reader or keep them to myself?" Theoretically, honesty is the best policy, but here is an area where all sorts of practical considerations can emerge that interfere with the workings of this norm. In no other single area of research does the reader rely so much on the integrity of the author of a research report.

This discussion of ethics may make it seem that producing honest, morally sound, and at the same time scientifically valid research is virtually impossible. And while ethics and good science sometimes conflict, it must also be pointed out that often they do not. Erikson has put it best: "It seems to me that any attempt to use masquerades in social research betrays an extraordinary disrespect for the complexities of human interaction, and for this reason can only lead to bad science" (1967, 373).

Chapter 2

Choosing and Formulating a Research Question

Defining terms
The role of values in choosing and formulating research questions
Factors influencing the choice of a research question
    Personal interests
        Personal experience
        Reading and intellectual pursuits
    Social concerns
    Chance
    Epilogue
Formulating a research question
    Learning about the subject: searching the literature
        Books
            Evaluating the reference
            Recording adequate information
        Scholarly journals
            Sociological abstracts
            Psychological abstracts
            Social science index
            Social science citation index
        Government documents
        Computer search
    Identifying the research impetus: reviewing the literature
        Testing theory
        Using theory to understand a research question
        Challenging prior research
        Clarifying an underlying process
        Attempting to account for unexpected findings
        Replication
        Seeing if a relationship in one area extends to another
Evaluating a research question
    Is it worthwhile?
    Is it feasible?
        What is the scope of the study?
        How much time is required?
        How much money is required?
        Are subjects available?
        Will subjects cooperate?
        Are the necessary equipment and facilities available?
    Is it ethical?

A prudent question is one-half of wisdom.
—Francis Bacon

One of the most difficult aspects of any endeavor is to begin, and research is no exception. The process by which a research problem is selected is, by its very nature, a creative process. It involves thinking about various ideas and issues, asking questions about them, and considering whether possible answers to these questions even exist. For most of us, it would be easier and certainly less painful if we could bypass this step and simply have someone tell us what to study. Creative thinking is hard work! However, this creative, largely intuitive searching process is a necessary and important first step in any research endeavor and one with which you need to be familiar.

The importance of studying this aspect of the research process is heightened by the fact that it is one of the least obvious steps in the research endeavor. As you begin to read published research, you will notice that almost all research endeavors begin with the research question. Just how this research question was chosen or formulated is seldom discussed. Thus, the reader is not given access to the creative processes that give rise to a particular question being asked in the first place. In fact, you may find already published research an inadequate model for helping you choose and formulate your own research question, for as we shall see, most published research does not guide you through the process of choice and formulation. And your own efforts to engage in this creative process may be infused with confusion and uncertainty. You may, for example, question whether you are going about the process of choosing and formulating a research question correctly. Accordingly, this chapter is about choosing and formulating research questions. Our task is to introduce you to the factors that can influence problem selection and formulation and to make this step in the research process more visible.

DEFINING TERMS

Before examining this selection and formulation process, it will be helpful to define what we mean by a research question and a research subject. The research question is just what it suggests—a question that can be answered by using the research process. It is important to note that not all questions capable of being devised by the human mind are answerable by scientific research. Questions of whether or not God exists, what the purpose of life is, how a person seeks the good, and other such broad philosophical questions are not answerable by scientific research. However, each of these questions might be translated into a question that would be answerable by the research process if we asked it in terms of what people think about the issue, how they act in relation to it, and so forth. In other words, questions about the *existence* of things that lie in the nonempirical world are outside the realm of science, but questions about people's opinions, attitudes, and actions toward these matters most definitely are within its province. It is difficult to know exactly what death is scientifically, but we can ask if and how attitudes toward life influence attitudes toward death.

Research questions are usually specific and encompass only a few variables. In contrast, a research subject is quite broad and general. Research subjects include friendship, interpersonal communication, juvenile delinquency, and marriage, just to name a few. There are many research questions that could be formulated on each of these research subjects. In general, we begin by identifying a research subject and then choosing and formulating a research question within that subject area. This process of choosing and formulating a research question within a research subject area is a filtering process that involves moving from the general to the specific.

THE ROLE OF VALUES IN CHOOSING AND FORMULATING RESEARCH QUESTIONS

We begin our discussion of this selection process with a controversial but important issue—the role of values in choosing and formulating research questions. The issue of value-free research in the social sciences is almost as old as the social sciences themselves. To illustrate, it might be helpful to look at the beginnings of just one social science: sociology. Sociology emerged from the widespread changes that the industrial revolution brought to Europe. Before the industrial revolution, societies could be characterized as tranquil and stable. But the industrial revolution threw societies into turmoil. Cities were growing very rapidly. This rapid growth was followed by an increase in crime. Social problems were becoming more prevalent. As a result, people were anxious for a way to explain and deal with these rapid changes. Sociology was the discipline that emerged to explain these social phenomena. We might say, then, that sociology's beginnings were not value-free, but arose in a context of societal problems and difficulties seeking solutions.

The idea of value-free sociology was introduced by Max Weber, who urged free and open research unrestrained by personal, social, political, and economic interests. It was this early challenge that gave sociology the autonomy required to make it a discipline in its own right. Even today, though, the issues of value-free sociology and value-free research remain with us and are discussed within the discipline.

We take the position that value-free sociology, or value-free science for that matter, is fiction, not fact. The commandment "Thou shalt not commit a value judgment" is simply not tenable. As we pointed out in Chapter 1, what a physiologist sees when he studies the brain is part of his own brain. If we recall Ian Mitroff's study of the moon rock scientists, we realize that our values *do* influence what we research and how we go about researching. As you have already learned, within any discipline, there are generally several paradigms or ways of looking at the reality being studied. There are different values for different paradigms, and the researcher's choice of paradigms is most likely influenced by his or her own values, background, and experiences, to say nothing of the restraints created by the fact that research is often by teams and with other people's money.

As scientists we cannot disrobe ourselves of our personhood, our selfhood. We cannot remove the cloak of culture when we enter the research setting. To even suggest that we can be value-free researchers in all phases of the research process is unrealistic. In truth, value-free research is impossible—so why pretend? Our fallacy as social scientists, though, is not that we are unable to isolate ourselves from our values. Rather, it lies in trying to kid ourselves that we can accomplish or have accomplished this end. If, as social scientists, we recognize that values are an integral part of who we are, both as persons and scientists, and we recognize what these values are, we are more ably prepared to see how they influence our choice of a research question and the way we choose to study that question. If we can see, for example, that our values are directing us toward a particular paradigm, we may not hold so tenaciously to that paradigm if research consistently fails to support it. In effect, recognizing our values places us in a more objective position. Value-free research cannot be our goal; value-aware research can. It is toward this end that we should strive.

FACTORS INFLUENCING THE CHOICE OF A RESEARCH QUESTION

Personal Interests

The role of values in the research process becomes even more apparent when we consider the single most important factor influencing the choice of a research question—personal interests. In general, scientists do research on questions that interest them. Certainly it is easier to endure the long research process if we are investigating a question that we personally like. Scientists who seek to uncover evidence of life after death, for example, most likely are personally fascinated by the subject. There is an old cliché in psychology that "researchers study their hang-ups." And such personal interest generally stems from either personal experience, or reading and other intellectual pursuits in a particular subject area.

Personal Experience. Much of what interests us evolves out of events that have happened to us. Robin Lakoff's research (1975) on language and women's place, for example, was born out of her own experiences and observations that language is sexist. As a result, she began to look at ways in which males and females use language in an effort to determine whether differences really did exist.

Phillip Goldberg's classic study (1976) on women's prejudices against women was also born out of his own personal experiences. Goldberg writes that in teaching his classes, he noticed marked differences between the males and the females. The women were bright, able, and hard-working, but they generally lacked intellectual aggressiveness. In contrast, the males were aggressive and quite willing to participate in classroom discussions. In Goldberg's words, "The girls could be counted on to do the work, the guys could be counted on to do the talking" (p. 155). Goldberg's evaluation of this situation was that women did not value themselves as they should. They were, he concluded, prejudiced against themselves—against women. As a result of this experience, Goldberg decided to devise an experiment that would allow him to test the hypothesis that women were prejudiced against women. Goldberg's thinking was confirmed.

One of the authors of this book also conducted an experiment that evolved out of a personal experience. The research concerned the effect of social class on tolerance for defeat (Guy and Allen 1975). The idea for this research was born out of a trip to a county fair. While at the fair, this researcher observed several dozen individuals put down quarter after quarter to play various games of luck and skill in hopes of winning a large stuffed animal. The question that came to mind was, "Just how long would someone be willing to try (tolerance) before he or she would give up (defeat), and what factors might affect this process?" The experiment devised to examine this issue required subjects to play both a game of luck and a game of skill. Tolerance for defeat was measured as the amount of time subjects were willing to play before giving up. As hypothesized, middle-class individuals were found to be more tolerant of defeat.

Reading and Intellectual Pursuits. There are many social phenomena that interest each of us but for which we have no direct experiences. We don't, for example, have to commit a criminal act to be interested in a specific type of criminal behavior. Sometimes our interests grow and develop out of our reading, studying, or various other intellectual pursuits (such as brainstorming). But that we would even choose to read or study in a certain subject area generally suggests an interest. And that interest will either blossom or wilt as we continue to read. If the interest grows, it is probably safe to assume that our curiosity has been further aroused and that we now have more questions than before. The more we read, the more we realize we do not know and the more curious we become. As you read in any subject area, it is a good idea to keep a file of questions that come to mind. Many of these questions will be researchable and could provide a basis for future research. If you are faithful in recording such "meteoric moments of mental magic," reading can be a valuable avenue for identifying new research questions.

Social Concerns

Still another factor affecting the choice of a research question is the social concerns of the day. There are those social scientists who prefer to do research in areas that demonstrate immediate social applicability. The issues must be socially and politically relevant. The last decade, for example, has witnessed an influx of research in the area of aging. This wave of interest has been due in large part to the increased attention the government has given to the elderly as a group. With both the birth and death rates dropping, the average age in the United States has been steadily increasing. Today, the elderly comprise a large segment of our population. In recognition of this segment, a great deal of research has been aimed at understanding this aspect of the life cycle.

Chance

One additional factor that can influence the choice of a research question deserves mention—chance. Sometimes we just happen to be in the right place at the right time. Many students who are pursuing master's or doctoral degree programs, for example, find themselves doing research in a particular area because they just happened to be paired with a particular professor. You may find yourselves doing research in a subject area because you just happened to get into a particular section of a methods class. If chance is the overriding factor in your choice of a research question, perhaps your interest in the question will be stimulated as you steadfastly pursue knowledge.

Epilogue

It is interesting to notice that spontaneity plays an important role with each of these selection factors. Quite often the research question does not evolve through our concerted efforts to be creative. Creativity is difficult to force. Rather, it emerges quite unexpectedly through the avenues of personal interests, personal experiences, intellectual exercises, social concerns, or chance. You should not construe this to mean that you could not sit down and derive a research question through creative processes. You probably could. But when research questions can emerge so naturally, you only need to be aware of these creative moments and take note. Most likely some of your best research questions will just come to you when you least expect it. Don't fight it; try to capitalize on it by maximizing the chances for such moments.

FORMULATING A RESEARCH QUESTION

Learning about the Subject: Searching the Literature

Let's assume that you now have decided on a research subject and that you are ready to choose and formulate a research question. It perhaps goes without saying that you will not be able to manage an entire research subject. As we have already learned, research subjects are generally quite broad and seldom sharply defined. To say, for example, that you are interested in doing research on marriage is much too broad. Even to say that you wish to do research on marital happiness is too broad, but it provides a better starting point than just marriage. In effect, it becomes necessary to focus on some small aspect or at least some manageable aspect of the research subject. For example, you might elect to examine the effect of children on marital happiness or the relationship between retirement and marital happiness. As we have indicated, this process of moving from research subject to research question is a filtering process. This process of sifting and fine-tuning will result in a research question that is both narrow and concrete.

This filtering process, though, is not automatic. Even though you may be able to identify a subject (e.g., marital happiness) that you would like to research, you are probably not knowledgeable about the research that has already been conducted on this subject. Consequently, you may be at a loss to initiate this filtering process. You may have some difficulty narrowing down the research subject to a specific research question. To be able to formulate a research question, then, you need to make some discoveries. You must first discover what research has already been done (re-search) and then use this information as a basis for deciding exactly what you want to do. We call this process of discovering a *search of the literature*. Primarily, this search of the literature generally requires the use of several types of reference materials including books, scholarly journals, government documents, and any other relevant sources.

Books. Often, students prefer to begin their search of the literature by looking for books related to their research subject. No doubt, this is partly because books are so familiar to us. As a child, you probably made frequent trips to the public library. As a college student, you have probably used the books in your library in writing English term papers.

A list of the books in any library can be found in the library's card catalog. Card catalogs are organized in three ways: (1) by subject, (2) by author, (3) by title. If you know very little about a research subject and are seeking to make discoveries, the most useful of these indexes will be the subject index. (See Figure 2.1.) The subject index provides a listing of all books organized by subject headings. For example, if you were interested in the subject marital happiness, this might be one subject heading in the subject index. Using the subject index, though, can be just like using the Yellow Pages—frustrating! No single subject heading will provide all relevant references. You will need to make a list of related subject headings and look for each of them. With respect to marital happiness, for example, you might also look under the subject headings marriage, family relationships, and divorce. Also, individual references will sometimes provide you with additional subject headings. In fact, most of the time, when additional subject headings are appropriate, they are listed on the card catalog.

The remaining two card catalogs differ only in that the organizing information is either the author's name or the title of the book. If you discover, for example, that a particular author has written one book related to your research subject, you may wish to check the author index to see if he or she has written any other related books.

EVALUATING THE REFERENCE   As you locate the catalog cards for books that are subject-appropriate, you will have to decide which

**FIGURE 2.1
Catalog Card
Indexed by Subject**

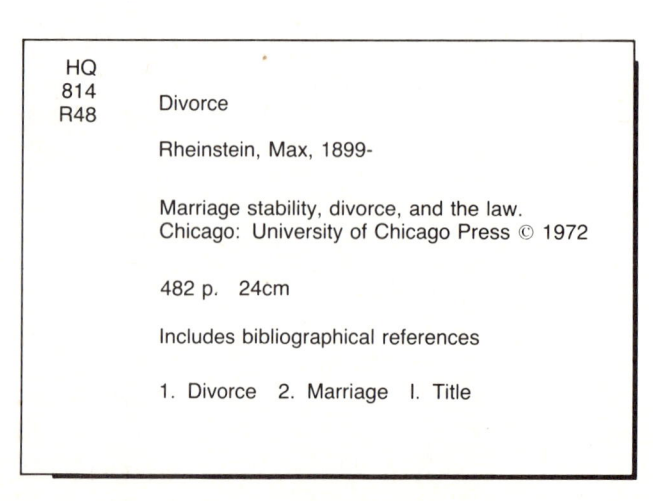

```
HQ
814
R48        Divorce

           Rheinstein, Max, 1899-

           Marriage stability, divorce, and the law.
           Chicago: University of Chicago Press © 1972

           482 p.   24cm

           Includes bibliographical references

           1. Divorce   2. Marriage   I. Title
```

references to retain and which to eliminate. This is particularly so if you have retrieved an overabundance of book references. Carol Williams and Gary Wolfe (1979) list seven factors to consider when deciding on whether to retain or reject a reference. Most of the time the card catalog will provide you with enough information to evaluate these factors.

1. *The book is out of date.* Generally speaking, five years ages a reference. And unless the work either is considered a "classic" in the area or stands as the only research in the area, more current references should be sought.
2. *The book is too elementary.* Most of the time, for example, you would not use introductory texts as main sources.
3. *The book is too advanced or technical.* If you found a book that described the marriage relationship in mathematical terms, you might decide to skip the reference. You might choose, though, to consult this reference at some later point when you have done more reading.
4. *The book treats an aspect of the subject you do not wish to cover.* A book on long-distance marriages—in which the two partners' careers force them to live in separate cities—would probably be discarded unless you were researching the influence of this factor on marital happiness.
5. *The author and publisher information suggests that the book may not be sufficiently authoritative.* Greater familiarity with the subject may be required to make this judgment.
6. *You have already consulted the book.*
7. *The book contains information you already have from other sources.*

RECORDING ADEQUATE INFORMATION   If, after considering each of these factors, you believe that the reference can be useful to you, you will need to make out a bibliography card. (See Figure 2.2.) In making out this card, be sure to include all information that would be required to find this

FIGURE 2.2
Bibliography Card

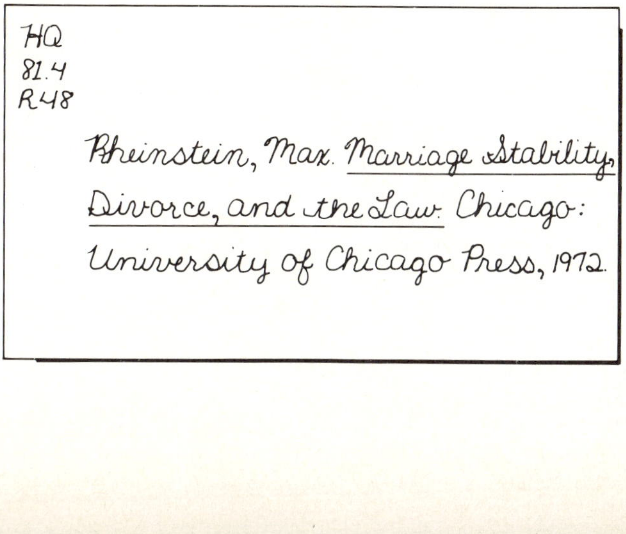

```
HQ
81.4
R48

    Rheinstein, Max. Marriage Stability,
    Divorce, and the Law. Chicago:
    University of Chicago Press, 1972.
```

book later in your library: (1) call numbers, (2) author(s), (3) title, and (4) date of publication. In addition, you should record any other information that would be required for footnotes or bibliographical references in your paper—most notably the publisher and the place of publication.

Scholarly Journals. Although the card catalog is often the first place students turn in trying to make discoveries about their research subject, it is not usually the most productive source. Quite frequently, the greatest amount of information is obtained from reading the scholarly journals. But herein lies a problem. There are hundreds of scholarly journals. Each is generally published several (two to six or even twelve) times per year, and each issue contains several articles. Consequently, when we talk of scholarly articles, we are talking about thousands of articles per year. If we went to the library with the intention of perusing these journal articles to find those which are related to our research subject area, it would take forever—and we would probably overlook many. Fortunately much of the guesswork and legwork has been taken out of this search. Just as the card catalog provides us with an indexing of published books, there are catalog-type sources that provide us with an indexing of the scholarly articles.

Sources that will be of substantial benefit to you in your search include the various *abstracts*. Abstracts are brief summaries of the major points of articles, usually written by the authors of the articles. Most likely, a search of the abstracts will be helpful to you regardless of the number of published articles on a subject. If there are very few articles on a particular subject, without the abstracts you may have trouble locating them. If there are many articles, you will need the abstracts to help you eliminate those which are not relevant. Two of the most used abstracts in the social sciences include the *Sociological Abstracts* and the *Psychological Abstracts*. Additional sources worth examining are various *indexes*. Indexes differ from abstracts in that they provide only bibliographical information—no brief summary. Two of the most used indexes include *Social Science Index* and *Social Science Citation Index*. Let's take a brief look at each of these abstracts and indexes. (See Figure 2-3 for sample entries.)

SOCIOLOGICAL ABSTRACTS   The *Sociological Abstracts* are a "collection of nonevaluative abstracts which reflects the world's serial literature in sociology and related disciplines" (*Sociological Abstracts*, 1981, preface). Each issue contains the following:

> Table of contents
> The citations and abstracts themselves
> Supplements
> A. IRPS (The International Review of Publications in Sociology)
>   i. Book abstracts
>   ii. Bibliography of reviews

B. Abstracts of papers presented at major sociological association meetings
Indexes
A. Author
B. Source
C. Subject

In addition, some issues contain abstracts of conference papers.

Sociological Abstracts assigns each article a four-digit code that serves to classify it. There are thirty-three major classifications into which articles may be coded. And for each major classification, there are subcategories that provide even further refinement. These major classifications are listed in Table 2.1. An article is classified in the section of *Sociological Abstracts* to which it is viewed as being most relevant. If two sections seem equally relevant, it is placed in the section where it will be most noticed.

Sociological Abstracts provides three indexes of articles: subject, author, and source. The subject index is a listing of assigned article codes organized by subject headings. The author index is a listing of authors and accession numbers by titles. As an additional aid, a cumulative index (of subjects, authors, and sources) is published at the end of each year. The subject index of this cumulative volume is composed of approximately five thousand key terms that appear in boldface type. Each entry appears with an informative or descriptive phrase to give the reader some idea of the article's content.

Let's suppose that you wished to locate the published research on marital happiness. You might begin by examining the listings in each issue classified under "The Family and Socialization." Following this search, you might use the subject index in the cumulative index volume to make sure that you didn't miss any references. If a particular journal seems appropriate (e.g., *Journal of Marriage and the Family*), you might check the source index for a listing of the articles in that journal.

If, from reading the brief summaries of these articles, you feel that an article is relevant, you should make a bibliography card. Information recorded should include author, title of article, journal name, volume number, date, and pages. On each bibliography card, be sure to record the code assigned to the article by *Sociological Abstracts*. As you move from each of the five yearly issues of *Sociological Abstracts* to the cumulative index for that year, some repetition of references is inevitable. If you have recorded the assigned codes, you may find that you have already examined many of these references, and you will not lose time looking them up again.

PSYCHOLOGICAL ABSTRACTS *Psychological Abstracts* are similar to *Sociological Abstracts*, providing brief summaries for the articles published in some 950 journals that are international in scope. Each issue is divided

TABLE 2.1 Classifications for *Sociological Abstracts* and *Psychological Abstracts*

Sociological Abstracts	*Psychological Abstracts*
methodology and research technology	general psychology
sociology: history and theory	psychometrics
social psychology	experimental psychology (human)
group interactions	
culture and social structure	experimental psychology (animal)
complex organizations (management)	
social change and economic development	physiological psychology
	physiological intervention
mass phenomena	communication systems
political interactions	developmental psychology
social differentiation	social processes and social issues
rural sociology and agricultural economics	experimental social psychology
	personality
urban structures and ecology	physical and psychological disorders
sociology of the arts	
sociology of education	treatment and prevention
sociology of religion	professional personnel and professional issues
social control	
sociology of science	educational psychology
demography and human biology	applied psychology
the family and socialization	
sociology of health and medicine	
social problems and social welfare	
sociology of knowledge	
community development	
policy, planning, forecasting, and speculation	
radical sociology	
environmental interactions	
studies in poverty	
studies in violence	
feminist studies	
Marxist sociology	
clinical sociology	
sociology of business	
visual sociology	

into sixteen major classifications, each of which is further subdivided for finer distinctions. These sixteen classifications are listed in Table 2.1. Additionally, an index volume is published every six months and a cumulative index volume every three years. These index issues provide both subject and author listings. The subject listings are similar to those in *Sociological Abstracts* and are identified by boldface type. As in *Sociological*

Abstracts, the index volume provides only a brief description of the study along with the code assigned by *Psychological Abstracts.* Again, if you think that the reference can be useful, you should record the necessary information on a bibliography card.

SOCIAL SCIENCE INDEX   *Social Science Index* is an index to 263 social science periodicals. This index first appeared in June 1974 and is published four times a year. *Social Science Index* continues the indexing of seventy-seven periodicals previously covered by the *Social Science and Humanities Index,* which is no longer published. This index consists of author and subject entries in one alphabetical list. Book reviews are organized separately. Both the author and subject entries appear in boldface type.

SOCIAL SCIENCE CITATION INDEX   One additional index to the scholarly journals that can be quite beneficial deserves our attention, as it is somewhat different from the previously cited sources. The brochure of the *Social Science Citation Index* (*SSCI*) reports that it "indexes every article and every significant editorial item from every issue of over 1000 of the world's most important social science journals. In addition, *SSCI* selectively covers another 2200 journals indexing only those articles perceived as relevant to the social sciences." *SSCI* provides two indexing schemes: citation index and permuterm.

Citation indexing is based on the premise that an author's references (citations) to previously published material indicate a subject relationship between his or her current article and the older publications. In effect, articles that cite the same references usually have subject relationships with each other. Using this basic assumption, *SSCI* groups together all newly published articles that have cited the same earlier publication. Thus, the basis for organizing references is the author's own use of references.

Permuterm indexing uses the descriptors provided by the authors in the titles of their articles. The author's titles are taken just as they are published, and every significant term is used as a retrieval term. Every term in the title is paired (permuted) with every other term in that title to create a series of two-level indexing terms for each article. Thus, this procedure, like the other, indexes the articles just as they are described by their authors.

Although *SSCI* is complete and comprehensive, you should not use it to the exclusion of *Sociological Abstracts, Psychological Abstracts, Social Science Index,* or other relevant sources. Cataloging references around citations and title key words is certainly not foolproof. These techniques will not always uncover all relevant research. Consequently, other sources need to be examined. In fact, if there are relevant older references that several articles keep citing, you will probably not know this until you

FIGURE 2.3
Samples of Entries from Abstracts and Indexes

The Family & Socialization

This entry was taken from "The Family and Socialization" section of one of the five issues of *Sociological Abstracts*. This is the only entry of this article that provides bibliographical information and an abstract. The author, source, and subject indexes found in this same issue will refer to this article by its accession number which is in the upper-left corner.

8507129

Demaris, Alfred (Auburn U, AL 36849), **A Comparison of Remarriages with First Marriages on Satisfaction in Marriage and Its Relationship to Prior Cohabitation,** UM *Family Relations*, 1984, 33, 3, July, 443–449.

¶ Marital satisfaction of 122 remarried vs 187 first-married white couples aged 20–45 living in Gainesville, Fla, was examined & compared on the basis of questionnaire responses. Additionally, remarriers were compared to first marriers with respect to cohabitation before marriage & its effect on current marital satisfaction. No significant differences were found between first-married & remarried individuals in either marital satisfaction or the propensity to cohabit before marriage. Cohabitation was associated with significantly lower satisfaction among individuals in first marriages, while, among remarried persons, cohabitation made no difference in current marital satisfaction. 3 Tables, 20 References. Modified HA

Subject Index

This entry was taken from the subject index of the cumulative index volume. Notice that the accession number matches the code of the above entry. In order to obtain the bibliographical information for this article, the above abstract would have to be located in one of the five yearly issues.

Marriage/Marriages/Marital

major depression, middle-aged women; social setting/income/marital status/employment/adversity/religiosity; community survey; depressed/normal women, Sweden; O7271

marital breakdown; childlessness, birth timing; General Household Survey data, divorce records; married females, GB; O7021

marital mobility/homogamy, Spain; spouse's parents' education/occupation; questionnaire survey; Madrid & Guadalajara 1975/76; O6662

[marital satisfaction, Moscow, USSR; self-diagnostic questionnaire tested; O7150]

marital satisfaction; remarriage vs first marriage, prior cohabitation; questionnaires; white couples, aged 20–45; O7129

marriage alliance, kinship; literacy; ethnographic data; Angkola Batak, Sumatra, Indonesia; O6307

Developmental Psychology

This entry was taken from the "Developmental Psychology" section of one of the issues. This is the only entry of this article providing bibliographical information and an abstract. The author and subject indexes will list this article by its assigned code only.

840 Perlman, Daniel; Gerson, Ann C. & Spinner, Barry. (U Manitoba, Winnipeg, Canada) Loneliness among senior citizens: An empirical report. *Essence,* 1978, Vol 2(4), 239–248.—Reports an empirical study of loneliness among 158 senior citizens (average age 70 yrs) in Canada, each of whom completed a self-administered questionnaire. Greater loneliness was associated with less friendship contact, fewer close friends, social anxiety, ineffectiveness in influencing others, low marital satisfaction, and low life satisfaction. Lonely respondents watched more TV, would have liked more planned activities, and had difficulty getting transportation to places where they wanted to go. Furthermore, loneliness was linked with poor hearing ability, poor health, and having a lower income. Finally, being lonely was correlated with a variety of recently experienced emotions (e.g., feeling restless, bored, and angry). (French summary) (14 ref)—*Journal abstract.*

Subject Index

This is an entry taken from the subject index of the three-year cumulative index volume. Notice that the assigned code matches the number of the above entry. In order to get the bibliographical information for this article, the above entry would have to be located.

Marital Problems [See Marital Relations]
Marital Relations [See Also Marital Conflict]
analysis of Catholic family triads with 14–17 yr old daughters, application of circumplex model of family & marital systems, 7841
attitudes toward change in marital relationships, permanence of relationships, counseling implications, 8442
bases of power & communication processes, family planning & birth control decision making, husbands & wives, 12388

•
•
•

family systems approach to marital & family conflict, reduction of extreme itching, 16 yr old female and her parents, 12935
females as perpetrators & victims of domestic & other violence, 10623
[friendship contact & number of friends & social anxiety & ineffectiveness in influencing others & marital & life satisfaction, loneliness & amount of TV watching, aged, 840]

(Continued)

FIGURE 2.3
(Continued)

high achievement in late adolescent task development, subsequent marital adjustment, married college students & student spouses, implications for developmental counseling model, 883

Social Sciences Index

Excerpted entries from *Social Sciences Index*.

Marini, Margaret Mooney
  Age and sequencing norms in the transition to adulthood. bibl *Soc Forces* 63:228–44 S '84
  Women's educational attainment and the timing of entry into parenthood. bibl *Am Sociol Rev* 49:491–511 Ag '84

Marital age
  Age at marriage, role enactment, role consensus, and marital satisfaction. S. J. Bahr and others. bibl *J Marriage Fam* 45:795–803 N '83; Discussion. 46:985–8 N '84
  Early marriage as a career contingency: the prediction of educational attainment. G. D. Lowe and D. D. Witt. bibl *J Marriage Fam* 46:689–98 Ag '84
  Out of sequence: the timing of marriage following a premarital birth. J. D. Teachman and K. A. Polonko. bibl *Soc Forces* 63:245–60 S '84
  Professional women and marriage. S. M. Allen and R. A. Kalish. bibl *J Marriage Fam* 46:375–82 My '84
  The social and demographic correlates of divorce and separation in the United States: an update and reconsideration. N. D. Glenn and M. Supancic. bibl *J Marriage Fam* 46:563–75 Ag '84

Marital instability. *See* Divorce

Marital satisfaction
  See also
  Kansas marital satisfaction scale
  Age at marriage, role enactment, role consensus, and marital satisfaction. S. J. Bahr and others. bibl *J Marriage Fam* 45:795–803 N '83; Discussion. 46:985–8 N '84
  Agreement, understanding, realization, and feeling understood as predictors of commu-

...nicative satisfaction in marital dyads. A. Allen and T. Thompson. bibl *J Marriage Fam* 46: 915–21 N '84

Excerpted entries from *Social Science Citation Index*®. Notice the link to the *Sociological Abstracts* reference. (Copied with the permission of the Institute for Scientific Information, © 1985.)

ARMSTRONG D			VOL	PG	YR
WEINMAN J	MED EDUC		18	164	84
80 MED ED PRIMARY HLTH					
ATKINSON P	SOCIAL SC M		19	949	84
82 ANN NEUROL 12 169					
SEE SCI FOR 1 ADDITIONAL CITATION					
ATKINSON JB	ARCH PATH L		106	341	84
82 RISE INT ORG SHORT H					
BAER GW	AM HIST REV	B	88	1250	83
83 MAY INT PERS MAN ASS					
BURKE MJ	J APPL PSYC		69	482	84
83 POLITICAL ANATOMY BO					
BELLABY P	SOCIOL REV	B	32	433	84
CHALFANT HP	SOCIAL FORC	B	63	610	84
MAGNER LN	AM SCIENT	B	72	218	84
SOFFER RN	AM HIST REV	B	89	445	84
WARREN CAB	CONT SOCIOL	B	13	622	84
83 POLITICAL ANATOMY BO		CH 3			
ARMSTRON D	SOCIAL SC M		18	737	84
84 ACQUIRED IMMUNE DEFI					
WEBER J	LANCET	B	1	714	84

begin to read the literature. Thus, *SSCI* will likely be more useful after you have gained some degree of familiarity with the literature.

Government Documents. Most libraries reserve an area for government documents, which might include U.S. Census reports, the findings of studies commissioned by various government agencies, statistics published by various government offices, and the like. Some of these documents might be useful for your research. For example, if you were researching some aspect of marital happiness, you might wish to have the latest statistics on the percentage of the U.S. adult population who are married, divorced, and single. Certainly, you should consider using this section of your library.

Computer Search. If, by now, you have the idea that a search of the literature is no small job, you are right. If this search is done thoroughly and correctly, you may have to spend several days or even weeks in the library. But some of this time can be saved by an innovation of today's modern technology. If you do not wish to conduct a self-search of the published literature, you may conduct a computer search. Computer searches generally identify relevant references by using key terms from the articles' titles and abstracts (brief summaries). The data bases for these computer searches are the abstracts and indexes we have already discussed (*Sociological Abstracts, Psychological Abstracts, Social Science Index, Social Science Citation Index*, etc.). The information in these sources has simply been stored in computer memory. Retrieved references can be sorted alphabetically by author or chronologically by year. The fee for such searches can range from $10.00 to possibly $500.00 or even more. Most institutions that perform such searches will ask the requester to place a price ceiling on the search. Most large university libraries are generally equipped to perform such searches. In addition, the indexing publications (*Sociological Abstracts, Psychological Abstracts*) perform such searches, and information on how to obtain such a search through these publishing organizations can be found in most issues of these publications.

Identifying the Research Impetus: Reviewing the Literature

The filtering process has begun. In searching the various indexes (card catalog, abstracts, etc.) for research related to your research subject, you have retained some references and rejected others. This filtering process has allowed you to narrow the research subject. You may, for example, have retained those references relating marital happiness and retirement but discarded those references concerned with the effect of children on marital happiness. In effect, filtering has allowed you to eliminate certain aspects of the research subject. But you are not yet ready to formulate the research question. In order to accomplish this task, you need to know more than just what research has been done. You need to be familiar with the knowledge communicated through this body of research. In other words, you now need to read or review this literature. Reviewing the literature will help you to identify the established findings on your chosen research subject. Understanding and organizing these findings will help to provide the impetus for your own research question.

By research impetus we mean the motivating forces or factors that lead to a specific research question. One purpose of research is to further knowledge, and your research should be no exception. No single research endeavor stands alone. In the social sciences, it has become customary to begin research by citing previous research. To this extent, the impetus for all research is some previous research. As you review the research literature, you should read with the idea of linking your research to previous research. This linking will help to provide the impetus for your research and thus lead to the formulation of your research question.

There is no single research impetus that adequately accounts for the bulk of research questions formulated in any research subject area. Rather, there are several motivating factors out of which research questions are formulated, and each is important in its own right. Selltiz et al. (1976) have identified several such factors, including (1) testing theory, (2) using theory to understand a research question, (3) challenging prior research, (4) clarifying an underlying process, (5) attempting to account for unexpected findings, (6) replication, and (7) seeing if research in one area extends to another. Let's see how each of these factors can provide the impetus for a specific research question.

Testing Theory. Sometimes the primary impetus for a specific research question is to test theory. We will talk about theory in detail in Chapter 3. At this point, it might be helpful to think of theory as a set of postulates, logically linked to provide a plausible explanation of some social phenomena. Let us illustrate with an interesting study. In late September in the early 1950s, a newspaper carried the following headlines on a back page: "Prophecy from Planet. Clarion Call to City. Flee That Flood. It'll Swamp Us on Dec. 21, Outer Space Tells Suburbanite." The story followed:

> Lake City will be destroyed by a flood from Great Lake just before dawn, December 21, according to a suburban housewife. Mrs. Marian Keech of 847 West School Street says the prophecy is not her own. It is the purport of many messages she has received by automatic writing. The messages, according to Mrs. Keech, are sent to her by superior beings from a planet called "Clarion." These beings have been visiting the earth, she says, in what we call flying saucers. During their visits, she says, they have observed fault lines in the earth's crust that foretoken the deluge. Mrs. Keech reports that she was told the flood will spread to form an inland sea stretching from the Arctic Circle to the Gulf of Mexico. (Festinger et al. 1956, 30)

This newspaper account was read by Leon Festinger, a psychologist, who thought that Mrs. Keech and her followers would provide an interesting study on attitude change. Festinger had been working on a theory of attitude formation and change that he labeled cognitive dissonance theory. Cognitive dissonance theory suggests that when individuals are faced with two or more obverse facts (one fact does not follow from the other), either the facts must be made to agree or attitude change will occur. Festinger viewed Mrs. Keech and her followers as an ideal group for testing his theory. If the flying saucer was to land on a designated date as Mrs. Keech predicted and yet it did not land, cognitive dissonance should result, according to Festinger. And the group could resolve this dissonance by either changing the facts or by changing their attitudes and beliefs. By concocting stories of communication with extraterrestrial beings, two of Festinger's graduate assistants were able to join the group. (We will reserve judgment about the ethics of this project until later.) As participants, they were able to observe the natural behaviors of all group members and to record the changes that group members underwent as they waited for the flying saucer. Their observations and written accounts provided substantial support for Festinger's theory of cognitive dissonance.

Festinger's theory of cognitive dissonance has been repeatedly tested since its inception in 1957. Festinger and Carlsmith (1959) devised an ingenious laboratory test of this theory. Students participated in an experiment requiring them to work on a boring task. Upon completion of the task, each student was asked to inform the incoming student that the task was pleasant and even exciting. For communicating this information, some students were paid $1.00 and others were paid $20.00. Festinger and Carlsmith reasoned that the students paid $1.00 should experience greater cognitive dissonance, as $1.00 was not sufficient reward to justify the bold lie. The experimental findings confirmed the hypothesis and thus provided a test of the theory. In any field, when theory is constructed, one must test it by means of numerous research endeavors. Such research is essential if we are to know the extent to which the theory is supported.

Using Theory to Understand a Research Question. Sometimes the impetus of research is not to test theory per se, but simply to use theory as an aid in understanding and answering a research question. In effect, it provides a perspective through which the research question can be viewed. To illustrate, in the late 1950s and early 1960s, Thibaut and Kelly (1959) and Homans (1961) independently formulated theories on interpersonal attraction. Both theories explain interpersonal attraction in terms of the rewards exchanged and the costs incurred. Specifically, a person (P) is attracted to other (O) when, in the course of interacting, O offers P more rewards than costs. When a person's profits (rewards minus costs) are directly proportional to investments, the result is distributive justice, a concept discussed by George Homans (1961).

Out of this research on distributive justice grew equity theory, which suggests that individuals compare their inputs to their outcomes and expect to get as much as they give. If the outcome is not proportional to the input, dissatisfaction results. Shafer and Keith (1980) have conducted an interesting study in which they use equity theory as a basis for understanding depression among married couples. Specifically, they have applied equity principles to the study of performance in certain marital roles or tasks. In marriage, they reason, there generally exists a division of labor that provides role expectations for both husband and wife. These expectations include not only role performance but also the quality of that performance. Shafer and Keith suggest that both husband and wife make determinations about the fairness of their own and their partner's role performances. They propose that marriage partners who perceive inequity in the performance of marital roles will feel more psychological distress than partners who perceive equity. They further propose that marriage partners who perceive that they are overbenefited will feel less psychological distress than partners who perceive that they are underbenefited. Their findings support the first proposition and are in the stated direction of the second. Thus, they conclude that equity theory is helpful in understanding depression among married couples.

Challenging Prior Research. Frequently the impetus of research is simply to challenge some previous research. Recognized research seldom goes unchallenged. As we have already discovered, social scientists are different enough that they quite often see things differently. When this is the case, research often serves to challenge. Research, for example, has clearly demonstrated sex differences in nonverbal communication. That is, males and females have been shown to use nonverbal cues differently (Henley 1977). These sex-specific models of nonverbal behavior have been labeled *genderlects*. Lamb (1981) has challenged such research, suggesting that though a few forms of nonverbal behavior may be sex-specific, "in general, they reflect patterns of power and control between the sexes, which are found in all human groups regardless of sex composition" (p. 43). Consequently, Lamb believes that these modes of nonverbal cues are perhaps more appropriately labeled *powerlects*. Lamb believed if he could demonstrate these patterns of nonverbal behavior in same-sex groups, he would have evidence of powerlects instead of genderlects. His findings show that females are just as consistent as males in using these forms of control with members of their own sex, suggesting that power rather than sex is the important factor in these nonverbal and paraverbal modes of communication.

Clarifying an Underlying Process. Sometimes, independent research endeavors that test similar hypotheses produce inconsistent and even contradictory findings. Since there is usually any number of logical and plausible explanations for these differences, research is often undertaken in an effort to clarify. Self-disclosure research provides an excellent example of such research inconsistencies. Self-disclosure can be described as the communication of intimacy or the act of revealing personal information to others. Research on self-disclosure has generally assumed self-disclosure to be a reward or positive outcome. This assumption would suggest a positive relationship between self-disclosure and attraction. That is, the more revealing the self-disclosure, the greater the attraction between the people concerned. However, existing research on self-disclosure and attraction is actually inconsistent. Although several studies demonstrate a positive relationship between self-disclosure and attraction, there are other studies that suggest a negligible or nonsignificant relationship and still others that indicate a negative relationship between these two variables.

Gilbert and Horenstein (1975) designed a study aimed at clarifying these inconsistencies. Their insight into the inconsistencies was derived from an earlier study by Gilbert (1972) in which a negative relationship between self-disclosure and attraction had been demonstrated. That is, subjects were found to be more attracted to a person (a confederate) who disclosed him- or herself less. Gilbert noted, though, that the low disclosure consisted of mild positive content (a woman's feelings about her brother who was getting married), while the high disclosure consisted of negative content (a woman's negative feelings about her mother and herself). Drawing from this observation, Gilbert and Horenstein suggested that perhaps the inconsistencies in the research on self-disclosure and attraction might be due to previous studies' failure to distinguish between the degree of intimacy (high or low) and the valence (positive or negativeness) of self-disclosure and their relationship to interpersonal attraction. With this in mind, a total of eighty males and females were assigned to one of four experimental conditions: (1) high positive, (2) low positive, (3) high negative, and (4) low negative. Their findings showed that subjects demonstrated the greatest degree of attraction when the disclosure content was positive, regardless of the degree of intimacy of the disclosure.

Attempting to Account for Unexpected Findings. Sometimes research efforts produce the unexpected. The patterns that emerge from the data are unforeseen. When such findings emerge, we label them serendipitous (unexpected, unanticipated). But it is not enough to just note the occurrence of serendipitous findings. Further research is often undertaken to determine whether or not these findings will reoccur. In 1976, Inbar and Adler published an article entitled "The Vulnerable Age Phenomenon: a Serendipitous Finding." The "vulnerable age phenomenon" refers to the finding that "children in about the 6 to 11 year-old bracket may be more vulnerable to crises in their environment than either younger or older youths" (Inbar 1976, 5). This finding surfaced in a cross-cultural study of immigrants. The impetus to search for this finding was a case study by Martan (1972) investigating the school achievements of children as a function of the impact of the Israeli educational system on youths. Martan expected to find a negative relationship between age of children and successful schooling (measured as the percentage having attended college). That is, a greater percentage of the younger children as compared with the older children would be more likely to attend college. This expectation was based on the notions that younger children learn a new language faster than older youths and that language problems for adolescents translated into school failures. Contrary to expectation, a positive relationship was found between age of children at immigration and chances of attending college. Specifically, younger children were less likely to attend college than older youths.

Martan's serendipitous finding served as a starting point for Inbar and Adler. Since Inbar and Adler were already planning a cross-cultural study of immigrants, they decided to look for the vulnerable age phenomenon. (See Table 2.2.) And, in fact, their study also demonstrated this phenomenon. Following this study, Inbar sought even further evidence of the vulnerable age phenomenon in two additional studies. In both studies the phenomenon was again documented. Inbar and Adler (1976) explain this phenomenon as a function of stress resulting from school transfers. While older children can articulate their problems, younger children sometimes have difficulty. Thus, the problems encountered by grade-school children often go unnoticed. When serendipitous findings occur, new research is needed. Without new research, we cannot know if the finding is reliable (will occur again) or is simply one of chance.

Replication. If the social sciences are to establish a rigorous body of knowledge, research must be replicated. It is simply not enough to say that one study produces fact. Any study has its limitations—of time, places, people. We might ask, for example, for any study, "Would the findings hold for another group of people? For another place? For another time?" Inbar (1976) attempted to replicate the vulnerable age phenomenon to see if it would hold for another group, in another place, at another time.

In the social sciences, as we have learned, replication is generally the exception, not the rule. However, there have been some studies where the research impetus was to replicate the findings of an earlier

TABLE 2.2 Percentage of Immigrants' Children Admitted to College by Age at Time of Immigration and Birth-Order

Age at Time of Families' Immigration	Percentages Admitted to College First-Born	Later-Born
0–5	40%(N=5)	24%(N=42)
6–11	00 (N=16)	16 (N=61)
12–15	22 (N=23)	26 (N=42)
16+	36 (N=25)	21 (N=24)
Total	23%(N=69)	21%(N=169)

Source: M. Inbar. *The Vulnerable Age Phenomenon* (New York: Sage Publications, 1976), p. 10. Adapted, used with permission.

study. In 1933, for example, Katz and Braly conducted what is now a classic study on stereotypes. The subjects for this study were one hundred Princeton students. Each student was given a list of ten ethnic groups and forty-eight traits and was asked to check those traits which seemed typical for each group. In addition, they were asked to choose for each group the five traits that seemed most typical. If students' selection of traits had been completely random, each trait would have been selected only 6 percent of the time. However, many of the traits that were chosen more often yielded stereotypic views of the different ethnic groups. Moreover, the same traits were not selected for each group. Hence, Katz and Braly conclude that stereotypic images do exist.

The Katz and Braly study was replicated in 1951 by Gilbert and again in 1969 by Karlins, Coffman, and Walters. Both replications also used Princeton University students. Most apparent from these replications were the changes in stereotypes over this thirty-five-year period. The stereotypic image of Americans became less positive while the stereotypic image of blacks and Jews became more positive. (See Table 2.3.) In fact, Karlins, Coffman, and Walters argue that stereotypic images are fading. While these studies were aimed at replicating the Katz and Braly findings, Kutner (1973) conducted a study aimed at replicating the Katz and Braly methodology. Kutner's study is also one of challenge. Primarily, Kutner suggests that if replications of ethnic stereotypes are to be conducted, an updating of the adjective checklist is needed. Replicating the methodology of Katz and Braly, she produced an updated list of traits. Kutner's research produced nineteen new descriptive traits, and of these, thirteen subsequently appeared among the five traits most frequently mentioned as typical of the ethnic group under study. Thus, Kutner concludes that perhaps stereotypes are not fading as much as previously thought. Rather, the Katz and Braly checklist is not meaningful to today's images.

Seeing If a Relationship in One Area Extends to Another. Often, our knowledge base is expanded by attempting to see if a relationship observed in one area can also be observed in another. Piaget's research on the cognitive development of children serves as an excellent example. Piaget argued that cognitive processes in children develop in stages. This stage theory of cognitive development suggests that children and adults organize their world differently. This differential organization has been demonstrated, for example, through conservation experiments. For example, in a conservation-of-volume experiment, a child is first shown two identically shaped beakers filled with water to an identical level. The water in one of the beakers is then poured into a third beaker, which is narrower and taller. Naturally, the water level in the third beaker is higher than in the original beaker. The child is then asked, "Which beaker holds more water, or do they hold the same amount of water?"

TABLE 2.3 Percent of Princeton College Students Assigning Traits to Ethnic Groups

		% checking trait					% checking trait		
	N:	100	333	150		N:	100	333	150
Trait	Year:	1932	1950	1967	Trait	Year:	1932	1950	1967
AMERICANS					**ITALIANS**				
Industrious		48	30	23	Artistic		53	28	30
Intelligent		47	32	20	Impulsive		44	19	28
Materialistic		33	37	67	Passionate		37	25	44
Ambitious		33	21	42	Quick-tempered		35	15	28
Progressive		27	5	17	Musical		32	22	9
CHINESE					**JAPANESE**				
Superstitious		34	18	8	Intelligent		45	11	20
Sly		29	4	6	Industrious		43	12	57
Conservative		29	14	15	Progressive		24	2	17
Loyal to family ties		22	35	50	Shrewd		22	13	7
Industrious		18	18	23	Sly		20	21	3
ENGLISH					**JEWS**				
Sportsmanlike		53	21	22	Shrewd		79	47	30
Intelligent		46	29	23	Mercenary		49	28	15
Conventional		34	25	19	Industrious		48	29	33
Tradition-loving		31	42	21	Grasping		34	17	17
Conservative		30	22	53	Intelligent		29	37	37
GERMANS					**NEGROES**				
Scientifically minded		78	62	47	Superstitious		84	41	13
Industrious		65	50	59	Lazy		75	21	36
Stolid		44	10	9	Happy-go-lucky		38	17	27
Intelligent		32	32	19	Ignorant		38	24	11
Methodical		31	20	21	Musical		26	33	47
IRISH					**TURKS**				
Pugnacious		45	24	13	Cruel		47	12	9
Quick-tempered		39	35	43	Very religious		26	6	7
Witty		38	16	7	Treacherous		21	3	13
Honest		32	11	17	Sensual		20	4	9
Very religious		29	30	27	Ignorant		15	7	13

Source: M. Karlins, T. Coffman, G. Walters, "On the Fading of Social Stereotypes: Three Generations of College Students," *Journal of Personality & Social Psychology*, 1969, Vol. 13: 1–16.

Whereas adults and older children recognize and respond that they both hold the same, preoperational children (under age seven) identify the narrow cylinder as holding more water.

With these conservation experiments in mind, Acker and Tiemens

(1981) performed an ingenious experiment by making an analogy to television. The appearance of an object on television is changed by zooming in or cutting to a close-up without changing the actual size of the object. Adults recognize a zoom or a cut as simply a change in camera perspective. However, given the findings of Piaget's and others' research, we might suspect that preoperational children perceive the transformation as representing a change in the object itself. In effect, this was the proposition set forth and tested by Acker and Tiemens. In addition to the conservation of television images, they used traditional conservation tasks. Their findings showed that when a zoom is used, children more readily perceive the object as growing large. Can you imagine the implications for advertising, especially for toys?

If you think of the research impetus as the motivating factor or force leading you to a specific research question and if you review the literature with this in mind, the task of formulating a research question will become easier. Remember, reading is a creative endeavor. Ask questions as you read. You cannot play a passive role even in this phase of research.

EVALUATING A RESEARCH QUESTION

Let's assume that you now have formulated a research question. At times this process has been frustrating and tedious. You are probably quite relieved to have progressed to this point. But wait! The process is not yet complete. We must now evaluate this question in an effort to determine whether it is both reasonable and desirable to pursue. To make this evaluation, we need to ask and answer several questions.

Is It Worthwhile?

This first question is not really a new one. We have considered it, at least indirectly, throughout this chapter. As you identified and read the relevant research literature, you were trying to formulate a research question, which, when answered, would make a contribution to knowledge. The potential contribution of any research question is not always obvious. Consequently, you should not make this decision hastily. If you bounce your research question off another person, don't be too discouraged or even necessarily swayed by such comments as, "Oh, everybody knows the answer to that. It's just common sense." As we have seen in Chapter 1, common sense is not always a reliable teacher. It does not always guide us either wisely or correctly. As a general rule of thumb, if you are convinced that knowledge in the field will be furthered by answering a particular research question, it is most likely worthwhile.

Is It Feasible?

The issue of feasibility is a broad one and can only be dealt with by asking and answering several further questions. Consider the following:

What Is the Scope of the Study? We have tried to stress that the process of choosing and formulating a research question is a filtering process. We begin with a research subject. We end with a research question. The broad and general nature of a research subject encompasses too many issues and too many concepts. It is simply not realistic to think that we could manage all of these issues and concepts in a single research endeavor. Take, for example, the research subject of factors influencing intelligence. It would be ambitious of us to assume that we could identify most of the important factors and examine them in a single project. Inconsistent and contradictory findings on this research subject have resulted in research introducing several factors: (1) sibship size, (2) birth order, (3) physiological condition of mother, (4) treatment of children by parents, (5) social class, (6) race, and (7) marital disruption, just to name a few. To consider all of these variables would be demanding for the research novice. Even the experienced researcher would be facing quite a challenge. In effect, the scope must be narrow enough that the research is manageable. Generally, a research question that considers no more than three or four concepts should be sufficient. This does not necessarily mean you will only collect data on these three or four concepts. You may collect data on several other concepts for answering a second or even third research question. If you use a questionnaire, for example, it may be constructed to answer several research questions. But for any specific research question, you certainly do not have to use every question on the questionnaire. Once again, the key is manageability.

How Much Time Is Required? Reading the research literature does not always give you an adequate appreciation of the time required to do research. When you read a study that prints into seven or eight pages, you may think, "Oh, I'll bet that didn't take very long." But the natural flow of the published research narrative can be quite deceptive. Almost everything takes more time than we think. Recall from Chapter 1 our reference to Humphreys's research on impersonal sex in public places. In discussing his research, Humphreys (1976) notes that the time investment for this study was approximately three and one-half years. The observation of impersonal sex acts (conducted part-time, as he was also a graduate student) took two years. Another six months of full-time work was invested in administering interview schedules to over one hundred respondents. And still another year went into data analysis. Carefully planned research takes time. The several steps in the total research process cannot be passed over lightly. It takes time to:

1. Identify the relevant literature on a research subject
2. Read this relevant literature
3. Formulate the research question
4. Locate measures for the concepts to be studied
5. Locate the groups to be studied
6. Collect the data
7. Code all of the data if stored in a computer *and enter data*
8. Analyze the data
9. Write the research report

These are just a few of the more obvious tasks to be performed. If you can establish even an approximate time schedule, you can pace your progress. Don't be disappointed if you find you cannot follow it to the letter. Such a schedule is only meant to provide guidelines and to give you some idea of the time required.

How Much Money Is Required? Research can be quite costly, and for most researchers, the sky is not the limit! Consider the following possible expenditures:

> Photocopying articles when reviewing the literature
> Requesting articles from other libraries when your library does not carry the reference
> Purchasing or renting equipment (e.g., a tape recorder)
> Paying subjects
> Having a questionnaire or interview schedule typed or copied
> Purchasing computer time for data storage and analysis

These are only some of the costs that might be incurred. There may be many others. When Festinger was studying the doomsday group, for example, he had to fly two of his graduate assistants to the group's meetings. Costs are very real and the researcher needs to examine this factor before beginning any research endeavor.

Are Subjects Available? If subjects are not available, nothing else really matters: the research cannot be done. There are research questions that require unique groups of individuals. If you wanted to study "swinging" activity among adults, you would have to locate a group of swingers. If such a group could not be found, you would have to choose another research question. If you were interested in studying "long-distance marriages," you would probably have to exert a great deal of energy and ingenuity to locate the appropriate couples. For most research questions, subjects can be found, although the search may be time-consuming and even costly. But if you are sufficiently interested in the research question and have the time and resources to locate individuals, subject availability should not be an insurmountable problem. If you find that subjects are not readily available and the time and resources required to locate subjects are not realistic, you will probably want to consider another research question.

Will Subjects Cooperate? If you find that subjects are available, you will next need to determine whether you can obtain their cooperation in your research endeavor. Suppose you learn, for example, that a "swinging" group does exist in your area. However, after contacting several group members, you realize that you will not be able to gain their cooperation. You might then decide to abandon the research question and choose another. Sometimes institutional officers deny a researcher permission to question or interview students, employees, or others whom they presume to control. In many cases, the official may have exceeded his or her actual authority. One researcher, for example, was denied permission to interview black students at a state university campus. The researcher simply ignored the officer, went to the campus, and interviewed the required informants at the student center. Quite honestly, the university officer had no right to deny the researcher normal access to the public facilities of that institution. In some instances, administrative authority cannot be countered. It is sometimes difficult to gain entrance into public schools. And if the research question deals with a hypersensitive issue (such as sex), entrance is doubly difficult, if not impossible. In effect, if the cooperation of those in authority cannot be gained, the researcher may need to redirect his or her research.

Are the Necessary Equipment and Facilities Available? The testing of some research questions requires sophisticated equipment that can be quite expensive. For example, if the test of your research question requires conducting an experiment, you will need a laboratory facility and possibly a tape recorder, television, public address system, and other items. If such facilities and equipment are not available, the research question may have to be abandoned.

Is It Ethical?

We cannot leave the area of evaluation without addressing the issue of ethics. Specifically, is the test of the research question ethical? Is the researcher being honest with his or her subjects, or does he or she intentionally deceive them? If deception is used, could it potentially harm the subjects? Does the treatment of subjects in any way harmfully alter their perceptions of self? Are their personal rights violated? The researcher should exercise a sense of responsibility toward his or her subjects. In fact, a principle of "reciprocal responsibility" should be operating. An individual who agrees to participate in any research endeavor is placing trust in the researcher. The researcher, in turn, should not violate that trust.

Chapter 3

Guiding the Research Process: The Role of Theory

The relationship between theory and method
    The dubious state of theory in everyday life
    Theory leads the process of research
    Theory is modified from findings
The nature of social theory
    What is a theory?
    Definitions
    Hypotheses
    Induction and deduction
    The discovery of grounded theory
    The process of deductive theory construction

Major theoretical paradigms in social research
    The functionalist paradigm
    The conflict paradigm
    The behaviorist paradigm
    The symbolic interactionist paradigm
        The self
        The act
        Social interaction
        Objects
        Joint action
    The ethnomethodological paradigm

Science is a graveyard of theories.
—Gregory Stone

THE RELATIONSHIP BETWEEN THEORY AND METHOD

Theory is to methods what a roadmap is to driving. Without it, all roads look the same, you can never tell for sure where you are, you waste a lot of time making wrong turns and getting lost, and when you get where you're going, you may not know it. These same problems plague the research process, and the answer is almost as simple as it is in driving. Theory is the researcher's roadmap, and it is indispensable.

In this chapter we detail the relationship between theory and methods, show how theory leads the process of research, how methodology is generated from theory, how theory is modified from research findings, and how different kinds of theories give rise to very different kinds of methodological techniques.

Astonishingly, not nearly enough attention is ordinarily given to the role of theory in guiding and directing research. We frequently give lip service to theory and then forget it in our enthusiasm for the technical side of methods and in the day-to-day difficulties of executing a research project. For example, in university curricula, most departments have separate theory and methods courses, suggesting by implication, if not by design, that the two are different enterprises. C. Wright Mills has placed this problem into context better than anyone:

> Two schools of sociological study have flourished in America. . . . One of them makes a fetish of "Method," the other of "Theory." The Higher Statisticians break down truth and falsity into such fine particles that we cannot tell the difference between them; by the costly rigor of their methods, they succeed in trivializing man and society, and in the process their own minds as well.
>
> The Grand Theorists, on the other hand, represent a partially organized attempt to withdraw from the effort plainly to describe, explain, and understand human conduct and society: they verbalize in turgid prose the disordered contests of their reading of eminent nineteenth-century sociologists, and in the process mistake their own beginnings for a finished result.
>
> In the practice of both these leading schools, contemporary Social Science becomes simply an elaborate method of insuring that no one learns too

much about man and society, the first by formal but empty ingenuity; the second, by formal but cloudy obscurantism. (1953, 5)

Careful attention to the delicate interrelationship between theory and methods overcomes these problems, and the reader of this chapter should emerge with a better understanding of how to conduct a research project so that the extremes Mills talks about are avoided. Better, more persuasive, and more useful research will be the result.

The Dubious State of Theory in Everyday Life

To many people who pride themselves in being commonsense thinkers, theory is a dubious enterprise. Americans have historically disdained theory, regarding themselves as practical people who are not interested in what they consider to be the rarefied atmosphere of theory. Unfortunately, all practical acts, all commonsense notions about how human beings behave, how society operates, and so forth, are laden with theoretical propositions. Someone has said that the person who prides himself on being atheoretical is usually the slave of some long-dead theories.

A clear-cut example of what we mean occurred on January 17, 1977. On that date a firing squad in the state of Utah executed Gary Gilmore, a convicted murderer. It seemed like common sense to many people that executing a murderer is a regrettable but nonetheless necessary and effective way of dealing with violent crime. It is a practical answer, apart from theory. In actual fact, however, execution is far from an atheoretical act. The theory informing capital punishment is almost three hundred years old and goes something like this: Human beings are rational creatures who weigh their acts in terms of a calculus of pleasure and pain. They attempt to maximize pleasure and minimize pain. In weighing the costs of an act, they will refrain from doing something they know will cost them their lives, and so capital punishment obviously must act as a deterrent to the commission of capital crimes. This so-called commonsense formulation, believed fervently by any number of people, is actually a reformulation of a theory that is at least four hundred years old and has been shown to be correct only in highly restricted circumstances, certainly not the ones that obtain in the commission of capital crimes. Most murders are emotionally charged crimes of passion in which there is little if any rational weighing of calculuses of pleasure and pain. Furthermore, given the typical time lag between crimes and punishment, whatever chance this theory has of being true is typically destroyed by circumstances that are built into the U.S. criminal justice system.

By the same token, many people who pride themselves on being practical thinkers feel that it only makes sense that if you give people long terms on the rock pile they will think twice before doing whatever it is that got them there in the first place. Unfortunately, such a practical and workable plan is not atheoretical either. Not only does it suffer from many of the theoretical assumptions that rational thinkers have built into arguments favoring capital punishment, but it is also hampered by the deficiencies in learning theory. One would think that if people are treated harshly and punitively, they would indeed think twice before acting that way again. The evidence, however, is not overwhelming, for it seems that for every person who is taught a lesson by harsh treatment, there are many more who are hardened, embittered, and made even worse by the same treatment.

On the other hand, the "progressive" and "enlightened" thinker about crime and punishment is often the slave of bankrupt theories too. It was once fashionable to prove one's reputation as a clear thinker by advocating rehabilitation. The criminal is obviously a victim of society, and with proper programs, virtually all criminals can be salvaged, shown the error of their ways, and brought back into the fold of reasonable human beings. This idea, no matter how humane and decently motivated, is not atheoretical either, and the theory that underlies it is equally suspect. The theory that supports rehabilitation is the very old notion (at least since Rousseau) that holds that human beings are pure and innocent, and it is society and its demeaning evils that corrupt them. Treated right, people will act right. Treated wrong, they will act wrong. No matter how much we might wish to believe this idea, research has simply not shown an enormous array of support for that theoretical proposition.

Our point in this short excursion into the emotionally charged issue of crime and punishment is simply this: the business of theory cannot be avoided in favor of "practical" approaches to the problems of life any more than the laws of economics can be avoided by taking a vow of poverty. Theoretical propositions underlie everything that we do, certainly everything we think, and must be faced rather than avoided.

Theory Leads the Process of Research

Theory, then, leads the process of research by setting forth a logically coherent series of interrelated propositions that might account for some phenomenon in which an investigator is interested. For example, let us suppose that as a result of a course in marriage and the family, you have gotten interested in why there is so much divorce in the United States these days. Perhaps you yourself came from a broken home and feel that in your case, at least, economic pressures were responsible for the breakup of your parents' marriage. You want to know, then, whether the general theory that economic pressures cause broken homes is true or not. You have not yet generated a theory but simply have an idea about a relationship between two variables. What do you do next? A search of the literature might reveal that quite a bit has been written about this relationship and that the issue is a lot more complicated than you thought. Other variables are suddenly brought to your attention that might have some effect on what you are now beginning to see as a very complex relationship. Conflict, theory, exchange theory, and even Marxian theory may have ideas worthy of consideration. Out of this welter of theoretical material, you can then begin to develop a specific hypothesis that may be tested by appropriate methodological techniques.

Theory Is Modified from Findings

The whole idea of research is to find out the solutions to puzzles; that is, answers to questions our minds and our experiences inevitably pose about life around us. Riddles, if they are worth asking, don't usually have simple answers. We began this chapter by quoting Greg Stone's observation that science is a graveyard of theories. He means that there is no theory capable of answering all the questions the human mind is capable of devising. Theories come and go; questions persist. Nothing is more useful than a good theory, but social reality is an infinitely flexible and elusive process for which no single explanation is ordinarily satisfactory, and which will change over time anyway. This means that the process of building an edifice of theory, although necessary, is never complete. What we find modifies what we thought was the case. In our preceding example, we may find, for example that there is no absolute relationship between divorce and economic hardships. For example, we might, in the course of our research on the question, run into the astonishing fact that the divorce rate during the Great Depression was very low. That must mean that economic hardships, in and of themselves, do not cause divorce. Noting what happened during the Depression doesn't invalidate the idea altogether, however; it simply means that whatever theory we are guided by must be modified by what we discover in the course of the research. We must necessarily begin with a theory, for how else will we know what to make of the facts we uncover during the research process? But those very facts, informed and directed by theory, usually lead to the modification of the theory. To use our earlier analogy of theory-as-roadmap, it seems that while you must have a roadmap to guide you through research, you don't assume that your roadmap is accurate. Rather, be ready to modify it as you discover new territory not on the map. If you find that someone has cut a new road, that doesn't necessarily mean the map was wrong—just that it wasn't complete or as up-to-date as we would like our maps to be. As it turns out, the analogy was not too far off after all, for maps (theories) must constantly be updated by what we find—not that they are useless or that we would want to start our journey without one.

THE NATURE OF SOCIAL THEORY

What Is a Theory?

A lot of confusion surrounds the seemingly simple question "What is a theory?" Although there is what Wittgenstein called a family resemblance among most definitions of theory, the definitions themselves differ rather widely. For us, the term *theory* is most often confused with a variety of related terms such as *concept, typology, model, proposition, assumption, assertion, hypothesis, paradigm,* and so forth.

It might be well to begin by stating what theories are *for*, and in doing so we will begin to get at what they *are*. The primary purpose of a theory is to account for or explain a particular phenomenon. It is this explanatory function that distinguishes a theory from other related concepts. Without theory we would have no way of even beginning to know the meaning of what we have found in our research. This function of theory, then, is to account for or to explain the findings of research. With that function as background, here are a few definitions of what a theory is from various scholars who have written about it:

> A theory is a set of logically interrelated propositions in the form of empirical assertions about properties of infinite classes of events or things. (Gibbs)

> There is general agreement that a theory is a set of propositions or theoretical statements. (Hage)

> A theory ought to create the *capacity* to invent explanations. (Stinchcombe)

> A theory is an integrated set of relationships with a certain level of validity. (Willer)

These differing definitions all have in common the idea that theories state, in as logical terms as possible, a set of general statements that explain or account for some phenomenon the researcher is interested in.

Theories are usually stated in the form of propositions and are worded in terms of *concepts*. A concept usually begins as a kind of mental image. We have an idea about the social world, but in order to articulate it enough to begin the research process, we must translate this idea into a concept or a series of concepts. Let's say that we want to study the relationship between crime and poverty. We all know what crime and criminals are. And we surely know what poverty is. Or do we? Just what do we mean when we use such terms? To think about relationships, we first have to translate vague ideas into concepts, and then define these concepts very carefully for the purposes of research. Actually, most of the ideas we have about the social world are about relationships, not about things. Has anyone ever seen his own father? We immediately say yes, but on closer reflection, as Durkheim pointed out many years ago, what we really "see" is a person we have labeled in that way to denote a certain relationship between us and him. In other words, we have a certain *concept* of father, just as we have a whole series of other concepts that we largely take for granted. But in doing research, we try as best we can to take *nothing* for granted. We are going to have to define each concept carefully and use it consistently so that we will not be measuring apples and oranges.

In everyday life, concepts are important, but the degree of precision in their use is not always necessary. If someone says, "It's cloudy outside," we don't generally ask, "What do you mean by *cloudy*?" But the researcher is in roughly the same situation as the weather bureau. Their work (like ours) necessitates a rather precise definition about such fuzzy terms as *cloudy*. For example, pilots need to know exactly what the weather is doing, and fuzzy concepts just will not do. What kinds of clouds are we talking about? Cirrus clouds? Cumulus clouds? Stratus clouds? Cumulonimbus clouds? Just knowing that it's "cloudy" without knowing what kind of clouds we're talking about can literally kill you if you are thinking of launching your airplane into the wild blue yonder.

By the same token, our research endeavors are going to hang considerably on how well we are able to define our concepts. The process of conceptualization, then, is central to precise research, and going through this process will help to stimulate additional thinking that will clarify just what the researcher wishes to find out. We know that two people who have a legal contract between them called marriage live together in a certain relationship. But for many types of research questions, just knowing that they are "married" might not do at all. There are many different kinds of relationships within marriage, and for some studies (not all) it could make a crucial difference what kind we are talking about. For example, what is the relationship between the stability of a marriage and its intensity? Most people think that stable marriages are good ones. But what do we mean by *stable*? What do we mean by *good*? It turns out that if by *stable* we mean "lasts a long time" (and how long is long?), it is inversely related to intensity (and how intense is intense?). Passion and intensity in marriage, as lots of studies have shown, often lead to low stability, and high stability often involves low intensity (Kiser 1984). For some research studies, such splitting of conceptual hairs is irrelevant, but for others it is essential, and which it is going to be depends on the nature of the study, the kind of theory being used, and many other considerations. At any rate, conceptualization is the process by which fuzziness gets turned into sharpness, and such considerations often make or break a research project.

Definitions

Concepts involve definitions, but definitions are even more precise than concepts. Suppose we want to study the average duration of marriage among American Indians. We have a pretty good conceptual idea of what we want to get at, but we will have to define our basic terms in a very precise way, and that may get tricky. Just what, for example, is an Indian? Even the Bureau of Indian Affairs does not know for sure and uses different definitions for different purposes. The definition may range all the way from a person with a certain percentage of Indian ancestry to a person who is merely regarded as an Indian by those around him. We might say that this is the difference between a genetic definition and a social one. For some purposes, again, it may not make much difference, but for others, it can make a lot.

Some studies have been ruined simply because the definitions they used were so faulty. One such study tried to get away with defining "unemployed" as anyone who worked less than full-time (Wallis and Roberts 1962). If you do that, you get a disparity of more than 10 million between the Census Bureau's figures of unemployment in the United States and those found by this study. The authors may have had good reasons for employing such a definition, but their work wound up causing even more argument and confusion about the extent of the unemployment problem in the country (Simon 1978). Problems of definition are exactly why the data of one "expert" can be very much different from the data of another. There is nothing inherently wrong with different research about the same phenomenon coming up with such different results. However, we will always want to be clear about just what definition we are using and, even more important, why we are using it.

Hypotheses

We have devoted an entire chapter of this book to hypotheses because they are so important to the research process. It will be enough here to define them and show their relationship to theory. Ideas, in the form of defined concepts, must be arranged for research purposes into hypotheses we can test. Hypotheses are always derived from theory. Technically, a hypothesis is an expectation about the nature of things according to theory. It is a statement of what we ought to find if our theory is correct. To use a grim example, from racist theories we might derive the hypothesis that blacks, being intellectually inferior to whites will do badly on intelligence tests. Of course, the aforementioned problem of concept and definition will come into play in building such a hypothesis because we must define carefully what we mean by *intelligence* and *intelligence test* and also deal with the theoretical problem of whether performance on an intelligence test is actually a measure of intelligence. Actually, emotional theories like those about racial inferiority are rarely tested fairly because the authors of such theories usually seek to prove their theory and assume that any data that do not fit it must be wrong. This problem occurs in other theories too, and we must always guard against using research as an ideological tool to prove pet theories. (More about this problem later in the chapter.) Theory is the good-faith, intellectually honest enterprise of keeping an open mind but not an empty one. We have ideas and theories, naturally, if we are good researchers, but we must not become so enamored of the theory that we will do anything to prove its correctness. This is intellectually dishonest. A good hypothesis is both carefully stated and tough-minded in the sense that ideally we want hypothesis to be a fair and rigorous test of theory. Done well, good hypotheses enable us to ask further questions (rather than close the door) and to modify theory as we mentioned in our previous discussion.

Induction and Deduction

The theory game is played logically in one of two ways, and it is important for researchers to know which way their theory asks them to move. These two forms of developing theory are called deductive and inductive. Much of what we have been discussing as theory in this chapter is actually deductive. It is the hallmark of the traditional view of how scientific research proceeds. In deductive theory we move from the general to the specific, and in inductive theory from the specific to the general. Deductive logic moves from general theories to specific facts, and inductive logic moves from facts to theories. Deductive logic is the logic of theory testing in the narrow and conventional sense, and induction is the discovery of what is called grounded theory. Deductive theorizing asks us to come up with a theoretical formulation that we will then translate into hypotheses and test in order to find out whether the facts confirm or disconfirm the theory. In short, we move from the general to the specific.

With deductive theorizing, we have an idea of what we are going to find to begin with, and then we develop a research design to confirm or deny our suspicions. With induction, we readily admit that we do not know what we are going to find until we get there. Instead, we first find out what the facts are and then arrange these facts into patterns that will move toward a theory.

Deduction is an indispensable part of knowledge. We arrange our lives all the time in terms of tiny little syllogisms that we presume to be true and do not really think twice about unless something tells us they are wrong. For example, let us say the class in which you are using this text meets on Monday, Wednesday, and Friday. You awake one morning, note that this is Wednesday, and therefore deductively conclude that you will be having class today. If you then hike off to class, you might discover that a single fact will ruin your theory, no matter how logical it seemed. You go on Wednesday, only to discover that your theory must be revised in light of the fact that your professor has come down with the flu and will not be meeting class today.

In a sense, as Julian Simon has observed, empirically established facts have much more of a claim to be called "knowledge" than theories do. When logic and facts collide, it is usually logic that gives way (hence our quotation at the beginning of the chapter: "Science is a graveyard of theories"). Many theories have been killed by a single little fact that stood in their way. Simon tells the story of a famous World War II navy airplane that theoretically (according to the engineers) would not fly at all. When a model was made and flown despite the theory to the contrary, the theory had to be revised. It is difficult to hold on to a theory that a plane cannot possibly fly after it has logged several million miles in the air (Simon 1978)!

Unfortunately, things are not always so clear-cut in the social sciences, but that is why theories are so important. A theory can be destroyed by one strategically located fact, but all the facts in the world will not add up to meaningful knowledge without the interpretation, synthesis, logic, and larger framework that are the province of theory.

Deductive logic depends on the validity of this basic premise. Induction depends on the accuracy of its facts. The famous Greek form of deduction, the syllogism ("All men are mortal; Socrates is a man; therefore Socrates is mortal"), is wholly dependent upon the accuracy of its premises, a point satirized by Ambrose Bierce in his book *The Devil's Dictionary* (1906):

> The basis of logic is the syllogism, consisting of a major and a minor premise and a conclusion—thus:
>
> *Major Premise:* Sixty men can do a piece of work sixty times as quickly as one man.
>
> *Minor Premise:* One man can dig a post-hole in sixty seconds: therefore—
>
> *Conclusion:* Sixty men can dig a post-hole in one second.

Obviously, the conclusion is a bit distorted by the inaccuracy of the major premise: there just might be a point at which adding men to a work detail does not add to the time saved in doing a job. The mental picture of sixty men trying to dig the same hole may begin to cast doubt on the accuracy of the major premise.

Scientific deduction, then, has the advantage of being able to begin the research with some idea of what one is going to find and to tie findings to some coherent logical system. The problem with deductive logic is that its premises must be scrutinized very carefully, for one inaccuracy means that all conclusions that flow from it will be wrong.

The Discovery of Grounded Theory

Theoretical induction leads to the discovery of what Glaser and Strauss (1967) call "grounded theory." The idea here is to begin not with theory, but with a general conception of how to do social research. This conception has observation and description as its most important techniques, and out of such work then emerges theory. We seek here to discover theory from data systematically obtained from the process of doing social research. The theory is then "grounded" in the sense that it was generated from data rather than having arisen from speculation, philosophizing, or some other abstract source.

Theory generated in this grounded way cannot usually be completely refuted or replaced by another theory, precisely because it is too closely linked to data. Such theory will be modified and reformulated in the endless cycle we spoke of earlier, but the complete refutation of it will not usually be possible because it is empirical and not merely logical.

Research built on inductive grounding will have a format considerably different from the deductive kind. Instead of the researcher's finding and verifying facts alone, the entire research endeavor will be conceived to lead toward a more general meaning so that the research accounts for and interprets what it has found and has a basis for doing so.

Grounded theory proceeds on the assumption that the adequacy of a theory cannot be assessed apart from the empirical process by which it is generated. This procedure stands in stark contrast to deductive theory, which begins as an exercise in logic and then depends for its test on the facts that are found. Actually, a hard-and-fast division between the two is somewhat arbitrary because it is often the case that grounded theory that arises from inductive logic later winds up being wisdom that can be tested by conventional techniques deductively. This interplay is one of the most important features of the dynamics of theory and methods. The most important thing to keep in mind is that researchers must always know what they are doing and which way they are working as they deal with theory.

The Process of Deductive Theory Construction

Theory construction is a highly specialized and often exceedingly complex pursuit, and a number of excellent books have been written about it (Zetterberg 1965; Blalock 1973; Gibbs 1972). Here we will briefly draw on Kinloch's excellent summary of the formal process by which deductive theories are formulated (1977):

1. The first step is delineation of the theory's underlying causal relationships. As we have pointed out, this explanatory framework is basic to the theory's explanatory structure. The para-

digm should be made as explicit as possible, especially the causal relationships within it that are assumed to be explanatory. The delineation of this model of assumed relationships is the initial and major step in the theorizing process.
2. The next step involves definition of the concepts in the paradigm as clearly and as fully as possible. Means of concepts are often assumed rather than defined, leading to ambiguity and possible confusion.
3. The logical relationships between these concepts implied by the theory's paradigm then require definition in the form of axioms and/or propositions. Further propositions may be logically deduced if the method of axiomatic deduction is followed.
4. The concepts are then operationalized in the form of variables, and the logical relationships between these variables are deduced from the above axioms and propositions in the form of hypotheses.
5. The methodology implied by these variables is then developed in order to test these hypotheses through empirical indexes. This methodology is then applied as rigorously as possible to test the hypotheses empirically.
6. The data are then analyzed according to techniques, statistical or otherwise, derived from the theoretical system just developed.
7. Having analyzed the data, the theorist needs to interpret the significance of the results in reference to the theory he or she has developed. The theory may be interpreted on the basis of those results or in reference to them, depending on the approach to theory construction accepted.
8. Finally, having completed the above steps, the theorist attempts to evaluate the theory on theoretical and/or empirical grounds depending, once again, on the particular approach to theorizing accepted.

The point of this summary is that theory and method are not separate entities but are tied together and should be evaluated as a single unit. To try to understand a methodological technique without understanding the theoretical paradigm from which it derives is like trying to understand automobile tires without having any understanding of automobiles.

MAJOR THEORETICAL PARADIGMS IN SOCIAL RESEARCH

In Chapter 1, the importance of paradigms in social research was mentioned and discussed. We learned that research is done in order to understand as much as possible about a given problem. But how is the problem derived in the first place? How do we know what to study and how do we know when we have found something important? This is what paradigms do. As fundamental images of subject matter, they set the theoretical and methodological terms of our focus.

The social sciences are full of differing paradigms (Ritzer 1975). Its theories develop out of paradigms, so no theory begins *tabula rasa* (with a clean slate). Unlike theories, paradigms do not give us answers, but they tell us where to look for them. In the course of doing this, naturally they direct our attention *away* from other possible places that might contain answers, and those places await the direction of other paradigms to find them. Paradigms, then, are obviously critical because where we look for answers largely determines what we will find. There is an old story about a man who loses a coin in his house but looks for it outside, under a street lamp, because the light is better there. In a sense, that is what paradigms force us to do, and while that may seem ridiculous, in many ways it is better than looking in the dark. This is why the more lampposts (paradigms) we can devise, the better our chances of finding the millions of answers we seek to complex social questions.

At the present time, there are four major paradigms competing for allegiance in the social sciences. Since most of the theories used by researchers arise from one of these four paradigms, we will discuss them briefly.

The Functionalist Paradigm

The functionalist paradigm (sometimes called structural-functionalism) originated in the work of organicists of the nineteenth century and claims to be the earliest scientific conceptualization of society. Society, from this point of view, is a system of interrelated parts in which the relationship between the part and the whole are the focus of analysis. Everything that happens happens because it contributes to the whole. Behavior is system-determined and system-sustaining. This paradigm, which is contained in the writings of such sociological masters as Emile Durkheim and Ferdinand Tonnies, focuses on the glue that sticks the individual and society together. It is highly deterministic; that is, it views all social phenomena as determined by societal forces that play on people and produce their behavior. In short, there is virtually no room for such ideas as freedom, will, or choice. At the level of analysis at which the functionalist paradigm operates, it can be a very powerful way of understanding social phenomena.

For example, if a researcher were studying crime or suicide rates he or she might wish to organize the data in terms of theories drawn from a structural-functional paradigm. What social conditions seem to affect crime rates? Do they go up during periods of high unemployment and down during times of prosperity? Is divorce affected by larger society conditions? Suicide? We chose these examples because each of these conditions is indeed affected by structural changes in society. What about delinquency and drug abuse? Do the rates of these behaviors vary with changes in the structure of society? What kinds of changes have made it more difficult for many people to be clear on the difference between right and wrong? In fact, are these terms themselves dependent upon the structure of society? Again, probably so, and this paradigm can be very useful in developing theories to explain various phenomena. Functionalism always turns our attention to the interdependent relationship between parts of society and often produces astonishingly insightful ways of understanding what is around us.

In an important article published in 1949, for example, Robert K. Merton used a functional paradigm to explain the continuing existence of urban political machines even in the face of almost everyone's view that they were bad. If they continued to exist, argued Merton, perhaps they fulfilled at least a latent—that is, an unintended or unrecognized—positive function in urban communities. Merton argued quite persuasively that political machines provided centralized authority to get things done when a decentralized local government could not, offered concrete help to the poor, and performed many services needed by people but considered not worthy or even illegal by formal public agencies.

By the same token, Herbert Gans (1972) has used a functional paradigm to organize his research on the intractable nature of poverty. Why does poverty continue to exist in a society where there is plenty to go around and where almost everyone believes poverty is bad? Gans decided that perhaps poverty exists because it is useful to society as a whole. He demonstrates this point by listing thirteen positive functions that the poor provide for the rest of society (from Herbert Gans, "The Uses of Poverty: The Poor Pay All." *Social Policy* (July–August 1971, pp. 20–24):

1. The existence of poverty ensures that society's "dirty work" will be done. Every society has such work: physically dirty or dangerous, temporary, dead and underpaid, undignified and menial jobs. Society can fill these jobs by paying higher wages than for "clean" work, or it can force people who have no other choice to do the dirty work—and at low wages. In America, poverty functions to provide a low-wage labor pool that is willing—or, rather, unable to be unwilling—to perform dirty work at low cost. Indeed, this function of the poor is so important that in some Southern states, welfare payments have been cut off during the summer months when the poor are needed to work in the fields. Moreover, much of the debate about the Negative Income Tax and the Family Assistance Plan has concerned their impact on the work incentive—the incentive of the poor to do the needed dirty work if the wages therefrom are no larger than the income grant. Many economic activities that in-

volve dirty work depend on the poor for their existence: restaurants, hospitals, parts of the garment industry, and "truck farming," among others, could not persist in their present form without the poor.

2. Because the poor are required to work at low wages, they subsidize a variety of economic activities that benefit the affluent. For example, domestics subsidize the upper-middle and upper classes, making life easier for their employers and freeing affluent women for a variety of professional, cultural, civic, and partying activities. Similarly, because the poor pay a higher proportion of their income in property and sales taxes, among others, they subsidize many state and local governmental services that benefit more affluent groups. In addition, the poor support innovation in medical experiments.

3. Poverty creates jobs for a number of occupations and professions that serve or "service" the poor and protect the rest of society from them. As already noted, penology would be minuscule without the poor, as would the police. Other activities and groups that flourish because of the existence of poverty are the numbers game, the sale of heroin and cheap wines and liquors, pentecostal ministers, faith healers, prostitutes, pawn shops, and the peacetime army which recruits its enlisted men mainly from among the poor.

4. The poor buy goods others do not want and thus prolong the economic usefulness of such goods—day-old bread, fruit and vegetables that would otherwise have to be thrown out, secondhand clothes, and deteriorating automobiles and buildings. They also provide incomes for doctors, lawyers, teachers, and others who are too old, poorly trained, or incompetent to attract more affluent clients.

In addition to economic functions, the poor perform a number of social functions:

5. The poor can be identified and punished as alleged or real deviants in order to uphold the legitimacy of conventional norms. To justify the desirability of hard work, thrift, honesty, and monogamy, for example, the defenders of these norms must be able to find people who can be accused of being lazy, spendthrift, dishonest, and promiscuous. Although there is some evidence that the poor are about as moral and law-abiding as anyone else, they are more likely than middle-class transgressors to be caught and punished when they participate in deviant acts. Moreover, they lack the political and cultural power to correct the stereotypes that other people hold of them and thus continue to be thought of as lazy, spendthrift, etc., by those who need living proof that moral deviance does not pay.

6. Conversely, the poor offer vicarious participation to the rest of the population in the uninhibited sexual, alcoholic, and narcotic behavior in which they are alleged to participate and which, being freed from the constraints of affluence, they are often thought to enjoy more than the middle classes. Thus many people, some social scientists included, believe that the poor not only are more given to uninhibited behavior (which may be true, although it is often motivated by despair more than by lack of inhibition) but derive more pleasure from it than affluent people (which research by Lee Rainwater, Walter Miller, and others shows

to be patently untrue). However, whether the poor actually have more sex and enjoy it more is irrelevant; so long as middle-class people believe this to be true, they can participate in it vicariously when instances are reported in factual or fictional form.

7. The poor also serve a direct cultural function when culture created by or for them is adopted by the more affluent. The rich often collect artifacts from extinct folk cultures of poor people; and almost all Americans listen to the blues, Negro spirituals, and country music which originated among the Southern poor. Recently they have enjoyed the rock styles that were born, like the Beatles, in the slums; and in the last years, poetry written by ghetto children has become popular in literary circles. The poor also serve as culture heroes, particularly, of course, to the left; but the hobo, the cowboy, the hipster, and the mythical prostitute with a heart of gold have performed this function for a variety of groups.

8. Poverty helps to guarantee the status of those who are not poor. In every hierarchical society someone has to be at the bottom; but in American society, in which social mobility is an important goal for many and people need to know where they stand, the poor function as a reliable and relatively permanent measuring rod for status comparisons. This is particularly true for the working class whose politics is influenced by the need to maintain status distinctions between themselves and the poor, much as the aristocracy must find ways of distinguishing itself from the nouveaux riches.

9. The poor also aid the upward mobility of groups just above them in the class hierarchy. Thus a goodly number of Americans have entered the middle class through the profits earned from the provision of goods and services in the slums, including illegal or nonrespectable ones that upper-class and upper-middle-class businessmen shun because of their low prestige. As a result, members of almost every immigrant group have financed their upward mobility by providing slum housing, entertainment, gambling, narcotics, etc., to later arrivals—most recently to blacks and Puerto Ricans.

10. The poor help to keep the aristocracy busy, thus justifying its continued existence. "Society" uses the poor as clients of settlement houses and beneficiaries of charity affairs; indeed, the aristocracy must have the poor to demonstrate its superiority over other elites who devote themselves to earning money.

11. The poor, being powerless, can be made to absorb the costs of change and growth in American society. During the nineteenth century, they did the backbreaking work that built the cities; today, they are pushed out of their neighborhoods to make room for "progress." Urban renewal projects to hold middle-class taxpayers in the city and expressways to enable suburbanites to commute downtown have typically been located in poor neighborhoods since no other group will allow itself to be displaced. For the same reason, universities, hospitals, and civic centers also expand into land occupied by the poor. The major costs of the industrialization of agriculture have been borne by the poor who are pushed off the land without recompense; and they have paid a

large share of the human costs of the growth of American power overseas, for they have provided many of the foot soldiers for Vietnam and other wars.

12. The poor facilitate and stabilize the American political process. Because they vote and participate in politics less than other groups, the political system is often free to ignore them. Moreover, since they can rarely support Republicans, they often provide the Democrats with a captive constituency that has no other place to go. As a result, the Democrats can count on their votes, and be more responsive to voters—for example, the white working class—who might otherwise switch to the Republicans.

13. The role of the poor in upholding conventional norms (see the fifth point, above) also has a significant political function. An economy based on the ideology of laissez faire requires a deprived population that is allegedly unwilling to work or that can be considered inferior because it must accept charity or welfare in order to survive. Not only does the alleged moral deviancy of the poor reduce the moral pressure on the present political economy to eliminate poverty but socialist alternatives can be made to look quite unattractive if those who will benefit most from them can be described as lazy, spendthrift, dishonest, and promiscuous.

These insights about poverty are just one of many pieces of research that have been informed by the functionalist paradigm.

The Conflict Paradigm

Functionalist paradigms are by their very nature preoccupied with questions of order and stability. Everything is seen as functional and therefore, in a sense, a desirable part of the whole. (Why would anyone tamper with a functioning organism?) The inability of such a paradigm to handle questions of conflict and change has of course generated other paradigms that see the world quite differently. The conflict paradigm, often associated with the work of Karl Marx, views social life as a continuous series of struggles between competing factions of individuals, groups, and classes. What may appear to be a nicely functioning whole is actually a seething caldron of antagonisms. To the proponents of this paradigm, conflict appears to be the organizing principle of life. Conflict is everywhere. Those with money versus those without, age versus youth, workers versus management, men versus women, whites versus blacks—the list of opposing sides is endless. Most of this conflict revolves around the competition over material things. Economic determinism is a basic assumption of the conflict paradigm. People get along only on the surface because beneath that surface is a heated competition over a host of scarce resources.

If we were to apply a conflict paradigm to an understanding of crime, suicide, divorce, and poverty, we might come up with quite different insights into the nature of these problems. Rather than being seen in structural-functional terms, they become understandable in terms of the inherent nature of conflict. People commit crime out of economic necessity, or because they live in a capitalist society that has always cared more about ends (money) than means (moral and ethical ways of acquiring it).

Conflict and functional paradigms do have certain characteristics in common. Both are structurally based paradigms that tend to look at whole societies. But whereas functionalism tends to see society as based on consensus, integration, and cooperation, conflict paradigms see it as based on competition, domination, and power.

It should be obvious that exactly the same data set could be interpreted in entirely different ways when looked at through the lens of a conflict paradigm or through a functional paradigm. This is the role of theory, and much care will have to be taken to ensure that the methods chosen are consistent with the assumptions of the paradigm underlying them, as different paradigms lead to quite different methodologies. Functionalism uses an empirical methodology based on the amassing of certain social facts collectively derived. Rates are evidence of these social facts, and so statistical formulations are helpful in coming up with data that will fit a functionalist paradigm. Comparative and experimental methods are also used in functional analyses along with the technique of historical induction in which we collect various historical facts and then weave them into a structural-functional view of the society that existed at the time. Society is an evolutionary outgrowth of previous structures that were changed through time and circumstance. Conflict theory, while emphasizing the technique of historical induction, reaches quite different conclusions with it—conclusions that are consistent with the assumptions of the conflict paradigm. The Marxist method of the dialectic is also commonly employed in methodologies emanating from conflict paradigms.

The Behaviorist Paradigm

The behaviorist paradigm, which has had great influence in psychology but also in the other social sciences, views external conditions as the source of all human behavior. Stimulus/response, conditioning, and learning theories are all within this paradigm.

The most famous stimulus/response theorist of recent vintage is B. F. Skinner, whose work has become extremely controversial. There are three major assumptions on which the work of Skinner and other reinforcement theorists rests: (1) behaviorism, (2) associationism, and (3) hedonism (Deutsch and Krauss 1965). Behaviorism stresses that behavior is the basic subject matter of social science and that the researcher should deal only with phenomena that are observable. So-called "internal" states and processes are excluded in favor of direct observation of the concrete properties of human behavior. Behaviorism arose as a revolt against the subjectivism of the late nineteenth century in which psychologists used terms like *instinct*, *will*, and *sensation*, as basic explanations for complex social behavior as well as simple behavioral acts. Primarily through the work of John Watson (1878-1958), behaviorism stressed that psychology should deal only with observable phenomena that are open to inspection by everyone. One can see the stimulus and one can see the response. Everything else is pure speculation and magic.

Associationism is an old idea that holds that the primary units of the mind are paralleled (or associated) with outer behavior. In other words, what we see as outward conduct is matched precisely by some inner version of the same thing. The behaviorists rejected the notion of mental units but retained the principle of association, substituting for mental states the conditioned response as the basic unit of analysis (Deutsch and Krauss 1965, 78-79). Because inside and outside were now regarded as basically one unit, the entire analysis could focus on external, observable behavior, and the person's inner life could effectively be ignored.

Reinforcement theories are further supported by the assumption that the human being is an economic creature driven to seek pleasure and avoid pain. This idea, which is the basis for what has come to be known as *exchange theory*, sees people's behavior as a simple response to their conditioning about costs and rewards. Behavior can be understood as attempts to maximize rewards and minimize costs (Homans 1961, 13).

In recent years Skinner has increasingly left laboratory work to others and has become something of an advocate of the use of behaviorism to solve social problems and reorganize society. He advocates the use of behavioral principles to develop what he calls a "technology of behavior, which would use behavior modification to discourage antisocial conduct and reward through reinforcement desired conduct" (Schellenberg 1978, 106). Skinner's work remains controversial, but it has been very influential.

The methodological implications of the behavioral paradigm are quite clear. The social scientist strives for complete objectivity, looks only at behavior, tries to use highly controlled, experimental (or preferably laboratory) techniques, and shuns any forms of research that would recognize a subjective element in human beings.

The Symbolic Interactionist Paradigm

While conflict theory and functionalism largely either leave human beings out of their analyses or else regard them as puppets in systems, the symbolic interactionist paradigm makes a social version of them the heart of its analysis. Conflict and structure both separate the individual and society almost into polar camps. Symbolic interactionism steadfastly refuses to separate them, insisting instead on the reciprocal relationship between the two.

Originating in the early 1900s in the United States, symbolic interactionism rapidly became one of the most dominant paradigms in sociology and especially in social psychology. George Herbert Mead (1863–1931) is generally considered to be the father of the symbolic interactionism paradigm. Rejecting any attempt to separate the individual and society or to reduce one to the other, Mead built a paradigm based on the idea that all social systems, structures, societies, and the like, arise out of the *interaction* between acting human beings.

Mead taught in the Department of Philosophy at the University of Chicago at the turn of the century. His philosophy was known as *pragmatism,* and it is necessary to know something of this school of thought to grasp the major difference in the symbolic interactionist paradigm. Pragmatism was a radical departure from traditional modes of philosophical thinking. Arising in the context of the impressive achievements of science, pragmatism held that the majority of philosophical problems should be recast in the light of scientific knowledge, especially evolutionary theory. Charles Darwin's work, mentioned earlier, led Mead to take seriously the idea of process, which had been considerably neglected prior to Darwin. Nature was regarded as being fixed, consisting of unalterable substances that existed independently of one another (Desmonde 1970). The substances of which nature was supposedly composed were regarded as eternal. The task of philosophy was to determine just what these eternal forms were and to show how human life was affected by them.

Darwin's work demolished this fixed conception of the universe and led to the acceptance of the idea of process and change. The developing social sciences were heavily influenced by this idea, as the work of Mead quickly showed. Organisms and their environment were not to be construed as separate entities, but the mutually dependent relationship between them was to be stressed. In addition, the reciprocal influence of organism and environment included an analysis of the shifting reconstruction that each was accomplishing on the other. Our current problems of pollution are a good example of this conception of the universe. People are reshaping the very environment in which they live through the products of industrial technology. As the environment changes, corresponding changes in human beings occur, and our heightened awareness of this process leads to efforts to restructure the environment in ways that are more livable and less destructive.

Mead did not refer to his own system of social psychology as *symbolic interactionism*. That term was coined later by Herbert Blumer (a student of Mead's at the University of Chicago at the time of Mead's death in 1931) in reference to what he believed were the essentials of Mead's position. Instead, Mead called his social psychology *social behaviorism,* and an understanding of why he chose that term will help us comprehend the strands of thought with which he was dealing, and his opposition to the behaviorist paradigm.

By destroying the dualism between a person's mind and body, Darwin's theory gave support to those paradigms that regarded human beings as part of a natural, evolutionary process. One of these was behaviorism, which we have already encountered. Mead agreed with the behaviorists that behavior is the basic datum of social psychology. From that point, however, Mead's thinking departed from theirs in some highly critical ways. First, Mead contended that the behaviorists' description of individual conduct stripped the organism away from the context in which its behavior occurred. The total behavior of an acting human organism includes not only those external, directly observable aspects but also covert, internal ones that are *accessible*, albeit indirectly. The behaviorists, according to Mead, tended to reduce human behavior to the model of billiard balls, acting and reacting against one another with no regard to the meaning their actions have for them (Desmonde 1970, 57). The behaviorist model of stimulus/response, action, and reaction could be regarded as meaningful in the case of human beings only when weighed against a total social situation.

Mead also rejected the behaviorists' image of human organisms as passive. Whereas a dog, rat, or pigeon may await an activating stimulus and then respond, human beings from the beginning of their lives are continually active (Dewey 1922). People dynamically select the stimuli they are going to respond to and do not simply react to perceptions. In this sense human beings in many ways determine their own environment. Objects in the social world may be put there in an effort to elicit a certain type of behavioral response, but in the final analysis what they are depends on how they are acted on by people. A table or a chair is created in order to be used as something to eat at or sit on. In a pinch, however, a human being might well decide to forgo the conventional responses toward those objects and chop them up for firewood.

The program of the behaviorists, as empirically sound as many of its tenets are, needs to be revised somewhat in the light of the special abilities of human organisms. Mead proposes, then, in contrast to psychological behaviorism a kind of social behaviorism in which human acts are taken to be social responses and not mere organic movements. Human movements, for example, usually begin with an idea. The idea, even though it is relatively covert, is an essential phase of the act. If we regard ideas and other mental processes as behavioral in their own right, then a behavioristic introspection is possible, because people—unlike rocks, trees, or pigeons—can be asked about their ideas and the role these play in their behavior. An empirically based social psychology is therefore possible, even though some aspects of social acts are not directly observable.

Human consciousness, rooted in the ability to communicate symbolically, means that human beings can learn new responses and new meanings without having gone through the trial/error, stimulus/response operant conditioning that the behaviorists offered as an adequate account of human functioning. Watching another person burn his or her fingers by putting them into a fire can mean that we might want to avoid such an exercise ourselves, even though we have never actually experienced the pain. The meaning of any event, then, is not necessarily in the direct experience of it but rather in the response we make toward it. This is why the same stimuli can mean radically different things to different people because they respond to the stimuli from different social perspectives. During the Vietnam War, for example, peace symbols came to elicit radically different responses from people. Any other symbol is subject to the same kind of differing response.

Human social life, then, consists of a series of symbolic interactions with the world people experience themselves as being in. And it is crucial to this paradigm to note that this process of interaction is collective, plural, and social—not individual. Meaning arises as a joint activity, even though the entire process may take place within the person's own "skin." Thinking, for example, is a social process—a kind of internal conversation—that takes place within people but involves considerably more than themselves. Mind, as Mead pointed out, emerges in communicative interaction with others and continues to have a life only with regard to these others. In this sense those who are defined as mentally ill are not so much out of *their* minds as they are out of the minds of others whose response they are no longer able to mobilize with their actions. Because mind is a social process that occurs in interaction, the components of interaction are essential to an understanding of even the most mental of all human activities. This understanding squares with Mead's definition of mind:

> Mind arises in the social process only when that process as a whole enters into or is present in the experience of any one of the given individuals involved in that process. . . . It is by means of reflexiveness—the turning-back of the experience of the individual upon himself—that the whole social process is thus brought into the experience of the individuals involved in it; it is by such means, which enable the individual to take the attitude of the other toward himself, that the individual is able consciously to adjust himself to that process, and to modify the results of the process in any given social act in terms of his adjustment to it. Reflexiveness, then, is the essential condition, within the social process, for the development of mind. (1934, 134)

For Mead, then, mind is simply the ability of one organism to take another into account as its action develops. Human beings, in fact, do that all of the time, and this ability considerably changes the way the social scientist ought to study them, a point we will make later in our discussion of field methods where the symbolic interactionist is most in evidence.

The major advocate of the Meadian tradition in social psychology has been Herbert Blumer. Primarily through Blumer's work (especially his teaching), Mead's ideas have stayed at the forefront of modern social science and the methodological implications of the symbolic interaction paradigm have been articulated. Much of Blumer's work has been critical of the remainder of social psychology for not taking into account Mead's trenchant observations on social life. Like Mead, Blumer believes that human society consists of an interpretive process through which meanings are used to give events their particular character. Blumer has summarized five of Mead's key concepts that social science must take into account: the self, the act, social interaction, objects, and joint action. We will discuss each of these five points briefly.

The Self. Mead saw the human being as an organism having a self, and "the possession of a self converts the human being into a special kind of actor, transforms his relation to the world, and gives his action a unique character. In asserting that the human being has a self, Mead simply meant that the human being is an object to himself" (Blumer 1969, 62). This self transforms human action into something quite different from animal behavior. People can act back on themselves in the same or similar terms as they act toward others and others act toward them. They can judge, analyze, evaluate, define, and guide their own conduct. Furthermore, the self is viewed as a *process* and not a structure. This idea separates interactionist thought from the personal approach that stresses cognitive structures as the source of human action.

Much of psychology has identified the self with a structure or organization. Freud's notion of the ego qualifies as such a structured view. But Mead insisted that a self is a social process characterized by the prospect of reflexivity. To be an object to one's own behavior changes the individual from one who merely responds to internal or external demands to one who acts toward the world, interpreting and organizing action on the basis of that interpretation:

> To illustrate: a pain one identifies and interprets is very different from a mere organic feeling and lays the basis for doing something about it instead of merely responding organically to it; to note and interpret the activity of another person is very different from having a response released by that activity; to be aware that one is hungry is very different from merely being hungry; to perceive one's "ego" puts one in the position of doing something with regard to it instead of merely giving expression to the ego. As these illustrations show, the process of self-interaction puts the human being over against his world instead of merely in it, requires him to meet and handle his world through a defining process instead of merely responding to it, and forces him to construct his action instead of merely releasing it.

This is the kind of acting organism that Mead sees man to be as a result of having a self. (Blumer 1969, 63–64)

The Act. Because human beings have selves, human action is built up in the process of coping with the world rather than being released out of preexisting structures. Despite all the material available socially and culturally to persons (or perhaps because of the wide variety of such material), acts must be put together by the self-reflective organism each time they are done. This means that human behavior is a continual accomplishment, not a mere routine carried out under the influence of some direct stimulus. Among the things that human beings indicate to themselves are their needs, wants, goals, and feelings; the expectations of others; the rules of the group; the nature of the situation they are in; conceptions of themselves; recollections; and images of possible lines of action to be taken toward others. The person is not the mere recipient of these things but must handle them as behavior unfolds.

Blumer notes that viewing behavior in this way is directly opposite to those perspectives that tend to be used in the psychological and social sciences. Traditionally, human behavior is seen as the result of factors that play on the organism, as though the resulting conduct were a mere response to activating mechanisms. Human beings are rarely seen as having selves but rather are viewed as mere vehicles through which other forces express themselves.

Social Interaction. Human beings respond to one another in two ways: symbolically and nonsymbolically. In nonsymbolic interaction people respond directly to one another's gestures. In symbolic interaction, however, they respond to their interpretations of one another's acts. Most human interaction is of the symbolic variety. It consists of defining and interpreting the acts of ourselves and others and acting on the basis of such definitions. The definitions may well be wrong, but people are nevertheless condemned to a world of meanings in which their actions must be constructed out of their definitions of what is going on.

Social interaction is therefore a process to be understood in its own right, not simply another variable to be plugged into schemes that lodge determinants of behavior in attitudes, values, feelings, or the organization of personality. Human interaction is a positive shaping in its own right and cannot, according to Blumer, be simply inserted beneath other factors that are deemed more important. Anyone who has had the opportunity to observe a wide variety of social situations is aware that the nature of the unfolding interaction is a highly significant process that in large measure accounts for the differences that occur in these situations.

A recognition of how social life involves the dual process of definition and interpretation enables social psychologists to deal with both permanence and change in the same analytic framework. Established patterns such as the family, religion, and economic systems exist and are sustained only through the continued use of some framework of interpretation. The defining acts of members of society regularly confirm various social arrangements, and change occurs when the definitions change. Relationships as varied as cooperation, conflict, domination, exploitation, consensus, and disagreement all hold this definitional basis in common. According to Blumer, an emphasis on social interaction overcomes the narrow tendency in social psychology to construct a general model of human interaction on the basis of one particular type of relationship. Conflict, exchange, and mutual expectations represent only a few of the many types of social interactions possible, and none of these by itself will serve as an adequate model of all human relationships.

Objects. We can easily observe that social life revolves around various kinds of objects that exist in the world. Blumer reminds us, however, that for Mead the concept of object had a very different meaning from that currently in use. Objects, for Mead, are *human constructs,* not self-existing entities with intrinsic properties. The nature of an object depends on how people act toward it. An object is anything that can be designated or referred to, including various physical classes of things such as buildings and cars but also—and importantly—social events such as a race riot or the activities of the middle class. The meaning of any of these classes of objects is not intrinsic to the object but flows from the nature of the social interaction that human beings have with the object. The object world, then, is created as human beings act toward it. We usually think of objects as *physical things,* but in social terms life consists primarily of the manipulation of *social objects,* which are the objects of *social acts.* A good example of a social object has been described by McCall and Simmons:

> A rather young man, in a park in the Bronx, is standing quietly but very alertly in the afternoon sun. Suddenly he tenses and scurries a few tentative steps to his right, still rather frozen, his gaze locked on a man only a few feet away. This other man makes a sudden movement with his right arm, and the first fellow breaks into sudden flight. Twenty or thirty yards away, still another fellow starts to run to cut him off, and the first man falls flat on his face, skidding and bounding roughly along the ground for several feet as a result of his great momentum. (1966, 51–52)

The acts being described here have created a social object—the stolen base in a game of baseball. It has no physical structure but is purely a social object, a kind of symbol created by the cooperative action of eighteen men laboring under a common rule. "A stolen base cannot be touched, smelled, or tasted, but it does exist, through the joint efforts of human actors" (p. 52).

Social objects such as the stolen base are all around us. In fact, most of the things we strive for—marriage, grades, academic degrees, positions in society, and so on—exist not in nature but only as social objects created jointly by the persons involved.

Joint Action. A final concept in Blumer's framework is the idea of joint action. Social objects and social acts are accomplished not by individuals acting alone but by people acting together. Individual lines of action must join. Marriage, sex, intimacy, and love all involve other people. The social realities that compose our lives cannot be understood as an outcome of individual acts, but can only be seen as a result of joint acts, undertaken in common with others. A fully developed social science, according to Blumer, must take this fundamental principle into account.

The Ethnomethodological Paradigm

As the interactionist perspective grew, inevitable offshoots and derivatives emerged. Drawing on different philosophical traditions, various schools developed. One of the most important of these is ethnomethodology (Garfinkel 1967). Based on the phenomenology of European thinkers such as Alfred Schutz and Edmund Husserl, ethnomethodology is founded on several assumptions. First, human behavior is to be understood subjectively from the standpoint of the experience of the acting individual. Second, there are as many different social worlds of reality as there are individuals. Third, social order and social action are seen as problematic constructions, even though they are taken for granted by the individual. Fourth, in the process of interacting with other people the individuals involved suspend many of their own commonsense assumptions and act as if they know and understand what the others are saying. Finally, these commonsense assumptions make up what we call human society (Lindesmith et al. 1975, 20).

Studying the commonplace, however, is not an easy task. The social psychologist must devise a strategy with which to make these scenes visible. Harold Garfinkel, who coined the term *ethnomethodology*, has done this ably with a series of small experiments designed to disrupt the usual routines of everyday life and, by so doing, make their features visible. The major feature of everyday life is the existence of a series of *background expectancies*. These consist of those taken-for-granted social understandings that are seen but unnoticed and are usually perceived only when they are violated (Garfinkel 1967).

The term *ethnomethodology* is a compound phrase taken from two words—*ethno*, meaning "people," and *methodology*, meaning "procedure." As a theory and strategy in social science, then, ethnomethodology focuses on the procedures people use to make sense out of everyday life.

Garfinkel reports that his standard procedure is to find a common routine in which people are engaged and then "see what can be done to make trouble." By observing how people respond, he can presumably uncover all the features and characteristics of these scenes. For example:

Case 1

The subject was telling the experimenter, a member of the subject's car pool, about having had a flat tire while going to work the previous day.
(S) I had a flat tire.
(E) What do you mean, you had a flat tire?
(S) She appeared momentarily stunned. Then she answered in a hostile way: What do you mean, 'What do you mean?' A flat tire is a flat tire.
(E) That is what I meant. Nothing special. What a crazy question! (Garfinkel 1967, 42)

Case 6

(S) How are you?
(E) How am I in regard to what? My health, my finances, my school work, my peace of mind, my . . . ?
(S) (Red in the face and suddenly out of control.) Look! I was just trying to be polite. Frankly, I don't give a damn how you are! (P. 44)

Case 7

My friend and I were talking about a man whose overbearing attitude annoyed us. My friend expressed his feeling.
(S) I'm sick of him.
(E) Would you explain what is wrong with you that you are sick?
(S) Are you kidding me? You know what I mean.
(E) Please explain your ailment.
(S) (He listened to me with a puzzled look.) What came over you? We never talk this way, do we? (P. 44)

The reactions of people to these violations of commonsense expectations demonstrate how much of social life is routine and based on a series of background expectations that ethnomethodologists are trying to specify. When these small rules of interaction are violated, the results are startling, immediate, and devastating.

In another procedure, Garfinkel had students spend time in their own homes with their families, acting as if they were merely boarders. They were told to conduct themselves in a polite and formal way, speak only when spoken to, and the like. Interestingly, some students found that they could not do this simple experiment because of the problems that arose. One student whose mother had a heart condition was afraid the shock might kill her.

For students who did try, the results were spectacular. Family members were stupefied. They sought to make the strange actions intelligible by providing accounts of the student's behavior, by acting angry or anxious, and by charging the student with being mean, inconsiderate, selfish, nasty, or impolite. One student embarrassed his mother in front of her friends by asking if she minded if he had a snack from the refrigerator before turning in for the night. The mother exploded: "Mind if you have a little snack? You've been eating snacks around here for years without asking me. What's gotten into you?" Family members responded routinely to these violations with the most savage attacks on the student (Garfinkel 1967, 47–48).

To the ethnomethodologist these experiments show how important commonsense social structures are. We act routinely in terms of shared assumptions about what reality is, and when these assumptions are challenged through behavior that does not validate them, the results are striking indeed.

Ethnomethodology is young and has few adherents at this time, although its influence among sociologically based social psychologists seems to be growing. Thus far, much of its theoretical work has been an effort to define itself and to distinguish it from other points of view, especially general symbolic interactionism. This attempt to carve out theoretical distinctions seems to be a common first stage in the development of competing paradigms.

Chapter 4

Choosing a Research Design

Research design defined
The relation of theory to the research design
The importance of the research design
Factors to consider in choosing a research design
   Who? (unit of analysis)
   When? (research time frame)
   Where? (research setting)
   Why? (research purpose)
      Explanation
      Description
      Exploration

What are the most crucial criteria for judging the adequacy of the design?
   Control
   Representativeness
   Naturalness
Three research designs
   Experiment
   Survey
   Field study
General considerations
The research design and data collection

If you is goin' anywhere in particular
Up here, ud'd better figger fust
How ta git thar
Cuz by jest goin'
Afore ya know where yere goin'
Ya might not wanta be.
—Anonymous

Let's begin by reviewing your progress. You have selected a subject area in which you wish to do research. You have spent time studying library materials to identify what has already been accomplished and to help in narrowing down the research subject to a research question. You have also used this relevant body of literature to formulate a plausible answer to the research question. This plausible answer constitutes your theory. Specifically, it defines the relationships you anticipate among the phenomena under study.

But theory is still theory. It remains a speculative or conjectural view of the way things work; it is not fact. And though logic and previously established fact may have been used to define the anticipated relationships, "the relations of logic are not necessarily the relationships of man" (Senn 1971, 23). The use of logic to formulate theory, then, is only a tool. Science insists that the knowledge derived through the use of this tool be tested in the real world (Senn 1971). But you have already discovered that theory is not directly testable. The abstract nature of stated relationships among concepts make such relationships and concepts vulnerable to multiple definitions (i.e., operationalization can take many forms). In fact, the more general the concepts, the more meanings and definitions there are to choose from. Thus, the researcher scientist must devise a strategy whereby the theory can be, at least indirectly, tested. *Research design* is the name we give to this strategy.

RESEARCH DESIGN DEFINED

By research design we mean the plan of procedures for data collection and analysis that are undertaken to evaluate a particular theoretical perspective. The research design involves the entire process of planning and carrying out a research study (Miller 1975). It is all the procedures or steps undertaken to ensure an objective test of the theory under investigation.

If you were presented with the pieces to a jigsaw puzzle and challenged to fit the pieces together, most likely your strategy for accomplishing this task would be something other than haphazard. Suppose the scene on the puzzle box were a red barn set in a wheat field under a blue sky. You might begin by sorting the pieces according to the major colors: blue, yellow-gold, and red. Or you might begin by identifying those pieces with a straight edge that provide the border for the picture. Such procedures suggest an organized approach to the puzzle's solution. Likewise, in attempting to evaluate a proposed answer to a research question, you should employ an organized approach. Before beginning you should outline the steps required to test the theory. These steps become your "blueprint," which serves to guide you in this test.

The principles of research design are those factors that influence the choice of a research design. Active researchers are frequently called on to make design decisions, and the factors that influence their choice of design are not always apparent. You can think of the principles or factors influencing design choice as different-colored puzzle pieces. As you consider the factors by answering certain relevant questions, your search for an answer to the research question will begin to take on some order. This order ensures a more objective approach to the research question. In addition to considering the factors that influence design choice, we will also relate these factors to the various research designs. This particular task can be somewhat tricky, though, since social scientists do not always agree on the labels they give to the various design alternatives. For this book, we have chosen to use the commonly applied labels: experiment, survey, and field study. This chapter will not describe in detail these three basic designs; that task will be saved for Chapters 8, 9, and 10. Primarily, this chapter is designed to help you think logically through a series of factors and to relate these factors to the design alternatives in such a way that you can make a reasonable and adequate design decision. The presentation of these factors is based on the premise that there are certain questions that can be asked and, when answered, offer concrete guidance in choosing the most adequate design. These factors also provide us with a basis for making comparisons between research designs.

THE RELATION OF THEORY TO THE RESEARCH DESIGN

The relation of theory to the research design, although basically quite simple, is of tremendous importance and deserves special comment. We have already established that theory is not directly testable. The concepts and the stated relationships among concepts must be reworked into variables (measurement of characteristics on which people differ) and stated relationships among variables (hypotheses) if they are to be tested.

In effect, the research design provides us with a plan whereby these transformations can take place. *Whereas theory guides our answer to the research question, the research design guides our test of this answer.* Thus, theory is instrumental in guiding our choice of a research design by identifying who or what is to be observed, how it is to be observed, and how these observations are to be interpreted. In fact, we must constantly be concerned with whether or not the research design fits the theory in order that our research will lead us to the relevant facts (Riley 1963). *The researcher simply must not get this process backward.*

THE IMPORTANCE OF THE RESEARCH DESIGN

To ensure the elimination of bias (the detection and correction of errors) as much as possible, science, as a way of knowing, requires a plan—a research design. Although a research design cannot guarantee reliable knowledge, it does provide an organized and stable approach to this mission in several ways. First, the use of a research design ensures that we are striving toward *objectivity*. Selective perception is not permitted. The researcher is obligated to examine a variety of cases, including cases that can disconfirm as well as confirm the theory being tested. Lombroso (1912), in his classic study of physical characteristics and criminal tendencies, did not do this. Lombroso believed that criminal behavior was inborn. To determine whether this position represented "truth," he developed a number of tests to measure the physical characteristics of convicted criminals. And true to his position, he found a number of recurring characteristics in criminals: shifty eyes, strong jaw, wispy beard, and receding hairline. However, Lombroso's fatal flaw was selective perception—that is, his failure to look for these same physical characteristics in the noncriminal population. Consequently, he did not really establish that these characteristics occurred more frequently in the criminal population—only that they did occur in the criminal population.

Second, the use of a research design ensures that our approach to knowledge is *systematic*. The researcher proceeds methodically, delineating in detail each step to be taken. Who or what is to be sampled? What is to be measured? How is measurement to be accomplished? How is measurement to be obtained? How is analysis to be done? And though no research design is a guarantee that the research process will be smooth, it is certain that it will be smoother.

Such a systematic approach suggests a third function of the research design. A research design ensures that the knowledge can be *replicated*. As we have already discovered, replication in the social sciences is not the rule. We might even say that it is the exception. That is, studies in the social sciences are seldom replicated. But the knowledge that the findings of a study can be checked and even rechecked is an essential characteristic. Having a research design makes this possible. The importance of a research design lies in the fact that it provides a means by which we are able to adhere to the scientific method in our quest for reliable knowledge. Without a research design, it is easier for our personal biases to get in the way in this search for knowledge. Thus, you might say that we employ a research design to keep from "straying off the straight and narrow."

FACTORS TO CONSIDER IN CHOOSING A RESEARCH DESIGN

We are finally ready to proceed from the realm of abstract ideas (theory) to concrete instances (research design). Many researchers feel uncomfortable with this transition, for they are more comfortable when ordering abstract ideas (formulating theory). However, there comes a time when we must choose a concrete version of an abstract question. Broadly speaking, the researcher has three designs from which to choose: the experiment, the survey, and the field study. In deciding which of these designs to use, several factors must be considered, including the following: *Who* will we study? *When* will we study them? *Where* will we study them? *Why* (for what purpose) will we be studying them? *What* is the most crucial criterion for judging the adequacy of the design? As you read about these factors and become familiar with the issues of concern, please remember that the answers to these questions will not dictate your choice of a research design. They will only provide concrete guidelines that aid in your choice.

Who? (Unit of Analysis)

As you have already seen, the social scientist is interested in social phenomena. The concept of social phenomena is quite broad and as such offers researchers tremendous latitude in who or what they can study. The unit of analysis chosen for study can be defined as the concrete research case used to address the research question. Basically, we can distinguish between four levels of the unit of analysis: (1) individuals, (2) groups, (3) organizations, and (4) social artifacts. Certainly, of these four, individuals most frequently serve as units of analysis. In other words, we usually describe social phenomena by studying the individuals who are a part of it. The *individual* as the unit of analysis can be characterized in many ways: student, worker, friend, spouse, parent, and so forth. Suppose, for example, you were interested in young people's attitudes toward popular dances. The individual would be the unit of analysis. If you were interested in whether males and females differed in their perception of competition and conflict, the individual would, again, be the unit of analysis.

It is worth noting, at this point, that although the individual serves as the unit of analysis, the write-up of analysis is not on this individual level. We are generally not interested in any given individual's attitudes or behaviors. We are interested in the attitudes and behaviors of an aggregate of individuals. Recall that one of the characteristics of science is that it is generalizing. We talk to people, but we are interested in them as social beings who interact with others. Thus, we tend to describe and explain social phenomena by grouping and summarizing the descriptions of individuals.

The *social group* may also serve as the unit of analysis in the study of social phenomena. Groups that might be studied, for example, include the family, friendship groups, cliques, and street gangs. When the group is used as the unit of analysis, the group's characteristics are usually derived from the characteristics of its individual members. Hoffman and Maier (1964), for example, were interested in studying how heterogeneous and homogeneous groups differ in their approaches to solving problems. In order to define heterogeneity or homogeneity of group membership, these researchers evaluated the degree of similarity and dissimilarity of the personality profiles of individual members. The characteristics of the individual members were then used to derive the characteristics of the group.

Organizations can also be treated as the unit of analysis. We may wish to study, for example, such organizations as churches or schools. We might, for example, be interested in the degree of bureaucratic structure within organized religion. In this instance, the unit of analysis would be the various church organizations as defined by denominations. When the organization is the unit of analysis, it is defined in terms of its organizational characteristics.

Finally, the unit of analysis does not have to be human; it may instead be a *social artifact.* Such units of analysis are sometimes called nonreactive measures (see Chapter 6), as they require neither participation in the social world under investigation nor the manipulation of that world. People, like other objects in the world at large, leave evidence of their presence. As a researcher, you can use this evidence to find out various things about them. Suppose, for example, you worked for a museum and were interested in learning which museum display was the most popular. Chicago's Museum of Science and Industry was interested in learning this. But the unit of analysis used to make this discovery was not human. Instead of questioning people directly about their favorite display, the researchers discovered that the tiles around the exhibit containing living, hatching chicks had to be replaced approximately every six weeks. Tiles in other areas of the museum lasted for years without replacement (Webb et al. 1981, 7–38).

Probably the most popular nonreactive measure used is content analysis, in which words, sentences, or topics frequently serve as the unit of analysis. Book content has been analyzed, for example, to understand sex-role stereotyping in U.S. society. Content analysis performed on grade-school readers (the classic Dick and Jane books) have shown a bias for placing women in domestic roles and men in career roles and thus helping to establish these stereotypic images in children's minds (Women on Words and Images 1972). Social artifacts, as the unit of analysis, can sometimes provide a data source not available through any other means.

Whatever the unit of analysis, there are primarily three ways in which this unit can be grouped: (1) real groups, (2) treatment groups, and (3) statistical groups. A *real group* is one that has an ongoing life of its own apart from the research setting. Such groups are formed by members' awareness of and involvement with one another, especially in a natural setting. The family is a good example of a real group. If you were interested in studying decision-making processes within the family, you would not think of randomly pairing a male, a female, and one or more children. The natural processes that function to create a family or any real group are germane to the issue. We shall see that this type of group is of special interest to researchers doing *field studies*.

In sharp contrast, the *treatment group* is an artificial group. It is one constructed by the researcher (usually an experimenter) for a specific purpose. Individuals grouped in this way generally have no relationship to one another outside the research situation. In fact, membership within a treatment group is often determined by the toss of a coin. Aronson and Mills's classic study (1959) of the effect of severity of initiation on liking for a group is an excellent example of treatment groups. Their study employed sixty-three college women who were randomly assigned to one of three groups: (1) severe initiation group, (2) mild initiation group, and (3) control group (no initiation). The women participating in the study were told that they were going to join a discussion group on sex, but in order to join, they were required to pass an initiation. In the severe initiation group, subjects were asked to read some very embarrassing material before judging the group discussion. In the mild initiation group, the material read was not very embarrassing. And in the control group, no reading was required. These three groups constituted the artificial or treatment groups. Membership was determined by the toss of a coin. As we shall see, such groups give the researcher tremendous power over the research situation and are of particular interest to the researcher using the *experiment*.

The third unit of analysis is the *statistical group*. In this type of group, the units need not be located in the same place or even be aware of each other. Statistical grouping results from all units possessing some characteristic central to the research question. Suppose, for example, we were interested in studying the differences in self-concept among adopted and nonadopted adolescents (Norvell and Guy 1977). The two statistical groups would be adopted adolescents and nonadopted adolescents. Comparisons of males and females, blacks and whites, marrieds and singles are all examples of statistical groups. The individuals composing these groups probably would not know each other or even be aware of each other. A subject's placement in one group or the other would be totally contingent upon possessing the defining characteristic. The more information obtained from each unit studied, the greater the possibilities for creating statistical groups. Primarily, the *survey design* uses this type of grouping.

When? (Research Time Frame)

Human behavior takes place in time and through time. Time is an important element for at least two reasons and as such should be considered in your choice of a research design: (1) Time helps in ordering the sequence of behavior and is an important determinant of causation. (2) Time positions behavior at some point along a continuum and thus raises the issue of generalizability for other positions along the continuum.

The study of social phenomena is conducted either at a single point in time or at several (two or more) points in time. Studies that examine social phenomena by obtaining data at a single point in time are called *cross-sectional*. Such studies portray events at a moment in time, as in a snapshot (Riley 1963). Such static studies are useful in defining the state of things as they are. Also they serve as important benchmarks for subsequent studies of process and change.

Studies that examine social phenomena by obtaining data at two or more points in time are called *longitudinal* studies. Political scientists who study the voting patterns of U.S. citizens over a five- or ten-year period are conducting longitudinal research. Economists who study change in spending and lending patterns in the United States over time are engaged in longitudinal research. Longitudinal and cross-sectional studies will be discussed at greater length in Chapters 8, 9, and 10. Right now, our concern is with understanding the role of time in the choice of a research design. Generally speaking, field studies are longitudinal in nature. The researcher is interested in observing natural groups over a period of time. The survey design can be either longitudinal or cross-sectional. Most experiments have a longitudinal quality in that data are collected at two points in time. But the period of time between the two data collections is usually short.

Where? (Research Setting)

Since human behavior also takes place in a particular setting, the research design must also take the setting into account. Every piece of research takes place in a setting that is unique with respect to time and space. Very simply put, the choice of setting reduces to two: the natural or the artificial, depending upon whether the research takes place in a real or a contrived setting.

Although the choice of a research setting seems quite simple and even obvious, it should be given careful thought and consideration. In truth, a number of factors need to be considered when choosing a research setting. Four of these are worthy of mentioning: (1) the nature of the research question, (2) the types of variables being studied, (3) the form of the hypothesized relationship among variables, and (4) the nature of rival hypotheses and the degree of control desired.

One factor affecting the choice of a research setting is the nature of the research question. Some research questions, for example, imply a definite concrete setting. If your research were concerned with trials, mental patients, or prisoners, you would probably go to a courtroom, a mental hospital, or a prison. Other research questions are less definite with respect to setting. If you were interested in studying conformity, competition, or conflict, your choice of settings would be much more varied.

A second factor is the types of variables being studied. Zeroing in on the independent variable, Ellsworth has written, "If the question or hypothesis concerns powerful or highly arousing events or strong feelings, the laboratory is usually not the most appropriate place to test it" (1977, 606). For example, if you were interested in fear, grief, or love, the laboratory would probably not be the most appropriate setting since the response range of these variables would be restricted to fairly low levels. In general, laboratory variables are weak and the more variables you try to control (manipulate), the weaker they are (Lewis 1975). Consequently, when control is more important than intensity, the laboratory is probably the preferred setting. When intensity is more important, the field is probably preferable. As for the dependent variable, the problem in the laboratory is one of subjects trying to "look good." Subjects know they are being studied and they want to look their best. Thus, they often respond in ways that they perceive to be appropriate and acceptable. Studies that involve socially undesirable behavior may often be better tested outside of the laboratory even in a situation where subjects do not know they are being observed by a social scientist. (We must be careful here, however. The ethics of such a procedure must be thought about carefully. We address this question in other sections of this book.)

A third factor to consider when choosing a research setting is the form of the hypothesized relationship among variables. "In general, laboratory studies are limited to studying immediately reactive variables such as self-esteem, liking, or commitment. Chronic self-esteem, lasting friendship, or long-term commitment may have quite different effects from their reactive counterparts. For long-term effects or the study of processes over time, a natural setting is certainly desirable" (Ellsworth 1977, 607). Suppose, for example, you were interested in studying interpersonal attraction or liking. You constructed an experiment in which paired individuals were asked to talk for fifteen minutes. One of the pair is always a member of the research team; the other is the true subject (stooge). In the course of the fifteen-minute conversation, the research team member has been instructed to offer fifteen comments providing reinforcement for the stooge ("You're so right." "That's very perceptive." "I fully agree."). Following the fifteen-minute conversation, the stooge is asked to fill out a brief questionnaire which, among other things, questions him on his feelings toward his conversational partner. Levinger and Snoek (1972) have noted that such studies of interpersonal attraction tend to be superficial. They deal with first impressions rather than with long-term relationships and with interpersonal attraction as a one-time event rather than as a continuous process. Levinger and Snoek have emphasized in their research that the important factors in a relationship differ from time to time. Thus, they argue for the natural setting to study the career (development over time) of a relationship.

A fourth factor to consider is the nature of rival hypotheses and the degree of control desired. No hypothesis stands alone as the sole explanation of some social phenomena. Alternative plausible explanations are the "stuff" of hypotheses. Certainly, it is in the researcher's best interest to eliminate as many of these rival hypotheses as possible in order to lend credibility to his hypothesis (Manhein 1977). Suppose, for example, your reading in methodology led you to this methodological research issue: the usefulness of a neutral point on a five-point response scale. Assume that the response alternatives on a five-point scale are (1) strongly agree, (2) agree, (3) neutral, (4) disagree, and (5) strongly disagree. Such a scale, as we shall see, is called a *Likert scale* (see Chapter 6). But for the moment, interest is in whether the presence or absence of a neutral position on the scale significantly affects an individual's score.

To test this hypothesis, you might consider having your subjects respond to the scale items twice: first with the alternatives strongly agree, agree, neutral, disagree, and strongly disagree. If you assigned weights to these response alternatives and then summed the weights to get each subject's two scores, you could compare the scores to determine if they were significantly different (statistical jargon). If different, your inference would be that the difference was due to the presence or absence of the neutral point. But there is another possibility: a rival hypothesis. The difference might be due to simply having taken the same test twice. To control for this rival hypothesis, you might decide to use two different tests whose content is similar. Although this eliminates the problem of taking the same test twice, it does not eliminate the problem of taking two tests. So there is still the possibility of a testing effect—that is, the difference observed between a subject's two scores is a function of testing (i.e., taking two tests) and not the presence or absence of a neutral point. Your choice of a research design would have to consider this rival hypothesis and maybe others and attempt to eliminate them (Guy and Norvell 1977). In general, then, we start with the relationship of interest and then scan the logical rivals to see which are plausible rivals in the particular instance; then we choose our research setting in such a way as to control for or measure the strongest contenders.

Why? (Research Purpose)

Once the researcher has answered the questions of who, when, and where (though not necessarily in this order), the important question of *why* must be dealt with. The question of why is concerned with the research purpose. But before considering specific research purposes, there are two frequently held misconceptions concerning purpose that need to be mentioned. First, it is an overgeneralization to assume that each researcher approaches a research question with a single purpose in mind. Although there may be only one purpose, it is not inconceivable or even improbable that the researcher would have two purposes in mind. Second, research purpose is not synonymous with research design. Although a certain purpose may seem more suitable and more frequently used with one design over another, purpose does not dictate design.

There are three general research purposes that seem applicable to the study of most social phenomena: explanation, description, and exploration.

Explanation. Explanation as a research purpose is concerned with why things are the way they are. We have named explanation first as it is the most advanced of scientific purposes. It is the purpose toward which all scientific research strives. To do research with this purpose in mind requires greater knowledge of the research question. Ultimately, the ability to explain gives one the ability to predict. And such predictive power assumes the ability to establish cause–effect relationships among variables. Killeffer (1969, 21) says, "Basic to the scientific method is the fundamental axiom that the physical universe is a rational, ordered one in which cause and effect are inevitably linked and where events fit together in logical patterns." In other words, we accept as self-evident that events are causally related and that we can discover the cause or causes of any event. In research, the variable said to be the cause is called the *independent variable*. The variable said to be the effect is called the *dependent variable*.

At this point, we might recall that strictly speaking, causal arguments cannot be verified empirically (Chapter 1). Causal inferences are not on the operational level; they are on the theoretical level. They involve purely hypothetical if–then statements that are inherently untestable (Blalock 1968). To put it even more bluntly, "There is no direct way to demonstrate that a relationship is causal. Nothing we can see, smell, or perceive in any way 'proves' that one thing caused another" (Orenstein and Phillips 1978, 129). Thus, we cannot establish beyond absolute doubt that the independent variable caused change in the dependent variable. We can only establish beyond *probable* doubt that the independent variable caused change in the dependent variable.

To establish beyond probable doubt that a cause–effect relationship exists, three essential criteria must be met. First, there must be a relationship between two variables. In particular, the two variables must covary (change together), and unless two variables do covary, we cannot infer that one is the cause of the other. Second, there must also be a time order to the variables. That which is cause must precede that which is effect in time. The third and final criterion is that we must be able to eliminate all plausible alternative explanations (rival hypotheses). Events are not such that a single cause produces a single effect. Probably any number of causes could produce a particular effect. In the example of the neutral position on a five-point scale, we identified two possible reasons for a particular effect. In theory, the number of possible causes is infinite. In practice, though, the most plausible causes can probably be identified. Consequently, if the research purpose is one of explanation (cause–effect), we must choose a research design that will allow us to make the best possible indirect test of cause-effect.

(We will want to remember here our discussion in Chapter 3. *Cause* and *effect* are terms that stem from one particular theoretical model (the mechanistic or positivistic one), and so if we search for causes methodologically, we will want to do so only because we are working with a theory that uses this idea. To the extent that cause is tied to explanation, it is also theory-derived, and theory-dependent. If the researcher is using other theoretical paradigms (such as symbolic interactionism) cause-and-effect are not a part of the search and analytical description becomes the appropriate methodological technique.)

Description. Studies whose primary purpose is one of description have one or two goals:

1. To portray accurately the characteristics of a particular individual, group, organization, or institution.
2. To determine the frequency with which something occurs or is associated with something else.

Description, as a research purpose, is concerned with delineating the way things are. Although the social scientist might like to be in a position to explain social phenomena, this is not always possible. Sometimes the present state of knowledge in an area makes explanation impossible.

Hence, an enormous amount of social research is conducted for the purpose of describing. Descriptive research concentrates on accuracy and completeness. In fact, studies having a descriptive purpose are typically more accurate and precise than studies having a causal and predictive purpose.

A familiar example of research with a descriptive purpose is the taking of the United States census. A U. S. census describes the people who live in the United States: the number of males and females, whites and non-whites, marrieds, singles, widowed, and divorced. Such an endeavor is primarily concerned with precision and completeness. Marketing researchers study people to learn what kinds of products they will buy. New products are not usually placed on the market blindly (and neither are commercials on television). Before a company invests a sizeable sum of money in a new product, they want to make certain it will sell. Consequently, they first poll the targeted population at which the product is aimed.

Exploration. Exploration, as a research purpose, is concerned with uncovering the way things are. Exploratory studies are undertaken primarily for four reasons:

1. To satisfy the researcher's curiosity and desire for a better understanding.
2. To test the feasibility of undertaking a more comprehensive study.
3. To develop methods to be used in a more comprehensive study.
4. To formulate a problem for more precise investigation or for developing hypotheses.

As social scientists, we sometimes display a tendency to underestimate the value of exploratory studies and to assume that such studies are not scientific. This is a gross inaccuracy and does injustice to exploration as a major research purpose. Granted, when exploration is the purpose, the level of scientific knowledge is usually not as advanced. However,

> The relative youth of social science and the scarcity of social science research make it inevitable that much of this research, for a time to come, will be of a pioneering character. Few well-trodden paths exist for the investigator of social relations to follow; theory is often either too general or too specific to provide clear guidance for empirical research. In these circumstances, exploratory research is necessary to obtain the experience that will be helpful in formulating relevant hypotheses for more definitive investigation. (Selltiz et al. 1976, 91)

Agreeing with this position, Hoover writes, ''We have barely figured out how to lay the foundation for a structure of theory to explain social behavior. People have muddled around for centuries trying to sort through significant connections'' (1976, 25). Science is a ''slightly elevated form of muddling'' by which these connections are often tried and tested and exploration is often a necessary first step.

What Are the Most Crucial Criteria for Judging the Adequacy of the Design?

It should be apparent by now that research design decisions are influenced by whom we study, when we study them, where we study them, and why we are studying them. But even given answers to these questions, three additional criteria remain that can help us in making our research design decision: (1) control, (2) representativeness, and (3) naturalness.

Control. When the researcher's primary concern is to establish unambiguously a causal link between two variables (as when explanation is the purpose), control is the most crucial criterion for judging the adequacy of the research design. By control, we mean the researcher's ability to manipulate all independent variables that could influence (causally connect to) the dependent variable. This would mean not only those independent variables which are central to the study but also those which are unknown or unobserved.

With the experiment, such control is established by making comparisons between a minimum of two groups that are initially ''alike'' in all ways but one—the independent variable. If these two groups are found to be different on the dependent variable, then the targeted independent variable is said to be the reason (cause). But how is such ''alikeness'' accomplished? One way is through matching the characteristics of subjects, which results in all such variables being held constant (i.e., such characteristics do not vary). Such a procedure, though, has distinct disadvantages. Consider this excellent example offered by Orenstein and Phillips:

> Imagine that we have a thousand potential subjects. Little Patricia is among them: She is black, highly intelligent, hates mathematics, is the first born child in her family, from a lower middle-class home, and a girl.
>
> Each of these characteristics may influence the dependent variable. Therefore, we must find another subject who is exactly the same on all six variables. Without an exact match, we cannot use Patricia as a subject. To find pairs of children who are matched on one or two variables is easy. To find pairs who are alike on many variables would require many more potential subjects than we normally have available. (1978, 6)

And it goes without saying that we could not match on every possible variable (e.g., number of brothers and sisters, religious background, parents' educational levels). Thus, many variables would remain uncontrolled. Just how these unmatched (uncontrolled) independent variables influence the dependent variable would not be known or even measurable. In effect, we could never really be sure we had eliminated all possible rival hypotheses. Because of these problems, another method of creating alikeness (equal groups) is needed. There is another method—random assignment of subjects to groups. In other words, a subject's membership in one group as opposed to another is determined by flipping a coin, just as in Aronson and Mills's study of mild and severe initiation. While random assignment of subjects to groups does not guarantee equivalent groups, it does make equivalence more likely. Campbell and Stanley (1963) concede that though randomization may be a less than perfect way of establishing initial equivalence between groups, it is nonetheless the most accurate way. Control through randomization is a frequent technique used in the experiment, and we will have more to say about this later.

Sometimes the nature of the research problem requires the use of independent variables that cannot be manipulated during data collection. If you were interested in whether males and females differed in leadership abilities, you would not flip a coin to decide a subject's sex: heads you're female and tails you're male. When control cannot be introduced at the point of data collection because of the nature of the independent variable, it is generally introduced at the point of data analysis. Such statistical control is quite frequent in survey research that seeks to explain since quite often the variables of interest in such studies cannot be manipulated during data collection (i.e., sex, race, marital status, social class, etc.).

Representativeness. When the researcher's primary concern is the accurate portrayal of characteristics or relations within a particular population, representativeness becomes the most crucial criterion in the choice of a research design. When this is the primary goal, the researcher must be able to identify the target population. He or she will then need to select a sample from that population whose characteristics mirror those of the population. Generally speaking, this means the use of probability sampling procedures (discussed in Chapter 7). Representativeness implies generalizability; that is, the ability to make inferences about the population from knowledge about the sample. Survey research whose primary purpose is to accurately characterize a population is generally most often concerned with representativeness.

Naturalness. When a researcher's primary concern is to understand the underlying processes of a particular social phenomenon or event, naturalness becomes the most crucial criterion in the choice of a research design. Generally speaking, it is the field study that is most concerned with the quality of naturalness. Here the researcher's concern is that behavior be uncontaminated by whatever sources: the researcher's presence, the subject's awareness of his or her subject status. There is no effort on the part of the researcher to manipulate or control subjects' behavior. Behavior is allowed to flow in natural sequence. For example, recall Festinger's research (1956) on the doomsday group (Chapter 2). Group members' unawareness of the identity of the graduate students allowed for the natural flow of behavior. Festinger's students were able to record behavior and events unobtrusively. Thus, events occurred in their natural sequence, uncontaminated by the subjects' knowledge of being researched. In the case of the doomsday group, this would not have been possible had the graduate students' true identity been revealed. And this would certainly be the case for many research endeavors.

THREE RESEARCH DESIGNS

Now that we have examined the factors that affect our choice of research designs, let's look briefly at the three research designs: the experiment, survey, and field study. Each of these three designs will be dealt with in detail in Chapters 8, 9, and 10. Here our intent is simply to relate the three designs to the five factors affecting our choice of research designs.

Experiment

Delbert Miller writes, "Experiments have always been associated with science and have been considered the most powerful tools" (1975, 22). The experiment is often held up as the standard for science—that is, the standard of what research *should* be like. This is not too surprising when we realize that the experiment provides a very convincing argument in the establishment of cause–effect relationships, and thus paradigms that use cause find it appealing. As Doby (1967) notes, the logic of causation and the logic of the experiment are the same. And as we have tried to demonstrate, this sameness serves to distinguish relationships that can be called associational from those which can be called causal. Ultimately, the experiment's strength in dealing with cause–effect relationships lies in the high degree of control (manipulation of independent variables) that can usually be achieved with this design. (See Figure 4.1.)

Experiments are sometimes labeled according to their setting: laboratory experiments and field experiments. In the laboratory the researcher has the greatest potential to manipulate independent variables and thereby control. But this gain in control costs the researcher in terms of naturalness. At some point, he or she must deal with the artificiality of the setting. "If theory is to eventually explain behavior in

**FIGURE 4.1
Flowchart of the Decision-Making Process for Experimental Design**

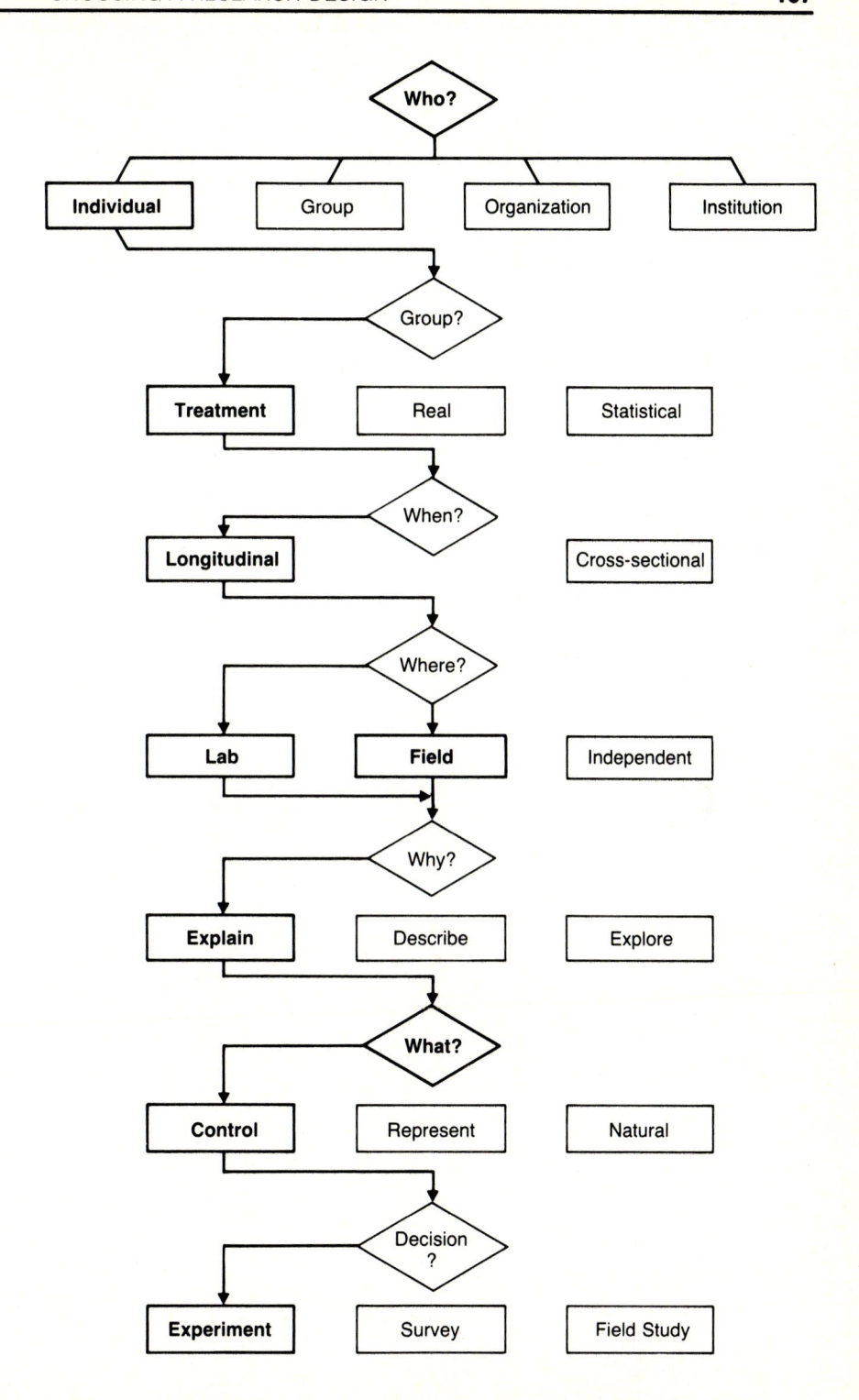

```
                            ┌─────────┐
                            │  Who?   │
                            └────┬────┘
          ┌──────────────┬───────┴───────┬──────────────┐
    ┌──────────┐   ┌──────────┐   ┌──────────────┐   ┌──────────────┐
    │ Individual│   │  Group   │   │ Organization │   │  Institution │
    └─────┬─────┘   └──────────┘   └──────────────┘   └──────────────┘
          │
          │         ┌─────────┐
          └────────►│ Group?  │
                    └────┬────┘
          ┌──────────────┼───────────────┐
    ┌──────────┐   ┌──────────┐   ┌──────────────┐
    │ Treatment│   │   Real   │   │  Statistical │
    └─────┬────┘   └──────────┘   └──────────────┘
          │
          │         ┌─────────┐
          └────────►│  When?  │
                    └────┬────┘
          ┌──────────────┤                ┐
    ┌──────────────┐                 ┌──────────────┐
    │ Longitudinal │                 │Cross-sectional│
    └──────┬───────┘                 └──────────────┘
          │
          │         ┌─────────┐
          └────────►│ Where?  │
                    └────┬────┘
          ┌──────────────┼───────────────┐
    ┌──────────┐   ┌──────────┐   ┌──────────────┐
    │   Lab    │   │  Field   │   │  Independent │
    └─────┬────┘   └─────┬────┘   └──────────────┘
          │              │
          │         ┌─────────┐
          └────────►│  Why?   │
                    └────┬────┘
          ┌──────────────┼───────────────┐
    ┌──────────┐   ┌──────────┐   ┌──────────────┐
    │ Explain  │   │ Describe │   │   Explore    │
    └─────┬────┘   └──────────┘   └──────────────┘
          │
          │         ┌─────────┐
          └────────►│  What?  │
                    └────┬────┘
          ┌──────────────┼───────────────┐
    ┌──────────┐   ┌──────────┐   ┌──────────────┐
    │ Control  │   │ Represent│   │   Natural    │
    └─────┬────┘   └──────────┘   └──────────────┘
          │
          │         ┌──────────┐
          └────────►│ Decision?│
                    └────┬─────┘
          ┌──────────────┼───────────────┐
    ┌──────────┐   ┌──────────┐   ┌──────────────┐
    │Experiment│   │  Survey  │   │  Field Study │
    └──────────┘   └──────────┘   └──────────────┘
```

spite of all extraneous variations of real life, then some research must take place in that complex real world'' (Liek 1972, 12). Decreasing artificiality, though, will mean a loss of control over many extraneous variables (noise, weather, etc.). We can summarize the two experimental designs as they relate to the various design factors:

LABORATORY EXPERIMENTS These experiments use treatment groups in contrived settings; they are strong on control, weak on naturalness and representativeness; they are most likely to be used in causal research. Although data are usually collected at two points in time, the time span between these points is relatively short.

FIELD EXPERIMENTS These experiments use treatment groups in natural settings; they achieve some control and some naturalness; they are most likely to be used for causal research. Although data are collected at two points in time, the time span between these two points is relatively short.

Survey

The survey design (see Figure 4.2) should not be considered any less scientific than the experiment. It simply serves different research needs. Generally speaking, survey research is used to obtain a considerable amount of information which can be generalized to an entire population. Although the survey can accommodate any research purpose (exploration, description, or explanation), it is usually used for description or explanation. When explanation is the primary purpose (causal connections), statistical controls are introduced at the point of data analysis since researcher manipulation of the independent variables is usually not possible.

SURVEYS Surveys use statistical groups that are independent of settings; they are especially strong on representativeness, though control and naturalness are not entirely sacrificed; While surveys are usually descriptive and causal, exploratory purposes should not be excluded. Surveys may be either cross-sectional or longitudinal, although most are cross-sectional.

Field Study

Of the three research designs discussed, the field study comes closest to approximating real life. (See Figure 4.3.) Here the researcher is primarily concerned with natural patterns of interaction and therefore does not attempt to exercise researcher control. The primary objective of such studies is not to generalize but to find fresh insights into the nature of a particular system or to find new ideas that might later be subjected to

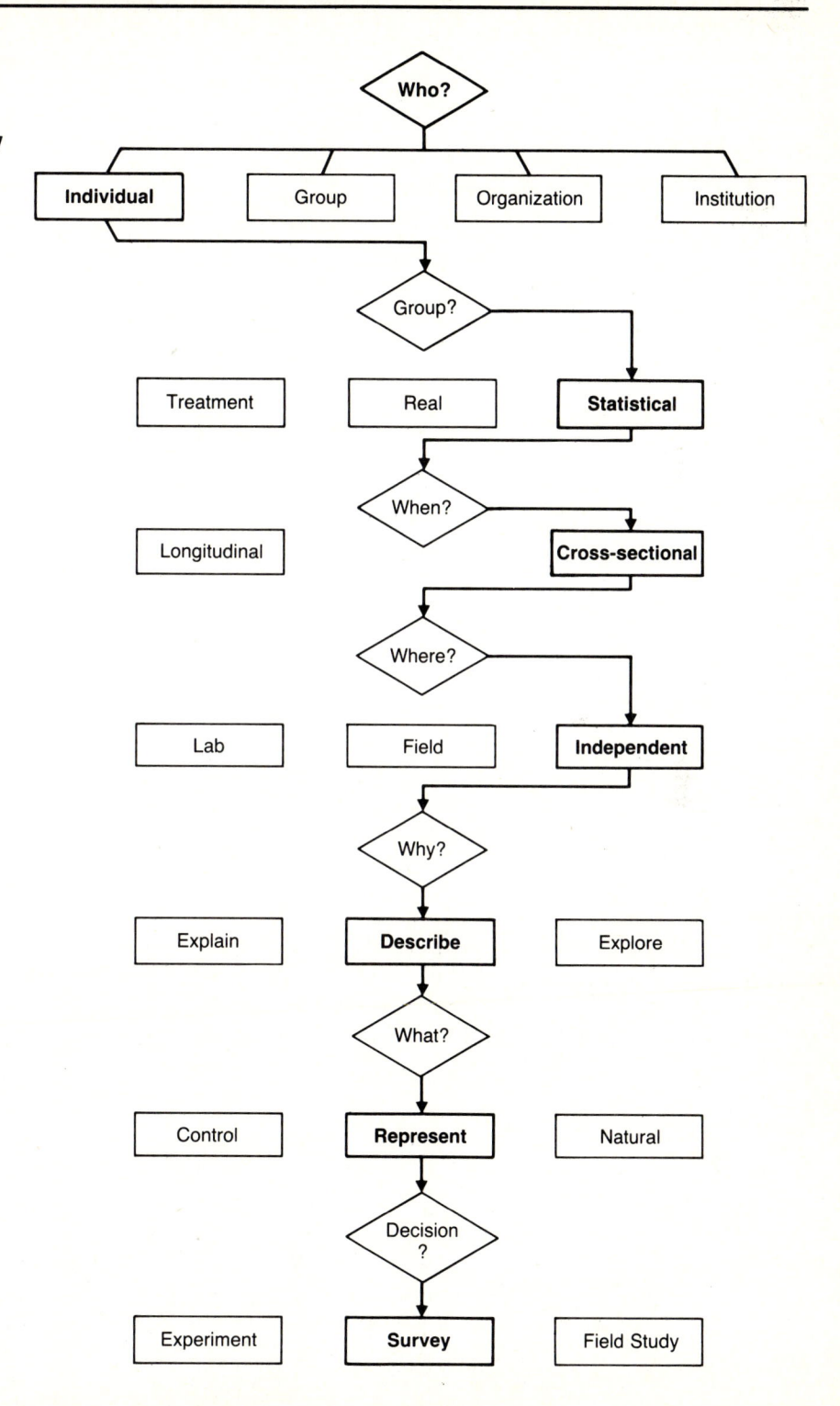

**FIGURE 4.2
Flowchart of the
Decision-Making
Process for Survey
Design**

**FIGURE 4.3
Flowchart of the
Decision-Making
Process of Field
Study Design**

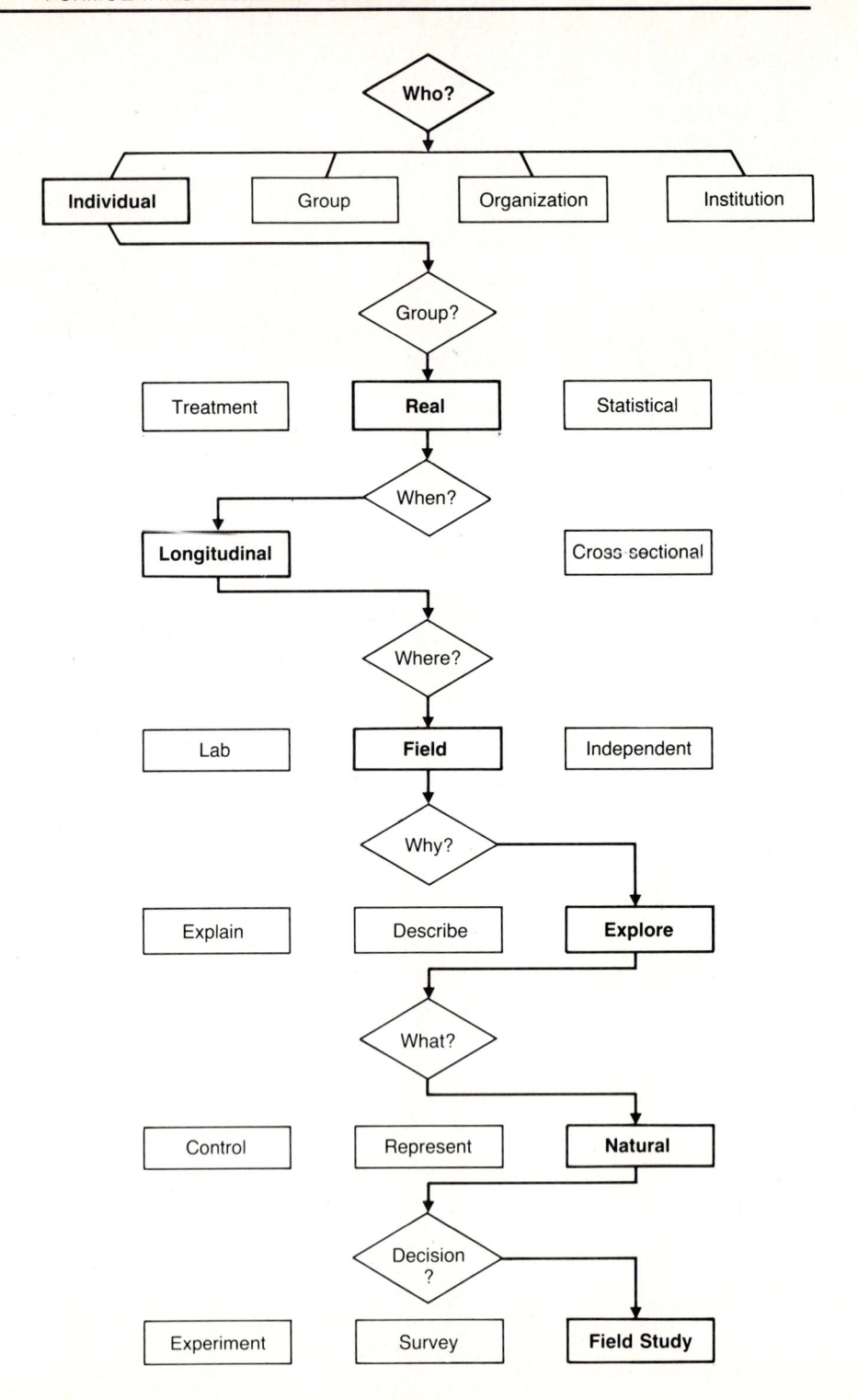

```
                          ┌─────────┐
                          │  Who?   │
                          └────┬────┘
        ┌──────────┬───────────┼───────────┬──────────┐
   ┌────────┐  ┌───────┐  ┌──────────────┐  ┌───────────┐
   │Individual│  │ Group │  │ Organization │  │Institution│
   └────┬─────┘  └───────┘  └──────────────┘  └───────────┘
        │
   ┌─────────┐
   │ Group?  │
   └────┬────┘
        │
┌───────────┐      ┌──────┐      ┌───────────┐
│ Treatment │      │ Real │      │Statistical│
└───────────┘      └──┬───┘      └───────────┘
                      │
                 ┌─────────┐
                 │  When?  │
                 └────┬────┘
   ┌──────────────┐   │         ┌───────────────┐
   │ Longitudinal │◄──┤         │Cross-sectional│
   └──────┬───────┘             └───────────────┘
          │
          └────────►┌─────────┐
                    │ Where?  │
                    └────┬────┘
        ┌──────┐      ┌───────┐      ┌────────────┐
        │ Lab  │      │ Field │      │Independent │
        └──────┘      └───┬───┘      └────────────┘
                          │
                     ┌─────────┐
                     │  Why?   │
                     └────┬────┘
        ┌─────────┐   ┌──────────┐   ┌─────────┐
        │ Explain │   │ Describe │   │ Explore │
        └─────────┘   └──────────┘   └────┬────┘
                                          │
                                     ┌─────────┐
                                     │  What?  │
                                     └────┬────┘
        ┌─────────┐   ┌───────────┐   ┌─────────┐
        │ Control │   │ Represent │   │ Natural │
        └─────────┘   └───────────┘   └────┬────┘
                                           │
                                      ┌─────────┐
                                      │Decision?│
                                      └────┬────┘
        ┌────────────┐  ┌────────┐   ┌────────────┐
        │ Experiment │  │ Survey │   │ Field Study│
        └────────────┘  └────────┘   └────────────┘
```

more rigorous testing. Such a design offers the researcher a great deal of freedom. Consequently, it is often used for purposes of exploration or description.

FIELD STUDIES Field studies use real groups in natural settings; they are strong on naturalness, weak on control and representativeness; they are most likely to be used in exploratory or descriptive research. Such studies generally take place through time and are therefore longitudinal.

GENERAL CONSIDERATIONS

In choosing a research design, apart from the five factors already discussed, some additional practical guides should be mentioned. Doby (1967) has identified five general considerations that need to be kept in mind when thinking about a research design. In Lewis's (1974) terms, "Different strokes for different folks." Most researchers have their favorite methods, which they will use over and over. Some researchers, for example, feel most comfortable with the experiment. Others prefer the survey or the field study. Obviously, one's feelings of expertise will play a role in design choice. Second, no set of factors points to a single correct research design. Any choice of design will represent a compromise dictated by the many practical considerations that go into social research. We all operate on limited time and money. Additionally, we must be concerned with the availability of subjects and the ethical appropriateness of how we study them. In effect, the best approach to a particular research question may not be possible.

Suppose, for example, you were interested in the effects of social isolation on the socialization of a child. You would not raise some children in isolation and others among people to answer this research question. But sometimes life's circumstances provide us with data on such research questions, as in the cases of Anna and Isabelle (Davis 1940, 1947). Anna and Isabelle were raised for the first six and one-half years of their lives in isolation. For a researcher to set about creating such data would be ethically reprehensible. When such data exist, though, we do make use of it. Third, no research design is a rigid blueprint to be followed without deviation. When the research is finished, it will be the rare researcher who can look back and say he or she followed the design to the letter. The research design is a series of guideposts to keep you headed in the right direction. You must always be flexible, as any research design will involve some "on-the-spot decision making" (Liek 1972), just as in putting together the pieces of a puzzle. Fourth, the research design does not guarantee definitive proof of your hypothesis. As you have already learned, in most cases multiple explanations will be plausible. Demonstrating your hypothesis does not rule out the alternative hypotheses and vice versa. The best you can do is make your own hypothesis look more or less plausible. Fifth, it is meaningless to argue whether or not a certain design is scientific. The question is not one of being scientific or not scientific but rather one of effectiveness of design. In fact, it may be preferable to sacrifice some science in favor of a more widely used procedure for the purpose of comparability to past research. This may be essential if the subdisciplines in the social sciences are to ever blend their knowledge (Hoover 1976, 25).

THE RESEARCH DESIGN AND DATA COLLECTION

Whatever the research design, there are only a few basic ways to collect data, and the most widely used techniques are observing behavior and asking questions. In addition to these firsthand data collection procedures, the researcher may use a third alternative: secondary and archival sources. Each of these data collection procedures will be discussed in detail in Chapters 8, 9, and 10.

Data collection is the tool or vehicle through which measurement is actualized. You have transformed concepts into variables since theory is not directly testable. But the creation of a variable is not the final step. Measurement is only realized through data collection. You may say, for example, that you wish to measure alienation with five statements. But then these statements become part of either a self-administered questionnaire or an interview schedule. You may wish to define leadership within a group as a function of the amount of talking one does, but then you must observe and record the amount of talking for each group member. Or you may decide to evaluate sexism in grade-school readers, but then you must use content analysis to determine the frequency of occurrence of traditional versus nontraditional sex roles for men and women.

Certainly the research design does not dictate the data collection procedures. But it is true that certain data collection techniques are more commonly used with certain designs. Field studies, for example, are more likely to use observational techniques and archival data, whereas surveys are more likely to use interviews or self-administered questionnaires. Experiments, in contrast, are more likely to use structured observations and self-administered questionnaires. (See Table 4.1.)

It is important to remember that no design requires that data collection be reduced to a single method. In fact, too much social science research has relied on a single data collection method (Webb et al. 1981; Denzin 1970). Both Webb et al. and Denzin advocate the use of more than one method of data collection in any given research endeavor. This use of more than one method in data collection is known as triangulation.

The term *triangulation* comes from surveying practices on topographic maps. The surveyor, wanting to locate a new object on a map, sets the map up at three known points on the ground, orients the map to coincide with the north direction, and sights on the new object. The surveyor draws a line along the sighting on the map from the known point toward the new object, then moves to the other two known points, again orients the map to the north direction, and draws two more sighting lines from the known point on the ground toward the new object. Usually, the three sighting lines will intersect with a small triangle called the *triangle of error.* The best estimate of the true location of the new object on the map is the center of the triangle, assuming that the three lines are about equal in error. This process is called locating the point by triangulation. Two sighting lines would intersect at one point, but this point is probably somewhat off. The third line permits a more accurate estimate.

In social science research this concept is applied by using a set of three different types of data collection techniques for a single research question. For example, suppose you were interested in high school students' attitudes and social priorities. Coleman (1961), in researching this issue, used three different data collection techniques. He combined (1) questionnaires on preferences and attitudes, (2) sociometric tests for identification of friendship groups, and (3) interviews of school personnel. The three kinds of information helped to reinforce and focus his conclusions: athletics and social activities rank far higher both in the students' value systems and in the attention they receive from school authorities than does academic performance. The picture was much more complete and the findings were more convincing because of the three-pronged attack on the problem (Webb et al. 1981). The use of triangulation in data gathering can serve to strengthen the overall research design.

TABLE 4.1 Choosing a Research Design

Research Design	Type of Unit in Setting	Time Frame	Purpose	Criteria Maximized
Experiment				
Lab	Treatment groups in contrived setting	Two points in time but short span between points	Causal	Control
Field	Treatment groups in natural setting	Two points in time but short span between points	Causal	Some control/ some naturalness
Survey	Statistical groups— independent of setting	Cross-sectional (although some are longitudinal)	Descriptive/ Causal	Representativeness
Field Study	Real groups in natural setting	Longitudinal	Exploratory/ Descriptive	Naturalness

Adapted from Golden 1976, 4.

Chapter 5

Hypotheses and Evidence

Hypotheses defined
Hypothesis construction as it relates to theory
    Hypotheses constructed from classical theory
    Hypotheses constructed from grounded theory
Hypotheses testing typology
    Research hypotheses
    Null hypotheses
Characteristics of hypotheses
    Hypotheses should be objectively worded
    Hypotheses must be specific and precise
    Hypotheses must be testable
    Hypotheses should provide an answer to the research question
Testing hypotheses

Triangulation
Use of evidence in hypothesis testing
    The persuasive power of evidence
    The effect of data sources on evidence
    The effect of the research design on evidence
    Replication in scientific research
The hypothesis cycle
    Hypothetical statements of relationship
    The test of a hypothetical relation
    Conclusion that affirms or disaffirms the hypothesis
    Start of a new hypothesis
    Serendipity in research outcome

Truth can be defined as the working hypothesis best suited to open the way to the next better one.
—Konrad Lorenz

HYPOTHESES DEFINED

The word *hypothesis* defines itself when we recognize its two major parts. *Thesis* means a proposition or statement that can be supported by argument and evidence. In higher education, for example, we require graduate students working on a master's or doctoral degree to make a statement about a research question and then to support it with evidence well enough to remove or at least reduce reasonable doubt. The Greek prefix *Hypo*, means "beneath" or "underlying."

A hypothesis, then, is a nonobvious statement that makes an assertion. The assertion may simply describe some phenomenon or specify a relationship between two or more phenomena. Such a statement becomes the basis for research that is designed to prove the truth of the statement. However, *hypothesis* implies that the true statement is not certainly known, or is hidden beneath appearances. The aim of a hypothesis, then, is to establish a testable base about a doubtful or unknown statement. A test of this statement discloses whether the hypothesis is tenable. As we have already learned, final proof is not possible, but successful research reduces doubt enough to convince other researchers.

William Stephens has defined a hypothesis as the smallest possible unit of description.

> It presumes to describe just one "fact," one thing. It can usually be stated in a single sentence. Those "descriptions" which take up entire paragraphs, pages, books—for example, theories, arguments, narratives, ramified explanations—are compounded of many hypotheses. The hypothesis is the essential unit, or building block, out of which the more complicated descriptions are made. (1968, p. 1)

Stephens offers the following examples of hypotheses:

1. Slums breed crime.
2. It is a cold day.
3. Economic development facilitates democratic government.
4. The older you are when you marry, the better your chances of making a go of it.
5. The earth is flat.

Stephens also offers an example of a statement packed with eight hypotheses:

> Women, as compared with men, are more active in church but less active in politics; mature earlier; live longer; drive fewer miles and have fewer accidents; threaten suicide more often but actually commit suicide less often. (1968, p. 1)

By now it should be fairly obvious that a hypothesis is a statement. But it is not just any kind of statement. It must be a statement that can be tested. It must be worded in such a way that it can be either rejected or not rejected, depending on the outcome of the test. Things are simple with hypotheses; you either have the evidence to support them or you don't.

The hypothesis stage of the research process, like all stages, is extremely important. Recall that to this point, we have chosen a research question and we have examined theory relevant to answering this question. We have given some thought to how we might test this answer by looking at alternative research designs. But even with all of this, the research process is far from complete. Theory is not directly testable, and although the research design provides us with a blueprint for testing, the theory must be reworded for such a test. We might say, then, that hypotheses are theories or parts of theories reworded into testable form. In this chapter, we will introduce you to the hypothesis stage of the research process. We will acquaint you with the different approaches to hypothesis construction, different types of hypotheses, and characteristics of hypotheses. Finally, we will examine the hypothesis testing process and some important factors to consider when testing hypotheses.

HYPOTHESIS CONSTRUCTION AS IT RELATES TO THEORY

Like all phases of the research process, hypothesis construction is not haphazard. Hypotheses must be carefully thought out and carefully derived. Generally speaking, this construction process will take one of two directions. Hypotheses may be constructed from classical theory or from grounded theory.

Hypotheses Constructed from Classical Theory

The ideal form of a scientific hypothesis is derived from formal or classical theory. Classical theory, as we have already learned, is stated logically. It is also based on extensive knowledge of the entire class of phenomena under study. But recall from our earlier discussion that formal theory cannot be directly tested. It is constructed with concepts that are abstract and operationally inexact. To remove the haze and render precision, we transform the concepts into variables. This transformation process is called measurement (discussed in Chapter 6). Hypotheses provide a means by which we can indirectly test formal theory. Thus, with this approach, the theory precedes the hypotheses. And this jump from theory to hypotheses is in many ways a leap of faith. Though the test of the hypotheses is said to be a test of the theory, we cannot know for certain how well we have tested the theory. Hence, it becomes imperative that we take painstaking care in constructing and testing hypotheses.

One highly respected formal theory in sociology from which hypotheses have been so derived is Max Weber's 1904 study of the relationship between the Protestant work ethic and the development of modern capitalism. Weber theorized that the developing capitalism of the European West was made possible through the influence of the Protestant work ethic (Weber 1958). As a leading authority on comparative religion, Weber noted that Protestantism in the Calvinist tradition supported a work ethic that stressed full dedication to any kind of productive work through body or mind, coupled with self-denial in the form of thrift and saving for ideal future goals. The combination of maximizing production and minimizing consumption produced a substantial surplus for reinvestment in productive enterprises. This encouraged capital formation and supported an expansion of industry, commerce, and economic growth.

One hypothesis that has been derived from Weber's theory is that in societies where the Protestant ethic is dominant, capitalism is encouraged and sustained. To test this hypothesis, we might compare predominantly Catholic countries such as Spain, Greece, Ireland, tzarist Russia, and the countries of South America with Protestant countries like England, Germany, France, Sweden, and the United States. And for the early industrial period from 1750 to 1900, this hypothesis seems to be supported. Since 1900, though, some major industrial societies have developed without the direct influence of a Protestant work ethic, including the Soviet Union, Japan, the Republic of Korea, and the Republic of China (Taiwan). Thus, for this later period of time, the hypothesis does not seem to be supported.

Hypotheses Constructed from Grounded Theory

Grounded theory is theory discovered directly from data as it is systematically obtained and analyzed in social research (Glaser and Strauss 1967, 1). We must stress two factors here. First, unlike classical theory, which must precede and imply the research hypothesis, the researcher does not develop grounded theory until after the data become organized sufficiently to suggest hypotheses. Thus, with this approach, the hypotheses precede the theory. Moreover, theory that is grounded in newly assembled or newly assessed data continues to evolve as the researcher is able to identify new hypotheses.

Although classical theory is abstractly formulated in a more or less elaborate logical system and classical hypotheses are logically derived from theory, only the hypotheses are tested with empirical data. In contrast, grounded theory and hypotheses are both implicit in the empirical data. And grounded theory continues to be modified step by step throughout the research process through the testing of various trial hypotheses as theoretical implications occur to the researcher. In many ways grounded theory is closer to the world of social interaction than is classical theory. Remember, hypotheses, by definition, are statements concerning nonobvious processes and relations. In a research quest where the primary elements are obscure or poorly defined, the researcher is generally less informed. The rapid evolution of grounded theory in the data analysis phase, from the first uncertain hunches to the more adequately supported theoretical explanations, is often a useful approach to hypothesis construction.

The Swedish sociologist Gunnar Myrdal applied the principles of grounded theory in his massive study of race relations in the United States in the 1940s. Starting with the general hypothesis that there was a profound contradiction between the exalted ideals of liberty, equality, and justice for all in the United States political tradition and the stark reality of systematic oppression of millions of black Americans, Myrdal employed a team of anthropologists, psychologists, sociologists, economists, political scientists, and professional educators to study the relationship between white and black Americans. These professional social scientists carried out careful separate studies of personal, social, institutional, judicial, and political systems in which this nation dominated by whites systematically excluded black Americans from equal participation in national, regional, and local affairs.

As the study progressed and the data were accumulated over several years, Myrdal developed and supported the hypotheses that white Americans (1) were uncomfortable about the unfair and oppressive treatment of black Americans, (2) could acknowledge the objective studies, and (3) were willing to make corrections in the system. Out of this information he also discovered a previously unrecognized agreement between what the white community was most ready to provide and what the black community was ready to receive. That was economic opportunity through education, training, and employment on equal terms at all social levels. Myrdal's hypotheses, grounded in practical affairs, such as black Americans' need for access to public and commercial facilities and to economic opportunities, were readily understood in all intellectual and professional circles. His voluminous book *An American Dilemma* (1958) was influential in legal, industrial, political, and religious circles, far beyond the impact of most publications in the social sciences.

Myrdal's evidence was thoroughly convincing because it covered the whole complex picture, and did so in meticulous objective detail and in clear, nontechnical language. This work was an important step in justifying the United States Supreme Court decision outlawing segregation in educational institutions in 1964, and for the civil rights acts that followed a decade later.

HYPOTHESES TESTING TYPOLOGY

Whether hypotheses are constructed from grounded theory or classical theory, generally speaking, they are classified as one of two types: research or null.

Research Hypotheses

The research hypothesis is a statement that describes or specifies a relationship between two or more variables. Stephens's hypotheses given earlier are examples of research hypotheses. Homans's well-known hypothesis on interaction and liking is also an example of a research hypothesis. This hypothesis asserts that an increase in interaction between individuals is positively associated with an increase in liking (Homans 1961, 64). Interaction is measured by reported frequency of contact by pairs of individuals in an interactive group. The degree of liking is measured by each individual's report of a degree of liking for the other individuals in the same group. And this hypothesis is generally supported by empirical research.

After long and detailed study of suicide rates, Durkheim demonstrated that the individual's social position affects vulnerability to suicide. As an underlying principle, he tested the hypothesis that there is an inverse relationship between the suicide rate and the individual's integration into society. Specifically, those less fully engaged with social ties have a higher suicide rate. Although suicide occurs with only 10 to 30 persons per 100,000 population per year, the rate tends to be higher with unmarried adults than with married adults of the same age. The suicide rate is higher with childless men than with married fathers. The suicide rate is also higher with Protestant individuals who bear greater individual responsibility in their lives than with Catholic communicants who get more personal support from the agencies of the Catholic church. Durkheim called this type of suicide "anomic suicide," indicating an effect of reduced social guidance.

Null Hypotheses

The null hypothesis negates or nullifies the descriptions or relations specified in the research hypothesis. We could, for example, transform Stephens's research hypotheses into null hypotheses:

1. Slums do not breed crime.
2. It is not a cold day.
3. Economic development does not facilitate democratic government.
4. Age does not influence one's chances of making a successful marriage.
5. The earth is not flat.

In Homans's research, the null hypothesis would be that there is no relationship between the extent of interaction and degree of liking. With Durkheim's research, the null hypothesis would be that there is no relationship between suicide rate and an individual's integration into a society. In other words, the null hypothesis negates the assertion or suggests that two variables do not vary together in any observable pattern.

Statisticians Neyman and Pearson (1967) have suggested that researchers should always begin with the null hypothesis. The reasons for this are largely a function of the nature and limitations of statistical procedures used to test hypotheses. When we test a hypothesis, *one* case can make it false and so we would reject it. In contrast, even if we identify millions of cases that would make a hypothesis true, we can never really accept it since we can't be 100 percent certain of the next case. The very next case could make the hypothesis false, and then we would have to reject it. If we test the null hypothesis and are able to reject it, though, the rejection points us in the direction of the research hypothesis. That is, rejecting the null hypothesis lends support to the research hypothesis.

CHARACTERISTICS OF HYPOTHESES

We have said that a hypothesis is a nonobvious statement describing or specifying a relation among objects. And it should be stated as simply as possible since a primary purpose of a hypothesis is to find the most direct and most basic relation between objects. The Thomas theorem—"If men define situations as real, they are real in their consequences"—can even operate as a hypothesis (1931, 572). In the social sciences, mental constructs do serve as objects. A belief in human love, or faith in a social institution, for example, has observable consequences for the way men and women treat each other—for example, the transactions that people execute through banks each month in paying periodic bills. Hypotheses, when properly constructed, should have certain characteristics. Let's take a look at some of these important characteristics.

Hypotheses Should Be Objectively Worded

In the social sciences, a hypothesis might encompass social values concerning property, money, security, social prestige, and other concepts, but the researcher should constantly strive to exclude personal values, hopes, and wishes from the wording of hypotheses. As we have already indicated, research is not value-free. Since researchers are ordinary human beings, their values follow them into any research endeavor. Since we cannot divorce ourselves from our values, our goal must be value-aware research. If we are aware of our values, we will be sensitive to their potential influence on our research. And one way of controlling this influence is to strive for objectively worded hypotheses. The following hypothesis, for example, is value-laden: "The more deserving employees receive the higher incomes." This hypothesis, if supported by evidence, might be used to justify an existing wage scale in a large bureaucracy. But the word *deserving* is a value word that may be arbitrarily applied by the sponsor based on the race and sex of the employee. A more applicable hypothesis in this case might be, "individuals whom the employer favors receive higher incomes, regardless of their production on the job."

Consider the following hypothesis: "Social adjustment is improved in retirement communities if there are good facilities for sports." This hypothesis suggests that men and women in their seventies have the same social values of competition and performance expertise that are common in the researcher's own age group and social class. Older people may prefer a slow pace and may even be satisfied with a lower level of performance than is assumed for younger energetic professionals. The hypothesis betrays the personal values and biases of the researcher. Consider one last example. Suppose you were to hypothesize that people's interest in the town where they lived would be reflected in their knowledge of the names of the town's office holders, including the auditor, surveyor, city engineer, chief of police, and others. Again, the hypothesis betrays the researcher's personal bias suggesting that interest in a town is accurately reflected through political knowledge and awareness. People may love their town and yet know little about its politics. Their love for the town may be demonstrated in other ways.

Hypotheses Must Be Specific and Precise

The elements in a research hypothesis should be as exact as possible. That is, each must have a single unambiguous meaning. A long-time subscriber to the British humor magazine *Punch* once wrote to the editor stating, "*Punch* is not as funny as it used to be." The editor responded with: "It never was!" This critic's hypothesis is simply not precise enough. It could be the isolated judgment of one reader. Moreover, the time frame is unspecified. At what earlier time was *Punch* funnier? Is "funny" an objective quality or a subjective quality? Subjective internal feelings are not comparable. However, *Punch* is designed to amuse, and it might be possible to establish an ordinal scale of the degree of amusement. Did the reader laugh more loudly or more heartily or more quickly at earlier issues? This also would be difficult to test since the humor of *Punch* often hinges on awareness of current events and fashions. A joke or cartoon that was amusing ten years ago might not have any meaning for a contemporary trying to evaluate old issues. Specificity and precision in hypotheses are important. A loose hypothesis—even though it may be supported by data—is both meaningless and inaccurate.

The hypothesis "Education is positively related to income" is simple, and we might agree that the terms *education* and *income* are readily understood. However, gross bias against employing certain minorities or the convention of withholding young married women from the work force makes this hypothesis inapplicable to a large segment of the population where no income is earned. A better form of this hypothesis would be, "For employed persons, education is positively related to income." And even this hypothesis would prove rather poor if a third of the work force, such as all working women, was generally confined to low-paying and low-skill jobs. The women would tend to be held in a narrow range of income variation so that regardless of variation in education, women employees tended to remain at a fairly uniform income. In effect, the hypothesis would not be supported. With so many irregularities in the distribution of income, particularly as it relates to years of formal education, the serious researcher would be wise to avoid such a loose and imprecise hypothesis. Educational patterns by sex and ethnic identification and by type of occupation would be more productive when relating education to income.

Hypotheses Must Be Testable

As a researcher, you cannot test what you cannot see, hear, touch, taste, or smell. You cannot test the existence of God, heaven, or hell. You cannot prove beyond reasonable doubt the existence of angels or the devil. Scientific hypotheses, to be tested, require sense data. In constructing a puzzle, when you pick up a puzzle piece and attempt to fit it in a particular position, you are testing the hypothesis that the piece fits in an identified location. Every attempt to position a piece of the puzzle is a test of a hypothesis. And notice that each test requires the use of sense data. When you attempt to fit the puzzle piece in a particular location, you observe visually whether or not it belongs there. If the piece does not fit, you reject the hypothesis. If it does fit, you do not reject the hypothesis.

Recent research efforts have begun to toy with the idea of testing hypotheses that have been heretofore untestable. The hypothesis "There is life after death" would seem to be untestable by our previously established criteria. However, several individuals have attempted to test this hypothesis by recording accounts of individuals who have been declared clinically dead and then revived. Verbatim accounts of such experiences have shown common threads running through them. Although such evidence does not remove all doubt (for example, the question of whether clinical death is "really" death or merely "close to death"), it has been interpreted by some as supportive of this hypothesis.

Even if sense data are available, a particular hypothesis may not be testable if you cannot find ways to accurately measure the variables to be included. Changing times, for example, often impose difficult restrictions on research unless the researcher establishes comparable records for a well-distributed series of time intervals. Davies and Kandel (1981) faced such time restrictions in their research on the influence of parents and peers on adolescents' education plans but were able to overcome them. These researchers used questionnaire data from a linked triad of respondents made up of an adolescent, one of the adolescent's parents, and the adolescent's closest school friend. The adolescent indicated her or his own educational aspirations and his perception of the parent's educational aspirations for him. The parent indicated her or his educational aspirations for the child. The best friend indicated her or his own educational aspirations. With a sample of more than 700 triads, the researchers demonstrated that parental influence was much stronger than peer influence. In fact, for boys, peer influence was insignificant. This research also demonstrated that the parental influence was greater than assumed by the child's perception of the parent's aspirations for her or him. This hypothesis was testable because the researchers found stable ways to measure the variables and to demonstrate the hypothesized relationship.

Hypotheses Should Provide an Answer to the Research Question

The test of a hypothesis should provide a direct answer to the research question. This does not mean that the hypothesis is supported. A direct answer may deny the research hypothesis and suggest alternative answers. But in any case, the research question is not left unanswered. In a research study comparing offense rates of delinquent and nondelinquent boys, it was hypothesized that the rates of law violation would be lower for church-attending boys when compared with non-church-attending boys based on the positive moral influence of church attendance. The evidence was clearly in the opposite direction. Church-attending boys reported significantly higher rates of law violation (Sandhu and Allen 1976). Though the answer suggested was not supported, the hypothesis did provide an answer. Rejection of the suggested answer compelled—as it often does—consideration of alternative hypotheses for later study. One alternative hypothesis consistent with this finding is that church-attending boys have additional opportunities through group associations to develop antiestablishment norms and behaviors as a kind of extension of the adolescent's resistance to parental authority. This hypothesis, too, provides an answer, although it may not be supported when tested.

Bridges (1980) tested a set of hypotheses derived from a theory that marginal industries employ more women while the more productive wealthier core industries employ more men. Using U.S. Census data from 1970 through 1976, he found strong support for only one of his six hypotheses: "Women are less likely to be employed in primary and secondary industries with high levels of fixed assets per worker" (p. 73). Bridges found only slight support for a second hypothesis, that women were underrepresented in industries providing higher wages to male workers. There was no support for four other hypotheses that were relevant to and implicit in the theory linking marginal industries with female employment. While the hypothesis does not have to be supported, it must provide an answer—whether that answer be one of support or denial.

TESTING HYPOTHESES

The primary reason for testing a research hypothesis is to minimize doubt about assertions or stated relationships. And the test of a hypothesis is said to succeed if and only if it is objective. That is, the variables and the process by which they are related are based on concrete observable events that are stable and can be consistently measured by a fixed standard.

If you see a social scientist working at a computer terminal and you ask her what she is doing, she might respond, "Massaging the data." We have also heard social scientists jokingly claim, "If at first you don't succeed, massage again." While a scientist may "work" the data to *avoid* drawing erroneous conclusions, she would not "work on" the data to *aid* her in drawing such conclusions. While all scientists dabble in data, it is not their intent to dabble in deception. Suppose, for example, you were interested in establishing the extent to which students at City University take math courses. If you position yourself outside the math building and survey as many students as you can flag down, you will probably conclude that students at City U take a lot of math. If you position yourself outside the history building and ask the same question, you may reach an entirely different conclusion. Both procedures lack objectivity.

Testing a hypothesis objectively means looking at *all* evidence—both positive and negative—weighing the positive and negative evidence, and then making a decision. It does not mean looking at *some* of the evidence and then making a decision. If we could be so selective when testing hypotheses, we would never state an incorrect hypothesis. We would confirm everything we set out to confirm!

Any successful test of a research hypothesis must provide a clearly positive or negative result. If the result is inconclusive, the test fails, though the hypothesis is not affected. Suppose we hypothesized that years of education beyond high school is positively related to a rise in social class. But we only recognized two social class levels: lower and upper. The hypothesis could be supported only for cases where years of education coincided with a shift across the boundary from lower class to upper class. If the upper class is defined by wealth and income, and is confined to less than 3 percent of the population, such shifts would be quite rare and the measure would ignore substantial improvements within the very broad lower class associated with higher education.

If a hypothesis is stated in universal terms, a single conclusively established negative case can disprove it. It was popular in the early years of the present century to say that there was no social class structure in the United States. Lloyd Warner conducted a long and meticulous study of a single small town in New England where he clearly identified three major social class divisions, each of which could be subdivided into lower and upper parts (Warner and Lunt 1941). The researchers interviewed extensively at all social levels in the community and verified social standing and resources in public records in the community. The respondents recognized and affirmed their own and others' social class position with sufficient consistency to support the hypothesis of a recognized social class structure. Recognized membership in the upper class was based on "old money" and social position inherited from earlier generations. The lower-upper class depended on substantial "new money" earned from business enterprise and investment by people in the current generation. At least in terms of specific urban communities, it seems that there is a recognized social class structure in the United States within the limits of definition and respondent perceptions. These findings were confirmed in several other communities.

In an absolute sense, no hypothesis is conclusively supported because new theoretical developments or new instruments may bring the conclusion into question and plausible alternative test results may have the same effect.

TRIANGULATION

Recall from Chapter 4 that triangulation means going at a problem from several methodological directions at the same time. By combining several approaches to data collection, it provides a more conclusive test of the hypothesis. If a researcher has three measures of perceived interpersonal communication between husband and wife, based on careful analytic interviews with the husband, the wife, and their marriage counselor, the data would be useful for testing hypotheses on variable consensus levels in relation to other variables. Such variables include length of marriage, personal satisfaction with the relationship, and orientation to other family members. School performance could be measured from the student's self-report, the school records, and the teacher's evaluation. The degree of agreement of the three sources could be related to the student's self-concept, socialization level, and patterns of interpersonal relations with peers.

Kinsey used the triangulation principle to support his working hypothesis that sensitive data could be secured. In taking the self-reported histories of sexual behavior of thousands of men and women, he wanted to assure that these personal data could not be linked to any individuals who gave them. He developed a three-phase system to separate the respondents' identity from their history of sexual behavior. First, Kinsey developed an elaborate code of special symbols for the different forms of sexual behavior in which the symbols had no apparent relation to the act reported. The histories were recorded in these codes, known only to the interviewers. Second, the respondents were assigned unique numerical codes that were stored separately from their names. Only the code numbers were tied to the encoded histories. Third, Kinsey kept all records in heavy metal safety file cabinets with three-combination locks. Finally, the materials were kept separately for each interviewer so that only one member of the research team could establish the identity of the source of her or his own protocols. Kinsey's hypothesis of complete security of the identity of his informants would have been disconfirmed if any identity had been revealed. But over the several years of the study, there was never a case in which these intimate and potentially embarrassing details were disclosed.

USE OF EVIDENCE IN HYPOTHESIS TESTING

The Persuasive Power of Evidence

The ultimate test of any scientific hypothesis is that the evidence must be totally convincing to people who are both judicious and well informed. An ideal example of this quality of evidence is the proof of Leverrier's hypothesis that there was an eighth planet in our solar system. Leverrier's hypothesis was based on the analysis of irregularities in the motion of the seventh planet, Uranus, which far exceeded the limits of measurement error in astronomic observations. Given such irregularities, Leverrier predicted the approximate position of the new planet and requested a search for it in September 1846. Observations at the Berlin Observatory taken twenty-four hours apart disclosed a twenty-one-inch angular movement in a faint object previously listed as an eighth magnitude star. This hard evidence settled the question forever. We can now predict the position of the eighth planet, Neptune, at a given time as it advances a little over two angular degrees per Earth year in its orbit around the sun.

The power of evidence in the area of medical sociology is demonstrated in the discovery of the cause of the highly infectious and often fatal puerperal fever. A young German physician, Semmelweiss, was concerned about the high morbidity and equally high mortality resulting from "childbed fever" in the obstetrics ward of the Vienna Hospital. Keeping detailed and meticulous records, he was able to determine that the infection rate was highest among mothers attended by doctors or medical students who came directly from the room where they had been dissecting cadavers. Semmelweiss met resentment and resistance from physicians senior to him who were professionally offended that a junior colleague should accuse them of infecting their own patients. Semmelweiss persevered and was able to demonstrate a reduced rate of infection in maternal deliveries attended by doctors or internists who thoroughly scrubbed their hands and arms with strong soap between the dissecting room and the obstetric ward. Such evidence gradually persuaded obstetricians and surgeons to scrub their hands and arms thoroughly and to boil their instruments before touching the insides of their patients.

The Effect of Data Sources on Evidence

In social science research, the source data requirements vary enormously with the scope of the research objectives. If the research concerns a widespread social characteristic, such as United States culture, it becomes apparent that culture includes social institutions, social identity, local, regional, and national history, and many well-differentiated kinds of technologies, social systems, and specialized communication systems. Source data regarding popular culture in the United States would require a good representative sample from the entire country. When such a sample is not available, researchers should carefully limit their claims to the population actually represented in their sample and search for any corroborating data developed by other researchers. Studies of the characteristics of criminals, which are commonly based on samples of prisoners in penal institutions, fall far short of the study of crime in general. Prison populations are largely made up of working-class offenders who have very limited social or financial resources. The more skilled, more resourceful, and wealthier law violators are not likely to be found in prison populations and therefore would not be included in any study of patterns of criminal involvement or patterns of criminal careers based on observations of prison records and interviews with prison inmates.

If a social phenomenon is thought to be fairly uniform in a society, a dense, well-controlled sample from a limited area may be very convincing because of the power of the evidence. Farnworth and Horan (1980) wanted to evaluate the effect of race on treatment in the criminal justice system, based on the dynamics of such treatment in the court process of case handling. Their sample included 12,454 nontraffic violations in eighty-three counties tried in the North Carolina court system from January 1967 to April 1969. The hypothesis was: "Extensive authority vested in social control institutions creates an unequal distribution of power conducive to exploitation of society. Least powerful groups are most subject to that authority. Low social power is characteristic of minority racial groups, females, and the young." A second hypothesis was: "Those with high resources are more likely than those with low resources to avoid and to resist negative labeling." The researchers found that for white defendants the private attorney avoids conviction much more successfully than the court-appointed attorney. In contrast, the private attorney does not help the case of the black defendant as compared with the court-appointed attorney for the black defendant.

The severity of the offense has a negative effect on the probability of conviction, and the negative effect is significantly greater for white than for black defendants. The occupational level negatively affects probability of conviction for white but not for black defendants. Prior court involvement increases probability of conviction for black but not for white defendants. At every step in the legal process, the lower-class person is more likely to feel the sting of the law enforcement process (Farnworth and Horan 1980, 385). The great strength of this evidence derives from a combination of a large number of cases, the large number of political units, the extended block of time, and the authenticity of the court records. The primary hypothesis, that social groups low in power are less able to escape conviction and imprisonment, is consistent with the overrepresentation of black inmates in state prisons.

The Effect of the Research Design on Evidence

Research designs vary greatly from simple to complex. A simple research design is demonstrated in a study of differential attitude change comparing medical and surgical students at a three-year interval at the University of Pennsylvania teaching hospital (Eisenberg et al. 1983). An eight-item questionnaire was given in July 1977 to sixteen medical and eighteen surgical students in the first year of training, and again to twenty-three medical and twelve surgical students at the end of the third year of training. The questions were Likert-scaled on five points: strongly agree, agree, undecided, disagree, and strongly disagree. Two questions were scored on each of four substrate variables: (1) confidence in subordinates' capacity; (2) information exchange; (3) allowing subordinates to share in decision-making; (4) ability of subordinates to be responsible for their own actions. The nonparametric Mann–Whitney ranks test indicated that on all four dependent variables, the surgical students were similar to the medical students on the first test but had shifted significantly toward authoritarian attitudes on the second test. This design is too simple to provide strong evidence on medical and surgical students' attitudes: (1) only a single class-year of students was tested; (2) these respondents could not be independent of each other in attitude formation; (3) the real difference developed from score ranks could be in doubt because of the very narrow range of variability for a set of two attitude questions.

An example of a more elaborate design concerns the hypothesis that family size influences asset accumulation (Smith and Ward 1980). The data came from a three-year longitudinal data file of 494 families from 1967 to 1970. This analysis showed that in the early years of marriage, changes in the husband's income produced large changes in family consumption, a negligible effect on savings, and a partly compensatory decrease in the wife's work effort and income. The young worker receiving a big pay increase revises standards upward, increases consumption, and reduces savings. In contrast, pay raises for the more mature worker result in a savings increase. Young families pressed harder by a poor capital market adjust by the wife's working more and by reducing consumption. The pressure of children keeps family consumption stable or reduced, owing to reallocation of the parents' time. The mechanism of more children is to reduce both the hours worked by the wife and family consumption, with a net reduction in savings. Only if the husband gets a higher wage rate does the family consume more. For example, in the research period (1967–1970), a child in the first year of marriage reduced savings by $1181.00 and family consumption declined by $414.00. But by the ninth year of marriage, children have a positive effect on savings because of a smaller decline in female earnings and working hours. In this study, the elaborateness of the research design permitted more detailed data analysis and thus a better grade of scientific evidence.

Replication in Scientific Research

If a social scientist confirms a hypothesis of a close relationship between two variables, other researchers should be able to repeat the research under similar conditions and obtain similar results. Sherif's hypothesis on the formation of group norms (1948) was replicated in his own research many times. He was able to show that verbally announced judgments of the amount of movement of a point of light in a completely dark room varied from person to person in a group of observers, but that the judgments over a large number of observers were normally distributed. Individuals with extreme judgments of movement above or below the group mean would tend to reduce these judgments toward the group mean on hearing others' judgments in later experimental sessions. Other researchers have repeated these experiments under similar conditions, and the hypothesized process of norm formation in small groups is well established among social psychologists and other social scientists.

Replication is used both to confirm and to reject hypotheses. Durkheim reclassified his data on suicide statistics many many times in his search for a convincing explanation of the social principles affecting suicide. He could exclude poverty as an explanation for suicide in several different tests by showing low suicide rates in areas where income was the lowest. He rejected the hypothesis that increased geographic north latitude increases the suicide rate by a number of comparisons showing that suicide did not consistently vary in cities of similar size at different north latitudes. He excluded the effect of cities by measuring suicide rates at increasing distances from the city center and found no uniform effect. When he tried a series of tests on the effect of social involvement, he did find consistent differences in which persons less bound to others in social and relational ties had higher suicide rates. Durkheim's conclusions have been subject to extensive reanalysis and criticism, but they stand as a major landmark in the development of social science precisely because of his careful and exhaustive replications of many plausible hypotheses. Replication is essential to the hypothesis testing process, as it provides a means of increasing the body of evidence.

THE HYPOTHESIS CYCLE

Hypothetical Statements of Relationship

The hypothesis cycle starts with a proposition in verbal or mathematical form that makes an assertion or describes a relationship among variables. The hypothesis often applies a new approach to answering a question that the scientist believes could give a more adequate understanding to the research question. The Western Electric studies began with the hypothesis that there was some optimal level of illumination that would be associated with maximum output by workers repeating the assembly of telephone relays from a set of simple parts. The hypothesis implied that insufficient illumination would cause a reduction of daily output per worker and that illumination exceeding the optimum level would waste electrical power and fixtures. The hypothetical form is: "The graduated change in level of illumination, if recorded in relation to daily output per worker for one week, will demonstrate the degree of change in output related to a measured change in illumination." Similar hypotheses were ready for research regarding the effect of graduated changes in room temperature and humidity.

The Test of a Hypothetical Relation

As a part of the experimental control to test the hypothesis of the effect of illumination on worker productivity, a group of workers had to be separated from workers in the rest of the large factory. They were placed temporarily under the control of the researchers. The workers were told that these researchers would be making various changes to determine the best conditions for work and that they should cooperate to the best of their ability. When more lights were installed in the initial test, there was an increase in worker output over a one-week period. The hypothesis was confirmed. Illumination was again increased, and again production increased. The replication was confirmed.

If the hypothesis of a direct correlation between light level and output were correct, production should be lower if the illumination was reduced. Consequently, the researchers reduced the light level for the next week, but instead of decreasing, production increased again. The hypothesis was now clearly in doubt. The researchers reduced illumination to the original level, and again production increased for the week. Then they reduced illumination to a level where it was actually difficult to see. Production declined under these adverse conditions, but was still above the original level before the tests started.

Conclusion That Affirms or Disaffirms the Hypothesis

From the carefully recorded results of the experiment with the light level, the researchers began to realize that within rather wide limits, workers can adjust to variation in light level and vary their output independently. It was clear that setting the illumination level in itself had no fixed effect on worker output. And they assumed that the same would be true if room temperature or humidity were similarly varied.

Start of a New Hypothesis

The testing of a research hypothesis can have three outcomes. First, it may be confirmed. If it is, the test conditions can be tightened to establish whether it will still be confirmed under more rigorous conditions. The researcher can try to find the limits of applicability of the hypothesis. Second, the hypothesis may be contradicted. If so, the researcher needs to reexamine the theory and the assumptions from which the hypothesis was derived. The contradiction of the hypothesis throws new light on the theory and on the system of elements included in the theory. Third, the outcome of the test may be ambiguous, giving only partial or weak confirmation or denial of the hypothesis. In this case, the researcher should improve the testing conditions or attempt to improve the power of the test instrument. The outcome of the initial test of a new hypothesis is often confounded by misconceptions of the researcher that can be identified and corrected only by reordering concepts, definitions, focus, and method, until more definitive and useful results are obtained.

In the Western Electric studies, when the manipulation of light levels gave contradictory results, the researchers reexamined their test situation to see what other factor could account for the improved production levels in the telephone relay assembly room. They saw that the only other change in the work setting was the substitution of the researchers for the regular bosses. The regular bosses had been rather formal, distant, and demanding in relation to the workers. They would reprimand or discharge a worker who showed a poor attitude or lacked regularity or sustained working speed. In marked contrast, the researchers had a very different relation to the workers. It was much more friendly and permissive since they had to persuade the workers to cooperate with the test conditions. The workers responded by trying hard to do what the researchers seemed to want them to do. In addition, the workers in the relay assembly room gained a special status in relation to other workers in the factory because they were privileged to work under less stringent supervision and were indeed getting extra work breaks of varying lengths. The factory was known as the Hawthorne Plant, and the positive response patterns of the experimental group have become known as the Hawthorne effect, or alternatively as the guinea pig effect, which is less fitting since guinea pigs are not particularly responsive to the personal influence of the researcher.

The researchers at the Western Electric plant went on to test a series of hypotheses. They supported the hypothesis that the workers' group was the primary influence in establishing and enforcing work production norms. These worker-derived norms were in contravention of company policy and a contradiction to the employer's assumption that company rules and close supervision were the primary causal factors in motivating and controlling worker productivity.

Serendipity in Research Outcomes

Recall from Chapter 2 that *serendipity* is a specialized term used in the description of scientific research procedures to note the unexpected discoveries that researchers often uncover in their attempt to find something else. Often the original planned research goal is based on faulty theory, and the misdirected search turns up something far better by accident. The practical value of this effect for the researcher is to encourage the development of theory in spite of inadequate prior information, and the development of a research design in spite of doubt about instruments and direction. An element of profound doubt shrouds all scientific research precisely because the operation of the target system is not known. Researchers, working in partial or total ignorance, will certainly stumble and fall in much of their research efforts.

Resourceful researchers combine background knowledge, imaginative theorizing, and inventive research techniques and instrumentation to resolve major problems. In some cases the researcher must develop or adapt new instruments as demanded by the nature of the problem. The serendipitous clue usually comes from close observation or seeming irregularities in the data, combined with a willingness to be flexible in both thought and action. The researcher must be willing to modify assumptions, theory, and technology to incorporate new and seemingly radical hypotheses to see the implications of the new and unorthodox information.

The most dramatic examples of serendipitous research events occur in the exact sciences. The Curies stumbled on the phenomenon of radioactivity in matter when they discovered that samples of pitchblend ore bearing radium caused action on unexposed photographic film. The ore samples were on top of an iron door key, on top of the box of new film in a desk drawer. When they developed the film, the outline of the iron key appeared on the negative. They immediately realized that the energy source was something from the pitchblend, which led to intensive research into the atomic energy field. Quasars or radio stars invisible to optical telescopes were discovered from unexpected small squiggles in the traces of longer-wavelength radio emissions from optically visible stars in radio telescopes.

There have also been examples of serendipity from research efforts in the social sciences. We have already mentioned Merton's realization that he was on the wrong track in trying to estimate the influence of a national news magazine on the general public through the influence of high-value readers. When he reorganized his research approach, he was able to show that the influence in social communities comes from persons specializing in specific topics and that media sources exercised their influence indirectly through opinion leaders widely dispersed through all levels and regions of the community. As researchers we need to be open both to seeking and to establishing new knowledge.

Section II

Measurement, Data Collection, and Analysis

Chapter 6

The Process of Measurement

The meaning of measurement
Why measure?
   To describe properties
   To determine relationships among properties
Levels of measurement
   Nominal level of measurement
   Ordinal level of measurement
   Interval level of measurement
   Ratio level of measurement
Single indicators as measures
Scales as measures
   Rating scales
      Graphic rating scales
      Itemized rating scales
      Comparative rating scales
      Precautions that should be taken with rating scales
   Questionnaire-based scales
      Thurstone scales
      Likert scales
      Guttman scales
      Semantic-differential scales
Comparison of scaling techniques
Nonreactive measures
   Physical traces
   Historical and public records
   Content analysis
The theory of measurement
   The true quantity
   The measured quantity
   Types of errors
      Systematic error
      Random error
   Sources of measurement error
      Instability in the property
      Instability in measuring instruments
      Transient personal factors
      Situational factors
      Variation in administering research instruments
      Item sampling error
      Clouded instruments
      Mechanical and processing errors
Evaluating the adequacy of a measure
   Validity
      Face validity
      Content validity
      Concurrent validity
      Predictive validity
      Construct validity
      Discriminant validity
   Reliability
      Test–retest reliability
      Split-half reliability
      Internal consistency: Cronbach's alpha
   The relation between validity and reliability

Aristotle could have avoided the mistake of thinking that women have fewer teeth than men by the simple device of asking Mrs. Aristotle to open her mouth.
—Bertrand Russell

Given a research question, a theory that provides a plausible answer to the question, and a chosen research design, we are now ready to begin thinking about measurement. You will recall that theory is composed of concepts that are logically linked. Since theory is not directly testable, these concepts must be transformed into variables. Measurement is the process by which this transformation takes place. But alas, here lies one of the true challenges for social research. Some of the concepts that interest social researchers are relatively easy to measure because there is broad consensus on how to evaluate their underlying properties. For example, age of individuals, education, and income are concepts that are relatively simple to measure since the properties are concrete and easy to assess. But social scientists are also interested in many other concepts whose properties are more difficult to evaluate. Love, friendship, motives, cooperation, communication, social cohesion, socialization, stratification, and conflict are but a few of the thousands of concepts that social scientists have attempted to measure and with only varying degrees of success. Consider, for example, the concept of religiosity—a difficult concept to measure. But the issue of how much a person participates in religious activities is much easier and tells us something about the first concept too.

In this chapter we will introduce you to measurement—the process by which concepts are transformed into variables. We will identify various types of measuring techniques, alert you to various sources of measurement error, and familiarize you with methods for evaluating the effectiveness of your measures.

THE MEANING OF MEASUREMENT

We will accept S. S. Stevens's definition of measurement: "Measurement is the assignment of numerals to objects according to a rule" (Stevens 1946; also see Lachenmeyer 1973; Kerlinger 1979). If you have ever visited a large hotel, you know that to assign room numbers in some fixed order is easier for everyone than to assign numbers at random regardless of floor or order. The same type of reasoning applies to the assignment of numbers for measures. Social scientists usually try to express their measures in terms of numbers to remove as much confusion and ambiguity as possible. The necessity of using numbers in research is also because much research is concerned with comparison of quantities, and for this, the mapping of properties in terms of some kind of number sequence is indispensable.

WHY MEASURE?

Why do we want to measure social phenomena? What value is there in trying to transform concepts into variables? These are important questions, and we will try to answer them by mentioning two primary objectives of the measurement process.

To Describe Properties

In the study of social relationships, many of the concepts we deal with can be described in purely verbal terms without the use of more systematic measurements. We can say, for example, that industrial societies are becoming more complex and that cross-cultural exchanges between people have accelerated in recent years. But such statements can be better focused and better used as a basis for decision, if more exact measures are included. Similarly, we can be much more informative in describing a city if we use such measured properties as the approximate population for a given year, the distribution of population by age and sex, the number of vehicles, and the number of industries. Other descriptive measures for quantification might include the literacy level, the extent of health and leisure facilities, increases or decreases in education, public services, and the city's requirements for water, energy, and other resources. Numerical representations of level of employment, personal and corporate income, and the level of development of public institutions for education, finance, and communication media permit a much better and more specific description of a city, a nation, or a region (Stinchcombe and Wendt 1975, 37).

Social scientists also devise measures to describe the properties of social events. The idea of social class, for example, can be studied more effectively if we can determine an ordered hierarchy of social class based on measures of income, education, life-style, and patterns of consumption. In fact, many of the most socially significant properties of our lives are conceived mainly in terms of an arbitrary system of measurement. Consider, for example, the importance of a paper-and-pencil test of perhaps 150 questions including factual statements, and logical and number problems scored according to the proportion of correct answers.

The score may be converted into an intelligence quotient (IQ) equaling 100 if the score is average for persons of the same age, or below 100 if the score is under average and above 100 if the score is higher than average for the standard of a given age group. Now we can give an operational definition of intelligence: "Intelligence is whatever it may be that the intelligence test measures" (Blalock 1968, 8). The measure of IQ, in other words (or any concept for that matter), depends entirely on social acceptance and on researchers' willingness to use it. The measured property is "real" because we act as if it is real. As you proceed in this chapter, try to be aware of the implications of this simple notion, as they are profound and far-reaching.

To Determine Relationships among Properties

Measurement also permits comparisons, determinations of change, and decision-making in research. Do husbands and wives see social roles in their own family in the same way? A well-designed measure of male and female roles given to both spouses can demonstrate the degree to which they share perceptions. Do blacks and whites with equal qualifications have equal opportunity for promotion in industry and government? Do men and women of equal qualifications get equal career opportunities? Careful measurement of level of qualification in relation to the attained position in pay and status permits us to answer this question (Torgemson 1958, 10).

LEVELS OF MEASUREMENT

Now that we have established what measurement is and that it is essential in social research, we are ready to examine different measurement techniques. But before doing that, it is important that we be familiar with the classification of measurement. A widely accepted classification has been constructed by Stevens (1946) in which he identifies four levels: nominal, ordinal, interval, and ratio. The use of the word *levels* is both intentional and appropriate. As we shall see, Stevens's classification describes measures in terms of basic mathematical properties, and the properties are cumulative as we move from one level to the next.

Nominal Level of Measurement

The nominal level of measurement is primarily a classification system. Quite simply, it is the assignment of names or numbers to categories, the names or numbers having no mathematical meaning. Many of the properties that will interest us are of this type. Sex, race, marital status, political preference, and religious preference are excellent examples. Sex, of course, has two categories, to which we assign the labels *male* and *female*. But there is no underlying mathematical meaning imputed to these categories. We cannot order them nor can we add them together in the same way we can add a quarter and a nickel. Even if we assigned numbers to these categories (males = 1; females = 2), adding these assigned numbers together to get three makes no sense.

There are two criteria that the categories in any nominal set must meet. First, they must be mutually exclusive so that each case is counted in only one category. Second, they must be logically exhaustive so that every case does belong in one of the categories of the set.

The fact that nominal-level measures have no mathematical properties does not mean that mathematical operations are inappropriate. We may not be able to order or average the categories, but mathematical functions can be performed with a category and used to compare across categories. The most frequent mathematical operations used on nominal-level measures are the calculation of frequencies (e.g., number of males = 15; number of females = 10), simple proportions (males = 15/25 or 0.60; females = 10/25 or 0.40), and percentages (males: 0.60 = 60%; females: 0.40 = 40%).

Ordinal Level of Measurement

Unlike nominal-level measures, ordinal-level measures are characterized with the most basic of mathematical properties. Ordinal scales incorporate a rising order of inequality between categories or scale points. (See Figure 6.1.) This inequality feature means more of something, comparing any higher-scale point with a lower-scale point. However, the distance between scale values is of unspecified size. Thus, we can talk in terms of "greater than" or "less than," but we do not know how much greater or how much less. To illustrate, if soap bars are sold in small, medium, and large sizes, we know that the large bar is larger than the medium bar and that the medium bar is larger than the small bar. But we do not know how much larger, and the difference between small and medium and between medium and large may not be the same. We know nothing about the exact size of any of these bars, only their relative rank in terms of size. All ordinal-level measures incorporate this mathematical property of order or rank. Here are three examples of ordinal measures, each with five ranks:

	Weight		*Military Rank*		*Education*
5	very fat	5	general	5	masters or higher
4	fat	4	colonel	4	college graduate
3	average	3	major	3	some college
2	thin	2	captain	2	high school
1	very thin	1	lieutenant	1	grade school

**FIGURE 6.1
The Difference Between Large and Medium is Not Necessarily Equal to the Difference Between Medium and Small**

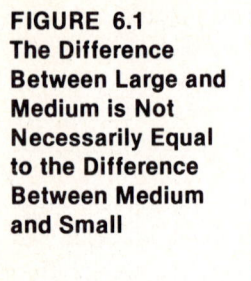

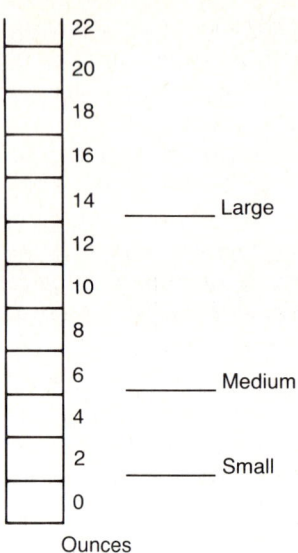

```
22
20
18
16
14 ____ Large
12
10
 8
 6 ____ Medium
 4
 2 ____ Small
 0
Ounces
```

For such measures, the ranks are assigned (1) according to the number of categories (in each of these examples, five categories) and (2) in ordered sequence (from less to more of a property).

Interval Level of Measurement

In addition to the mathematical property of order, interval scales assume an equal distance between points representing order. In an interval scale the distance between the points on a measuring instrument is known, and this distance between points is equal. On a Fahrenheit scale, the distance between a reading of 50 and 51 degrees is the same as the distance between a reading of 51 and 52. This is because, as with all interval scales, each unit is exactly equal to every other unit, regardless of position in the series. However, we cannot say that 100 degrees Fahrenheit is twice as hot as 50 degrees Fahrenheit since an interval scale does not have an absolute or real zero position. The placement of zero on this scale is arbitrary since the best we can do is operationally define the absence of the property being measured. On a centigrade scale, for example, zero, the absence of heat, is operationally defined as the temperature at which water freezes. Thus, 0 on a centigrade scale is equivalent to 32 on a Fahrenheit scale since this is the Fahrenheit temperature at which water freezes.

Many of the measures constructed by social scientists are interval measures. Scales constructed to measure feelings, beliefs, and behaviors generally have arbitrary zeros. In the measurement of attitudes toward death, for example, we may assume that the difference between a score of 2 and 3 is the same as the difference between a score of 6 and 7. However, the absence of attitude or neutrality still requires an arbitrary placement of 0.

Ratio Level of Measurement

Ratio measures incorporate both of the mathematical properties already mentioned (order and equal intervals) and one additional property: the presence of a natural or absolute zero. The ratio level of measurement is based on an ordered series of equal intervals, beginning with an absolute or natural zero. Since the zero on a ratio scale is absolute, it always means absence (none) of the property being measured. A checking account at the bank, for example, has a natural origin of zero. A deposit of $25.00 makes the balance $0.00 plus $25.00, or $25.00. A second deposit of $75.00 makes the balance $100.00 (assuming no checks have been written and no withdrawals made). Now the balance is four times as much as it was following the first deposit. Notice with an absolute zero, the numbers on the scale indicate the actual amount of the property being measured, and this makes possible mathematical operations with ratios. The ratio of 100.00 to 25.00 is 100/25 or 4/1. Thus, we can say $100.00 is four times as much as $25.00. Age is a ratio-level measure, as the moment of birth represents a natural zero. Thus, when a person is sixty years old, we can say she has lived twice as many years as a person who is thirty.

Our measurement of concepts will include all four of these levels. For most concepts, there is no single correct measure. In fact, most concepts can be transformed into variables in many different ways. And the different measures of a given concept may even be at different levels. The measure chosen for any given concept will depend in large part on (1) what measures are currently available, (2) what has been used in past research, and (3) what has been proved adequate. Several measurement techniques have been introduced to help us construct adequate measures. These include single measure indicators and scales.

SINGLE INDICATORS AS MEASURES

Some of the most widely used measurements in social research are indicators that yield indirect measures of some property. The best common example is a clock. A direct measure of time depends on the apparent movement of the sun from the eastern horizon to the north–south meridian, directly overhead. A division of the angle of the sun's movement into sixths would correspond to the hours from sunrise to noon, and in similar measure from noon to sunset. The clock is designed to coincide exactly with the Earth's daily rotation, driving the hour hand around the dial twice each day. Once the clock is set, it continues to synchronize or keep time with the Earth's rotation, and the rotation of the hand indicates the rotation of the Earth.

We could put together a clock to measure anything indirectly. The Bureau of the Census in Washington, D.C., maintains a population clock, which indicates the estimated population of the United States moment by moment. With 0.5 percent natural increase, and more than 215 million people, the United States increases one unit of population (excess of births over deaths) about every thirty seconds. Visitors can see the population grow by three to four persons while they watch for just two minutes.

A single measure indicator can be constructed in just two steps: (1) a decision on what observations are used to measure a concept and (2) a procedure for combining these observations operationally (Coleman 1964, 77). The number of law violations reported to the police can provide an approximate indicator of the annual crime rate. It is limited as an indicator, though, since as many as half of the violations against persons are not reported, and an unknown number of paper violations, such as underreporting income on taxes and falsifying financial records, are never exposed. Entertainers use decibel meters to record the loudness of and timing of applause as an indicator of appreciation of a show overall.

Many different kinds of figures can serve as indicators if we know how to interpret them. For example, the United States railroads reported about 2,500 derailments per year in the late 1970s. Since nearly all rail movements are of freight, these accidents typically were of little concern to the public, except when dangerous chemicals and fuels were released. However, they may be regarded as an indicator of the condition of the roadbeds and of the relative condition of the United States railroad industry. Many large rail lines have gone into bankruptcy, and most are in severe financial difficulties. These facts, taken together, provide a single measure indicator that is significant for employment, public safety, and sectors of the national economy, including farms, factories, and certain elements of national defense, all of which depend on rail service for their operations.

There is currently some interest in establishing dependable single measure indicators of United States society to help identify changes, trends, and problem areas. The Senate passed the Full Opportunity and Social Accounting Act of 1967, which responded to a need for a concise picture of conditions in health, education, housing and vocational opportunity, arts, humanities, and other areas of life (Land and Spilerman 1975, 9). As indicators of social change, a series of surveys has already been conducted to measure such concepts as life-cycle fertility, duration of marriage, prestige of public employment, political participation, alienation and discontent, schooling, income, and attitudes (Duncan

1975, 111). Such single measure indicators are one means of transforming concepts into variables.

SCALES AS MEASURES

The term *scale* refers to a special type of measurement in which numbers are assigned to positions, the assignment indicating varying degrees of the property under consideration. We can think of a scale as a standard measurement procedure providing the basis for agreement among social scientists that assessment of a property is appropriate (Nunnally and Wilson 1975). When a concept is measured using a scale, the result is usually a single score for an individual. The score represents the degree to which an individual possesses the property being measured. There are many different types of scales in social research. In the following pages, we will present some of the more frequently used including rating scales and questionnaire-based scales.

Rating Scales

Generally speaking, rating scales all have one feature in common. The person or object being rated is placed in one of an ordered set of categories where numerical values are assigned to categories. Rating scales can be used to secure individuals' ratings of themselves or someone else's ratings of them. For the most part, self-rating is more accurate, as most individuals are in a better position to evaluate their own feelings, behaviors, and skills. However, this assumption is only true if individuals are aware of their own feelings and behaviors and are willing to reveal them. Three of the more commonly used rating scales are the graphic rating scale, itemized rating scale, and comparative rating scale.

Graphic Rating Scales. Graphic rating scales are those constructed with (1) a designated number of ordered scale points and (2) a written description for every or every other scale point. It may help to think of a graphic rating scale as analogous to a ruler. The points are positioned at equal intervals, and a written description is supplied for most or all points. The rater is instructed to select the one written description (and hence the corresponding scale point) that most closely approximates his or her position. Miller (1975) has devised a battery of twenty graphic rating scales for evaluating important norms and patterns within national cultures. All of his graphic rating scales have six positions ranging between two contrasting poles. (See Figure 6.2.)

Itemized Rating Scales. Itemized rating scales are composed of a series of ordered statements to which point values have been assigned. Although

**FIGURE 6.2
Graphic Rating Scale**

3. Concern for and trust of others

1	2	3	4	5	6
High concern for others. Respect for the motives and integrity of others. Mutual trust prevails.		Moderate or uneven pattern of concern for and trust of others.		Lack of concern for others and lack of trust.	

4. Confidence in personal security and protection of property

1	2	3	4	5	6
High confidence in personal security. Free movement night and day, for both sexes. High sense of security of property. Locking of homes is optional.		Moderate confidence in personal security. Confidence of men is high in personal security but women are warned to take precautions. Movements of women restricted to daytime. Simple property precautions essential.		Low confidence in both personal security and protection of property. Men and women restrict all movement at night to predetermined precautions. Many property precautions obligatory. Extensive use of locks, dogs, and guards.	

5. Family solidarity

1	2	3	4	5	6
High solidarity with many obligations of kinship relations within large, extended family system.		Relations of solidarity within a limited kinship circle with specified obligations only.		Small, loosely integrated, independent family with highly specific individual relations.	

6. Independence of the child

1	2	3	4	5	6
Child is raised to be self-reliant and independent in both thought and action.		Child is given specified areas of independence only.		Child is raised to be highly dependent and docile.	

raters may read through the statements and check all of those with which they agree, generally they are instructed to check only one statement. The statements vary in terms of intensity, the middle statement expressing a relatively neutral position. The statements may also vary in length from one sentence to several sentences including illustrations. The clearer the distinctions among statements (and therefore scale positions), the more reliable the scale. The Survey Research Center at the University of Michigan frequently uses itemized rating scales when conducting national surveys. Since these surveys generally cover a broad range of topics, it is not feasible to measure all concepts with a battery of statements, each of which requires a response, as the questionnaire would become much too long. The 1968 survey, for example, included the following itemized scale (Survey Research Center 1973, 540). Respondents were asked to choose the statement closest to their own view.

1. The Bible is God's word and all it says is true.
2. The Bible was written by men inspired by God but it contains some human errors.
3. The Bible is a good book because it was written by wise men but God had nothing to do with it.
4. The Bible was written by men who lived so long ago that it is worth very little today.

Comparative Rating Scales. Comparative rating scales are those that ask the rater to position self or other on a scale where the position is judged relative to some other individual or group. This type of scale differs from an itemized scale in that an itemized scale does not require that the rating be made in direct reference to someone else. The position assigned by the rater is based on his or her knowledge of the referent. For example, when a professor is asked to evaluate a student seeking admission to graduate school, there is frequently a question requesting a rating of the student's ability to do graduate work:

Of the students you have known, is this student in the top:
1. 5%
2. 10%
3. 25%
4. 50%

To make this evaluation, a teacher must have a clear picture of this student in relation to other students she or he has worked with.

Ziller (1969) has developed a comparative scale for measuring social self-esteem where social self-esteem is conceptualized as relative to the social reality of the individual (Ziller et al 1969). (See Figure 6.3) The self-esteem measure consists of six circles displayed horizontally, followed by a list of "people" such as (1) doctor, (2) father, (3) friend, (4) nurse, (5) self, and (6) someone you know who is unsuccessful. There are six such lists, all including self. Respondents are asked to place each person in a circle. The further to the left one places self, the higher one's self-esteem.

Precautions that Should Be Taken with Rating Scales. Some precautions should be taken when using rating scales because there is potential for systematic error (error that occurs over and over) whether the rating is made by self or other. Potential errors include (1) halo effect, (2) generosity error, and (3) contrast error. *Halo effect* refers to the tendency to create a generalized impression of a person and to carry this impression over from one rating to the next. If, for example, a rater evaluates a person as aggressive and believes that aggressive people are dominant, independent, and assertive, this person would also get high marks on these characteristics. Thus, the halo effect introduces high association among

FIGURE 6.3
A Measure of Self-Esteem

Directions: The circles stand for people. Mark each circle with the letter standing for one of the people in the list. Do this any way you like, but use each person once and do not omit anyone.

List for student form of the measure:
- F— someone flunking;
- K— someone you know who is kind
- H— happiest person you know
- S— yourself
- Su— a successful person you know
- St — strongest person you know

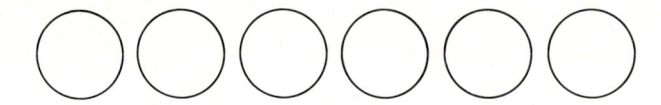

○ ○ ○ ○ ○

Five sets of social objects in the **student form** of the instrument:

a) doctor, father, friend, mother, yourself, teacher;

b) someone you know who is a good athlete, a good dancer, someone who is funny, someone who gets good grades, yourself, someone who is unhappy;

c) an actor, your brother or most like a brother, your best friend, yourself, a salesman;

d) someone you know who is cruel, a judge, grandmother, a housewife, a police officer, yourself, your sister or most like a sister;

e) doctor, father, nurse, yourself, someone you know who is unsuccessful.

Source: Robert C Ziller, Joan Hagey, Mary Dell Smith, Barbara Long, 1969 "Self-Esteem: A Self-Social Construct." *Journal of Consulting & Clinical Psychology* Vol 33 No 1 p 84–95. Extract from Col 2, p 85. By permission of the American Psychological Association.

rated traits. The *generosity error* refers to the rater's tendency to overestimate the positive traits of those persons he or she likes. *Contrast error* is a tendency for raters to see those rated as opposite self.

The halo effect can be controlled by using more than one rater. If raters independently make evaluations, their evaluations can be compared and the average or middle rating might be used. The generosity error and the contrast error can be controlled by avoiding extreme scale point descriptions or extreme statements. One additional means of controlling for these types of errors is to use a different type of scale—a questionnaire-based scale.

Questionnaire-Based Scales

By questionnaire-based scales, we simply mean the use of multiple statements that are tallied so as to create a single composite score. The use of the phrase *questionnaire-based* is not meant to imply that rating scales are not included on questionnaires. This phrase is only meant to suggest that questionnaire-based scales are formatted much like questionnaires in that multiple statements are used. With questionnaire-based scales, respondents are asked to respond to every statement. By using a battery of statements to create a composite score, the researcher is also in a better position to avoid the errors noted with rating scales. Several questionnaire-based scales have received wide acceptance in social research, including Thurstone, Likert, Guttman, and semantic-differential.

Thurstone Scales. Of the questionnaire-based scales, the Thurstone scaling technique is the most elaborate. (See Figure 6.4.) To construct a Thurstone scale, a set of statements is arranged along a continuum where the scale points vary from one to eleven. The location of each statement along the continuum is achieved by asking a panel of judges to evaluate the statements along that continuum. We should stress that judges are responding to the statements, not on the basis of their own feelings, but rather on the basis of the statements' meaning. The final scale consists of some two dozen statements (approximately two statements for each scale position) whose positions on the scale have been agreed upon by the judges. We have summarized the steps that must be followed to create this type of scale:

1. You must first choose the concept you wish to measure. You might be interested, for example, in measuring attitudes toward women's liberation, group marriages, or death. If so, the concept selected is ready to be transformed into the variable (measurement).
2. Once the concept has been selected, you must construct or collect a wide variety of statements about the concept. These statements may be collected from newspapers, magazines, books, individuals, or self. The statements should represent a wide variety of opinions since the end result is to identify statements that can be positioned at each of the eleven scale positions.
3. Approximately 100 statements are assembled on file cards. Only one statement should be placed on each card, as the identification process to follow is made easier by this procedure.
4. A panel of 200–300 judges is solicited to sort these cards into eleven piles. The eleven piles are labeled A through K, with A representing the most negative statements, K the most positive, and F neutral. The statements placed in each pile are assumed to be an equal distance from statements placed in the other piles as estimated by the judges. In other words, those statements placed in pile A are assumed to be an equal distance from those statements placed in pile B, which are assumed to be an equal distance from those statements in pile C, and so on.
5. Judges who performed their task carelessly are eliminated together with those statements that received widely different ratings from the 200–300 judges.

6. The scale values for each statement are then calculated by computing the median scale values. The spread of judgments about the median is also computed. Some researchers prefer using the mean and the spread of scores about the mean. Use of the mean or median will depend upon the size of the panel of judges. If a large panel is used, the two measures should give approximately equivalent results. If the panel is small, the median will probably be more appropriate. Calculation of either the mean or the median assumes conversion of the scale to a number continuum where A = 1, B = 2, C = 3, and so on.
7. Final selection for the scale is made from those statements which have a small spread and are equally spaced along the scale. Equal representation should be given to each of the intervals. With two statements per interval, the final scale would contain twenty-two statements. If there are many statements from which to choose, clarity and brevity of wording may serve as additional criteria for selection.
8. The scale is administered by having respondents check only those statements with which they agree, and a respondent's score is the mean scale value for all the statements he or she has endorsed.

Likert Scales. Shortly after the development of the Thurstone scale, Rensis Likert (1932) offered an alternative to it. (See Figure 6.5.) Basically, there are three differences between Thurstone and Likert scales, and we will look at each. The first difference is in the statement format and the instructions given to the respondents. With the Thurstone scale, no scale weights are given with the statements and respondents are asked to check only those statements with which they agree. With the Likert scale, respondents are asked to indicate the degree of agreement or disagreement for all statements on the instrument using a five-point scale. In other words, five response categories are provided for each statement: strongly agree, agree, neutral, disagree, strongly disagree. On an a priori basis, the researcher must determine the direction

**FIGURE 6.4
Thurstone Scale**

Attitude Toward the Church

This is a study of attitudes toward the church. On the following page you will find twenty-four statements expressing different attitudes toward the church. Put a check mark (✓) if you agree with the statement. Put a cross (×) if you disagree with the statement. If you cannot decide about a statement, you may mark it with a question mark. This is not an examination. People differ in their opinions about what is right and wrong on this question. Please indicate *your own attitude* by a check mark when you agree and by a cross when you disagree.

FIGURE 6.4
(Continued)

Scale Value		
3.3	1	I enjoy my church because there is a spirit of friendliness there.
5.1	2	I like the ceremonies of my church but do not miss them much when I stay away.
8.8	3	I respect any church-member's beliefs but I think it is all "bunk."
6.1	4	I feel the need for religion but do not find what I want in any one church.
8.3	5	I think the teaching of the church is altogether too superficial to have much social significance.
11.0	6	I think the church is a parasite on society.
6.7	7	I believe in sincerity and goodness without any church ceremonies.
3.1	8	I do not understand the dogmas or creeds of the church but I find that the church helps me to be more honest and creditable.
9.6	9	I think the church is a hindrance to religion for it still depends upon magic, superstition, and myth.
9.2	10	I think the church seeks to impose a lot of worn-out dogmas and medieval superstitions.
4.0	11	When I go to church I enjoy a fine ritual service with good music.
0.8	12	I feel the church perpetuates the values which man puts highest in his philosophy of life.
5.6	13	Sometimes I feel that the church and religion are necessary and sometimes I doubt it.
7.5	14	I think too much money is being spent on the church for the benefit that is being derived.
10.7	15	I think the organized church is an enemy of science and truth.
2.2	16	I like to go to church for I get something worth while to think about and it keeps my mind filled with right thoughts.
1.2	17	I believe the church is a powerful agency for promoting both individual and social righteousness.
7.2	18	I believe the churches are too much divided by factions and denominations to be a strong force for righteousness.
4.5	19	I believe in what the church teaches but with mental reservations.
0.2	20	I believe the church is the greatest institution in America today.
4.7	21	I am careless about religion and church relationships but I would not like to see my attitude become general.
10.4	22	The church represents shallowness, hypocrisy, and prejudice.
1.7	23	I feel the church services give me inspiration and help me to live up to my best during the following week.
2.6	24	I think the church keeps business and politics up to a higher standard than they would otherwise tend to maintain.

(positive or negative) of each statement. Each of the five alternatives is assigned a weight from 1 to 5 such that agreement with favorable statements will be treated equivalent to disagreement with unfavorable statements:

	SA	A	N	D	SD
Favorable statement	1	2	3	4	5
Unfavorable statement	5	4	3	2	1

It is a good idea to have both positively and negatively worded statements. Sometimes when all of the statements are worded in only one direction, a *response set* develops. By response set we simply mean a tendency to answer all statements the same. If all the statements were positively worded, for example, a respondent might pencil in *agree* for each statement without reading any of the statements carefully.

A second difference between Likert and Thurstone scales is in the scoring. Whereas Thurstone scales are scored by computing the mean (or median) value of those statements endorsed, Likert scales are scored by simply summing the weights for all statements. With a twenty-statement Likert scale, for example, we would expect a minimum score of 20 and a maximum score of 100. Both of these values assume that all twenty statements are answered.

A third difference between Thurstone and Likert scales is in the method used to choose the statements. With Thurstone scales, this is determined through a panel of judges. With Likert scales, no panel of judges is needed. Instead, a large number of statements (approximately 100) are administered to a group of respondents who are assumed to be representative of those for whom the scale is being constructed. Responses are analyzed to determine which statements best differentiate between the low- and high-scoring individuals. And the best statements are those which differentiate between high and low scorers. Those statements for which high and low scorers respond similarly are eliminated.

Likert also specifies that an objective check of each statement can be obtained by correlating each statement with the total cumulative score. This check will serve not only to determine whether the statements are discriminating between low and high scorers but also to determine whether the numerical values are properly assigned. A negative correlation indicates that the numerical values are not properly assigned and that the 1 and 5 ends of the scale should be reversed. If a zero or near-zero correlation results, the statement does not differentiate between low and high scorers. Likert (1932, 46) gives four reasons for why a statement may prove undifferentiating:

1. The statement may involve a different issue from the one involved in the rest of the statements; that is, it relates to a different concept.

**FIGURE 6.5
Likert Scale**

Death Attitudes Scale

DIRECTIONS: This form measures your attitudes on a number of important issues. Each item is a statement of belief or attitude. At the right of each statement is a place for you to indicate your feeling. Please circle the symbols that best express your point of view. Please respond in terms of how *you* feel, not how you think others feel or what society wants you to feel.
WORK QUICKLY AND PLEASE RESPOND TO EVERY ITEM.

SA—Strongly Agree
 A—Agree
 ?—Neutral, don't know
 D—Disagree
SD—Strongly Disagree

 4 In many instances, married couples should be encouraged to use birth control devices.

   †SA   A   ?   D   SD

 7 Mercy-killing, assuming proper precautions are taken, will benefit people on the whole.
*9 Preventing conception by mechanical birth control devices is as wrong or almost as wrong as taking a human life after birth.
*10 Laws which provide the death penalty for crimes are morally wrong.
*11 Although my definition of God may differ from that of others, I believe there is a God.
*14 Physical or mental illness, no matter how severe or hopeless, should never be the basis for taking the life of the involved person.
*16 Killing during war is just as indefensible as any other sort of killing.
 18 As unfortunate as it is, killing during wartime may be justifiable.
 19 The possibility that God exists today seems very unlikely.
 23 If a mother's life is seriously endangered, forced abortion of the fetus may be necessary.
 26 Life after death seems an improbable occurrence.
*27 I find the prospect of my eventual death disturbing.
 29 There is some sort of existence after our present life ends.
*30 Forced abortion of the fetus is wrong, regardless of the health of the mother or the social conditions involved.

* The items are negative and their weights must be reversed for purposes of scoring.
† The same response alternatives are used with all items.
R. A. Kalish, "Some Variables in Death Attitudes," *Journal of Social Psychology* 59 (1963): 137–145.

2. The statement may be responded to in the same way by practically the entire group. [E.g., Likert found that some two thousand students responded to the following statement in practically the same way: "Should the United States repeal the Japanese Exclusion Act?"]
3. The statement may be so expressed that it is misunderstood by members of the group. This may be due to its being poorly stated, phrased in un-

familiar words, or worded in the form of a double-barreled statement [E.g., "I feel my age, but it does not bother me"].
4. It may be a statement of fact which individuals who fall at different points on the continuum will be equally liable to accept or reject (E.g., "Everyone dies, including me"].

Since the development of the Likert scale in 1932, the basic scoring procedure has remained the same. However, for reasons not always specified, researchers have often found it desirable to modify the number of response alternatives accompanying each statement and to change the wording used to describe these alternatives. In general, the number of response alternatives has ranged from two to seven. But the wording used to describe these alternatives has experienced greater change. Rotter (1972) has attempted to shed light on these various alternatives by determining the extent of agreement connoted by the various descriptions. (See Table 6.1.) He also (1) identified descriptions representing equivalent counterpoints of agreement and disagreement and (2) selected end points of the scale that approached totality or the entire range of agreement–disagreement. Rotter recommends seven response alternatives for use with Likert scales:

Totally Agree	+3
Agree Very Much	+2
Tend to Agree	+1
Neutral or Don't Know	0
Tend to Disagree	−1
Disagree Very Much	−2
Totally Disagree	−3

These seven-scale points were selected for three reasons:

1. These end points best anchored the range of agree–disagree.
2. The parallel counterpoints best represented equivalent distances from the neutral position.
3. The numerical values approximated an equal interval scale.

Although Rotter's research will probably not squelch the use of various response alternatives and arbitrary weights, it is an empirical effort to identify appropriate response alternatives and meaningful weights.

Guttman Scales. A third prominent measurement technique, developed and introduced in the 1940s, is referred to as Guttman scaling (Guttman 1950). Guttman scaling is a scoring technique that assumes an underlying cumulative continuum. In other words, knowledge of a total score allows us to predict perfectly a subject's responses to each individual statement. The statements assume an a priori order such that agreement

TABLE 6.1 Assessment of Terms of Agreement and Disagreement

Agreement	Disagreement
Absolutely Agree	Absolutely Disagree
Totally Agree	Totally Disagree
Agree Unconditionally	Disagree Unconditionally
Extremely Agree	Extremely Disagree
Intensely Agree	Intensely Disagree
Agree Strongly	Disagree Strongly
Agree Utterly	Disagree Utterly
Agree Greatly	Disagree Greatly
Agree Very Much	Disagree Very Much
Agree a Great Deal	Disagree a Great Deal
Agree	Disagree
Mostly Agree	Mostly Disagree
Do Not Agree	Do Not Disagree
Tend to Agree	Tend to Disagree
Agree Somewhat	Disagree Somewhat
Agree Slightly	Disagree Slightly

Adapted from: G. Rotter, "Attitudinal Points of Agreement and Disagreement," *Journal of Social Psychology* 86 (1972): 211–218.

with any particular statement assumes agreement with the statements preceding it. Let's take, for example, a series of simple mathematical equations:

(1) $1 + 1 = 2$
(2) $2 \times 3 = 6$
(3) $48/12 = 4$
(4) $\sqrt{25} = 5$

For these four equations, we are assuming an a priori order. Of all mathematical processes (except counting), addition is considered to be the simplest and is usually the first learned. Multiplication is considered more difficult than addition; division more difficult than multiplication; and square root more difficult than division. If these four items were administered to a subject and one point was scored for each correct answer, a maximum score would be 4. Similarly, if a subject could answer none of these four, a minimum score of 0 would be obtained. With a minimum score of 0 and a maximum score of 4, perfect prediction is possible, as it is readily apparent that either none or all of the problems were answered correctly. With a score of 1, 2, or 3, though, if prediction is to be consistently accurate, it must be founded upon some sound assumptions. The ability to predict accurately lies in the assumed cumulative character of the items. If the solutions to problems 2, 3, and 4 assume prior learning (problem 1), it is reasonable to predict that a subject who receives a score of 1 answered correctly only the first problem. Likewise, if a subject receives a score of 2, we would predict that he or she answered problems 1 and 2.

Because the reliability of the scale depends upon our ability to reproduce perfectly statement responses, a method of checking the degree of reproducibility is needed. Guttman has worked out such a method. It is accomplished with the *coefficient of reproducibility (r)*. Mathematically the formula can be represented as follows.

$$r = 1 - e/nk$$

Where: e = number of errors in predicting
n = number of subjects
k = number of statements on the scale

For example, with a four-statement scale, the following predictions would be made for scores of 4, 3, 2, 1, and 0.

Score	Statement Responses
4	+ + + +
3	+ + + −
2	+ + − −
1	+ − − −
0	− − − −

Any other series of plusses and minuses for a subject would constitute an error. If a subject with a score of 3 had scored + + − + our prediction would have created an error, as we would have predicted the above order (+ + + −) for a score of 3. The coefficient of reproducibility ranges between 0 and 1.00, where 0 indicates no predictability and 1.00 indicates perfect predictability. Scalability is said to exist if the coefficient of reproducibility is equal to or greater than 0.9. If the coefficient of reproducibility does not reach 0.9, the scale is questionable and we should reexamine the order of the statements. However, reordering the statements is not always the answer. A low coefficient of reproducibility may not necessarily be the result of faulty ordering but rather may be the result of a multidimensional set of statements (i.e., more than one concept being measured with the set of items) (Guttman 1950). With a low coefficient of reproducibility it is sometimes difficult to determine whether the set of statements was actually multidimensional or whether irrelevant statements were included in the pool.

Paul Wallin (1953) has developed a Guttman scale for measuring women's neighborliness. (See Figure 6.6.) The scale consists of twelve

FIGURE 6.6
Guttman Scale

A Guttman Scale for Measuring Women's Neighborliness

Variable Measured: The neighborliness of women under sixty years of age.

Description: This instrument is a unidimensional Guttman scale consisting of twelve items. The scale items can be simply scored for any sample by counting each *GN* (greater neighborliness) answer as 1 and each *LN* (lesser neighborliness) as 0. The possible range of scores is 12 to 0.

Where Published: Paul Wallin, "A Guttman Scale for Measuring Women's Neighborliness," *The American Journal of Sociology* 59 (1953): 243–46. Copyright 1953 by the University of Chicago.

Reliability: The coefficient of reproducibility of the scale from two samples of women was .920 and .924.

Validity: Face validity.

1. How many of your best friends who live in your neighborhood did you get to know since you or they moved into the neighborhood? Two or more (*GN*); one or none (*LN*).
2. Do you and any of your neighbors go to movies, picnics, or other things like that together? Often or sometimes (*GN*); rarely or never (*LN*).
3. Do you and your neighbors entertain one another? Often or sometimes (*GN*); rarely or never (*LN*).
4. If you were holding a party or tea for an out-of-town visitor, how many of your neighbors would you invite? Two or more (*GN*); one or none (*LN*).
5. How many of your neighbors have ever talked to you about their problems when they were worried or asked you for advice or help? One or more (*GN*); none (*LN*).
6. How many of your neighbors' homes have you ever been in? Four or more. (*GN*); three or less (*LN*).
7. Do you and your neighbors exchange or borrow things from one another such as books, magazines, dishes, tools, recipes, preserves, or garden vegetables? Often, sometimes, or rarely (*GN*); none (*LN*).
8. About how many of the people in your neighborhood would you recognize by sight if you saw them in a large crowd? About half or more (*GN*); a few or none (*LN*).
9. With how many of your neighbors do you have a friendly talk fairly frequently? Two or more (*GN*); one or none (*LN*).
10. About how many of the people in your neighborhood do you say "Hello" or "Good morning" to when you meet on the street? Six or more (*GN*); five or less (*LN*).
11. How many of the names of the families in your neighborhood do you know? Four or more (2); one to three (1); none (0).
12. How often do you have a talk with any of your neighbors? Often or sometimes (*GN*); rarely or never (*LN*).

statements and can be scored by counting each GN (greater neighborliness) answer as 1 and each LN (lesser neighborliness) as 0. The coefficient of reproducibility of the scale from two samples of women was 0.920 and 0.924. The scale is included here in its entirety.

Semantic-Differential Scales. The semantic-differential scaling system, one of the oldest measuring devices, depends on a collection of opposite-pair adjectives with 7 to 11 scale points related to a specific concept (Snider and Osgood 1969). The opposite-pair adjectives are selected to gauge three aspects of the concept being measured: evaluation, potency, and activity. The instrument may include up to nine such semantic-differential scales for each of these dimensions, and each scale is marked from 1 to 7 or 1 to 11. Statements may also be reversed to avoid response sets. For instance, on the question "How do you view football?," the following adjective pairs might be used:

EVALUATION Dimension

Bad	Good
Boring	Interesting
Harmful	Beneficial

POTENCY Dimension

Weak	Strong
Cheap	Expensive
Unimportant	Important

ACTIVITY Dimension

Slow	Fast
Quiet	Loud
Simple	Complex

The semantic-differential scale correlates well with other scales and appears somewhat more straightforward and direct in its approach to the rating problem. There is greater flexibility in the selection of opposite adjective pairs. As with other scale techniques, a semantic-differential scale should be pretested in a pilot group to assess the validity of terms and the need for change.

COMPARISON OF SCALING TECHNIQUES

With the proliferation of scaling techniques for measurement, you might begin to question the relationship of one scaling technique to another. Do the different scaling techniques yield similar results? Veevers (1971) attempted to answer this question by investigating drinking attitudes and drinking behavior using Thurstone scales, Likert scales, itemized rating scales, and graphic self-rating. One hundred thirty-three items were developed from the literature on alcohol use, and sixty-seven judges from diverse backgrounds were asked to evaluate the statements. Twenty-one statements were selected and split into two equivalent scales, with one statement common to both scales. The graphic self-rating was determined by having subjects indicate a position by circling a number on a continuum. The subject's own drinking behavior was measured by the Alberta Quantity Frequency Index (AFQ Index) developed by Maxwell (1958). Respondents were categorized into six groups ranging from abstainers to heavy drinkers. Veevers concludes that with the exception of the graphic self-rating, all of these scaling techniques yield essentially the same results.

NONREACTIVE MEASURES

By now you may have the impression that the researcher conventionally applies a scale of some sort to individuals or groups in order to measure. Certainly, such measures have drawbacks. Respondents, for example, may counterfeit their true response patterns to fit the researchers' expectations, or answer when they may not know or care. Or the researcher may distort the world in terms of personal biases. Researchers do use other measures to help circumvent such problems. Nonreactive measures permit the world to speak for itself in its own way. Such measures are called nonreactive because the source of inquiry is operating on its own environment without being changed or affected by the researcher's act of measurement.

Physical Traces

An unannounced head count of those attending religious services at a large sample of churches would give a better estimate of church attendance than members' estimates and reports of their own attendance in response to an interview. Photographs taken from the air provide evidence for counting and estimating crowd size, and this kind of evidence is sometimes more trustworthy than official reports. For example, the reported size of crowds turning out for public celebrations varies by a factor of ten between police, news reporters, and the organizers' estimates. The historical shifts in patterns of consumption and evidence of change in cultural interest are reflected in the trash dumps of some cities. Many of the discarded items are dated, and the chronology is suggested by their depth in the layers of refuse.

Historical and Public Records

The vast array of historical records, both recent and ancient, is an almost infinite source for productive research. Durkheim (1964), almost a century ago, used contemporary newspaper and government records from many countries and cities to compare suicide rates by marital status, by occupation, by religion, and by time of year to show that the rate of suicide is partly a negative function of people's involvement in society (Durkheim 1964). Rogoff (1953) used the occupations entered in marriage license applications by grooms for themselves and their fathers as evidence in intergenerational occupational mobility. Newspapers often maintain complete files of all past issues of the newspaper for the researcher who wants to find detailed information on the records of local athletic teams, the quality and amount of reported social activities, labor and commercial activities, changes in process and product emphasis, from one decade to the next. To find a sample of firstborn six-year-olds, a researcher checked birth announcements in the local paper files six years earlier, noting the sex of the child and the names of parents. Checking these with current telephone listings indicated which children were still in town, and a telephone call determined whether the child was firstborn.

Many kinds of social processes demand a span of time such as two, three, or four decades or in some cases a century for proper measurement. For example, suppose we wanted to examine the changes in the intergenerational rate of reproduction. Birth registration has been fairly complete and constant in certain cities. What has been the trend, comparing 1920, 1940, 1960, and 1980 for the age of the mother at first and last birth? What has been the trend in lot size for private homes, changes in occupational specialities, and the pattern and frequency of telephone communications? What are the primary trends in government service, influence, and intervention, comparing local, state and national levels? All of these questions can be approached through the use of a variety of public and private records.

Content Analysis

Content analysis is a form of measurement applied to text of various kinds. Such text may be anything in written form, such as personal letters, newspaper reports, government documents, advertising, transcriptions of recorded conversations, movie scripts, children's essays, period literature, technical journals, plays, song lyrics, magazines, and sacred writings. And the possible kinds of measurements that can be achieved with content analysis are just as diverse. Item counts include the number of reports published in a given time period on political, military, social, or economic events (Berelson 1982). Quantity may be given by estimates of word count. In analyzing factors stressed in newspapers, the number of column inches may indicate relative importance of subject matter. This may be weighted by prominence of display on the early pages of the newspaper or as a lead article in a journal.

Topical analysis combines an identified range of topics with a frequency count, but the primary aim is usually to make inferences about the culture. Thomas and Znaniecki (1918) collected several hundred personal letters between Polish immigrants in Chicago and their relatives in Poland. Znaniecki translated these from Polish into English. Their content analysis demonstrated the kind of family ties and the unaccustomed personal problems the immigrants had in making the transition from the highly supportive culture of the rural Polish village to the impersonal and nonsupportive culture of Chicago. The letters also demonstrated explicit pressures on relatives still in Poland to come to the United States to reunite the families. Support of this cultural transplant is still evident in Chicago and other cities where Polish workers were so eagerly sought by U.S. industrialists.

THE THEORY OF MEASUREMENT

Like other processes in social science research, the measurement processes we have been discussing are guided by theory. The theory and set of assumptions underlying measurement are always open to question, but in plain honesty, we must state what they are and then allow you, the reader, to draw your own conclusions about how plausible the theory really is. The following discussion concerns the theory underlying measurement.

The True Quantity

Research always aims at the actual, real, or true dimensions of the concept being studied. In other words, it assumes an empirical paradigm (see the discussion of paradigms in Chapter 1). A city has an actual population at any given moment in time. It is this actual population that a demographer considers in making projections about increases or decreases in the future size of the city. Presumably, but more problematically, a marriage can be assessed at any given time as to its relative strength. Such elements as the degree of commitment of each spouse to the other and to the family, the support and influence of close relatives, the pressures of work and community, and the resources of each spouse to meet the varying demands of the marriage could all be brought together in an instrument that would give at least a rudimentary measure of how strong the marriage actually is. The size of a city may be easier to measure than the strength of a marriage, but similar, if not identical, principles go into both.

To evaluate or measure the true properties of a concept, we work from sense data that have exact quantities. For this four things are required: (1) a conceptual model that defines the case, (2) an empirical definition of its properties, (3) actual cases that fit the concept, and (4) a recognition of what the indicators will tell us when we have seen them (Riley 1963, 328). It is important that the language used in assigning numbers to properties be consistent and applied under a set of rules (Cirourel 1964, 15). However, despite our efforts, we can never be sure the measurement we make is the measure of the true quantity.

The Measured Quantity

Basically, a measure of some concept is a logical construct that can only approximately map reality. For example, the smaller a set of numbers, the more accurate a count is likely to be. If we say there are three boys "out there," or seven horses, the accuracy of these statements is pretty good. But as the count increases, the true quantity is more open to doubt. When frequency counts are in the thousands, we find real difficulty in verifying their accuracy. In counts of millions, we are taking things very much on faith. When it comes to ratios and proportions, the numbering system becomes quite inexact. One divided by three, seven, and nine cannot be exactly expressed in decimals. Generally, then, the use of numbers to represent a measure is an approximation. "The notion that any correction beyond what we have the instruments and art to make is a mere fiction of the mind, useless and incomprehensible," said Hume 200 years ago, and his statement is as reasonable today as it was then.

TYPES OF ERRORS

Given that measurement can only approximate reality, there is likely some difference between the true quantity and the measured quantity. In effect, error is virtually inevitable. "Everyone makes mistakes." This old saying should be forever chiseled into the front of our minds when we seek to measure. However, knowing what kinds of mistakes are most likely to be made is going a long way in reducing them.

Error tends to balloon and magnify in the successive steps of the research process and quickly invalidates any evidence the scientist may claim to find. The most important and immediate task of the serious researcher is to control and reduce measurement error to a practical minimum.

Systematic Error

Systematic error is a form of bias in the measurement process that usually distorts the data in one direction. In other words, systematic error will result in respondents' scores being consistently too high or consistently too low. A weighing scale misadjusted by two pounds when nothing is on the platform systematically makes all weighings two pounds too heavy. Systematic error may be induced with human subjects by cues from the researcher or by the makeup of the research instrument. A scientist who, for example, is attempting to prove a hypothesis may faithfully record favorable results while sometimes neglecting to record unfavorable results. This would result in systematic error favorable to the scientist's hypothesis. Systematic error will also result from respondents' either knowing or guessing the desired outcome. Whenever there is a choice, the respondents will often select the choice believed to be the most favorable or most popular. The respondent easily controls the impressions given, and most respondents make the impression positive (Phillips 1973, 42). In fact, many respondents exaggerate their position on a question beyond what is habitual for them when they know they are under observation.

Random Error

Random error is a form of bias in which distortions in the measurement process result in fluctuations on either side of the true quantity. A large volume of small random errors tends to balance out in positive and negative fluctuations around the true values. If the random errors are very large, they may make the whole research project useless because they conceal the central tendency with a very wide margin of error. If there are only one or two pieces of data, random errors on each may completely distort the facts. Increasing the number of items helps to distribute such errors more uniformly on both sides of the true average.

Suppose we measured the social activity of college students at a university by recording the number of persons each individual talked with in the course of a regular weekday at school. A sample of 300 students is randomly selected from the total of those attending the university. The total population of 15,000 students would report some exact number of conversation partners, and this population average would probably be slightly higher or lower than that reported by the 300 students actually sampled. The difference in the count recorded for an unbiased sample and the count that would come from the population is random error resulting from the sampling selection process. A relatively small random sample cannot exactly match the exact distribution of the whole population.

SOURCES OF MEASUREMENT ERROR

There are several common sources of measurement error, whether they are systematic or random. An awareness and understanding of these error sources can help you to avoid these pitfalls.

Instability in the Property

Measurement processes are degraded by a broad variety of factors, including instability in the property being measured (Selltiz et al. 1976; Miller 1975). In other words, many of the social properties we might wish to measure are inherently fluctuating. An individual varies considerably from day to day and from hour to hour. Response to any standard stimuli will lag more or less in time and will fluctuate in intensity or depth of response. The researcher can measure several times, hopefully at representative levels of the intensity cycle, but the respondent's constant shifting makes the evaluation irregular and masks the "true quantity." Social phenomena with rather long time cycles (e.g., the socialization process over the human lifetime) challenge the skill of the researcher to keep track of all the relevant variables.

Instability in Measuring Instruments

In all research, the measuring instrument contributes systematic error to all measurements. It is the researcher's duty to check and recheck the instruments whenever they are used, to guard against contamination of the data. Electrical and electronic circuits fail without any external indication of change. Settings and control switches are bumped into the wrong position. A researcher unknowingly administers the wrong form of a survey instrument, and the respondents are unaware. Questionnaires can easily become outmoded in three to five years so that responses to items on racial attitudes, sexual behavior, or political concerns are not at all comparable to those of the earlier studies or to the intent of the researcher.

A researcher who uses the same instrument over several years is likely to undergo basic changes in orientation and judgmental standards. The instruments become too familiar, and the researcher may skip rapidly over details that received more meticulous attention in the earlier phase of the research. Control of measurement error demands that the researcher guard against such lapses and gradual changes. This problem is partially resolved by keeping organized notes and records of all events in the research process, and through frequent review of definitions, rules, and conventions of research, plus conferences with colleagues and assistants to revalidate the primary measures.

Transient Personal Factors

Errors of the personal type result when respondents are careless in reading and responding to questions. Carelessness can generally be attributed to such factors as fatigue, hunger, or general bad mood. When such personal factors are present, the result will be wide differences in the quality of responses. The responsible researcher will try to verify the appropriateness of each respondent's answers.

Situational Factors

In everyday activities, temporary but major events may be significant for the researcher. Among many that we could consider is noise. An interview can succeed well only in a fairly private environment. The researcher must provide suitable accommodations or check to be sure that the interviewee's situation provides such a place. For example, empty classrooms and main offices in public schools are poor places to interview teachers or students. But the school authorities usually know of a more adequate place if the interviewer explains the need. Other situational factors might include a poorly heated or cooled facility, inadequate lighting, uncomfortable desks, and interruptions.

Variation in Administering Research Instruments

Measurement can easily be flawed by careless administration of the instrument. Researchers have been known to leave a set of questionnaires for supervisors to administer without clear instructions, and the supervisors may then turn them over to an assistant who merely lets anyone who wishes fill one in. Each copy of a questionnaire should carry sufficient instructions, including specification of those for whom the instrument is intended. For instruments given to groups, the researcher should have a well-prepared paragraph explaining the project at least enough to orient and motivate the respondents. This should be read exactly the same way to each group. The researcher should remain available to answer any question that might arise. He or she should take notes on the apparent mood and spirit of the respondents. The date, time, and place should also be recorded, and note should be made of any comments about the research. The researchers should review the instruments as they are turned in for omitted items and should correct oversights where possible.

Item Sampling Error

Any measurement assumes a sampling of items randomly drawn from the universe of possible items. If we are interested, for example, in measuring self-esteem, we know that the items chosen to measure this concept are not the *only* items that could have been used. Had other items been chosen, our measurement would probably be somewhat different. With Thurstone scales, for example, we begin with one hundred statements. The final scale, though, has only twenty or so statements. If we had selected a different set of twenty from the original hundred, no doubt our measurement would be somewhat different. Or if we had started with a different set of one hundred statements, our measurement would be different. This difference is labeled item sampling error.

Clouded Instruments

Instrument error is a prime source of difficulty in developing convincing evidence on a social property. Exact measurements of temperature are slightly affected by the temperature of the thermometer. A cool thermometer slightly cools the mouth of the patient and slightly reduces the temperature reading from the correct value. A dipstick inserted in a container of fluid to measure the depth itself displaces fluid and falsifies the reading to varying degrees. This error would be small using a large stick in a ten-liter pot, and it would be large in a teacup of fluid. The precision possible in all measuring instruments is limited, and this is particularly true of instruments used in the social sciences (Kaplan 1964; Lachenmeyer 1973).

The basic requirement for an instrument applied in scientific research is that it permit clear, consistent, and relatively invariant values of a particular property when applied in the same way to the same object. Therefore, the instrument should be stable and inelastic when operated on the property it is designed to measure.

Mechanical and Processing Errors

In every phase of data processing, there is a constant threat of errors, large and small. Duplicated data cards are unintentionally retained in the deck. In very large decks of data cards, it is easily possible to leave out a large number of cards unless there is constant verification and rechecking to control against such an omission. In typing, transforming, and reproducing data, there is a human tendency to transpose numbers, decimal points, and letters unawares. One of the more humorous cases of data processing error was reported for the 1950 Census of Population:

> Our first clue was the discovery in the 1950 Census of Population of the United States of startling figures about the marital status of teenagers. There we found a surprising number of widowed 14 year-old-boys and, equally surprising, a decrease in the number of widowed teen-age males at older ages. The numbers listed by the Census were 1670 at age 14; 1475 at age 15; 1175 at 16; 810 at 17; 905 at 18; and 630 at age 19. Not until age 22 does

the listed number of widows surpass those at 14. Male divorces also decrease in number as age increases, from 1320 at age 14 to 575 at age 17. Smaller numbers of young female widows and divorcees are listed—565 widows and 215 divorcees at age 14. (Coale and Stephan 1962, 338)

After some careful searching and some shrewd detective work, it was finally determined that a shift in columns during keypunching was the source of the error. And although the proportion of error was small, it was sizable enough to be detected.

The more transformation and recordings, the greater the potential for error through oversight, transposing, and mishandling. Most calculations should be performed twice to guard against such errors. Coded data should be thoroughly verified, code by code, against source documents. Careful editing and proofreading are mandatory, as the data and derived measures move step by step through the research process. The best that can be hoped is that through thorough and continued verification the total amount of error will be reduced to 1 percent. Whether it is, in most cases, will never really be known. The error problem is particularly serious when data are transformed to ratio form because small errors, both random and systematic, can be seriously magnified in ratio transformations.

EVALUATING THE ADEQUACY OF A MEASURE

Validity

The validity of a measure refers to whether or not a measurement actually measures what it purports to measure. Does a certain scale, for example, really measure attitudes toward death? Is the wearing away of tiles on a floor really a measure of the popularity of a museum display? We have indicated throughout this chapter that measurement is the process whereby concepts are transformed into variables. Concepts, we know, exist on an abstract level; variables exist on a concrete level. And the gap between concept and variable may be quite large. What we are really concerned with is whether the concept and variable are synonymous. A measure is said to be valid if the true quantity (concept) and the measured quantity (variable) are one and the same. Although we know, in theory, that there is a true quantity for any concept, we also know, in reality, that this true quantity cannot be identified. If validity is the degree to which the true quantity and the measured quantity match and if the true quantity cannot be identified, then validity cannot be directly tested. There is, in fact, *no* direct test of validity. Hence, we do the next best thing; we establish validity through indirect tests. There are several techniques that can be employed to establish validity, and these result in different types of validity. Some of the more frequently used include face, content, concurrent, predictive, construct, and discriminant validity.

Face Validity. Face validity refers to the apparent reasonableness of the measure. A medicine flask with a false bottom would have face validity, even if the buyer had no idea how much fluid should be contained in a four-ounce flask that it resembles. A measure with face validity has no obvious characteristics that make it appear incorrect for the property it is to measure. A twenty-dollar bill in U.S. currency bearing Lincoln's picture lacks face validity as a measure of dollars because Jackson's face belongs on the twenty-dollar bill. If a counterfeit twenty-dollar bill bore Jackson's face, and was generally true to the engraving and printing standards of regular currency, it would have face validity. An instrument is said to have face validity if, *on the face of it,* it appears to measure what it purports to measure. This technique is primarily an "eyeballing" technique and does not require stringent statistical procedures.

Content Validity. Content validity indicates that the measuring device does incorporate the essence of the property it purports to measure. Tape measures, when stretched taut, have the property of linearity on a relatively inelastic line. Color samples of paint may incorporate rectangles of the actual paint, in which case they have high content validity in "measuring" color intensity and hue to be found in the actual commercial paint. But if the colors were printed in printer's ink to resemble the actual colors in the bulk paint, they would probably fall short of content validity. A questionnaire aiming to measure interpersonal adjustment in family relations would have content validity if it stuck realistically to questions relating to interpersonal adjustment. Content validity would be reduced if extraneous, unrelated questions were included (Nunnally and Wilson 1975).

Concurrent Validity. Concurrent validity has to do with existing conditions and existing relationships. If a measure of alienation consistently identifies criminal offenders and psychiatric patients already known to be highly alienated against individuals and society, then the measure has concurrent validity. If a measure of mechanical aptitude were given to an appropriate sample of high school students and it failed to identify those who actually had high mechanical aptitude by other good criteria, and indicated high aptitude for those who had none, it would lack concurrent validity. It would not agree with what we already know and thus could not be trustworthy in testing other populations (Williamson et al. 1977).

Predictive Validity. Predictive validity is established for a measure when it consistently predicts correctly the quality or property that it is constructed to measure. Many law schools consider applicants partly on the basis of their scores on a standardized legal aptitude test. It incorporates the kinds of questions and problems used in legal work, court trials, and jurisprudence. If results on this test consistently identify those who later succeed well as law students, then it has predictive validity. Generally, in the social sciences, we are well satisfied with a measure that has predictive validity.

Construct Validity. A construct is an idea developed in the social scientist's mind that is used to define and identify objects and events. Constructs help to organize thinking and promote understanding on an abstract level. *Social cohesion* is a construct defining the force that binds individual members to a group. Cohesion is presumed to increase as members devote more time, energy, and resources to cooperating with others to achieve group goals. A measure would have construct validity if, at the real-world level, it varied with other measures in ways suggested by the theory. For example, if our measure of social cohesion varied with measures of members' time, energy, and resources in the presumed ways, we would say our measure had construct validity.

Many widely used constructs in sociology are of doubtful construct validity. One such construct is the causal effect of the broken home on juvenile delinquency. Extensive research on this connection indicates that the broken home as such need not lead to delinquency since many delinquents come from intact homes and the proportion of delinquent children among all children from broken homes is not consistently high. In short, the broken home as a construct to measure delinquency has rather low validity (Nunnally and Wilson 1975).

Discriminant Validity. A measure is said to have discriminant validity if the measure consistently identifies or differentiates the construct being measured from other constructs. If a measure correlates too highly with other measures from which it is supposed to differ, the measure is lacking in discriminant validity. We would not, for example, expect to find a strong relationship between education and social isolation. Dean (1961), in seeking validation of his alienation scale, found a correlation of -0.07 (0.00 is no correlation at all) between social isolation and education, which is evidence of discriminant validity.

Reliability

Reliability in a measure means consistency of measurement. That is, a measuring device is said to be reliable if it gives the same or almost exactly the same results on repeated measures of the same object, assuming that the object itself is stable. A linear measuring tape that shrinks and expands both with temperature changes and with the strength of the pull on the tape would be unreliable. A questionnaire containing indecisive questions to which the same subject would answer differently depending on his mood at the time would also be unreliable because of the inconsistency of response. An interviewer who varied the depth and wording of questions depending on the widely variant quality of his or her own reaction to the respondent would be unreliable as a measuring instrument since the measures would indicate the interviewer's unique pattern of personal preferences more than the objective characteristics of the respondents. It is not uncommon for measures to reveal more of the character and preferences of the researcher than of the objects of research (Hirschi and Selvin 1967). Several techniques for establishing reliability have received wide use. Three of the most frequently used are test–retest, split-half, and internal consistency.

Test–Retest Reliability. One technique for assessing reliability is to make repeated measures of the same object, perhaps with different testers. If the differences are very slight (usually determined through correlation techniques), the instrument is considered reliable. If the differences are relatively large, the instrument is considered unreliable. In the case of questionnaires, the test–retest application permits comparison of results if the researcher can assume that there was no marked learning between the repeated measures. Test–retest also assumes stability in the property tested, and when the subjects are human beings, they may be much more or much less responsive if they completed the questionnaire at different times in the week (Lachenmeyer 1973).

Split-Half Reliability. If the measurement is relatively long and the items are well mixed in sequence, the items may be divided into two halves and the responses comprising each half may also be used to give a measure of reliability. Frequently these two halves are created by assigning the odd-numbered items to one half and the even-numbered items to the other. It is not a good idea to assign the first 50 percent of questionnaire items to one half and the second 50 percent to the other. Transient personal factors and item difficulty might influence the reliability coefficient. If the correlation between pairs of subscores for the split-half is large, the test is judged reliable. If the results are highly varied, the correlation coefficient will be low (i.e., close to zero) and the measure is judged unreliable (Williamson et al. 1977).

Internal Consistency: Cronbach's Alpha. A questionnaire-based scale can be tested for internal consistency by comparing the variation for any single item with the variation of the entire set of questions. This measure, called Cronbach's alpha, ranges from a maximum value of 1.00 to 0.00. An alpha value of less than 0.25 shows very little consistency for a single item to vary in the same way as the total set of questions of which the item is a part. There should be at least five questions in the set to make this measure meaningful. An alpha value of 0.8 would show a relatively high consistency or internal agreement between an item and the set. The alpha coefficient is defined as follows:

$$\alpha = \frac{n}{n-1}\left(1 - \frac{\Sigma S_i^2}{S_x^2}\right)$$

Where: n = the number of questions in the set
S_i^2 = the variance of a single item
S_x^2 = the variance of the total set

If an item has a low alpha value, it should be dropped out of the set, and the alpha, when recomputed with the reduced set will be higher. In addition, the instrument will measure more effectively.

The Relation between Validity and Reliability

Before leaving validity and reliability, a word must be said about the relationship between these two. Quite obviously, validity and reliability are not the same thing. Whereas validity is concerned with whether or not we are measuring what we say we are measuring, reliability is concerned with the stability of a measure from one measurement to the next. If the measured quantity matches the true quantity, we know we have achieved validity. If a measure is consistent from one measurement to the next, we know we have achieved reliability. Validity, though, is not directly testable. We cannot know for certain that the true quantity matches the measured quantity. On the other hand, reliability is directly testable. We can determine the degree to which a measure is consistent from one measurement to the next. Unfortunately, in the social sciences, we usually demonstrate the tendency to reason, "If a measure is reliable, that is enough." We frequently attempt to establish reliability—but seldom validity. Hence, many of the measurements used in the social sciences must rest on face validity. Our failure to establish validity probably stems in part from the fact that it cannot be directly tested, whereas reliability can be directly tested. Quite honestly, though, this is a mistake. If a measure is valid (if the measured quantity represents well the true quantity), we will get the same results from one measurement to the next. In essence, a measure that is valid will also be reliable. However, the reverse is not always true. A measure that is reliable is not necessarily valid. Bathroom scales that are set at two pounds instead of zero will consistently weigh everything two pounds too heavy. The measurement is not valid, but from one weighing to the next, the weight registered will be consistent. Consequently, it is reliable. As social scientists, we need to expend greater energy establishing the validity of our measures. Reliability will be a natural consequence.

Chapter 7

Sampling

Some basic definitions
Why sample?
The representativeness of a sample
    The 1936 election
    The 1948 election
    The 1968 election
    The 1976 election
Sampling theory: How it works
    The population distribution
    The sample distribution
    The sampling distribution of sample means
Sampling plans
    Probability samples
        Simple random samples
        Systematic samples
        Stratified samples
            Proportional stratified samples
            Disproportionate stratified samples
        Cluster samples
        Multistage sampling
    Nonprobability samples
        Convenience samples
        Purposive or judgmental samples
        Snowball samples
        Quota samples
    Combining probability and nonprobability sampling techniques
What size sample?
    z score transformation
    Confidence interval estimates
    Determining sample size

By a small sample we may judge of the whole piece.
—Cervantes

SOME BASIC DEFINITIONS

Sampling is a method of selecting some part of a group to represent the total (Warwick et al. 1973, 33). In research, the total group is called the *population*, while that part of the total that is selected is called the *sample*. Sampling in the social sciences can take place at several different stages of the research process, including (1) the selection of research units, (2) the selection of research sites, and (3) the choice of indicators by which the researcher wishes to measure the theoretical concepts. Choosing the population (whether it be sites, individuals, groups, institutions, or indicators) and the method of sampling this population are very important steps in research. In this chapter, we examine the sampling process closely.

WHY SAMPLE?

The objective of sampling is to estimate population values from information contained in a sample. Suppose, for example, we wanted to know what proportion of people in the United States are happily married. We would probably select a sample of married Americans from the population and identify the proportion in the sample that report happy marriages. We might then reason that the proportion for the population is the same as that calculated for the sample. At first glance, such a procedure might seem careless. After all, if we really want to know something about a particular group, why not study everybody? But research would be tedious and often impossible if it always required that we study an entire population. It is also not very practical. Populations are usually too large, too obscure, or too inaccessible to study in their entirety. In our study of married Americans, for example, think of the hurdles we would encounter in trying to get information from all married couples. And if we were interested in studying some topics, such as prostitution or "swinging," the population would probably be both obscure and inaccessible. Thus, to facilitate our research efforts, we study samples and generalize to the total population. Sampling is a definite plus in our research endeavors and for several important reasons. Let's look at some of the reasons.

1. *Sampling reduces the length of time needed to finish a study.* If we were to conduct research using an entire population, the larger the population, the more time we would need to finish the study. Data collection takes time. And once collected, the data must be analyzed. Consider the Population Census Survey, which is conducted once every ten years: data collection for the population of U.S. households takes approximately two months. But even more time-consuming are data coding and analysis. Some of the data collected from the 1980 census, for example, will not even be available until 1983.
2. *Sampling helps cut research cost and thus permits more diligent follow-up.* Generally speaking, the more people included in a study, the greater the cost. Every unit studied adds some cost to research, whether in data collection or data analysis, or both. And if that population is also geographically dispersed, there are even more costs. Consider the costs incurred by the federal government for the 1980 census—one billion dollars! By sampling from the population, one can reduce the cost of research substantially. In addition, more time can be devoted to locating and collecting data from all those units selected for the sample.
3. *Sampling allows for better supervision, record keeping, and training of researchers.* With fewer people to be studied, there is more time to invest in other phases of the research process. There is more time to train and supervise researchers. Such training, as we have already discovered, is important to the total research endeavor—especially if we are paying close attention to being as objective as possible in the collecting and coding of data.
4. *Sampling is almost as accurate as studying the entire population, and sometimes even more so.* It seems reasonable that studying an entire population would be more accurate than studying only a part of it. And although it may seem logical that studying a part of something could be about as accurate as studying the total, it seems absurd that it could be *more* accurate. Yet errors can spring from several sources. We may choose to study an entire population and then find ourselves scurrying with insufficient time for training, supervision, and record keeping. The resulting errors may be greater than the errors we would have sustained had we studied a sample. Recognizing this potential problem, the Bureau of the Census follows its decennial (every ten years) census with a sample survey for purposes of evaluating the data collected from the total population.

Without a doubt, sampling procedures have aided scientific research. Most likely, a considerable amount of research is conducted that would otherwise be impossible. But obviously not just any sample will do. If we estimate the proportion of happily married Americans by sampling only friends and acquaintances, for example, the estimate will probably be wrong. Using a sample value to estimate a population value is useful only if we can estimate correctly.

THE REPRESENTATIVENESS OF A SAMPLE

The best way to ensure that sample values correctly estimate population values is to select a *representative* sample. The results obtained from such a sample are what we would have found had we studied the entire population. Thus, representativeness ensures the generalizability of the research conclusions (Kidder 1981, 78). Establishing the representativeness of a sample can be tricky; ideally, we would need to compare our sample characteristics with the population characteristics. But when the population characteristics are difficult or impossible to obtain, this is not practical. In fact, a sample is sometimes selected and an estimate computed because a population characteristic is not known and cannot be determined. Consequently, the representativeness of a sample is often assumed rather than proved. We can strengthen the integrity of the assumption of representativeness, though, by considering two important factors.

The first factor is *the degree of precision with which the population is specified*. Confidence in representativeness increases if the population is well defined. The empirically defined population from which the sample is taken is called the sampling frame. We might, for example, be interested in studying all individuals currently enrolled in at least one credit hour in a U.S. college or university. Although this population might be difficult to access, it is defined. By the same token, if we wanted to study potential buyers of microcomputers, the population is less well defined. When a sample is selected from an unknown population or a poorly defined population (i.e., sampling frame), it is labeled biased. Usually such samples are controlled by unconscious selection procedures. Though such procedures may be thought of as "random," they probably are not. Smith, in his discussion of this problem, writes, "There are studies showing that if subjects are asked to sample 'randomly' from a universe of pebbles, they will unconsciously make biased selections—some will tend to pick smoother pebbles, others tend to pick larger pebbles, and some choose particularly colored pebbles" (1981, 269). This tendency for people to have unconscious response biases is so well known to professional sampling experts that most respectable research organizations will not allow their interviewers to make any sampling decisions. Sometimes interviewers make the mistake of drawing a sample from a working population without having clearly identified the theoretical population to which they wish to generalize. The resulting bias is usually unmeasurable (we have no way of knowing how much), and our ability to generalize from sample to population becomes questionable.

The second important factor is *the heterogeneity or homogeneity of the population*—that is, how similar (homogeneous) or dissimilar (heterogeneous) population units are. The more alike the units of a population, the smaller the sample can be and still be representative. But remember, to identify the degree to which the population units are the same or different, the population must still be well defined.

An analysis of public opinion surveys is helpful in understanding the extent to which samples can represent populations. This is no easy task since changes in public opinion are largely unpredictable—responsive to external forces that are themselves unpredictable. Widely held general opinions, such as "Females are weak and need male protection," are not likely to change very rapidly. But opinions on specific topics and persons, such as presidential election polls, can shift dramatically from week to week in response to current events, and selecting a representative sample becomes a challenge. Because political polling was so instrumental in developing the art and science of sampling, a comparison of the political polls predicting the presidential elections in 1936, 1948, 1968, and 1976 is informative in understanding how sampling evolved.

The 1936 Election

In 1936, *Literary Digest* made a prediction that left its editors with egg on their faces. They predicted that Alfred M. Landon would win the presidency over Franklin D. Roosevelt by a landslide—in fact, by nearly 15 percentage points! Needless to say, *Literary Digest* was wrong even though they polled nearly *2 million* voters. (As we said, the size of a sample may have little to do with its accuracy.) *Literary Digest*'s fatal mistake resulted from its definition of the population. Its sample was selected from a population defined with telephone directories and automobile registration records instead of from a listing of all registered voters in the United States. And while this sampling frame might have been sufficiently workable in the 1920–1932 elections, it was not workable in 1936. In the midst of the Great Depression, there was an unprecedented number of poor voting citizens who could not afford automobiles or telephones in their homes. Thus, they were not represented in the polls and the sample did not provide a representative cross-section of U.S. voters.

Apparently, a majority of the poorer people (who were not included in the sample) voted for Roosevelt, while a majority of the richer people (who were included in the sample) voted for Landon as *Literary Digest* predicted. The sample was representative of rich voters, but it was not representative of all voters, rich and poor alike. A second survey was conducted in the same year by George Gallup, who correctly predicted that Roosevelt would win the election. Gallup succeeded where *Literary Digest* failed because his sample better ensured that all U.S. voters, both rich and poor, were represented in the poll.

The 1948 Election

Even though Gallup was very successful in predicting the 1936 election, he and most other political pollsters failed to predict the victory of Harry Truman over Thomas Dewey in the 1948 election. A combination of factors was responsible for this fiasco. First, regardless of the fact that public opinion steadily shifted toward Truman over the course of the campaign, most pollsters ended their polling too soon. Second and perhaps more important, the 1948 polls exposed the serious shortcoming of nonprobability sampling techniques. We will discuss this topic later in the chapter.

The 1968 Election

The 1948 election prompted a number of academic researchers to experiment with probability sampling techniques, and their findings showed such samples to be amazingly accurate. In the 1968 election, for example, the Gallup Poll predicted that Richard Nixon would receive 43 percent of the vote and the Harris poll predicted 41 percent. Nixon's actual vote was 42.9 percent. Furthermore, both of these predictions were made using a sample of only 2,000 of the approximately 73 million voters from the population. Contrast this to the sample of 2 million voters used by *Literary Digest* to make an incorrect prediction in the 1936 election. Good sampling, at least on such discrete matters as for whom a person is going to vote, does work!

The 1976 Election

The results of the 1976 election polls seem to have rectified whatever harm the history of political polling brought to sampling. In the 1976 presidential election, Gerald Ford received 48.9 percent of the two-party vote, while Jimmy Carter received 51.1 percent. The week before the election, George Gallup, Louis Harris, Burus Roper, and the *New York Times* in collaboration with CBS conducted national polls. Regardless of the respondents who were undecided during the polling, the poll estimates were accurate. Discounting the "undecideds," the *Times*–CBS polls predicted 48.9 percent for Ford and 51.1 percent for Carter. The other three polls deviated from the actual vote by 0.6 to 1.6 percentage points. And again, approximately 2,000 voters were found to be representative of the nearly 80 million citizens voting. (Of course, polling companies are only one election away from disaster at any time, so they must be very careful in order to keep public confidence.)

The conclusion to be drawn here is that studying a sample can be as accurate as studying an entire population. In fact, despite early difficulties, public opinion polls have actually compiled a very good track record. The obvious question here then is, How is this possible? How can a sample provide us with as much or almost as much accuracy as the population? Let's take a look at how this works.

SAMPLING THEORY: HOW IT WORKS

If all members of a population had the same characteristics and were the same in every way, there would be no need for sampling. One unit would represent the entire population. But human beings, at least, are heterogeneous—different from each other in many ways. Any given human population, then, is composed of varied individuals. And any sample drawn from that population must contain essentially the same variations that characterize the entire population if we are to infer that the sample is representative of the population. To make such an inference, as we have already indicated, theoretically, we would have to compare the sample value to the population value to determine how similar they are. But most of the time the population value is neither known nor obtainable. Thus, we are left in the position of trying to determine whether a sample value is representative of an unknown population value. To overcome this obstacle, we employ statistical inference. *Statistical inference* describes the process of inferring a population characteristic from a sample characteristic. The use of statistical inference requires the consideration of three different and distinct distributions: the population distribution, the sample distribution, and the sampling distribution of sample means.

The Population Distribution

The population distribution is a map or plot of all of the unique values for the variable under study and the frequency of occurrence of each value. If we are studying many variables, we have many populations—in fact, one for each variable. For example, if we were studying housing sales in a large metropolitan area for 1978, we might be interested in (1) selling price, (2) mortgage price, (3) square footage, and (4) number of rooms. For each of these variables, there is a population distribution, and each has it own unique shape. Given every member of a population and a

FIGURE 7.1 Population Distribution for "Number of Rooms"

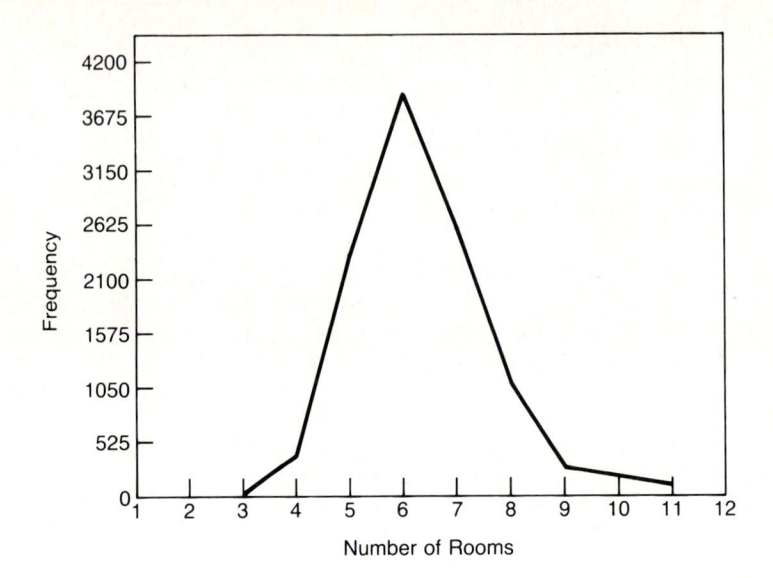

value for the variable being considered, the exact shape of each population can be determined by plotting all unique values and the frequency of occurrence of each. The shape of the population distribution for the variable "number of rooms," for example, might appear as we have pictured it in Figure 7.1. From this population distribution, we can see that there are a few houses selling that have only three rooms and a few houses selling that have eleven rooms, but most houses selling have six rooms. The population distribution for the variable "selling price" might appear as it is pictured in Figure 7.2. From this distribution we can see

FIGURE 7.2 Population Distribution for "Selling Price"

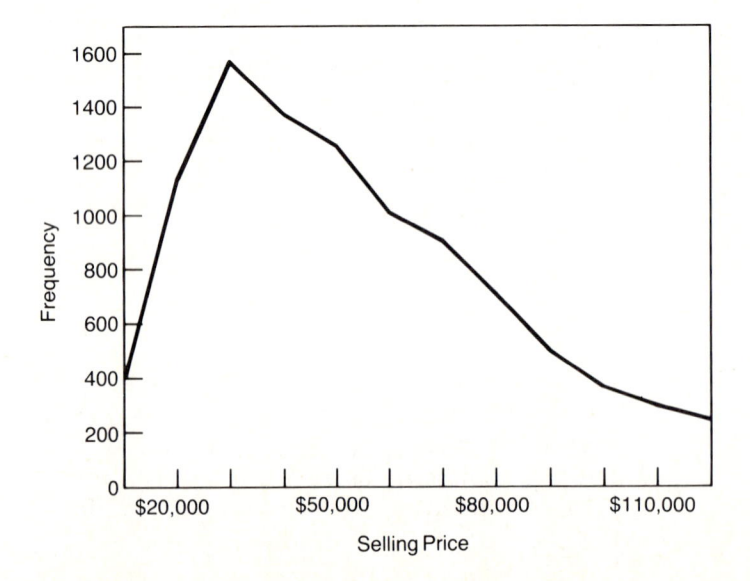

SAMPLING 181

that there are a few houses selling for $10,000 and a few houses selling for $120,000 but most houses are priced between $30,000 and $40,000. Most of the time, though, we do not deal directly with populations since most are so large and/or obscure that it is impossible to evaluate every unit.

The Sample Distribution

The sample distribution is the distribution that we deal with directly. The sample distribution refers to the way in which the variable as measured is distributed in the sample. We have reproduced in Figure 7.3 the sample distribution for the variable "number of rooms" for a sample of size 100. If the sample is representative of the population, the two distributions should be similar in shape and, theoretically, the sample distribution and the population distribution should have the same mean and the same standard deviation. The difference between the population distribution and the sample distribution is that the population distribution is a mapping or plotting of all units or members, whereas the sample distribution is a mapping of only a part of the population. Notice, for example, that Figure 7.3 has the same approximate shape as Figure 7.1. Similarly, Figure 7.4 has the same approximate shape as Figure 7.2. But although they are similar, they are not exact. And unless they are exact, there is sampling error. Regardless of how careful we are, errors in sampling will always result just from the "luck of the draw." Suppose, for example, we selected three samples from our population of housing sales in a large metropolitan area. The variable of interest is "selling price." Let's assume that the population of housing sales in this area for 1978 is 10,000, with a mean selling price of $36,762.67 and a standard deviation of

FIGURE 7.3 Sample Distribution for "Number of Rooms"

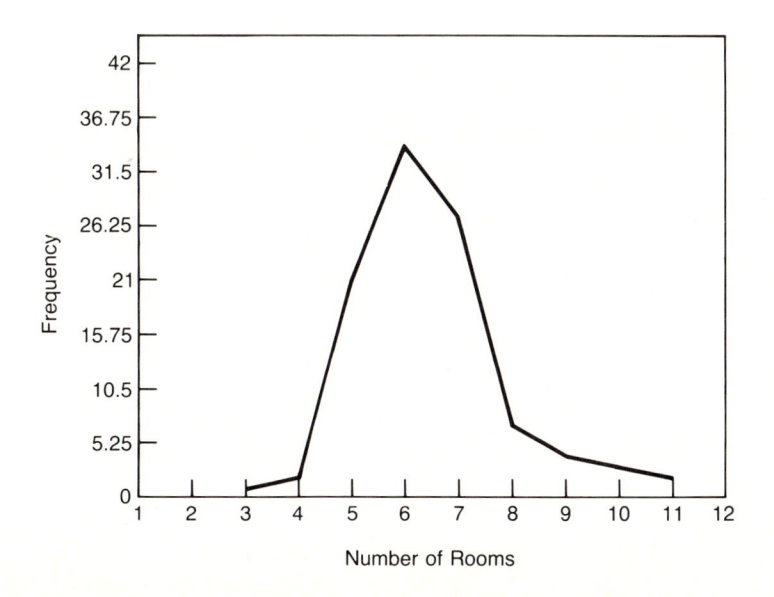

**FIGURE 7.4
Sample Distribution for "Selling Price"**

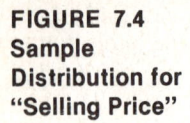

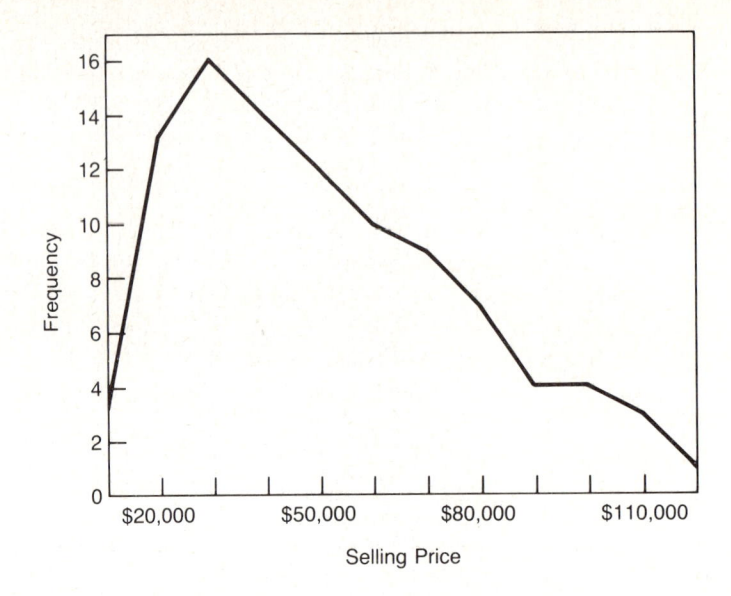

15,078.88. Each of the three samples drawn includes 100 sales records. We calculate the mean selling price of a house for each of these three samples:

Sample 1: $36,133.19
Sample 2: $38,268.22
Sample 3: $35,159.56

Notice the error encountered by sampling. The magnitude of the error can be computed as the difference between the population mean and a sample mean. And this error cannot be completely eliminated because the luck of the draw will always result in some differences from one sample to the next, regardless of how many samples we draw.

The Sampling Distribution of Sample Means

One way of tackling sampling error is to (1) select several samples, (2) calculate the mean for each sample, and (3) average these sample means. In other words, we calculate the mean of the sample means as an estimate of the population mean. This procedure helps to eliminate variability associated with the luck of the draw. For our three samples, if we average the means, we get $36,520.32, which *is* closer to the true population mean (i.e., there is less error). Theoretically, the more sample means we have to include in this averaging process, the closer we will get to the true population mean.

If we were to draw many many samples of a designated size (in our

**FIGURE 7.5
Sampling
Distribution of
Sample Means**

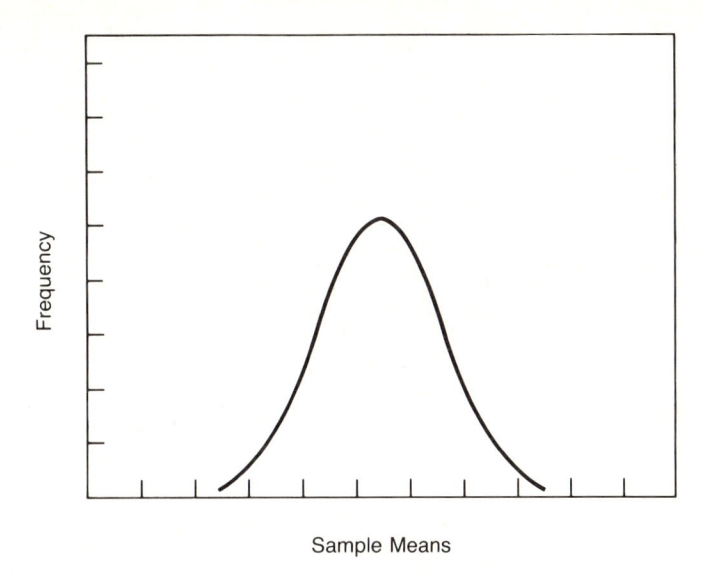

[Bell curve graph with Frequency on y-axis and Sample Means on x-axis]

case, size 100) from this population and calculate the mean for each sample, these sample means could themselves be treated as a distribution. In fact, we could draw every possible sample of some designated size (e.g., 100), calculate the mean for each sample, and then map or plot these means. Such a plot even has a special name: the sampling distribution of sample means. And any sampling distribution of sample means will always have three important characteristics (Figure 7.5).

1. *This distribution will take the form of a normal distribution regardless of the shape of the population distribution.*[1] Even if the variable in the population is distributed in a nonnormal fashion (as is selling price), the distribution of sample means will be normal. A note of caution here, though: the more the population distribution deviates from normal, the larger the samples must be in order to produce a distribution of sample means that is normally distributed.

2. *The mean of the sampling distribution will equal the mean of the population from which the samples were drawn.* Recall from our earlier example that when we averaged our three sample means, the average was closer to the true population mean than any single sample estimate. And if we were to draw every sample of size 100 from this population, calculate the mean

---

[1] By normal we mean a symmetrical bell-shaped curve. All normal distributions have four properties: (1) They are symmetrical. (2) The curve never touches the base line since theoretically scores could extend in either direction to infinity. (3) The scores tend to cluster toward the center. (4) The mean, median, and mode are all equal and all in the center of the curve.

for each, and average these estimates, this average would not only be closer, it would be *equal* to the population mean.

3. The third characteristic has to do with the standard deviation or spread among the sample means comprising this distribution. *The standard deviation of the sampling distribution of sample means will equal the standard deviation of the population divided by the square root of the sample size:*

$$\sigma_{\bar{x}} = \sigma/\sqrt{n}$$

Notice from this formula that unless we draw samples of size 1, the standard deviation of the sampling distribution will be less than the standard deviation of the population. In effect, the plot of sample means forms a closer knit distribution than the population distribution. This is because when we increase the number of population members that comprise a sample, we also decrease the likelihood of drawing a sample with a mean extremely different from the population mean. In our three samples, while there was variation between sample means, no single sample mean was really extreme. Restated, as we increase sample size, we can expect less variation from one sample mean to the next. In fact, if every sample included every population unit, there would be *no* variation between sample means; they would all be the same.

It is generally costly in both time and resources to draw just one sample, let alone many samples. And drawing all samples to create the sampling distribution of sample means is simply not practical. Thus, in any research endeavor, we usually select only one sample from the population. But we also know that our sample is just one of many, many (in fact an infinite number) samples of this size that could be selected from the population. For example, when we draw one sample of 100 housing sales records from the population of 10,000 sales records, we know that in the population there are many, many more samples of size 100 that could be drawn. In short, the real importance of the sampling distribution of sample means lies in the fact that it can be used to determine the probability or likelihood of drawing just one sample with a particular sample mean from the population. (For more on the sampling distribution of sample means, see Chapter 13.)

SAMPLING PLANS

In modern sampling theory, a basic distinction is made between probability and nonprobability samples. The distinguishing characteristic of probability samples is that the researcher can specify for each unit in the population the likelihood that it will be included in the sample. In the simplest case, each unit of the population has the same chance of being included in the sample. It is because of this known probability of inclusion that we can determine sampling error—or variability associated with the luck of the draw. In contrast, with nonprobability samples, there are population units that have no chance or that have an unknown chance of being included in the sample. In other words, a restriction on the definition of the population is implied. If a complete listing of the population is not possible, then we cannot specify the population and the concept of sampling error or variability associated with the luck of the draw is not meaningful.

Suppose, for example, in our study of housing sales, we had decided to make our sample all those houses that sold in the month of January. Certainly, with this procedure, not all housing sales have a known chance of being included in the sample. And because they don't, we cannot identify the probability of any single housing sale being included. The difference between the population mean and the sample mean is no longer just a function of sampling error or variation associated with the luck of the draw. Now we have introduced a selection bias (month of January) as well. And we do not know to what extent the difference in the population mean and the sample mean is a function of one or the other. If we calculate what we think is the sampling error, as we would with a probability sample, these two types of error will be entangled. They simply cannot be separated, and thus the concept of sampling error no longer makes sense. In other words, for nonprobability samples, we cannot determine our sampling error. Although this limitation might be troublesome, it is not fatal. In fact, there are a number of research situations in which nonprobability samples are really more practical and more useful.

Probability Samples

Simple Random Samples. Simple random sampling is the basic probability sampling design, and it is incorporated in all of the more elaborate designs. A simple random sample is defined as a sample in which every member of the population has an equal and independent chance of being selected. If, for example, in our population of 10,000 housing sales records, a simple random sample of 100 is to be selected, the probability of any population unit's being included in the sample is 100/10,000, or .01. Randomness in the sample selection process can be accomplished with one of two methods: lottery or a table of random numbers. Both methods require a listing of the population units. With the lottery method, every member of the population is represented on a piece of paper and dropped into a lottery cylinder. The pieces of paper are mixed well and the sample is drawn. With a table of random numbers, we begin by assigning all population units a unique number (0 to N). Our starting point in the sample selection process is a random number (i.e., one that is randomly selected from a table of random numbers). Numbers from a table of random numbers are read in order (up, down, or sideways—the direction is not important as long as we are consistent). When a number that appears in the table corresponds to a number on the population list, that unit is included in the sample. This procedure is continued until the desired sample size is reached. Notice that with either of these methods, the selection of any given unit does not restrict the selection of other units.

Systematic Samples. A systematic sample is one that approximates a simple random sample. To obtain a systematic sample, we begin with a listing of all elements in the designated population. We then determine the desired sample size and divide it into the population size to give us our increment value, labeled N. The sample selected is composed of every Nth element from the population. If, for example, we wanted a sample of 100 housing sales and if the number of units in the population equaled 10,000, we would divide 10,000 by 100. In effect, every 100th element in the population would be selected for the sample. But in order to ensure randomness, the first selection must be determined by some random process such as a table of random numbers or lottery. A word of caution here: it is a good idea to begin with a randomly ordered population list. Consider, for example, what might happen if we ordered the sales by month of sale. If a disproportionate number of sales occurred in the months of June to August as compared with March to May, our listing of the population would ensure the inclusion of a larger number of sales for the summer months. The ordering itself would introduce a selection bias such that every sale would not have an equal chance of being included. Those homes selling in the June-to-August period would have a greater chance of being included than those selling in the March-to-May period. This selection bias can be eliminated by beginning with a population list that is randomly ordered. All in all, systematic random sampling is much easier than simple random sampling, even though many researchers treat systematic and simple random samples as one and the same (Walizer and Weiner 1978, 435–436).

Stratified Samples. The stratified sample is still another modification of a simple random sample. But with stratified samples, the population is divided into layers, or strata. Stratification is especially useful when a population is characterized as heterogeneous but consists of a number of homogeneous subpopulations or strata. When a population is homogeneous, little or no benefit is obtained from stratification. Suppose, for example, we wished to study a factory employing 4,000 workers from different ethnic backgrounds: black, white, Asian, and Hispanic. We decide to study a sample of 800 workers. If we want each ethnic group to be represented in the sample, we might divide the workers into strata according to their ethnic classifications and select from each stratum. Basically, there are two ways to determine the number of elements being sampled from each stratum: proportional and disproportional.

PROPORTIONAL STRATIFIED SAMPLES Of the stratified samples, proportional stratified samples are perhaps more frequently used by researchers. With this procedure, the number of items selected from each stratum will be proportional to the size of the stratum in the population. In our example of factory workers, if the black workers comprise 30 percent of the population of workers, they should also comprise 30 percent of the sample. The following simple equation can be used to identify the number of elements to be selected for each of the stratum in the sample.

$$n(I) = N(I)/(N)(n)$$

Where:

$n(I)$ = the size for the Ith stratum in the sample
n = the sample size
$N(I)$ = the size of the Ith stratum in the population
N = the population size

If we were to apply this formula to our example, the solution would be as follows:

$$\text{black workers} = 1{,}200/(4{,}000)(800) = 240$$
$$\text{white workers} = 1{,}600/(4{,}000)(800) = 320$$
$$\text{Asian workers} = 560/(4{,}000)(800) = 112$$
$$\text{Hispanic workers} = 640/(4{,}000)(800) = 128$$

Total sample size = 240 + 320 + 112 + 128 = 800

This type of sampling design assures representativeness with respect to the property forming the strata and decreases the chances of excluding members of the population because of the classification process. However, it requires accurate information on population proportions for each stratum. And if stratified lists are not available, it may simply be too costly to prepare them (Miller 1975, 57).

DISPROPORTIONATE STRATIFIED SAMPLES With disproportionate stratified samples, the sample size of each stratum is not proportionate to the size of each stratum within the population. The size of each stratum is based on analytical considerations or convenience. One simple and practical approach is to select an equal number of items or respondents from each stratum regardless of size, cost, or variability. In our sample of 800 factory workers, for example, 200 workers would be selected from each of the four strata.

This method is more efficient and a better predictor than the proportional stratified sampling technique for comparison of strata. But it is less efficient for determining population characteristics.

Cluster Samples. Cluster sampling is still another form of simple random sampling. Like stratified sampling, it requires the grouping of population units. Unlike stratified sampling, the units are grouped by clusters instead of homogeneous strata within the population. Using our example of factory workers, we might choose a sample that included all workers (regardless of ethnic background) in the quality control division of the factory. Rather than selecting individuals, we are randomly selecting divisions.

Cluster sampling is not costly if the clusters are geographically defined. It requires listing only the selected clusters. The characteristics of the clusters as well as those of the population can be estimated, and the same clusters can be used for subsequent samples since clusters, not individuals, are selected. On the other hand, cluster sampling yields larger errors for a comparable sample size than other probability sampling techniques, and it requires that each member of the population be uniquely assigned to one and only one cluster. The inability to do this may result in the duplication or omission of individuals.

Multistage Sampling. The four probability sampling designs discussed thus far provide the fundamental selection techniques for the multistage sample system—so called because the selection process takes place in a series of stages. A form of random sampling is used in each of the sampling stages, and in some cases, sampling units are selected with probabilities proportionate to their size in the population. The Bureau of the Census, for example, uses multistage sampling in conducting the surveys that it prepares before and after the census in some areas in the United States. For such surveys, the sampling stages might look as follows:

Stage 1: Random selection of regions
Stage 2: Random selection of neighborhoods within regions
Stage 3: Random selection of households within neighborhoods

Each stage of the multistage procedure may involve any of the possible sample designs already discussed. This method of sampling has a wide range of applications, but in general it is most useful in sampling a large number of units, especially when cost saving is important (Cangelosi 1979, 235). If the units are geographically defined, travel and field research costs will be lowered. On the other hand, sampling errors are likely to be larger than the sampling errors with simple or systematic random samples of the same size.

In sum, probability sampling can be quite simple or extremely complex. It can be time-consuming or time-saving. It can be expensive or inexpensive. Whatever the situation, however, it remains the most effective method for selecting population units because it avoids conscious or unconscious biases in the sample selection process and thus permits the estimation of sampling error.

Nonprobability Samples

In general, nonprobability samples are used for those research situations in which probability samples would be extremely expensive and/or when precise representativeness is not essential. Furthermore, if a population cannot be defined because no listing of the population is available, the researcher will be forced to use a nonprobability sample (Nachmias and Nachmias 1976, 430). With nonprobability sampling techniques, though, we will never be able to specify the probability of each population unit's being included in the sample, and thus we have no assurance that every unit does, in fact, have some chance of being selected. The major problem with nonprobability samples, then, is that there is no formal procedure for generalizing from sample to population since sampling error cannot be determined. And since generalizability is so important, researchers are often advised to use nonprobability samples with caution and primarily when probability methods are not feasible (Walizer and Weiner 1978, 437; Kish 1965, 19). Nonprobability sampling techniques include convenience, purposive (judgmental), snowball, and quota.

Convenience Samples. A convenience or accidental sample is one in which the researcher selects those respondents who are "close at hand." Using a convenience sample saves time, money, and effort. Thus, what is lost in accuracy is gained in efficiency. A common example of a convenience sample is data collected in a classroom setting. Only those students enrolled in the selected classrooms have any chance of being included.

Haphazard or volunteer subjects samples, such as those used by archaeologists or historians, are also convenience or accidental samples. When news reporters conduct street surveys, they are using convenience samples. In effect, they simply talk to whoever is available. Researchers who use such samples draw conclusions from whatever units are available. But since generalizability is questionable, caution should be exercised in drawing conclusions from such samples.

Purposive or Judgmental Samples. Sometimes a researcher selects a subgroup that, on the basis of available information, can be judged to be representative of the total population. Choosing the first three days of the month as typical days for auditing ledgers or picking a typical village to represent a national rural population is an example of a purposive sample. Purposive or judgmental samples are used by researchers because they reduce the cost of preparing the sample since ultimately units can be selected so that they are close together. However, again, variability and sampling error cannot be measured or controlled. Hence, such samples require strong assumptions or considerable knowledge of the population and the subgroup being selected (Miller 1975).

Snowball Samples. The use of snowball samples has actually snowballed in recent years as more researchers are making use of this technique. The term is taken from the analogy of a snowball, which begins small but becomes bigger and bigger as it rolls downhill. In the first stage of sampling, only a few respondents are identified as having the required characteristics and are interviewed by the researchers. But these respondents are used as informants to identify others who also qualify for inclusion in the sample. The second stage is interviewing these new persons, and so on. This sampling technique is particularly useful in observational research and in community studies. Snowball sampling is also useful for the study of obscure or hidden populations. Studies of prostitution, abortion, or homosexuality, for example, often fare better with this sampling technique.

Quota Samples. A quota sample is a nonprobability sample similar to a stratified sample. Quota sampling generally requires that each stratum be represented in the sample in the same proportion as in the total population (Bailey 1978, 81). In the United States, for example, when the government wants to admit immigrants from different countries, it stipulates that the number of immigrants from a specific country should be proportional to the number of U.S. Americans originating from that country. This method of sampling is not costly and introduces some stratification effect. On the other hand, it also introduces observer bias in the classification of subjects and nonrandom selection within classes (Miller 1975, 58). Quota samples are most successful in controlling for objective variables such as socioeconomic status rather than subjective variables whose measurement depends on the judgments of the interviewers.

Combining Probability and Nonprobability Sampling Techniques

It is possible to combine probability and nonprobability sampling techniques in the same design if sampling is done in a series of stages. One or more of the stages are accomplished using the principles of probability sampling, while other stages are accomplished by using the principles of nonprobability sampling (Kidder 1981, 438-439). Let's examine how this might work. Suppose we wanted to study unemployment rates in different regions of the United States. We could use a multistage probability sampling technique to choose the counties in each state and the neighborhoods within each county. For the final stage of choosing respondents within each neighborhood, though, we could use a nonprobability quota sample controlling for, say, ethnicity and race.

Such a design is relatively inexpensive, especially with the use of a quota sample in the final stage. On the other hand, we benefit from probability sampling at least in the earlier stages of sampling areas and neighborhoods. Using probability samples at the earlier stages gives the researcher added security at relatively little cost.

A second example of combining both probability and nonprobability samples demonstrates how these two broad types of sampling techniques can be combined yet a little differently. Suppose we were to select different regions of the United States for the study of unemployment rates and then draw a probability sample of respondents from within these regions. The purposive sample of regions might be based on the knowledge that for a long period of time some regions were considered prosperous with a low rate of unemployment, while other regions were considered poor. Within each of these regions, we might use a probability sampling technique to choose neighborhoods and respondents within each neighborhood.

One way of looking at this type of design is to think of the typical regions as defining a population. If a probability sample of this population were taken, the mathematical theory of probability sampling would be completely applicable, and we could measure our sampling error. We could then generalize the inferences regarding this restricted population to the national population, subject to the assumption that the typical regions were still typical of their respective states. So long as this assumption was valid, it seems likely that such a sampling plan would produce the most dependable sampling results at a low cost.

WHAT SIZE SAMPLE?

Beginning students of social research are often stumped when it comes to determining sample size. Students generally suspect that there is some minimum sample size needed to represent the population from which they are sampling in order to generalize findings. And by the same token, they realize there is some maximum sample size beyond which additional sampling does not improve generalizability. Thus, the question becomes: Just how small is minimum and how large is maximum? A sample may be one population unit, all but one unit, or any number in between. And since most samples will probably be some number in between, guidelines are needed to aid in this decision-making process. Let's take a look at what goes into this decision.

z Score Transformation

Recall from our earlier discussion of sampling theory that we were interested in establishing the representativeness of our particular sample mean. To establish representativeness, we must be able to locate the position of our sample mean on the curve of sample means. In short, we are primarily concerned with the position of our sample mean relative to the population mean and the likelihood of drawing a sample (of a designated size) from the population whose mean is a certain value. To locate our sample mean on this curve (sampling distribution of sample means), though, we must transform the mean to a z score. In other words, we must transform the mean to a score that represents the number of standard deviation units it is from the population mean. And this transformation requires that we know the mean and standard deviation of the sampling distribution of sample means. This transformation score is computed as follows:

$$z = \frac{\overline{X} - \mu}{\sigma/\sqrt{n}}$$

Again, our primary concern is with whether or not the z score transformation of our sample is less or greater than $+/-1.96$ since $+/-1.96$ represents the scores bounding off 95 percent of the area under the curve (see Figure 7.6). If our mean is located within this 95 percent area, we will reason that the difference between our sample mean and the population mean is just chance fluctuation resulting from the luck of the draw. Therefore, the sample mean is viewed as representative of the population mean and the sample representative of the population. If our sample mean is located outside of this 95 percent area, we will reason that the observed difference is not likely to be chance fluctuation since the luck of the draw doesn't often result in a sample with so *extreme* a mean. Therefore, we will conclude that the sample mean is not representative of the population mean and the sample is not representative of the population.

Confidence Interval Estimates

By rearranging this formula, we can also compute something known as a confidence interval estimate. When a sample value is computed to represent a population value, it is called a *point estimate*. Our sample mean, for

**FIGURE 7.6
Standard Normal Curve**

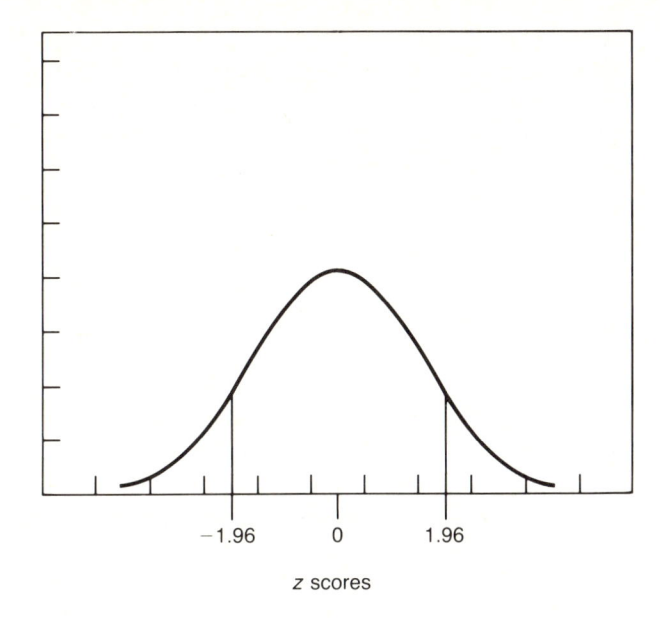

−1.96   0   1.96

z scores

example, is a point estimate of the population mean. A confidence interval estimate is a probabilistically constructed range about a point estimate that provides an interval estimate of a population value (in our case, the population mean). The probability associated with this estimate indicates the likelihood that the statement concerning the population value is true (Cangelosi 1979, 156–157). Suppose, for example, a sewing machine company stated in its pamphlets that it was 95 percent confident that the average life of the company's machine is between 3 and 5 years under heavy usage. Restated, the true population value (i.e., life of the sewing machine) should be between 3 and 5 years for 95 out of every 100 of the company's sewing machines. This probability of 95 percent is derived by bounding off 95 percent of the area under the curve from the other 5 percent. As we have already indicated, for the standard normal curve, the scores establishing the 95 percent level of confidence will always be +/−1.96 since the curve is fixed. If we want to be more certain, say 99 percent, the boundaries become +/−2.58 since these are the scores that bound off 99 percent of the area from the other 1 percent. Notice that to be this confident, the interval is widened to include more values. The interval itself is either right or wrong.

The concept of confidence intervals is also evident in Figure 7.6. Recall that in order for us to have reasoned that our sample mean was not representative, we said that it would have to be as low as 33,807.21 or as high as 39,718.13. Actually, this reasoning makes use of confidence intervals in that these two values establish the boundaries for the interval estimate. And we can say that we are 95 percent confident that the true population mean is within this interval since 95 out of every 100 samples of some designated size drawn from the population will have a mean within this range. We computed these lower and upper values by establishing the two scores located approximately two standard deviations below and above the mean. We chose two standard deviations below and above since $+/-1.96$ (approximately 2.00) is the standard score providing the boundaries setting off 95 percent of the area under the curve:

$$\bar{X} - 1.96\sigma/\sqrt{n} < \mu < \bar{X} + 1.96\sigma/\sqrt{n}$$

If you look closely at this rearranged formula, you might notice that given a fixed level of confidence (95 percent or 99 percent) and a fixed standard deviation (*s*), there is only one way we can improve our precision in estimating the population value from the sample value (i.e., narrow our interval estimate), and that is by increasing our sample size. If, for example, we increased our sample size from 100 to 1,000, notice what happens to the interval: 35,828.07–37,697.27. And if we increase our sample size to 5,000, notice what happens to the interval: 36,344.71–37,180.64. In fact, with a second rearrangement of this formula, we can solve for *n* (sample size). (See Figure 7.7.)

Determining Sample Size

Suppose we decided in advance of conducting our study just how much precision we desired. That is, we decided what size interval we would be willing to tolerate around the population mean. We will call this *e* (for error). If we also knew or could estimate the population standard deviation and we decided on a level of confidence (e.g., 95 or 99 percent), we could determine the sample size needed to obtain the specified precision at the desired level of confidence since the formula for determining sample size is just another rearrangement of the *z* score formula (see Figure 7.7).

FIGURE 7.7 Determining Sample Size

We begin with:
$$z = \frac{\bar{X} - \mu}{\sigma/\sqrt{n}}$$

By substitution:
(*e* is the maximum error we are willing to tolerate in prediction)
$$e = \bar{X} - \mu$$

Thus:
$$z = \frac{e}{\sigma/\sqrt{n}}$$

Solving for *n*:
$$n = \frac{z^2\sigma^2}{e^2}$$

SAMPLING

For example, to estimate the population mean within $1,000 (+/−$500) at the 95 percent level of confidence, we would have computed the sample size as follows:

$$n = \frac{(1.96^2)(15{,}078.88^2)}{1{,}000^2}$$

$$n = 874$$

To be within $500 (+/−$250 on either side) of the population mean at the 95 percent confidence level, we would need a sample of size 3,494. Notice that the sample size must be quadrupled just to narrow the interval width by $500. Thus, with a sample of 874, we can be 95 percent confident that the sample value is within $1,000 (+/−$500) of the population value. But with a sample of 3,494, we can be 95 percent confident that the sample value is within $500 (+/−$250) of the population value. As a researcher you would have to decide whether the increased precision is worth the additional time and cost required to collect the sample.

Although this formula provides us with a quick and simple answer to "What size sample?," there still remain several issues and questions to be considered. First of all, the designated sample size suggested by this formula is based on a single variable. And even the simplest of research projects makes use of more than one variable. Usually we want to estimate several characteristics from the same sample, and the sample size needed to achieve the desired precision for one population characteristic may be smaller or larger than the size needed to achieve the desired precision for others. But this problem can ordinarily be solved by selecting a sample large enough that each of the most important characteristics is estimated with sufficient precision at the desired level of confidence. Suppose, for example, we conducted a survey collecting 100 variables. We could conceivably identify 100 potential sample sizes—one for each of the 100 variables. Using this approach, our final decision on sample size would equal the largest estimate. Such an approach would be conservative in that we would be collecting a sample size that for most variables was even larger than that required for the designated precision and level of confidence. However, computing 100 potential sample sizes is not very practical. A more practical approach would be to identify those variables central to the study and compute estimates of sample size based only on those. We would then collect a sample whose size equaled the largest estimate.

A second issue and unanswered question that remains is, What if all the important variables are not variables for which we can compute means and standard deviations? What if, for example, we are concerned with such variables as sex (male, female) or marital status (single, married, widowed, divorced)? For these variables, mean and standard deviation make no sense. In such cases as these, we employ a variation of the z score formula that uses the standard deviation of the distribution representing a plot of such discrete or categorical responses. Such distributions require that we consider dichotomized categorical responses. With a variable like marital status, for example, we would need to identify four population distributions: (1) married versus not married, (2) single versus not single, (3) widowed versus not widowed, and (4) divorced versus not divorced. For such variables, the most conservative estimate (i.e., the largest sample size needed for any such categorical responses) will be computed when the proportions associated with each of the two categories are $p = (1-p) = .5$. This is because the maximum value for population variance will be reached at these values since the product of p and $(1-p)$ is a maximum value: $(.5)(.5) = .25$; $(.6)(.4) = .24$; $(.7)(.3) = .21$; etc. Consequently, for any and all categorical variables, we can always estimate the maximum sample size needed by assuming equal proportions (i.e., .5) for variables with dichotomized categorical responses. While we will sometimes wind up with a sample larger than necessary, it will never be too small—given a designated level of confidence and a desired range of precision.

A third issue and unanswered question is, Doesn't this formula for determining sample size consider sampling error? The answer is yes. In fact, when we establish the degree of precision desired (i.e., the interval around the population value), we are actually specifying how much sampling error we are willing to tolerate. This is an extremely important point given our earlier discussion of sampling error. In effect, since sampling error can be computed for probability samples, we can readily use this procedure to determine sample size. However, with nonprobability samples, since it is not possible to determine sampling error, this formula is simply not meaningful. In fact, with nonprobability samples, there are no quick and easy formulas for determining sample size. Thus, with nonprobability samples, a decision on sample size must be based on other considerations.

One of the primary considerations when nonprobability samples are used is, How are the results to be analyzed? It is important to estimate how many times the sample may have to be subdivided during data analysis and to ensure an adequate sample size for each subdivision. Generally speaking, the minimum sample size should equal ten times the maximum number of subdivisions. Beyond data analysis, the primary considerations become cost and time. Researchers are always cautioned to select an adequate sample that will be cost- and time-efficient.

A sound rule taught to beginning students of research is "Use as large a sample as possible." The smaller the sample, the larger the error, and the larger the sample, the smaller the error. But large samples are not championed because large numbers are good in and of themselves. They are championed to give the principles of randomization a chance to work (Kerlinger 1979). To some extent, sample size does depend on population size. Some populations are quite small—for example, all Catholic popes in the Vatican. For such studies the entire population is fewer than fifty and we would probably study the entire population. Other populations are quite large—for example, all voting U.S. citizens—and a sample of 2,000 or 3,000 would be necessary. But regardless of the sampling technique used, sampling bias is not affected by sample size. Certainly *Literary Digest* was not saved by having used a large sample in its election poll. Generally speaking, for most research endeavors, samples will be adequate if within the limits of 30 and 500. Samples of less than 30 are usually too small, while samples of greater than 500 are seldom necessary.

Chapter 8

The Experiment

"Deviance in the Dark"
Creating equal groups
    Matching as a means of creating equal groups
    Random assignment of subjects to groups
    Matching versus random assignment
Technical considerations concerning the independent variable
    Manipulating the independent variable
    Preventing unintended differences in treatment
    Criteria for causality revisited
        Time order
        Relationship between variables
        Rival hypotheses
Two experimental designs
    Pretest/posttest control group design
    An important note
    Posttest-only control group design
Laboratory versus field experiment
Field experiment
    "From Jerusalem to Jericho"
    Control in the field experiment
    Control in evaluation research
Internal validity
    History
    Maturation
    Testing
    Instrumentation
    Regression effect
    Experimental mortality
External validity
True experiment versus quasi-experiment
Quasi-experiment

> *No amount of experimentation can ever prove me right;*
> *but a single experiment can prove me wrong.*
> —Albert Einstein

"DEVIANCE IN THE DARK"

The setting is a college classroom building. The event is a student casually perusing a cluttered bulletin board. After a few minutes of careful reading, she spots a notice seeking students' participation in a research study. The notice includes a telephone number for interested students to call. Upon calling, our student is told that the study in question is on "environmental psychology." She is given an address to go to and a time for her participation. Upon arrival, a man ushers her into an empty room and asks her to fill out a series of written forms. Twenty minutes later, he returns and takes her to a totally dark chamber. The chamber or room is approximately ten by twelve feet. Both the walls and floor are padded, and the ceiling is out of reach. The only light in the room is a pinpoint of red light over the door for emergency exiting.

Our student is told that she will be left in the room, along with seven other students, for approximately one hour. She is told that there are no rules as to what to do. She is also told that at the end of the hour she will be escorted from the room alone, hence providing no opportunity to meet face-to-face with the other participants. The student slips off her shoes, empties her pockets, and enters the room.

The research question addressed by Kenneth and Mary Gergen and William Barton in their study "Deviance in the Dark" (1973) began just this way. Their question: "What do people do under conditions of extreme anonymity?" (p. 129). In other words, what do people do with each other when the normal sanctions that govern their behaviors are severed? Will they willingly forsake these sanctions for alternate ways of interacting? Or will they continue to behave in normative ways despite the knowledge that there is no way to reward or punish subjects appropriately for their behavior? With this question in mind, Gergen and his colleagues hypothesized that extreme anonymity would free subjects of the routinized behavior we have come to expect in today's society and thus enable them to act in any way deemed mutually acceptable.

Approximately fifty individuals participated in the Gergen et al. study. Subjects were primarily students between the ages of eighteen and twenty-five. Participants were divided into groups of eight, half males and half females. All voice communications were tape-recorded during the one-hour sessions. The pinpoint of red light above the emergency exit was enough to videotape all movement using infrared cameras.

In addition to the dark chamber condition, Gergen et al. created a second condition. Some groups of subjects spent one hour in the chamber with the lights left on. In both conditions, each subject was asked to write down his or her impressions of the experience after being removed from the chamber.

The data collected in this study confirm the researchers' hypothesis. In fact, the differences between students in the dark-room condition versus the lighted-room condition proved to be quite enlightening. First, subjects in the lighted room kept a continuous stream of conversation going from the start to the finish of the session. In the dark room, talk slacked off dramatically after the first thirty minutes. Second, subjects in the lighted room quickly found a place to sit (seldom closer than three feet to any other subject) and remained seated in the same position for the entire hour. In fact, the research team wrote that they could predict with 90 percent accuracy within the first five minutes where a subject would be seated in the last five minutes of the session. In contrast, subjects in the dark room moved about fluidly, making it impossible to predict with greater than 50 percent accuracy where a subject would be from one five-minute period to the next.

All dark-room participants accidentally touched one another, while less than 5 percent of the lighted-room participants did. Approximately 50 percent of the dark-room subjects reported that they hugged one another, and 80 percent stated that they felt sexual excitement. In marked contrast, none of the lighted-room subjects hugged each other, and only 30 percent acknowledged being sexually aroused.

The written impressions of the dark-room subjects only serve to confirm even more the lack of normative structure under a condition of extreme anonymity. One student wrote:

> As I was sitting Beth came up and we started to play touchy face and touchy body and started to neck. We expressed it as showing "love" to each other. Shortly before I was taken out, we decided to pass our "love" on, to share it with other people. So we split up and Laurie took her place. We had just started touchy face and touchy body and kissed a few times before I was tapped to leave.

In contrast, the subjects in the lighted room were less likely to explore the chamber and more likely to report boredom.

From the data collected in this study, Gergen et al. conclude that intimacy is quite natural, at least for people aged eighteen to twenty-six. When freed from the normative constraints of everyday life, people in this age group developed very immediate and close relationships.

What we have just described is an experiment. As we learned in Chapter 4, the experiment is a research design that uses at least two groups in either a contrived or a natural setting, and it is a design that is higher on control than representativeness. We shall discuss each of these points later in the chapter.

The experiment can be thought of as the one research design that epitomizes the standard of science. As we indicated in Chapter 4, this is largely because the logic of causation and the logic of the experiment are one and the same. The goal of an experiment is to determine whether two or more variables are *causally connected*. Recall from Chapter 4 that a variable is any characteristic on which individuals or groups differ. In the experiment just described, for example, the researchers were interested in whether the condition of extreme anonymity would cause changes in behavior typically governed by norms. In this experiment, *extreme anonymity* is the *independent variable*—the *presumed cause*, while *behavior* is the *dependent variable*—the *presumed effect*.

In addition to labeling the variables in an experiment, we also label the groups. The group receiving some treatment is the *experimental group*. The comparison group is the *control group*. In the experiment just described, the group spending one hour in the dark chamber is the experimental group, while the group spending one hour in the lighted chamber is the control or comparison group.

As you begin to reflect on the experiment just narrated, several questions will probably come to mind. How did the researchers decide who would be in the experimental group versus the control group? How could the experimenters be sure that the observed behavior differences between the two groups were really a function of extreme anonymity? Is this experiment truly characteristic of real life? Can these kinds of research findings be generalized to the larger population? In our discussion of the experimental design, we shall attempt to answer each of these questions, and we hope our answers will begin to broaden your understanding of this design.

CREATING EQUAL GROUPS

The logic of the experimental design requires that all groups must be initially equal. In short, this means that if 50 percent of group 1 is male, then 50 percent of group 2 should also be male. If 85 percent of group 1 is single, then 85 percent of group 2 should also be single. If the average age of group 1 is twenty, then the average age of group 2 should also be twenty. As we shall see, if we cannot assume equal groups before the experiment begins, we cannot establish beyond a probable doubt that any observed differences between groups are a function of the independent variable.

Suppose, for example, in the "Deviance in the Dark" experiment, that the researchers had not bothered to establish equal groups. Now the *cause* of the observed difference in behavior between groups would be in question. Would the difference between groups be a function of the independent variable (light versus dark) or a function of one or more of the differences that existed initially between these two groups? Unfortunately, there would be no way of knowing, and under such conditions the experimental data would not provide us with many (if any) answers.

Matching as a Means of Creating Equal Groups

One method of creating equal groups is through matching—a process of identifying two similar subjects who are alike on a number of measured characteristics and placing these subjects in separate groups. If, for example, we selected a student who is single, female, twenty-two, black, and a psychology major with a 3.6 grade-point average to go in group 1, we would need to find another student matching on all of these same characteristics to go in group 2. Although it may be relatively easy to find pairs of subjects matching on one or two characteristics, it becomes next to impossible to create such matches on a half-dozen or more variables.

Matching creates an exact equivalence only on the measured and matched variables. Regardless of how careful we are to match on every conceivable variable that may be causally connected to the dependent variable, there remain unmeasured and uncontrolled variables whose influence may be crucial. Suppose, for example, five years after the "Deviance in the Dark" experiment, someone discovered that eating chocolate significantly affected behavior. Suppose chocolate was shown to lift people's inhibitions. If we were reflecting back on the "Deviance" experiment, we might now begin to wonder whether group 1 had eaten more chocolate one hour before the experiment. Perhaps group 1's more liberal behavior was actually a function of all subjects digesting chocolate before participating in the experiment. Although this hypothesis may seem somewhat preposterous, the fact remains that without measuring this variable and controlling for it, we would have no way of knowing the extent to which chocolate was responsible for the observed difference between groups. In short, the problems inherent in the matching process suggest that there must be a more efficient way to establish equality.

Random Assignment of Subjects to Groups

A second means of establishing equal groups is through random assignment. The random assignment of subjects into groups means that the placement of each subject in a group is based on chance. In other words, the decision to place a subject in group 1 versus group 2 is based on, for example, the flip of a coin—heads you are in group 1; tails you are in group 2. By using such a method, every subject has an equal chance of being in any given group, and the process is not based on human decision. Also, by using this process, we can safely assume that our groups are approximately equal. In other words, when we identify the proportion of males in group 1, it should be approximately the same for group 2. When we identify the proportion of singles for group 1, it should be approximately the same for group 2. When we compute the average age for group 1, it should be approximately the same for group 2.

We don't want to leave you with the impression that randomization is the panacea for all experiments. Certainly, there are risks. With chance operating, we could conceivably end up with all the singles in one group and marrieds in another. Or we could end up with all the older subjects in one group and the younger subjects in another. Although the probability of this happening is pretty remote, we must recognize that it could happen.

To safeguard against such a problem, our best strategy is to measure our subjects on a number of easily obtained variables that could prove influential. If our groups do not differ markedly on these variables, they probably do not differ markedly on others.

Matching versus Random Assignment

While matching creates an *exact equivalence,* randomization creates an *approximate equivalence.* However, the exact equivalence created with matching is only with respect to the set of measured variables used in the matching process. In contrast, the approximate equivalence created with random assignment is in reference to *all* variables—those identified and measured and those unidentified and unmeasured. If two years after the "Deviance in the Dark" experiment chocolate was discovered to be causally linked to behavior, the "Deviance" findings would not be affected. Even without knowledge of this variable, the random assignment of subjects to groups suggests that the average number of ounces of chocolate ingested by group 1 the hour before the experiment was approximately the same as for group 2. Trading an exact equivalence for an approximate equivalence may seem unreasonable, but it is a good trade when we realize that the equivalence applies to all variables—those unidentified and out of sight as well as those identified and measured.

TECHNICAL CONSIDERATIONS CONCERNING THE INDEPENDENT VARIABLE

Once subjects have been assigned to either the experimental or the control group, we can turn our attention to the treatment—the manipulated independent variable. The second step in an experiment is applying different treatments to the various groups. In the ideal experiment, the treatment to which subjects are exposed should differ in only one way, although in reality this is not always the case. Let's see how this works.

Manipulating the Independent Variable

As we have already indicated, the experiment begins with at least two groups that are alike in every way. Once equality is established, the researcher is in a position to decide what each subject will experience next. In the "Deviance in the Dark" experiment, for example, the researchers decided which subjects would experience the dark room and which subjects would experience the lighted room. The research team did not ask each subject which setting they preferred. Subjects were given no choice in the matter. In fact, they were not even aware that any other condition existed. And in making this decision, the researchers actually manipulated the *independent* variable.

Manipulation of the independent variable has the effect of giving the researcher total control over the research setting. With this kind of control, the researcher can be reasonably certain that the only difference between the two groups is the difference he or she introduces (i.e., the independent variable). (Obviously the control of every single possible variable is impossible, as we will show in a moment.)

It perhaps goes without saying that some variables cannot be manipulated. If, for example, you wanted to know whether or not males and females react differently to a particular type of film presentation, you cannot randomly assign sex. Sex is a more or less permanent attribute that does not lend itself to this kind of manipulation. There are actually a number of such nonmanipulative variables used by sociologists—marital status, age, race, and occupation, just to name a few. These variables are not easily manipulated in a laboratory setting. And this is no doubt a factor contributing to the low usage of the experimental design within sociology.

Preventing Unintended Differences in Treatment

Total control over the research setting does not guarantee identical experiences for all persons involved. Each subject enters the research setting cloaked in personal experiences, and these experiences will no doubt contribute to what he or she sees. To illustrate, a subject who is afraid of the dark will probably not have exactly the same experience as a subject who loves the dark. However, this is not a major methodological flaw. In fact, it is usually not even a problem. It is not really necessary that all subjects have exactly the same experiences. As long as subjects' *differences in experiences* are not systematically related to whether they are a part of one group versus another, the difference is inconsequential. Restated, the differences between individuals' experiences must not be systematically related to the independent variable. Unsystematic differences are nothing to worry about. In fact, we expect subjects' individual experiences to be somewhat different.

Criteria for Causality Revisited

As we have already noted, while the experiment does a good job of testing cause–effect models, this test is not direct. In effect, we are able to *infer* a cause–effect link from three essential pieces of information: time order, relationship between variables, and rival hypotheses:

Time Order. First, there must be a time order to the variables. Specifically, this means that the independent variable must precede the dependent variable in time. In the "Deviance in the Dark" study, the independent variable (lighted room versus dark room) preceded in time the dependent variable (behavior). Time order is crucial if we are to say that one thing caused another. Something that occurs later in time cannot be the cause of something that occurred earlier. By manipulating the independent variable, we can ensure that the time order to the variables is correct.

Relationship between Variables. A second essential piece of information needed to infer cause–effect relationships is establishing a relationship between the independent and the dependent variable. If one variable is to be considered the cause of the other, then these two variables must vary together in some kind of pattern. As one goes from the lighted chamber to the dark chamber, for example, behavior becomes more diverse.

Rival Hypotheses. In the "Deviance in the Dark" experiment, Gergen et al. begin with the notion that extreme anonymity has some influence on behavior. In fact, they suggest that it can alter behavior significantly. But you and I know—or at least suspect—that other things can also alter behavior. Perhaps intelligence is an important variable. If so, we might hypothesize that people with high IQs are more likely to experiment with alternative behaviors, normative or otherwise. To eliminate this hypothesis, we must select students whose IQs are the same. A second plausible alternative hypothesis might suggest that religiosity influences the extent to which people are willing to experiment with alternative behaviors. To eliminate this alternative, we would have to select students with similar levels of religiosity. As we have already noted, we can accomplish this through matching or through random assignment.

The logic of eliminating these alternative hypotheses is extremely important to the experiment. It is, in fact, this elimination process that makes cause–effect statements possible. To begin with, Gergen et al. cannot definitely show (beyond absolute doubt) that extreme anonymity causes behavioral changes in participating students. As we learned in Chapter 4, cause–effect models are actually theoretical. Because cause–effect links exist only in theory, there is no *direct* test of such models. Hence, we must test cause–effect models indirectly. This indirect test is really a process of eliminating rival hypotheses. The more rival hypotheses we can eliminate—with our hypotheses still in the running—the more confident we can be that a causal link exists. In fact, the more alternatives we can eliminate, the better our hypothesis looks.

TWO EXPERIMENTAL DESIGNS

To introduce you more fully to the experimental design, let us now examine two simple but frequently used experimental designs.

Pretest/Posttest Control Group Design

$$\begin{array}{cccc} R & Y1 & X & Y2 \\ R & Y3 & & Y4 \end{array}$$

In this experimental design, two groups are created and each is tested twice. The R's in this model indicate that subjects have been randomly assigned to groups. By randomly assigning subjects to the two groups, we can assume that these two groups are initially equal in every respect. And although we cannot test for this equality on an infinite number of variables, we do establish it for the dependent variable. The Y represents our observed measurement of groups 1 and 2 on the dependent variable. Once measured, the researcher introduces a difference between the two groups. This is accomplished by manipulating the independent variable. The X in the above model represents the treatment or the independent variable introduced to group 1. Notice that no treatment is given to group 2. It is the introduction of this treatment to one group and not to the other that results in creating a difference between the two groups, which were initially equal. Finally, we take a second measurement of the dependent variable for both groups. If a comparison of groups on this second measurement now demonstrates a difference between the two groups, we can reason that the difference is due to the one difference we introduced—the independent variable.

Let's now examine these rather abstract procedures within the context of a real example. Suppose, as a researcher, you were interested in the extent to which microcomputers aided in the learning of mathematics in seventh grade. You gain permission from the Board of Education to use a school of seventh-graders, and you are ready to begin the design of your experiment. First, you realize that you will need two seventh-grade groups—those who will be using micros and those who will not. Second, you realize you must make these two groups initially equal. You do this by randomly assigning the seventh-graders to one of the two groups—heads you're in the computer group; tails you're in the noncomputer group.

Once our two groups have been established, we test these groups on their mathematics skill. Random assignment suggests that this test should demonstrate no differences between groups. This testing represents our pretest—our first measurement of the dependent variable. Now we introduce the treatment. One group learns math with the aid of micros; the other learns math without the aid of micros. At the end of the semester, we test our groups again on the dependent variable. This testing represents our posttest—our second measurement of the dependent variable. Since an entire semester has passed for both groups, we expect both groups to change some (more about this later). However, if our treatment is effective, we are expecting a greater change from the experimental group over the control group. If the group using micros scores considerably higher than the other group on the skill test, we can conclude that the measured difference is a function of using micros in the math classroom.

An Important Note

As we have already noted, although random assignment ensures equality between groups, there may be other subtle differences. What about differences introduced by the teacher, the course content, or the time of day? We might want to ensure that both groups take math at the same time of day, and we will probably want to use the same book in both classes. We will also want to instruct both teachers as to how they should behave toward students. However, as you can see, students' experiences are not always going to be the same. And, as indicated earlier, it doesn't really matter. As long as the differences in students' experiences are not systematically related to whether they are a part of one group versus the other, there is no real problem with different experiences.

Posttest-Only Control Group Design

$$R \quad X \quad Y_1$$
$$R \quad \quad Y_2$$

In the posttest-only control group design, as in the previous design, two groups are created and subjects are randomly assigned to one of these two groups. However, unlike the previous design, no pretest is run. The random assignment of subjects to groups allows us to assume equality between groups, and no pretest is run to confirm it. As in the previous design, the researcher manipulates the independent variable and thereby introduces a difference between groups. Following manipulation of the independent variable, both groups are measured on the dependent variable. If a difference can be established, this difference is attributed to the independent variable.

By now you may have realized that the "Deviance in the Dark" experiment is a posttest-only control group design. Recall that in this experiment the researchers randomly assigned subjects to one of two groups—the dark chamber or the lighted chamber. No measure of conformity to normative behavior was taken prior to the manipulation of the independent variable (such a measure would probably be difficult!). Instead, once the dark-room or lighted-room condition was established, behavior was observed. In effect, the researchers created a posttest-only control-group design.

LABORATORY VERSUS FIELD EXPERIMENT

So far, our discussion of the experimental design has focused on what we might label laboratory experiments. The researcher creates an environment in which he or she has virtually total control. And in so doing, he or she has created what Orenstein and Phillips (1978) label the laboratory drama. This drama, if staged well, has all the properties of a well-rehearsed play.

But a drama is not real, and neither is a laboratory experiment. This fact has made the laboratory experiment fall prey to heavy criticism. Are laboratory experiments realistic and, if so, how realistic? Just how realistic, for example, is the extreme anonymity condition created by Gergen et al.? Is the laboratory drama generalizable? Can we correctly generalize that under conditions of extreme anonymity in a real-world setting, individuals would behave similarly to the subjects in this drama?

To answer these questions, we must take a closer look at the concept of realism as it is used in the social sciences. Laboratory experiments do not need to seem "real" in the conventional sense. That is, it is not necessary for laboratory situations to exactly parallel situations as they are found in the real world. To understand why this is so, let's take a look at the now-classic experiment of Solomon Asch.

Three decades ago Asch (1952) devised an experiment whereby a real subject and a number of stooges (confederates who were members of the research team) are asked to judge which of three lines most closely matches a reference line in length. The task was not designed to be tricky. Over repeated trials, the correct answer was actually quite obvious, and without others present, subjects almost always guessed correctly.

However, in the laboratory setting, with the stooges, the real subject gives his or her answer only after all of the stooges have given their incorrect answers. Will the real subject over repeated trials give the obvious and correct answer, or will he or she conform to the unanimous but incorrect response of the stooges?

Aronson and Carlsmith (1968) note that the Asch study involves little down-to-earth realism since situations similar to this are not likely to occur in the real world: "In everyday life, it is rare to find oneself in a situation where the direct and unambiguous evidence of one's senses is contradicted by the unanimous judgment of other persons." In addition, the task itself is rather trivial—one that is not likely to occur outside of the laboratory. Nevertheless, Aronson and Carlsmith argue that the Asch experiment does demonstrate considerable realism. The subjects are involved in the laboratory situation, and they do take the task seriously. Subjects sweat and squirm. They appear troubled and anxious. The situation is real for them. In short, the contrived situation poses a real choice of conforming or not conforming.

FIELD EXPERIMENT

One way of increasing mundane realism in the experiment is to take it out of the laboratory and into a natural setting. Let's illustrate with an example.

"From Jerusalem to Jericho"

In Darley and Batson's study "From Jerusalem to Jericho" (1973), they note that "Helping other people in distress is, among other things, an ethical act." We learn very early in life that one should help others who are in distress. And as these authors note, the classic story on helping appears in the New Testament:

> ... "And who is my neighbor?" Jesus replied, "A man was going down from Jerusalem to Jericho, and he fell among robbers, who stripped him and beat him, and departed, leaving him half dead. Now by chance a priest was going down the road; and when he saw him he passed by on the other side. So likewise a Levite, when he came to the place and saw him, passed by on the other side. But a Samaritan, as he journeyed, came to where he was; and when he saw him, he had compassion, and went to him and bound his wounds, pouring on oil and wine; then he set him on his own beast and brought him to an inn, and took care of him. And the next day he took out two denarii and gave them to the innkeeper, saying, 'Take care of him; and whatever more you spend, I will repay you when I come back.' Which of these three, do you think, proved neighbor to him who fell among the rob-

bers?" He said, "The one who showed mercy on him." And Jesus said to him, "Go and do likewise." (Luke 10:29–37 RSV)

After reading this story carefully, Darley and Batson began to reflect on the types of persons the priest, the Levite, and the Samaritan were. After some consideration, Darley and Batson came up with a list of characteristics out of which three hypotheses were derived:

1. People who encounter a situation possibly calling for a helping response while thinking religious and ethical thoughts will be no more likely to offer aid than those persons thinking about something else.
2. Persons encountering a possible helping situation when they are in a hurry will be less likely to offer aid than persons not in a hurry.
3. People who are religious for intrinsic reasons or whose religion emerges out of questioning the meaning of their everyday lives will be more likely to stop to offer help to the victim.

To test these hypotheses, seminary students were asked to participate in a study on religious education and vocations. During the first testing session, personality questionnaires measuring types of religiosity were administered. In a second, individual session, each subject began his participation in one building and was asked to report to another building for his final participation. While in transit, each subject passed a slumped "victim" planted in an alleyway.

The dependent variable for this study was whether and how each subject would help the victim. The independent variables for this study were (1) the degree to which each subject was told to hurry to the other building and (2) the talk he was to give when he arrived. Some subjects were instructed to talk on jobs in which seminary students would be most effective. Others were instructed to talk on the parable of the Good Samaritan.

Control in the Field Experiment

There is a price to be paid for increased mundane realism, and that price is researcher control. (Another price is an ethical one. See the discussion on this in Chapter 1.) In the Good Samaritan study, for example, of the forty-seven subjects scheduled to participate, seven were eliminated and three of these seven because of contamination. (Contamination refers to unexpected events over which the researcher has no control, which can alter the ways in which the dependent variable behaves.) What brought about the uncontrollable problems resulting in contamination? In the researchers' own words:

> ... we found the spot. A short dead-end alley ran between the building which housed the psychology department and a partially condemned old building in which some members of the sociology department had their offices. ... We asked the faculty members to help us by taking a longer route to their office which avoided the alley. They graciously complied. ... Service traffic was harder to control because it was sporadic. One morning about ten minutes before the first subject was to be sent through the alley, we found a telephone truck sitting squarely in the middle of the alley, with no phone men in sight. A frantic search produced one of the service men, who rather quizzically but amiably moved his truck out of sight. The janitor also presented a problem. On the second day of running, just as the subject entered the alley, he came out of a side door and cheerily called over to our "victim" huddled ready and waiting, "Feeling better today?" One subject's data, $2.50, and over an hour of experimenter time evaporated. (p. 209)

In a field experiment, the setting is not usually under complete control of the experimenter. And this lack of complete control can be crucial to inferring cause–effect links. In short, while we have increased mundane realism, we have probably sacrificed some degree of control.

Control in Evaluation Research

The problem of control so evident in the field experiment also finds its way into the area of evaluation research. The term *evaluation research* is used to refer to a whole range of studies conducted to test whether or not a particular "program" is having the desired effect.

As Orenstein and Phillips note, government reports provide some of the best evidence of the difficulties of the field experiment.

> Between 1962 and 1972, according to its own estimate, the Federal government spent 179.4 million dollars on experimental job training programs for the poor. A major goal of these projects was to find out if people who are retrained earn more money and are raised above the poverty line. The results of the many studies done were summarized for the Joint Economic Committee of Congress. The report concludes that most of the studies were so ill-conceived that they can support few reliable conclusions; in other words, we have not learned much about the question that prompted the research. (1978, p. 53)

The most frequent methodological blunder in these government-financed evaluation studies was failure to use a control group. Instead of randomly assigning welfare recipients to either a training or a no-training group, the researchers used no control group. And without a control group, very little, if anything, can be concluded. Even if a difference is observed for a single group from one time period to another, we have no way of knowing if the difference is any less than or greater than what might have been observed in a control group. Without a comparison group, the findings are meaningless.

Another methodological flaw in these government-financed studies noted by Orenstein and Phillips was the failure to follow subjects for a long enough time. Benefits from training may not be so noticeable in a period as short as six months or even a year. It make take several years for a person to move up and stabilize in an occupational slot. If long-term differences are to be observed, subjects must be followed for a longer period of time.

INTERNAL VALIDITY

In their classic book *Experimental and Quasi-Experimental Designs for Research*, Campbell and Stanley write that "Internal validity is the basic minimum without which any experiment is uninterpretable." *Internal validity* refers to whether or not we can appropriately draw the inference that the independent variable has caused some change in the dependent variable. (See Figure 8.1) Presumably, such a causal inference is possible because we have established initial equality between groups (i.e., matching or random assignment) and thereby eliminated any plausible alternative explanations. However, no matter how careful we are, certain subtle but uncontrolled variables creep in, serving to threaten internal validity. This threat essentially suggests that plausible alternative hypotheses or competing explanations may be responsible for any observed difference between groups.

Stanley and Campbell (1963) have identified a number of threats to internal validity, and we will discuss six of them here: history, maturation, testing, instrumentation, regression effect, and experimental mortality.

History

History refers to the specific events occurring between the first and second measurement of the dependent variable in addition to the manipulated independent variable. If events occur that could potentially alter the second measurement of the dependent variable, we would have no way of knowing how much of the observed change is a function of the independent variable versus these specific events.

Let's suppose that you wish to conduct a study to evaluate the influence of media message on wearing seat belts while driving. You design an experiment with three experimental groups and one control group. In the three experimental groups, you vary the intensity of the media message. Your experiment will involve the collection of data over a six-month period. In the fourth month of your experiment, the governor of the state is seriously injured in an automobile accident in which he was not wearing his seat belt. Your experimental findings are now potentially contaminated with this specific event. In short, you have no way of determining the extent to which this event is influencing your measurement on the dependent variable. However, if subjects have been randomly assigned to groups, you can safely assume that the effect of this specific event is the *same* for all groups. In other words, this specific event would alter both groups' scores in the same way, so that even though the scores might be different from the pretest, they would still be the same. Hence any observed difference between groups can be interpreted as a function of the treatment.

Maturation

Maturation refers to the process within respondents operating as a function of the passage of time per se—for example, growing hungrier or growing older. In our hypothetical study on the effect of computer-aided instruction on the math skills of seventh-graders, maturation was certainly at work. During the course of the semester, each child was getting older. With increases in physical age, we can usually expect an increase in mental skill. With maturation at work, we may not be able to determine whether the observed differences in math skill are a function of age or a function of computer-aided instruction. If, however, subjects are randomly assigned to groups, we can expect any age effect to be the same for both classes. In other words, while maturation only would change both classes' scores, the classes would still be equal. Hence, any observed difference between classes can be attributed to the manipulated independent variable (computers versus no computers).

Testing

Testing refers to the effects of pretest scores on posttest scores. If subjects are taking a test for the second time (or an alternative form of a previously taken test), will they do better than subjects taking the test for the first time? The answer to this question is yes, they probably will, and hence this influence serves as a potential source of contamination on the second measure. In short, we may not know whether scores on the second measurement are being influenced by what subjects remember about the first measurement. If subjects have been randomly assigned to groups, any testing effect is neutralized since we would expect it to be the same for each group. Any observed difference can be viewed as a function of the independent variable.

Instrumentation

By *instrumentation* we mean that changes in the calibration of a measuring instrument or changes in the observers or scorers used may produce changes in the obtained measurements. In other words, the instrument may not be measuring what you intend it to measure, or a second group of observers recording measures may not be using the same criteria for making judgments as the first group.

Suppose you are doing an experiment on dieting and your experimental design calls for weighing your subjects. If your scales are faulty, weighing all subjects five pounds too heavy, you have introduced a potential contaminating effect resulting from instrumentation. As with previous threats to internal validity, though, the effect of instrumentation is neutralized if you have randomly assigned subjects to groups.

Regression Effect

By *regression effect* we mean the tendency for people who score at the extremes on a first test to move toward a middle position on a second test. Suppose, in our hypothetical study on computer-aided math instruction for seventh-graders, we had chosen to create our two classes on the basis of math performance on the pretest. Since we have reason to believe that computers will aid greatly in math skill, we decide to place our poorest students in the computer class. At the end of the semester, our posttest demonstrates a reduced difference between the groups. Can we conclude that computers greatly aided the poorer students in their learning of math skills? The answer is no.

People who score very well on a test usually do so because they know the material and because there is a little bit of good luck involved. People who perform very poorly on a test usually do so because they do not know as many answers and because there is a little bad luck involved. On a second testing, the law of averages suggests that the good scorers will not score quite as good and the poor scorers will not score quite as bad. In other words, both groups should move toward some middle ground. If we had divided the seventh-graders on the basis of pretest performance, we would not be able to separate regression effects from the effects of the treatment. However, if we randomly assign subjects to groups, the regression effect should be the same for each group. Hence, any observed difference can be attributed to the independent variable—in this case, microcomputers versus no microcomputers.

Experimental Mortality

Mortality refers to the dropout rate in a study. Subjects can drop out of an experiment for a number of reasons—people get sick, move, or even die.

FIGURE 8.1
Internal Validity

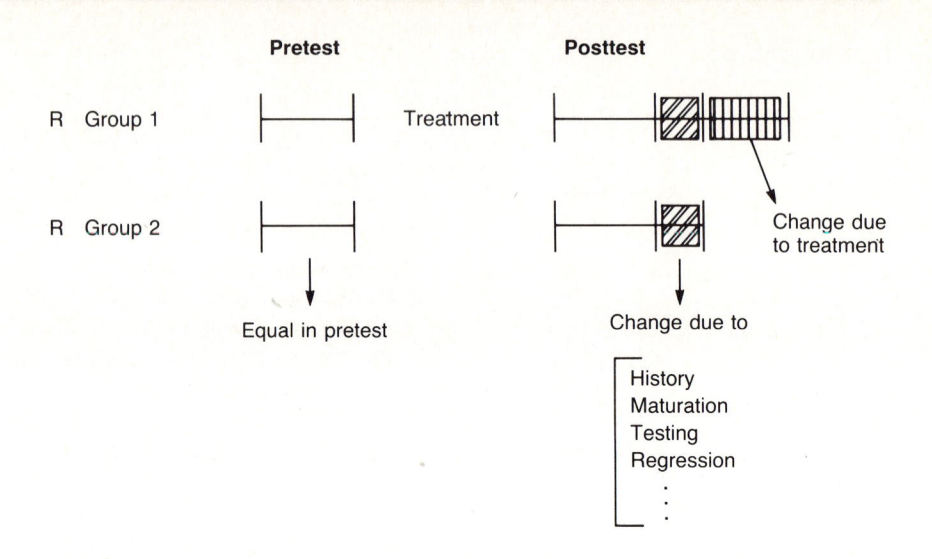

```
                    Pretest                    Posttest
R  Group 1         |------|    Treatment      |------|▨▥
                                                        ↘ Change due
                                                          to treatment
R  Group 2         |------|                   |------|▨
                        ↓                          ↓
                  Equal in pretest           Change due to
                                             ⎡ History
                                             ⎢ Maturation
                                             ⎢ Testing
                                             ⎢ Regression
                                             ⎣ ⋮
```

If subjects have been randomly assigned to groups, we can generally assume that the mortality rate for all groups will be roughly the same. Hence, any observed difference can be attributed to the independent variable.

EXTERNAL VALIDITY

External validity refers to the generalizability of the study—the ability to generalize the findings of a single study to the larger population. High external validity requires that subjects be randomly selected from the larger population. Recall from Chapter 7 that a random sample ensures the representativeness of a sample. Since random samples are rarely used in experiments, external validity is rarely high in the experiments. In most experiments, the sample of subjects is composed of volunteers, and it seems unlikely that these volunteers are representative of the larger target population. In fact, given the nonrandom nature of the sample, it is usually not possible to establish representativeness.

Failure to draw a random sample of subjects from the target population and hence ensure external validity is certainly not fatal in the case of the experiment, particularly when we remind ourselves of what the experiment is trying to accomplish. The experiment is a test of causal models. This is an important step in theory development and one that needs to come before generalizability. Often, in designing research, we labor under the false impression that external validity (generalizability) is perhaps even more important than internal validity. In reality, internal validity must come before external validity. Without internal validity, we cannot establish the causal link we are trying to test. Without the ability to establish this causal link, we are only generalizing contaminated findings. Even without generalizability, the experiment is making an important and significant contribution to our understanding of social phenomena.

TRUE EXPERIMENT VERSUS QUASI-EXPERIMENT

Generally speaking, there are two basic forms of experiment—the true experiment and the quasi-experiment. As we have already seen, in every true experiment, three elements must be present. First, there must be at least two groups (one experimental and one control). Second, there must be an intentional manipulation of the independent variable. Third, subjects must be randomly assigned to groups. In the quasi-experimental design, the researcher cannot directly manipulate the independent variable and subjects are not randomly assigned to groups. Hence, comparisons are established by *ex-post facto* means.

Because of our inability to use random assignment in quasi-experimental groups, internal validity poses quite a threat. If we cannot find some means of establishing initial equality, we have no way of separating the effects of the manipulated independent variable from these contaminating sources. Hence, cause–effect statements become more difficult to make, but they can be made.

QUASI-EXPERIMENT

The strict requirements of experimental designs in laboratory and natural settings are so difficult to achieve at times that other possibilities must be entertained if the researcher wishes to complete a project at all. For this reason, a quasi-experiment is sometimes called for. A quasi-experiment differs from a true experiment primarily because it lacks the randomness and control characteristic of a true experiment. Remember that in a true experiment it is essential that subjects be assigned to groups in a random fashion. But when this is impossible, we may be able to salvage the situation after all by using an experimentlike procedure.

Quasi-experiments are also sometimes called *ex-post-facto* experiments, and their most important distinguishing characteristic is, as Simon suggests, the fact that some force *clearly unrelated to the independent variable* causes the variation in the dependent variable (1969, 121).

The multitude of research studies on smoking and health offers an example of both the uses and the deficiencies of quasi-experiments.

Ideally, if we wanted to experiment with the effects of smoking, we would get a group of nonsmokers, randomly assign them to smoking and nonsmoking status, and then watch to see who developed health problems and who did not. Obviously, we can't do that (forcing people to take up smoking is not only ethically reprehensible but probably impossible!). In other words, people have already chosen to smoke or not to smoke, so we can't randomly assign the independent variable to our experiment. Therefore, we have to go at this in another way and put up with the less-than-perfect results of our choice.

We could forgo studying people at all and do studies on rats and mice—after all, you can force *them* to smoke, with few problems. (Note that we said *few,* not *none.*) But, of course, the problem there is that conclusions about people drawn from animal experiments are always suspect because people aren't animals.

What we can do to overcome some of these obstacles is to find a group of smokers and a group of nonsmokers, and then assign them to our experimental and control groups not randomly, but selectively by attempting to match them on the basis of every single variable we think might have something to do with health problems *except smoking* and hope that the careful matching cancels out the effects of those variables. Then we can see whether or not the smoking group had more incidence of health problems. This is not perfect and is not a true experiment, but it does help us study something that otherwise would be difficult to study.

Another way to go after this quasi-experiment would be to find a culture in which smoking had been recently introduced after a long period of not smoking and see whether health records could be compared. In other words, the quasi-experiment seeks to match the experiment for groups that are, in effect, self-selected. The results are not perfect, but they can help us understand some things that would be difficult to study with a true experiment.

Quasi-experiments are often used with natural field study designs, since they have much in common with the assumptions of a naturalistic methodology. For an excellent book on the entire matter, we refer you to Thomas Cook and Donald Campbell's *Quasi-Experimentation: Design and Analysis Issues for Field Settings* (1979).

Chapter 9

The Survey

The survey defined
   The United States Census
   Public opinion polling
   Marketing surveys
Planning your survey design
   Define your research objectives
   Identify the unit to be researched
   Sample the population
   Choose an appropriate setting
   Choose the time frame for your research
      Cross-sectional studies
      Longitudinal studies
         Trend studies
         Panel studies
         Cohort analysis
Constructing a questionnaire
   Describe the information you seek
   Decide on the type of questions you will need
      Open-ended questions
      Closed-ended questions
   Create a first draft
      Questionnaire content
      Structure of questions
      Number of questionnaire items
      Ordering the questions
   Question format
      Spacing
      Using boxes for recording responses
      Contingency questions
      Matrix questions
   Review and revise your questionnaire
   Write a cover letter and introduction
   Pretest your instrument
   An illustration
Self-administered questionnaires
The mailed questionnaire
Face-to-face interviews
   Effects of interviewer characteristics
Tips for interviewing
Telephone interviews
The interview versus the self-administered questionnaire
Strengths and weaknesses of survey research
Using secondary data to supplement interview data

Do you ever get the feeling that the only reason we have elections is to find out if the polls were right?
—Robert Orben

THE SURVEY DEFINED

Have you ever been asked to evaluate a course and its teacher at the end of a school semester? If you agreed to such a request, you were probably given an evaluation form to fill out. If you completed this form, you have participated in a *survey*. You should recall from Chapter 4 a list of factors that characterize the survey design. First, surveys use *statistical groups* that are *"independent of settings."* In a course evaluation survey, for example, it doesn't really matter where the survey form is filled out, although the classroom is usually the designated place. And the data generated by these forms are usually analyzed (grouped statistically) by such characteristics as classification, grade-point average, and expected course grade.

Second, surveys are especially strong on *representativeness*, though control and naturalness are not entirely sacrificed. While course evaluation surveys, for example, usually aim to look at a total population (in our example, a class of students), such ambitious surveys are the exception rather than the rule. The popularity of the survey rests largely with its potential for representativeness—that is, its ability to evaluate large populations using relatively small samples. With the survey it is possible to examine a small segment of society (a research sample) and from that small segment make certain inferences about the population from which the sample was originally taken. In short, if a survey is carefully designed and executed, the results yielded from a sample can be an amazingly accurate portrayal of the original population, although we can never totally rule out the possibility of misleading or inaccurate findings.

Third, while surveys are usually *descriptive or causal*, exploratory purposes should not be ruled out. Surveys can be used to collect data that explore, describe, or explain some social phenomenon. Demographic information that might be collected for any one of these purposes includes sex, marital status, education level, income, political preference, and religious preference. Surveys can be used to explore, describe, or explain respondents' knowledge about a particular subject, their past or current behavior, or their attitudes and beliefs concerning a particular subject. Student journalists, for example, gathering information on proposed legislation aimed at raising the national drinking age, might wish to probe into respondents' previous knowledge of the drinking age controversy. In effect, the survey technique has been used to research a wide variety of topics including attitudes toward criminal offenders, political orientation, knowledge of taxation laws, consumer trends, and NFL teams that might make it to next year's Super Bowl.

Finally, surveys may be either *cross-sectional* or *longitudinal*, although most are cross-sectional. With cross-sectional surveys, data are collected at one point in time. With longitudinal surveys, data are collected at several (at least two) points in time. We will have more to say about this a little later.

In this chapter, we will examine the survey design and its many variations. We will take a look at the steps involved in designing a survey and in constructing a questionnaire. We will also look at the primary methods used to collect questionnaire data and compare their relative advantages and disadvantages. Finally, we will look at secondary data as an additional or alternate source of survey data. Let's begin, though, by looking at three rather different examples of the survey: the U.S. Census, public opinion polling, and market surveys.

The United States Census

Once every ten years, the United States Bureau of the Census conducts a special survey aimed at collecting demographic data on *all* persons within this country. From these data emerge demographic statistics—descriptive statistics that deal with the quantitative aspects of a population, including such characteristics as sex, age, and racial/ethnic background, economic and health characteristics, and geographic distribution. The U.S. Census is the largest survey attempt conducted in the United States, and it has been required by law since the writing of the Constitution in 1790.

The main purpose of this decennial survey is to gather data essential to the functioning of our government. (Technically, and constitutionally, the main purpose of the United States Census is to allow for apportionment of the House of Representatives. All other uses are ancillary to this.) Federal funds, for example, are often distributed according to census counts—those areas having high population counts (as tabulated by the census) will receive more funds than those areas having low population counts. Other uses the federal government has for census data include calculating economic indicators, projecting the future of agencies such as Social Security, and formulating domestic policies such as federal housing legislation.

The usefulness of the census data is not limited to the federal government. Numerous social scientists have also found them to be extremely valuable to their research. However, using the entire body of census data can be quite cumbersome and certainly cost-prohibitive. Hence, the Census Bureau also prepares samples of the original (nationwide) population data. These samples range from 25 percent of the total population (one out of every four Americans) to a mere 0.04 percent (one out of every 10,000 Americans). These samples are recorded on magnetic computer tapes and are made available to anyone wishing to use them.

Since the Census Bureau's basic questionnaire is relatively short (twelve demographic questions and eight housing questions) and hence does not allow for collecting extensive information, the bureau has also developed a more extensive questionnaire, which is distributed to every twentieth person. In other words, selected persons (one out of every twenty Americans) representing a cross-sectional sample of the entire population are asked to fill out a longer form (twenty additional demographic questions and twenty additional housing questions). Since the cost of collecting census data by the government restrains the number of questions that can be asked of the population, this carefully selected sample allows the Census Bureau to collect a greater variety of information that can be viewed as representative of the total population.

Although this massive decennial survey is an admirable task, it is not without problems. As you might suspect, data collected once every ten years soon becomes outdated in a rapidly changing society. Since data collection is really needed more frequently than once every ten years, a multistage sampling design is also used to conduct a monthly Current Population Survey. (See Chapter 7 for a discussion of multistage sampling.) And the sampling methodology used for this survey is even more rigorous than for the decennial census (Spiegelman 1968, 22). First, interviewers are selected and trained more carefully than for the decennial census. Additionally, the interviewers gain a greater level of expertise since they work over extended periods of time. What's more, the data generated by the Current Population Survey is usually more up to date than that collected in the decennial survey. However, since the current population survey is generated using a sample, we cannot be certain that it is as accurate as the decennial population survey, which uses the total population.

Public Opinion Polling

We have become quite accustomed to the idea of public opinion polling through the works of such well-known polls as Gallup, Harris, and Roper. But unlike the U.S. Census, polls rarely (if ever) make use of a total population. Instead, opinion pollsters attempt to select a sample of interviewees who seem to be typical of the overall population with respect to identified social and economic characteristics. This need to obtain a sample that is typical of the total population makes random sampling an important and compelling consideration. Whenever possible, opinion polling should include some form of random sampling. With random sampling, each member of the population is assured a *known* chance of being included in the sample (see Chapter 7). Hence, this form of sampling gives the best assurance that the sample will be characteristic of the entire population (Weisberg 1977, 19).

But not all opinion polls use random samples. In fact, nonrandom samples are quite frequently found in opinion polling. One nonrandom sampling technique frequently used in public opinion polls involves the selection of natural cases occurring so rarely that a random sample simply would not be feasible. Examples of such nonrandom samples might include mothers of quintuplets and impeached politicians. A second type of nonrandom sample used in public opinion polls involves the collection of data from available or willing participants. Examples of such haphazard samples, as they are often called, include customers in a restaurant or students hanging out in the student center. A third nonrandom sample that is often used as a quick check of rapidly changing data by public opinion pollsters is quota sampling—the establishment of quotas within a sample that are based on the population proportions for relevant characteristics (Bogue 1981, 85). When it is necessary to use nonrandom samples, it is essential that checks and controls be used since nonrandom sampling techniques often result in bias.

We do not want to leave you with the impression that bias is limited to nonrandom samples. This is certainly not the case. As we stressed in Chapter 7, bias can occur even when random samples have been selected if you are not careful. Recall from Chapter 7 our discussion of the *Literary Digest* presidential poll of 1936. *Literary Digest* pollsters were not guilty of failing to draw a random sample. They did in fact select a *random* sample through telephone directories and automobile registration records. Based on the responses obtained, the magazine predicted a clear victory for the Republican candidate Alf Landon, although Franklin Roosevelt won by a whopping majority. The *Literary Digest* sample failed because it excluded millions of the poor and unemployed of the Great Depression who could not afford either telephones or automobiles. In short, the *Literary Digest* sample proved to have a built-in bias despite the random selection process because the sample was selected from a base that excluded a large proportion of the population—primarily the Democratic voters.

Marketing Surveys

Have you ever wondered how manufacturers decide which products to market and which to scrap? How do manufacturers know, for example, that cheese grits will sell or that flavored potato chips will be a family favorite? How do they know that perfume will be more appealing if packaged in container A instead of B, or that two-ply toilet paper will be more marketable than single-ply paper? Before manufacturers put a new product on the market, they want and need to know how consumers will react to that product. Marketing research is conducted with the goal of predicting such consumer reactions. To identify these reactions, though, marketing researchers almost always use nonrandom samples. Have you ever been stopped while shopping and asked to answer a few questions or to take a "taste test"? Such haphazard or convenience samples provide a quick and inexpensive way of gathering product-evaluation data.

Until recently, marketing researchers have shown little interest in the theory and testing of social science hypotheses. Their primary interest has been limited to predicting the marketing future of specific products. Although marketing researchers are often accused of studying superficial problems to the neglect of theory and hypothesis testing, market surveyors have been able to provide those who make marketing decisions with accurate and reliable predictions.

PLANNING YOUR SURVEY DESIGN

Define Your Research Objectives

Now that we have examined the survey through several concrete examples, let's look specifically at the steps that you must take when designing your own survey. When beginning any type of survey, your first step is to clearly define your research objective(s). What do you want to know by administering this survey and why do you want to know? Surprisingly, this is often the single most difficult step in the research process for most researchers and particularly beginning researchers. One thing that may help in this definition process is the formulation of a *thesis statement*. This thesis statement should have several important characteristics. First, it should generally be one sentence in length. Second, it should contain a subject and a verb and should not be written as a fragmented or run-on sentence. Third, this statement should define the objective of the survey. If, for example, the purpose of your survey is to describe the attitudes of students under twenty-one toward the proposed federal minimum drinking age, then the thesis statement should state this purpose. If the purpose of your survey is to determine how students who support the minimum drinking age differ from those who do not, then the thesis statement should state this purpose. If your purpose is to investigate the relationship between students' ages and their opinions on the minimum drinking age, then this purpose should be stated in the thesis statement. The thesis statement is invaluable insofar as it provides a means of precisely defining your research subject, and you should give considerable thought to its development. Some examples of thesis statements for survey research follow.

1. This paper has two major objectives—to examine (1) determinants of education, political consciousness, and collectivist orientation, and (2) the role of education in explaining the collective orientation of blacks and women.
2. In this paper we focus on the effects of school size on rates of student participation in school activities.
3. In this paper we will investigate whether the trend of the 1960s and early 1970s toward more egalitarian sex-role attitudes continued into the late 1970s despite a general conservative drift in social and political sentiment.

As you can see, the research objective can be very clearly defined in one complete sentence. Once you have constructed your thesis statement, your research should have clear direction, and your project should then flow from this statement in a logical and coherent fashion.

Identify the Unit to Be Researched

The second step in planning a survey design is to identify the units that comprise the population you are researching. The unit of analysis for survey research can range from individuals, such as Harvard Law School graduates and their achievements five years after graduation, to entire nations and groups of nations, for example, comparing industrialized nations with Third World nations. Each respondent is one case in your data set. As researcher, you must become familiar with the range of units available (see Chapter 4) before deciding which to use in your own survey.

Sample the Population

The third step in planning a survey is to sample from the population with an eye to representativeness. As we have already noted, the popularity of the survey rests largely with its potential for representativeness. When careful probability (random) samples are selected, the sample characteristics can be generalized to the larger population. For a full discussion on sampling, see Chapter 7.

Choose an Appropriate Setting

The fourth step in planning your survey design is choosing an appropriate research setting. Generally speaking, the survey design is independent of setting. That is, the setting is usually unimportant to the data collection process. Self-administered questionnaires, for example, may be filled out individually in any quiet place or in large groups in a classroom or auditorium setting. Similarly, mailed questionnaires can be filled out almost anywhere. However, you may wish to create a standard environment. If you are conducting interviews, for example, you may ask respondents to come to one central location. In any case, a decision on setting must be made.

Choose the Time Frame for Your Research

The fifth step in planning a survey design is to choose the time frame for your research. In short, you must decide whether the data for the survey can be collected at one point in time using a cross-sectional design, or whether it should be collected at different points in time using a longitudinal design.

Cross-sectional Studies. In a cross-sectional survey, data are collected from a chosen sample at a single point in time. A cross-sectional survey is a single, unrepeated survey that produces prompt results and can be completed in a relatively short time. As we indicated in Chapter 4, such a survey is analogous to a still snapshot taken by a camera. While it does provide you with a good picture of the population at one point in time, it does not reveal any movement or change over time. The census, for example, gives us an instantaneous picture of the U.S. population at one point in time—really no more and no less. Without a doubt, cross-sectional surveys are the most frequently used in social science research primarily because of their low costs and their quick results.

Longitudinal Studies. Most topics of interest to sociologists are dynamic processes that are not static in time but tend to develop over extended periods. Research studies designed to measure events over a span of time are called longitudinal studies. With longitudinal studies, data are collected at several points in time during the survey period. Such research is analogous to a motion picture camera, which portrays an event in motion over a period of time. In short, longitudinal studies provide the researcher with data that can be analyzed in terms of change. Three common types of longitudinal designs are used by social researchers: trend studies, cohort studies, and panel studies. Let's take a brief look at each of these.

TREND STUDIES A trend study is actually several cross-sectional studies conducted successively over some designated period of time. Each survey is administered to a different sample of respondents but under similar conditions and using a similar survey instrument. These surveys are then analyzed to measure change over time. Many public opinion polls are administered repeatedly to determine changes in the opinions of the U.S. public. In an election year, for example, public opinion polls are constantly assessing the public's voting preferences. Such polls are conducted periodically up to the time of an election and change in public opinion is assessed and reported to the public.

If you choose to use a trend study, it is essential that you remember to standardize your variables since measures taken at one point in time are not necessarily compatible with measures taken at another point in time. If, for example, you were to compare the cost of an ounce of gold in 1958 with the cost of an ounce of gold in 1984, the comparison would be meaningless unless you standardized (controlled) for several important factors. Specifically, without standardization, you would not be able to differentiate between changes caused by internal factors or processes (e.g., the number of carats) from changes caused by external processes (e.g., the rate of inflation).

Another important factor to consider in trend studies is the extent to which the time periods included in the study seriously affect the outcome. Short-run attitudes on matters of high but temporary interest (such as the outcome of an election) must be studied over a period of weeks. Other types of changes, such as changes in the attitudes of high school students, must be studied over a period of years. The time frame to be analyzed should match the tempo of change over time in the subjects being surveyed.

One of the major advantages of trend studies is that they permit us to view changes or developing trends that occur within a given population. In addition, they allow for intelligent speculation about the reasons for trend shifts. The disadvantages of trend studies include the long period of time needed to complete the study and the unknown reliability and validity resulting from different samples and several researchers collecting data. Hence, when changes are documented by such surveys, it is sometimes impossible to pinpoint the source of change. The changes identified by trend studies may be real changes reflected in the population over time, or they may be spurious changes resulting from the research methods used (e.g., different subjects at each time interval). Consequently, in reporting results from trend studies, we do run the risk of misrepresenting the trend.

One variation of the trend study that helps to overcome this problem is the *retrospective* time series technique. With this technique a group of respondents are asked questions about specific events, experiences, or opinions that are now a part of their past. The biggest danger in this form of survey is memory distortion; one's recollection of the past is almost always tainted by the present. One means of overcoming this problem is the panel study.

PANEL STUDIES   A panel study is a specific type of trend study that requires repeated interviewing with the *same sample* (panel, or group of subjects) over an extended period of time. Like the trend study, its purpose is to measure change in attitudes or behavior over time. In many cases, the panel is given the same set of questions at regular time intervals over a specified time period. A panel, for example, might be given the same questionnaire asking about attitudes toward the military at six-month intervals for three successive years in an attempt to analyze the stability of attitudes toward the military.

The primary advantage of panel studies is that they do indeed tend to show the amount, direction, and timing of shifts in opinions or behaviors (Smith 1981, 410). However, while the panel study can be quite effective in many cases, it does have its disadvantages. First, the costs of a panel study are much higher than the costs of other types of studies. This is largely because the researcher must maintain contact with the same group of respondents. Second, more time is consumed in this type of research since maintaining contact with the same group of individuals over several years requires a great deal of time as well as money. Third, cooperation of respondents on a repetitive basis is often difficult to obtain. While most people will agree to participate in a study one time, fewer people are willing to participate several times over an extended period. Thus, when conducting a panel study, you can bet that your original panel size will probably be much larger than your final panel size. Fourth, respondents can be lost because of changing residences, job changes, vacations, and the like. And with both of these latter disadvantages, results may become biased.

COHORT ANALYSIS   Cohort analysis is a method of analyzing the experiences of cohorts throughout their lives for some specific period of time. Such studies begin with a cohort—a group of persons who share some common characteristic. Examples of cohorts might include all persons born in 1955, or all persons who received their baccalaureate degrees in 1984. Data collection for such studies would generally require measuring attitudes, behaviors, opportunities, and so forth, for a sample of members of this cohort group over an extended period of time.

Cohort analysis is a very good method for exposing long-term trends. We could, for example, examine the opportunities open to women with Ph.D.'s by identifying female doctoral candidates from selected universities during the five-year interval 1961–1965 and comparing their professional experiences with those of women graduating in the later intervals of 1966–1970 and 1971–1975. A longitudinal study of different cohorts would allow us to compare age-specific patterns of behavior and achievement for successive groups.

Cohort analysis is frequently used in demographic research. It permits prediction of changes within a population and allows the development of rather precise estimates of longevity for successive age cohorts.

CONSTRUCTING A QUESTIONNAIRE

Once the survey has been planned, you are ready to identify the data needed to accomplish your research objective. A questionnaire is a data collection instrument containing a select group of questions chosen because of their relevance, carefully worded for clarity, and carefully formatted for printed copy. A questionnaire is essential to the collection of survey data. When constructing your questionnaire, you should always seek to reach two specific goals. First, the questions you ask should produce the data you need to gather. This task seldom proves to be as easy as it sounds. Second, to be reliable, the questions you ask must tap the same type of information in each person participating. Like the first goal, this is also easier said than done. Meeting both of these goals will require a great deal of effort on your part. However, the task will become easier if you will follow these six essential steps in questionnaire construction:

1. Describe the information that you are seeking.
2. Decide on the type of questions needed.
3. Write a first draft of the questions to be asked.
4. Review and revise the questions.
5. Document the procedures for using the questionnaire.
6. Whenever possible, pretest the questionnaire in a pilot study.

Let's take a quick look at each of these steps.

Describe the Information You Seek

The first step in questionnaire construction, describing the information which you seek, is probably the single most important step in developing your survey instrument. By adequately describing the data you seek, you have provided a starting point for planning the organization and composition of the questions to be included. Such a description of the data, particularly if you are a beginning researcher, will help you to exclude any irrelevant questions and will prevent you from omitting data that is essential for your research.

Decide on the Type of Questions You Will Need

The second step in questionnaire construction is deciding on the type of questions you will need to reach your research objective. In determining the type of questions to ask, you should consider the educational and social levels of your respondents and your plans for data analysis. In general, your questions will be either open- or closed-ended.

Open-Ended Questions. The open-ended question requires respondents to answer in their own words. If, for example, you were to ask some high school students what constitutes sex appeal, they might respond with a variety of characteristics such as attractive smile, nice clothes, dynamic personality. In short, the respondents answer the questions in their own words, and sometime later, these responses are categorized. This process of categorization serves to organize the responses into coded data for analysis and interpretation. But these categories are not presumed before starting the research.

In general, open-ended questions are most useful when you expect an issue to provoke a wide range of responses or when responses are likely to be very detailed and you do not wish to limit the possible range. However, open-ended questions should not be mistaken or substituted for the kind of involved exploration and probing that characterizes intensive interviews—a whole different research method. Nor should they be expected to produce revealing or provocative in-depth responses. In fact, the heavy use of open-ended questions can lead to disappointment if your respondents neglect to respond or give only brief, superficial answers.

As you might have already suspected, coding open-ended questions can present a unique set of problems, particularly if two or more persons are involved in coding these responses. Simply put, coders must be well trained to code responses in a consistent manner. If two coders categorize the same response in two different categories, the data analysis becomes meaningless. In short, reliability of the research results demands agreement among all coders as to the categorization of responses. Therefore, it is advantageous to review the coding of open-ended responses with the coders prior to data analysis. We shall have more to say about this in Chapter 11.

Closed-Ended Questions. Closed-ended questions are structured to offer a list of acceptable answers from which respondents may choose. This list of answers should cover all significant alternatives without any overlap between categories, and may include a catch-all category for respondents whose answers are not provided among the choices. While this catch-all category may change with the nature of the question, it usually takes the form of "other" or "don't know." The wording of closed-ended questions should also be clear, definite, and impartial.

The biggest advantage of closed-ended questions is the relative ease of coding and analyzing data. Because each categorical response can usually be given a numeric code, the data can quickly be entered into a computer. The major disadvantage of such questions is that the categories typically do not contain all possible responses, and you therefore run the risk of forcing your respondents to fit (though somewhat incorrectly) into predesigned categories.

Create a First Draft

The third step in questionnaire construction is to create a first draft of your questions, giving special attention to both content and format (question layout). Since both of these issues are very important to your finished product (the questionnaire), let's take a brief look at each.

Questionnaire Content. Relevance is the key word in questionnaire content, and considerable thought needs to be channeled into your content. Your questionnaire content will be determined in part by the theory from which the survey springs, in part by your research objective (the task described in your thesis statement), and in part by the requirements of the statistical procedure(s) to be used (see Chapters 12 and 13). The questions you choose to include must satisfy both the requirements of your study and the limitations of your respondents. Last but not least, the questions you choose must measure the concepts they are designed to measure (see Chapter 6 on measurement). Issues related to questionnaire content include the (1) structure of questions, (2) number of questions, and (3) order of questions.

STRUCTURE OF QUESTIONS All questions must be relevant, clear, and to the point. In most cases, the educational level of most of your respondents will not be as high as yours. Consequently, your respondents will probably not share your professional vocabularies. In short, the vocabulary used in the questionnaire must be understandable and recognizable to your respondents. Sociologists, for example, use the term "delinquent," whereas teenagers talk about being "in trouble." Similarly, "higher education" may mean high school to a respondent and the completion of an undergraduate degree to a researcher. It is a good idea to contact someone familiar with your target population to inquire about the best terminology to use.

A good question is emotionally neutral, leaving the choice to the respondent. A biased question is emotionally colored, leaving little or no choice to the respondent. A biased question might be, "Don't you feel that Japanese-built automobiles are better made than American-built cars?" A much better (and neutral) question would be:

> Comparing cars built in the United States and those built in Japan, which do you think are better constructed?
>
> a. Japanese cars
> b. American cars
> c. They are built about the same.

The more sensitive the issue, the more care you should put in the composition of the questions. Questions dealing with issues such as deviant behavior, political issues, and personal relations can be particularly sensitive. In short, questions should be worded to minimize respondents' negative reactions.

NUMBER OF QUESTIONNAIRE ITEMS   A good questionnaire is limited to the minimum number of items needed to satisfy the research requirements. You must consider the amount of time respondents will need to complete your survey. If participation is voluntary and the survey is quite long, many respondents will not complete the form. As a general rule of thumb, you should make a rather lengthy list of potential questions and then carefully trim down the list. Pilot studies are good indicators of which questions can be dropped from the questionnaire and which should be left in. When conducting a pilot study, it is a good idea to include more questions than you intend to ask and then let the results of the pilot study assist you in further reducing your questionnaire. We will have more to say about pilot studies a little later.

ORDERING THE QUESTIONS   The order in which the questions appear on the questionnaire is also extremely important in questionnaire construction. The questions should appear in some logical pattern, and transitions should appear in cases where the logical flow is interrupted. The first (lead) question should be both interesting and noncontroversial to your respondents. Additionally, this first question should make your readers want to continue. More difficult or sensitive questions should appear toward the end of the survey, to be encountered by respondents after sufficient rapport has been developed.

Often, beginning researchers have a tendency to unknowingly group two questions into a single question. For instance, consider the question "Does your employer have lower salary categories for racial minorities and women?" A respondent might answer "yes" if lower salary categories apply for women but not minorities, or "yes" if lower salary categories apply for minorities but not women, or "yes" if lower salary categories apply for both minorities and women. In the first two conditions stated above, it is equally conceivable that a respondent would answer "no" to the question if the lower salary categories did not apply to both groups. In effect, two questions are being asked, and two questions should be written.

Question Format.   You may think that talking about questionnaire format is rather silly, and even wasteful of space in this book. However, we believe that once you start your own questionnaire construction, you will see things a little differently. The format of your questionnaire is extremely important because it invariably helps to set each respondent's mood. If the questionnaire appears disorganized, your respondents will become confused and their motivation to complete the questionnaire will be dampened. Among the important issues related to questionnaire format are (1) spacing, (2) boxes for response alternatives, (3) handling contingency questions, and (4) matrix questions. Let's take a brief look at each of these.

SPACING One way to communicate an air of order and organization is by spreading the questionnaire out and allowing some white spaces to slip in. If the questions are crammed together, your respondents may accidentally skip one or more questions or become confused by the clutter. Attractive spacing of questions will make your instrument easier to read.

USING BOXES FOR RECORDING RESPONSES For closed-ended questions, it is a good idea to use some kind of box for response alternatives. These boxes can best be created with parentheses or brackets. If, for example, you ask your respondents to indicate their sex, each response alternative, male and female, should be listed with a box. The use of boxes gives respondents a very clear idea of where they are to record their responses. Without a box, respondents may not know where you want them to put their answers.

CONTINGENCY QUESTIONS Sometimes there are questions whose relevancy depends on a respondent's answer to a previous question. Such questions are called contingency questions and must be clearly formatted on your questionnaire. Suppose, for example, you are doing marketing research on gold jewelry purchases. You might ask the following question:

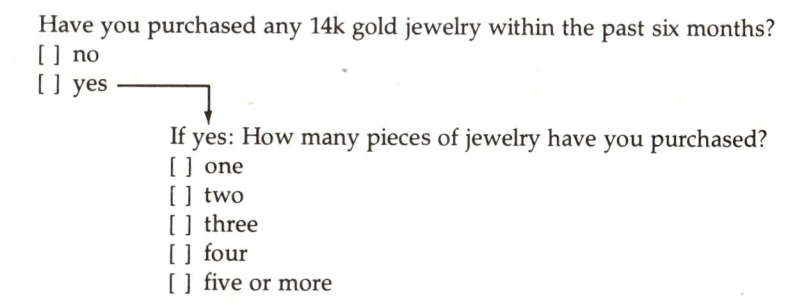

Have you purchased any 14k gold jewelry within the past six months?
[ ] no
[ ] yes

        If yes: How many pieces of jewelry have you purchased?
        [ ] one
        [ ] two
        [ ] three
        [ ] four
        [ ] five or more

Contingency questions must be formatted in such a way that your respondents will know to answer them only if their answer to a previous question warrants it. Again, the important thing is that you do not confuse your subjects. If necessary, add arrows and additional instructions before such questions to ensure clarity.

MATRIX QUESTIONS Sometimes you will have a series of questions whose response alternatives are all the same. For example, if you were assessing students' attitudes toward social statistics, you might have a series of statements whose response alternatives are in Likert format (see Chapter 6). In such cases, it is useful to construct a matrix of questions. This matrix format is illustrated in Figure 9.1.

The matrix format has several distinct advantages. First, it is space-efficient. It allows the placement of similar questions in a relatively small amount of space. Second, it is time-efficient. Generally, respondents will be able to answer questions put in this format in a reasonable amount of time. Third, it allows for direct comparisons of answers across questions. As respondents answer each question, they can look back to see how they have answered previous questions. This ability to examine previous answers, though, does have its disadvantages. In short, this kind of comparison can lead to a response set. If subjects agree with the first statement in the matrix, they may check "agree" for all similar statements without really reading the questions or without giving the questions much thought. When using matrix questions, you will need to check for response sets.

**FIGURE 9.1
Example of
Matrix Questions**

For each of the following statements, choose the response alternative that best describes your feelings. Response alternatives are STRONGLY AGREE (SA), AGREE (A), UNDECIDED (U), DISAGREE (D), and STRONGLY DISAGREE (SD).

		SA	A	U	D	SD
1.	Statistics should NOT be a part of the sociology curriculum.	[]	[]	[]	[]	[]
2.	I would take this course even if it were not required.	[]	[]	[]	[]	[]
3.	It is very difficult to pass statistics the first time.	[]	[]	[]	[]	[]
4.	Statistics frightens me.	[]	[]	[]	[]	[]
5.	Statistics is similar to other courses in the sociology curriculum.	[]	[]	[]	[]	[]
6.	I find math challenging and therefore am excited by the prospects of such a course.	[]	[]	[]	[]	[]
7.	Statistics is irrelevant to the discipline of sociology.	[]	[]	[]	[]	[]
8.	What I have heard about this course from others has primarily discouraged me.	[]	[]	[]	[]	[]
9.	Statistics can be learned if I am willing to work.	[]	[]	[]	[]	[]
10.	Statistics is a valuable skill to the sociologist.	[]	[]	[]	[]	[]

Review and Revise Your Questionnaire

The fourth step in questionnaire construction is reviewing and revising your questions. One misgiving that beginning researchers often have is that once the questions have been committed to paper, they need not be altered. This is simply not so. Generally speaking, questions will need to be revised—that is, refined for clarity, depth, and lack of ambiguity—again and again. As we have already stressed, you should seek comments from individuals who have had experience dealing with persons similar to your targeted population. If, for example, your targeted population is Jesuit priests, it would be advantageous to have a priest review your questionnaire. Look for technical defects at this step, and be sensitive to redundant questions. In addition, look for formatting problems that might result in confusion.

Write a Cover Letter and Introduction

The fifth step in questionnaire construction is writing an introduction to the questionnaire and, in the case of a questionnaire that is to be mailed, a cover letter. The primary purpose of a cover letter is to introduce the questionnaire to respondents and to explain what your research is all about. Additionally, the cover letter serves to legitimize the questionnaire in the eyes of your respondents. Your cover letter should strive to convey to each respondent the importance of his or her responses in the research endeavor and to emphasize the need for truthful and accurate answers. Your letter should also point out that there are no right or wrong answers and that all information given will be kept confidential.

Instructions for filling out a questionnaire usually appear before each new section. In general, the instructions explain how the questionnaire is to be filled out. Like the cover letter, the instructions should emphasize the need for honest answers and ensure respondents their anonymity. If only one choice is allowed for each question, the instructions should also make this clear. If any of the terms used in the construction of questions holds a special meaning or tends to be ambiguous, it needs to be clearly defined in the instructions.

Most problems can be avoided if the instructions are prepared carefully. In short, the instructions should be prepared well enough to meet the needs of your least sophisticated respondent. At the same time, you should keep instructions brief and to the point.

Pretest Your Instrument

The sixth step in questionnaire construction involves pretesting the questionnaire through a pilot study, which gives you the opportunity to discover unforeseen problems of administration, coding, and analysis. A pilot study is essentially a pretest of the survey instrument. It is conducted to test the instrument for ambiguous or misleading questions and to offer you the opportunity to evaluate the performance of the survey instrument prior to its general distribution. Often, the pilot study indicates that a question on the survey is not tapping the desired information. At other times, the pilot study will forewarn you that your instrument is too long or too complex for the average respondent to complete. The pilot study also provides an opportunity for you to test the statistical methodology of your survey and to determine if reorganization is needed. Finally, information yielded from the pilot study may suggest new channels of inquiry and inspire ideas about additional questions that can enrich your research.

An Illustration

To help you see all of the steps come together into a concrete product, we have included a composite illustration of a questionnaire. The questionnaire presented here was constructed by an undergraduate student for a senior research project in sociology. We have not selected this questionnaire because we think it is perfect. On the contrary, we know there are some problems with the instrument. Carefully examine the questions and take time to read the notes that we have provided as a partial critique of the instrument. A careful study of this questionnaire and the accompanying notes should help you as you begin your questionnaire construction.

Dear Respondent:

You have been selected to participate in a study concerned with people's perceptions of criminal offenders. There are no right or wrong answers to these questions. We would simply like to know how you feel about the situations and issues described in this survey.

Please take some time to fill out the accompanying form. Do not put your name on the survey form. There will be no attempt to identify any respondents.

Thank you for your cooperation.

Sincerely,

Questionnaire

Listed below are twelve criminal cases brought to trial. You are to assume the guilt of the persons involved. The "criminals" mentioned in these descriptions are not real persons, and any similarity in names or circumstances to any real persons is merely coincidental.[1] Two questions follow each brief description. You are asked to check one and only one answer for each question. Remember, there are no right or wrong answers to these questions.

FOR QUESTION NUMBER 1: You are to imagine that you are the judge in the courtroom. Each person described has been found guilty, and you must pronounce sentence.

FOR QUESTION NUMBER 2: You are to imagine that you are each person's neighbor. You know what he has done. How would you treat him, knowing his misdeed?

CASE NO. 1
Jones Meat Packing Company has engaged itself in a price-rigging scheme with Brown Meat Packers, Inc. Since these two companies together control a large segment of the meat-packing industry in central Louisiana, their actions have driven up the prices of meat considerably in the area. They have been found guilty of price-rigging.

1. Would you sentence them to[2]:
   [ ] a prison term of one year or greater
   [ ] a jail term of less than one year or probation[3]
   [ ] other treatment or no sentence
   [ ] can't say

2. In interacting with Jones and Brown, would you[4]:
   [ ] avoid associating with them
   [ ] continue to associate with them but with reservation
   [ ] continue the relationship as though nothing had happened
   [ ] can't say

CASE NO. 2
Michael Reed, a 20-year-old male, had been dating Karla, a 16-year-old female. On a date to Chaplin's Lake, Michael and Karla willingly and eagerly engaged in sexual intercourse. Karla's parents found out and were enraged, and they charged Michael with statutory rape.

1. Would you sentence him to:
   [ ] a prison term of one year or greater
   [ ] a jail term of less than one year or probation
   [ ] other treatment or no sentence
   [ ] can't say

2. In interacting with Michael Reed, would you:
   [ ] avoid associating with him
   [ ] continue to associate with him but with reservation
   [ ] continue the relationship as though nothing had happened
   [ ] can't say

CASE NO. 3
Debbie Carloss, a junkie, was picked up on skid row for possession of heroin. Although this was her first time for possession, she did have a couple of petty thefts on her record.

1. Would you sentence her to:
   [ ] a prison term of one year or greater
   [ ] a jail term of less than one year or probation
   [ ] other treatment or no sentence
   [ ] can't say

2. In interacting with Debbie Carloss, would you:
   [ ] avoid associating with her
   [ ] continue to associate with her but with reservation
   [ ] continue the relationship as though nothing had happened
   [ ] can't say

CASE NO. 4
Tom Grest, a 31-year-old male, was arrested after an attack where a good deal of force was used in the sexual assault of a 21-year-old female. Grest was found guilty of rape.[5]

1. Would you sentence him to:
   [ ] a prison term of one year or greater
   [ ] a jail term of less than one year or probation
   [ ] other treatment or no sentence
   [ ] can't say

2. In interacting with Tom Grest, would you:
   [ ] avoid associating with him
   [ ] continue to associate with him but with reservation
   [ ] continue the relationship as though nothing had happened
   [ ] can't say

CASE NO. 5
Patrick Dowen was drunk when he strangled his girlfriend at the culmination of an argument. Dowen was found guilty of second-degree murder.

1. Would you sentence him to:
   [ ] a prison term of one year or greater
   [ ] a jail term of less than one year or probation
   [ ] other treatment or no sentence
   [ ] can't say

2. In interacting with Patrick Dowen, would you:
   [ ] avoid associating with him
   [ ] continue to associate with him but with reservation
   [ ] continue the relationship as though nothing had happened
   [ ] can't say

CASE NO. 6
Paul Hill met Ray Boulder in a public restroom where the two men engaged in a voluntary homosexual act. They were found guilty of homosexuality.

1. Would you sentence Paul Hill and Ray Boulder to:
   [ ] a prison term of one year or greater

[ ] a jail term of less than one year or probation
[ ] other treatment or no sentence
[ ] can't say

2. In interacting with Paul Hill and Ray Boulder, would you:
[ ] avoid associating with them
[ ] continue to associate with them but with reservation
[ ] continue the relationship as though nothing had happened
[ ] can't say

CASE NO. 7
Keven Cross was picked up for robbery after he held up a liquor store, threatening the proprietor with a Saturday night special.[6]

1. Would you sentence him to:
[ ] a prison term of one year or greater
[ ] a jail term of less than one year or probation
[ ] other treatment or no sentence
[ ] can't say

2. In interacting with Kevin Cross, would you:
[ ] avoid associating with him
[ ] continue to associate with him but with reservation
[ ] continue the relationship as though nothing had happened
[ ] can't say

CASE NO. 8
Harold Pitt is a local business executive arrested by police for drunk driving after a New Year's Eve party.

1. Would you sentence him to:
[ ] a prison term of one year or greater
[ ] a jail term of less than one year or probation
[ ] other treatment or no sentence
[ ] can't say

2. In interacting with Harold Pitt, would you:
[ ] avoid associating with him
[ ] continue to associate with him but with reservation
[ ] continue the relationship as though nothing had happened
[ ] can't say

CASE NO. 9
Ralph Dorn is a 29-year-old male who exposed himself to several coeds walking on campus during the day. He was charged with exhibitionism.[7]

1. Would you sentence him to:
[ ] a prison term of one year or greater
[ ] a jail term of less than one year or probation
[ ] other treatment or no sentence
[ ] can't say

2. In interacting with Ralph Dorn, would you:
   [ ] avoid associating with him
   [ ] continue to associate with him but with reservation
   [ ] continue the relationship as though nothing had happened
   [ ] can't say

CASE NO. 10
Ann Greene was picked up in her car for possession of an ounce of marijuana. It was her first offense.

1. Would you sentence her to:
   [ ] a prison term of one year or greater
   [ ] a jail term of less than one year or probation
   [ ] other treatment or no sentence
   [ ] can't say

2. In interacting with Ann Greene, would you:
   [ ] avoid associating with her
   [ ] continue to associate with her but with reservation
   [ ] continue the relationship as though nothing had happened
   [ ] can't say

CASE NO. 11
William Tracy was a bookkeeper for the First National Bank in Summerville. In an ingenious scheme, Tracy manipulated the books in such a manner that he was able to borrow over $15,000 from the bank over a three year period. Tracy was found guilty of embezzlement.

1. Would you sentence him to:
   [ ] a prison term of one year or greater
   [ ] a jail term of less than one year or probation
   [ ] other treatment or no sentence
   [ ] can't say

2. In interacting with William Tracy, would you:
   [ ] avoid associating with him
   [ ] continue to associate with him but with reservation
   [ ] continue the relationship as though nothing had happened
   [ ] can't say

CASE NO. 12
Mary Ross passed a bum check while she was mildly under the influence of alcohol.

1. Would you sentence her to:
   [ ] a prison term of one year or greater
   [ ] a jail term of less than one year or probation
   [ ] other treatment or no sentence
   [ ] can't say

THE SURVEY

2. In interacting with Mary Ross, would you:
   [ ] avoid associating with her
   [ ] continue to associate with her but with reservation
   [ ] continue the relationship as though nothing had happened
   [ ] can't say

For each of the following statements, choose the response alternative which best describes your feelings. Response alternatives are STRONGLY AGREE (SA), AGREE (A), UNDECIDED (U), DISAGREE (D), and STRONGLY DISAGREE (SD).

		SA	A	U	D	SD
1.	The courts mollycoddle criminals.	[ ]	[ ]	[ ]	[ ]	[ ]
2.	All persons are treated equal under the law.	[ ]	[ ]	[ ]	[ ]	[ ]
3.	Rehabilitation should be the goal of our criminal justice system.	[ ]	[ ]	[ ]	[ ]	[ ]
4.	The answer to the rising crime rate is to build more prisons.	[ ]	[ ]	[ ]	[ ]	[ ]
5.	A defendant who can hire a good defense lawyer will get off easier than someone who cannot afford such a lawyer.	[ ]	[ ]	[ ]	[ ]	[ ]
6.	Most adult criminals cannot be rehabilitated.	[ ]	[ ]	[ ]	[ ]	[ ]
7.	If a person with a past criminal record were to move next door to me, I would not want to know about it.	[ ]	[ ]	[ ]	[ ]	[ ]
8.	If I were on a jury, I would consider sentencing a defendant to death if he/she were convicted of first degree murder.	[ ]	[ ]	[ ]	[ ]	[ ]
9.	Alternatives to a prison term should be considered when the defendant is a first offender.	[ ]	[ ]	[ ]	[ ]	[ ]
10.	A person should always obey the law, even if the law is not a good one.	[ ]	[ ]	[ ]	[ ]	[ ]

PLEASE GIVE THE FOLLOWING BACKGROUND INFORMATION ON YOURSELF. THIS DATA WILL BE USED FOR STATISTICAL PURPOSES ONLY.

Sex: [ ] male   [ ] female

Age: _____ (in years)

Marital status: [ ] single
                  [ ] married
                  [ ] divorced, separated, or widowed

Number of children: _____

Religious affiliation: _____

Education level: [ ] never completed high school
 [ ] graduated from high school
 [ ] some college
 [ ] graduated from college
 [ ] graduate degree

Are you currently employed?
[ ] no
[ ] yes

    If yes: What is your current position? _____

Notes

1. Including a disclaimer in a questionnaire concerning names and real-life circumstances is a good thing to do—especially for circumstances such as described here.
2. When constructing a questionnaire such as this, there is a risk that respondents' answer to the first question related to each case will affect their answer to the second question. If you have questions such as this, you should make it a point to check for response sets.
3. Two of these response alternatives reflect two real alternatives: a jail term of less than a year or probation and other treatment or no sentence. Because these four alternatives have been combined into two, some information is lost and some ambiguity is introduced. If, for example, a respondent checks the third alternative, you have no way of knowing if he or she prefers "other treatment" or "no sentence."
4. Case No. 1 refers to "them," but it is unclear as to who "them" really is. It may be Mr. Jones and Mr. Brown or it may be both the Jones and Brown Corporations. To make things clearer, it would be better to ask "Would you sentence Mr. Jones and Mr. Brown . . . ?"
5. The rape described in Case No. 4 is more stereotypical in its description than it is typical of the rape cases that generally come before the courts. When this survey was administered, this case received the strongest formal and informal sanctions by respondents. If the question had portrayed a more typical rape case, the responses might not have been so strong.
6. This question presumes the respondent knows what a "Saturday night special" is. It might have been better to have replaced "Saturday night special" with "sawed-off shotgun."
7. Case No. 9 assumes that everyone will know what "exposed" himself means. But in constructing a questionnaire, it is best to be as simple as possible. We might want to use a more descriptive term like "took down his pants in front of several women." Try very hard not to use language that some strata of society will not understand.

SELF-ADMINISTERED QUESTIONNAIRES

By definition, a self-administered questionnaire is one given to respondents with the assumption that each respondent can read the questions, has the knowledge and interest to answer them, and has a pencil, a place, and time to complete the instrument. Respondents may complete such a questionnaire in a group or individually.

If you are dealing with respondents in a public setting where all can be presumed to be aware of and concerned about a problem, a convenience sample can often be used. In such instances, a questionnaire is distributed in random locations and at times when typical members are passing by. As part of an aroused group, they may have higher than usual motivation to answer. Some examples might include students on a university campus concerned about an unexpectedly large increase in tuition or fees, or people in an area devastated by a windstorm. If the questionnaire is distributed at a group meeting, such as a school class or public assembly, respondents may be encouraged to answer more frankly because of group support than they would if they were alone.

THE MAILED QUESTIONNAIRE

Mailed questionnaires are used extensively in social science research because they are capable of reaching sample respondents living in widely dispersed geographic areas at relatively low costs. With the mailed questionnaire, respondents answer and return the questionnaire only if they are motivated to do so. Therefore, it is especially important that a persuasive cover letter be enclosed with each questionnaire. The word processor is a powerful tool in creating personal letters, and you should consider using one if it is available to you. You should also make responding to your questionnaire as easy as possible by minimizing the costs in both time and money for your respondents. Using a short questionnaire and a self-addressed return envelope, for example, will tend to increase your response rates.

With the mailed questionnaire, one of your prime concerns will be maximizing your response rates. Response rates may be well below 50 percent for a mailed survey. However, this return rate can definitely be increased with follow-ups. Professional researchers often use up to four mailings (i.e., follow-ups) to increase their return rate. If you plan to use the mail-back procedure, it is imperative that you develop a method for checking the address of each respondent returning the questionnaire. Without such a code, you will not be able to determine who has returned the questionnaire and who has not. One method that you might use is to print a number on the questionnaire or envelope so that you are able to match up the return numbers with those on the original mail-out list. Often a blank questionnaire is mailed out along with the reminders, just in case the first questionnaire has already been "filed." Besides serving as a reminder to fill out the questionnaire, the repeated mail-back procedure demonstrates to your respondents how much you value their responses. Repeated appeals to answer the survey can also serve to persuade initially reluctant respondents to fill out the questionnaire.

Mailed questionnaires have several advantages. First, they are less costly to conduct. Since there is no difference in the cost of collecting data within your own city or across the nation, mailed questionnaires are frequently used to collect data from across the United States. Second, there is little personal bias involved with the mailed questionnaire because respondents are able to answer the questionnaire by themselves and at their own convenience. Hence, they have no one to influence them and more time to consider their answers. Third, there is a standardization of the questions asked in the mailed survey since all respondents are given the same printed questions. Since there is no personal meeting with a researcher, respondents cannot be influenced by face-to-face interaction. Fourth, training requirements for assistants are minimal since there is little or no researcher–respondent interaction.

Several disadvantages are associated with mailed questionnaires. First, you can never really know for certain who filled in the questionnaire. Was it the person to whom it was sent, or was it a friend or a relative? Second, out-of-date mailing lists may result in questionnaires that cannot be delivered, forcing you to make special provisions when this occurs. One way of handling this problem economically is to arrange with the post office for return-postage-guaranteed envelopes. When this type of arrangement is made with the post office, return postage is paid only on those envelopes actually returned.

With mailed questionnaires, every return must be scrutinized to ensure that it was not falsely or frivolously filled in. It is your responsibility as researcher to do everything possible to remove contaminated and spoiled returns.

FACE-TO-FACE INTERVIEWS

In a face-to-face interview, a researcher (or research assistant) contacts respondents personally to answer the research questions. Questions are asked orally by the researcher, although charts, cards, or other visual aids are sometimes used during the interview process, and they are answered orally by the respondents.

Face-to-face interviews have several distinct advantages, and knowing these may help you decide whether this procedure is best for your study. First, in a face-to-face interview, the interviewer can clarify questions that seem confusing or that are misinterpreted by respondents. If a respondent clearly misunderstands a question, such clarifications are essential or data may be lost. When confusing or misinterpreted questions call for clarification, it is important that clarifying remarks be standardized. Without such control, you can never be sure whether your respondents are responding to the question or the clarifying remarks. Second, the interview typically produces a higher response rate than does the mailed questionnaire. This is most likely because it is a lot more difficult to turn someone down face-to-face than to turn someone down by throwing away a printed questionnaire. Third, the presence of an interviewer usually serves to decrease the number of "don't know" and "no answer" responses. With the interview, you can gently probe respondents for a position. Fourth, in addition to asking questions, the interviewer can observe. These observations may include general reactions to the respondents' dress, grooming, and mannerisms as well as the physical surroundings.

Although the advantages of interviewing will probably outweigh any disadvantages, several disadvantages should be mentioned. First, interviews are very time-consuming. Interviewers must be trained, and this training must make use of the final interview schedule to ensure that the intent and spirit of the research project are being positively served. The success of the interview ultimately depends on the interviewer's skill, persuasiveness, and persistence. Second, interviews are costly in time and resources. While the per-case collection cost in a mailed questionnaire is about equal to five first-class postage stamps ($1.10 in 1985), or about a third of an hour's labor at minimum wage rates, each interview is likely to cost an average of three hours' labor at minimum wage rates. This includes time in contacting and scheduling and rescheduling interviews, travel time to the interview location, and an hour or more to complete the interview. In general, a brisk, short, well-planned interview has a better chance of succeeding than a long, rambling one does. The latter is prone to interruption, and if it is interrupted, the spirit of the interview may be difficult (even impossible) to recover. Sometimes funded researchers find it advantageous to pay interviewees to come to a central site for interviews. Although this procedure may reduce net costs somewhat for the interviewer, it frequently raises the cost for the interviewee and hence the rate of refusals.

In sum, the interview is superior for gaining extensive information, verified by extended discussion and probing in problem areas. If the interviewer is well matched to the respondent for sex, age, background, and interests, the flow of information is usually enhanced. For many respondents, the research interview is rewarding in itself. For most of us, personal contact is inherently rewarding if the partner is pleasant, responsive, and considerate.

Effects of Interviewer Characteristics

Untrained, inept, or insensitive interviewers can easily defeat the objectives of data collection by scheduled interview. Thus, the interview method is more risky than the questionnaire method unless you give serious attention to your choice of interviewers. Dress, appearance, and social background are very important, and generally should be similar to that of your respondents. Perceived common background and interests will usually put respondents at ease. In doing research on working women's attitudes toward feminism, for example, it would be a mistake to send a strong-willed traditional male to do the interviewing. And in doing research on the fertility rate in large-city black neighborhoods, black female interviewers would probably be more successful.

Interviewers should be well rehearsed on the basic research objectives and knowledgeable in the practical aspects of the research subject. Training sufficient to assure self-control and resilience in the give and take of interviewing is essential. Interviewers must also have good conversational skills and good social skills to deal smoothly and pleasantly with a wide variety of respondents. Finally, interviewers must be skilled in turning the conversation in the right direction, shifting to the next subject when one subject has been satisfied, and terminating the interview gracefully.

Tips for Interviewing

Interviewing is an art, so hard-and-fast rules do not always apply. However, we would like to share with you a few tips that we believe can prevent problems.

- Try to establish a friendly relationship with the respondent, who is usually greatly affected by the interviewer's presence. As the interviewer, you should create a comfortable atmosphere for the respondent by being pleasant, courteous, well groomed, neat, and low-keyed. In addition, giving some interesting information on the research project can help to set the tone of the interview.
- Conduct the interview in a comfortable, private place to avoid distraction from other activity and interruptions from callers. A private office is preferred over a home since interviews often encounter intrusive family activity.
- Keep the interview on the subject as required by the interview schedule. Avoid any discussion of the respondent's personal affairs or concerns with politics, religion, or any extraneous matters. If such subjects are introduced by the respondent, show polite interest, then get back to the interview question or go on to the next question. The main flow of information should be from

the respondent to the interviewer. A good interviewer does very little talking but stimulates relevant conversation from the respondent.

- Especially sensitive issues should be introduced late in the interview, after the respondent has developed a rhythm of communication and has become accustomed to the interviewer's style and manner. Lead up to sensitive matters by asking routine questions. Sensitive issues might include death of family or friends, sexual and criminal behavior, and close personal matters such as health, career security, and past failures. Always show sympathetic interest and understanding. With proper attention from the interviewer, the respondent may feel relief at being able to talk about traumatic personal matters.
- Avoid giving the respondent the idea that you can help to solve any personal problems. You are only there in the capacity of an interviewer engaged in social science research.
- Avoid making any suggestions to the respondent except those implied by the interview schedule and the research objectives. As interviewer, you should repeatedly review these objectives, making sure that all are included when there is opportunity.
- If the research objective requires discussion of family relationships, income, and age, you should anticipate that such issues may be difficult for the respondent to discuss. Here, generalities may be helpful, such as the statement that all families have problems to varying degrees, with relations between spouses, and between parents and children, and the elderly. This provides an opening and a little bit of planning time for the respondent to discuss family matters.
- If it becomes apparent that the respondent is lying or concealing or falsifying facts, do not worsen the situation with hard or incisive questions. Be tactful in moving on to other subjects without harming the interview relationship.
- It is permissible to accept minor hospitality such as an offer of coffee, tea, or a soft drink. In such cases, consume the drink discreetly and without much delay in order to proceed with the interview.
- Recording the interview must be limited to what is agreeable to the respondent. The most complete method is the tape recorder, and it is soon forgotten once the interview is under way, provided the respondent is willing. If a tape recorder is permissible, use a sensitive microphone incorporated in the recorder and keep the machine to one side or out of sight. It is usually too distracting to the interviewer to take notes during the interview, so cultivate the skill of remembering necessary details, and outline them

completely as soon as the interview is ended. A concise and well-organized interview schedule will help keep the interview on track and will help reduce the volume of unnecessary information. If the interviewee asks you not to include or use some information from the interview, you should cooperate and honor the request since the interview is voluntary.
- End the interview with some light, routine questions and with pleasant or amusing matters that are appropriate to the situation and the time.
- At the end of the interview, thank the respondent for donating time and effort to your research project. It is appropriate at this time to ask if the respondent is interested in seeing a copy of the research report. Some respondents will greatly appreciate such an offer.

TELEPHONE INTERVIEWS

One alternative to the face-to-face interview is the telephone interview, which can greatly reduce the cost and inconvenience of reaching and personally interviewing respondents. Such interviews can cover a wide geographic area at relatively low costs, even when compared with local travel costs. With telephone interviews, there is also less need to match the characteristics of interviewer and respondent. And in fact, rather extensive information can be obtained, though the contact is less close and less intense than the direct personal interview. As with the face-to-face interview, interviewers should rehearse with the actual research interview schedule. A thorough critique of each interviewer's approach, explanation of the project, plea for cooperation, and skill in following the schedule are very helpful in improving the quality and success of telephone interviews. It is estimated that telephone interviewing is about 43 percent as costly as face-to-face interviewing (Rubin 1983, 267).

The telephone interview should include only brief, simple questions, with fewer questions than the direct interview schedule, and far fewer than the self-administered questionnaire. While you might think that direct personal interviews are more reliable, surveys using the same items by telephone and by direct personal interview have yielded very similar results, suggesting that randomly selected telephone numbers is a cost-effective alternative to the direct interview. As in any data collection procedure, some telephone interviews are lost because of interruptions on the respondent's end, and some are lost because of respondents' reluctance to discuss sensitive issues by telephone.

THE INTERVIEW VERSUS THE SELF-ADMINISTERED QUESTIONNAIRE

Both questionnaires and interviews rely on the validity of verbal reports, but there are important differences between these two procedures. Information obtained from questionnaires is limited to the respondents' written answers to a prearranged printed set of questions that are given directly to respondents or sent to them by mail. In the interview, the interviewer and respondent are in direct contact during the time of the information exchange. In the face-to-face interview, the interviewer can observe the respondent's reaction to questions and to the surrounding situation. In short, the interview requires more skill in sustaining personal relations and in eliciting information. And while it also takes far more time and money, the quality of information just may compensate for the added expense.

STRENGTHS AND WEAKNESSES OF SURVEY RESEARCH

Although we have discussed the strengths and weaknesses of the questionnaire and the interview schedule, we believe it would be worthwhile to look at the strengths and weaknesses of the survey in general. Like all research designs, the survey is not perfect. Although it does have its strengths, it also has its weaknesses.

First, the survey is particularly useful for describing the characteristics of a large population. A carefully developed questionnaire administered to a random sample allows us the opportunity to describe the population from which the sample was taken.

Second, large samples are feasible, especially when the survey is self-administered. Large surveys are really not unusual, and when the questionnaire has a sizable number of items, the sample must be large for purposes of statistical analysis.

Third, surveys permit standardization of measurements. Once questions are worded, this wording becomes a standard in that every respondent is exposed to it. In essence, exactly the same wording of questions is presented to all subjects.

Survey research has a number of weaknesses. First, surveys frequently rely on respondents' memories, which may make relevant data less assessable by the researcher. When memory is a factor, the data are only as good as the respondent's memories.

Second, respondents' motivation and ability vary widely, and this variation can affect results. With survey data and especially the self-administered questionnaire, motivation is a key factor in getting all questions answered. Since this answering process requires substantial energy on the part of subjects, motivational levels must be kept high.

Third, survey research is weak on validity and strong on reliability. Surveys are poor approximations of direct observations. Hence, our measures are not always going to be good indicators of whatever they are supposed to measure. On the other hand, they are strong on reliability in that the measures used tend to produce the same results over repeated measures. However, validity is also essential and needs to be examined more often than it is.

USING SECONDARY DATA TO SUPPLEMENT INTERVIEW DATA

Secondary data is an inclusive term that refers to documents, records, reports, and books from a variety of sources that are already in existence, as well as *the use of existing data sets from previous surveys that can be used for other purposes.* Major surveys take a considerable amount of time and money to do right, and as a result, many researchers have neither the time nor the money to construct their own data set from scratch. Using secondary data, the researcher can acquire a set of data collected from some other survey and, by careful analysis, often use the responses to that survey to figure out a population's response toward other questions. This has led Phillips to define secondary data analysis as "the analysis of available data with a framework that differs from that used in the original study" (1985, 260).

An enormous volume of such material exists, including government archives at the national, state, and local level, reports by commercial, industrial, journalistic, and professional organizations, and by individual private researchers working for a wide variety of commercial and business interests. Much of these data are available in major libraries or can be obtained at a fraction of the cost of a new survey.

One of the major sources of secondary data for sociological purposes is the census. As indicated earlier, the census is taken completely every ten years with a variety of smaller studies done between periods. It asks a variety of questions, which can be used then for other kinds of purposes. Questions asked of households concerning the number of persons living there, whether they are headed by a male or a female, whether or not the members are married to each other, and so forth, can tell us a considerable amount about changes in the U.S. family.

Similarly, every four years the national election sends forth a host of survey researchers armed with questionnaires, asking the populace questions aimed at uncovering attitudes perceived as affecting voting behavior. Secondarily, however, these same studies can be used to construct creatively a wide variety of studies of things that have virtually nothing to do with voting behavior. Because surveys have become big business in politics, these data sets are often quite sophisticated in their sampling techniques, reliability coefficients, and so on, and offer the limited-budget researcher an enormously appealing source of information to be used for other research purposes. In fact, Daniel Yankelovitch (1981), a political pollster of some talent, secondarily analyzed much of his previous work on political attitudes in order to come up with an entire book, *New Rules*, which is not about politics at all but about larger changes that have taken place in American values. One might say that secondary data analysis is a way by which the researcher "spins off" new uses for research data in the same way that technological spinoffs occur everyday (we got nonstick cookware as a by-product of the space program, for example).

Every single day researchers across the land are punching computer cards, administering questionnaires, conducting interviews, and engaging in other research projects for countless purposes. The trick is to get these researchers to let you use their data for your purposes. It can be expensive or cheap (it can even be free), and the cooperative spirit in research can be appealed to in such a way that researchers can even trade data sets so that each can get more than he or she could acting on his own. Given the expense of conducting research from the ground up, it is not at all surprising that secondary data analysis has become such an important subject in contemporary research.

Secondary analysis of data is not without pitfalls, however. When using resources that were collected for some purpose other than what you are interested in, you must take time to evaluate the validity and applicability of such existing sources. There is nearly always some relevant published information to relate to these new research projects. Generally, the value of new research is to demonstrate the nature and extent of changes since the publication of earlier data. Comparison with earlier sources is useful in analyzing changes in the population pyramid and forecasting changes in the composition of the labor force. Ongoing crime problems such as shoplifting may benefit from analysis over time.

Our preoccupation in this book with connecting theory and research, however, also calls for a special set of cautions the researcher needs to take when subjecting data to secondary analysis. Secondary data rarely afford a perfect match to the research design requirements of the new study. Research projects are always constructed according to some theoretical notions of the researcher, and questions are constructed accordingly. This is because words are never neutral; some theoretical biases are always embedded into the very nature of the questions that are asked. (This is why smart respondents sometimes respond to a question by asking back, "Why do you want to know?") Therefore, it will be of prime importance for the researcher to know what kinds of theoretical underpinnings guided and directed a particular research project. Why did the researcher ask the particular questions he or she asked? How were the questions asked? What did the researcher want to know? These questions help establish the theoretical direction and assumptions of the research and let you know whether or not the answers are consistent with the research you are doing.

When a researcher uses secondary data, he or she is *still* responsible for the methodological inadequacies of that data. This is a crucial *ethical* problem because the tendency is either not to know how the original data were collected or, since there is nothing you can do about it after the fact, use it as though it were valid. Time is a crucial variable, too, for a significant change often occurs in terminology and cultural values if several years have intervened between the time of the earlier material and the current research. Such differences must be identified and adjusted if the secondary data are to be applied correctly.

Some researchers rely on the legitimacy of official sources of data, when in fact every data source, including highly placed ones, often has serious shortcomings. For example, material from the U.S. Department of Labor is sometimes regarded as highly reliable. However, a close check on the quality and method of the original data gathering and analysis may show serious deficiencies. Again, it is the responsibility of the researchers to defend the data they are using secondarily, just as if it were being collected and used for the first time. If, as will be frequently the case, the validity and reliability of the data cannot be determined, the conscientious researcher will candidly note that the data are subject to limitations of method and standards prevailing at the time they were produced.

Chapter 10

Field Research

The nature of field research
    "Knowing about" versus "knowing"
    The concept of "field"
    Quantitative and qualitative research
    The attitude of the qualitative researcher
    Paradigms consistent with field research
Major research strategies in field research
    Participant observation
        Complete participant
        Participant-as-observer
        Observer-as-participant
        The complete observer
    Getting started
        Casing and approaching
        Entering into relationships
    Presenting self and study
    Sampling strategies in field research
    Watching and listening
    What to watch for
    Watching without listening and listening without watching
Recording and analyzing field observations
    Strategies for recording
    A note on the use of tape recorders
    Different types of notes
    Files, files, and more files
    The analysis of qualitative data
    Strategies for writing
Ethical issues in field research

No one will go far wrong who remains in close touch with and seeks to understand a body of concrete phenomena.
—George Homans

THE NATURE OF FIELD RESEARCH

Of the ways of collecting data we have discussed thus far, field research offers perhaps the most striking departure. Experiments can be performed in a laboratory, surveys and questionnaires can be administered almost anywhere. But field research, by definition, can only be done where the phenomenon the investigator is interested in studying takes place naturally.

A simple definition of field research, then, would be that it is a technique of studying behavior in the natural setting of its occurrence. We do not bring subjects to us; we go to them. We do so because of a set of theoretical understandings concerning the relationship between the investigator and the investigated. It will be important for us to come to grips with this understanding before we can talk about specific strategies for doing field studies.

"Knowing About" versus "Knowing"

One important characteristic of the modern world is that we increasingly know *about* far more than we *know*. There is nothing intrinsically wrong with this; indeed, there is much of the world which we could never do more than know about. We read research and reports about people whom we have never seen, often from the vantage point of authors who have never seen them either. We know about people in terms of categories they have been placed in by others: journalists, geographers, sociologists, intellectuals, artists, novelists, and so on. Such portraits, which represent much of our knowledge, are important and indispensable, but they are also likely to contain significant errors. Because of the distance between the researcher and his or her subject matter, what is known about is often a stereotype at worst or an oversimplification at best. Field research is an attempt to remedy this problem by grounding our studies in the field of their natural occurrence.

Although there is a long-standing debate among researchers about whether this type of research is "scientific" or not, we can look upon it simply as a way of respecting the nature of a certain subject matter. For when we study human beings, because the researcher is also a human being, we have the possibility of not only knowing about, but also of "knowing." By this we mean we can identify the distinctly human concerns of human beings, their feelings, emotions, loves, hates, and jealousies, as well as their age, sex, and socioeconomic status.

No one has stated what we are trying to say better than Lillian Rubin, a sensitive field researcher who has written much about life in the working-class family:

> I am aware that both the methods of this study and the style of presentation are vulnerable to criticism from colleagues in the social sciences. The small sample not randomly chosen makes generalizations suspect. The anecdotal presentation raises the questions of representativeness in the use of data. The only answer to these criticisms lies in the quality of the work itself—in the ability to persuade by appealing to a level of "knowing" that exists in all of us but is not very often tapped; in its ability—to borrow a phrase from psychology—to generate an "aha experience."
>
> We have hundreds of representative studies of one aspect or another of family life—important and useful studies. We have attitude studies and behavior studies; but few that make the link between the two. We have probability statistics on marriage, divorce, sexual behavior, and much, much more; but they tell us nothing of the experience of the flesh-and-blood women and men who make up the numbers. This is not a failure of those studies; they are not designed to do so. Still, they leave us with only a fragment of knowledge. Therefore, we need also social science that is so designed—qualitative studies that can capture the fullness of experience, the richness of living. We need work that takes us inside the family dynamics, into the socio-emotional world in which people are born, live, and die—real people with flesh, blood, bones, and skeletons. (1976, 13–14)

The Concept of "Field"

The concept of "field" is a bit cloudy, for people often use the term in different ways. When someone asks you what "field" you are studying, they mean something a bit different from what we mean when we talk about "field research." The main component of the concept of field as the term is used by researchers is that it *locates* the research in a particular place—the place in which the phenomenon being investigated occurs. If we want to study the routines of secretaries in an office, we will have to go to an office. If we wish to investigate the round of life lived in a nursing home, we will have to find ourselves one and go there. If we want to study the world of urban police officers, it will be necessary for us to gain access to the scenes in which they live and work.

Our principal concern in this chapter is that field research *not* be taken as the equivalent of laboratory research, merely conducted in a different place (Schatzman and Strauss 1973). Experimental research (even when it is conducted in the "field"), laboratory research, and even to some extent survey research are primarily interested in controlling variables as precisely as possible so that careful manipulations can be made to produce some kind of information. While the idea of control itself is open to some question, the kind of research we are discussing under the heading of "field research" is simply not amenable to that kind of treatment. We will want to understand behavior *as it occurs.* The researcher will not, in most instances, try to control it because to do so would be to violate the naturalistic principle that governs this type of activity.

The basic idea of field research, simply put, is that in order to know our subjects, whether they be prostitutes or presidents, delinquents or Druids, popes or pimps, we must see them where they live and enter, as best we can, into their round of life.

Quantitative and Qualitative Research

Most of our preconceptions about research are probably of the kind we speak of as "quantitative." Quantitative research is often (incorrectly, we believe) associated exclusively with the scientific method. It attempts to make generalizations based on precisely measured quantities. The question that informs quantitative research is "how much?" Many of the chapters in this book address themselves to quantitative research, and for many problems you will be working on, such an approach is indispensable. On the other hand, quantitative research is not suitable for all types of problems in the social sciences and is often associated with our previous discussion of "knowing about" rather than "knowing." This is one of the shortcomings of the natural science model of social science we discussed in Chapter 3. The techniques used for "knowing about" are not the same techniques we would use for "knowing."

To bridge this gap, we need another technique, more suitable to the natural, everyday world that human beings occupy as they live their daily lives. Field methods are often associated with this second form of research, sometimes called "qualitative." Just as the word *quantity* asks the question "How much?," the word *quality* asks the question "What kind?" Qualitative research wants to know what kinds of things people are doing, what kinds of processes are at work, what kinds of meanings are being constructed, what kinds of purposes and goals inform the participants' acts, what kinds of problems, constraints, and contingencies they see in the worlds they occupy. Bogdan and Taylor define qualitative research this way:

> Qualitative methodologies refer to research procedures which produce descriptive data: people's own written or spoken words and observations. This approach directs itself at settings and the individuals within those set-

tings holistically; that is, the subject of the study, be it an organization or an individual, is not reduced to an isolated variable or to an hypothesis, but is viewed instead as part of a whole. (1975, 4)

While one often encounters the view that qualitative and quantitative are not opposing ways of doing research, it must be stated in all candor that they do represent different ways of approaching a research project and they are not easily translated back and forth. Therefore, we will want to be especially cautious about the assumptions made in the theories we are using, for some types of theories demand quantitative data, while others insist that only qualitative data will be suitable. As we have learned, theories are basically answers we give to questions we ask of the world, and the type of data that will test this answer depends in large measure on the nature of the question.

Those who caution us not to see these types of strategies as opposing are correct when they point out that the two can be, and often are, combined in various research projects. But the researcher must exercise some care that the imperatives of theory not be compromised in an attempt to produce counting for the sake of counting, statistics because they look impressive, or interviews because they are fashionable.

Quantitative data can lead us to a field for further qualitative study, as when we encounter statistics about the divorce rate and decide to do a qualitative study of a divorced men's self-help group in order to feel something of the experience of divorce. Or we may get interested the other way around, as when we first do a descriptive, qualitative study of joggers and then later firm up the research with some quantitative data on numbers, demographic characteristics, and so forth.

The Attitude of the Qualitative Researcher

What stance does the qualitative researcher assume when doing research in the field? This is an important question because the wrong stance can destroy the possibility of ever finding out very much about or from the people who live there. Much of what follows will help you understand the attitude we are suggesting, but the matter is of such importance that a special introduction seems to be in order.

First, as David Matza has pointed out, the attitude must be one of *appreciation* rather than *correction* (1969, 15–40). Appreciation is the basic goal of trying to understand something rather than either advocate it or stamp it out. Appreciation requires an understanding of the subject's own viewpoint. It does not require an acceptance of that viewpoint, but it does require some empathy with it. The development of an *interior* view of the world one is investigating can be cultivated through this attitude of appreciation; it is unlikely to emerge if the stance is one of correction.

This is a rudimentary point, but necessary because so much of scientific research, especially in the social sciences, is collected with an ax to grind. Some groups fund studies of pornography in order to find out how to stamp it out. Other studies are commissioned to find out how to get rid of crime. Although these may be lofty moral goals, the researcher who adopts such a correctional perspective is unlikely to find out very much in the field from the people most directly involved (i.e., pornographers and criminals). This is not to say the researcher does not or cannot have values like anyone else. It does mean that since the researcher's primary goal is to understand the life of the people being studied, his or her values will have to be subordinated to theirs, at least for the purposes of the study.

This subordination of oneself in field research means that the attitude of the qualitative researcher is a relatively *humble* one. Field researchers are typically on someone else's turf, not their own, and their attitude must be that the subject knows more about the world he or she occupies most of the time than the investigators do, at least at the beginning of the research. (Later, if the research is successful, the investigators may know more about that world as a whole than any single participant in it does.)

It has always seemed to us that this is why professors, who are used to playing the role of expert, tend to be such poor field researchers and often give the task over to students. Good field research involves taking on almost the exact opposite of the professorial role. Whatever the researchers believe they know about a phenomenon initially awaits confirmation or refutation from the people they are studying. The field researcher, then, is often an interloper, and it will be necessary to avoid any conduct that might be interpreted as arrogant or elitist.

Paradigms Consistent with Field Research

Of the theoretical paradigms we discussed in Chapter 3, only a few are fully consistent with field methodology. Symbolic interactionism by its very nature emphasizes field methods almost to the exclusion of other kinds, while structural-functionalism does not generally believe that field research is very useful since the "field" is merely an outcome of the work of larger, macro-level units anyway. Conflict theory has something of the same bias against field research because the accounts and meanings people build up around their own lives are often regarded by conflict theorists as smokescreens or false consciousness that obscures the economic substrate of human relationships. On the other hand, some conflict theorists might say that field studies can be useful adjuncts to other types of research within that paradigm by helping to understand the personal costs of exploitative economic systems by examining the lives of people within it.

All of this is to say that field research, like any other type of research methodology, must be carefully coupled with theoretical concerns. Theory, as we have mentioned before, is more than simply questions or propositions, it is a whole constellation of assumptions, propositions, and metaphysical commitments that lead us in one direction or another methodologically. To understand this relationship through the concept of paradigm is to know that not just any method can be used with any theory. Sensitivity to this issue is often what separates mediocre from brilliant research.

MAJOR RESEARCH STRATEGIES IN FIELD RESEARCH

Participant Observation

Participant observation is probably the best-known technique of field research, and it has been most popular with sociologists and social psychologists working within the paradigm of symbolic interactionism. There are actually several variations of participant observation, and we will discuss these in a moment, but the classical meaning of the term refers to a researcher entering a setting he or she wants to study and actually participating in the very scene he or she is observing, analyzing, and writing about. The researcher is at the same time actor and audience; player and sociological spectator.

This research method has a long and honored tradition within sociology. Howard S. Becker's study of jazz musicians (1963) was conducted as participant observation, with Becker actually a member of the jazz group he was studying. Festinger's research on the doomsday cult (1956) was one of participant observation, in which two graduate assistants became members of the group waiting for the destruction of the world and the arrival of the flying saucer that was to save the handful of believers. Humphreys's controversial work, *Tearoom Trade* (1970), which investigates homosexual encounters in public rest rooms, employs the methodology of participant observation, with Humphreys getting his information by assuming the role of watch queen, a lookout who warned of the approach of "straights" or police. None of the participants in the "tearoom" doubted the watch-queen role played by the researcher, who did indeed give warning when necessary.

The impetus for this approach to research occurred in the United States primarily around the turn of the century when the "Chicago School"—the sociology department at the University of Chicago, their students and disciples—developed directional observational studies under the influence of Robert Park. Park was a former journalist who saw sociology as a superior form of journalism because it gave what he liked to call "the big picture." Park considered himself an empiricist in the finest sense of the word and exhorted his students to get dirty in the "real world" of human beings. You will get the flavor of Park from the following quote:

> You have been told to go grubbing in the library, thereby accumulating a mass of notes and a liberal coating of grime. You have been told to choose problems wherever you can find musty stacks of routine records based on trivial schedules prepared by tired bureaucrats and filled out by reluctant applicants for aid or fussy do-gooders or indifferent clerks. This is called "getting your hands dirty in real research." Those who thus counsel you are wise and honorable; the reasons they offer are of great value. But one thing more is needed—first-hand observation. Go and sit in the lounges of the luxury hotels and on the doorsteps of the flophouses; sit on the Gold Coast settees and on the slum shakedowns; sit in the Orchestra Hall and in the Star and Garter Burlesk. In short, gentlemen, go get the seats of your pants dirty in real research. (Park, as quoted in Lofland 1971)

And get dirty they did. Graduate students under the influence of Park began to pile up an impressive array of firsthand observational field studies. Nels Anderson wrote *The Hobo*, a study of homeless men. Frederick Thrasher produced *The Gang*, a study of delinquent boys. Zorbough wrote *The Gold Coast and the Slum*. These were just a few of the many pieces of work produced in the early days of the methodology of participant observation. They became classics of their genre and got field research off to an impressive start.

The essence of participant observation, then, is to place oneself *within* the process of conduct without disrupting it and to take the perspective of the participants. By actually participating in the social worlds they are describing, the researchers not only observe events but also experience the emotions and concerns of the people they are trying to understand. Park used to say rather indelicately that "you can't understand people unless you can also smell them."

Here are some formal definitions of participant observation from people who work within its tradition:

> Participant observation is used here to refer to research characterized by a period of intense social interaction between the researcher and the subjects, in the milieu of the latter. During this period, data are unobtrusively and systematically collected. (Bogdan and Taylor 1975, 5)

> The strategy to be described now is called, variously, participant observation, field observation, qualitative observation, direct observation, or field research. All these terms refer to the circumstance of being in or around an on-going social setting for the purpose of making a qualitative analysis of that setting. This may not be the person's sole purpose for being present, but it is at least an important one. (Lofland 1971, 93)

> The concept of participant observation . . . signifies the relationship which the human observer of human beings cannot escape—having to participate

in some fashion in the experience and action of those he observes. (Blumer 1969, vi)

Participant observation is a commitment to adopt the perspective of those studied by sharing in their day-to-day experiences, such that it is clear that they are being studied, or the investigator may conceal his scientific role and attempt to become a "normal" member of the community, cult, organization, tribe, or club being studied. (Denzin 1970, 185)

These definitions, even though they are varied and emphasize slightly different things, should give you a feel for just what the participant observer is trying to accomplish, although the term *participant observation* is actually an umbrella that tends to cover a wide variety of field methods and researcher roles.

Although each of these definitions gets at the crux of the strategy, none covers all the possible roles a participant observer can play in conducting a piece of research. For example, Gold, expanding on a formulation first used by Junker, has shown that there are at least four roles that the participant observer can take, and only one of them is in the classic tradition of "participant" (Gold 1969, 30–39). We will present these four roles and discuss some of the dilemmas associated with each.

Complete Participant. The complete participant in Gold's view is a disguised observer. Like a CIA agent, he infiltrates a group he is interested in studying, gains access to the world they inhabit by posing as one of them, and then collects research information without telling them what he is really up to. This is what Festinger's two graduate assistants did when they joined the doomsday cult. This is also what Humphreys did in his study of the "tearoom traders" we mentioned before. But there are at least two problems with this strategy: one ethical and one substantive to the study itself. The ethical problem is rather obvious. The complete participant must deceive the people he is studying by pretending to be only what he appears to be to them: namely, a colleague in their world. Instead of being himself in the role, he is something other than that because of his dual commitments and the perceived necessity of hiding the observer self from other participants in the scene. Gold gives a good example: "Playing the role of potential convert to study a religious sect almost inevitably leads the field worker to feel not only that he has 'taken' the people who belong to the sect, but that he has done it in ways which are difficult to justify. In short, he may suffer severe qualms about his mandate to get information in a role where he pretends to be a colleague in moral, as well as in other social aspects." (p. 34)

The ethical problem of deceit is joined by the research problem of becoming so immersed in the role that the observer half of the role is lost. By going completely native, incorporating the role comprehensively in the self, the observer may find that even writing his findings may be troublesome. At the very least, the researcher who chooses this variety of participant observation will find himself in a position where ethical issues demand attention, and where the need for cooling-off periods will be frequent lest the researcher lose himself completely in the role of participant to the exclusion of everything else.

Participant-as-Observer. In this form of participant observation, both the field-worker and the people he or she is studying are aware of the researcher's true purposes in participating in the world of their activity. This mutual awareness resolves the problem of deceit, but it does not completely resolve the dilemmas posed by the dual roles the researcher continues to play. The researcher tries to develop a certain intimacy with persons who are a part of the scene being studied in order to gain information from them; but the process of accomplishing that can jeopardize the research in one of two ways. First, the informant may become so identified with the field researcher that it becomes difficult to continue to function as an informant. To view oneself as being "studied" may change in some subtle ways the nature of one's own views and experiences. Second, in this role, as in the previous one, the researcher may "go native" and run the risk of losing the observer role. In other words, the problems of the known participant-as-observer have to do with the difficulties posed by trying to balance the requirements of two roles. None of this is to say that such a balance cannot be struck, but merely that it is difficult to do, and the researcher must be on guard constantly lest the balance fall too much one way or the other. Sensitive researchers, in fact, often do pull off the roles of participant-as-observer and in the process produce fine studies.

Observer-as-Participant. The observer-as-participant role involves the researcher's going to the scene of the study to collect information without in any way trying to carry off the pretense that he or she is a participant. This role is usually taken on when the field research is studying a series of processes that require short interviews on the scene with persons in the know. Often it is part of a mixed strategy and is used to fill in pieces of information not obtainable in any other way. Many of the participant problems we have mentioned are resolved since the researcher does not try to participate, but many of the advantages of participation are lost too. The danger here is that because the researcher is not really a part of the scene under investigation, the informants are likely to misunderstand the researcher, and he or she is likely to misunderstand them.

The Complete Observer. This role is sometimes called nonparticipant observation. The complete observer does not try to participate, but merely observes. The persons being observed usually do not know they are being watched. Nonparticipant observation means observing situations in terms of what can be understood purely from the outside. This strategy is usually employed as an adjunct to participant observation but has been used for large segments of research as the basic methodological technique. Some of the work of Erving Goffman is of this type.

Sometimes nonparticipant observation is used in the initial phases of a research project in order to determine many of the practical elements of a research setting, such as the time when events occur, the physical arrangements of places and things, and the appearance of participants. These elements can be ascertained best by simply being in a place and watching what goes on without a question being asked and even without the researcher's being regarded as part of the setting by the participants. (Obviously, this depends on what you are studying. If a mafia council session happens to be the setting, you are unlikely to be able to be a nonparticipant observer.) As an initial strategy, however, nonparticipant observation can be indispensable because it allows time to discover the basic outlines of the field we are studying and to find out what kinds of questions and actions will help find what we want to know. Such knowledge can prevent many disrupting errors when the researcher reaches the point in the study when he or she actually joins the group and begins to relate to it as a participant.

The researcher who chooses the complete observer role exclusively, however, is likely to miss a great deal that is going on and to violate the main rationale for doing field work in the first place.

It is impossible for us to say just what role a researcher ought to adopt in any particular instance. This is part of the art of methodology and will depend both on ethical and substantive questions. The rationale for some form of participation in the scene that is being studied is clear. Just how that is to be accomplished in any given research project will depend on a variety of contingencies involved in the project itself.

Getting Started

Suppose you have decided that the project you are going to research can best be understood through some form of field research. You may have decided this for a variety of reasons, such as the fact that you are working within a paradigm such as symbolic interactionism that is closely aligned with the field tradition, or perhaps because you want to fill in with qualitative materials data you have collected in some other way, such as with surveys or questionnaires. How do you get started?

In field research, the answer to this question is fairly simple, although not always easy to translate into action. Having identified a general topic of inquiry, and based on the idea that it will be impossible to know in advance or to impute to that topic all the important questions that could inform it, the researcher will need to find some persons who are actually involved in the activity and go to where it occurs. For example, the researcher may be interested, as John Irwin was, in finding out about surfing in California (Irwin 1977). It was necessary to find a group of people involved in surfing and then go to a beach where this activity went on, so as to observe, listen, talk, and even surf a bit himself.

The sequence goes something like this:

> Once the researcher has his focus of interest, he must locate a site that contains people and social activity bearing upon that interest; then, he must enter the site, establish an identity and relations with the host, watch the people and their activity, listen to the symbolic sounds that will make meaningful much of what goes on there, record his experiences, convert these experiences into data, analyze them, and validate his new understanding. (Schatzman and Strauss 1973, 18)

Let's discuss these steps one at a time. How does the researcher get a focus of interest? The identification of a problem may occur through a variety of channels, as we have already noted in Chapter 2. The researcher may simply be personally interested in a particular problem. Or, after the researcher has researched some other problem, another pops up that demands resolution even before the first can be fully understood. The research problem may be general or specific, but whatever it is, it will await the actual field experience before it is firm in the researcher's mind. This point requires some elaboration.

While it is true that theory guides the research process, we are discussing theory in a slightly different way. In qualitative research we often do not want to test a previously constructed theory, but rather to find theory grounded in an empirical context (Glaser and Strauss 1967). Theory in this sense is not a set of deductive propositions that require testing in order to be validated, but rather theory that emerges inductively from the research in the field itself. This is the real advantage of field methods, for it creates the possibility of either new theory or the validation of old theory from the actual field of its occurrence. No other method allows this.

If we wish to seek grounded theory, then, it will be impossible to formulate hypotheses and to know exactly what the theory is until we find out in our experiences in the field just what questions are important and which are not. To know in advance what kind of questions to ask (which is the role of theory, typically conceived) is often to impose a question on a research setting that is not really part of that setting. Therefore, fidelity to the integrity of the field itself is going to demand that the researchers not make their mind up too soon about what questions are important. This is not to say that the researchers should go into the field with an empty mind. It is to say that they should go into the field with an open one. Only in that way can they know when previous conceptions are not valid and new ones are.

To meet this charge, researchers will want to have a special kind of relationship to prefield library research. As in other research methods, they will want to read everything they can about the scene they are going to study, not to narrow or close their mind, but to open it to possibilities that subsequent field experience will either expand or contract with specific information. Having read everything practically possible, the researchers will then be in a good position to discover what is the forte of field research: that much of what has been written, both in the professional and popular literature on almost any topic of sociological interest, is wrong in key respects. The attitude of the field researcher, which we mentioned previously, means that when discrepancies arise, he or she will be in a position to recognize them and make a grounded choice on what is correct.

By this time, the field researcher will have whetted his or her appetite for the task at hand. What to do next? Schatzman and Strauss, who have written one of the finest small volumes on field research, suggest that entering the field is a crucial first step and usually involves the following: (1) casing and approaching, (2) entering into relationships, and (3) presenting self and study. We will discuss these one at a time.

Casing and Approaching. "Casing the joint" is usually the first step in deciding both whether and how to do a study involving participant observation. The field researcher does this for several reasons. First, he or she will want to find out if the site selected is really suitable to the study at hand. Second, given that the site is excellent for the study to be undertaken, is it at the same time feasible in terms of such things as size, resources, and area to be covered? Finally, casing will assist the researcher in deciding on suitable tactics for both gathering information and gaining access to the field setting.

Whether the researcher is studying an organizational setting such as a hospital or a social movement such as a feminist rally, casing gives an opportunity to learn much in advance, such as the rhythms and temporal movements of a place. This is invaluable information, for it will let the researcher know the best times to visit (and when to stay away), as well as local site persons who will make good contacts later. Involved in this first contact with the field of study is also some astute knowledge of the power relationships among persons in the setting. To know the pecking order within any group or organization is not only to shortcut a lot of potentially wasted time, but also to improve the chances of gaining maximum access to the field.

Whether the researcher ought to identify himself or herself and the study at this point in the process is open to some question. Usually it is not the right time, but sometimes a discreet inquiry about the possibility of a study can give the researcher a feel for the practical problems that he or she is going to encounter in doing the study. It is impossible to be precise about this; the researcher will have to exercise both tact and good judgment to know just when the time is ripe for presenting self and study to possible hosts in the field.

Entering into Relationships. It is almost impossible to overstate the importance of this next step in the process of conducting a field study. Whether the study gains valuable and useful information or the researcher is thwarted at every step will often depend on how this is handled. Indeed, if this step is botched, sometimes the study cannot be done at all! Once again, however, we encounter an area where the art of research is more important than its science. Sometimes persons who seem to be receptive hosts turn out to be resented by others whose cooperation the field researcher will also need to conduct the study. Sometimes the field researchers can be introduced in such a way that they appear to be investigators with an ax to grind within the context of the organization itself. This is especially a problem when a place of work is the site of the study.

However, if these problems are met with finesse, the researcher may actually discover what is often the case: that people are flattered to be a part of a good study, and even though they sometimes have axes to grind themselves, those things can be filtered out and much useful information gained. Even though the field researcher is, in a sense, invading the privacy of the people who are being studied, if a good relationship is cemented in the beginning, this can be an asset rather than a liability. Most people like to talk about the social worlds in which they are involved, and will not necessarily see the researcher as a threat if he or she (a) truly is not one; and (b) behaves in such a way to give assurances that the study will be conducted on the up-and-up.

To gain entry to the field is, of course, not the end of relationships between the field researcher and the people being studied; indeed, it is just the beginning. Theoretically, every person the researcher encounters and asks questions of will have to be dealt with, and it is important that the researcher keep the lines of communication open by not siding with factions within the group or being co-opted in any way. This can be a formidable task at times, for the tendency is clearly to try to use field researchers for intragroup purposes. It will take a considerable amount of dexterity to keep this from happening.

Presenting Self and Study. Finally, the field researcher will find it necessary to present both self and study to the people from whom he or she is acquiring information. While many field studies have been conducted that tried to conceal the true purposes of the research, we have never found that such a tactic made good sense either ethically or scientifically. The watchword here is *honesty*, and it is the time to give it in abundance. If the researchers do not level with the people they are studying at this stage, it is likely to come back to haunt them later. Once a field researcher's credibility is gone, it is not likely to be regained and it *is* likely to poison the climate in which the research is conducted. Sometimes a letter to the host agency is in order, but at other times a simple verbal description of the essentials of the study is sufficient.

It is important that researchers "get the story straight" because they may have to tell it many times to persons in the field, and it will create confusion and erode trust if they fail to communicate correctly the research process. This can be difficult, of course, because as we have already mentioned, the researchers at this point may not know exactly what it is they want to know. It is best to be honest about this too, so that the general idea is communicated.

Much of the above advice assumes that the researchers are studying an organization or a group with a formal structure. Gaining entry to an informal group can be either easier or more difficult, depending on the circumstances. Nevertheless, the tactics we have suggested still apply. It will still be necessary to be honest about the study one is conducting, keep relationships sound with informants, and communicate self and study correctly and openly. Often the communication comes later because of the nature of informal settings, groups, and processes, and the researchers can gain valuable information before the natural course of events calls for them to reveal self and study to informants.

Sampling Strategies in Field Research

Having gained entry to a field of inquiry, and some preliminary information from spending time observing, researchers will usually be confronted with the question of sampling. Obviously, it is impractical under ordinary circumstances to talk with everyone involved in a field of inquiry or to see everything that is going on. Therefore it will be necessary to be somewhat selective. Previously we discussed the principles of sampling and representativeness, but it is important to understand that these highly controlled principles do not ordinarily apply in field research. The reason for this is that most of the time the field researcher is not really interested in characterizing scientifically a group of people, but rather a social process or an interactional setting. What the researchers will want to do, then, is to observe and talk at various "sites" where the action is ongoing in order to get a feel for various dimensions of the process under investigation. Usually this means that they will want a sample of at least four things: time, space, people, and events (Schatzman and Strauss 1973, 39).

As noted in Chapter 4, time is an important component of any social process, and it will be necessary for the researchers to observe what is going on at various times within the life of a field being studied. For example, if the study is of an emergency room in a hospital, they will want to get a feel for the time rhythms all around the clock. Different shifts, different work schedules, various clientele, all are telling in terms of the processes the field researchers ordinarily want to investigate. What this means practically is that the researchers will want to draw observations from whatever the appropriate time segments of the field are, and this may involve 2 A.M. rallies into the field as well as the usual 9-to-5 routines.

The researchers will also want to draw a sample of places because the concept of field, while seemingly a unitary whole, is actually often broken into subunits, all of which are located in a different place. Locations, of course, mean different types of information, and sometimes different people, involved in the round of activity the researchers want to know about. Therefore, it is imperative that the relevant locations be experienced. What this means practically is that the researchers will want to be asking people more or less constantly where to be at a given time in order to find out what they want to know. To position oneself at different locations is frequently to gain a wholly new perspective on what is going on; conversely, to stay in the same place is to limit the amount of information one receives as well as to jaundice the view of the whole.

Sampling people must be dealt with in a very specific way because the field researcher is not really interested in the usual rationales for sampling human populations. The attempt in field research is not to be representative but to know what is going on. Some people will know far more about what is going on than others will, some will be better able to articulate their knowledge than others, and still others will want to speak. An example might be a study of a political convention. Talking to different people will be imperative to the success of the study, but talking to the *right* people will at times be even more important. This is because every human scene is composed of people who are differentially knowledgeable about the happenings of the place.

On the other hand, as McCall and Simmons suggest, some kind of quota sample is often necessary simply to make sure that persons from all relevant segments of the field are talked to in the study (1966, 64). To take our previous example of a political convention, it would be unwise to talk with only one faction or hear only one side of the issue. Obviously, research in the field is geared to hearing and seeing all sides of the action, and a researcher might want to intentionally seek out persons who represent various sides in a battle or a dispute. The particular categories that are relevant to an organization can simply not be known in advance, and the standard sociological list of demographic variables (age, sex, race, occupation, socioeconomic status) will come to be relevant or irrelevant only in terms of the contingencies of a particular case. Obviously, but not altogether facetiously, a study of Ku Klux Klan rallies is not likely to produce a nonwhite perspective, at least within the group itself. At other times, in other fields, race will be an important dividing line, as will sex, money, and a host of other things. To reiterate, this knowledge simply cannot be known in advance of direct experience in the field. The researcher's subjects, through their talk and his or her observations, will make it known which categories are important and which are not.

Finally, field researchers will want to get a feel for the different kinds of events that make up a round of life to the participants in a field setting. Human settings are composed of different kinds of activities: some usual and routine, some relatively rare, some bizarre. The researchers will need to be on hand enough to experience all of these in some measure, and knowledgeable people within the scene can often tell exactly what is going to happen when and where. One device for nailing this down in advance at least somewhat is a schedule, and this may be either a formally published one or informal cues concerning the timing and scheduling of events. To gain a feel for all of the categories of relevant events that make up the life of a field is important if the researchers hope to know about the setting they are studying.

Watching and Listening

Since most people do not know how to either watch or listen, this section is especially important because watching and listening is where we get virtually all of our information in field studies.

Obviously, when you go into a field for the first time, your senses are going to be bombarded by a variety of stimuli. This is why first days in the field should be given over to merely watching and listening without any systematic attempt to analyze or clarify what is being watched or seen. First impressions are often very important, not because they are correct but because they become points of reference later as one becomes more knowledgeable about what one has seen and heard. To let the vast and often contradictory stimuli of the field sweep over you is an important first step in learning what is important and what is not.

Obviously, watching is watching something, and it is not altogether clear to a newcomer to a field setting just what it is he or she is seeing. This is what we meant earlier when we said that researchers should go to the field with an open mind but not an empty one. Past experiences and theoretical interests will intertwine to let the researchers know what they are seeing. It is quite impossible to do a field study well without some theoretical direction. Depending on what the thrust of the research is, the investigators will want to approach the study with such elementary concepts as social structure, ideology, roles, social types, norms, and routines in mind so that they can begin at some point to do two things: (1) to make sense out of the enormous range of input they are receiving from the field setting itself and (2) to know if, when, and how these ideas apply to the scene being viewed. As Norman Denzin (1970) has pointed out, the research act is itself a form of interaction, and all the matters we are discussing will emerge between the observer and the observed.

What to Watch for

While the theory and questions being used in a study will circumscribe partially the objects of interest to the investigators, it is possible to list a group of things the researchers will probably organize their observations around. John Lofland has suggested six basic categories, arranged from the most microscopic (1971, 14–15). These are starting points and will focus attention in places where it will produce the most results:

1. *Acts*—Action in a situation that is temporally brief, consuming only a few seconds, minutes, or hours.
2. *Activities*—Action in a setting of more major duration—days, weeks, months—constituting significant elements of persons' involvements.
3. *Meanings*—Both the verbal and non-verbal productions of participants that define and direct action.
4. *Participation*—Persons' holistic involvement in, or adaptation to, a situation or setting under study.
5. *Relationships*—Interrelationships among several persons considered simultaneously.
6. *Settings*—The entire setting under study conceived as the unit of analysis.

These concepts are hardly sacred, but they do give a starting point for watching that can be quite fruitful. In other words, one way of conceiving of the act of watching is to ask, What are the characteristic acts, activities, meanings, participation, relationships, and settings, the forms they assume, and the variations they display?

This is only one of many different schemes of things that the researcher will want to watch for. Kenneth Burke discusses what he calls the "pentad" and suggests that a discussion of human social acts requires an analysis of the relationship between five elements, each of which is an answer to a certain type of question.

1. Act—An answer to the question "What is going on?" Are we dealing here with a communion, a political campaign, an orgy, an airline flight? Crucial to the question of qualitative research is an answer to the question of acts.
2. Actor—An answer to the question "Who is doing this?" We mean "who" not in the sense of the psychological characteristics of the actors, but rather what characters they come to represent, what roles they play, how they perform in the acts that are ongoing.
3. Agency—An answer to the question "How?" All acts are conducted through certain means, and it will be important to notice

what kinds of means, props, or other supporting devices are used to begin, maintain, or end acts.
4. Scene—An answer to the question "Where?" Everything that goes on goes on somewhere, and obviously in field research the characteristics of the scene itself will have an important bearing on what is happening. The researcher will look for physical characteristics and how they influence action, and how these elements of scene work with the rest of the elements we are discussing.
5. Purpose—An answer to the question "Why?" Again, we mean this not in the sense of depth psychology of the actors, but rather the constructed purposes of the people acting in the scene itself. Why do they do the things they do? What are the avowed and imputed purposes that give a rationale for the activities under investigation? Usually a variety of purposes will emerge in a study, and the investigator will want to pay close attention to how they relate to one another and to the rest of the action. (Burke 1962)

Watching without Listening and Listening without Watching

At times in the field the overwhelming nature of the sensory input the field researcher is receiving can lead to a certain obscuration of subtle elements crucial to the activity being studied. For this reason, it can be useful at times to try to watch without listening in order to catch many of the nonverbal elements that comprise any interactional setting, and at other times it will be useful to listen without watching. (Even closing your eyes can be a useful tactic.)

Listening without watching has another, less literal meaning also, and this deserves some elaboration. Good field research requires getting into the subjects' skin and seeing the world from their point of view. George Herbert Mead (1934) spoke of this process as "role-taking," that human ability to see the world through the eyes of another. It is the process that makes human communication possible and is crucial to good field research. By listening without watching, then, we mean apprehending the world within the symbolic vocabulary of the participants in that world without imposing preformed categories on the scene being studied. To listen in this sense, then, means to *really* listen to what people are saying and what it means from their point of view. This can be especially difficult to do because the sociologist has in mind a set of research problems that he is eventually going to try to make sense out of, using the field as data. However, in the initial stages at least, it will be well to avoid this as much as possible in an effort to understand what things really mean to the people being studied. The developing framework of the investigator must be predicated on empirically grounded listening and watching. This is the essence of good field research, and it will be destroyed if the researcher "listens" too quickly, thereby failing to grasp just what the world looks like to the people in it.

Several types of listening are possible. The researcher may simply eavesdrop by keeping quiet and listening to what is going on without in any way trying to elicit comments or ask questions. This form of listening has many advantages, especially during early days in the field when the researcher does not yet know what kinds of questions to ask. But as Schatzman and Strauss point out, a point of diminishing returns is reached and the researcher will need to engage in some type of conversation in order to fully understand the activity being watched. When that is necessary, the researcher may engage in either conversational interviewing or formal interviewing. In the former, the researcher generally makes short inquiries as part of an ongoing conversation that he or she is a part of either as a participant or as a person in the same setting. It is a strategy that does not require disruption and that maximizes the amount of information to be gained while minimizing the amount of time necessary to gain it.

The timing of these types of questions tends to be right too, for they are situated in the context of what is being studied, so it is easy to ask the right question at the right time. A formal interview can often lose that timing and, unless it is re-created, the interview is not very productive. There usually comes a time, however, when some type of "formal" interview needs to be conducted. This is because the number of questions and the depth of the questions need a setting where the researcher can sit down with an informant and probe in detail for the exact information the investigator wishes to know. This can, theoretically, be done anywhere, but we have found that if it is done in the field setting itself, the results are much more productive. For example, one of the authors was recently involved in a study of emergency-room physicians. Although watching, eavesdropping, and small conversations sandwiched between events were all exceedingly useful, there came a time when it was necessary to sit down and talk at length with emergency-room physicians. We chose a small room adjacent to the emergency room and conducted extensive discussions (conversations, to be sure) about specific things we either did not understand or wished to probe in depth.

As you can see, watching and listening take many forms and are generally part of a mixed strategy at different times during the research process. No single watching or listening strategy will be correct for all situations, and it takes a considerable amount of artistic flexibility to know when and where to employ what strategy. First days in the field are often difficult, and the first research project an investigator conducts will reveal a great deal about what strategy fits where.

Whichever listening and watching strategy is adopted, it is important to make the informants know that their ideas are valuable and that the investigator wants them to be themselves as they communicate with him or her. A certain sensitivity to human problems and to the difficulties of communication can go a long way toward eliciting the best responses from subjects.

Simply listening to people talk in field settings can produce some of the most amazing social science data. For example, sociologist E. E. LeMasters conducted a participant observation study of a tavern in Wisconsin frequented primarily by blue-collar, working-class men. The insights he gathered were fashioned into a powerful statement about working-class life entitled *Blue-Collar Aristocrats* (1975). In one of the most interesting sections of the study, LeMasters reports on the comments men made about women in the bar:

> It is difficult, if not impossible, to talk with men at The Oasis Bar about the opposite sex without feeling that they view women with suspicion and distrust . . . .
>
> One man said: "The trouble with American women is that they don't know their place. I was in Japan after World War II and by God those women know who's boss. You tell one of them babes to jump and all they ask is 'how high?' But an American woman will say, 'why?'"
>
> "What in the hell are they complaining about?" one man asked. "My wife has an automatic washer in the kitchen, a dryer, a dishwasher, a garbage disposal, a car of her own—hell, I even bought her a portable TV so she can watch the goddamn soap operas right in the kitchen. What more can she want?"
>
> These men have an ambivalent attitude toward rape. While they do not approve of males using force to obtain sexual favors from a female, at the same time they believe that many forcible rape charges are fictitious—that the woman 'had it coming to her'.
>
> "By God," one man said, "if I were on a jury the woman would have to prove her case. A lot of women lead a man on until he can't control himself and then they yell rape. Bullshit, I say."
>
> The men at The Oasis are also skeptical about statutory rape. Many of them feel that the age of consent for girls is too high—eighteen in this particular state. "They should tattoo their birth date right on the girl's belly at birth," a plumber said. "Then a man would know whether they're old enough or not."

It is easy to see from this brief glimpse of a participant observation study how powerful data can be when given in the subjects' own words. Such data still have to be interpreted, but having them grounded in a field context is a long step toward making sure that interpretations are accurate and valid.

RECORDING AND ANALYZING FIELD OBSERVATIONS
Strategies for Recording

As you have seen from our discussion thus far, the basic tools of field methods are the senses with which every human being is automatically equipped. Eyes and ears are indispensable to good field research, but in this section we want to note some practical ways the senses can be augmented so that later analysis will be possible. We are talking here about recording observations.

Obviously, field researchers are not going to be able to remember everything they see and hear. Recording is therefore a practical necessity, and most of the time this means note-taking. The image of the field researcher with pencil and pad ready immediately comes to mind, but this is only one of several possibilities, and it is not always the best one. Certainly a pencil and a pad are important, but they have at least two disadvantages: (1) It is quite impossible to record in a transcript manner what you are seeing. Inevitably the note-taker who tries to do this will leave out important elements of the process he or she is observing or will even forget to observe in the enthusiasm for "getting it all down." (2) The process of taking notes can often interfere with the spontaneity of the occasion itself. In short, the researcher's informants may be put off by the presence of a person playing the role of a stenographer, and this will destroy the reason for doing field research in the first place.

For these reasons, note-taking must be done carefully. To the extent that the researcher wishes to use notes in the presence of informants, developing a kind of shorthand will be helpful. This shorthand will be highly personalized, but it must be readable later and remind the researcher what he or she has seen and heard. Often field researchers will decide not to take notes in the field at all but rather to systematically reconstruct a set of notes as soon as possible after observations in the field were made. Memory is directly related to the passage of time, so the note-taking must be done quickly. What really happens in this case is that the real "notes" are taken in the field researcher's head as his or her experiences are unfolding, and then transcribed in written form at a kind of one-person "debriefing" session later. Notes done in this fashion can be very effective, and the presence of the pad and pencil does not get in the way of what is being observed, either to the researcher or to the informants. Either way, the content of notes should include both a kind of running description of what has been seen, along with first-impression interpretations as they come to mind. Some persons would argue that interpretation ought to come later, but this misconstrues the relationship between the observer and the observed. Much of what is seen is tied to interpretation, and the field researcher who does not interpret will not "see" much of what is going on. The recording of such interpretations can also be useful later when the analysis of the notes will inevitably show a time sequence in which the observer's own reactions can be assessed along with what has been observed. Some things appear to be one thing at first and are later revealed to be something else. Without a record of the researcher's initial interpretations, such movements cannot be documented.

Making a full set of field notes is a time-consuming process. For every hour spent in the field observing, as many as three hours may be spent constructing notes that will be useful later in the analysis. Usually the researcher will want to begin by reconstructing events as they were seen and heard. These should be accompanied by analytical interpretations, which will almost always come to mind as the notes are being constructed. Most people who write about their work in the field also feel strongly that a set of field notes ought to include their own personal impressions and feelings. Obviously, researchers are also participants of one kind or another, and therefore their own feelings are important parts of the data being collected. Such information can be extremely useful, both in putting together the analysis itself and in communicating to future audiences the nature of the work. (Audiences often want to know as much about the personal feelings and emotions of the researcher as about the findings of the study.) This is legitimate territory, and investigators would be remiss if they ignored it.

A Note on the Use of Tape Recorders

Much of the tediousness of field research can be minimized by the use of any of the small tape recorders now available at modest cost. With certain cautions in mind, they can speed up virtually every stage of the research process, from doing part of the listening for the researcher, to acting as note-taking machines in place of a pad and pencil, to being a check against faulty memory later when the data is being analyzed.

For the purpose of recording the sounds that occur naturally in the field, a tape recorder can be invaluable. Later, sights that accompanied the sounds will be easy to recall while listening to the tape, and not as much will be lost as would be with a notebook. The tape recorder need be no more intrusive than a pad and pencil; in fact, we have often found that it is less intrusive because the researcher can give full attention to what is going on without having to stop and write on the pad.

The problem with tape recorders, of course, has to do with the inhibiting effect they sometimes have on participants. In the post-Watergate era, the tape recorder is suspect in many settings, especially bureaucratic ones, and this must be assessed very carefully before the researcher tries to employ the device. If fields of activity that involve deviant or even criminal activity are the site of the research, obviously tape recorders can be threatening and even the suggestion of their use can jeopardize the entire project.

Good sense should dictate the choice of whether to tape or not, and ordinarily the researcher will want to request permission from hosts before taping for any purpose at all. Sometimes the recorder can be used for interviewing specific events but permission to tape the sounds of ongoing activities will be denied; at other times the reverse situation obtains. Either way, getting permission beforehand is the sensible way to avoid difficulties later.

Although using the tape recorder for interviews is convenient, beware of turning it into a substitute for other research skills. Good interviewing involves asking the timely and trenchant question, being sensitive to the concerns of the informant, listening to what the person has to say, and so on. The tape recorder obviously does none of this for you; it is merely a device to facilitate recall later, once you have done all of these things well during the conduct of the interview.

After interviews are conducted or research sites are observed, the tape recorder can come into its own even more as an adjunct to the research process. For example, many research sites involve travel from where the researcher is located, and we have often dictated observations (in effect, a set of field notes) into the recorder on the way home. This does two things. First, it avoids much of the drudgery of paper-and-pencil note-taking after observations have been made. Second, it ordinarily makes it easy to put together the notes, observations, feelings, and impressions very shortly after they were made. When played back later, these impressions and observations can be invaluable during the analysis and writing phases of the research. Some field researchers like to transcribe their tapes later (especially if they have secretarial assistance!), and it can be helpful to see on paper what is heard on the tape. We do not feel, however, that the researcher should rely on transcriptions alone, especially on tapes made by someone else, for tone of voice, inflection, background noise and remarks, as well as a host of other factors can qualify written words in a variety of ways that might well be lost if the researcher merely read the transcripts. Transcribing can be tedious and expensive work, however, and this must be weighed against the sometimes marginal benefits of having a fully written record of what is on the tapes.

Different Types of Notes

Schatzman and Strauss suggest that field notes are of three different types, possibly contained within the same set, but analytically distinct enough to deserve different types of designations. These three types are observational notes, theoretical notes, and methodological notes (1973, 100–101).

Observational notes are statements that describe events experienced primarily through watching and listening. They are not designed to interpret as yet, but merely capture as much as possible what is being said and done in the presence of the participant observer. The observational note is basically organized around the Burkian pentad of Who?, What?, Where?, When?, How?, and Why?, as mentioned earlier. It may be an observation of an episode, an extended interaction, or some other happening, but it is to be recorded as accurately as it happened as possible. Obviously, if we use a tape recorder, the tape captures much of this, though some details may need to be filled in by the researcher augmenting the taped record with experiences that are not auditory. The observational note can be a paraphrasing, but more often it is a literal recording of exact words, phrases, and important statements made by participants in a scene being studied.

Theoretical notes, in effect, are notes the researchers make to themselves about the importance of what they have seen as they observe. They are attempts to derive the meaning of what is seen as it is experienced for the analytical purposes the researchers have in mind. It is the note that records the sparkling insight, the link between analytical inference and basic data. The theoretical note might contain hypotheses to be supported or refuted later, tentative interpretations, suggested conclusions, or the wildest of speculations. Here the investigators are talking to themselves about the analysis that, after all, is the purpose of the study, and, unlike the observational note, it may or may not make sense if shared with the persons being studied.

Methodological notes are statements that "keep house" on the study being conducted. They are notes to the researcher to do this or that, how to proceed next, whom to interview when, what to look for where, and so forth. They are also, importantly, notes that try to record the researcher's own role in the study, and this is important because the field study, more than any other types of sociological investigation, must be reflective about its own involvement in the research process. Because the researcher is also a participant, leaving this important set of observations out of the study would do violence to the whole concept of doing social science in this way.

Files, Files, and More Files

As field research is going on, the researcher will be collecting not only notes, but also other material that will be important in analyzing and writing the results of the research. These materials include documents and written data from or about the scene being studied, tables, charts, graphs, newspaper clippings, articles, tapes, and anything else that bears on the research. These can then be filed according to concepts, topics, analytical uses, relation to other data, and the like.

In addition to various types of files, we have found that a useful piece of information to keep when doing field research is a log. This log would be a chronology of events from the first time the research began to percolate in the mind of the researcher to the finished product. This "biography" of the project itself is extremely useful, for it gives both practical and intellectual time sequences for all the major events in the research. The log can then be drawn on heavily for both analysis and writing, as well as for interesting postscriptive uses after the research is over.

The Analysis of Qualitative Data

How do researchers organize this mass of data they have accumulated, this flotsam and jetsam of experience, into some coherent picture of the world being studied? This is what analysis is all about, and it is, without question, the most difficult part of qualitative research. Unfortunately, it is not really possible to set down on paper a step-by-step operational procedure that will produce qualitative analysis. Unlike quantitative research, field research does not lend itself to that sort of certainty. For that reason, our discussion will be more on the order of tips and hints, understanding full well that a researcher's own project and the contingencies built into it will in large measure determine the exact nature of the analysis. Because qualitative data are experiential and definitional, standard measures and highly controlled processes of analysis are not possible. We sound apologetic at this point, but the reader should not really get that impression. Field research is a calculated strategy to give up precise, quantified rigor in exchange for grounded insights that, at their best, sparkle with meaning. Field research, then, looks for different kinds of things and finds them through different kinds of strategies. The fact that the analysis cannot be done so patly (although analysis is seldom pat even in quantitative analysis) is not a liability, but rather a strength. It is a measure of what priorities we have set and what assumptions we have made in charting a particular research course.

Given that analysis cannot be very cut-and-dried in qualitative research, what nevertheless do the researchers do when they reach this stage of the project? To begin, they will look for naturally occurring classes of things, persons, and events, and the properties that characterize them. In short, they will look for similarities and dissimilarities: the ways in which data begin to stack up as alike or different. At first, they will want to use these naturally occurring categories to make simple statements, which can later be abstracted as much as necessary into larger propositions. The files we created earlier come into play here. What the researchers will want to do early in the process is to shuffle the data as many different ways as possible, until similarities begin to fall out and hidden relationships become revealed. There is much serendipity in all of this, and it is not unlikely that the more the researchers look, the more different things will emerge from the same batch of data.

Naturally occurring categories are to be found in all data. For example, in Erving Goffman's field study of mental patients and mental hospitals, it became clear early in the study that his problem—the process by which persons become identified as mentally ill and what happens to them after they have been identified as such—could be understood in terms of four basic analytical categories into which his data naturally fell. He talked of these as various phases of the career of the mental patient: the pre-patient, in-patient, post-patient, and re-patient phases. They dealt, in turn, with how a person comes to be a mental patient, what happens to him after he is admitted to a mental hospital, what is involved with being an ex-mental patient, and what happens to the patient who is re-admitted after having already once been in a mental hospital. These phases of the patient career fell out of the data rather naturally; all it took to recognize them was a perceptive researcher who, after spending a long time in the field, could see these naturally occurring phases in terms of an analytical problem that emerged early in the study (Goffman 1981).

A variety of concepts that are involved in all human relationships can also be used to tease out of data particular characteristics that bear on a problem. For example, the ideas of hierarchies, formal and informal relationships, time sequences, subordinate and superordinate relationships, personal and impersonal relationships—all can be useful ways of finding out if a set of data is concealing information pertinent to a line of inquiry.

We have sometimes talked about field research primarily as though a single researcher were involved in a single project. We have done this for the sake of simplicity of presentation, but often research is done by members of teams, and during the phases of analysis we are discussing here, the advantages of having several people on the team really come to the fore. Here members of the research team can talk with one another about what kinds of naturally occurring events they believe the data fall into, and the observations of one will often spark a dialogue that will result in a process of cross-fertilization as enormous insights are generated.

In the absence of a team of colleagues to discuss the data with (or even in addition to them), a researcher will often do what Schatzman and Strauss call audience conjuring. That is, he or she will mentally create an audience to talk with, even to the point of beginning the writing with a particular audience in mind to whom the researcher wishes to communicate. By engaging in this kind of dialogue early on, one can level out of data relationships that might remain obscure if the dialogue were totally with oneself.

Somewhere in the process of analyzing data, the researcher might also want to try his or her ideas out on a live audience. This can be a relatively simple matter if the researcher (as is typically the case) also happens to be a member of the academic community, for there are all sorts of forums available for the presentation of work-in-progress. Meetings, seminars, symposia, or simply classes one is teaching can be useful forums for such presentations. The feedback can be invaluable, although the researcher, knowing what he or she is doing best, will not want to be open to just any idea, but rather to those that fit the style and methodology of field research the best. Knowledgeable colleagues who are attuned to the type of research you are doing will be the best sources, but the comments of all can be useful either to give new ideas or to confirm old perceptions and lines of analysis.

The data must be constantly consulted during the analytical phases to discover whether they are really saying what you think they are saying. Other people can be helpful in this process, but in the final analysis, you, the researcher, must rely on your own senses, especially in view of the fact that you, not someone else, were the observer in the project. An important audience to eventually check one's analysis against is members of the group or scene where the observations were done in the first place. Some researchers talk about this as "host verification," while others speak of the "membership test of validity." Either way, the important thing is to remember that while any given member of the group being studied may not understand all the purposes of the research, they can tell you whether or not you have captured the essence of a scene and in what important respects you have missed significant aspects of what you have studied. We would not go so far as to say that a negative response from a host should disqualify the analysis, but we do feel that the researcher should take such responses seriously and know exactly why they are being discarded in favor of some perception held by the researcher.

Clearly, if the people you have studied do not even recognize what you are saying about them and the world they inhabit, some or all of the study ought to go back to the drawing boards. This is not to say, of course, that there will be a one-to-one correspondence between their experience of the world and the investigator's rendering of it. There are good reasons for such a disparity, for the framework of social science research is essentially different from a framework used by persons in everyday life. On the other hand, as we said before, the researcher ought to be confident that he or she knows exactly why there exists a disparity and be able to account for that as well as congruence between the study and the studied.

Strategies for Writing

Good field research is written in a lively, engaging manner, and it is unlikely that a poor writer will ever make a good field researcher unless he or she has considerable help from members of a research team who do know how to write. Unfortunately, like many of the other skills associated with qualitative research we have discussed in this chapter, good writing ability is difficult to teach, and a person often either has it or doesn't.

Yet, the sheer excitement of being involved in important field research can be a tremendous stimulus to good writing. Every conceivable type of writing style can be found among field researchers, but the important thread that runs through all of them is that they have the capacity to reproduce in the reader a sense of being "there" and of knowing far more about the phenomenon than he or she did before he read the research.

Some people write methodically as the research unfolds; others do best when they are up against deadlines and must produce a large volume of materials in a hurry. Either way, one has to recognize how one's best work is done and then conduct the writing in harmony with one's own style. For people who have a difficult time writing, their research often suffers from what John Lofland calls "analytic interruptus," a premature closing off of the research process because they just could not get it down on paper the right way. We feel that writing skills are best developed in use and the researcher needs to write, even if the finished product is not acceptable on first or even later drafts. The most encouraging news we can offer about the writing problem is that it seems to get easier the more you do it, and the difficulties are offset frequently by exhilaration when it comes out right:

> It [writing] may be accompanied by moodiness, irritability, despair, or even existential crisis. But take heart—it can also be punctuated by profound moments of sudden insight, by the rushing release and coalescence of ideas, and by intense excitement, such that one works almost around the clock for days on end, unable to stop. Such experiences are sometimes called "writing highs" and may not be dissimilar to other kinds of "highs." (Lofland 1971, 14)

Some researchers find writing difficult because they simply cannot let go of the project. Writing necessarily involves some sense of moving toward a conclusion, and obviously when a researcher finally publishes a study, he or she is going to be held responsible for its quality. We know any number of scholars who, for this reason, polish work practically forever, accomplishing either very little or sometimes nothing at all because they simply could not let go of the project. Another problem with social science research is that it is often dated so quickly, so the researcher is reluctant to let it go before getting that last bit of fresh material. Unfortunately, this is typically a no-win situation, and at some point the analysis must be closed off and published.

ETHICAL ISSUES IN FIELD RESEARCH

Because all social research occurs within a social environment, it is intensely and inherently ethical. The traditional view in the sciences that scientific activity is itself neither moral or immoral but rather amoral has taken something of a beating in recent years. Even though one can make a case for that fact that "pure" scientific procedures are not in and of themselves moral questions, the uses of such research and the researchers themselves are intensely moral, so much so that any such theoretical distinction seems almost beside the point. The best possible safeguard against the immoral and unethical uses of social science research is constant awareness of the possible compromises where and when they occur. During the earliest stages of the research process, when plans are being formulated and strategies are being conceived, is the best time to consider the ethics of the research. Then, all during the process, we will want to monitor our conduct with this in mind.

As we have already indicated, the best strategy is honesty with persons who are being observed in field studies. To make clear in general terms what the study is about and what the researcher wishes to acquire is both good social science and elementary courtesy. We cannot really conceive of a legitimate research question that would necessitate deception and could not be gotten through honesty. In a comment on the use of disguised observation in sociology, Erikson echoes our feeling:

> It is unethical for a sociologist to deliberately misrepresent his identity for the purpose of entering a private domain to which he is not otherwise eligible; that is, it is unethical for a sociologist to deliberately misrepresent the character of research in which he is engaged. (1967, 372)

Erikson closes with an additional reason why we should not deceive people we are studying, and it is a sentiment we also share: "It seems to me that any attempt to use masquerades in social research betrays an extraordinary disrespect for the complexities of human interaction, and for this reason can only lead to bad science."

Chapter 11

Data Reduction and Organization

The meaning of datum/data
Why we organize and reduce data
The role of the computer in data reduction
An introduction to the computer
Preparing the data for computer input
  Coding the data
  Developing a codebook
    Deciding on numeric codes
    General requirements
  Coding nonstandard responses
  Checking for coder reliability
  Coding missing data and nonresponses

Formatting the data for computer input
Keypunching the data
  The transfer sheet
  Edge coding
  Optical scanning sheets
  Direct keyboard entry
Editing the data for errors
  Possible punch cleaning
  Contingency cleaning
Storing the data

Simplify, simplify.
—Henry David Thoreau

Rhonda Reason is a junior sociology major taking Methods of Social Research. Since course requirements include conducting a term research project, Rhonda has been keeping her eyes and ears peeled for a research question. After several weeks of looking, listening, reading, and thinking, Rhonda has become interested in whether or not males and females choose sociology as a major for the same or different reasons. Rhonda begins by formulating her research question: "Are males' and females' reasons for majoring in sociology the same or different?" Rhonda then goes to the library to do a more extensive search of existing literature. After several sessions with a variety of books and journals, Rhonda formulates a theoretical position and a hypothesis that suggests that males' and females' reasons for majoring in sociology are not different. Now it is time to devise a test of this hypothesis. After careful and thoughtful evaluation, Rhonda decides to use the survey design. With decisions made on how to measure each variable, Rhonda constructs her questionnaire. The questionnaire covers a lot of territory: personal information (age, sex, race, marital status, father's occupation, mother's occupation, etc.); attitudes toward people, work, and sociology; previous majors and double majors; and reasons for majoring in sociology, just to name a few. In fact, Rhonda's questionnaire consists of exactly fifty questions. Now Rhonda must decide *whom* she will ask to fill out this questionnaire. Ideally, she would like to solicit the help of all sociology majors. But with 875 majors, this admirable plan would cost too much in time and money. So Rhonda decides to draw a random sample of 400 majors and mail each selected major a copy of her questionnaire along with explicit instructions on how to complete it. Although 400 may seem like a somewhat ambitious number, Rhonda knows about poor return rates from mail questionnaires. Even so, she is hoping for a 50 percent return on the 400 questionnaires mailed out. In due time (and after two follow-ups), Rhonda does receive 150 questionnaires—not as good as she had hoped, but typical of mail questionnaires!

THE MEANING OF DATUM/DATA

What Rhonda has stacked in front of her are known in the social science world as *data*. In the social sciences, we use the term *data* to refer to any observations or information collected during the research process. We should distinguish, at this point, between *datum* and *data*. *Datum* is the singular of *data*. The term *datum* is used to refer to any single observation or any single piece of information—a subject's age, a subject's sex. Generally speaking, we are concerned with many observations or many pieces of information. Hence, we generally use the term *data*. Rhonda, for example, has 150 questionnaires, each with fifty pieces of information. That multiplies out to 7,500 pieces of information. And these 7,500 pieces of information comprise Rhonda's data.

WHY WE ORGANIZE AND REDUCE DATA

You may not have conducted a survey like Rhonda's, but if you have completed the data collection phase of your research project (whether survey, experiment, or field study), you also should have in your possession a collection of information, and this collection of information represents your data. And the imminent question now becomes, "What's next?" To answer this question for both you and Rhonda, let's take a look at some of the options available to Rhonda. She could begin by reading through the 150 returned questionnaires, and when she has finished, she will have read all 7,500 pieces of information. Though this option is admirable, if she were to choose it, what would she really know? How much of the information could we expect her to retain? Would she have a tendency to remember those pieces of information which support her hypothesis and forget those which do not? Perhaps it goes without saying that this is not the most plausible option for either Rhonda or you to adopt. Rhonda could also begin by grouping like pieces of information together. Of the 7,500 pieces of information, for example, 150 represent age. Another 150 (each) represent marital status, sex, race, and so on. If Rhonda were to organize her data by variables, she would be constructing a number of distributions—in fact, one for each variable. A *distribution* is simply a listing of all values for some designated variable. To illustrate, the distribution of ages would consist of the 150 values representing age—one for each subject unless, of course, someone did not answer this question. Since Rhonda has fifty variables, she also has fifty distinct distributions. But even with these kinds of groupings, there still remains more information than Rhonda can make sense of. And with fifty distinct groupings, Rhonda would lose the ability to examine two variables in relation to each other. While Rhonda could examine the distribution of ages and the distribution of males and females, for example, she could not examine the distribution of ages for males apart from the distribution of ages for females.

While it might be possible to identify some merit in both of the above methods, what Rhonda really needs is an even better method—one that will permit her to organize and reduce the data to a more meaningful and intepretable level. One plausible procedure for accomplishing the desired level of organization and reduction is to put the data in *matrix form*. Suppose, for example, Rhonda were to take a large piece of paper (about the size of poster board) and label fifty columns across the top, one for each variable. Then she numbers 150 rows, one for each subject. If she now copies her data from the questionnaires onto this piece of paper, she will have transformed her data to matrix form, where each row represents a subject and each column in that row represents a variable response belonging to that subject. The data might appear as in Figure 11.1. While Rhonda still has fifty distributions since each column (variable) is a distribution, she can also identify smaller distributions—the distribution of females' ages or the distribution of males' ages. By now you should begin to see that data organization and reduction is a method of transforming data in order to facilitate the search for meaningful patterns. Without data organization and reduction, data would remain an overwhelming and meaningless mass of information.

**FIGURE 11.1
Rhonda's Data Matrix**

?#	Age	Sex	MS	Father's Occ.	Mother's Occ.	Reasons/Major
001	21	F	S	history teacher	librarian	Like to work with people
002	18	M	S	carpenter	housewife	Because of interest in aging.
003	19	M	M	minister	housewife	Complement psychology major.
004	20	F	M	accountant	pharmacist	Not sure.
005	20	F	S	professor	math teacher	Understand self better.
006	21	M	S	lawyer	housewife	Like to work with people.
007	18	F	M	doctor	doctor	Have an interest in marriage/family counseling.
008	19	M	S	electrician	housewife	Want to go into counseling.
009	20	M	S	lawyer	lawyer	Want to go into counseling.
010	23	M	M	doctor	lawyer	Tried everything else.
.						
.						
.						
200	24	F	M	lawyer	professor	Like to work with people.

THE ROLE OF THE COMPUTER IN DATA REDUCTION

Let's consider for just a moment the steps that Rhonda might go through in order to compute the average age of her sample, using only her hands, eyes, and brain. Rhonda begins by reading the age on the first questionnaire (the questionnaire numbered 001) and remembering this numeric value. In other words, Rhonda *reads* this value and stores it in her *memory*. Now Rhonda reads the age written on the second questionnaire. But instead of storing this age in memory, Rhonda decides to add its value to the first age and store their sum. You see, Rhonda has already determined that she cannot quickly and efficiently memorize 150 ages and then add these ages together. So she begins with a sum of zero, reads into memory the first age, and adds that age to her initial sum (zero). The sum, at this point, is really just the first age (0 + first age = first age). This sum is then stored in memory, and Rhonda reads the second age. This second age is added to the sum, and the new sum is stored in memory. Now Rhonda reads the third age and adds its value to the current sum. This process is repeated 150 times since Rhonda has 150 ages. Once all ages have been input, Rhonda divides the sum by 150 to obtain the average age, and this value is *output*—perhaps written down. This process has been diagramed for you in Figure 11.2.

Can you imagine what data organization and reduction would be like if the only tools at your disposal were your hands, eyes, and brain? Computing the average age for Rhonda's 150 respondents turned out to be quite a task. But suppose Rhonda now decides to compute the average age for males and then the average age for females. She would first have to sort the 150 ages into two distributions—ages belonging to males and ages belonging to females (a fairly simple task using her data matrix)—and then compute the average age of each distribution. Now let's further suppose that Rhonda needs to know the average age by marital status, race, and college classification. The sorting process must begin again for each of these variables before average age can be computed. The sorting possibilities for age alone are endless, not to mention the sorting process for other variables (average income, occupational prestige, and GPA by sex, marital status, college classification, etc.) with which we might do this very same thing.

In a nutshell, data organization and reduction with only our hands, eyes, and brain would be extremely time-consuming and laborious. In addition, human beings engaging in such tasks are highly susceptible to fatigue and boredom, and both of these factors are likely to result in increased errors. Rhonda can compute the average age of her sample by adding up all the ages and dividing the sum by 150. But the more averages Rhonda computes, the more likely she is to make a mistake. Even if Rhonda were to use a calculator to help her brain, the numbers would have to be entered into the calculator for each average computed. And with each value entered, the potential for error increases.

**FIGURE 11.2
Diagram of Steps Needed to Compute an Average**

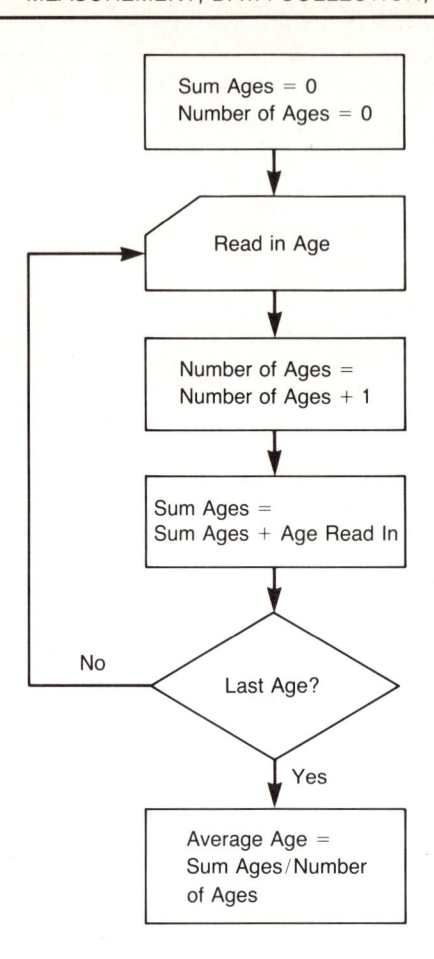

```
Sum Ages = 0
Number of Ages = 0
        ↓
   Read in Age  ←──────┐
        ↓              │
Number of Ages =       │
Number of Ages + 1     │
        ↓              │
Sum Ages =             │
Sum Ages + Age Read In │
        ↓              │
     Last Age? ── No ──┘
        │
       Yes
        ↓
Average Age =
Sum Ages/Number
of Ages
```

With the advent of the computer age, data analysis in research has taken on an entirely new meaning. Computers are very good at repetitive tasks like sorting and adding, the same tasks that cost you and me increasingly higher error with each repetition. What's more, computers can work at incredibly high speeds—speeds that no human can approach—and they can do this without sacrificing accuracy. To be more precise, computers can compute at speeds approaching one-fourth the speed of light! This speed is so incomprehensible to the human mind that someone has described it with this comparison: If you were interacting with a computer—you giving the computer data, the computer giving you data, back and forth—it would take you each time, in the computer's time frame, *eight years* to respond!

Despite the extraordinary nature of these marvelous machines, computers are not loved by all—not even by all social scientists! There are some people who have always feared that computers would take over the world. Remember the movie *2001*? The only villain was HAL the computer. While this early image still lingers with us, it is an image which needs to be dispelled. The fact is that a computer is not really a machine to be feared. In actuality, a computer is a very simple-minded machine. It knows only two things: yes and no. You see, a computer is just an intricate pattern of circuits that are either opened or closed, representing yes or no. Anything else a computer "knows" is the result of human programming. If you think you have caught the computer in an error, you probably need to think again. Since computers are programmed by humans, they do exactly what humans tell them to do.

To a social scientist, the computer, with its ability to perform repetitive tasks at incredibly high speeds, can be an invaluable tool. Complex analyses of both large and small data sets that were heretofore impossible have now become run-of-the-mill. Complex analyses that might have taken months, even years, can now be done within minutes or hours. With the aid of the computer, social scientists can examine their data more carefully and more thoroughly than ever before thought possible. In reality, the marvel of the computer lies not in any power it holds for itself but rather in the power it can give to those of us who are willing to use it in our research.

AN INTRODUCTION TO THE COMPUTER

Since computers are programmed by humans, it should come as no surprise to learn that they work very much like the human brain. Let's recall for a moment the steps that Rhonda went through in order to compute the average age of her sample. The ages were *input* one at a time into her *memory*. Once in memory, a *control center* triggered another part of her brain to do some *arithmetic*. Once the arithmetic was done, another age was read in. When all 150 ages had been read into memory, a control center triggered the final arithmetic operation, and the answer was *output*. The basic components of a computer are the same as those used by Rhonda's brain to compute average age: (1) memory, (2) control unit, (3) arithmetic–logic unit, and (4) input–output (i/o) unit. A diagram of these four components is given in Figure 11.3. It is these four components that communicate with one another to process data. Let's take a brief look at each.

The *memory* is that part of the computer where data are stored. Most memories contain thousands of locations that are capable of storing thousands of pieces of information. Generally speaking, two types of information are stored in a computer's memory. The first type of information you are already familiar with: it is the data (represented in matrix form) to be analyzed. The second type of information stored in a computer's memory is a set of instructions or codes that tell the computer

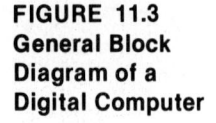

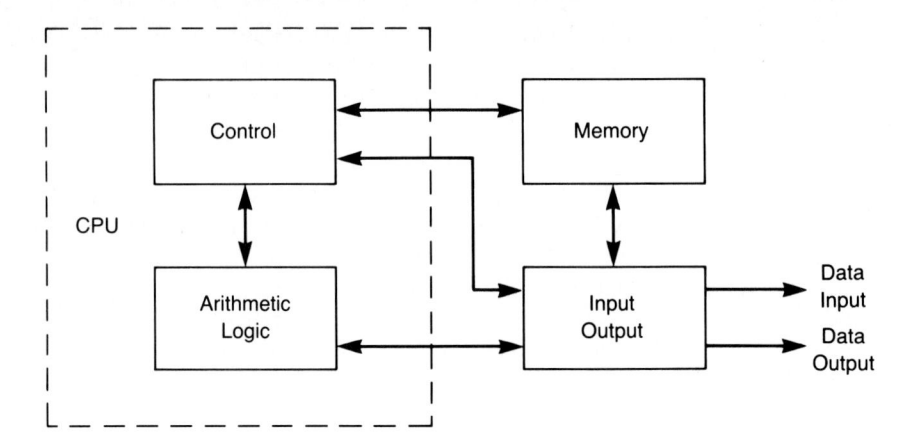

**FIGURE 11.3
General Block
Diagram of a
Digital Computer**

what to do with the data. Instructions, for example, may tell the computer how to sort the data or how to compute an average (e.g., average age). When instructions tell the computer what to do with the data, they are labeled a *program*. In other words, a program is a sequence of instructions that causes data to be processed in some unique way. Both types of information (programs and data) are stored in the computer's memory.

The *control unit* is that part of a computer which is responsible for a program's being executed automatically without outside help. More specifically, the control unit sequentially examines the instructions in a program and issues signals to other sections of the computer, which carry out the instructions. Each instruction is retrieved from memory by the control unit, interpreted, and then executed one at a time until the program is completed. As each instruction is examined or decoded, the control unit generates timing and control signals that tell other sections of the computer what to do to carry out the operation specified by the control unit.

The *arithmetic-logic unit* is that section of the computer that actually processes the data. Two main types of processing are carried out: arithmetic operations, such as addition and division, and logic operations, such as AND and OR. For example, if we wanted to identify married females, we would ask the computer to sort out those cases where sex equals female AND marital status equals married. If we also wanted to compute the average age of these respondents, we would store the appropriate "add" and "divide" instructions in memory. The control unit would then retrieve each instruction, interpret each, and send signals to the arithmetic-logic unit that would result in the ages being added together and their sum being subsequently divided by the number of ages. The control section and the arithmetic-logic unit are very closely related. They operate together and are often viewed as a single unit. When the control unit and the arithmetic-logic unit are thought of as one, we use the term *central processing unit* (CPU). In other words, the CPU is the control unit and the arithmetic–logic unit combined.

The *input/output (i/o)* section of a computer is the set of logic circuits that permits the central processing unit and the memory to communicate with the outside world. All information that transfers into and out of the computer must pass through the i/o section. The i/o acts as an interface between the computer and any device that permits input and/or output. And there are a wide variety of input and output devices. Data may be entered into the computer, for example, through a typewriterlike *keyboard*. Data can also be entered using *cards, disks,* and *magnetic tape*. Data can be output on a *cathode-ray tube* (CRT) or printed by a *typewriter*. Data can also be output to a high-speed *line printer, cards, disks,* or *magnetic tape*. You should note that input and output devices are not mutually exclusive. In fact, as you can see from this discussion, several devices can be used for both input and output.

PREPARING THE DATA FOR COMPUTER INPUT

Coding the Data

Whenever data are input into a computer for storage, analysis, and retrieval, they must be transformed into a highly condensed form in order to conserve space and simplify analysis. This transformation process is known as coding. By "coding" we mean the assignment of numbers to all data (pieces of information). If you reexamine Rhonda's data pictured in Figure 11.1, you will quickly notice that some variable responses are represented as numbers while others are represented as letters or phrases. When Rhonda recorded each respondent's age, for example, she used a number, since age is a number. On the other hand, when Rhonda recorded each respondent's sex, she used a letter, and when she recorded "primary reason for majoring in sociology," she used a phrase. Rhonda's decision to use an M or F for sex and a phrase for "primary reason" was based upon the fact that there is no clear-cut and universally understood numeric representation for these variables. Now, while Rhonda or you or I could look at her data matrix (Figure 11.1) and understand fully its contents, several response identifiers could be more efficiently represented. All primary reasons, for example, could have been coded as numbers, and these numbers could have been placed in the matrix to represent respondents' answers. This transformation of responses to numeric codes results in a highly condensed data form that conserves space and, as we shall see, simplifies data analysis. If Rhonda's data matrix were transformed to numeric form, it might appear as in Figure 11.4.

When such variables as sex, race, marital status, and college

FIGURE 11.4
Rhonda's Data Matrix in Numeric Form

?#	Age	Sex	MS	Father's Occ.	Mother's Occ.	Reasons/Major
001	21	2	2	78	47	1
002	18	1	2	39	99	2
003	19	1	1	69	99	1
004	20	2	1	57	61	4
005	20	2	2	78	78	5
006	21	1	2	76	78	1
007	18	2	1	82	82	6
008	19	1	2	49	99	7
009	20	1	2	76	76	7
010	23	1	1	82	76	8
.						
.						
.						
.						
.						
200	24	2	1	76	78	1

classification are to have some numeric representation, then we must assign it. A conventional procedure in the social sciences for coding sex, for example, is to code males as 1 and females as 2. Please notice that these numbers do not mean anything mathematical. They are simply being used to identify or designate a person's sex. Now you might want to reason that using a one-digit number to code sex is really no more conservative or efficient than using M or F. While it is true that alphabetical codes are sometimes used to represent response alternatives, they are *not* recommended. When alpha (alphabetical) codes are used, they eventually have to be transformed to numeric codes for purposes of data analysis since most statistical software (i.e., statistical programs—instructions) has been written to expect numeric input. Hence to eliminate one unnecessary step and thus simplify data analysis, it is preferable to code all data with numbers.

Developing a Codebook

Before coding any data, the trained researcher will begin by developing a codebook. The codebook is an outline of what is to be coded and how it is to be coded. It is a list of variables and the numeric values being used to represent each variable response. Let's face it, researchers are human and they do forget things. When 1 means 1 as in age, there is no problem with memory. But when 1 means ''male'' (as in sex) or ''I like to work with people'' (as in primary reason for major), there may be a memory problem. If you set your data aside for four weeks, will you remember that 1 represents "male" or that 1 represents "I like to work with people"? The codebook provides you with written instructions for transforming each variable response into a numeric value and serves as documentation for what you have done.

Deciding on Numeric Codes. How do you decide on the numeric codes to be used? First, you will probably look to convention and note how these same variables have been coded in past research. In addition, you should consider your own theory and hypotheses to be tested. As a general rule of thumb, it is preferable to code all variables at the highest level of measurement possible. If, in the process of data analysis, you find you need to regroup and recode a variable, it will be easy to do so. Suppose, for example, you are interested in studying some facet of socialization throughout the various life stages—infancy, childhood, adolescence, young adulthood. Instead of coding actual age, you decide to code each subject into one of these life stages. In effect, you define an age range for each life stage and code your subjects on the basis of their ages. If, in the course of analyzing your data, you decided to alter the age ranges defining each life stage and thereby also alter the life stage into which some subjects fall, you would not be able to do it. If you had coded age initially, you could now play with the ranges as much as you liked. In other words, coding your data at the highest possible level of measurement will give you the greatest flexibility in your data analysis.

General Requirements. In developing the coding scheme for your set of variables, two general requirements must be met. First, your coding categories must be mutually exclusive. That is, there should be *no* values that could be coded in more than one category. Second, your coding categories must be logically exhaustive. That is, they should allow for classification of *all* categories or values that appear in the study. No category or value identified through the study should be omitted or left out. Let's examine these characteristics more closely by again looking at Rhonda's data. Two of the questions on Rhonda's questionnaire are:

1. What is your sex?   (1) male   (2) female
2. What is your primary reason for majoring in sociology?

If you look closely at these two questions, you will notice that they are really very different. Whereas the first question has two response alternatives from which each subject must choose, the second question has none. Recall from Chapter 9 that the first question is a closed-ended question; the second is an open-ended question. Closed-ended questions are *precoded*—that is, the response alternatives and their assigned numerical values are determined before the data are collected. Variables like sex, race, marital status, and education are usually precoded. Open-ended questions, on the other hand, are not often precoded primarily because we do not know what the range of response alternatives will be. Instead, open-ended questions are *postcoded*—that is, the response alternatives and their assigned numerical values are determined after the data are collected and after we have had a chance to view the response alternatives given. Postcoding requires that you read through all answers received on an open-ended question and develop a categorical scheme for those answers. Rhonda's question, for example, on "primary reason for majoring in sociology" is going to require postcoding since there is really no way that Rhonda can determine prior to data collection all the various responses that will be given. Hence this question and similar questions will require a close examination of the data once the data are collected.

Coding Nonstandard Responses

Despite the care and energy invested in developing the codebook and despite the type of questions asked (precoded or postcoded), there will probably be some respondents who give answers that seem to defy the categories and coding scheme. To standardize coding and reduce error associated with unexpected responses, it is a good idea to let one person (someone designated as *editor*) go through the questionnaires and edit the data—that is, make coding decisions on all nonstandard answers. If there is a great deal of data and it would be too time-consuming to have one individual examine each questionnaire, then the editor should be on hand as the questionnaires are coded to handle such situations as they arise. In effect, the editor's job is to ensure clarity so that coders have only to make standard decisions that can clearly be based on the codebook.

Checking for Coder Reliability

Checking the reliability of coders is also a vital part of the coding process. Just as one coder should always make the same decisions about how a question is to be coded each time he or she confronts it, so should different coders always code the same responses in the same way. To ensure a high level of coder reliability, the coding staff should be thoroughly trained on all coding procedures. This training process should include some testing to determine the extent to which coders agree on how a response should be coded. In addition, it is a good idea to monitor coders at all times. Preferably monitoring should be done by the editor. We stress again, the presence of an editor will help to ensure that nonstandard responses are treated the same by all coders.

Coding Missing Data and Nonresponses

No matter how carefully your questions are constructed or how hard you try to obtain complete data, there will probably be some questions left blank by some respondents. It is a good idea to assign a specific numeric code to nonresponses since no code is really a code—a blank—and can result in error and ambiguity. And when the computer reads blanks using the same instructions it uses to read numbers, the blanks become zeros. In other words, blanks are read as zeros, and for those variables having a legitimate code of zero, nonresponses or missing data have been miscoded. Suppose, for example, one of the questions on Rhonda's questionnaire is "What is your annual income?" Since income is a sensitive question for many respondents, there will probably be several individuals who choose not to answer. There may be others who do choose to answer this question and whose income is zero dollars. If Rhonda does not code (i.e., leaves blank) nonresponses, they will be read as zeros. Hence respondents not answering this question will appear to have an income of zero dollars, and it will be impossible to separate those individuals having no real income from those refusing to answer the question.

To avoid ambiguity and this unnecessary source of error, it is a good idea to identify some numeric value or values that will represent missing data. A conventional procedure in the social sciences is to assign a 9 or a group of 9s (e.g., 99, 999, 9999) to represent missing data. The number of 9s assigned is contingent upon the largest valid code for the specified variable. Suppose, for example, you are trying to determine your missing values code for income. If the largest income reported by your respondents is $10,000, you would use 99999 to code missing data. On the other hand, if the largest income reported is $5,000, a code of 9999 would be sufficient. Each missing value code should be a number composed of 9s that is larger than the largest valid code for the specified variable.

FORMATTING THE DATA FOR COMPUTER INPUT

Once each piece of information in the data matrix has been assigned a numeric code, we are now ready to consider our data format. By *data format* we mean specification of the precise form the data will take for computer input. And these specifications are an essential part of our codebook. Of the input devices available, the most frequently used by beginning researchers is the computer *card*. Hence, we will begin our discussion of data format by taking a brief look at the computer card's design. The computer card is a heavy piece of paper that forms a matrix

**FIGURE 11.5
Computer Card**

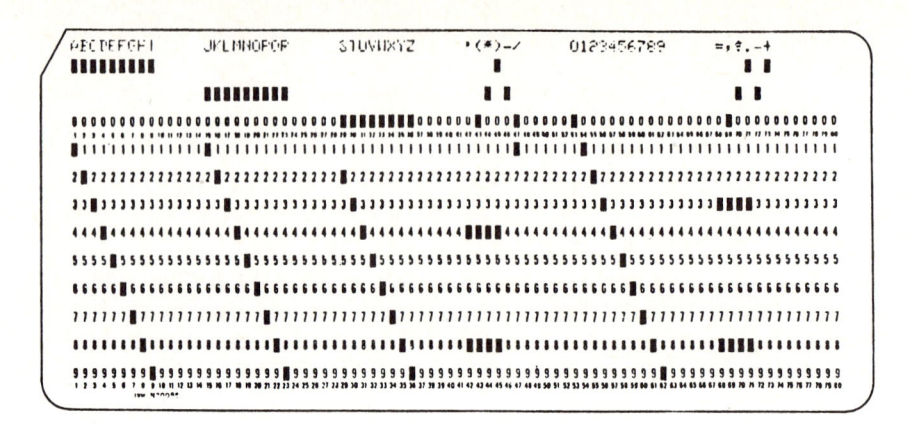

of eighty columns and twelve rows. This card is pictured in Figure 11.5. While the number of columns on this card is easily identified, the number of rows is not quite so obvious. Ten of the rows on the card are marked with the numbers 0 through 9. There are two additional, unmarked rows just above the zero row.

When holes are punched in this special card (using a keypunch machine only), it becomes readable to a computer. Each column on this card is a card location, and only one character (i.e., single-digit number, alphabetical letter, or special character) can be punched per card column. For each single-digit number (0–9), alphabetical letter, and special character, there is a predefined pattern of holes. This predefined pattern allows for any character (single-digit number, alphabet letter, or special character) to be punched into one column using one or more of the twelve rows in that column to create the appropriate punch pattern. A numeric punch, for example, is a single-hole punch. This means that there will be only one hole punched in the column you designate to store a number 0 through 9. If you want to put a 0 in column 1, only the 0 will be punched out. If you want to store a 5 in that column, only the 5 in that column will be punched out. Restated, any single digit number will consist of only a single punch. An alpha character, on the other hand, is a two-hole punch in a single column. In other words, there will always be two holes punched in any column in which you store an alphabetical character. The pattern of these two-hole alpha punches is derived by dividing the alphabet into three sets. The first nine characters in the alphabet (*A–I*) are in the first set, the second nine characters (*J–R*) in the second set, and the last eight characters (*S–Z*) in the third set. A punch in one of the first three rows (of the designated column) indicates the alphabetical set. A second punch using rows one through nine (of the designated column) indicates the alphabetical character in that set. If, for example, the letter *A* were punched in column one, we should find punches in row one (unmarked row) and row four of that column. These two punches tell us that the character punched in column one is the first letter in the first alphabetical set—or the letter *A*. Figure 11.5 also shows the punch patterns for special characters. Interestingly enough, special characters can be anywhere from a one- to a three-hole punch in the designated column. In sum, any single digit or character (alpha or special) can be punched in a single column. The computer's representation of that character will be either a single- or multiple-hole punch. In either case, the character is housed in a single column.

Suppose, for example, you wanted to store "subject's sex" in column one. If the subject is female and you are using the numeric codes of one equals male and two equals female, a hole would be keypunched in the row labeled two of column one. Since you have twelve rows for each column to use in creating the appropriate punch pattern, you can punch any single digit, alpha, or special character in any column. When variable response alternatives require more than one digit, they are coded onto computer cards by assigning a specific set of contiguous columns to a variable. A set of contiguous columns assigned to a variable is called a *field*. To keypunch an age of 37, for example, after punching the numeric code for sex in column one, we would punch a 3 in column two and a 7 in column three. Although fields may vary in width (number of columns), each must be large enough to allow one column per digit for the largest number to be coded in that field. Suppose, for example, we had one subject whose age was 102. In order to code *this* age we would need a field of three columns. This means we must reserve a specific field of three contiguous columns for age. For those subjects whose age is represented by two digits, the two digits must be *right-justified* in the field. Age 37, for example, becomes 037 or blank-37. If you fail to right-justify this age and keypunch 37-blank, the computer will read the blank as zero and you will have a respondent whose age appears to be 370!

Let's suppose you have conducted a short telephone survey, making 200 successful calls and collecting seven pieces of information per call:

1. Respondent number (questionnaire number)
2. Sex of respondent
3. Marital status
4. Age
5. Husband' education
6. Wife's education
7. TV on? (yes or no)
8. Channel

You now have in your possession 1,600 pieces of information, and in order to make some sense of this data, you must examine them for meaningful patterns. This will require data organization and reduction. Since you plan to input the data into the computer, you begin by developing a codebook. Your codebook for these variables might look like Figure 11.6. Your record length for these data is twenty-one since we have used twenty-one columns per card. Now suppose we were to keypunch all 200 surveys to computer cards and then spread these cards out as in Figure 11.7. You should notice that any given variable always occupies the same column or sequence of columns on each card. Questionnaire number, for example, is always in columns 1 to 3. Sex is always in column 5. Now, if you can imagine the card images disappearing, you are left with rows and columns of data. These rows and columns form our data matrix, where the columns identify all the variables and the rows identify the subjects. If these same data were stored on magnetic tape or disk, we would have this same matrix. Each row or line of data (on tape or disk) is the equivalent of a card image. And the column representations for disk or tape are identical to the column representations for cards. In their card image form, the data are referred to as a *deck*. In their tape or disk form, the data are referred to as a *file*.

**FIGURE 11.6
Codebook for Short Questionnaire**

Variable Name	Values	Column(s)
Questionnaire ID #	0–200	1–3
Sex of Respondent	1 = male 2 = female 9 = missing	5
Marital Status	1 = single 2 = married 3 = divorced 4 = widowed 5 = cohabit 9 = missing	7
Age	18–78 99 = missing	9–10
Husband's Education	in years 99 = missing	12–13
Wife's Education	in years 99 = missing	15–16
TV on?	1 = no 2 = yes 9 = missing	18
Channel?	1–36 99 = missing	20–21

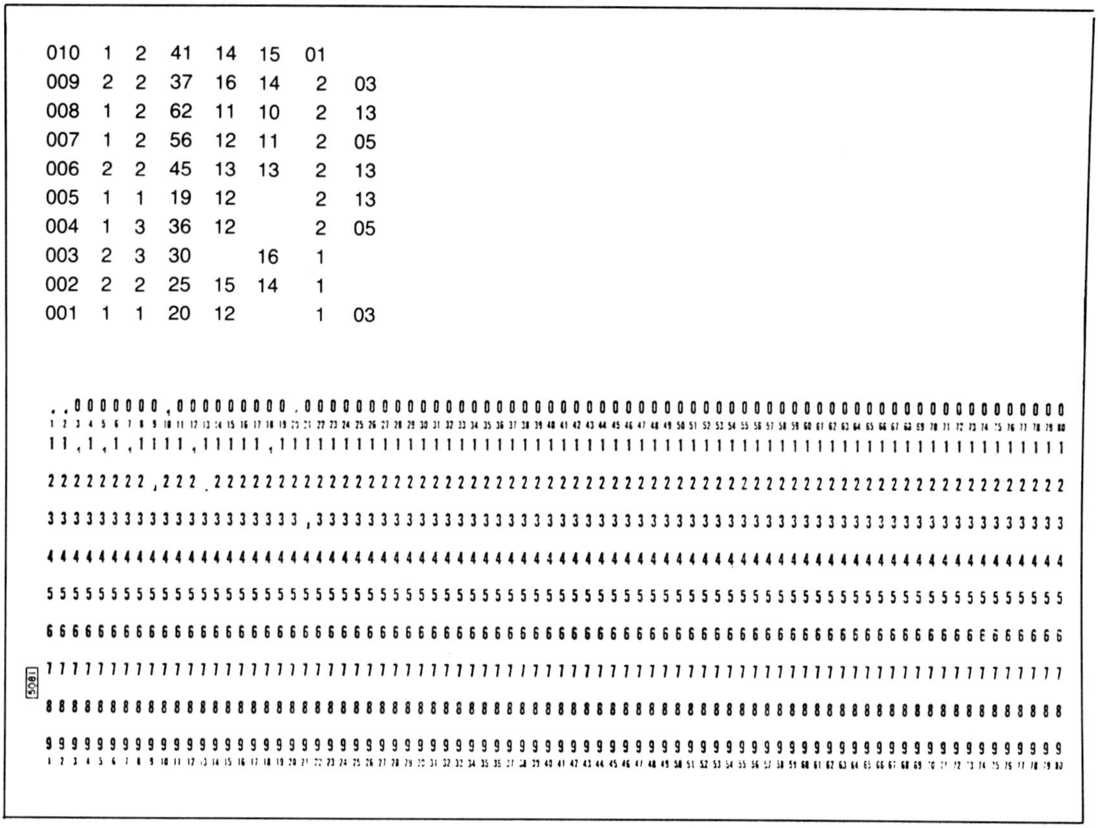

```
010  1  2  41  14  15  01
009  2  2  37  16  14  2  03
008  1  2  62  11  10  2  13
007  1  2  56  12  11  2  05
006  2  2  45  13  13  2  13
005  1  1  19  12      2  13
004  1  3  36  12      2  05
003  2  3  30      16  1
002  2  2  25  15  14  1
001  1  1  20  12      1  03
```

FIGURE 11.7
Data Matrix
Created with
Computer Cards

KEYPUNCHING THE DATA

With numeric codes assigned to all response alternatives and card space allocated, we are now ready to consider having the data keypunched. There are several ways to integrate the coding and keypunching procedures, including transfer sheets, edge coding, optical scanning sheets, direct keypunching, and direct keyboard entry.

The Transfer Sheet

The conventional method of data processing involves first writing the numeric codes on *transfer sheets (or code sheets)* and then having a keypunch operator keypunch from the transfer sheets. A transfer sheet is a sheet of paper that is ruled off in eighty columns of a computer card. Each line of a transfer sheet represents a computer card. This transfer sheet is pictured in Figure 11.8. To use a transfer sheet, you would simply write the numeric values to be keypunched onto the transfer sheet in the appropriate columns. These sheets are then given to a keypunch operator, who will punch a card for each line of data on the sheet. If, for example, you give the keypunch operator five filled transfer sheets, he or she will return to you one hundred cards (twenty cards per sheet since each line is a card equivalent).

Once the cards are keypunched, they are run through a card verifier. Although a card-verifying machine looks very much like a keypunch machine, it performs a very different task. Whereas a keypunch machine punches holes in cards, a verifier reads the holes that have been punched. The verifier operator begins the verifying process by loading the punched deck (not blank cards) into the verifier, which then simulates the repunching of the cards from the transfer sheets. If the verifier operator types a number that does not match, a red light will illuminate and the machine will come to an abrupt halt. The operator will have two more tries to match the number. If he or she fails, the card is notched over the questionable punch. All notched cards must be repunched. When all corrections have been made, the cards are returned to the researcher.

Edge Coding

One coding technique that eliminates the need for transfer sheets is edge coding. With edge coding, the card column specification for each variable (i.e., 1–80) along with a blank line are written in the outside margin of each page. Once the data are collected, the numeric codes are transferred to these spaces and the cards are punched directly from these codes.

Optical Scanning Sheets

Sometimes it is possible to print a questionnaire on a specially formatted and specially prepared form known as an optical scanning sheet. When such sheets are used, the respondents read the questions and shade in a small area (representing their choice of answers) with a number 2 pencil. These sheets are then read through a machine (optical scanner), which reads these marks and produces a punched deck. Although the use of op-

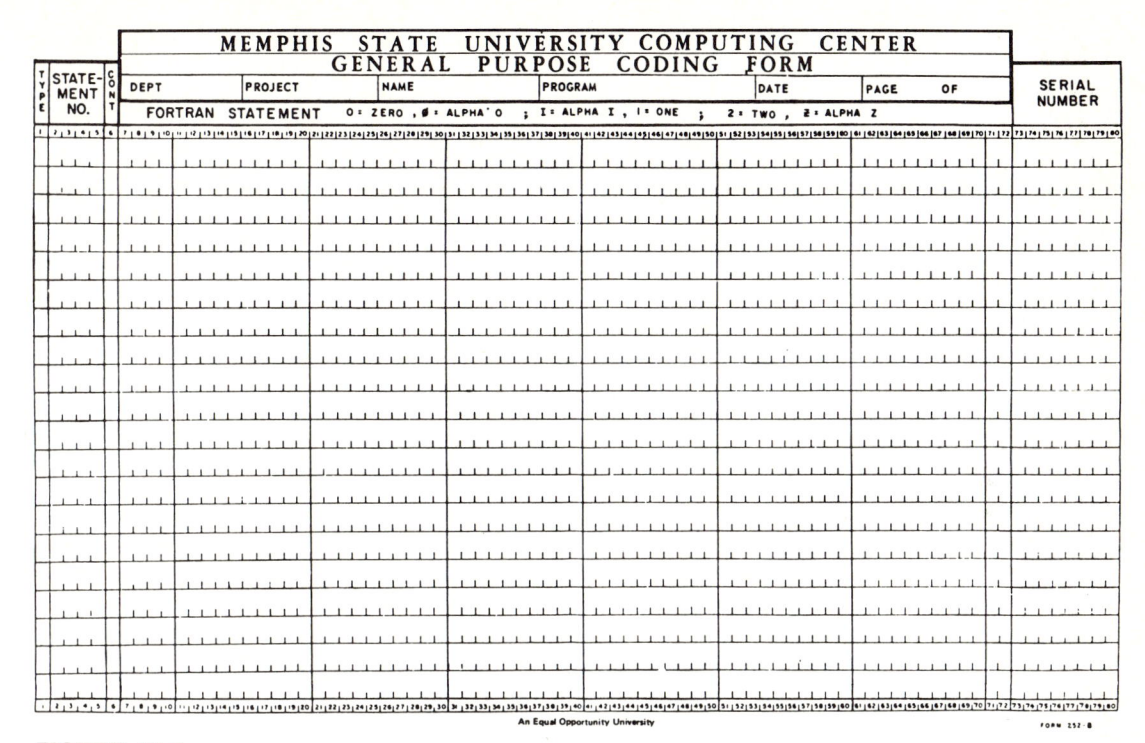

FIGURE 11.8
Transfer Sheet

tical scanning sheets is faster and more accurate, an added cost for the special forms is required. In addition, shaded areas that are only partially filled in or lightly filled in are not likely to be read. And this is a problem you will detect only after you have begun your analysis with the punched cards.

Direct Keyboard Entry

An increasingly popular and seemingly more expeditious data entry technique is direct keyboard entry. With this technique, a coder sits before a video terminal displaying a coding form. The video screen displays case one, variable name one, and prompts the coder for the numeric code. The coder keys in the code, and the screen then prompts for the code for variable two of the same case. The terminal will prompt for each variable in order until all data on the questionnaire have been entered. Once all data for that questionnaire have been entered, the data will be stored to the data file and the computer begins again—prompting for variable one, case two.

In sum, the keypunching procedure that you choose to use should be based on your needs and resources. Not everyone, for example, will have access to optical scanning forms or to software that allows for direct keyboard entry. By assessing your needs and establishing the options available, you will be able to determine the most efficient keypunch procedure for your research.

EDITING THE DATA FOR ERRORS

Although transferring your data from questionnaires to computer cards is a necessary and important step, it is not your last step in data organization and reduction. You are now ready to examine your data for errors. This process is known as *data cleaning*. Now, you might be thinking that this step is a duplication of effort—especially if an editor has been available to make decisions and nonstandard responses and if the computer cards have been verified. But no matter how carefully the data have been coded and keypunched, some errors are inevitable. Since we humans are not perfect, the coding and transfer process is not likely to be perfect.

Data cleaning can be accomplished with two procedures, both of which are essential to this process: possible punch cleaning and contingency cleaning.

Possible Punch Cleaning

Take a quick look at the codebook developed for our telephone survey, Figure 11.6. You will notice that for each variable listed, specific numeric codes are assigned. The variable sex, for example, has three legitimate codes: 1 for males, 2 for females, and 9 for missing data. If we were to find a case where sex has the code 6, we would know that an error had been made since 6 is not a legitimate code for this variable. On the other hand, the variable age has many more than three legitimate codes. In order to identify illegitimate codes, we must first have some knowledge of the youngest and oldest persons in the sample. The best way to detect errors of this nature is to use possible punch cleaning.

There are two methods which can be used to accomplish possible punch cleaning. First, there are computer programs that are designed specifically for this purpose. With such programs, you simply specify all possible punches that can be found in each card column and check for a legitimate punch. When illegal punches are found, the computer will let you know. To correct the punch, you will need to examine the original questionnaire. This document can be identified by matching the identification code on the card to the identification code on the questionnaire.

If a special program is not available for possible punch cleaning, an alternate procedure for accomplishing the same task is to create a frequency distribution for each variable being checked. A frequency distribution is simply a listing of all unique variable values and the number of times each value appears in the sample. If, for example, we wanted to examine our sex codes with a frequency distribution, we might have the following:

1	male	75
2	female	120
6		1
9	missing	3

This frequency distribution tells us that we have 75 males and 120 females in our sample. We also have three cases for which we have no information on sex. The one case having a code of 6, though, we know is incorrect. Thus, while we have identified an incorrect punch on sex, we have not identified the case number. We will now need to go into the data file and locate the appropriate case before a correct can be made.

From a data cleaning standpoint, direct keyboard entry has the edge over the other keypunch techniques. When special programs are used in direct keyboard entry, the program will ask you to identify those codes considered appropriate for each variable. If you attempt to input a value that is incorrect, the computer will not accept it. Such programs provide greater assurance that the data will be coded and keyed correctly.

Contingency Cleaning

A second type of data cleaning that is more complex but often essential is contingency cleaning. This technique identifies the appropriate coded responses contingent or dependent on responses assigned on another variable. Recall, for example, the strange data produced in the 1950 census of the population (see Chapter 6). Two variables were involved: age and marital status. We expected some fourteen-year-olds, and we expected some married persons, but we didn't expect these two characteristics to belong to the same persons. To our surprise, there were quite a few fourteen-year-old males and females who were married. What's more, the percentage of married males and females declined with age! This is not the pattern we would expect. In fact, it is just the opposite. These counts suggest to us that something is definitely wrong, as fourteen-year-olds are usually not married.

**FIGURE 11.9
Cross-Tabulation
of the 1950 Census
Data**

Age	S	M	D
14	1670		1320
15	1475		
16	1175		
17	810		575
18	905		
19	630		

Contingency cleaning may be accomplished through computer programs designed especially for this purpose or through the use of the cross-tabulation procedure. By cross-tabulation we mean a cross-classification of two variables and a count of the number of observations in each cell. To discover the error in the 1950 census, for example, we might use a cross-tabulation like the one in Figure 11.9.

It perhaps goes without saying that no data cleaning method will be 100 percent successful in identifying all errors. Even after both methods are used, errors may be later discovered. For example, you may discover that a male was coded as a female or that a twenty-seven-year-old was coded as 37. Possible punch cleaning and contingency cleaning can only identify those punches which are outside of some specified range. These techniques cannot detect wrong punches that fall within the specified range.

STORING THE DATA

Once the data have been keypunched, we must now concern ourselves with storage. This is a particularly important issue since data analysis is not a one-shot deal. In fact, the process of data analysis may take place over a period of weeks or possibly months.

When data are punched on cards, these cards may be used to process the data or they may be used to transfer the data to the medium of tape or disk. Regardless of the storage medium used, it is important to remember that storage is more than housing the numeric codes. It is also important to keep accurate written records of all variables, numeric codes for all variable response alternatives, and card and column locations. If data transformations are performed, this information should be written down and kept as part of data documentation.

As we have seen, one of the primary purposes of a computer card deck is to provide a medium whereby the data can be input into the computer's memory. The computer card deck also serves another very important function: it is a medium whereby the data can also be stored. Data stored on cards can also be transferred to magnetic tape or to disk for storage. Of these three, disks are the ideal form of storage, as they are quickly and easily accessed. Of the three mediums, though, disk is the most expensive. The most economical form for data storage is magnetic tape. Tapes are capable of storing thousands of pieces of information. If you choose cards as your medium for storing your data, you should keep your cards in a pressurized cabinet especially designed for computer cards. Such storage is both necessary and essential since computer cards, like any card made of paper, are highly susceptible to warpage. Once warped, the cards will not read through a card reader.

With our data in numeric and matrix form and prepared for computer input, we are now ready to consider how we will process the data—that is, what statistical procedures will we be running in order to ferret out any patterns in our data? We are now ready to look ahead to Chapter 12, ''Analyzing Data.''

Chapter 12

Analyzing Data: Descriptive Statistics

The role of statistical methods in the research process
Discrete and continuous data
Discrete frequency distributions
  Definition
  Handling missing data
  Graphing the discrete frequency distribution
    Bar graph
    Pie chart
  Grouping discrete data
Continuous frequency distribution
  Definition
  Graphing the continuous distribution
    The histogram
    The polygon
Descriptive summary measures

Measures of central tendency
  Defining the mode, median, and mean
    Mode
    Median
    Mean
  Comparing the mode, median, and mean
  Applying the mode, median, and mean
Measures of variability
  Defining range and semi-interquartile range
    Range
    Semi-interquartile range
  Defining the variance and standard deviation
    Variance
    Standard deviation
  Applying the variance and the standard deviation

> *Two statisticians were drafted into the army and found themselves fighting on the front lines. Simultaneously spotting an enemy, both soldiers raised their rifles and fired. Statistician 1 fired a foot too far to the right. Statistician 2 fired a foot too far to the left. Turning to each other with pride and smiles plastered all over their faces, they shook hands and congratulated each other.*
> On the Average, the Enemy Soldier Was Dead
> —Richard P. Runyon

While every stage of the research process is fascinating, we think that you will find the data analysis stage to be especially so. Prior to this stage, the substance of your research has only been conjecture. You have identified a research question. You have tentatively answered this question by developing hypotheses within the framework of theory. And you have collected data to test these hypotheses. But as yet, you have no definitive answers. It is in the data analysis stage of your research that you gain such answers to your research question.

The basic intent of data analysis is to examine a body of data for the hypothesized relationships and to exhibit the results in a clear and understandable manner. This important and essential examination can take two general forms: qualitative analysis and quantitative analysis.

Heated debates comparing qualitative to quantitative methods have fueled the fires of social science research discussions for many, many decades. Despite often polarized views, we believe that these two broad categories represent different approaches to a research problem and are therefore both essential to the research process. As we learned in Chapter 10, the word *quantity* asks the question "How much?" while the word *quality* asks the question "What kind?" More to the point, some types of theories demand quantitative data while others insist that only qualitative data be used. Since theories are really answers we give to research questions, the type of data that will test these answers depends largely on the nature of the research question. Hence, if your research calls for qualitative data, we hope you will use that kind. If quantitative data seems more appropriate, then this should be your choice. And remember, there is nothing wrong with using both types of data. Since we have already taken a detailed look at qualitative methods of analysis in Chapter 10, we will not repeat our discussion here. Instead, we will begin our detailed examination of quantitative methods.

THE ROLE OF STATISTICAL METHODS IN THE RESEARCH PROCESS

It is often acknowledged that numbers provide a level of precision that is unequaled by any descriptive vocabulary that we might choose to use. Suppose, for example, we were to describe a room as large. Such a description could certainly be labeled as vague because the descriptive adjective *large* is vulnerable to multiple interpretations, each influenced by individual perceptions of space. In other words, the descriptive adjective *large* is not precisely defined. If, on the other hand, we were to describe a room as eight by fifteen meters, there would be no misconception about the size of the room or its comparison with similar measures of space.

As a second example, suppose we wanted to study the effects of drug addiction on academic grades within college. If we chose to describe our research findings with definitive adjectives, we might have the following: "Drugs are bad." "Drugs are harmful to students' grades and general college performance." While such descriptions would tell our readers that we have identified a social problem, they would not provide a precise account of the problem. What's more, they would not give any accurate indication of the severity of the problem. On the other hand, if we were to collect data from students and then analyze this data *statistically*, we could present exact information on the number of students taking drugs, the amount of drugs being used, the frequency of use by age, sex, and ethnic background, and the grades of those taking drugs in each of the age, sex, and ethnic categories.

The simple little examples just given demonstrate clearly the importance of *statistical methods*—the methods used in collecting, presenting, and interpreting data. Such methods are absolutely essential if meaningful information is to be extracted from a *large* body of data. Two main approaches comprise the subject matter of statistics. One is the *descriptive approach*—describing characteristics of a population or sample. The other is the *inferential approach*—generalizing sample characteristics to a total population.

Quantitative research findings are normally presented in statistical form along with a discussion linking the reported findings to theory. To understand and fully evaluate the information provided by your data, you must have a good working knowledge of the various statistical procedures available to you. With your research objective in mind, you must decide whether your research is descriptive or inferential. From your reading of published research, you will find that most researchers use both types of procedures, beginning with a descriptive summary of characteristics and moving to inferential statistics for the test of hypotheses. Since both descriptive and inferential statistics are integral to the research process, we will devote a full chapter to each. In this chapter, we will address the subject of descriptive statistics. Chapter 13 is devoted to the issue of inferential statistics.

DISCRETE AND CONTINUOUS DATA

Recall from Chapter 11 that every set of data is comprised of *variables* and *variable values*. Each variable and its corresponding values constitute a *distribution*. Remember Rhonda's questionnaire, which included such variables as age, sex, race, marital status, father's occupation, mother's occupation, attitudes toward people, work, and sociology, previous majors, and reasons for majoring in sociology? The collected values for each of these variables were described as a distribution. In fact, Rhonda had as many distributions as she had variables. Suppose Rhonda is ready to analyze her data. Before she can properly begin this process, she must identify each variable by *type*.

Each of Rhonda's variables (or all variables, for that matter) can be classified as either discrete or continuous. *Discrete* variables are those variables which can assume only a limited or finite number of values. In Rhonda's data set, for example, sex, race, and marital status are discrete variables because each assumes a finite number of values (e.g., sex—male and female; marital status—single, married, widowed, divorced, separated). Although sex and marital status represent nominal-level variables (see Chapter 6), discrete variables may be measured at any level of measurement (nominal, ordinal, interval, ratio). Number of children in a family and number of sales in a company are also examples of discrete variables, but measured at the ratio level. In general, if it is possible to list or count every single value that a variable can assume, the variable is said to be discrete.

Sometimes, though, the number of values a variable can assume is so great that it is impossible to even identify them all, much less list them. Such variables are called *continuous* variables. Again, using Rhonda's data set, age can be viewed as a continuous variable. Other continuous variables include income, time, weight, and height, to name a few. In general, if between any two values a variable assumes, there are other values the variable can assume, the variable is said to be continuous.

DISCRETE FREQUENCY DISTRIBUTIONS

Definition

The most common method for summarizing the values of a discrete variable is the *frequency distribution.* We will define a frequency *distribution* as a listing of all variable values and a count of the number of times each value occurs. Let's illustrate the discrete frequency distribution with a study on marital status data for the male and female employees of a very large retail store. Our data are represented in Table 12.1. If you examine this table closely, you should notice three important things. First, all values for the variable marital status are represented. Second, the frequencies for each variable value (single, married, divorced, separated, and widowed) are listed. Third, the corresponding *percentage* for each frequency has been computed. Percentage transformations convert any set of frequencies to the standard base 100 by (1) adding all cases in the independent category (for example, males) (2) dividing that total into the frequency for each discrete variable value, and (3) multiplying the computed value by 100. This procedure gives the rate per 100 or, in the Latin form, percentum. To illustrate, for the 120 divorced males, for example, these computations would be as follows:

$$120/1000 = 0.12 * 100 = 12\%$$

By comparing the percentages of married males and married females, we can easily demonstrate that a higher percentage of females than males are married. Additionally, the percentage of separated males exceeds the percentage of separated females by a factor of 4 (i.e., 40 percent for males versus 10 percent for females). There is also a much higher percentage of single females (25 percent) than males (8 percent). These kinds of com-

TABLE 12.1 Frequency Distribution of Employees' Marital Status by Sex (without Missing Data)

	Males		Females	
	f	%	f	%
Single	80	8	125	25
Married	300	30	200	40
Divorced	120	12	100	20
Separated	400	40	50	10
Widowed	100	10	25	5
TOTAL	1,000	100%	500	100%

parisons simply would not be apparent if we compared the frequencies because the two groups differ considerably in size. In short, the conversion of frequencies to percentages applies the useful statistical technique of *standardization*, which makes data sets of different sizes directly comparable.

Handling Missing Data

As we have often indicated, the road to research is not paved with perfection, and you will frequently be reminded of this as you begin your data analysis. During data collection, for example, it is not uncommon for some respondents to skip one or more questions on the questionnaire. When this happens, you must have some method of dealing with this missing information. Assume, for example, that for the data just examined, there were actually 110 males and 41 females who did not answer the question on marital status. In other words, while each of these 151 subjects completed almost all of the questionnaire, they for some reason (inadvertently or intentionally) did not answer this question. Rather than lose these subjects entirely (and thus lose all of the data they have provided for all other questions), we can recompute our percentages to recognize missing data. Table 12.2 reflects an added column showing the *adjusted percentages*—computed from only those respondents answering the marital status question (i.e., adjusted for missing data). These percentages are identical to those presented in Table 12.1. In contrast, the *unadjusted percentages* are computed from a base of total respondents, including nonrespondents. In effect, nonrespondents comprise a residual category of unknown data that must be excluded from data analysis (but noted).

TABLE 12.2 Frequency Distribution of Employees' Marital Status by Sex (with Missing Data)

	\multicolumn{3}{c}{Males}			\multicolumn{3}{c}{Females}		
	f	Unad. %	Ad. %	f	Unad. %	Ad. %
Single	80	7	8	125	23	25
Married	300	27	30	200	37	40
Divorced	120	11	12	100	18	20
Separated	400	36	40	50	9	10
Widowed	100	9	10	25	5	5
MISSING	110	10	MISS	41	8	MISS
TOTAL	1,100	100%	100%	541	100%	100%

Unad. = unadjusted
Ad. = adjusted

Graphing the Discrete Frequency Distribution

Bar Graph. Although the discrete frequency distribution provides a simple and meaningful picture of the data represented, it is not always easy to read and interpret. This is especially true when your reading audience has little statistical training. On such occasions, it is a good idea to use a graphic display because this kind of presentation increases readability and understanding. The bar graph is probably the most popular kind of graph used to depict the distribution of a discrete variable. A bar graph, like all graphs, is a pictorial presentation of a discrete variable. The specific characteristics of a bar graph will become apparent as we construct one.

The first step in creating a bar graph is computing the frequency distribution for the targeted variable. In our case, this has already been done for marital status. Second, we must create the vertical and horizontal coordinates of the graph. While not etched in stone, you will generally find that the frequency values are plotted along the vertical axis and the discrete variable values along the horizontal axis. Rectangular bars are then used to plot the frequency (represented as height on the vertical axis) of each discrete variable value. A bar graph for the data in Table 12.1 is presented in Figure 12.1. One of the most distinguishing characteristics of a bar graph is the obvious spaces separating the bars. These spaces are intentional and designed to reflect the discrete (noncontinuous) nature of the discrete variable values being plotted.

**FIGURE 12.1
Bar Graph of
Marital Status
Distribution by Sex**

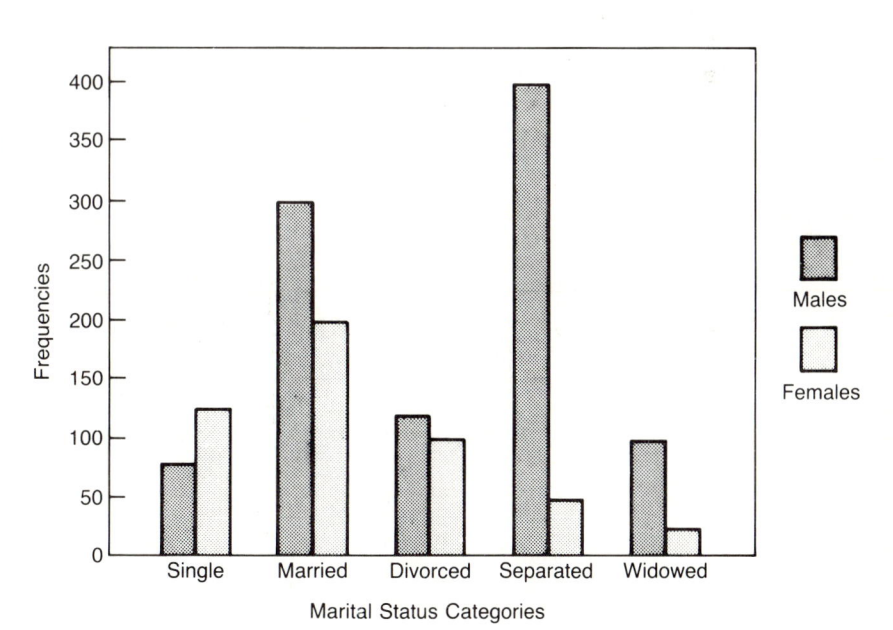

Pie Chart. Our marital status distribution could have also been graphically displayed with the pie chart. The pie chart is a circular graph usually used to show the relative proportions of a conceptual whole. This chart is applied to nominal-level (discrete) variables so that there is no presumption of order—that is, greater than or less than. Figure 12.2 displays the marital status distribution for males using a pie chart.

Grouping Discrete Data

As we have already indicated, discrete variables do not have to be nominal. They may be measured at any level of measurement. But if we were creating a frequency distribution for a discrete variable measured at the ordinal, interval, or ratio level, our procedure might need to be a little different from the one just described. Suppose, for example, we wanted to create a frequency distribution for number of children in a family. The raw values for this variable are listed in Figure 12.3. While we could list each unique value (just as they appear in Figure 12.3), such a listing could easily get out of hand with a large number of values. To overcome this problem, we might choose to group the variable values. If we choose this option, there are four essential steps that we must follow.

1. Compute the range—the difference between the largest and smallest number of children in a family plus 1. For our example, the highest number of children in a family, 12, minus the smallest number of children in a family, 0, plus 1 produces a range of 13.
2. Divide the number of intervals desired into the range to obtain

**FIGURE 12.2
Pie Chart of Marital Status Distribution for Males**

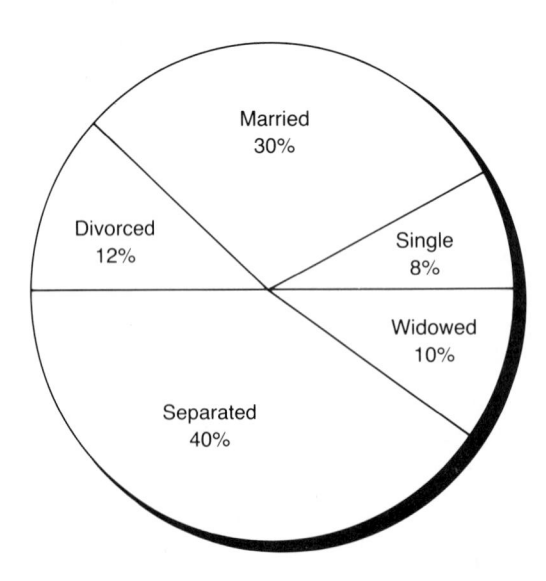

FIGURE 12.3
Distribution of "Number of Children in Family" Variable

Unordered	Ordered
0	0
12	0
6	1
7	1
4	1
4	2
3	2
2	2
1	3
1	3
10	3
0	3
3	4
5	4
9	5
3	6
2	7
1	9
2	10
3	12

the interval width—the number of unique scores in each interval. Using our example, the range, 13, is divided by 7, the desired number of intervals, to yield an interval width of 2 (some rounding may be necessary). Hence, our distribution of "number of children in family" is organized into 7 intervals of size 2.
3. Specify the end points of each interval. For our first interval, the end points would be 0–1. For our second interval, they would be 2–3.
4. Tabulate the frequencies for each interval.

The frequency distribution for this data is presented in Table 12.3. The bar graph giving a pictorial view of this data is presented in Figure 12.4.

TABLE 12.3 Frequency Distribution for "Number of Children in Family" Variable

Interval	f
12–13	1
10–11	1
8–9	1
6–7	2
4–5	3
2–3	7
0–1	5

FIGURE 12.4
Bar Graph of "Number of Children in Family" Distribution

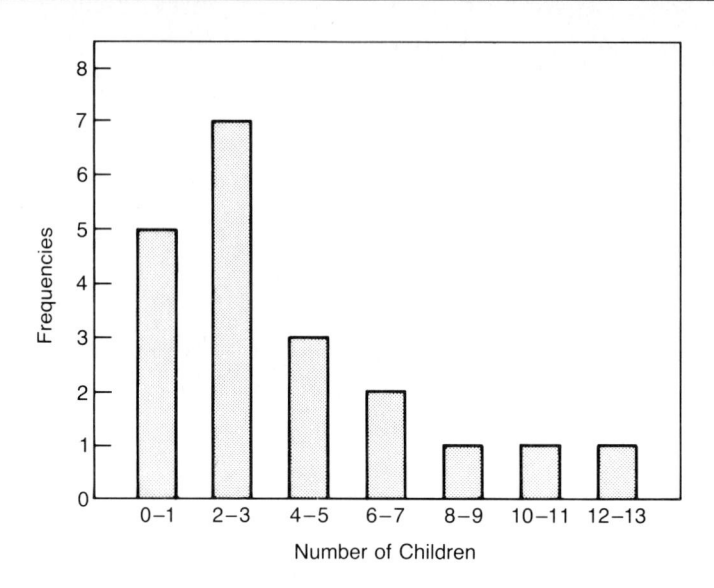

CONTINUOUS FREQUENCY DISTRIBUTION

Definition

Now suppose that we want to create a frequency distribution for the thirty-one ages listed in Figure 12.5. Since age is a continuous variable, our procedure again will need to be somewhat different from that used for discrete variables. As with discrete data (except nominal), we begin by finding the range. Second, we divide this range by the number of intervals desired, rounding any fraction upward to the nearest integer. This integer represents the *interval width* or the number of unique values in each interval. In our present example, the highest age, 31, minus the lowest age, 22, plus 1 gives a range of 10. If we choose to divide our age distribution into five intervals, we divide 10 by 5, yielding 2. Hence, for this distribution, we have chosen to use five two-year intervals. (If this division had produced a fraction, we would have rounded upward to the nearest integer.) Third, we specify the end points for each interval. Our age distribution organized into five two-year intervals is shown in Table 12.4. If you examine this distribution closely, you should notice at least one glaring problem. Since age is a continuous variable, there is really no interval for recording ages between 30 and 31, 40 and 41, 50 and 51, and so on. In our age distribution, for example, there are two ages that cannot be placed in any of these intervals: 21.25 and 30.75, and to place these variable values we had to round them off—21 and 31. In order to place every possible value (i.e., age) within one of these intervals, these so-called gaps must be eliminated. After all, this is a continuous variable! We eliminate these gaps by creating *upper* and *lower boundaries*. In effect,

FIGURE 12.5
Distribution of Ages

20
21.25
23
23
24
24
25
25
25
25
25
26
26
26
27
27
27
27
27
27
28
29
29
29
29
29
29
29
30.75
31

the upper boundary of one interval becomes the lower boundary of the interval just above it. Generally these boundaries are defined as halfway between two whole numbers. The frequency distribution for age has been re-created in Table 12.5, where we have computed the upper and

TABLE 12.4 Frequency Distribution of Ages Organized into Six Two-Year Intervals

Intervals	*f*	%
30–31	2	6.4
28–29	9	29.0
26–27	9	29.0
24–25	7	23.0
22–23	2	6.4
20–21	2	6.4
TOTAL	31	100.0

TABLE 12.5 Frequency Distribution of Ages with Boundaries and Midpoints

L.L.	Interval	U.L.	Midpoint	f	%
29.5	30–31	31.5	30.5	2	6.4
27.5	28–29	29.5	28.5	9	29.0
25.5	26–27	27.5	26.5	9	29.0
23.5	24–25	25.5	24.5	7	23.0
21.5	22–23	23.5	22.5	2	6.4
19.5	20–21	21.5	20.5	2	6.4

lower boundaries for each interval. In addition, we have computed the midpoints of each interval. As we shall soon see, the *midpoint*, defined as the average of the two boundaries, can be used to graph a continuous frequency distribution.

Graphing the Continuous Distribution

The Histogram. The histogram represents a plot of continuous data. By using the vertical axis for frequencies and the horizontal axis for the interval boundaries, we can create a graphic display of our age distribution. For the histogram, like the bar graph, the frequencies are represented with bars. However, for the histogram, the bars are plotted somewhat differently. Specifically, the bars are plotted around the lower and upper boundaries of the interval. Since the upper boundary of one interval is the lower boundary of the interval above it, each interval shares one stern of the bar with another interval. Figure 12.6 illustrates our age distribu-

FIGURE 12.6 Histogram of Age Distribution

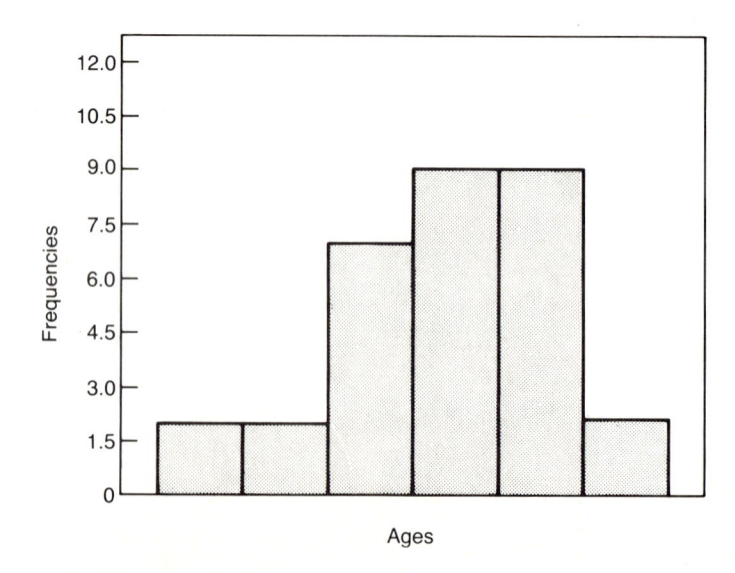

**FIGURE 12.7
Polygon of Age Distribution**

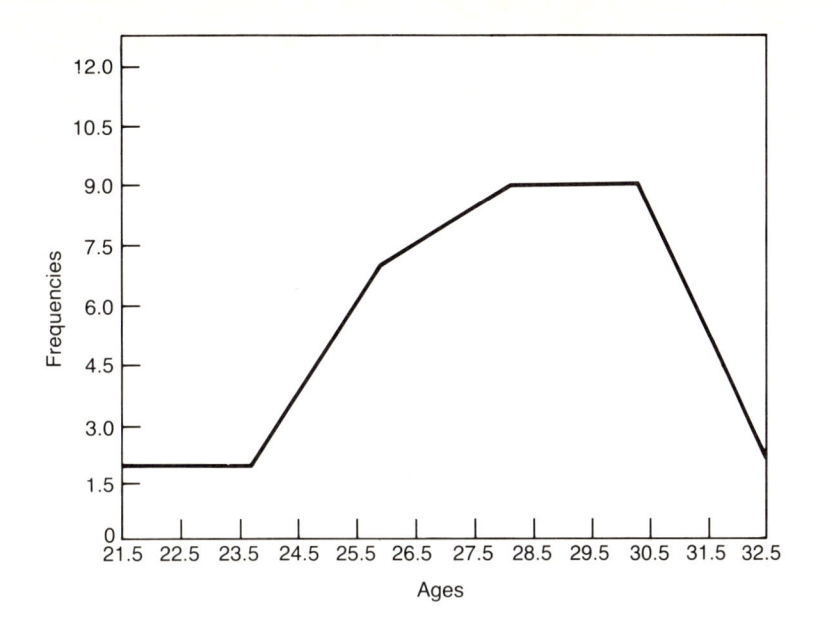

tion graphed with a histogram. By removing the vertical lines separating the adjoining bars, the graph actually gives the appearance of a continuous variable. In this instance, the histogram presents an outline of the distribution of frequencies for each age interval.

The Polygon. The polygon is another means of graphing a continuous variable. Like the histogram, the polygon assumes a continuous variable plotted along the horizontal axis. Unlike the histogram, though, the polygon graphs with points that are plotted above the midpoints of each interval, and these points are then connected with line segments. These points and lines together show the frequency distribution pattern. Figure 12.7 illustrates the age distribution graphed with a polygon. With a polygon, the connecting line is sometimes dropped to the base line at each end, presupposing the termination of the scale for this distribution.

DESCRIPTIVE SUMMARY MEASURES

Social scientists use frequency distributions and graphic displays because they know that this kind of presentation will reduce misunderstanding and increase readability. In addition to these data summary techniques, there are some valid and viable alternatives that are more economical of space and, for analytical purposes, even more precise.

Two types of such summary measures can be used to describe the values in a distribution. The first, measures of central tendency, indicates how the scores "bunch up" in the middle of a distribution. The second, measures of variability, indicates how widely the scores in a distribution vary above and below the center of the distribution. Let's take a look at both types of measures.

Measures of Central Tendency

Three measures of central tendency are frequently used to describe the center of a distribution—the mode, median, and mean. The use of these measures can help you to convey an accurate and economical picture of any distribution. Let's begin our discussion of these three measures by defining each. To help clarify these definitions, we will illustrate each measure using the ages listed in Figure 12.5.

Defining the Mode, Median, and Mean

MODE   The mode is the most frequently occurring score in a distribution. This measure of central tendency is actually found by counting the number of occurrences for each unique variable value. In short, the variable value with the highest count is the mode. For our distribution pictured in Figure 12.5, the mode is 29, since 29 occurs more often than any other value (eight times).

You may be somewhat surprised to learn that the mode is not always located at the center of a distribution. In our distribution of ages, for example, the mode is at the high end of the age distribution, not in the center. What's more, a distribution may have more than one mode. If the frequency count for two or more scores in a distribution is the same, a distribution is described as either *bimodal* (two modes) or *multimodal* (many modes).

MEDIAN   The median is the score that divides an ordered distribution into two equal halves. Notice that this definition stipulates an ordered or ranked distribution. That is, before you can find the median, you must first order the scores from lowest to highest. For our distribution of ages (Figure 12.5), the median is 27. In this distribution the median is pretty easy to find because there is an odd number of scores (31). When there is an even number of scores in a distribution, the median is computed as the average of the middle two scores. If, for example, we were to add one age, 55, to our age distribution, the median would become the average of the two middle scores, which in this case would produce the same value: (27+27)/2 or 27.

MEAN   The mean is the balance point of a distribution. It is the arithmetic average or the value obtained by adding all the scores in a distribution and dividing the sum by the number of terms. For our distribution of thirty-one ages, this means 20 + 21.25 + 23 + . . . + 29 + 30.75 + 31 = 797/31 = 25.7.

Comparing the Mode, Median, and Mean. Now that we have defined these three measures of central tendency, let's compare them. In general, we can say that the mode represents "most," the median represents "middle," and the mean represents "average." Of these three measures, the mean is by far the most precise and the most sensitive. In fact, the mean is so precise and so sensitive that it will change if only *one* value in a distribution is changed. Suppose, for example, we were to add 25 points to the largest term in our age distribution (Figure 12.5). Our new distribution appears in Figure 12.8.

As you can see, the mode is still 29 and the median is still 27. However, the mean has changed from 25.7 to 26.5. If you are paying close attention, you have probably realized that we could have altered a

**FIGURE 12.8
Distribution
of Ages**

20
21.25
23
23
24
24
25
25
25
25
25
26
26
26
27
27
27
27
27
27
28
29
29
29
29
29
29
29
29
30.75
56

score, which would have changed the mode and median. We could, for example, have changed the 26s to 27s and the mode would be 27. Or we could have changed the 27s to 26s and the median would be 26. In short, any single change in a distribution will change the mean, whereas only specific changes will alter the mode and median. Hence, the mean is viewed as the most sensitive of these three measures.

Applying the Mode, Median, and Mean. Although the mode is not used much in social science research, it does play an important role in other substantive areas. In fact, the mode is especially useful in marketing research. A shoe store owner, for example, might like to know the most popular (modal) sizes in women's shoes so she can order accordingly. A marketing research team might like to know people's favorite (modal) colors so they can advise their firm to package products accordingly. In marketing research, the mode seems to be synonymous with popular.

The fact that the median is not affected by the size of extreme values does makes it a very useful measure of central tendency for some purposes. The median is an especially important measure when there are a few extreme scores in a distribution. Since extreme scores pull the mean in their direction, the mean of such a distribution is somewhat distorted. In such instances, the median is really more representative of the central tendency than the mean. The distribution of annual incomes in the United States is a good example of a distribution with extremes. While most Americans' earnings are on the lower end of the income continuum, a few Americans do earn millions of dollars. Since all incomes are used to compute the mean, the mean is pulled in the direction of these extreme incomes. Thus, the average income for American earners will appear larger than it really is. For such lopsided distributions, the median is a more representative measure of central tendency than is the mean.

Despite the uses for the mode and median, the mean remains the most important measure of central tendency. The sensitivity of the mean makes it a good indicator of the size of the terms in a distribution. In a very general sense, the higher the mean, the higher the terms in a distribution tend to run. The mean is also used to compare locations of distinctive groups on the same scale. When we say, for example, that the mean test score for females is larger than the mean test score for males, we are really saying that females did better on the test. In addition to these descriptive uses, you will soon discover (in Chapter 13) that the mean is a very useful measure in inferential statistics.

Measures of Variability

While measures of central tendency are concerned with how the scores in a distribution are grouped together, measures of variability are concerned with how the scores in a distribution are spread apart. Four measures of variability are frequently used in the social sciences: range, semi-interquartile range, variance, and standard deviation. Of these four measures, we will find variance and standard deviation to be the most valuable. However, an understanding of range and semi-interquartile range will give us a greater appreciation of the more useful measures.

Defining Range and Semi-Interquartile Range

RANGE   The simplest measure of variability is the range—the difference between the lowest and highest values in a distribution plus 1. For the distribution of ages pictured in Figure 12.5, the range is 12 (31 − 20 plus 1) because there are twelve unique scores in this spread (i.e., 20, 21, 22, 23, 24, 25, 26, 27, 28, 29, 30, 31).

Although the range does convey some meaning concerning the spread of scores in a distribution, it is really a rather crude measure of variability and hence rather unstable. To illustrate, we have already noted that the distribution of ages pictured in Figure 12.5 has a range of 12. But when we added 25 points to the highest age (Figure 12.8), the range became 27—considerably larger. By changing one value, we actually doubled the range. In effect, we have identified the primary limitation of the range. This measure of spread is only sensitive to the highest and lowest values in a distribution. It is insensitive to any variation between these two extremes, making it rather unstable.

SEMI-INTERQUARTILE RANGE   To overcome the instability of the range as a measure of variability, the semi-interquartile range may be used. This measure of variability is found by computing the difference between the score at the 75th percentile (labeled the third quartile) and the 25th percentile (labeled the first quartile) and then dividing this difference by two. The semi-interquartile range includes only the two interior quartiles, or 50 percent of the total distribution. By excluding the two exterior quartiles, we do eliminate most extreme scores, but the measure remains somewhat crude. Like the range, it is still computed from only two scores in a distribution.

Defining the Variance and Standard Deviation.   Given the insensitivity and instability of the range and the semi-interquartile range, we need to find a measure of variability that will overcome these limitations. If we were to identify the criteria or the conditions that would produce the ideal measure of variability, we might come up with the following list.

1. It should be sensitive to every score in a distribution. Unlike the range and the semi-interquartile range, which are affected by only two scores, we want a measure of variability that is affected by every score in a distribution. Ideally, our measure of variability should be so sensitive that a change in only one score would also result in a change in variability.

2. This ideal measure of spread should produce a small value when the scores in a distribution are close together and a larger value when the scores are farther apart. Consider, for example, the scores in the following distributions:

Distribution A	Distribution B
1	100
2	200
3	300
4	400
5	500

At a glance, you can quickly see that the scores in Distribution A are closer together than those in Distribution B. Hence, we would also like our measure of variability to reflect this obvious difference.

3. It should be independent of the number of scores in a distribution. In other words, our measure of variability should not be affected by the number of scores in a distribution. Consider the following distributions:

Distribution A	Distribution B
3	3
3	3
3	3
3	3
3	3
	3
	3
	3
	3
	3

Distribution B has ten scores, while Distribution A has only five. Yet, if you look at the scores comprising each of these distributions, it should be fairly obvious that their variability is the same. This sameness should be reflected in our measure of variability.

4. This ideal measure of variability should be independent of the mean. That is, it should not get smaller as the mean gets smaller and larger as the mean gets larger. Again, consider the following two distributions:

ANALYZING DATA: DESCRIPTIVE STATISTICS

Distribution A	Distribution B
3	5
3	5
3	5
3	5
3	5

Quite obviously, Distribution A has a mean of 3 while Distribution B has a mean of 5. Despite this difference in the two means, it is also obvious that there is *no* variation in either distribution. Hence, both distributions should have the same variability. Put another way, Distribution B should not have a larger variability score merely because its mean is larger.

Given these four characteristics, what measures of variability can we identify that satisfy all? As it turns out, there are actually two measures of variability that satisfy all four conditions—the variance and the standard deviation.

VARIANCE The variance can be defined as the mean of the squared deviations from a distribution's mean. In other words, it is the sum of the squared deviations from the mean divided by the number of squared deviations. In formula form, the variance can be expressed as:

$$S^2 = \Sigma \frac{(X - \overline{X})^2}{N}$$

To gain a better understanding of this definition (and formula), let's compute the variance for the following three distributions:

Distribution 1	Distribution 2	Distribution 3
3	0	1
3	2	2
3	2	3
3	5	4
3	6	5
$\overline{X} = 3$	$\overline{X} = 3$	$\overline{X} = 3$

To compute the variance for any one of these three distributions, we must carry out the following steps:

1. Compute the $\overline{X}$ for each distribution. For our three distributions, the means are all the same—3.

2. Subtract the $\bar{X}$ from every term in the distribution. For our three distributions, we would have the following:

Distribution 1		Distribution 2		Distribution 3	
X	X − $\bar{X}$	X	X − $\bar{X}$	X	X − $\bar{X}$
3	0	0	−3	1	−2
3	0	2	−1	2	−1
3	0	2	−1	3	0
3	0	5	2	4	1
3	0	6	3	5	2

3. Square each deviation from the mean, and then add up these squared deviations:

X − $\bar{X}$	(X − $\bar{X}$)²	X − $\bar{X}$	(X − $\bar{X}$)²	X − $\bar{X}$	(X − $\bar{X}$)²
0	0	−3	9	−2	4
0	0	−1	1	−1	1
0	0	−1	1	0	0
0	0	2	4	1	1
0	0	3	9	2	4
0	0	0	24	0	10

4. Divide the sum of the squared deviation by the number of terms in the distribution. The obtained value is a mean. In fact, it is the mean of the squared deviation from the mean—or variance.

Distribution 1	Distribution 2	Distribution 3
0/5 = 0	24/5 = 4.8	10/5 = 2

If you study these three distributions and their variances, you will soon discover that this measure of variability meets our earlier stated criteria. It appears to be sensitive to all the scores in a distribution. The more "bunched up" the scores are, the smaller its value. The more "spread apart" the scores are, the larger its value. It is independent of the number of terms in a distribution and independent of a distribution's mean. How do we know all of this? Let's make some careful comparisons.

If you look again at the terms in each of these three distributions, you should easily see that the terms in Distribution 1 are closer together than those in Distributions 2 and 3. In fact, the terms comprising Distribution 1 are all identical. On the basis of our previously established criteria and this observation, we would expect Distribution 1 to have the smallest variance—and it does! Additionally, the variance appears to be independent of the number of terms in a distribution and independent of a distribution's mean. Again, a quick glance at our three distributions will confirm that all three distributions have the same number of observations and the same mean. If variance were affected by a distribution's size and mean, we would expect these three distributions to have the same variance. Since all three distributions have different variances, we can surmise that our measure is independent of these characteristics. If you are still not convinced of the validity of these criteria, you should create some distributions of your own and try computing their variances.

STANDARD DEVIATION   Before we impute meaning to this measure of variability, let's consider one additional measure of variability—standard deviation. The standard deviation can be defined as the positive square root of the variance. Using our three previously cited distributions:

Distribution 1	Distribution 2	Distribution 3
variance = 0	variance = 4.8	variance = 2.0
SD = $\sqrt{0}$	SD = $\sqrt{4.8}$	SD = $\sqrt{2}$
SD = 0	SD = 2.2	SD = 1.41

Since the standard deviation is derived from the variance, we can safely assume that this measure of variability also fulfills our earlier established criteria. In addition, the standard deviation has one advantage that the variance does not have. Unlike the variance, the value of the standard deviation has the same underlying scale as scores in the distribution. To understand why this is so, we must reconsider briefly our procedure for computing variance.

As you will recall, the second step in computing the variance requires that we subtract the mean from every term in a distribution. If you look closely at the three distributions of *deviations from the mean*, you should quickly discover that each of these distributions (of deviations) sums to zero. This is not just a coincidence. For any distribution (regardless of size), the sum of the deviations from the mean is *zero*. If you're not convinced, create some distributions of your own, calculate the mean of each, and sum the deviations from the mean. The sum of the deviations from the mean will always be zero.

Because the sum of the deviations from the mean is always zero, we cannot use this sum to compute the variance. In short, if we did use this sum, the variance would always be zero—sum of deviations/N. To circumvent this problem, the mean deviations must be altered. You will recall that we altered the mean deviations by squaring each of them. And except for those rare cases where all the terms in a distribution are the same (e.g., Distribution 1), the sum of the squared deviations is a positive number.

Although squaring the mean deviations does eliminate one problem (i.e., a sum of zero), it also creates another problem. Squaring these deviations inflates (increases) the value of each deviation. When the squared deviations are summed, the sum is also inflated, and when this sum is divided by the number of terms in the distribution, this value (variance) is also inflated. In short, the value of variance is not based on the same underlying scale as the scores comprising the distribution. To correct for this inflation, we use the mathematical procedure that represents the reverse of squaring—square rooting. By taking the square root of the variance we have the standard deviation—a measure of variability whose value can be interpreted within the context of the original distribution's scale.

Applying the Variance and the Standard Deviation. Imagine that you are in the library looking for research references that are relevant to your research topic, "Changing Attitudes toward Sexual Behavior: 1980 to the Present." As you begin to page through the *Journal of Sexual Facts*, you notice an article that appears to be pertinent. This article, you soon discover, is on the differences among age groups with respect to attitudes toward sexual behavior. You decide to read a little further. In the methods section of the paper, the authors indicate that they are using an attitude scale whose scores can vary between 10 and 50, where 10 represents a negative attitude and 50 a positive attitude. In the results section of the paper, the authors submit that sexual attitudes vary little if any across age groups. The data supporting this declaration are also presented in table form:

Age Intervals	*Mean Attitude Score*
50–59	23.93
40–49	24.26
30–39	25.00
20–29	24.51

You glance at this table and immediately see that the means are close together, giving some credence to the authors' conclusions. But you are still somewhat troubled. Something seems to be missing. Aha! Suddenly, it comes to you like greased lightning! While you can survey the means for each age category, you cannot determine how representative these means are of their respective distributions. Without this information, you feel you really cannot evaluate the research findings.

Now suppose you actually had access to the raw attitude scores by age group and the distributions were as follows:

Ages 20–29	Ages 30–39	Ages 40–49	Ages 50–59
23	20	10	10
25	20	11	10
26	22	15	11
27	22	17	15
27	27	19	15
28	28	21	20
28	28	37	31
28	31	40	45
29	33	41	46
29	33	43	48
30	36	46	49

From a close examination of these scores, it is apparent to you that the means have been computed correctly. However, the distributions look different. In fact, the mean equivalences are clouded by the very obvious differences in the scores of the four distributions.

What's missing from the authors' presentation is the standard deviation for each of these distributions. Since the standard deviation is a measure of average distance from the mean of a distribution, we can use it to assess the representativeness of each mean. In fact, we could easily do without the distribution of raw scores if we had access to the standard deviation for each of these four distributions.

Computing the standard deviation for each of these distributions, we obtain:

Ages 20–29	Ages 30–39	Ages 40–49	Ages 50–59
$s = 2.0$	$s = 5.6$	$s = 14.0$	$s = 16.7$

From the standard deviations, it is apparent that the means of Distributions 1 and 2 are more representative of their respective distributions than are the means of Distributions 3 and 4 for theirs. In fact, the scores in Distributions 3 and 4 are so spread out that neither mean appears representative of the scores listed.

While the mean gives us some information about the center of a distribution, by itself it is not enough. Similarly, while the standard deviation gives us some information about the spread in a distribution, alone it is not complete. When taken together, the mean and the standard deviation, like love and marriage, render an unmatched union.

Variance and standard deviation, like the mean, are not limited to descriptive purposes. Both measures, as we shall soon see, are also an integral part of inferential statistics.

Chapter 13

Analyzing Data: Inferential Statistics

The normal curve
The standard normal curve
The standard normal curve as a probability distribution
The t test for two independent samples
The F test—three or more independent samples
Correlation and regression
   Simple correlation and regression
      The adequacy of the fit
         The standard error of the estimate
         The correlation coefficient
         The squared correlation coefficient

A composite example
Multiple correlation and regression analysis
   The adequacy of the fit
      The standard error of the estimate
      The multiple correlation coefficient
   Plotting the residuals
   Autocorrelation
   Colinear data
A composite example

Then there is the man who drowned crossing a stream with an average depth of six inches.
—W. I. E. Gates

Most students have difficulty with the inevitable chapter in methods books on statistics, and unfortunately, this one may be no exception. Inferential statistics is not a subject for the queasy, but neither is it an impossible task. We have assumed that you have some familiarity with statistical procedures, and while this chapter is an overview of how to analyze data using statistical inference, the student who has difficulty might wish to refer to an elementary statistics text for more basic information than that which informs this chapter.

In our discussion in Chapter 12 we focused on those quantitative measures which are used to *describe* the characteristics of a sample. In short, we suggested that this description would usually take the form of a frequency distribution, a measure of central tendency, and/or a measure of variability. While such descriptive information concerning one's sample is always useful, it is seldom enough by itself since such information applies only to the sample on which it is computed. In most research situations, the sample is not our main concern. Rather, our primary concern is for the population from which the sample has been drawn, and the sample is merely the vehicle for learning about the population.

Our concern for the population over the sample introduces an interesting and rather provocative dilemma. As we have already learned (see Chapter 7), in most research situations we do not have access to the total population. On the contrary, we usually have access to only a part of a population—a sample. If we do not have access to a total population, how, then, can we identify its characteristics? In effect, we cannot actually *identify* them. We can only *infer* them from our knowledge of the sample characteristics. The term *statistical inference* is used to describe the process of inferring the characteristics of a population from the characteristics of a sample. This process of statistical inference is made possible through the use of probability distributions.

A *probability distribution* is a list or map of all the possible outcomes that can occur for a designated phenomenon and the likelihood of occurrence for each outcome. Suppose, for example, that the total number of housing sales in Memphis, Tennessee, for 1978 was 10,000. This number represents the population of housing sales. Now suppose we were to draw a sample of 100 sales records from this population. Although we may compute the mean selling price for this sample, our real concern is for the population mean. Since we cannot actually identify the population mean, we would like to infer that its value is the same as the sample mean. To make this inference, we need to examine the probability distribution for this particular variable.

If we could draw an infinite number of samples of size 100 from this population, compute the mean of each sample, and plot these means, this plot of sample means would constitute a probability distribution. From this distribution, we could determine the likelihood of occurrence of our one sample mean. However, such a probability distribution would be almost impossible to compute since it would require extensive knowledge of the population. In fact, we might as well compute the population's characteristics as create this probability distribution! Fortunately, we have been saved from all of these computations. We can use a *theoretical distribution* (instead of a finite distribution) to map all possible outcomes. To understand fully how this is possible, let's first take a look at one theoretical distribution—the standard normal curve—and then examine how this curve can be used as a probability distribution.

THE NORMAL CURVE

In the eighteenth century, a Frenchman, Abraham de Moivre, presented a mathematical solution for mapping (plotting) an infinite number of outcomes. Moivre's formula actually computes the number of times (Y, defined by height of curve) a specific event (X) will occur. This calculation is based on two familiar characteristics of a distribution: the mean and the standard deviation. If Moivre's formula were used to calculate the Y's (the number of times each specific event occurs) for an infinite number of X's (all possible events), the line defining this shape would be a *curve*. And if the phenomenon represented by this curve is normally distributed, the figure produced is that of a normal curve. The normal curve is pictured in Figure 13.1. Every normal curve possesses the following characteristics:

1. It is *symmetrical*. The left half of the curve is a mirror image of the right half. If the curve were folded in the middle, one half would be identical to the other.
2. It is *bell-shaped*. This means that the scores tend to cluster about the center. And as we move away from the center, the frequency of scores decreases.
3. The *mean, median, and mode of the distribution are the same.* Restated, the point of balance for the distribution (mean) is also the point that divides the distribution into two equal halves (median) and the point at which the greatest number of scores occur (mode).

FIGURE 13.1
The Normal Curve

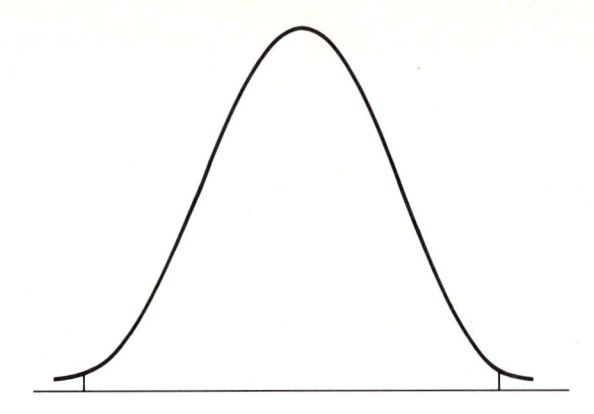

4. It is *asymptotic*. It is made up of an infinite number of scores on the X axis, each of which has a corresponding Y value that never touches the base line. As we move away from the mean in either direction, the frequency of Y values decreases and approaches zero. But zero is never reached, as there is always some likelihood that a value more extreme than the last will occur.
5. *The total area encompassed by the curve is equal to 1.00.* Thus, the Y value for any given X divides the curve into two parts, with some portion of the area falling below that value and some portion falling above. For example, the mean divides the distribution into two equal parts, so we can say that 50 percent of the area lies below the mean and 50 percent of the area lies above it.

Given Moivre's formula for a normal curve and a set of X values, we could calculate the corresponding Y value for each X to derive the actual points on a curve. Once we had calculated these points, we could identify the frequency of occurrence of any given score within a distribution. However, our task would not be an easy one since these calculations would have to be redone for each set of X's as changes in the mean and standard deviation would alter the location and shape of the curve. Fortunately, these individual calculations can be avoided by transforming the original distribution of scores into *standard form*.

THE STANDARD NORMAL CURVE

The standard normal curve is based on a distribution of scores in z form. Any distribution that is converted to z score form will have a mean of 0 and a standard deviation of 1.00. Although the z score values theoretically extend to infinity in either direction, the majority of cases fall within the range of +/−3. Any set of interval scores can be transformed to z score form by the following formula. Figure 13.2 illustrates this transformation.

**FIGURE 13.2
z Score
Transformation**

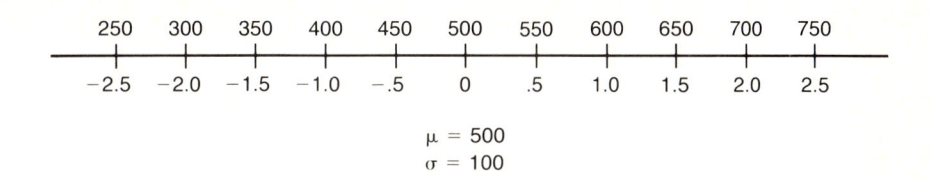

```
    250   300   350   400   450   500   550   600   650   700   750
    ──┼────┼────┼────┼────┼────┼────┼────┼────┼────┼────┼──
   -2.5  -2.0  -1.5  -1.0  -.5    0    .5   1.0   1.5   2.0   2.5
```

$\mu = 500$
$\sigma = 100$

Where: X = any individual score in a distribution
$\overline{X}$ = the mean of the distribution
s = the standard deviation of the distribution

You should notice that a z score transformation is a linear transformation in that it does not change the relative position of any score. In short, all normal distributions converted to z score form will be identical and have identical properties:

1. Their centers will all be located at the same point on the scale—0.
2. They will have the same spread since they all have the same standard deviation—1.00.

If Moivre's formula were used to calculate the Y values for a set of X's in z score form, the result would be a standard normal curve. Since all distributions in standard normal form look the same, individual calculations are no longer necessary. And since the area associated with each z score never changes, tables have been prepared for us (see Appendix B).

The utility of converting observed scores to z score form and the importance of a table describing the proportion of area under the curve associated with z scores rests on the assumption that the likelihood or probability of the occurrence of any given score can be established using such a theoretical distribution. In effect, the z score transformation can be used to evaluate whether an outcome is usual or unusual—that is, likely or not likely to occur by chance. Let's turn our attention now to understanding how such a theoretical distribution can be used to establish probabilities.

THE STANDARD NORMAL CURVE AS A PROBABILITY DISTRIBUTION

If we knew the *frequency* associated with each unique sample mean that could be computed on samples of some fixed size drawn from a population, we could use this information to determine the *probability* (i.e., likelihood) of drawing a sample with a specific mean:

PROBABILITY = number of successful events/total number of events

$$\text{RESTATED: PROBABILITY} = \frac{\text{number of samples (size } n\text{) with a particular mean}}{\text{total number of samples (size } n\text{) with any mean}}$$

However, just as a population is usually *infinite* in size, so is the number of samples of some fixed and designated size that can be drawn from a population. And given an infinite number of samples of some designated size, we can calculate neither the *absolute count of successful events* nor the *absolute count of total events*. To accommodate this limitation, we simply restructure our definition of probability within the framework of *proportions* instead of *absolute counts*. Probability, redefined, is *the proportion of successful events (e.g., proportion of samples with a certain mean) relative to the proportion representing the total number of events—samples with any mean (always 1.00).*

$$\text{PROBABILITY} = \frac{\text{proportion of events representing success}}{\text{total events expressed as a proportion}}$$

Restated, the area under the curve is simply read as a proportion. As we have already established, the total area under the curve is set equal to 1.00, and any part of the total is some proportion less than 1.00. By determining the proportion of area between any two values relative to the total area (i.e., 1.00), we have identified the likelihood of drawing a sample whose mean is within some specified range.

Let's suppose that we have a population of ten unique terms. Let's further suppose that the mean of this population is 5.5 and the standard deviation is 1.94. Now let's draw all possible samples of size 2 from this population and compute each sample's mean. These samples and their means are pictured in Figure 13.3.

Graphing these sample means, we obtain the distribution pictured in Figure 13.4. The horizontal axis on this graph represents the values of the sample means. The vertical axis represents the number of times a sample mean of a specified value occurs.

1. The probability of drawing a sample with a mean of 5.5 is 1/9.

$$p = \frac{\text{number of successful outcomes}}{\text{all possible outcomes}} = \frac{5}{45} = \frac{1}{9}$$

2. The probability of drawing a sample with a mean between 4.5 and 6.5 is 21/45.

$$p = \frac{21}{45} = .4667$$

**FIGURE 13.3
Samples of Size 2
Drawn from
Population of
Ten Unique Terms**

1,2	2,3	3,4	4,5	5,6	6,7	7,8	8,9	9,10
(1.5)	(2.5)	(3.5)	(4.5)	(5.5)	(6.5)	(7.5)	(8.5)	(9.5)
1,3	2,4	3,5	4,6	5,7	6,8	7,9	8,10	
(2)	(3)	(4)	(5)	(6)	(7)	(8)	(9)	
1,4	2,5	3,6	4,7	5,8	6,9	7,10		
(2.5)	(3.5)	(4.5)	(5.5)	(6.5)	(7.5)	(8.5)		
1,5	2,6	3,7	4,8	5,9	6,10			
(3)	(4)	(5)	(6)	(7)	(8)			
1,6	2,7	3,8	4,9	5,10				
(3.5)	(4.5)	(5.5)	(6.5)	(7.5)				
1,7	2,8	3,9	4,10					
(4)	(5)	(6)	(7)					
1,8	2,9	3,10						
(4.5)	(5.5)	(6.5)						
1,9	2,10							
(5)	(6)							
1,10								
(5.5)								

3. Now suppose we were to view this sampling distribution as a map of all possible outcomes that would occur if samples of size 2 were drawn indefinitely. The area under the curve represents all possible outcomes—1.00. To identify the probability of getting a sample mean between any two identified values (for example, 4.5 and 6.5), we would simply read the area under the standard normal curve between these two means. In order to read a portion of area under the standard normal curve, these two identified means must be converted to z form. Using the z score formula and by substitution, we obtain:

**FIGURE 13.4
Sampling
Distribution of
Sample Means**

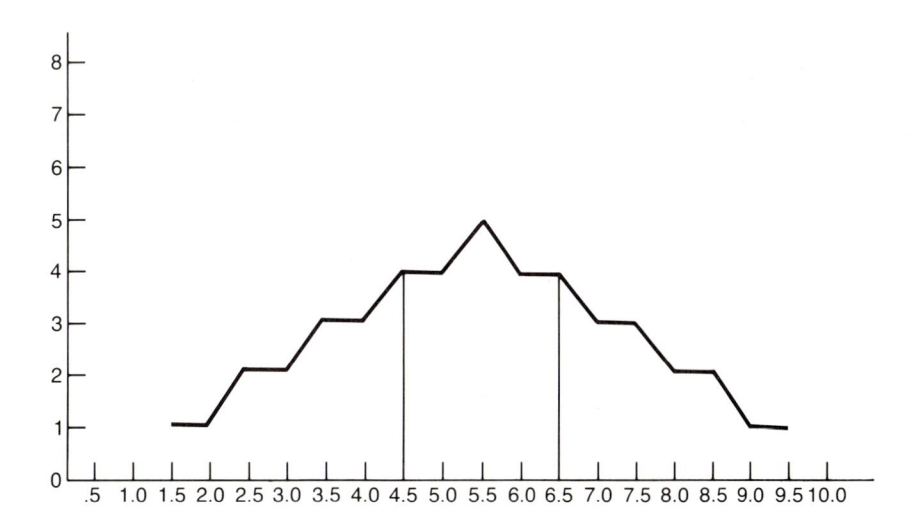

$$z_{4.5} = \frac{4.5 - 5.5}{1.94} = -.52$$

$$z_{6.5} = \frac{6.5 - 5.5}{1.94} = +.52$$

5. The area between $-.52$ and $+.52$ equals .3970. From reading this area, we would conclude that the probability of drawing a sample from the identified population with a mean between 4.5 and 6.5 is approximately .40, or 40 samples out of every 100.
6. Notice how close this probability is to the one calculated from the finite set of discrete outcomes (.4667). If our population were larger and we were drawing samples larger than size 2, the curve of samples means would smooth out and these two probabilities would be even closer in value.
7. Also notice that probability is still the ratio of successful outcomes to all possible outcomes—but now both the numerator and the denominator are expressed as proportions. In essence, this is the way we must proceed when dealing with continuous variables since it is usually not feasible to express all possible outcomes as a finite set.

$$p = \frac{\text{successful outcomes (expressed as a proportion)}}{\text{all possible outcomes (expressed as a proportion)}} = \frac{.40}{1.00} = .40$$

To illustrate the standard normal curve as a probability curve, let's now return to a sampling problem introduced in Chapter 7, that of determining the extent to which a sample mean represents a population mean. Let's assume that the population of housing sales in Memphis, Tennessee, for 1978 is 10,000, with a mean selling price of $36,762.67 and a standard deviation of $15,078.88. Suppose we draw a sample of 100 selling prices and compute the mean for this sample. Although we are working with a sample, our primary concern is not for this sample. What we really want to know is whether this sample mean represents the population mean. Restated, we are really concerned with the probability of drawing a sample whose mean does not deviate *too much* from the population mean.

1. First we must ask, How much is *too much*? How much deviation from the population mean will we allow and still reason that this sample mean is representative?
2. This question has been answered for us, albeit arbitrarily. From a z score table we can determine that 95 percent of the area under the sampling distribution curve (or any standard normal curve, for that matter) falls between a z score of $+/-1.96$.

**FIGURE 13.5
Boundaries that Separate 95% of the Area under the Curve from the Other 5%**

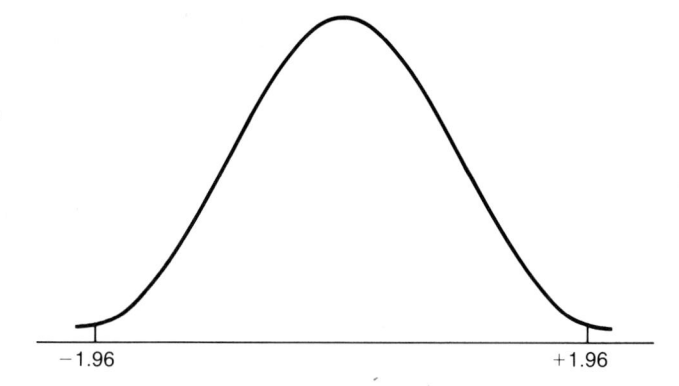

−1.96   +1.96

3. Therefore, we know that 95 out of every 100 samples ($p = 95/100$) drawn from the specified population (or any population) will have a mean whose z score transformation locates them between $z = +/-1.96$. Only 5 out of every 100 samples drawn randomly from this population will have a mean whose z score transformation locates them outside this range. These two regions are pictured in Figure 13.5.
4. If our particular sample mean has a z score transformation that falls within the bounds of $+/-1.96$, we can refer to this outcome as the "expected" outcome since 95 out of every 100 samples will have a mean whose z score transformation locates them within this range just by the luck of the draw (i.e., sampling fluctuation). Therefore, we can reason that our sample mean is not really different from the population mean; at least not any different than we would expect by chance, or luck of the draw (i.e., sampling fluctuation).
5. If our sample has a mean whose z score falls outside of the bounds of $+/-1.96$, we can identify this as an atypical or unusual outcome—one that does not often happen just by the luck of the draw. Thus, we can reason that the difference is not likely one of chance and that the sample mean is probably different from the population mean.[1] For our example, the sample mean would have had to be as low as $33,807.21 or as high as $39,718.13 for us to reason that it was probably different from the population mean.

---

[1] In statistical terms, this is known as the .05 level of significance. If the probability of asserting that there is a difference between means is equal to or less than .05 then the difference is said to be significant at the .05 level.

You might be wondering why we go to all this trouble to determine whether a sample's mean is representative of a population's mean when we know the population mean. After all, the z score formula requires it! Well, most of the time we do not *know* the population mean and/or standard deviation. When we draw one sample from the population, we are actually hypothesizing with respect to the population mean. Suppose, for example, you decided to study a sample of students on your campus. You select a random sample of 200 students. Since campuses usually maintain statistical information on their student bodies, you know that certain pieces of information are available. You should be able to obtain the average age of the student body or the average GPA. Given these population averages, you can check to see if your sample is representative with respect to these variables. While we may not be able to establish representativeness with respect to all variables, establishing it for some variables can make us feel more comfortable about our sample.

Generally speaking, we have little difficulty identifying population values. In fact, we frequently use published research and/or secondary data sets such as the U.S. Census for obtaining these values. In general, if our sample mean is close to the hypothesized value, we are comfortable in reasoning that our sample represents the population under study.

In sum, theoretical distributions are probability distributions in that they represent a map of all possible outcomes, and the likelihood of any given event can be established by using this map—that is, the likelihood that an event is happening by chance. This procedure is the essence of inferential statistics. And in fact, inferential statistics rests on our ability to use theoretical distributions for evaluating probability.

THE *t* TEST FOR TWO INDEPENDENT SAMPLES

Perhaps the most usual situation that you will face as a researcher is one in which you are interested in drawing two samples from a population instead of one. These samples are generally drawn on the basis of some identifying characteristic. For example, you might draw one sample of males and one sample of females in order to compare males and females with respect to some other variable. Once the samples are drawn, you compute the two means. You then compute the difference between the two sample means ($\overline{X}_1 - \overline{X}_2$). Since both samples come from the same population, you expect this difference to be zero:[2]

---

[2] The Greek letter μ is the symbol used to represent the population mean.

$$\overline{X}_1 = \mu$$
$$\overline{X}_2 = \mu$$
Therefore: $\overline{X}_1 = \overline{X}_2$ and $\overline{X}_1 - \overline{X}_2 = 0$

However, in reality, you know that these two $\overline{X}$'s will probably not be exactly the same (due to sampling fluctuations). Our concern, then, is with *just how different* these two means really are. If they are not too different, we can reason they really did come from the same population and are therefore equal. If they are too different, we must reason they did not come from the same population and are therefore not equal. In order to make this evaluation, the difference between these two means, like the single sample mean, must be standardized and located on a standard normal curve of an infinite number of such mean differences. This standardized difference between sample means is called a *t* score (instead of a *z* score), which can vary between zero and infinity. A *t* score of zero means no difference between $\overline{X}_1$ and $\overline{X}_2$ (although the evaluation is actually based on the sizes of the two samples involved).[3]

If the *t* score is so large that it falls outside the boundary separating 95 percent of the area under the curve from the other 5 percent, we must reason that the two means are different and therefore not equal. If the *t* score falls within these 95 percent boundaries (a difference of chance—sampling fluctuation), we can reason that the means are not really different and therefore are equal.

Let's illustrate with an example. Suppose that after your first research methods exam, you wanted to compare the mean exam score for males with the mean score for females. The data for this comparison might appear as in Table 13.1.

The *t* score for the difference between these two means is .16—a score that easily falls within the 95 percent range (the *t* score separating the 95 percent area from the other 5 percent for this data is 2.101). Therefore, we can reason that this is a difference that occurs by chance and that the mean test scores for males and females are not really different.

---

[3] While *z* is a fixed distribution, the *t* distribution is not. When we do not know the population standard deviation, we must substitute our best guess for this value. Our best guess is the standard deviation of our sample. However, because of sampling fluctuation (sample standard deviation varies from one sample to another), the *t* curve is not a fixed shape. Hence, evaluating a *t* score must take into consideration degrees of freedom—the number of values in a sample that are free to vary.

TABLE 13.1 Exam Scores by Sex

Males	Females
89	92
92	78
76	73
81	81
93	64
68	97
71	83
78	91
73	73
86	83
$\overline{X} = 80.7$	$\overline{X} = 81.4$
$S = 8.945$	$S = 10.035$

THE F TEST—THREE OR MORE INDEPENDENT SAMPLES

In our discussion of the *t* test, recall that the two independent samples were drawn on the basis of some identifying characteristics such as sex. Oftentimes, the identifying characteristic used to draw the random samples is such that more than two independent samples will be drawn. For example, if marital status were the identifying characteristic, we might have three independent samples: (1) married, (2) single, and (3) divorced. When you want to compare simultaneously sample means for more than two samples, the *t* test can no longer be used since it can compare only two sample means at a time. However, the *F* test can make comparisons between more than two sample means and is an appropriate test for this purpose. This simultaneous comparison between more than two sample means is accomplished by calculating two different estimates of the population variance (σ^2).[4]

1. One estimate of σ^2 is obtained by calculating the variance for each of the independent samples and then taking an average of these estimates. This, in fact, is our best estimate of the population variance since one way to eliminate variability in a statistic (in this case, variance) from one sample to the next is to draw several samples and take an average of the statistics. Hence, an average of several estimates of the variance provides us with our *best* estimate of the population variance.

---

[4] The symbol σ^2 is used to represent the variance of the population.

2. A second estimate of σ^2 is obtained using the sample means. We begin by treating the same means as a distribution and then calculate the variance for this distribution of sample means. But since this variance is calculated on sample means, it is actually an *estimate of the variance of the sampling distribution of sample means*. Recall, though, from our earlier discussion that there is a relationship between the variance of the population and the variance of the sampling distribution of sample means:

$$\sigma_{\bar{x}}^2 = \sigma^2/N$$

Where: $\sigma_{\bar{x}}^2$ = variance of the sampling distribution of sample means
σ^2 = variance of the population
N = sample size

Since we have an estimate of σ^2 (just calculated from our sample means) and we know the size of the samples drawn, we can obtain our second estimate of the population variance.

The first estimate of the variance is labeled the *within variance*, as it is based on variance *within* samples. The second estimate of the variance is called the *between variance*, as it is based on variance *between* sample means. The *F* test, then, is simply a comparison of this second estimate to the first estimate. This comparison is accomplished by taking the ratio of the second variance estimate to the first.

$$F = \frac{S_B^2}{S_W^2}$$

If the between variance estimate is equally as good an estimate as the within variance estimate, this ratio will be approximately 1.00 (i.e., the two variances will be approximately equal), and we can safely reason that the sample means were computed on samples drawn from the same population. Therefore, all the sample means are equal. If this ratio is considerably larger than 1.00, then we have reason to believe that at least two of the sample means are far apart in value and one or more is probably outside of the actual population spread. Thus, the sample means are not equal. This concept is pictured in Figure 13.6.

To illustrate, let's suppose that we are interested in comparing mean exam scores for married, single, and divorced students. Now we

FIGURE 13.6   Suggested Spread when the Within and Between Variance are Equal:

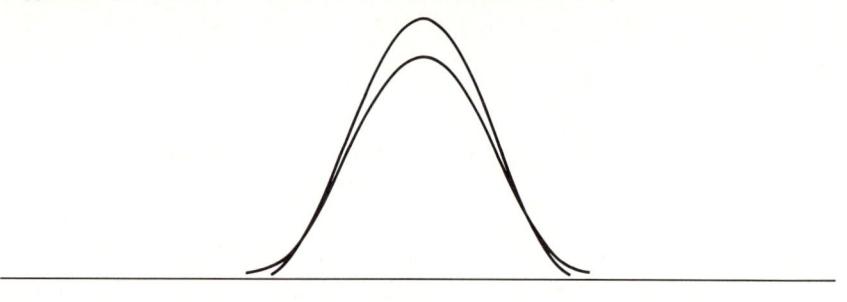

Suggested Spread when the Within and Between Variance are Not Equal:

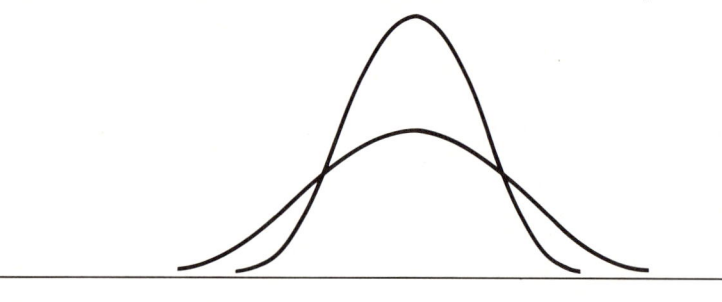

When the Within and Between Variance are NOT Equal, in Reality, Two or Three Populations:

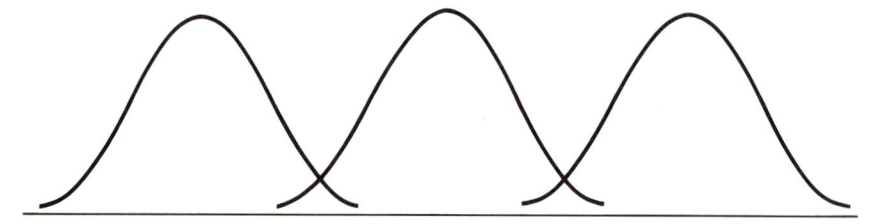

have three independent samples and three means to compare simultaneously. The data for these comparisons appear in Table 13.2.

The within-variance estimate computed from these three samples is 92.45. The between variance computed from these three sample means is 28.67. As with z and t, this F must be evaluated, and it is evaluated on a theoretical distribution known as F. If our F falls within the 95 percent area (easily occurs by chance), then we will reason that the three means are not different. If this F falls outside the 95 percent area (does not often occur by chance), then we will reason that the three means are not different. As it turns out, this F is well within the 95 percent area. Therefore, we can conclude that the three means are not different—in other words, no different than what we would expect by chance (sampling fluctuation).

TABLE 13.2 Exam Scores by Marital Status

Single	Married	Divorced
89	92	73
92	78	81
81	76	71
93	64	83
68	97	78
73	91	86
73	82	
$\overline{X} = 81.29$	$\overline{X} = 82.86$	$\overline{X} = 78.67$

CORRELATION AND REGRESSION

Correlation and regression are statistical procedures that make use of bivariate data—that is, pairs of measurements. When using correlation and regression, the essential feature of the data is that one observation can be paired with another observation for each value in the data set. Generally speaking, both variables should be measured at the interval or ratio level of measurement. As we shall soon see, correlation is primarily concerned with describing the degree of relationship between two variables, whereas regression is concerned with estimating one variable from another.

Simple Correlation and Regression

Let's begin our discussion of simple correlation and regression with an example. Assume that we have a normally distributed population of achievement test scores with a mean of 75 and a variance of 16. Now suppose we were to draw one test score at random from this population and make a guess as to its value. Although we could conceivably guess any value, realistically our best guess would be the population mean. The reason for this can be stated in terms of the *two* properties of the mean:

1. Our average error will be zero since the sum of our errors will be zero.
2. This guess will produce the smallest error variance. In fact, since μ is our best guess and since σ^2 is the average of the squared deviations from μ, the population variance and the error variance are one and the same.

Realistically though, we are looking for a procedure whereby we can make predictions with even fewer and smaller errors.

Suppose, for example, we could divide the original population of achievement scores into two subpopulations: one of males and the other of females. Now let us also assume that the mean achievement score is 73 for males and 77 for females. When we draw one achievement score and make a guess as to its value, we now have one additional piece of information: the sex of the individual making the score drawn. Given this additional piece of information, we now have three options with respect to our prediction:

1. We can make a blind prediction (any guess that comes to mind).
2. We can guess the population mean ($\mu = 75$).
3. We can guess the subpopulation mean (if male, 73; if female, 77).

In effect, our best guess is actually the mean of the subpopulation. In other words, we use the information we have about sex to make our prediction about test score. In essence, this is the meaning of regression. Regression can be defined as using one variable (X) to predict another (Y) (in this case, using sex to predict achievement score) where the predicted Y (Y') value is the mean Y ($\overline{Y}$) for the designated value of X. If the score drawn belongs to a male, then a guess of 73 will be closer to the true score than will be a guess of 75, the population mean, since the average male score is 73. In other words, regression is a statistical procedure through which we can analyze the relationship between a dependent or criterion variable and an independent or predictor variable.

In this example, the independent variable is a nominal level variable. In regression, though, both the independent and dependent variables are usually interval. The independent continuous variable (X) can be thought of in the same way that the independent discrete variable (X, in our example, sex) can be thought of. Each value of X (even though there are an infinite number of X values) can be conceptualized as a category. For every X value (conceptualized as a category), there is a normal distribution of Y's, and each Y distribution has its own mean. When we identify a value (category) of X, our predicted Y value is the mean Y ($\overline{Y}$) of the normal distribution of Y's for the designated value (category) of X. Figure 13.7 demonstrates the logic of this procedure.

Let us now draw upon a second example to demonstrate in greater detail the use of interval level variables. Suppose we are interested in predicting freshman GPAs from ACT scores. Assume an infinitely large population of GPAs. Now suppose we could divide this population into thirty-six subpopulations—one for each ACT score. For any value of ACT, there is a normal distribution of GPAs with a mean. The predicted GPA for a designated value of ACT is the mean GPA for the normal distribution of ACT at that value of ACT.

Realistically, it is not possible to gain access to an entire population of Y scores. Therefore, it is also impossible to identify all the Y values that make up the normally distributed Y subpopulation for a designated value

**FIGURE 13.7
Logic of
Regression
Analysis**

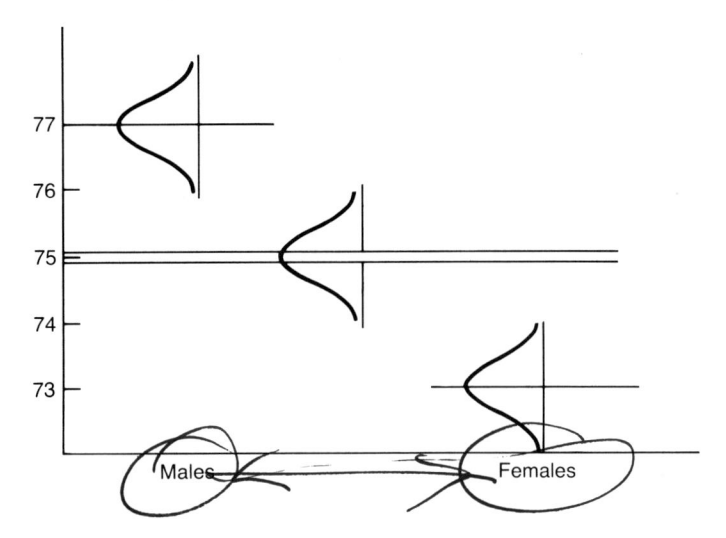

of X. Hence, the predicted Y's for all values of X are determined by using the formula for a straight line:

$$\text{Predicted } Y (Y') = \alpha + bX$$

Where: α = Y intercept – the point where the line crosses the Y axis – the value of Y when X = 0

b = slope of the line – rise/run – the increase in Y for a unit increase in X

X = the designated value (category) of X

By using this equation, any predicted Y will be the mean Y of the normal distribution of Y's for the designated value (category) of X. This concept is pictured in Figure 13.7. Each point on this line (and there are an infinite number of points just as there are an infinite number of X values) represents the Y value for the corresponding value of X displayed on the horizontal axis. Using the hypothetical data presented in Table 13.3, we will solve these equations. For this example, the regression equation would be:

$$Y' = -1.67 + .16X$$

A scatterplot of these data is presented in Figure 13.8. From this scatterplot, you should notice that the points lie almost in a straight line. In fact, most of them are pretty close to the line drawn through the points. In addition, the following observations can be made:

MEASUREMENT, DATA COLLECTION, AND ANALYSIS

TABLE 13.3 ACT and GPA Scores

X ACT	Y GPA
15	0.75
24	2.25
30	3.25
34	3.75
18	1.25
20	1.50
26	2.50
28	2.75
16	0.80
31	3.25

1. The points on the line represent the predicted Y's—the predicted GPAs.
2. The plotted points represent the actual Y values—the actual GPAs.
3. The distance between any plotted point and its corresponding point on the line is a *residual* or error in prediction.
4. Intuitively, you should see that in this example, our error will be small, since the points on the line and the plotted points are quite close.

The Adequacy of the Fit. Even though we can now look at the actual Y's (GPAs) and the predicted Y's (GPAs) and see that they are indeed close

**FIGURE 13.8
Scatterplot of
Raw Data**

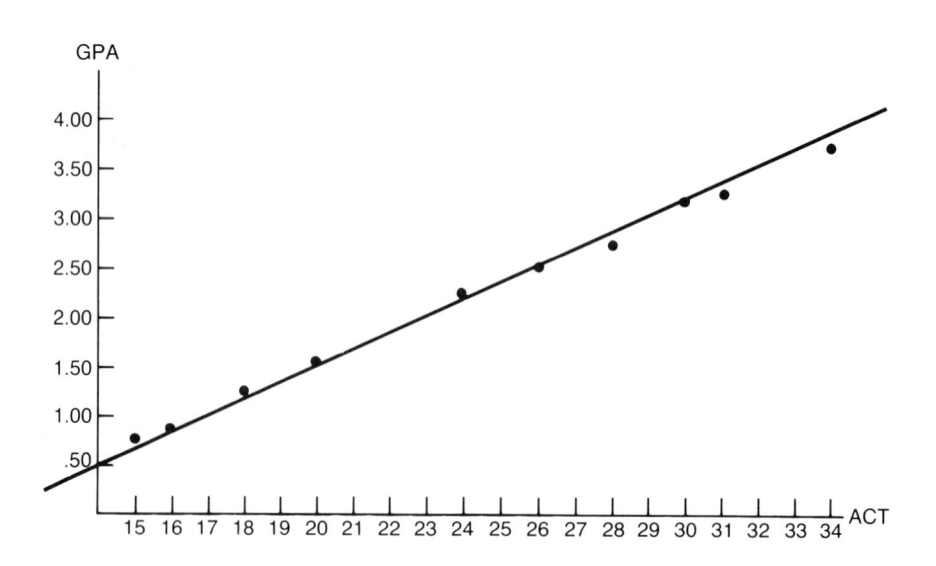

(residuals are small), such a subjective evaluation does not provide sufficient evidence that the equation ($Y' = -1.67 + .16X$) yields a good prediction and therefore is an adequate fit to the data. Consequently, more objective measures of how well an equation "fits" the data should be used. There are several such measures. Let's take a brief look at each.

THE STANDARD ERROR OF THE ESTIMATE   One measure of the adequacy of the fit of this regression equation (i.e., closeness of plotted points to the regression line) is the standard error of the estimate, which is really the standard deviation of the residuals. This statistic provides a measure of the average distance of each residual (error in predicting: $Y - Y'$) from the mean residual of zero. If the regression equation were perfect, every prediction would be perfect. Thus, every predicted Y would equal every actual Y. In effect, all residuals would be zero. Thus, the standard deviation of these residuals would be zero. Intuitively, you should recognize that the smaller the standard error (standard deviation of the residuals), the better the predictions and thus, the better the regression equation.

THE CORRELATION COEFFICIENT   A second measure of the adequacy of the fit of the data to the regression line (that is, the closeness of the plotted points to the regression line) is the correlation coefficient. The correlation coefficient is a measure of the strength of the relationship between two variables, X and Y. That is, it is a measure of the degree to which these two variables vary together. The correlation coefficient varies between 0 and $+/-1.00$. The extreme values ($+/-1.00$) represent perfect correlations. That is, X and Y covary (vary together) perfectly. Stated another way, the plotted points and the predicted points (points on the regression line) are identical, and we will be able to predict perfectly every time. A correlation of $+1.00$ means the relationship between X and Y is positive. As one variable increases in value, the other variable also increases in value. Or as one variable decreases in value, the other variable also decreases in value. A correlation of -1.00 means that the relationship between X and Y is negative. As one variable increases in value, the other variable decreases in value. A correlation of zero means no relationship at all. Hence we have no ability to predict one variable from the other.

Finally, we can test the significance of the correlation coefficient by testing the null hypothesis of no relationship between Y and X in the population—that is, $r = 0$. In effect, the null hypothesis is that the correlation coefficient is zero or nearly zero. This hypothesis is tested with the F statistic. The greater the proportion of variance explained, the larger the value of F. Thus, in a very general sense, the larger the value of F, the greater the likelihood of rejecting the null hypothesis (that is, the greater the likelihood of a relationship between Y and X and the greater the likelihood of X explaining variation in Y).

THE SQUARED CORRELATION COEFFICIENT Another measure of the adequacy of the fit of the data to the regression equation is the squared correlation coefficient, which represents the proportion of variance in Y (the dependent variable) that is explained by X (the independent variable). The squared correlation coefficient varies between 0.00 and $+/-1.00$. When the squared correlation coefficient is 0.00 (no ability to predict), zero percent of the variance in the dependent variable is explained by the independent variable. When the squared correlation coefficient is 1.00 (perfect ability to predict), we know that 100 percent of the variance in the dependent variable is being explained by the independent variable.

A Composite Example. To illustrate simple correlation and regression, let's look at a composite example. Suppose we wanted to predict the selling price of a house from the number of square feet in the house. We will make our prediction from our sample of 100 sales records taken from the population of 10,000 housing sales in Memphis, Tennessee, for 1978. We begin with the following prediction equation:

$$Y' = \alpha + bX$$

Where: Y' = predicted sales price

X = square footage

Now let's examine a scatter diagram of the two variables (X and Y) with price on the vertical axis and square footage on the horizontal axis. This scatter diagram is pictured in Figure 13.9. It is generally a good idea to plot the data before running the regression analysis because this simple visual aid can frequently identify potential problems with the regression analysis. In particular (and this will be discussed at greater length in the next section) we are concerned with the assumption of linearity. As you can see in this scatter diagram, these data form a generally linear pattern from the lower left-hand quadrant of the plot to the upper right-hand quadrant. However, if the plot had indicated a curved or curvilinear relationship, then a straight line (regression line) would not be appropriate for describing this relationship. One of our assumptions in regression is linearity, and even though a curvilinear relation is in a more general sense linear, a straight line is an inappropriate manner in which to describe a curved relationship.

Using the appropriate formulas, suppose we were to obtain the following relationship:

FIGURE 13.9
Scatter Diagram of Square Feet and Selling Price

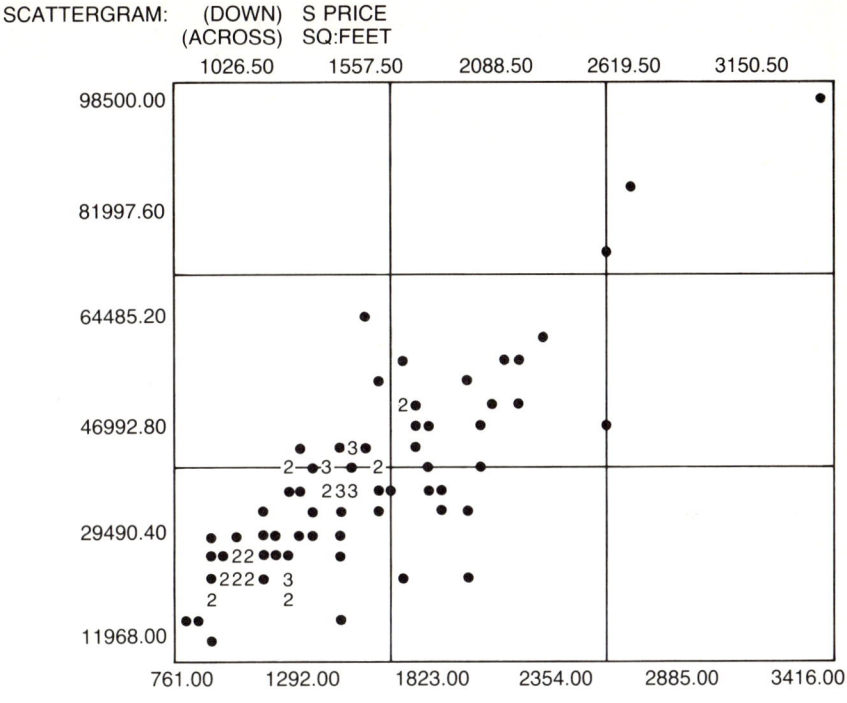

```
SCATTERGRAM:   (DOWN)  S PRICE
               (ACROSS) SQ:FEET
               1026.50    1557.50    2088.50    2619.50    3150.50
      98500.00                                                    •

      81997.60                                           •
                                                         •

      64485.20                         •
                                          •        • ••
                                     2•      •• •
      46992.80                    •3•    ••
                               2—•3—•—2                      •
                                 233 ••    ••
      29490.40        ••  ••• •
                      ••22 •••    •
                      •222• 3   • •
                      2     2
      11968.00     ••
                    •
           761.00    1292.00    1823.00    2354.00    2885.00    3416.00
```

STATISTICS..
CORRELATION (R) = .82907
R SQUARED   = .68735
SIGNIFICANCE   = .00001
STD ERR OF EST   = 8179.99018
INTERCEPT (A)   = −1743.83193
SLOPE (B)   = 26.57758

PLOTTED VALUES = 96   EXCLUDED VALUES = 0   MISSING VALUES = 4

$$\text{Predicted } Y (Y') = -1{,}743.8 + 26.58 \text{ (SQFOOT)}$$

Where: −1,743.8 = Y intercept

26.58 = slope of the line or an increase in $26.58 for each additional square foot

If the square footage of a house is 1,550, we would predict a selling price of $39,455.20.

$$Y' = -1{,}743.8 + 26.58(1550) = \$39{,}455.20$$

Now let's also suppose that the correlation coefficient for our data is .829, which is a fairly high correlation. The F statistic for this r is 206.6. With an F of this size, we know that only one time out of 10,000 would such an F

occur by chance. Hence, we can reason that our F is probably not a chance event. This r is significantly different from 0. In short, we reject the null hypothesis that $r = 0$. The correlation coefficient squared (r^2) is .687, indicating that a little over 68 percent of the variance in selling price is explained by square footage. That leaves only 32 percent of the variance in selling price unexplained by this variable. In short, this regression equation is doing an adequate (though not perfect) job of predicting selling price from square footage.

Multiple Correlation and Regression Analysis

Few things in life are perfectly and uniformly related. No single variable is generally the sole predictor of something else. Thus, a more realistic approach to explaining any phenomenon is to look for several variables that work together to explain something else. For example, suppose condition and age of house are also good predictors of selling price, and suppose both of these along with square footage are better predictors than any one is singly. *Multiple regression* is simply an extension of simple linear regression in that we are now using two or more independent variables to predict the dependent variable.

To understand how multiple regression works, let's consider the following example. Let's assume that we have a normally distributed population of housing selling prices with a mean of $40,000 and a variance of $20,000. Now suppose we could divide this population into four subpopulations: (1) older homes in below-average condition, (2) older homes in above-average condition, (3) newer homes in below-average condition, and (4) newer homes in above-average condition. For this example, let's assume older homes are homes fifteen years old or older and newer homes are homes less than fifteen years old. If we were to draw one sales record from this population and make a guess as to the selling price, we would now have *two* pieces of information to help us with our guess: (1) age (older or newer) and (2) condition (below or above average) of the house sold. And our best guess would be the mean of the subpopulation of the normal distribution of Y's for the designated combination of X's. In other words, we use information that we have about age and condition to make our prediction about selling prices. In essence, this is the meaning of multiple regression. Multiple regression can be defined as "using two or more variables ($X_1, X_2, \ldots X_k$) to predict another (Y) (in this example, using age of home and condition to predict selling price of a house) where the predicted Y (Y') is the mean Y ($\overline{Y}$) for the designated combination of X values (categories). Restated, multiple regression is a statistical technique through which we can analyze the relationship between a dependent or criterion variable and a set of independent or predictor variables.

If, for example, we were to draw a newer home in above-average condition, our predicted selling price would be $65,000 since the average selling price of a new home in above average condition is $65,000. In other words, a guess of $65,000 every time will be closer to the actual price (that is, fewer and smaller errors) than will be a guess of $40,000, the population mean. In effect, fewer and smaller errors result from the fact that the sum of the squared deviations from a distribution's mean is a minimum value (smallest sum).

In the example just given, the two independent variables were nominal or at best ordinal. In regression analysis, both the independent and dependent variables are assumed to be interval. Independent continuous variables (X_1 and X_2) can be thought of in the same way that the independent discrete variables (age of home and condition) can be thought of. Each combination of X_1 and X_2 values (even though there are an infinite number of X_1 and X_2 values) can be thought of as a category. For every combination of X_1 and X_2 values (conceptualized as a category), there is a normal distribution of Y's—each of these Y distributions having its own mean. When we identify the desired combination of X_1 and X_2 values, our predicted Y (Y') value becomes the mean Y ($\overline{Y}$) of the normal distribution of Y's for the designated combination of X_1 and X_2 values.

Let's now reexamine our two independent variables—age of home and condition—but this time treated as interval variables. We are still interested in predicting selling price of home from age of home and condition. Now let's suppose we could divide this population into subpopulations—one for each combination of age and condition. Again, for every combination of age and condition, there is a normal distribution of selling prices each with its own mean. And the mean selling price of this normal distribution is the predicted selling price for the designated combination of values on age and condition. This concept is pictured in Figure 13.10. The predicted Y (selling price) for a four-year-old home in good condition, for example, is the mean $\overline{Y}$ (Y) for the normal distribution of Y's (selling price) for this particular combination of X_1 and X_2 (that is, four-year-old home in good condition).

As in simple linear regression, it is not always possible to gain access to an entire population of Y scores. Similarly, it is not possible to identify all the Y values that make up a normally distributed Y subpopulation for a designated combination of X_1 and X_2. As it turns out, the mean Y's ($\overline{Y}$'s) for all values of X (when there are just two independent variables—X_1 and X_2) are determined by using the formula for a plane:

$$\text{Predicted } Y (Y') = \alpha_{y.12} + b_{y1.2}X_1 + b_{y2.1}X_2$$

Where: $\alpha_{y.12}$ = y intercept or the value of Y when X_1 and X_2 are zero

$b_{y1.2}$ = the increase in Y for a unit increase in X_1 at a constant value of X_2

**FIGURE 13.10
Predicted Selling Price for Four-Year-Old House in Good Condition (Aerial View)**

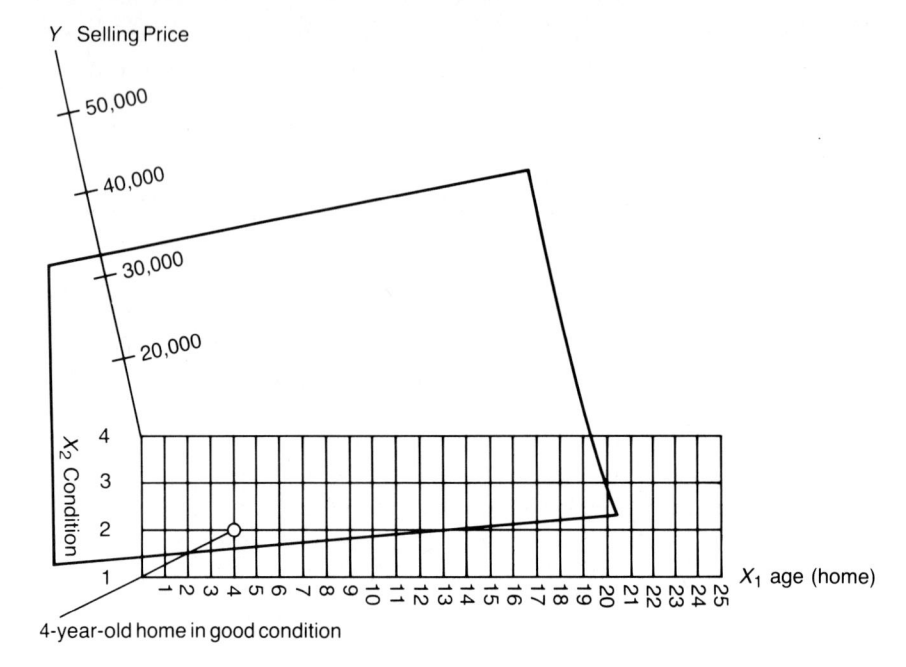

$B_{y2.1}$ = the increase in Y for a unit increase in X_2 at a constant value of X_1

X_1 = the first independent variable

X_2 = the second independent variable

Multiple regression models can be extended to include k independent variables. When the regression equation contains three or more independent variables, the regression model cannot be pictured geometrically, although it does have a definite algebraic equation. We should also mention that the betas in the multiple regression equation will not ordinarily be the same as those obtained in the two variable case. In the two variable case (one independent and one dependent variable), the beta obtained ignores all other independent variables. That is, other variables are not held constant. In contrast, the betas in the multiple regression equation are referred to as partial betas since they represent slopes that are computed controlling for each of the remaining independent variables included in the regression equation.

Finally, we want to introduce you to a standardized beta. The standardized beta represents the value that would be computed if both the X and Y variables had been entered into the regression equation in z score form. Such betas are extremely useful in that they provide a means by which we can compare the relative contributions of each independent variable (that is, to explaining variance in the dependent variable). With the standardized regression equation there is *no* intercept since in standard form this value is always zero.

In Figure 13.11 we present a graphic display of the two variable multiple regression equation. The points on the plane are the predicted Y's—in our case, the predicted selling prices. The plotted points are the actual Y's—the actual selling prices. The distance between the plotted points and the points on the plane represent our error in predicting.

The Adequacy of the Fit. As with simple linear regression, we can use several objective measures to determine the degree to which the data fit the multiple regression equation.

THE STANDARD ERROR OF THE ESTIMATE Like the simple linear regression equation, if the regression equation could predict perfectly, the standard error would be zero. If the regression equation were perfect, every prediction would be perfect. Thus, every predicted Y would equal every actual Y. All residuals $(Y - Y')$ would equal zero. Consequently, the standard deviation of these residuals would be zero. Again, the smaller the standard error (standard deviation of the residuals), the better our ability to predict—hence, the better the regression equation.

**FIGURE 13.11
Graphic Display of Regression Plane**

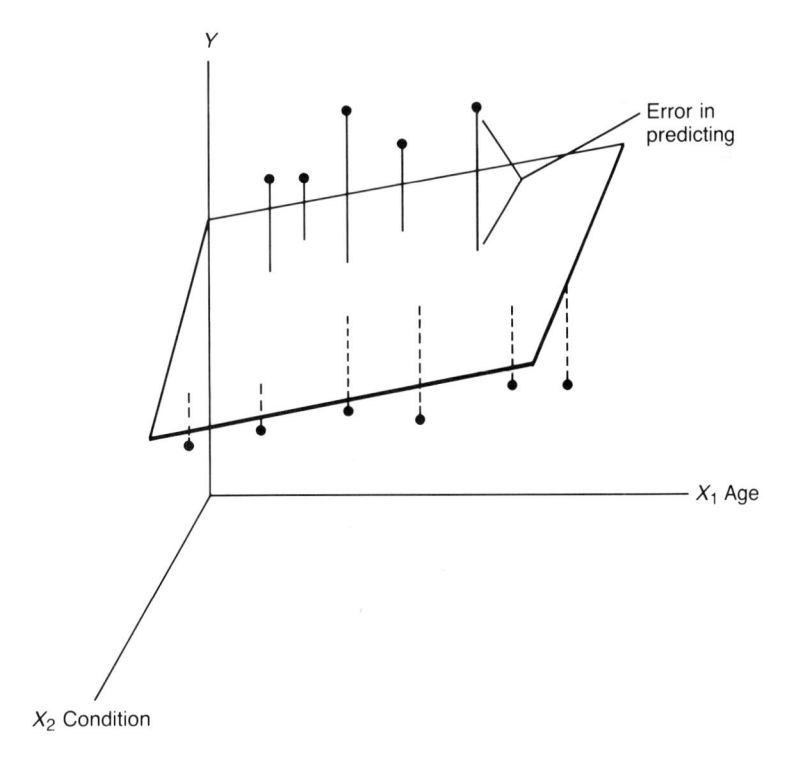

THE MULTIPLE CORRELATION COEFFICIENT A second measure of the adequacy of the fit of the data to the regression plane (that is, closeness of the plotted points to the regression plane) is the multiple correlation coefficient. It represents the zero order correlation between the actual Y's and the predicted Y's. Multiple correlation coefficients range between 0 and $+/-1.00$. A correlation of $+/-1.00$ indicates that the regression equation is perfect—that is, it will predict perfectly every time. A correlation coefficient of zero indicates that the regression equation will not be able to predict at all.

The squared multiple correlation coefficient represents the proportion of variance in the dependent variable that is being explained by the regression equation—that is, by the independent variables acting together (in our case, by the two independent variables acting together).

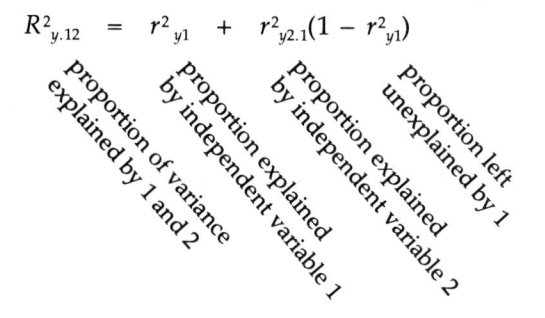

$$R^2_{y.12} = r^2_{y1} + r^2_{y2.1}(1 - r^2_{y1})$$

- proportion of variance explained by 1 and 2
- proportion of variance
- proportion explained by independent variable 1
- proportion explained by independent variable 2
- proportion left unexplained by 1

PLOTTING THE RESIDUALS A third measure used for detecting model deficiencies in a multiple regression analysis is examination of the residuals. The ith residual is defined as:

$$e_i = Y_i - Y_i'$$

These residuals can be standardized as follows:

$$z_e = \frac{e - \bar{e}}{S_e}$$

Since the mean error (e) is zero, this equation reduces to:

$$z_e = \frac{e}{S_e}$$

These residuals in standard form have a mean of zero and a standard deviation of 1.00. An appropriate graph of residuals will often expose gross model violations when they are present. Some of the more commonly used plots are those in which the standardized residuals (e_i) are plotted as the *ordinate* (i.e., vertical axis) against:

1. The fitted value, Y'
2. The independent variables, $X_1, X_2, \ldots, X_k$
3. The time order in which the observations occur

In general, when the model is correct, the standardized residuals tend to fall between -2.00 and $+2.00$ and are randomly distributed about zero. The residual plot should show no pattern of variation. Residual plots can help to identify several problems including the following:

1. Residual plots can help to identify *outliers*—that is, extreme values.

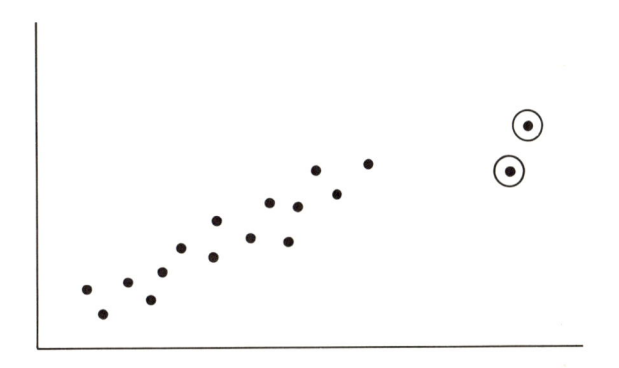

2. Residual plots can help to identify *heteroscedasticity*—that is, fluctuations in variance from one residual to another.

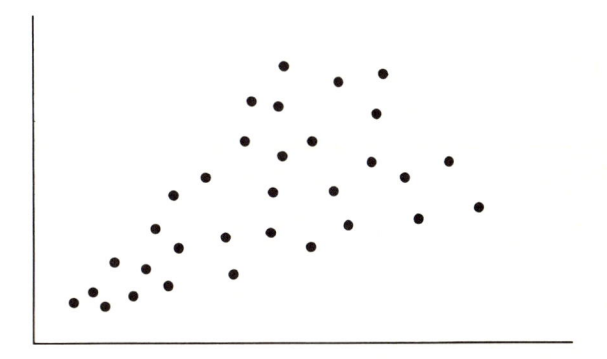

(Can be removed by adding or transforming variables.)
3. Residual plots can detect a *linear relationship between residuals and the variable on the horizontal axis.*

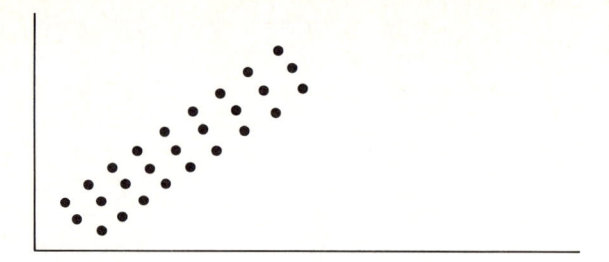

(Can be removed by adding variables.)
4. Residual plots can detect a *curvilinear relationship*.

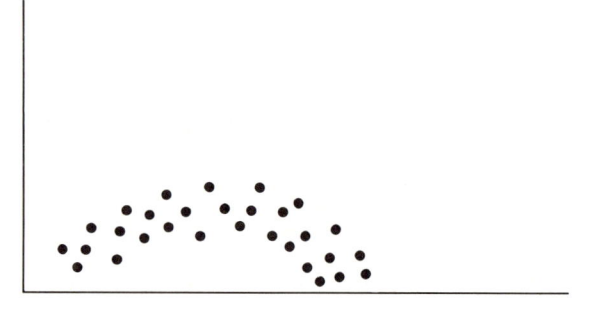

(Can be removed by adding or transforming variables.)

AUTOCORRELATION One of the standard assumptions in any regression model is that the error terms associated with each of the observations are uncorrelated. Correlation among the error terms suggests that there is additional explanatory information in the data that has not yet been exploited in the current model. When the observations have a natural sequential order, the correlation is referred to as autocorrelation. A characteristic pattern that would suggest autocorrelation would be one where several successive residuals would be positive, the next several negative, and so on.

The Durbin-Watson statistic d is a popular test of autocorrelation in regression analysis. There is an approximate relationship between d and r: $d = 2(1 - r)$. The Durbin-Watson statistic d has a range from 0 to 4. When r is close to 0, d is close to 2. Thus, the closer d is to 2.00, the firmer the evidence that there is no autocorrelation.

COLINEAR DATA Interpretation of the multiple regression equation depends implicitly on the assumption that the explanatory variables are not strongly interrelated. When there is complete absence of linear relationships among the explanatory variables, they are said to be orthogonal. In most regression applications, the explanatory variables are not orthogonal. Usually, though, the lack of orthogonality is not serious enough to affect the analysis. However, in some situations the explanatory variables are so strongly interrelated that the regression results are ambiguous. There are several ways to detect multicolinearity:

1. There exist high intercorrelations between the describing variables.
2. There are large variances in the estimates of the regression coefficients.
3. There is a large R^2 coupled with statistically nonsignificant regression coefficients.
4. There are large changes in the values of estimated regression coefficients when new variables are added to the regression.
5. The computer program is unable to compute regression coefficients (because of inability to compute the inverse of the correlation matrix).

There are also several ways to correct for multicolinearity:

1. We can collect additional data.
2. We can remove the variables that are causing trouble from the regression equation.
3. We can combine variables into a summary measure (less often approved).

The sequence of steps in multiple regression analysis can be summarized as follows:

1. Test the null hypothesis of no relationship between all independent variables acting together and Y (that is, the test of significance for the multiple correlation coefficient).
   a. If there is no relationship, then there is no need to go any further; we do not reject the null hypothesis.
   b. If there is a relationship, then we will also want to test for the influence of each independent variable.
2. Solve for the regression equation, identifying the Y intercept and the unstandardized and standardized betas. The signs of the slopes will tell us the direction of the relationship, and their sizes are an indicator of the amount of change in Y produced by a unit change in X. The F test will tell us whether or not these slopes are significantly different from zero (a horizontal line). The unstandardized slopes, though, should not be used as an indicator of the relative impact of each independent variable on the dependent variable Y. (A change in the units of measurement would change the slopes.) Thus, we calculate the standardized equa-

tion where both the "effect" of variable X_1 on Y and the "effect" of variable X_2 on Y are expressed in the same units of measurement, and thus, can be compared for their "relative" importance in determining Y.
3. Plot the residuals (generally standardized residuals against the standardized predicted Y's) as a measure of the adequacy of the fit.
4. Examine the residuals for autocorrelation.
5. Examine the independent variables for colinearity.

A Composite Example. Now let us return to the example that was presented in the section on simple linear regression. In our discussion of simple linear regression, we used square footage to predict the selling price of a house. As you will recall, this single variable appeared to be a fairly adequate predictor of selling price. However, this model has one problem that we have not yet mentioned—autocorrelation in the residuals. The Durbin-Watson statistic for this equation is 1.58—indicative of autocorrelation for our sample size. This autocorrelation is the result of a definite pattern found among the residuals. In effect, our one independent variable equation tends to overestimate the selling price of low-priced houses and underestimate the selling price of high-priced houses. The presence of autocorrelation suggests that there is probably a better regression equation. In addition, given that only 68 percent of the variance in selling price is explained with this one variable, we might want to examine our options. We could, for example, look for another single variable that performs better than square footage. Or we might try the number of rooms in a house or an amenities index based on the presence or absence of such features as carpet, central air conditioning, and built-in kitchen appliances.

A scatterplot of the amenities index and selling price is pictured in Figure 13.12. As you can see, the pattern is linear. The correlation coefficient is .683, which is lower than the correlation between square footage and selling price. This is our first indicator that this variable will not perform as well as square footage. The squared correlation coefficient is .466, indicating that a little over 46 percent of the variance in selling price is explained by the amenities index. In fact, this variable does not explain as much of the variance in selling price as the first variable, square footage. Additionally, there is still autocorrelation in the residuals (Durbin-Watson = 1.67), and the pattern producing this correlation is essentially the same. The lower-priced houses are overestimated and the higher-priced houses are underestimated.

Looking at these two correlation coefficients and the amount of variance each explains in the dependent variable (68 percent and 46 percent, respectively), you might think that we now have two good variables if taken together. In fact, if you tried to add together the amount of

FIGURE 13.12
Scatterplot of Amenities Index and Selling Price

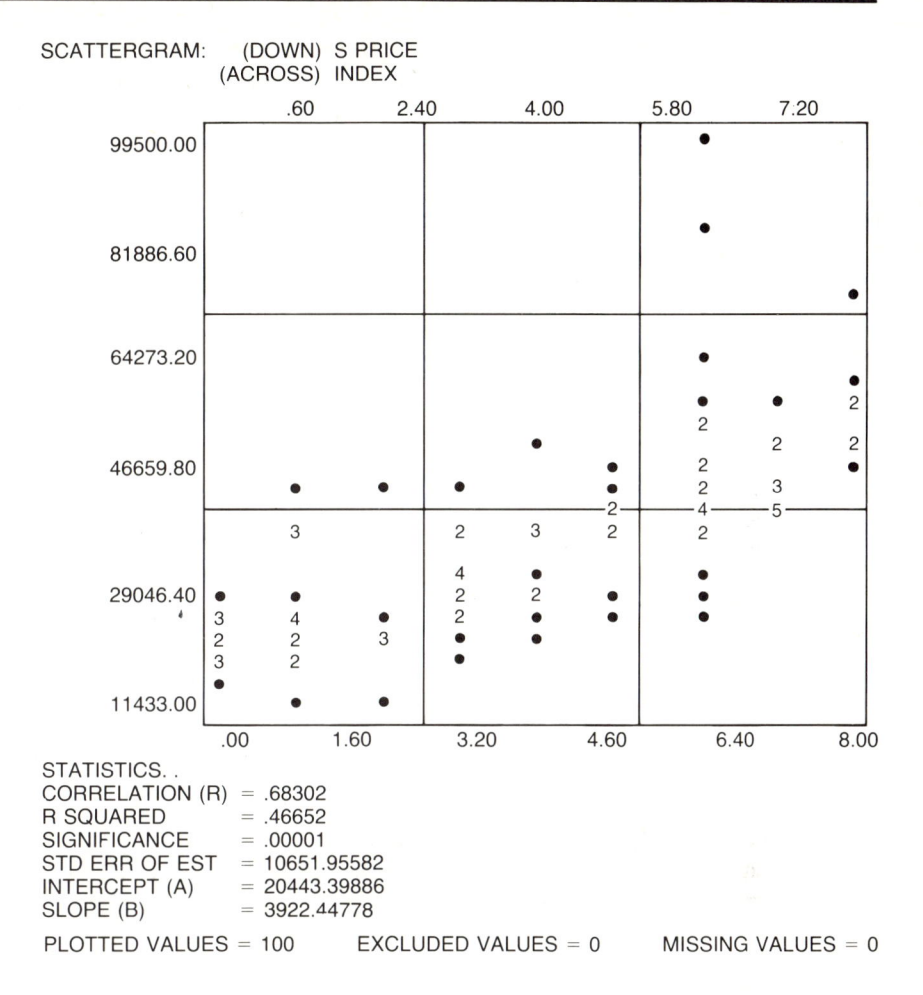

```
SCATTERGRAM:   (DOWN) S PRICE
               (ACROSS) INDEX
                   .60      2.40      4.00      5.80      7.20
         ┌─────────────────────────────────────────────────────┐
99500.00 │                                        •            │
         │                                                     │
         │                                                     │
         │                                                     │
81886.60 │                                        •            │
         │                                                                •│
         │                                                     │
64273.20 │                                        •            │
         │                                                            •  •│
         │                                                     2          2│
46659.80 │           •         •         •        •            │
         │                                        •        2       2     2│
         │                                             2        3       5│
         │           3                   2   3    2                      │
29046.40 │•                              4        •            │
         │ 3         •        •          2   2    •   •        │
         │ 2         4        2          2   •    •   •        │
         │ 3         2        2     3    •   •    •   •        │
         │•                              •                     │
11433.00 │           •        •                                │
         └─────────────────────────────────────────────────────┘
          .00      1.60      3.20      4.60      6.40      8.00
```

STATISTICS..
CORRELATION (R) = .68302
R SQUARED   = .46652
SIGNIFICANCE   = .00001
STD ERR OF EST = 10651.95582
INTERCEPT (A)   = 20443.39886
SLOPE (B)   = 3922.44778

PLOTTED VALUES = 100   EXCLUDED VALUES = 0   MISSING VALUES = 0

variance each variable explains, you would get over 100 percent (which, of course, is not possible). However, we could only add these two percentages together if there were no relationship between square footage and our amenities index. In other words, these two independent variables would have to correlate at zero. Intuitively, you should know there is a relationship between these two variables. In fact, these two variables correlate with each other at .61. In effect, what this means is that square footage and our amenities index are explaining some of the same variance in selling price. Hence, we need to identify that portion explained by each. That is, we need to identify that proportion of the variance in selling price left unexplained by square footage that can be explained by the amenities index. In other words, we need to place both of these variables in the regression model at the same time, and that requires a multiple regression model.

We will begin with two independent variables, square footage and our amenities index. The test of this model is displayed in Table 13.4. Our dependent variable is still selling price of a house. The multiple R for this equation is .856. Notice that this correlation indicates a stronger relationship between these two independent variables taken together and selling price than either variable taken singly. However, this relationship is only slightly stronger than the relationship between square footage and selling price. The R^2 is equal to .732, indicating that 73 percent of the variance in selling price is explained by the variables square footage and amenities index taken together. The test of significance for the multiple R^2 produces an F of 126.96—providing still further evidence that one or both of these variables is explaining variance in the dependent variable, selling price. Both betas produce significant F's, indicating that both

TABLE 13.4 Multiple Regression Model

Two Independent Variables

Variable	Unstandardized Beta	Standardized Beta	F
Index	1,545.00	.2,705	15.47
Square footage	21.16	.6,600	92.06
(alpha)	−254.95		

$R^2 = .856$ $F = 126.96$ Standard Error = 7,614.95

Six Independent Variables

Variable	Unstandardized Beta	Standardized Beta	F
Stories	−3,014.70	−.006	1.09
Square footage	24.77	.768	108.09
Car cover	3,324.80	.111	4.18
Condition	−4,734.50	−.169	9.90
Amenities index	1,016.00	.175	4.30
Age of home	−73.86	−.007	
(alpha)	8,578.65		

$R^2 = .805$ $F = 55.13$ Standard Error = 6,618.79

Four Independent Variables

Variable	Unstandardized Beta	Standardized Beta	F
Square footage	23.00	.713	123.84
Car cover	3,218.60	.108	3.97
Condition	−4,692.70	−.168	9.77
Amenities index	1,353.80	.234	12.46

$R^2 = .800$ $F = 81.92$ Standard Error = 6,627.23

variables are significant in the equation. For the amenities index, the unstandardized beta suggests that for each amenity added, we can add $1,545 to the selling price of the house. For square footage, the unstandardized beta suggests that for every square foot added, we can add $21.16.

By comparing the standardized betas, we can also determine the relative importance of each variable in the equation. In effect, square footage has a little over twice the effect of the amenities index on selling price. Additionally, there is no evidence of colinearity even though the two independent variables correlate at .61. This correlation is not enough to create colinearity. When we compare the standard error of this equation to the standard error of the first, we find it is smaller. However, the Durbin-Watson d statistic still suggests autocorrelation among the residuals (1.577). The pattern creating this autocorrelation remains the same. We are underpredicting the selling price of the higher-priced houses and overpredicting the selling price for lower-priced homes.

To facilitate our search for the best regression equation and to eliminate autocorrelation in the residuals, let's try a six-independent-variable model. The six independent variables being introduced to predict selling price of a house include (1) square footage, (2) amenities index, (3) condition of house, (4) age of house, (5) number of stories, and (6) number of bathrooms. The test of this model appears in Table 13.4.

The multiple correlation coefficient for this equation is .897, and the squared multiple correlation coefficient is .805, indicating that these six variables taken together account for a little over 80 percent of the variance in selling price of a house. Since this model is significant ($F = 55.129$), we will proceed to test each of the independent variables to discern if each is making a significant contribution to the prediction equation. These tests are pictured in Table 13.4. As you can see from the F tests of the beta weights, two variables are not significant—number of stories and age of house. Additionally, although the standard error is smaller (6,618.79) than for our previous model, the Durbin-Watson d statistic still reflects evidence of autocorrelation ($d = 1.64$). To make this model clearer and simpler, the two insignificant variables need to be removed. Consequently, a new model is constructed that includes only four independent variables: (1) square footage, (2) amenities index, (3) condition, and (4) number of bathrooms. The test of this model appears in Table 13.4.

Notice that the multiple R for this equation is .894—a difference of only .003 from the previous six-variable equation. In effect, removing the independent variables "number of stories" and "age of home" has little effect on the fit of the data to this equation. The R^2 is .800, indicating that 80 percent of the variance in selling price is explained by these four variables taken together. A look at the F tests for each of the betas indicates that all four independent variables are significant. Additionally, by examining the standardized betas, we can see the relative importance of these variables: (1) square footage, (2) amenities index, (3) condition of house, and (4) number of bathrooms. The standard error of this equation is also reasonable—6,627.23. There is no evidence of colinearity among the independent variables. In addition, the plot of the standardized residuals against the standardized predicted Y's appears random. However, there still remains the problem of autocorrelation in the residuals (Durbin-Watson $d = 1.58$). This pattern is again such that the low-priced houses are overestimated and the high-priced houses are underestimated. In short, it may be that the variables available to us are limited in some way. It may also be that other variables, such as quality of neighborhood, racial mix, and crime rate, need to be included in our model. In any event, it is reasonable to say that we have not yet found the most adequate model.

Section III

Using Data to Answer Research Questions

Chapter 14

The Interpretation and Consequences of Research Data

Back to paradigms
   The role of theory in the interpretation of data
   Modest versus immodest interpretations
   The ethical nature of interpretation
      An example: The effects of pornography
The consequences of research
   Personal consequences
   Reactions from colleagues
   Reactions from the people you study
   Consequences for the enemies of people studied
Inductive and deductive interpretations
   The logic of interpretation
   Telling how the study was done
   A final word

In science as in love, concentration on technique is likely to lead to impotence.
—Peter Berger

Even though it may not seem so, the analysis and the interpretation of data are two quite different things. As you have just seen, the analysis of data collected in a research project involves separating complex material into its constituent parts and showing the relationship between these parts. Interpretation, on the other hand, is the broader task of coming to grips with the meaning of research and is the process by which the research project is finally tied back to the theory from which it evolved. This is the part of research that we feel is most often neglected both in actual research and in methods texts that discuss how research is done. All one has to do is attend enough dissertation defenses or meetings of social scientists who present their work in order to see that the larger question of "What does it mean?" is often lost in the enthusiasm for putting together a "proper" piece of research. This question of meaning is the one laypeople are often most interested in, for methodological slickness does not make up for a research project that people regard as meaningless. In this chapter, we will redress that inadequacy and show how social research is filled with fascinating meanings and implications, and how best these meanings can be teased out of research findings and presented in a coherent and interesting way.

BACK TO PARADIGMS

The Role of Theory in the Interpretation of Data

Research is seldom any better than the theory that guides it. This point we took some pains to make in Chapter 3, and without belaboring it too much, we wish to rejuvenate that notion and discuss it briefly.

You will recall from the discussion in Chapter 3 that a paradigm is

> a fundamental image of the subject matter of science. It serves to define what should be studied, what questions should be asked, how they should be asked, and what rules should be followed in interpreting the answers obtained. The paradigm is the broadest unit of consensus within a science and serves to differentiate one scientific community (or subcommunity) from another. It subsumes, defines, and interprets the exemplars, theories, methods, and instruments that exist within it.

In other words, theory and method, fact and framework of interpretation are tied together in an inextricable mix. There is no such thing as an independent fact. All pieces of data must be tied to theory or they have no meaning at all. A fact awaiting interpretation is like a windshield wiper waiting to be switched on. Facts are paradigm-dependent, and different paradigms rearrange the criteria for accepting something as "truth." So, if the researcher wishes to know something, he or she will have to pay some attention to the body of theory that gives rise to the questions the research will ultimately try to answer.

For example, there has been in sociologically based research in social psychology a continuing preoccupation with questions of the self. In fact, probably no other single concept has given rise to so much research. On the other hand, while all of this research seems to have a family resemblance, the families can hardly talk to each other when it comes to the question of interpreting the data each derives from its research! This is because the theories and intellectual traditions from which the concept of self arises are so divergent. There are paradigms that see the self as being an indwelling property of the individual that is reflected in that person's behavior. Such paradigms use paper-and-pencil tests in an effort to reveal who and what people really are (Kuhn 1962). Interpretations of these data then are tied to the basic assumption that a methodological technique is designed to *uncover* something that is already there. There are other paradigms, however, that see the self as a construct that arises out of the interactions one has with others. From the standpoint of this imagery, paper-and-pencil tests could not possibly reveal anything more than the current self the respondent is establishing before the researcher because there is nothing there to be revealed in the first place. Such a paradigm would lead to a very different kind of methodology. Instead of looking for strategies that *reveal,* one develops strategies that *describe* the kind of self that is being constructed and the techniques by which that construction is being accomplished (Goffman 1959). Interpretive strategies, then, necessarily follow the assumptions of the paradigm, and each researcher would interpret the data from the standpoint of the paradigm guiding the research.

On the other hand, as George Ritzer (1975) has pointed out, the greatest pieces of research ever conducted were almost always ones in which the practitioner "bridged paradigms," interpreting findings from the standpoint of several paradigms simultaneously in order to get a better view of findings. This is close to the concept of triangulation, which we have discussed elsewhere in this book—that is, getting at data from several different angles. It is in the interpretation section of a research project that triangulation, in its broadest sense, is most appropriate. Using our example of the self in social psychology, we might note that the creative researcher, even though his or her work is obviously guided by a paradigm that has been carefully elucidated in the project, might wish to examine what his or her finding would be like if interpreted from the standpoint of alternative paradigms. This obviously requires some amount of intellectual honesty and dexterity, for most researchers are tied to the methods of their paradigm so thoroughly that the way of seeing dictated by the underlying assumptions of their paradigm often becomes a set of blinders rather than a set of lenses. (Every set of lenses obscures as well as reveals.)

Nevertheless, researchers should always ask themselves how many different ways a given piece of research can be read. In this sense, data are like flights into space: at lift-off a variety of details on the ground are revealed, but as you gain altitude, old perceptions fall away and new ones come into play. Finally, from orbit, one can see a wide variety of features that could not be seen from down low. This example is instructive because it also points out that there is no perspective that does not also conceal, and things begin to look very different when perspectives are switched. Which is the superior perspective depends on what kind of problem you are working on. For example, the view from orbit is terrific for long-term weather forecasting, but not worth a darn if you want to see the features of a flower planted near the launch pad.

In social science research we have a similar problem. Each of the techniques discussed in this book has strengths and weaknesses, long suits and shortcomings. The sensitive researcher overcomes the weaknesses of given methods as much as he or she can, but in the final analysis some weaknesses simply go with the methodological territory one is in, and, as a result, interpretations need to be fairly modest.

Modest versus Immodest Interpretations

For example, trying to make sweeping generalizations from data derived from the technique of participant observation and from its guiding interactionist paradigm is always risky, for the close description, involvement in depth, and firsthand knowledge of a given social world do not usually allow one to generalize too freely to other worlds that were not a part of the researcher's study. Conversely, survey researchers who operate out of a structural-functional paradigm must exercise some restraint in getting too specific about the detail of various social worlds they have not seen firsthand.

These cautions are really caveats about intellectual honesty. Creative interpretation and even a measure of speculation are one thing; arrogance and bluster are quite another. The former are to be cultivated, the latter abhorred.

It is obviously in the researcher's own interests to be relatively modest in the way in which he or she interprets and presents data. Leaps of speculative faith, defined as such, and offered to the reader with appropriate qualifications and cautions are certainly a part of a provocative research project. But throwing caution to the wind in one's enthusiasm to get as much attention as possible for a piece of research to which you have committed a considerable amount of effort can backfire overnight. Unfortunately, social research in this area is hardly immune to the common tendency in our society for persons (especially the press) to seize upon the weakest statement in a research project and trumpet it as the project's most important finding. This is why modest interpretations are generally better, lest readers wind up making much more out of a finding than the researcher would. On the other hand, risks of being provocative (lots of publicity, making a "name" for yourself, etc.) can be worth it too, and it is up to the individual researcher, in the last analysis, to defend what he or she has done.

The Ethical Nature of Interpretation

Aside from the risks to the researcher in making interpretative leaps that are unwarranted, there are also a number of ethical issues involved in the process of presenting research findings which, in our judgment, need far more attention than they currently get. In this section, we will discuss what we regard as some of the more important ethical issues facing the interpreter of social research findings. We are dealing here specifically with the ethical nature of *interpretation* as opposed to the many other ethical issues facing researchers as they plan and execute research projects. Those questions we have addressed in other sections of this book.

The first ethical problem in interpretation consists of the dilemma facing every researcher whose research is sponsored by an outside agency. Implicitly or explicitly, the sponsors of research have some kind of agenda in mind, and that is why they hired the research done in the first place. How is the researcher to maintain integrity in the face of the overwhelming power of money or political favor or any number of inducements that might be dangled in front of him or her in order to get the research to say what the sponsoring agency wants it to say? It is the matter of interpretation where such issues may often arise, for as we have said, facts do not speak for themselves and can be arranged in an almost infinite number of ways in order either to contribute to or demolish various ideologies the sponsor may have in mind. The problem is getting to be so great, in fact, that increasingly researchers in the social sciences are not even funded to do direct research projects, but are merely contracted to do some piece of technical work (e.g., draw a sample, conduct interviews), and the funding agency then completes the research and draws its own conclusions.

On the other hand, sponsoring agencies by and large still hire research projects because part of their ideological interests are best served by being able to give at least the impression of objectivity. In other words, what funders often want is not the truth of a particular bit of the social world but the imprimatur of legitimacy stamped on their policy, product, or agency decision by the social science community. Whether the sponsoring agency is a government body or the manufacturer of a product that comes in an aerosol can, the dilemmas posed for the researcher trying to keep his or her integrity intact can be enormous. What follows is an example from our not-too-distant past.

An Example: The Effects of Pornography. In 1967 the administration of President Lyndon Johnson decided, after what can safely be called centuries of debate, to fund a blue-ribbon commission to tell the country objectively whether or not exposure to pornographic material causes harm and whether or not access to such materials should be controlled. Commission members included seven university professors (including one social scientist), five lawyers, three clergymen, one nonacademic sociologist, one clinical psychiatrist, and a retired publishing house executive. When approved by Congress, the commission was directed to develop studies and recommendations around four areas. They were:

1. with the aid of leading constitutional law authorities, to analyze the laws pertaining to the control of obscenity and pornography; and to evaluate and recommend definitions of obscenity and pornography;
2. to ascertain the methods employed in the distribution of obscene and pornographic materials and to explore the nature and volume of traffic in such materials;
3. to study the effect of obscenity and pornography upon the public, and particularly minors, and its relationship to crime and other antisocial behavior; and
4. to recommend such legislative, administrative, or other advisable and appropriate action as the Commission deems necessary to regulate effectively the flow of such traffic without in any way interfering with constitutional rights.

Even as the commission began its work, the entire enterprise became embroiled in controversy. As Ray Rist (1975) reports in his comprehensive summary of the events that developed around the commission's work, members tried to proceed conscientiously with developing the kind of methodologies, data, and theoretical frameworks that would be appropriate to the questions they were asked to answer, but problems beset them from the outset. Although virtually all of the data and studies they developed pointed to an inescapable conclusion—that pornography has no harmful behavioral effects—by the time the report hit the public arena, both internal and external pressures had built to the point where rational debate no longer prevailed. Two members of the commission, a Catholic priest and the president of Citizens for Decent Literature, who was appointed by President Nixon to replace a member of the original commission who resigned, denounced the findings as degenerate and put out a minority report. Press leaks during the original deliberations about various methodologies used in trying to assess the effects of pornography were seized upon, and various scurrilous interpretations were created. In other words, the commission and its work had come to be a convenient whipping post for politicians who were looking for ways to convince the electorate that they were fighting for public morality and decency.

The Nixon administration, anxious to put distance between itself and the commission's findings, denounced the majority report as the product of "radical liberals" bent on destroying the United States by unleashing a torrent of smut. With the president leading the way, and an election at hand, other members of the Congress introduced various bills to denounce the commission findings. Finally, a week before the election, Nixon himself issued the following statement:

> I have evaluated that report and categorically reject its morally bankrupt conclusions and major recommendations.
>
> So long as I am in the White House, there will be no relaxation of the national effort to control and eliminate smut from our national life.
>
> The Commission contends that the proliferation of filthy books and plays has no lasting harmful effect on a man's character. If that were true, it must also be true that great books, great paintings and great plays have no ennobling effect on man's conduct. Centuries of civilization and ten minutes of common sense tell us otherwise.
>
> The Commission calls for the repeal of laws controlling smut for adults—while recommending continued restrictions on smut for children. In an open society, this proposal is untenable. If the level of filth rises in the adult community, the young people in our society cannot help but also be inundated by the flood. (Rist 1975, 266–67)

We have presented this brief example in order to illustrate in as bold relief as possible some of the dilemmas that face social researchers as they interpret their own studies and as others interpret them for themselves. It is apparent from the reaction to the commission's report that the accuracy, validity, generalizability, and other criteria of scientific methodology had precious little to do with the ultimate fate of the report. A variety of interests became party to the commission's work even before it became known exactly what they were doing or what their ultimate findings would be. This is characteristic of social science research on any number of topics, but especially controversial and emotionally charged ones. As Rist has suggested:

> Those who bring a social science orientation to commission endeavors, and who seek to address themselves to the issues within such an analytical

framework, confront others who do not accept the social science approach as appropriate. Those members of the Obscenity Commission who argued that the debate over sexually explicit material was not one of utility, but one of philosophy and ethics, illustrate this point: from the perspective of an alternative social reality, "mere facts" about the effects of sexually explicit material are irrelevant to the issue. (Rist 1975, 265)

But, of course, social science does not deal with "mere facts" either, as our discussion of theories and paradigms has shown. So it appears that participation by social scientists in the pornography controversy has the result of presenting "answers" to the questions it was asked from only a limited and partial perspective, which was doomed from the beginning to be unacceptable to a variety of interests. In retrospect, it seems that social scientists on the commission agreed to undertake a series of questions that social science could never really answer. Even though they carefully limited their interpretations of their findings to the data themselves, those data, like most in social science research, were inadequate to the whole range of questions that might be asked of them. For example, the members of the commission who studied the behavioral effects of the exposure of persons to pornographic literature acknowledged that their major finding—that no personal or social harm tended to result from viewing pornography—was subject to a variety of limitations. They noted that their research was one short-term exposure, and that the long-term effects could not be investigated on a commission that worked on that segment of the research for only two years. Furthermore, almost no research was available on the effects of pornography on children, obviously because of the major ethical obstacles to exposing children to pornography for research purposes. Finally, they noted that all of their research on behavioral effects was done with volunteers, and as we have noted repeatedly in this book it is difficult to generalize to nonwilling persons research findings that were obtained from studying willing ones. Nevertheless, even with those limitations, the commission chose to interpret the results of their studies as concluding that "no dangerous effects have been demonstrated on any of the populations which were studied" (Wilson 1975, 235).

The interpretation of the data by commission members was (it seemed to them) relatively modest. But like most interpretations, it really did go beyond the data at hand, even though they carefully couched it in qualified terms. Or, to put the matter another way, persons opposed to pornography could interpret the same data as concluding that social science has *not* proved that pornography is harmless.

Was it worth the effort for social science to get involved in the pornography controversy? The answer is not altogether clear. On the one hand, the research ... forced a wedge into the political construction of definitions of sexually explicit materials. Although many politicians denounced the Commission's findings and its recommendations, the Report, however briefly, opened a public debate over the issue of "effects" and its relation to the science-vs.-morals debate. (Rist 1975, 266)

Social science research seems at its best when its findings and tentative conclusions increase the level and quality of discussion in an open society. There is no question that the pornography commission's findings did just that. On the other hand, the commission's work opened far more questions than it was able to answer and seemed to hold social science up to be considerably less than it is often promised to be. In terms of the values of science, opening up more questions is usually a very positive development because it leads to further research, better understanding, and a refinement of both theory and methods. But in terms of the values of society where answers are sought after with an enormous emotional intensity, and decisions have to be made even on the basis of imperfect knowledge, social science seemed to fail to provide the necessary basis for making a decision about such crucial questions.

THE CONSEQUENCES OF RESEARCH

We selected the example of the pornography research because we thought it to be a particularly fruitful one for understanding the broader context in which the interpretation of social research occurs. All actions have consequences, and the research process, no matter how much we may want to make it seem like a neutral scientific enterprise, is fraught with consequential implications for the individual researcher, those whom the research is conducted on or about, and society in general.

Much of the impact of a study is beyond the control of the researcher, but much of it is controllable if we understand the most likely consequences that are to arise from it. The Loflands, whose analysis of the research process we will have occasion to refer to later, have noted that a researcher should anticipate and attempt to shape at least some of the more important consequences of a research project. They list several possible consequences in the following categories (Lofland and Lofland 1984).

Personal Consequences

Researchers, like other people, have to earn a living and get along with others. For this reason, research often has enormous personal consequences. At its best, the authors of a piece of research will be praised for their efforts, lauded for their interpretive skill, and rewarded in the marketplace of both ideas and money. Unfortunately, not all of the personal consequences may be positive. A piece of research done badly may stalk the authors and their reputation for the rest of their career. Researchers may feel that they have betrayed the people they were studying in some fundamental way or, like Robert Oppenheimer and his group of physicists who developed the first atomic bomb, that the research was used for negative purposes and had outcomes that were tragic. Social research is not always so dramatic in its potential for harm, but such potential is there, and many researchers have come to feel that they were guilty of a kind of "treason" (Heilman 1980; Thorne 1979). In qualitative research, especially, where close participation with the subjects of your research is both inevitable and generally positive, there can be the sense that the research did not have the consequences that were hoped for or even anticipated.

Reactions from Colleagues

Again, at best, the reactions of colleagues to a published piece of research can be among the most rewarding aspects of all the labor that goes into such an endeavor. One comes to be known as a person who contributed something substantial to the literature within an area, and even some measure of fame may come from the authorship of a solid piece of research. Let it be known, however, that even good research (sometimes *especially* good research) comes under the scrutiny and criticism of colleagues and may be panned, cut up, or even (heaven forbid!) reduced in the pages of some journal to intellectual rubble. Laud Humphreys's analysis of the homosexual "tearoom" has generated some of the most pointed and acerbic criticism ever aimed at a piece of social science research, and Humphreys has had to live with his work, for better or for worse, ever since it was published. Questions of intelligence, credentials, ethics, and prejudices are just a few among many sources of criticism that can be leveled against a researcher. Often the criticism is unfair. No researcher could have anticipated or dealt with all of the contingencies that were raised about a project, a point we saw vividly displayed in the example of the pornography commission. The slings and arrows of outrageous fortune are never more apparent than the fallout from a piece of research that becomes notorious. To engage in research is to put oneself in a position of some vulnerability, and so you might as well get prepared for something other than simply glowing reviews of your work. This point is just as valid for the student in a research methods class doing her first project and hoping to get an A, but ever in danger of getting something less, to the seasoned researcher who is publishing her tenth book.

Reactions from the People You Study

In qualitative research, the people you study will almost always have to be reported back to, and their reaction is likely to be an important factor in your later feelings about the project. There are numerous surprises here, for the people studied rarely respond to a piece of research the way the researcher thinks they will. They may be accepting, but not very impressed with the importance of the work, or they may be downright hostile. Lofland and Lofland have noted the following generalizations about reactions you are likely to get:

- Most people do not seem to care very much about scholarly analyses that are written about them. Many don't get around to reading them even when they are provided. There are harsh reactions and conflicts only in a minority of cases.
- Reports dealing with stable communities or ongoing groups are much more likely to generate a response from the participants than studies of more amorphous social situations or fluid groupings.
- The use of pseudonyms and a scholarly mode of writing tend to minimize the participants' interest in a report.
- The most interested and reactive participants appear to be members of elite groups in relatively small communities. (Lofland and Lofland 1984, 158)

In quantitative research it is not always quite so clear just what the impact will be on people you study. First, the actual groups that are interviewed or surveyed may not be identifiable in a statistical summary at all. Second, the impact of the study may be diffused, so that its results are quite subtle. There can be real ethical questions here. For example, to survey people with a fixed response questionnaire, force them to answer questions in preformed categories, and then use their responses as policy tools often means that a kind of shell game has been played in which social science research is used to imply a consensus about something when no such consensus may have existed at all. This is done all the time and can have enormous consequences on people's lives without very much of an opportunity for them to even know what has happened, much less do anything about it.

Consequences for the Enemies of People Studied

The groups you study in a research project are often asked to reveal aspects of themselves that could be at best embarrassing and at worst the ammunition with which their enemies can launch an attack. Julian Roebuck's study of southern "rednecks" (1983), for example, is a sensitive portrayal of a group under considerable pressure from various quarters, and his research, while sympathetic, could be used by a variety of the enemies of that culture to do it harm. Ethical considerations simply mandate that the author of a research project take every available opportunity to anticipate possible harm to subjects and ward it off.

INDUCTIVE AND DEDUCTIVE INTERPRETATIONS

The Logic of Interpretation

By definition, when we interpret, we move beyond "mere facts" to an arena that is more characterized by art than by science. We want to speculate, but from a base of factual material. We want to move from mere data to the larger plane of human meaning. There are two major ways of interpreting, just as there are two different ways in which the theory game is played, as we put it in Chapter 3. These two basic logics are inductive and deductive, and the nature of our interpretive efforts are going to depend in large measure on which of the two ways of analyzing data are used.

Remember that in deductive logic, we move from the general to the specific. It is in this form of theory and research that interpretation seems most tied to the premises of the general theory from which it sprang. If we have a theory about male–female relationships becoming more problematic in the twentieth century, for example, our data are going to be developed around a rather closely held set of theories and then "plugged into" those theories as they seem to fit. Interpretation is going to be a matter of assessing the fit between facts and theory, perhaps modifying the theory as things move along, or developing new methodologies to test new relationships that seem to be warranted from the emerging facts. Interpretation, in this process, is a matter of seeing the theory in a brighter light or altering it as that light seems to require. Interpretations that are inductively produced are much more difficult because their empirical grounding in a close analysis of a series of cases usually means that their generalizability is not as great. On the other hand, *because* they are empirically grounded, interpretations that move from an inductive form of logic may be much more powerful levers for interpretation than deductive ones because the facts from which they proceed seem to be so irrevocable.

One of the most brilliant pieces of research done in the past twenty years proceeds from an inductive base, and its interpretations of social reality are among the most provocative of our time. Daniel Yankelovitch, the head of a survey research polling firm (Yankelovitch, Kelly), used a series of interviews and questionnaires in order to assess basic changes occurring in the people's aspirations, goals, and lives. Published in a book called *New Rules*, Yankelovitch's interpretations are by far the most important part of his analysis. He takes mundane pieces of data and weaves them into a mosaic that is insightful, powerful, provocative, stimulating, and useful.

New Rules is a memorable piece of research because it is effective in what the Loflands call the *interpenetration* of data and analysis (Lofland and Lofland 1984). The analysis and interpretation have evolved *out of the data*. Much research seems to consist of a first section and last section that are theoretically and interpretatively interesting, but in between the data consist merely of either low-level descriptions (often characteristics of qualitative research) or reams of numbers (too often found in quantitative research). In this sense, interpretation and analysis are merely tacked onto a research project. It almost seems that the task of collecting and presenting data is so enormous that the researcher has not had time to reflect on, think about, or contemplate the meaning of his or her own work. To merely pile one fact on top of another is *not* research. Research consists of a full span of activities that includes planning, gathering, writing, reflecting, interpreting, and rewriting.

John and Lyn Lofland have put together one of the most exhaustive analyses of how the practice of social research is accomplished, and while their focus is on qualitative research, many of their suggestions about how to conduct the latter phases of a research project have relevance to *any* kind of research (Lofland and Lofland, 1984).

Telling How the Study Was Done

Much of the interpretation of a research project can be stimulated by simply describing how the study was done. This includes such things as the origins of the researchers' interest and how and why they undertook the kinds of methods they did. In creating a retrospective about such things, the study becomes situated in both an intellectual as well as a research context. Obviously, the researchers thought that the topic merited investigation, and the exercise of discussing it will make it clearer to both the reader and the investigators why the study was important. As it turns out, this retrospective analysis is usually very revealing if done honestly and leads to a host of interpretations of the problem that might not otherwise be possible. For example, such reflection enables the reader to have access to the process by which the problem became meaningful to the investigators, how it took form and shape in the researchers' minds, how they gained access to the information and settings necessary to do the project, what difficulties they encountered along the way, and how the project changed over time.

In addition, the researchers' own private feelings, doubts, and fears, the kinds of emotions the research generated, and how they were dealt with are extremely revealing and give rise to a host of interpretations not possible by presenting the technical part of a project without such a human dimension.

Describing the data-gathering stage can be equally illuminating. How much time was spent? How did the researchers decide what to look for, whom to talk with, what kind of techniques to use? What kind of techniques did they use to record your observations? What barriers did they encounter?

Retrospectives about data analysis are a gold mine of information for the reader as well as the researchers. How were data put together? How did the researchers decide what they meant? How did they reach their conclusions? What were their personal feelings about the research as it unfolded? With the 20/20 vision provided by hindsight, how would they have done it differently?

Giving some thought to the conceptual framework one chose to employ is also a key process in later interpretations of the meaning and import of a piece of research. Obviously, we either invest or borrow concepts, and the arrangement of these concepts is a major part of interpretation. Could different terminologies have been used? What would the research look like if they had been? This is one of the most fertile grounds for stimulating thought, and again, both the researchers and their reader can profit by such an exercise.

Distancing yourself from your work is crucial to the interpretive phase of a research project. After having worked on a piece of research for a long period of time (and this can sometimes mean *years*), it is wise to put everything aside, and come back to it later. Such a process of distancing can, at its best, create a fresh look at a piece of research that will enable the researcher to gain new insights into a project that was beginning to grow stale from too close a familiarity with it. Even if you don't change a thing, having done this means that everything will be settled in your mind with a certain maturity that grows out of looking at things from several different angles. Part of the distancing process may also involve sharing the research at various times with colleagues who can be depended upon to be constructive and helpful. One of the authors of this text makes it a habit never to publish a piece of research without sharing it during its developmental stages with a particular colleague in another state who over a long period of time has proved his dependability for constructive, sensitive criticism. Any number of research projects, at various stages of development, have been improved by doing this. Two heads really are sometimes better than one!

A Final Word

Despite all of our preoccupation in the social sciences with research techniques, it is important to remember that research is, first and foremost, simply a type of scholarship in which a curious mind, intellectual honesty, ethical considerations for subjects, a passion to know the truth, and a desire to communicate it effectively to an audience are all that is really needed. A certain humility about the process will also carry the researcher a long way. In a world where arrogances of all kinds abound, it is well to remember the words of Thomas Edison, one of the foremost minds of any century, who once observed that "the smartest man in the world still only knows 1/1,000,000 about anything."

Chapter 15

Writing the Research Report

Why write a research report?
Factors to consider when writing
   Aim of the report
   Readership
Characteristics of scientific writing
   Objectivity
   Accuracy
   Clarity
   Economy
Organization of the research report

Abstract
Introduction
Methods
Presentation of the results
Discussion section
References
Tables
Appendix
Rewriting the research report

I love being a writer. What I can't stand is the paperwork.
—Peter De Vries

WHY WRITE A RESEARCH REPORT?

At last, you are near the end of the research process. You have formulated a research question, identified an intriguing theory, chosen a research design, and collected and analyzed data. But this whole process will be in vain if you consider yourself finished. If you stop here, the discoveries you made will go unnoticed and will eventually be forgotten. As a responsible researcher, you owe it to yourself and to other researchers to report your findings. By sharing your research with others, you contribute to the growth of knowledge in the research area. But a research report means writing, and writing is often viewed as a difficult and boring task. The authors of this book, for example, have often heard students say, "The hardest thing about research is writing." Our response to this is, "The hardest thing about writing is knowing." If you are knowledgeable—that is, if you know your subject matter—you will have little difficulty writing. Of course, writing is difficult when you don't know your subject matter. You have nothing to write about!

We think you will find that writing the research report is one of the most exciting, challenging, frustrating, and satisfying tasks in the research process. With this report, you will bring all phases of your research into clear focus, stimulating new insights and new understanding. You will come to know and understand more fully and more clearly your research findings as you seek ways to express them to others. But the path to this expression is not always easy or smooth. It is not always easy to take a large amount of material and condense it into a few sentences or paragraphs. It is not always easy to explain lucidly complicated methodology or statistical analysis. In this chapter we will discuss the rudiments of the research report. This discussion is not designed to teach you to write. We believe the best teacher for this task is experience. Instead, we hope to sharpen and improve your present writing skills. Read and reread this chapter very carefully, and as you read, remember two things: *Don't be afraid to try,* and *there's always room for improvement.*

FACTORS TO CONSIDER WHEN WRITING

Aim of the Report

In general, the research report is written for other people. It is written to inform someone else of the research project and its results. For the student, it informs the professor and is the basis for a grade. For the young researcher seeking recognition and support, it is a chance to publish for professional credit. For the established professional, it is an opportunity to add to scientific knowledge and to communicate with colleagues and sometimes the public. Ideally, your writing should carry your readers through the research process as if they were personally experiencing each of the steps. In fact, the successful research report creates an air of sharing the research question and the search for meaningful answers. Above all, the research report should aim to convince your readers, by the combined weight of evidence and logic, of the credibility of your research. The report should move each reader to believe the results and to respect the procedure by which they were obtained.

Readership

Perhaps it goes without saying that the intended reading audience will influence the style and length of your final report. When a report is being written for a general reading audience, you cannot assume an exceptionally high level of specialized knowledge. Therefore, points must be made in more detail and technical terms must be more fully explained. In contrast, when a report is being written for the scientific community, you can generally assume a fair amount of specialized prior knowledge and therefore eliminate much of the explanatory detail and technical information. For either reader, the report must be well organized, well illustrated, and conceptually clear.

CHARACTERISTICS OF SCIENTIFIC WRITING

Before examining the components of the research report, let's take a brief look at some of its more important characteristics. Specifically, we wish to discuss the ways in which a report should reflect the goals of objectivity, accuracy, clarity, and economy.

Objectivity

Objectivity in writing means intellectual honesty in the research report. It means reporting those data which *disconfirm* the research hypothesis as well as those which support it. Such an approach ensures that the whole story is told, including acknowledgment of errors, problems in data collection, and conditions or events that may cast doubt on the research. Objectivity also means that you draw only those conclusions which are clearly supported by the data. In effect, when a hypothesis is repeatedly confirmed by well-conducted experiments, a firm conclusion can be made. When the data of just one experiment give support to a hypothesis, conclusions must be tentative with an eye for future testing.

Accuracy

Accuracy in the research report means a thorough checking and rechecking of all source materials. Error, omission, and carelessness will contaminate any report enough to make its value questionable. *This surely means failure.* You should keep meticulous records on authors, titles, publishers, and page references of relevant literature. And you should make repeated checks to ensure that errors are not generated as this information is moved from source to notebook to draft report to final form. Every person who processes the material is certain to inject some distortion into it. It is important that all such conversions, omissions, and alterations be found and corrected. This will mean checking and double-checking of original data. As a responsible research reporter, you should continually review the details of your research in order to identify and eliminate as many errors as possible. Only with such care and labor will the research report become error-free.

Clarity

Clarity is the ideal of all writing and is a skill that will sharply improve the chances that your research will have an impact on those who read it. Because research often involves new and unconventional methods, measurement, and theory, it is essential that it be communicated clearly. Although what is new doesn't have to be confusing, it often is, and you can be sure that such confusion will make it all the more difficult for you to persuade the reader of the accuracy and meaningfulness of your work.

How is such clarity achieved? The road to clarity lies in the process of thinking and rethinking the main statement of the problem, the theory, and the methodology. The statement of the research problem should be definitive, short, and declarative. Likewise, the hypotheses that must be tested should also be straightforward and declarative. The numerical data should be presented in simple and well-labeled tables. The written interpretations should address the data in the tables. Finally, you should draw only those conclusions which can be seen in the data presented.

Economy

Economy in report writing means telling the whole story without wasting words, space, or time. In the case of the research report that is published in a national journal, wordiness often means the loss of the article because publishers simply won't publish it! Some of the most influential pieces of research ever published have filled only five or six pages of journal space. Long, turgid, uneconomical writing, even if it is published, not only wastes journal space, but often alienates readers, who simply will not persist in reading to the conclusions.

A word about computers is necessary here, for it is certainly possible to generate, with the aid of a computer, dozens of tables from quantitative sources, and it is sometimes quite difficult to cut it off. Tables and computer-generated data must, like words, be there for a purpose, and the writer must exercise special care not to let them get out of hand. If these matters are not controlled, a long, rambling, overloaded report is produced. Such a strung-out report will generally exhaust the patience and the attention of all who come into contact with it. A short, direct, carefully organized report is much more effective and persuasive because the essential points are more readily identified and understood. Most finished reports can be compressed up to 25 percent with enormous gains in economy and effect.

ORGANIZATION OF THE RESEARCH REPORT

Enough said about research report characteristics. What about the organization of the report? While there are a number of different ways to organize the research report, we believe that the organization used by journals for publication is as good as any. Since publication is usually the goal of research, you will have to have experience with the preferred style. In addition, with this organization, you have an infinite number of resources (publications) to provide you with examples.

In general, the research report should include the following sections:

1. Abstract (summary of sections 2 through 5)
2. Introduction (includes a statement of the problem, a review of the relevant literature, and the hypotheses to be tested)
3. Methods (includes subjects, measures and procedures)
4. Results (includes statistical analysis, which provides the basis for the tests of the hypotheses)
5. Discussion (includes interpretation of the results)
6. References (includes an alphabetical list of all references)

7. Tables (presentation of data in table form)
8. Appendix (includes any additional relevant information, such as questionnaire forms, figures, and mathematical formulas)

Abstract

The abstract is a summary of your entire research report and, as such, cannot be completely written until everything else is written. The abstract, which is found at the beginning of your research paper, gives your readers a chance to discover what your research is all about. To give your readers the fullest possible account, your abstract should contain information on all of the following: statement of the research problem, research design, results, and conclusions. First, your abstract should provide your readers with a brief statement of the research problem. While you cannot state your entire theory, you should introduce the purpose of your research. Second, your abstract should briefly establish the basics of your research design. This means characterizing your subject population (number, age, sex, etc.) and describing your research design, test instruments, research apparatus, or data-gathering procedures. Third, your abstract should present your primary results. This means summarizing your data findings in terms of statistical significance. Finally, your abstract should present any conclusions drawn in your research. In other words, provide a brief statement of any inferences drawn from your results.

This may seem like a lot of information for an abstract, and you may think you are rewriting your entire paper for this one section. Well, this is not entirely so, because your abstract cannot be quite as long. Rather, it should be between one hundred and two hundred words. The brevity of the abstract makes it quite a challenge. You may find it difficult to condense what you have done into fewer than two hundred words. If you do feel this way, we want you to know that we sympathize. However, we challenge you to write this section as well as you can because many times it is the only section that is read. If you think you disagree with this, try to recall the number of articles that you looked at when doing your research and the number of articles that you actually read. What was the deciding factor?

The following is the abstract from "Ocular Breaks and Verbal Output" by Donald Allen and Rebecca Guy (1977). It is not presented as perfect. Rather, it is presented as a concrete example of what an abstract can look like.

> It has been assumed that ocular breaks during dyadic social intercourse are causally associated with the need to reduce the stimulus load for the person speaking. If Kendon's proposition to this effect is correct, dyadic partners should manifest a high incidence of ocular breaks in the speaking mode,

and a low incidence in the listening mode, since the load on the speaker is higher. Moreover, there should be a higher incidence of ocular breaks at those points in the verbal stream where alternatives of judgment, and the mental processes are expressed, since there is more uncertainty, and more stress suggested at these points. An analysis of 52 five-minute dyads indicates that a higher incidence of ocular breaks is associated with these conditions, and Kendon's proposition is supported.

Introduction

The task of actually writing the research report begins with the introduction. Here you will want to inform your readers of your research problem, your chosen theoretical position, and the hypotheses you plan to test. While economy is an essential element in any good research report, you should not begin by diving right into your research problem. Begin by setting the stage at some broader level. The following is the introduction from "Ocular Breaks and Verbal Output" by Allen and Guy. Again, this introduction is by no means perfect. If you had written it, you probably would have done some things differently. If we were writing it now, we probably would too. It is simply offered to you as a concrete example of this part of the research report.

> One of the richer event sources in the face-to-face social encounter is the movement and positioning of the eyes. In recent years, Soviet scientists have shown interest in eye movement as it relates to visual tracking (Gippenreiter, 1971), size estimation (Borozdina, 1969), and instrument reading (Kamishov and Lasarev, 1969). Goffman (1964) has characterized the social interaction relation as a kind of "eye-to-eye ecological huddle." Borden (1969) noted that the pattern of action in group behavior may be derived from records of the direction and duration of looking among members of the group. The eyes have been called the most important part of the body for transmitting emotion and other subtle messages (Fast, 1972; Knapp, 1972). Ekman and his associates also isolated the eyes as a special area for identifying facial affect.
>
> Several investigators have employed real time scoring of looking behavior in connection with other parameters of the social relation. Efran (1968) found that low-status students (freshmen) look more at high-status students (seniors) than they do at equal-status partners. Interview partners look at each other more when separated by a distance of six feet than when separated by a distance of two-and-a-half feet (Goldberg et al., 1969). Mehrabian (1972) identified a second effect of distance in relation to the degree of conviction a persuader could generate. Although he found little difference at the closer distance (four feet), at the greater distance (12 feet), males were more convincing with less eye contact, while females were more convincing with more eye contact.
>
> There is evidence that the duration and frequency of looking at the partner

in dyadic interaction creates a pressure on both actors. Argyle noted that people usually engage in direct eye-to-eye contact for short periods of three to ten seconds. If mutual glances are longer than this, anxiety is frequently aroused (Argyle and Williams, 1969). It has been established that eye contact is maintained for longer periods in the listening mode than in the speaking mode (Argyle and Dean, 1965; Allen and Guy, 1974). In this relation, it is apparent that the pressure of the demand for action is greater on the speaker than on the listener.

Kendon has identified four functions of eye contact in conversation: (1) cognitive, to reduce load when having difficulty encoding; (2) monitoring, to check the partner's reactions; (3) regulatory, to control the beginning and ending of verbal sequences; and (4) expressive, to signal the degree of interest, involvement, or arousal (Kendon, 1967). This research constitutes a partial test of Kendon's proposition that speakers break eye contact as a means of reducing the external stimulus load when they want to concentrate on what they are going to say.

The text reproduced here represents approximately half of the introduction to this article. If you read this part of the introduction closely, you should have noticed several significant things. First, the opening sentence does not reference a journal. Instead, it makes a general statement about face-to-face encounters and eye contact. If we were to characterize the research report from beginning to end, we could liken it to an hourglass. The research report begins at a broad level and becomes more and more specific as you present your own research. Then, as you interpret your own results, the research report broadens again. Second, notice that the literature review that is incorporated into this part of the introduction summarizes the current state of knowledge. It informs us of current relevant findings in the research area. Third, notice that the literature review is composed of a limited number of studies. It doesn't try to cite every article written on the subject.

In general, it is not necessary and usually not possible to cite all journal articles, books, and reports that have an apparent relation to the research being reported. Instead, you should select a limited number of studies that are closely related to your research. A half-dozen relevant references are far more effective than two or three dozen references, including many of only secondary interest. It is important that you have cited the works of researchers who have made recognized contributions to the research area. Be sure you have examined research in related fields. Every serious researcher should dig into related scientific and technical fields as required to support or fortify each research project.

The second half of this introduction sets the stage for the research being reported:

> In face-to-face conversation, the speaker simultaneously carries out a relatively complex set of behaviors associated with planning and emitting

intelligible verbal sequences, monitoring his partner, and suppressing his own potentially non-relevant motor behavior. As the work load becomes excessive, he can reduce it by closing off one or more of his receptors. A simple means of load reduction is to break eye contact with partner by shifting the gaze to some neutral and inactive background. If the ocular break is associated with excessive tension and system overload, we would expect the verbal stream to show certain traces of this effect in close association with the moment of ocular break. From an empirical viewpoint, one way to test this hypothesis is to identify vocabulary associated with ocular breaks, and to compare it with vocabulary not associated with this behavior. Vocabulary elements which we assume to indicate uncertainty and a slightly higher stress level include mental process words ("think," "hope," "know") and judgmental words ("bad," "good," "just," "probably"). The mental process words imply a reasoning process which is inherently doubtful in its outcome. This concept is most explicit in words such as "imagine" and "wonder." The judgmental words imply a mental process of comparison and evaluation between reference objects, or relating to their properties, and objects, or relating to their properties, and they provide a basis for a second test of the effect of such factors on the ocular break. The opposite assumption applies for verbal affirmation in the form of "yeah," "uh-huh," and "yea." The affirmatives tend to assert assurance and certainty, and to indicate that some conclusion or firm idea has been reached. The same reasoning should apply to the negative, "huh-uh" and "no." Affirmations and negations are expected to have reduced frequency in the vicinity of ocular breaks, as they compared to the frequency of these forms in other parts of the conversation record.

Fragmentation in the verbal stream generally indicates some uncertainty, awkwardness, and problems in composition, and we would therefore expect fragmentation to be positively related to ocular break. Verbal fragmentation includes stuttering, portions of words, phrases of sentences which are discarded, and conventionalized vocalizations sometimes called "fillers" where the speaker is apparently uncertain of what he wants to say ("ah," "er," and variants). Since fragmentation is a function of the composition of statements and strings or sequences of statements, the amount of verbal output should also be positively related to ocular break. These research expectations reduce to the following propositions:

1. Mental process words will occur with greater frequency in close association with ocular breaks in the conversational stream.
2. Judgmental words will occur with greater frequency with ocular breaks.
3. Affirmation will occur with reduced frequency with ocular breaks.
4. Word output is a function of pressure, and will correlate positively with the volume of ocular breaks.
5. Fragmentation of words and sentences, as an editing function, will correlate positively with ocular breaks and with word output.

Notice that the second half of this introduction addresses the research being reported. This does not mean a detailed description of procedures. But it does mean a look at the concepts integral to the reported research, definitions of these concepts, and the hypotheses to be tested. From the second half of the introduction presented here, you should recognize some presentation of theory. The theory presented may take one of two forms. It may be general theory, historically built up from philosophical and scientific writings. Or it may be specific theory formulated for an individual research project. In either case, the theory is your own formulation, carefully expressed in the idiom of research. In this introduction, for example, we see a more general theory that seeks to refine existing categories and to clarify doubtful general assumptions. This introduction ends (as should any introduction) with the hypotheses to be tested. In this example, five hypotheses are testable using an appropriate research design, and later sections of the research report should reflect evidence for or against these hypotheses.

Methods

As we discussed in Chapter 4, the research design is the plan by which your research is accomplished. The importance of this plan cannot be overemphasized since another researcher must use it in order to report, test, and prove your theory. Put simply, this plan must be described as simply and in as much detail as possible. The process of repeating research is called *replication* or repetition of the research, and either this procedure will verify the research and increase the support for the theory or it will fail, indicating that the theory is still in doubt. In short, the methods section includes a detailed account of all of the research procedures used to gain evidence for hypothesis testing, including (1) selection of subjects, (2) measurement, (3) data collection, and (4) data processing. Let's take a brief look at each of these important components.

The methods section usually begins by indicating the number of human subjects used and describing how these subjects were divided into groups. If your sample is supposed to represent a large theoretical population, the research report must describe fully the random selection process by which the sample was chosen. At the same time, the presumed character of the sampled population should be made explicit. If a table of random numbers is used to select telephone numbers from a city telephone directory, for example, then the population from which this sample is taken is confined to names listed in that directory. It does not include unlisted telephones, new institutions, and individuals not yet listed. If you are a meticulous researcher, you will recognize and estimate the true character of the population that you are sampling. If you decide to use some other method of random selection (systematic, stratified, multistage), then you must describe this sampling method, together with the number of cases drawn. And the number must be large enough, usually several hundred and sometimes several thousand, to represent reasonably well a large, heterogeneous population.

The methods section must also delineate carefully the measuring instruments used in your research. Measurements that are so elegant and so definitive in the natural sciences (e.g., mass, energy, velocity, volume, and distance) are scarcely known in the social sciences. This is partly because social scientists deal with such complicated factors as alienation, interpersonal attraction, conflict, or the efficiency of social organizations. While basic questions have long since been settled by definitive experimentation in the natural sciences, simple questions in the social sciences remain unresolved despite the advanced research facilities of our leading institutions. It is here that the contemporary researcher has the most profound problem but yet the greatest opportunity. Most current measures are implicit in statistical tests, and as the researcher, you must be careful to choose measures that satisfy the requirements of reliable statistical tests.

Finally, data collection and data processing techniques must be described in sufficient detail that another researcher could repeat them exactly in another research project with the same test objectives. If assistants were used, how were they trained? What was the chronology of the research operations? What was the sequence of contacts with agencies or individuals to be involved or concerned with the project? If instruments were used for measurements, they should be described in enough technical detail that equivalent instrumentation could be developed and applied elsewhere. In addition, relevant environmental conditions such as light, sound, and social conditions should be described in terms of their possible effect on the collection of data.

If instruments such as questionnaires and interviews were used, how were they applied? How did the presence and actions of a researcher seem to affect the respondents? Were gender effects recorded and taken into account? What provisions were made to elicit cooperation and responses from human subjects? What were the intrinsic rewards to human respondents? How and in what direction did these rewards affect subjects' responses? For example, if mailed questionnaires were sent to and intended for employed mothers of school-age children, what steps were taken to identify and exclude questionnaires filled out by unqualified respondents? Finally, what provisions were made to find and eliminate errors in coding the data and in preparing it for statistical analysis?

To give you a concrete example of these ideas at work, let's take a look at the methods section for our ongoing research example:

Subjects were students in equal numbers from two southern universities. The sample consisted of 52 5-minute recordings of conversations between dyads, generated in 6 experimental groups of 6 students each. Each group included three males and three females, and each member was paired once with either two or four others in the group. This produced 26 male-female dyads, 13 female dyads, and 13 male dyads. The effects of sex are not considered in this report of the research. There was either a slight or no prior acquaintance between conversing partners.

Video and audio recordings were made in a university television studio. The video portion was recorded through two cameras, at about 10 degrees from the normal, looking over the shoulder of each participant into the face of the other. The cameras were preset and prefocused to maximize the faces on the right or left half of the recording area, to provide good legibility on eye movement. For the recording, the pair was isolated in a small home-like "conference room" made up of studio flats, with pictures on the walls, and a settee along one wall. The partners were seated across the corner of a small square table. The ready lights on the television cameras were disconnected, and there was no visual or auditory signal in the experimental chamber to indicate that recording was in progress.

All participants were previously instructed to talk about anything they wished during the recording session. They were told that the object of the research was to determine the nature of conversation, and that any behavior normal to themselves and their regular habits of relating to others would be appropriate. Each pair started conversation spontaneously, and the start of the recording was controlled independently by the researchers at the recording console.

Data Processing

The audio record was transcribed and verified by two persons, one of whom was a participant in the transcribed conversation. The speech lines for the two actors were separated horizontally to provide separate areas for tracking facial behavior, including eye movement from the video record. Verbal segments on the tape were replayed until full agreement on content was reached. All audible elements were retained in the transcript, including word fragments, stuttering, and laughter by syllable count, in order to provide a veridical record for the accompanying facial behavior.

Two teams of two members each were used to transcribe the elements of the video record. All coders were pretrained on trial runs. In the team transcribing the actor on the right of the screen, one member closely observed the eye movements, while the second member, as reader, read the verbal transcript while listening to the audio replay of the conversation. The observer signalled the reader with continuous tactile pressure while the actor's eyes were fixed on the conversational partner, and removed this pressure when the actor's eyes were elsewhere. While tactile pressure was applied, the reader drew a continuing line above the appropriate words on the transcript.

The video was then run a second time to verify the ocular record for the two actors. Coding reliability was high ($r = .98$). Nearly all corrections involved advancing the "eye-line" to a point one word earlier in the transcript to compensate for occasional delays in responding to ocular shifts or to shifts in tactile pressure. The idea of switching teams for replay was tried and rejected because the second team merely introduced other errors into the second coding, whereas the original coding team could recognize and correct errors in the second run.

The verbatim record, together with codes for the beginning and end of ocular contact for the two actors, was transcribed to computer cards. The complete vocabulary list was extracted, counted, and ordered on the computer, together with data on the frequency and duration of eye contacts. We assumed that the verbal evidence of uncertainty and pressure would be found immediately after the start of each ocular break. For each ocular break for a speaker, up to five words were extracted, beginning one word before, and up to four words following the break, to improve the chance of identifying the relevant types of words. The retrievals did not always include the maximum of five words because the ocular break sometimes occurred near the end of an actor's output cycle.

As earlier noted, the methods section of the research report includes a description of the sample selected, the measurements used, and the data collection and data processing procedures. If you look closely at the methods section presented here, you should find all of these elements. First, it identifies the number of human subjects used and describes how they were divided into groups. Since a random sample was not selected, an elaborate discussion of sampling techniques was not necessary. Second, it describes how the research instruments were developed, prepared, and applied, and this description is in detail. Third, it describes what was done and in what sequence. Fourth, it delineates the verbal instructions that subjects received. Fifth, it describes the training and preparation necessary for coding the data. In short, this methods section provides the kind of detail that would be necessary if this research were to be replicated.

Presentation of the Results

The fourth section of the research report is the results section. The results that are of primary interest to your readers are the findings that relate immediately to your research hypotheses. As the researcher, you will probably want to search the data for those findings which support your theory and your hypotheses. It is important, though, that you examine the data with objectivity, looking at both the positive and negative findings. While positive findings do suggest the success of your research project and the correctness of your theory, they should be carefully reviewed and verified to establish the actual degree of support. If the evidence is clear and overwhelming, then a claim of success is justified. More often in social science research, though, the degree of support is actually limited and marginal. And along with this limited and marginal support, there may be some anomalous findings that call into question the relevance of the theory and the hypotheses. In fact, it is not uncommon for portions of the data to reject the theory by contradicting the hypotheses.

The maximum value of research comes from a thorough and correct evaluation of results in relation to test hypotheses. When the results are inconclusive, no conclusion should be drawn. The theory is not supported, and the research question remains open. If the theory appears to be overturned, you must report this without equivocation. Remember, research "fails" only when you fail to report results that are interpreted honestly and in line with the facts.

To get a more concrete picture of the results section of the research report, let's look at the results section of our ongoing research example.

> The record for the 52 5-minute conversation dyads included 6,714 words associated with ocular breaks and 46,581 words not closely associated with ocular breaks. There were 1599 ocular breaks by actors while speaking, averaging 15.4 ocular breaks per dyad-actor, with a standard deviation of 10.2. Words per break averaged 4.2. These data indicate that ocular break behavior is an intermittent phenomenon which occurs with sufficient frequency to permit testing the research propositions, without saturating the action.
>
> Preselected lists of 14 words each, for mental process and judgment, were shortened to 10 words each due to the low frequency of some words in the ocular break vocabulary or the total vocabulary. The results for mental process, as shown in Table 1, indicate a combined frequency of 39.1 mental process words per 1000 words in the ocular break vocabulary, compared to 23.8 of these words per 1000 words in the remainder of the vocabulary. This difference is statistically significant ($p < .0005$), and tends to support the proposition that ocular break is associated with a higher incidence of mental process words. The assumption that mental process words reflect uncertainty and pressure for the speaker is, of course, not directly tested. In the second test, for the effect of judgmental words, there was a rate of 36.0 judgmental words per 1000 words of ocular break vocabulary, and 26.4 judgmental words per 1000 words in the remainder of the vocabulary. This difference also is statistically significant ($p < .0005$), and supports the proposition that judgmental words have a higher frequency in the close vicinity of ocular breaks. Again, these data do not permit direct examination of the assumption that judgmental words indicate uncertainty or pressure for the speaker.
>
> The assumption that affirmation is closely related to certainty rests on somewhat firmer ground, intuitively, because a speaker in the process and act of affirmation is indicating certainty and resolution to some degree. We would expect a reduced rate of affirmations associated with ocular break, if eye break actually is more associated with uncertainty and pressure. Affirmation occurs in three forms in the natural vocabulary, as generated from the college students in the sample. The most frequent form of affirmation is "yeah," and the next most frequent is "uh-huh," with about 10 percent of the affirmations taking the prescribed form of "yes." The rate of affirmation

is approximately half as high in the ocular break vocabulary as in the remainder of the vocabulary, and the difference is statistically significant (p < .0005). The evidence is fairly convincing that affirmation is depressed in the four to five word segments which occur with ocular breaks.

The association of ocular break with word output, and with verbal fragmentation, is consistently in the direction proposed for each of the two actors, both in the first and the second half of each conversation, making two sets of 52 records each containing 2.5 minutes of conversation and facial behavior. The explained variance (R^2) ranges from a minimum of .07 through an average of .17 to a maximum of .42. The twelve within-actor correlations are consistent with the hypothesis, and when taken together, give rather convincing evidence that ocular break and fragmentation are positively associated with the volume of word output, which is assumed to be a function of pressure on the speaker. The negative correlations in Table 4 demonstrate the inverse relation of verbal output between dyadic partners, specifically within the 5-minute time frame. The inverse correlation also applies to the related factors of ocular break and verbal fragmentation.

If you have read this results section closely, you should notice at least two significant things. First, it is important to note that this section of the research report focuses on results—that is, research findings. Each hypothesis and the evidence providing a test of each hypothesis are presented. This evidence is evaluated statistically and conclusions are drawn. Restated, the evidence either supports or fails to support the hypothesis. Second, notice the absence of interpretations in this section of the research report. This is because the results section is not concerned with interpretation. It is concerned with the actual findings. The interpretations applied to these findings are presented in the discussion section of the research report.

Discussion Section

The fifth section of the research report is the discussion section. In this section you must provide a full explanation of your research findings. Remember, the connection of findings with theory is always indirect. The findings relate directly to the test hypotheses, not to the theory. Within this section, at least six specific tasks must be accomplished. Let's take a look at each of these.

Your first task in the discussion section is to explain to what degree the test hypotheses are supported by the data. The weight and direction of the evidence are reported together with reasonable arguments for your conclusions. All test hypotheses must be reviewed, preferably in the same order in which they were originally stated. In rare cases, you will be able to claim strong positive support for each hypothesis. If this is possible, you have taken a major step in convincing your skeptical readers. Such positive support is also likely to motivate some other researchers in the field to replicate your research to test whether the conclusions can be supported with the same kind of source materials and methodology in another setting.

The second task in the discussion section is to show the relationship between your test hypotheses and your theory. As we have already noted, this connection cannot be proved. It can only be made to appear plausible. However, you are now in a better position to support your theoretical statement based on your research procedures, findings, and hypotheses that are logically implied by the theory. Support for your theoretical statement depends on the harmony and mutual implications among all elements of your research operation. It is your responsibility to show care, veracity, and insight in all phases of your project, including the research report. And remember, if support for the test hypotheses is mixed, weak, or missing, you really have no support or confirmation for your theory.

Your third task in the discussion section is to indicate conservatively how the data justify the conclusions. Most good research begins with a reasonable question and ends with a reasonable doubt. Even in the rare cases where there appears to be complete and strong support for the theory, conservatism in making claims is certainly preferable. After all, research represents only one step by one person, presumably on an important and difficult question. The success claimed in the report is really dependent on its credibility when presented to skeptical readers. Further, it must hold up against challenges from many directions because it is the function of the research community to question and to challenge until reasonable doubts have been resolved. (And what is "reasonable" is often in doubt too!) If you are a serious researcher, you will come to expect questions, doubts, and denial from others until repeated tests of the theory can firmly settle the question. If the data support the test hypotheses only in part, then claims for support of the theory come clearly into question. As the research reporter, you should openly acknowledge that the research question remains open because the theory is not well confirmed—though it may not be wrong either.

A fourth task in the discussion section is to identify weaknesses in your research project. One of the primary contributions any researcher can make to an area of study is the presentation of research findings with candor and honesty. As the research reporter, you must identify and describe the weak elements in your project from beginning to end. Is there any evidence in light of the research experience that the theory was misconceived from the beginning? Certainly, you have made an important discovery if you have determined that a plausible and generally accepted theory is in error.

Robert Merton once began a major research project on the influence of the printed media on readers assuming, as most publishers and advertisers did, that the effect of printed materials is direct on general readers

(Merton 1949). The media tended to assume an uninformed readership for editorials and advertisements. Merton and his associates started field research with this theory, but soon found that local opinion leaders were the main source of influence in a small circle of acquaintances. In effect, the opinion leaders were the direct consumers of media persuasion. The bulk of the general readers reserved judgment on media appeals until they heard the opinions of an acquaintance who had a special interest and was presumably more knowledgeable about the policy, candidate, or product. Merton changed his theory to the two-step theory of median influence: (1) from publisher to topical opinion leader and (2) from opinion leader to concerned citizen. Merton's study is a good example of how theory is modified in the course of the research process. In short, as research reporter, you should review the main elements of the research process. You should explain areas where problems arose and areas where the information was incomplete, biased, or unknown. Questionnaire responses, for example, do not present facts from the empirical world, but only the claims of the respondent from his or her own viewpoint. It is important to notice such biases and limitations when writing the research report.

A fifth task of the discussion section is to suggest specific questions for further research. A research project is an attempt to learn more about an unknown phenomenon. It usually represents a unique venture and a substantial investment of time, effort, resources, and thought. On concluding a research project, you are in the position of expert. You have a great deal of knowledge on certain aspects of the theory and its relationship to the world. This is the time to outline related questions that require further research. Don't hesitate to recommend what else needs to be done to establish the research theory more completely. Is there some evidence that the research is on the wrong track, whereas the right track is now in view? If so, set forth an improved formulation of the theory. Are there weak areas in the research procedure? If so, identify them and indicate what is needed to avoid such weaknesses in future research.

The sixth task of the discussion section is to indicate new directions for research. The best research is often research that points the way to future study rather than having the last word on a given subject. Research is an ongoing process of discovery, not an attempt to corner the truth so that no one else will ever need study an area again.

The following is the discussion section from our research example. It should go without saying that this discussion section is presented as a concrete example, not as a perfect specimen.

> The findings presented here provide support for Kendon's proposition that the speaker breaks eye contact to reduce stimulus load as he concentrates on what he is going to say. As the speaker continues, we can identify nine elements of his task: (1) plan, compose and emit a syllable string; (2)

monitor his own speech; (3) evaluate what he hears against his intention; (4) edit and correct as he exceeds the limits of the intended effects; (5) monitor partner visually; (6) monitor partner aurally; (7) suppress environmental noise; (8) suppress internal noise; and (9) maintain somatic posture and somatic outputs. Overload appears to occur when the speaker encounters uncertainty, faulty memory, slips of the tongue, logical or grammatical contradictions, and errors in sequence.

The types of tests applied here appear to be consistent with the overload concept, and the selected sets of judgmental words, mental process words, and fragmentations are rather consistently associated with the speaker's ocular breaks for 36 students in 52 dyadic conversational pairs. At the same time, it must be recognized that speakers vary in verbal skill, and that verbal skill level is itself a primary dimension of success in social interaction, and in social transactions. Therefore, this line of research could well be extended to speakers with various levels of verbal skill, to determine more adequately the degree of relation between variance in the stimulus load and the incidence of ocular break.

A second problem arises in the definition of the ocular break. Many speakers make slight eye shifts within a small fraction of a second, returning to the fixed focal point (partner's face) within one or two syllables. We have assumed that the ocular shift from partner's face must endure for more than .5 seconds (about two words) to be counted as an ocular break which operates effectively to reduce stimulus load. Part of the rationale for this assumption was that the coding teams had difficulty making clear identifications of eye break in these tiny momentary shifts. Second, it was assumed that the relation of ocular break to the rest of the action would be more definitive and more demonstrable, if scoring were confined to clear and unmistakable breaks of significant duration. Accordingly, the significance of momentary eye shifts is not considered in this analysis. However, it should be assumed that this behavior does have effects, both on the speaker's action stream, and on the responses of the listener.

We conclude that there is good support for Kendon's proposition with regard to judgmental and mental process words. Their higher frequency in the vicinity of ocular breaks suggests that uncertainty in the verbal stream is associated with ocular breaks. The fact that affirmations are negatively associated with ocular breaks offers indirect support, if it is granted that affirmations tend to indicate the opposite of uncertainty. These conclusions are necessarily tentative, and they raise some new questions, but they appear relevant to the analysis of the functions of the ocular break.

References

The sixth section of the research report is the reference section. In this section, you must list every bibliographic reference used in the body of your paper. While the style for references should be consistent throughout your paper, there are several acceptable styles. The most widely used reference style is the author and year notation within the body of the text with references listed alphabetically by author and year at the end of the paper. This is called the *Harvard method,* and is used, for example, by the American Sociological Association and by the American Psychological Association journals. (This is also the method used in our research example.) To illustrate: "One authority stresses the relationship between research and theories in the middle range (Merton 1957)." The complete reference for this example would appear at the end of the research paper and would list author, year of publication, title, and source.

A second method of identifying references within a research report is the *serial method.* With this method, references are numbered in the order in which cited in the text, and they are then listed in that same order at the end of the article. This represents an older journalistic style by which the same references could be listed more than once at the end of the article. It is also less convenient for researchers who may be primarily concerned with the references and sources, since they are not listed in standard order.

A third method of identifying references is the *alphabet–number system.* With this method, the references are ordered alphabetically by author and then numbered serially. Only the reference number is inserted in the text. This method is slowly gaining favor because it saves space and results in less disruption of the text. With this method, if the Merton reference were the twelfth reference in the alphabetized reference listing, the text would read: "Merton stresses the relation between theory and method in the middle range (12)." Again, regardless of the method you choose, remember to be consistent. The reference section from our ongoing research example is included here to give you once again several concrete examples.

REFERENCES

Allen, Donald E., and Rebecca F. Guy
  1974 Conversation Analysis. The Hague, Netherlands: Mouton.
Argyle, M., and J. Dean
  1965 "Eye contact, distance, and affiliation." Sociometry 28:298–305.
Argyle, M., and M. Williams
  1969 "Observer or observed: A reversible perspective in person perception." Sociometry 32:396–412.
Borden, G., R. Gregg, and T. Grove
  1969 Speech Behavior and Human Interaction. Englewood Cliffs, New Jersey: Prentice Hall.
Borozdina, L., and U. Gippenreiter
  1969 "O funktsii dvishenni glaz pri zritel'nikh otsenkakh." Voprosi Psikologii 3:46–55.
Efran, J.
  1969 "Looking for approval: Effects on visual behavior of approbation from persons of differing importance." Journal of Personality and Social Psychology 10:21–55.

Ekman, P., W. Friesen, and P. Wentworth
 1972 Emotion in the Human Face. New York: Pergamon.
Fast, J.
 1971 Body Language. New York: Pocket Books.
Gippenreiter, U., and S. Smirnov
 1971 "Urovani sledyashchikh dvizhenii glaz i vzritel'noye vnimaniye." Voprosi Psikologii 3:31–45.
Goffman, E.
 1964 Behavior in Public Places. Glencoe, Illinois: Free Press.
Goldberg, G., C. Kiesler, and B. Collins
 1969 "Visual behavior and face to face distance during interaction." Sociometry 32:43–53.
Kamishov, K., and V. Lazarev
 1969 "Nyekotorie osobennosti peremeshinia vzora lechika pri shchitevanii pokazania proborov v real'nom polyetye." Voprosi Psikologii 4:44–56.
Kendon, A.
 1967 "Some functions of gaze direction on social interaction." Acta Psychologica 26:22–63.
Knapp, M.
 1972 Non-verbal Communication in Human Interaction. New York: Holt, Rinehart, Winston.
Mehrabian, A.
 1972 Non-verbal Communication. New York: Aldine-Atherton.

Tables

The seventh section of the research report includes all tables that support the results section. Although the tables are really a part of the results section, they are not placed directly in the body of this section. Instead, they are placed at the end of the paper in their own section to avoid disrupting the smooth flow of the text.

Each table in your research report should be typed on a separate sheet of paper. Each should be given a table number and a title. The table number is extremely important since this number is used to reference the table within the body of the text. The title is also important since it gives the reader some idea of what the table is showing. The information included in the table should be labeled with great care to ensure that it can be interpreted on its own without reference to the text. This means that if columns are headed by numbers or letters, there should be a legend with the table that identifies the meaning of those headings. In every case, the headings chosen should reflect relevant, mutually exclusive, and logically exhaustive categories within the context of the table. Generally, independent categories are distributed by column, and the dependent categories are distributed by row. If gender affects voting behavior, for example, columns should be headed *Female* and *Male* and rows should be marked by political party. Each table in your research paper must be referenced within the text. The following tables are taken from our research example.

TABLE 1 Mental Process Words Per 1000 Words With and Without Ocular Breaks in 52 5-Minute Conversation Dyads

Mental Process Words	With Ocular Break N = 6,714	Without Ocular Break 46,581
Believe	.9	.1
Enjoy	1.3	.2
Guess	1.6	1.3
Hope	.9	.4
Imagine	.6	.4
Know	19.3	14.2
Remember	.6	.4
Think	8.7	5.2
Want	3.8	1.5
Wonder	1.4	.1
Total	39.1	23.8

Note: $\chi^2 = 53.4$; df = 1; $p < .0005$, direction indicated.

TABLE 2 Judgmental Words per 1000 Words With and Without Ocular Breaks in 52 5-Minute Conversation Dyads

Judgmental Words	With Ocular Break N = 6,714	Without Ocular Break 46,581
All	4.8	3.8
Any	6.3	3.6
Bad	1.6	1.0
Every	2.0	.5
Good	2.5	2.7
Hard	1.2	.6
Kind	2.5	1.1
Just	7.1	5.6
Probably	1.6	1.6
Some	6.4	5.9
Total	36.0	26.4

Note: $\chi^2 = 19.6$; df = 1; $p < .0005$, direction indicated.

TABLE 3 Affirmation Words Per 1000 Words With and Without Ocular Breaks in 52 5-Minute Conversational Dyads

Affirmation Words	With Ocular Breaks N = 6,714	Without Ocular Breaks 46,581
Uh-huh	4.5	9.5
Yeah	5.7	12.5
Yes	1.7	2.0
Total	11.9	24.0

Note: $\chi^2 = 38.2$; df = 1; $p < .0005$, direction indicated.

TABLE 4 Correlation of Ocular Breaks. Verbal Fragmentation, and Verbal Output Within and Between Actors in 52 5-Minute Conversation Dyads, Replicated by Halves

	Actor 1 Ocular Breaks	Actor 1 Fragment	Actor 1 Verbal Output	Actor 2 Ocular Breaks	Actor 2 Fragment	Actor 2 Verbal Output
Actor 1						
Ocular Breaks	—	.45	.43	−.27	−.29	−.42
Fragment	.29	—	.33	−19	−.05	−.15
Verbal Output	.43	27	—	−.41	−.57	−.45
Actor 2						
Ocular Breaks	−.06	−22	−.55	—	65	.60
Fragment	−.33	1	−.52	.43	—	.63
Verbal Output	−.42	−25	−.58	.54	.60	—

Note: $r > .17$ are significantly greater than zero at $p = .05$. Entries above the main diagonal are the findings for the first half of the conversations; those below the main diagonal pertain to the second half.

Appendix

Although an appendix is rarely called for, it is helpful under certain circumstances. The criterion for including an appendix should be whether it improves your readers' chances of understanding, evaluating, or replicating your study. Some examples of suitable materials for an appendix might include (1) a new computer program specifically designed for your research and unavailable elsewhere, (2) an unpublished test and its validation, and (3) a complicated mathematical proof.

REWRITING THE RESEARCH REPORT

After completing the written report, you should edit the manuscript with great care, keeping in mind the variety of readers. Does the title correctly suggest the content of your report? Is the ordering of ideas correct, or could it be improved? Do all sentences make sense? Are the spelling and punctuation correct? Can the tables be improved by condensation or more informative titles and subheadings? Is the level of precision reasonable? (Two decimal places are sufficient for correlation and regression values, and are usually satisfactory for probability or confidence levels.)

If any portions of the research report are confusing, be sure you take time to rewrite them. Be careful to write all numerals and symbols clearly, with open space around them. Scruffy copy given to your typist delays the typing and invites errors and misreading. The easier the manuscript is for the typist, the better will be the finished product. At this point, then, the report should be typed in clean final form, complete with all sections. But don't breathe a sigh of relief yet. You are not finished! Your report is now ready for a preliminary review by several classmates, who can serve as knowledgeable and discriminating critics. Your classmates are in a good position to help you discover and correct defects that would bring negative comments from your instructor. Ask your classmates to be demanding of your text—to mark errors and make critical notes on their copy.

Your classmates' recommendations will represent several viewpoints, some of which may be contradictory. You should survey all comments, correct errors of typing, fact, and reference, and then begin to integrate those recommendations which best present the subject. This is not the time to hurry or save labor. Since your classmates have spent time identifying faults, weak arguments, and oversights, you should thoroughly recast the material so as to meet the criticism as fully as possible. This may require some further analysis of data and a reformulation of tables, discussion, and conclusions. Whatever the cost, it is time and resources well spent in order to bring the research report up to the highest possible standard. By now your paper is in its third or fourth draft and is ready to be retyped.

While the procedures described here may seem like a lot of work, they will help to ensure that yours is a worthwhile document. If you follow these steps persistently, you should produce a meaningful research report. Happy research writing, and may all your words be well chosen and wise!

Appendix A

Using SPSS: Statistical Package for the Social Sciences[1]

WHAT IS AN SPSS PROGRAM?

The letters SPSS stand for Statistical Package for the Social Sciences. This package is a highly developed and integrated system of statistical software available for most mainframe computer systems and at present one microcomputer system. SPSS allows persons without computer programming training to run a variety of statistical procedures with ease.

SPSS programs consist of a series of cards[2] that follow in a logical sequence and together direct the computer through the steps necessary to run statistical analyses on a given set of data. Typical functions that these cards direct include telling the computer where to find the data; telling the computer the names and locations of the variables to be used within the data files; various data transformations such as creation of new variables, recoding of existing variable values, and, of course, informing the computer of which statistical procedures to run on the variables.

SPSS is one of the most widely available statistical packages currently in use. Its English-like syntax and its excellent documentation render it easy to use for even a beginner writing SPSS programs. It is this ease in using SPSS, coupled with the wide availability of this package, that makes it worthwhile for the beginning researcher to learn.

---

[1] This appendix was co-authored by Colleen Claire Cook.

[2] Throughout this text, the word *card* will be used to represent either a physical card to be keypunched or a single line to be typed on the screen of a CRT terminal. Currently the trend is for greater usage of CRTs, and in many places there is a partial or total phasing out of the Hollerith card as a medium for communicating with the computer.

GETTING STARTED

Your SPSS program will be preceded and followed by cards that are used to process your program (i.e., instructions to the computer) through the computer. These cards, commonly known as Job Control Language (JCL), provide the computer with information such as the account number to be billed, the software to be used in the computer run, the name and location of the computer file(s) to be accessed in the run, and other pertinent information needed by the computer to execute your program. Since the information on these cards differs in both form and syntax from one computer installation to another, JCL will not be covered in this appendix. Obtain the necessary instructions concerning JCL from your instructor, or check your SPSS manual, which also has some helpful information on the topic.

Writing an SPSS program is really simple. All you must do is write the tasks to be accomplished in the order in which they are to be performed and then submit them to the computer. These task statements must be written according to the syntax rules recognized by SPSS. Fortunately, these syntax rules are English-like and can be written with ease by even a novice computer user.

SPSS statements always consist of two parts or fields: the control field and the specification field. The control field consists of the first fifteen columns of the card and contains the command words that identify the task to be accomplished. The specification field consists of columns 16 through 80 and provides the computer with specific information (e.g., identification of variables) needed to carry out the task called for by the command words. If more than one card is needed to complete such specifications, you need only tab over to column 16 of the next card and continue typing the specifications. When continuing onto a second card, you do not repeat the control word(s) in columns 1 through 15. It is the *omission* of the control word(s) that signals to the computer that a card is a continuation.

Generally speaking, there are three types of commands or instructions that together make up an SPSS program: data definition(s), task(s), and procedure(s). Each of these three types of instructions will be examined in the appendix.

DATA DEFINITION COMMANDS

Data definition commands are control cards whose purpose is to *define the data file*. Let's take a look at some of these control cards and their applications.

RUN NAME   TITLE OF RUN (LABEL UP TO 64 CHARACTERS)

The RUN NAME is an optional data definition command that allows you to print a header or title on the top line of each page of your SPSS output. The keyword for this command is RUN NAME. The specification field (16–20) can contain up to 64 characters of text that serves to describe your SPSS output.

VARIABLE LIST   V1 TO V4, V10

This data definition command informs the computer of the variables that will be used in the SPSS run and of the order in which they will be stored in the data file. Note that it is not necessary to list by name every variable in the data file if all the variables are not being used. Instead, you may list only those variables which are pertinent to the analyses.[3] Variable names may be up to eight alphanumeric characters in length, the first of which must be alphabetic and none of which may be an embedded blank. The TO convention is a shorthand notation for denoting a list of sequential variables found in the data file. Its use requires that the variable names end with a number (as in the above example). The computer will then generate the variable names using the numbers found within the sequence (e.g., V1, V2, V3, V4).

INPUT FORMAT   FIXED(4F1.0,5X,F2.1)

The INPUT FORMAT data definition command tells the computer where within the data file to find the variables named in the preceding VARIABLE LIST card. This card consists of the command words INPUT FORMAT in the control field and the keyword FIXED followed by some codes that help the computer locate the data your program needs to access.

The codes used in the INPUT FORMAT statement are based on codes adapted from the programming language FORTRAN and carry a meaning that is about the same as in the parent language. The F format describes to the computer the organization of the individual data values stored in the data file. The general formula for the F format is:

---

[3] There are occasions when it is both convenient and economical to include all variables in the variable list. If you plan to execute several runs of the same data set but want to use different variables each time, it would probably be advantageous to include all variables in the variable list. This will prevent you from having to rewrite the variable list statement for each new computer run.

nFw.d

where:

n = the number of times in succession this particular F code may be found

F = the letter *F*, which is always used with the F format

w = the width of the field or the number of contiguous columns that the variable occupies on a given card

d = the number of columns found to the right of the decimal

The X format is also frequently used in SPSS to instruct the computer to skip over columns. The general formula is:

nX

where:

n = the number of columns to be skipped

X = the letter *X*, which is always used with the X format

In the previous example, the 4F1.0 informs the computer that there are four variables found in succession, each of which occupies a width of one column and none of which has any places recorded behind the decimal. In the next code, the 5X informs the computer that it is to skip over the next five columns. Finally, the F2.1 tells the computer that the next variable has a width of two columns with one position to be implied behind the decimal.

DATA LIST   FIXED (1)/1 V1 1 V2 2 V3 3 V4 4 V10 10-11 (1)

An alternative to the combined use of the VARIABLE LIST and INPUT FORMAT statements is the SPSS definition command called the DATA LIST. In the example above, the DATA LIST card describes to the computer the same variables as in the previous VARIABLE LIST and INPUT FORMAT statements. The keyword FIXED informs the computer that the data file is in a fixed format, with each variable always occurring in the same position of a designated card (first, second, third, etc.). In this example, there is only one card per case, which is made known to the computer by the number 1 found in the parentheses. Had there been more than one card per case in the data file, that number would have been placed within the set of parentheses.

A slash follows the number of cards per case in the data file, and the number 1 following the slash informs the computer that we are now reading variables from card one. Variable V1, according to the DATA LIST card, can be found in column one of card one, V2 in column two of card one, and so forth. Note that V10, which occupies two columns with a decimal implied behind the first column, is located in the data file by identifying the beginning and ending column numbers and by indicating the number of columns to be implied behind the decimal within the parentheses immediately following the beginning and ending column notations.

There are advantages and disadvantages to both of these two variable identification alternatives. In cases where a variable format occurs repeatedly (as in the case of twenty successively occurring variables with the same F1.0 format), it is usually easier to use the combination VARIABLE LIST and INPUT FORMAT cards. On the other hand, the DATA LIST card is often conceptually easier than the FORTRAN-based INPUT FORMAT card for the beginning SPSS user to understand. In addition, the DATA LIST is usually easier to use with the formatting information provided in most data codebooks.

N OF CASES   **N or
UNKNOWN**

This data definition command tells the computer the number of cases that are to be found in the data file, with N representing the number of cases. If the exact size is unknown, or if the number of cases can change from one SPSS run to the next, you can use the SPSS notation UNKNOWN in lieu of the exact number. When UNKNOWN is specified, the computer will automatically count the number of cases for you.

                                 CARD
INPUT MEDIUM   **TAPE
DISK**

This data definition command specifies to the computer the type of device on which the data file is stored. Most systems accept the keywords CARD (specifying the same device as where the SPSS file itself is located), TAPE (specifying that the data file is stored on magnetic tape), and DISK (specifying that the data file is stored on disk). This notation is acceptable on most but not all systems. Check with someone familiar with the computer on which you will be working to determine the exact information needed.

READ INPUT DATA

This data definition command instructs the computer to begin reading the data. If the specification on the INPUT MEDIUM CARD is CARD, this instruction should be placed immediately after that card. Otherwise, the READ INPUT CARD should be positioned immediately following the first procedural card.[4] The READ INPUT DATA card has no corresponding specification field.

END INPUT DATA

This data definition command instructs the computer to end the reading of input data. Like the READ INPUT DATA card, this card has no corresponding specification field. This card is placed immediately following the READ INPUT DATA card.

FINISH

This data definition command informs the computer that the SPSS run is finished. It has no corresponding specification field and should always be the last SPSS command card in your program.

Two Optional Data Definition Cards

VAR LABELS   VN, VARIABLE LABEL/VN, VARIABLE LABEL . . .

The VAR LABELS data definition command assigns a variable label to the variables specified on the card. A maximum of 40 characters are allowed for each variable's label. All printable characters are permissible except the parentheses and the slash. Since each variable label is terminated with the slash, more than one variable can be placed on one VAR LABELS card. This is an optional card.

VALUE LABELS   VN (VALUE) VALUE LABEL (VALUE) VALUE LABEL /

The VALUE LABELS data definition command is used to tag on a label of up to 20 characters to some specified value or values of a variable. All characters except the slash and parentheses are acceptable. The slash is used to indicate the end of the value labels for a particular variable. Like the VAR LABELS card, many variables' values may be defined in one statement. An example of these two cards follows.

---

[4] Procedural cards will be discussed in a later section of Appendix A.

VAR LABELS   AGE, AGE OF STUDENT/SEX, SEX OF STUDENT
VALUE LABELS   SEX, (1) MALE (2) FEMALE/

On the first card, the variable AGE is given the variable label "age of student" and the variable SEX is given the label "sex of student." The two variable labels are separated with a slash. On the second card, the variable SEX is given two value labels: "male" for those coded as a 1 and "female" for those coded as a 2. These labels are not involved in any calculations but are peeled off by the computer and printed onto your output sheet verbatim.

TASK COMMANDS

Task commands instruct the computer to transform or manipulate the data in some way. This section will discuss four of the more commonly used task commands: the IF command, the SELECT IF command, the RECODE command, and the MISSING VALUES command. For a discussion of other available task commands, check your SPSS manual.

IF   VARN (LOGICAL EXPRESSION) SPECIFIED VALUE

The IF task command allows you to make data transformations on selected variables if a specified condition(s) is met. Most commonly, the IF statement is used to create a new variable and allows the researcher to either collapse data or transform values to accommodate specific statistical analyses to be run. For example, suppose we wanted to dichotomize students scheduling elementary statistics into two groups on the basis of major: those majoring in sociology and those not majoring in sociology. When major equals 1, our newly created variable equals 1, and when major is not equal to 1, our newly created variable equals 2.

Logical operators acceptable to SPSS include GE (greater than or equal to); LE (less than or equal to); GT (greater than); LT (less than); EQ (equal to); NE (not equal to); AND; NOT; and OR.

SELECT IF   (LOGICAL EXPRESSION)

The SELECT IF task command instructs SPSS to process only those cases which meet certain specified criteria. For example, if you wanted to run analyses using only females, you could SELECT IF SEX EQ 2. The same logical operators that are valid with the IF command are also valid with the SELECT IF command. When multiple SELECT IF commands are used, SPSS will include only those cases which meet all specifications delimited.

RECODE   VN (ORIGINAL VALUE = RECODED VALUE)

The RECODE task command allows you to change one value or a set of values of a variable to another value. The general format for accomplishing this transformation is to type in the command word RECODE in the control field, followed by the name of the variable(s) to be recoded and the changes to be made in the specification field. The changes to be made always take the form of "original value = recoded value."

MISSING VALUES VN (VALUE)

The MISSING VALUES task command is usually used to flag a specified value of a variable as a missing value. Very often a full field of 9s occupying all allotted columns for the specific variable is used to signify a missing value. For example, an F1.0 format would use the value 9 to denote missing values (assuming 9 is not a legitimate code); an F2.0 format would use the value 99; an F3.0 format would use the value 999, and so on. However, it is not essential that 9s be used to denote missing values. Any value that is not legitimate for a given variable may be used to represent that variable's missing values. SPSS allows you to use up to three specified values as missing values for any individual variable. These flagged values are often given special treatment using available options specified along with procedural commands.

PROCEDURAL COMMANDS

The third group of SPSS commands are the procedural commands. The procedural commands are those which instruct the computer to compute specified statistical procedures on your data. These commands are the heart of any SPSS program. While the data definition commands define and the task commands manipulate and transform your data for statistical processing, it is the procedural commands that test your hypotheses and produce the statistics that will be used in your analysis and interpretation of data.

We will cover several of the most commonly used procedural commands and their associated statistical tests in this appendix. These discussions should not be considered exhaustive. However, you should develop a good foundation for the use of the procedures with SPSS. Should you need to run one or more of these procedures, it would be advantageous to refer to the references at the end of this appendix for further information.

For the examples given in this appendix, we have used a data file labeled SOCISTAT. This file represents data collected from students who have scheduled social statistics at State University. A general survey is administered to students enrolled during the first week of each semester, and the survey results are entered into a data file used by the students in their SPSS computer runs. A copy of the data file and its codebook may be found at the end of this appendix. It should be noted that several of the variable values have been reconstructed in order to better illustrate some of the key concepts discussed in this appendix.

Using the FREQUENCIES Procedure Statement

FREQUENCIES is a univariate (one-variable) statistical procedure that will provide you with a frequency distribution of each variable in your program. You can use the FREQUENCIES command to create a frequency distribution for only one variable or for many variables. To do this you would simply type the name of the variable or variables behind the GENERAL= keyword, separated by commas if more than one variable is listed (e.g., V1, V2, V3, V4). If you wish to obtain frequencies on all variables, you may use the word ALL in place of each variable name.

Several descriptive statistics are available when using procedure FREQUENCIES. Special statistics (when available for a specific statistical procedure in SPSS) are run using a separate STATISTICS card, which immediately follows the procedural card to which it refers. A few of the most often used statistics available for procedure FREQUENCIES are the mean, median, mode, standard deviation, variance, and range. SPSS knows these statistics by numeric codes given in the specification field of the statistics card. To obtain frequencies and the statistics listed above, we would use the following commands.

```
FREQUENCIES    GENERAL = ALL
STATISTICS     1,3,4,5,6,9
```

The numeric codes used in the specification field of the statistics command represent codes for the mean, median, mode, standard deviation, variance, and range respectively.

Procedure FREQUENCIES also offers two special options that can be of tremendous use to the novice researcher. OPTION 7 allows the statistics requested on the STATISTICS card to be printed without a frequency distribution. In other words, by using OPTION 7, the computer will calculate and output the mean, median, mode, standard deviation, variance, and range without listing a frequency distribution for the variable(s) designated on the FREQUENCIES card. This option can be useful when you have a large number of variables or when you have a large number of unique values for a variable. OPTION 8, another useful option, allows you to obtain a histogram of a variable—a pictorial representation of how your data are distributed. Knowledge of the shape of the data for a given variable can serve to alert you to variables whose shapes are unique or unusual or which do not fall along the lines of a normal (bell-shaped) curve. These two options can be obtained by immediately following the STATISTICS card with an OPTIONS card.

    OPTIONS   7,8

The numbers 7 and 8 represent options for summary statistics only and a printed histogram respectively.

Example 1: Using Procedure FREQUENCIES to Clean Up Data. After any data are collected, they must be properly coded and keypunched for computer input. Since keypunching is a task performed by human effort, it is possible that keypunching errors will be made. Hence, before running any statistical analysis on a data set, we must first check the data for errors. The SPSS procedure FREQUENCIES is a very useful tool in discovering "stray" output—output that falls outside the range of legitimate values for a particular variable.

    Since procedure FREQUENCIES will provide you with a frequency distribution for any designated variable, an examination of the data distribution will warn you of values that are not legitimate codes. Using the data file SOCISTAT, we will use procedure FREQUENCIES to uncover any inappropriate data values for the variable AGE. If we find any stray data values, we will recode them to 99 and then flag them as missing values.

    The needed syntax for running procedure FREQUENCIES on the variable age is as follows.

    FREQUENCIES   GENERAL = AGE

Since we do not need calculated statistics or histograms to conduct this data cleanup, the STATISTICS and OPTIONS cards discussed earlier will not be used here. The complete SPSS run is shown in Figure A.1. Running this program on the data file SOCISTAT produces the output which appears in Figure A.2.

    Examination of the data for variable AGE shows one value that seems inappropriate: the student whose recorded age is 83. Since there were no elderly students enrolled during the semester in which this survey was administered, it is safe to assume that this value was recorded in error. Assuming that we do not have the original survey forms to verify the correct value for this student's age, we will discard the erroneous data by using the RECODE and MISSING VALUES cards.

    First we will recode the value of 83 to 99. To do this, we will use the following command.

USING SPSS: STATISTICAL PACKAGE FOR THE SOCIAL SCIENCES

FIGURE A.1
SPSS Program Listing

```
1.  RUN NAME        EXAMPLE PROGRAM FOR APPENDIX B- SPSS PROGRAMMING
2.  VARIABLE LIST   SEX,CLASS,MATH,GRADSKOL,AGE,ATTITUDE,
3.                  THEORY,LAB,TEST1,TEST2
4.  INPUT MEDIUM    UNIVACNAME='SOCISTAT.'
5.  INPUT FORMAT    FIXED (T10,F1.0,T13,F1.0,T17,F3.1,
6.                  T27,F1.0,T48,6F2.0)
```

ACCORDING TO YOUR INPUT FORMAT, VARIABLES ARE TO BE READ AS FOLLOWS

VARIABLE	FORMAT	RECORD	COLUMNS
SEX	F 1.0	1	10- 10
CLASS	F 1.0	1	13- 13
MATH	F 3.1	1	17- 19
GRADSKOL	F 1.0	1	27- 27
AGE	F 2.0	1	48- 49
ATTITUDE	F 2.0	1	50- 51
THEORY	F 2.0	1	52- 53
LAB	F 2.0	1	54- 55
TEST1	F 2.0	1	56- 57
TEST2	F 2.0	1	58- 59

THE INPUT FORMAT PROVIDES FOR   10 VARIABLES.   10 WILL BE READ
IT PROVIDES FOR   1 RECORDS ('CARDS') PER CASE. A MAXIMUM OF   59 'COLUMNS' ARE USED ON A RECORD.

```
7.  IF                (MATH LT 3.0) DVAR=1
8.  IF                (MATH GE 3.0 AND LT 9.0) DVAR=2
9.  IF                (MATH GE 9.0) DVAR=3
10. TASK NAME         FREQUENCY DISTRIBUTION FOR AGES
11. FREQUENCIES       GENERAL=AGE
```
GIVEN WORKSPACE ALLOWS FOR   1968 VALUES AND   787 LABELS PER VARIABLE FOR 'FREQUENCIES'

AFTER READING   78 CASES FROM SUBFILE NONAME , END OF DATA WAS ENCOUNTERED ON LOGICAL UNIT # 8

FIGURE A.2
Example Program Output

AGE

CATEGORY LABEL	CODE	ABSOLUTE FREQ	RELATIVE FREQ (PCT)	ADJUSTED FREQ (PCT)	CUM FREQ (PCT)
	18.	2	2.6	2.6	2.6
	19.	3	3.8	3.8	6.4
	20.	4	5.1	5.1	11.5
	21.	8	10.3	10.3	21.8
	22.	6	7.7	7.7	29.5
	23.	7	9.0	9.0	38.5
	24.	8	10.3	10.3	48.7
	25.	11	14.1	14.1	62.8
	26.	4	5.1	5.1	67.9
	27.	4	5.1	5.1	73.1
	28.	2	2.6	2.6	75.6
	29.	1	1.3	1.3	76.9
	30.	1	1.3	1.3	78.2
	31.	2	2.6	2.6	80.8
	32.	1	1.3	1.3	82.1
	33.	2	2.6	2.6	84.6
	34.	1	1.3	1.3	85.9
	35.	2	2.6	2.6	88.5
	36.	1	1.3	1.3	89.7
	37.	1	1.3	1.3	91.0
	38.	1	1.3	1.3	92.3
	40.	1	1.3	1.3	93.6
	41.	1	1.3	1.3	94.9
	44.	1	1.3	1.3	96.2
	50.	1	1.3	1.3	97.4
	51.	1	1.3	1.3	98.7
	83.	1	1.3	1.3	100.0
	TOTAL	78	100.0	100.0	

VALID CASES   78   MISSING CASES   0

RECODE   AGE (83=99)

Now that we have recoded this value to 99, we will flag the value 99 as the missing value. We do this using the following command.

MISSING VALUES AGE (99)

In this example, it might have been easier to have just flagged the value of 83 as a missing value without going through the added effort of recoding the value to 99. However, had there been another stray value within the data for variable AGE, it would have been more efficient to recode both values to 99. In addition, had other variables had stray output to be flagged as missing values, it would have been easier to recode strays uniformly using a full field of 9s rather than having to remember the unique missing values flagged for each individual variable.

We may now use the variable AGE in statistical calculations. By using special missing values options for those procedures that provide them, we are able to give special treatment to the missing data.

Using the CROSSTABS Procedure Statement

CROSSTABS   VARIABLES = VAR1 (MIN,MAX) BY VAR2 (MIN,MAX)

where

VAR1 = the (row) variable

VAR2 = the (column) variable

(MIN,MAX) = the minimum and maximum values for the row and column variables

The procedure CROSSTABS allows you to cross-tabulate data in order to create a joint frequency distribution for two or more variables. The cross-tabulation of data is an important and highly useful technique. To explain what cross-tabulation is, let us look briefly at a hypothetical example. Suppose there were two groups of licensed drivers for whom we had data: drivers with a history of driving while intoxicated (DWI) and drivers without such histories. We would like a joint frequency distribution (cross-tabulation) of drivers' DWI status by sex. A cross-tabulation of the data might look as follows:

	MALES	FEMALES
DRIVERS WITH DWI HISTORIES	6	4
DRIVERS WITHOUT DWI HISTORIES	12	9

From this table, we can surmise that there are six males with DWI histories and twelve without. Additionally, there are four females who have DWI histories and nine who do not.

Procedure CROSSTABS allows you to create such joint frequency distributions. Because of this feature, procedure CROSSTABS is often used in data cleanup as a supplement to the procedure FREQUENCIES discussed in Example 1.

Contingency tables such as those produced by procedure CROSSTABS are not limited to being a tool of descriptive statistics; they are often used to determine whether two variables are independent of each other. This is accomplished primarily with the use of the chi-square statistic.

To obtain the chi-square statistic in SPSS we use the numeric code 1 on the STATISTICS card immediately following the CROSSTABS procedural card. The chi-square statistic is used to determine whether two variables are independent. By convention (not requirement) the .05 significance level is commonly used among social scientists for making such determinations. If the chi-square (χ^2) statistic computed has a probability greater than or equal to .05, then we will conclude that the two variables are not independent. If the probability associated with the statistic is less than .05, we would reject the null hypothesis of no relationship (i.e., independence) between variables in favor of a working hypothesis stating a relationship.

Cross-tabulations are not limited to a bivariate (two-variable) relationship. A third, fourth, or even fifth variable can be incorporated into the tables. In SPSS this is done by altering the basic CROSSTABS syntax to the following format.

> CROSSTABS   VARIABLES = VAR1 (MIN,MAX) BY VAR2 (MIN,MAX) BY VAR3 (MIN,MAX)

A word of caution concerning the addition of variables into a cross-tabulation model: with every variable added to the table, there is an increased probability of empty or near-empty cells. Empty or low-frequency cell counts threaten the statistical validity of the chi-square statistic. It is a good practice in all but the largest of samples (e.g., cross-national samples of significant magnitude, or United States Census data) to include no more than three variables in any model.

Example 2A: Using Procedure CROSSTABS in Data Cleanup. In the previous example, the procedure FREQUENCIES was used to facilitate our cleaning up of erroneous data entries. As indicated previously, it is important that data be checked for keypunching and coding errors before using them for any statistical testing. One inherent limitation of the FREQUEN-

CIES procedures in data cleanup is that a data value must be an illegitimate value to be detected. For instance, suppose we have a data file that contained two variables—SEX and ADMIT (admittance to the maternity ward of a hospital). Sex has legitimate values of 1 (male) and 2 (female) for the variable SEX, and ADMIT has legitimate values of 1 (admitted to the maternity ward) and 2 (not admitted to the maternity ward). To find a value of one for either the variable SEX or ADMIT in the FREQUENCIES output would not cause us any concern. But suppose we ran a joint frequency count and found that both response values were recorded for the same respondent?

Use of the procedure CROSSTABS allows you to uncover errors of this nature (commonly called contingency errors because the error detected is contingent upon the two response values occurring jointly). By producing cross-tabulations, you can easily identify many contingencies (joint frequencies) occurring within the data that constitute legitimate values for both the variables involved but that, when occurring jointly, do not logically fit together.

Returning to the data file SOCISTAT, one contingency that we might run is a cross-tabulation of classification in college (CLASS) with the number of hours earned in college math. This output has been reproduced in Figure A.3. Most of the output in this table appears believable. One contingency, however, seems inappropriate—the freshman (code 1) who is recorded as having completed 33 hours of math credits. Although both the value of 1 for CLASS and 33 for MATH are legitimate codes for their respective variables, by university policy freshmen are defined as students having earned 29 or fewer hours of credit; thus we know that the case where these two variables occur jointly is in error.

Example 2B: Using Procedure CROSSTABS and the Chi Square Statistic. Traditionally males have been thought to be more ambitious than females in their career and educational aspirations. To examine this assumption, we will focus on males' and females' desires to continue into graduate school as recorded on the survey administered to our sample of statistics students. Is there really a difference between the males and females surveyed with respect to plans for going to graduate school?

> I. STATEMENT OF STATISTICAL HYPOTHESES
> 1. Working hypothesis: There is a significant relationship between sex and one's graduate school aspirations.
>
> 2. Null hypothesis: There is no significant relationship between sex and one's graduate school aspirations.
>
> II. STATEMENT OF STATISTICAL TEST, LEVEL OF SIGNIFICANCE, AND USE OF A ONE- OR TWO-TAILED TEST
> Chi-square test; .05 level of significance; two-tailed test.

FIGURE A.3
Cross-Tabulation of Classification by Math Hours Earned

```
                        DVAR
               COUNT  I
               ROW PCT I                                ROW
               COL PCT I                                TOTAL
               TOT PCT I    1  I     2  I     3  I
       CLASS          -I--------I--------I--------I
                   1  I    0  I     0  I     1  I     1
                      I   .0  I    .0  I 100.0  I    1.3
                      I   .0  I    .0  I  10.0  I
                      I   .0  I    .0  I   1.3  I
                     -I--------I--------I--------I
                   2  I    2  I     0  I     0  I     2
                      I 100.0 I    .0  I    .0  I    2.6
                      I   3.8 I    .0  I    .0  I
                      I   2.6 I    .0  I    .0  I
                     -I--------I--------I--------I
                   3  I    8  I     4  I     0  I    12
                      I  66.7 I   33.3 I    .0  I   15.4
                      I  15.4 I   25.0 I    .0  I
                      I  10.3 I    5.1 I    .0  I
                     -I--------I--------I--------I
                   4  I   28  I    12  I     5  I    45
                      I  62.2 I   26.7 I   11.1 I   57.7
                      I  53.8 I   75.0 I   50.0 I
                      I  35.9 I   15.4 I    6.4 I
                     -I--------I--------I--------I
                   5  I   14  I     0  I     4  I    18
                      I  77.8 I    .0  I   22.2 I   23.1
                      I  26.9 I    .0  I   40.0 I
                      I  17.9 I    .0  I    5.1 I
                     -I--------I--------I--------I
              COLUMN      52       16       10       78
              TOTAL      66.7     20.5     12.8    100.0
```

III. STATEMENT OF IMPORTANT SAMPLE STATISTICS
Sample size = 78

IV. ASSUMING THE NULL HYPOTHESIS IS TRUE, RUN PROCEDURE CROSSTAB
Refer to Figure A.4 for SPSS output.

Looking at the SPSS output, you can see that 18 males wished to go to graduate school and 2 did not. Additionally, 46 of the females are planning to go on to graduate school and 12 are not.

The percentages printed along with the raw cell counts may at first glance appear confusing. The key to understanding these percentages is found in the left uppermost corner. The word COUNT indicates that the raw score count is the first figure in each cell. ROW PCT in the second

**FIGURE A.4
Cross-Tabulation
of SEX by Graduate
School
Aspirations**

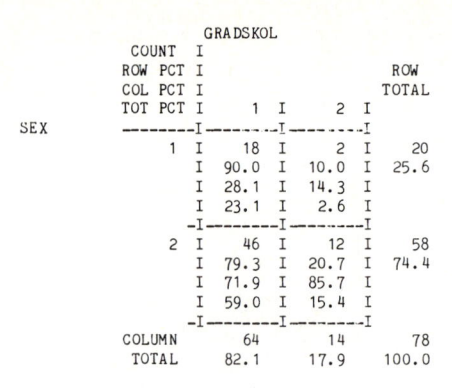

```
                         GRADSKOL
            COUNT   I
            ROW PCT I                         ROW
            COL PCT I                         TOTAL
            TOT PCT I    1   I     2   I
      SEX   --------I-------I--------I
             1  I      18   I     2   I    20
                I    90.0   I  10.0   I  25.6
                I    28.1   I  14.3   I
                I    23.1   I   2.6   I
                -I-------I--------I
             2  I      46   I    12   I    58
                I    79.3   I  20.7   I  74.4
                I    71.9   I  85.7   I
                I    59.0   I  15.4   I
                -I-------I--------I
            COLUMN       64        14        78
            TOTAL      82.1      17.9     100.0

    1 OUT OF    4 ( 25.0%) OF THE VALID CELLS HAVE EXPECTED CELL FREQUENCY LESS THAN 5.0.
MINIMUM EXPECTED CELL FREQUENCY =   3.590
CORRECTED CHI SQUARE =      .54221 WITH 1 DEGREE OF FREEDOM.   SIGNIFICANCE =   .4615
      RAW CHI SQUARE =     1.15391 WITH 1 DEGREE OF FREEDOM.   SIGNIFICANCE =   .2827
```

row of the left uppermost cell indicates that the second figure in each cell is row percentage computed using row totals. Now look at the cell that represents males (coded 1) who plan to go on to graduate school (coded 1); the second figure tells you that 90 percent of the males surveyed wanted to go to graduate school. COL PCT in the third row in the uppermost left corner indicates that the third value in each cell is column percentage computed using stands for column totals. In the same cell, 28.1 percent of those students wanting to go to graduate school (GRADSKOL being the column variable) were males. ROW PCT indicates the percentage of those cases in a designated row that fall into a particular cell, while COL PCT indicates the percentage of cases in a designated column that fall into a particular cell. TOT PCT indicates the percentage of all cases in the table that fall into a particular cell. In this same cell, for example, it is apparent that 23.1 percent of all students surveyed were males who wished to go to graduate school.

SPSS also provides us with row and column totals and the percentage of cases occurring in each row or column. As you can see, 20 students surveyed were male, comprising 25.6 percent of the sample, and 64 of the students surveyed wanted to continue beyond the B.A. degree, constituting 82.1 percent of those surveyed. Finally, the total number of students surveyed (78) is given, which represents 100 percent of the sample.

There are two chi-square statistics given for this table. The corrected chi square, which will always be a more conservative statistic when it is calculated for a table, is given whenever any cell counts are low enough to possibly bias the chi-square results. When a corrected chi square is given, you should use its associated probability in the decision-making process. The probability associated with the corrected chi square indicates that there is no significant relationship between sex and graduate school aspirations. If a corrected chi square had not been indicated on the output, we would have used the raw chi-square probability value, which has been calculated at .2827, also indicating no relationship.

In this example, our decision is to fail to reject the null hypothesis. We have found no evidence that sex and graduate school aspirations are related to one another.

Using the T-TEST Procedure Statement

In doing research, we are often concerned with discovering and evaluating the differences between effects. We might, for instance, be interested in the difference between GPAs for male and female students. The procedure T-TEST allows us to test for a difference between the mean GPAs for males and females. In other words, do the average GPA for males and the average GPA for females really differ beyond that which might be expected by chance?

The T-TEST, like the chi-square test you have already been introduced to and the statistical procedures that will follow in the appendix, is an inferential statistical tool. That is, it is used as a tool for making generalizations from a random sample to a larger population. The concept of a randomly selected sample is important for all of these tests since they are designed to work in cases where each member of the original population has a known chance of being selected for the sample. SPSS cannot determine whether or not your sample is randomly drawn. This is something you will have to ensure for yourself.

Assuming that your sample is randomly selected, the *t*-test will make it possible to determine whether the difference between the two groups' means is significant (i.e., indicative of a true difference found in the parent population rather than one found as a result of the luck of the draw). There are several types of *t*-tests available. Two of these tests, the *t*-test for two independent samples and the *t*-test for paired samples will be discussed here.

Suppose you were interested in knowing whether average spelling scores were significantly different for male and female children. Using a random sample of fourth-graders, you administered a spelling exam to them. It would seem logical that if the mean for the male students and the mean for the female students were close in value, then probably the difference found between these two averages would be a product of chance or luck of the draw. If, on the other hand, the difference between the mean score for the males and the mean score for the females was quite large, then it is more likely that the difference could not be attributable to chance factors. Running procedure T-TEST and using the GROUPS= option allows you to test for mean differences in male and females' average spelling scores.

The syntax for procedure T-TEST for two independent (uncorrelated) samples is as follows:

T-TEST   GROUPS = VAR1/VARIABLES = VAR2

where
                  VAR1 = the grouping (independent) variable
                  VAR2 = the dependent variable
GROUPS = AND VARIABLES = = keywords which represent the required syntax in the T-TEST command

Example 3A: Using Procedure T-TEST to Test for Differences Between Two Independent Samples. It might be assumed that males have a more positive attitude toward statistics than females do. If this is the case, then it seems reasonable to suggest that the males surveyed from our statistics class should rate their feelings toward statistics at a significantly higher level than the female class members. Is there really a difference in male and female attitudes toward statistics, one beyond what we would expect as a result of chance (sampling) fluctuation?

I. STATEMENT OF STATISTICAL HYPOTHESES
1. Working hypothesis: There is a significant difference between males and females with respect to attitudes toward statistics.

2. Null hypothesis: There is no significant difference between males and females with respect to attitudes toward statistics.

II. STATEMENT OF STATISTICAL TEST, LEVEL OF SIGNIFICANCE, AND USE OF A ONE- OR TWO-TAILED TEST
T-test for two independent samples; .05 significance level; two-tailed test.

III. STATEMENT OF IMPORTANT SAMPLE STATISTICS
Sample size = 78
Mean for males = 5.95   S.D. = 2.781
Mean for females = 6.069   S.D. = 3.145

IV. ASSUMING THE NULL HYPOTHESIS IS TRUE, RUN PROCEDURE T-TEST.
Refer to Figure A.5 for SPSS output.

It appears that for the 20 males surveyed, the calculated mean is 5.95 with a standard deviation of 2.781. Among the 58 females surveyed, the mean is 6.069 and standard deviation is 3.145.

The F value and its associated two-tail probability are given to test the assumption of homogeneity of variance. This assumption is supported if the two-tail probability associated with the F value is greater than .05 (assuming use of the .05 level of significance). If this probability is above the .05 level, we will choose to look at the part of the SPSS output labeled POOLED VARIANCE ESTIMATE to obtain our t statistic. If

FIGURE A.5
T-TEST for Independent Samples

```
GROUP 1 - SEX        EQ        1.
GROUP 2 - SEX        EQ        2.
                                                             *              * POOLED VARIANCE ESTIMATE * SEPARATE VARIANCE ESTIMATE
                                                             *              *                          *
             NUMBER              STANDARD      STANDARD     *   F   2-TAIL  *  T   DEGREES OF  2-TAIL  *  T   DEGREES OF  2-TAIL
VARIABLE    OF CASES    MEAN    DEVIATION       ERROR       * VALUE  PROB.  * VALUE  FREEDOM   PROB.   * VALUE  FREEDOM   PROB.
-------------------------------------------------------------------------------------------------------------------------------
ATTITUDE                                                    *              *                          *
    GROUP 1    20     5.9500      2.781         .622        *              *                          *
                                                            * 1.28   .565  * -.15     76       .881   * -.16    37.05    .874
    GROUP 2    58     6.0690      3.145         .413        *              *                          *
                                                            *              *                          *
-------------------------------------------------------------------------------------------------------------------------------
```

the probability associated with the *F* value is relatively close to .05, however, we would probably choose to use the *t* statistic calculated under SEPARATE VARIANCE ESTIMATE.

Since the two-tail probability associated with the *F* value is .565, we will choose to examine the *t* statistic found under the heading "POOLED VARIANCE ESTIMATE." The *t* calculated is −.15 with 76 degrees of freedom. The associated probability for this calculated *t* value is .881. Thus we can conclude that there is no significant difference in feelings about statistics among males and females. Hence we will not reject our null hypothesis and will assume that the small difference we have observed is one of chance (sampling fluctuation).

Example 3B: Using Procedure T-TEST to Test for Differences Between Paired Samples. Using the *t*-test for paired samples, our reasoning is basically the same with no difference. We are using paired (matched) subjects in our sample groups. For example, suppose a statistics instructor wished to test two different approaches to teaching statistics. After giving a preliminary mathematics achievement test on the first day of classes, she matches the students—pairs them according to their mathematical abilities. Then she follows by assigning one of each pair of students to Group A and the other to Group B. After grouping the students, she assigns the two groups to different lab times when she can teach each of the groups by a different method. At the end of the semester, she gives a comprehensive exam. The statistics teacher reasons that since students were grouped controlling for mathematical abilities, she should be able to determine whether there is a difference in the achievement of students in the two groups attributable to the method of instruction. If the mean of one of the groups is significantly different from the mean of the other group, then she can reason that the higher of the two mean scores is most likely the most effective teaching method. Using the T-TEST with the PAIRS= option will test this hypothesis.

The syntax for the T-TEST for paired samples is as follows.

T-TEST   PAIRS=VAR1 WITH VAR2/

where
VAR1 = the scores for group 1
VAR2 = the scores for group 2
PAIRS = = a keyword which represents the required syntax on the T-TEST command

Refer to Figure A.6 for SPSS output.

Using the ONEWAY Procedure System

In the last section, you saw how the T-TEST procedure can determine whether there are significant (as opposed to chance) differences in two group means. One limitation of the T-TEST is that it allows an independent variable to be categorized into only two groups. While the variable SEX does divide nicely into two groups, many variables do not. When the independent variable has more than two categories (or groupings), you may still test for differences between group means by using a different procedure: the ONEWAY analysis of variance. Like the T-TEST, the ONEWAY analysis of variance will allow you to determine whether the mean differences you have identified are likely the results of chance.

Suppose, for example, you were interested in determining if there is a significant difference in attitudes of grocery store employees at three large chain stores near your home. You administer an employee satisfaction survey to random samples of employees selected from the employee rosters of each of the three chain stores. You then use procedure ONEWAY to determine if there is a significant difference in the mean attitudes of employees at each of the three stores.

It should be noted that a significant F score (the F score being the ratio of the between-the-groups variance to the within variance) only reveals whether or not there is a significant difference between means. It does not reveal where the differences between means lies. The difference could be found between all three groups of employees, or it could be that there is an extreme difference between the attitudes of one store's employees as opposed to the attitudes of the other two groups of

FIGURE A.6
T-TEST for Dependent Samples

VARIABLE	NUMBER OF CASES	MEAN	STANDARD DEVIATION	STANDARD ERROR	(DIFFERENCE) MEAN	STANDARD DEVIATION	STANDARD ERROR	2-TAIL CORR. PROB.	T VALUE	DEGREES OF FREEDOM	2-TAIL PROB.
TEST1		41.9744	6.200	.702							
	78				-.3333	5.344	.605	.583 .000	-.55	77	.583
TEST2		42.3077	5.404	.612							

employees. There are other tests that can be run in conjunction with the ONEWAY procedure to help determine where the differences lie. These tests will not be discussed in this appendix; for information on such tests available in SPSS see the SPSS Manual.

The syntax for procedure ONEWAY is as follows.

ONEWAY   VAR1 BY VAR2 (MIN,MAX)

where
    VAR1 = the dependent variable
    VAR2 = the independent (grouping) variable
    (MIN,MAX) = the minimum and maximum values for the independent variable

Example 3C: Using Procedure ONEWAY to Test for Differences Between Three Group Means. Among the questions on our survey, one concerns the number of math hours that each respondent has earned in college prior to entering statistics. In trying to better understand the conditions under which students will enter a statistics course with a positive attitude, we might ask, "What effect does a student's prior math background have on his/her initial attitudes toward statistics?" To answer this question, we must again look at the variance found among different groups of students, but this time we will look at the differences found among three groups arbitrarily defined for the purpose of this example. We will group the students into the following categories: (1) students with 0 to 2 hours of completed math credits, (2) students with 3 to 8 hours of completed math credits, and (3) students with 9 or more hours of math credits. This grouping will be accomplished through the use of the RECODE card illustrated earlier in this appendix. The variable MATH (in its recoded form) will be our independent variable, and the variable FEELINGS will be our dependent variable.

    I. STATEMENT OF STATISTICAL HYPOTHESES
1. Working hypothesis: There is a significant difference in attitudes toward statistics for students with varying math backgrounds.

2. Null hypothesis: There is no significant difference in attitudes toward statistics for students with varying math backgrounds.

    II. STATEMENT OF STATISTICAL TEST, LEVEL OF SIGNIFICANCE, AND USE OF A ONE- OR TWO-TAILED TEST
Oneway analysis of variance; .05 significance level; two-tailed test.

    III. STATEMENT OF IMPORTANT SAMPLE STATISTICS
Sample size = 77

    IV. ASSUMING THE NULL IS TRUE, RUN PROCEDURE ONEWAY.
Refer to Figure A.7 for SPSS output.

FIGURE A.7
ONEWAY Analysis of Variance

```
VARIABLE   ATTITUDE
BY VARIABLE  DVAR
```

ANALYSIS OF VARIANCE

SOURCE	D.F.	SUM OF SQUARES	MEAN SQUARES	F RATIO	F PROB.
BETWEEN GROUPS	2	4.7394	2.3697	.252	.7781
WITHIN GROUPS	75	706.1452	9.4153		
TOTAL	77	710.8846			

The SPSS output demonstrates that the calculated between-group sums of squares is 4.7394, the within-groups sums of squares is 706.1452, and the total sums of squares is 710.8846. When divided by their respective degrees of freedom (found in the second column of the table), the between-groups means squares (variance) is 2.3697 and the within-groups means squares (variance) is 9.4153. The calculated F ratio is .252 with an associated probability of .7781.

The small between-groups variance when compared with the much larger within-groups variance indicates that most of the difference found in students' feelings toward statistics occurs within these groupings rather than between these groupings. That is, the greatest amount of variation found within our data is found *among* the students with similar math backgrounds rather than between the students with dissimilar math backgrounds.

When reading an F probability given in procedure ONEWAY output, anything less than or equal to .05 is statistically significant (assuming, of course, that the .05 level of significance has been established by the researcher). Since the probability associated with the F statistics is .7781, (clearly above the .05 cutoff point), we can assume that there are no significant differences in the attitudes of the three groups of students with varying math backgrounds. In other words, we have no evidence that background in math influences attitudes toward statistics.

Using the ANOVA Procedure Statement

The analysis-of-variance (ANOVA) technique is not limited to one independent variable. SPSS will allow for a maximum of five independent variables in one design, using the procedure called ANOVA. The ANOVA procedure will print out an analysis of variance table similar to the one you received with procedure ONEWAY. Additionally, it will print cell means and sample sizes. The syntax for implementing the procedure ANOVA using two independent variables is as follows.

    ANOVA   DVAR BY IVAR1 (MIN,MAX) IVAR2 (MIN,MAX)

where
- DVAR = the dependent variable
- IVAR1 = the first independent variable
- IVAR2 = the second independent variable
- (MIN,MAX) = the minimum and maximum grouping values of the independent variables used in the procedure

Using the SCATTERGRAM and the PEARSON CORR Procedure Statements

A scattergram is a pictorial representation of the joint values for a two-variable relationship. This pictorial representation comes in the form of a graph, with the scales of the graph contingent upon the minimum and maximum values specified for the two variables. A scattergram is frequently used by researchers to obtain a clearer picture of what their data look like. Examining a scattergram, for example, can warn researchers of outliers (extreme values that may distort statistical findings) or allow them the opportunity to ensure that the data fall in a linear pattern (an assumption that is often crucial to the statistical analyses being performed).

Rarely are scattergrams used by themselves; more often they are used in conjunction with other statistical procedures—specifically, correlation and regression. Correlation is defined as the degree to which variation (or change) in one variable is related to variation (change) in another variable. A correlation coefficient is an index that summarizes the strength of the relationship between two variables and also allows you to compare the strength of the relationship obtained between one pair of variables and a second pair.

The correlation coefficient r varies from -1.00 to $+1.00$ with either -1.00 or $+1.00$ representing a perfect correlation. An r of $+1.00$ indicates that either as one variable increases in value, the other variable also increases, or as one variable decreases in value, the other variable also decreases. An r of -1.00 indicates an inverse relationship. That is, as one variable increases in value, the other variable decreases in value. Both indicate perfect predictability. If we know the value for one variable (designated as X), we will be able to predict the value of the other variable (designated as Y). This fact will become more important in the next section when we discuss regression. An r of 0 indicates no linear relationship and means that knowing the value of one variable does not allow us any prediction power in estimating the other variable. Most of the data that you will use in real research situations will produce an r

greater than −1.00 and less than +1.00, indicating that while X gives you some power in predicting the value of Y, it does not provide perfect prediction power. The strength of the predicting power is determined by how close the calculated r is to −1.00 or +1.00. The closer the r is to either of these values, the stronger the relationship and hence the greater your predicting power.

The benefits of using the SCATTERGRAM procedure in conjunction with the PEARSON CORR can be seen in the case of a low correlation coefficient (i.e., an r that is close to zero). The low correlation coefficient may indicate no relationship between the two variables, or it may indicate a different type of relationship (e.g., a curvilinear relationship). The only way to rule out the possibility of a nonlinear relationship is through examination of the scattergram produced by plotting the two variables.

If there is a linear relationship between two variables, another useful statistic is the correlation coefficient squared (r^2). This statistic is a measure of the proportion of variance in the dependent variables that is explained by the independent variable. You can obtain this statistic by specifying a 2 on the STATISTICS card. To obtain r and r^2 using the SCATTERGRAM procedure, the syntax is as follows.

```
SCATTERGRAM    VAR1 (MIN,MAX) WITH VAR2 (MIN,MAX)
STATISTICS     1,2
```

where
- VAR1 = the variable plotted on the horizontal axis
- VAR2 = the variable plotted on the vertical axis
- (MIN,MAX) = the minimum and maximum values you want to include in the scattergram for each variable

There are times when you may choose to omit certain values from the scattergram. One use of the scattergram is location of extreme deviations (outliers) that may significantly distort the picture presented in the graph. In such cases, you should set the minimum and maximum values for the two variables so as to exclude the unwanted values from the graph.

To obtain the correlation coefficient using the PEARSON CORR card, the syntax is as follows.

```
PEARSON CORR   VAR1 WITH VAR2
STATISTICS     5,6
```

Two additional statistics that the SCATTERGRAM procedure can yield are the slope of the best-fitting line (commonly known as the regression line) and the Y intercept of that line. These statistics, which become important when you are doing regression analysis, can be obtained by adding statistics 5 and 6 to the STATISTICS card illustrated above. A second means of obtaining these statistics will be introduced with the NEW REGRESSION card discussed in the next section.

Example 5: Using Procedures SCATTERGRAM and PEARSON CORR in Testing Hypotheses. With the trend toward older students returning to college, there is a lack of data concerning the attitudes and performance of these returning students. Specifically, we might wish to determine whether there is a relationship between a student's age and his or her attitudes toward statistics.

I. STATEMENT OF STATISTICAL HYPOTHESES
1. Working hypothesis: There is a relationship between students' ages and their attitudes toward statistics.

2. Null hypothesis: There is no relationship between students' ages and their attitudes toward statistics.

II. STATEMENT OF STATISTICAL TEST
Pearson Product Moment Correlation (r)

III. STATEMENT OF IMPORTANT SAMPLE STATISTICS
Sample size = 78

IV. ASSUMING THE NULL HYPOTHESIS IS TRUE, RUN PROCEDURES SCATTERGRAM AND PEARSON CORR.
Refer to Figure A.8 for SPSS output.

Looking first at the correlation coefficient calculated for the bivariate relationship, we can see an r of $-.3474$. This appears to be a rather weak relationship, and if we were to accept this correlation coefficient without any further investigation, we would likely state that there is little relationship between students' ages and their attitudes toward statistics. However, before making such a decision, it is important that we look at a scattergram of the variables in order to rule out the possibility of a nonlinear relationship among the variables.

In examining the scattergram for the variables AGE and FEELINGS, it is apparent that there is indeed a nonlinear relationship present among the variables: attitude scores are low among the younger students, then rise steadily among students in their early to mid-twenties, and then decline steadily after age 25. Obviously the correlation coefficient cannot tell us why this curvilinear relationship exists; all it can do is indicate the extent to which two variables vary in a linear pattern. But as we have seen, the relationship present among the variables is not linear in form, a fact we were not able to confirm prior to examination of the scattergram.

FIGURE A.8
SCATTERGRAM

```
                 19.65      22.95      26.25      29.55      32.85      36.15      39.45      42.75      46.05      49.35
         .+----+----+----+----+----+----+----+----+----+----+----+----+----+----+----+----+----+----+----+----+----+----.
   10.00 +            2   3   4        I                     I                     I                              +  10.00
         I                              I                     I                     I                              I
         I                              I                     I                     I                              I
         I                              I                     I                     I                              I
    9.00 +        3   3   3   6        I                     I                     I                              +   9.00
         I                              I                     I                     I                              I
         I                              I                     I                     I                              I
         I                              I                     I                     I                              I
    8.00 +        2   2   2 * 2        I                     I                     I               .              +   8.00
         I                              I                     I                     I                              I
         I                              I                     I                     I                              I
         I                              I                     I                     I                              I
    7.00 +    2 *           2          I                     I                     I                              +   7.00
         I------------------------------------------------------------------------------------------------------------I
         I                              I                     I                     I                              I
    6.00 +        4              2 *   I                     I                     I                              +   6.00
         I                              I                     I                     I                              I
         I                              I                     I                     I                              I
         I                              I                     I                     I                              I
    5.00 +        2              2     I                     I                     I                              +   5.00
         I                              I                     I                     I                              I
         I                              I                     I                     I                              I
         I                              I                     I                     I                              I
    4.00 +  * 2                      * *I *                  I                     I                              +   4.00
         I                              I                     I                     I                              I
         I------------------------------------------------------------------------------------------------------------I
         I                              I                     I                     I                              I
    3.00 +*   * 2                      I     2 * *           I                     I                              +   3.00
         I                              I                     I                     I                              I
         I                              I                     I                     I                              I
         I                              I                     I                     I                              I
    2.00 +*  *                         I          *  *  *    *     I    *              +   2.00
         I                              I                     I                     I                              I
         I                              I                     I                     I                              I
         I                              I                     I                     I                              I
    1.00 +                              I           *  *  *    I* *                     *  *+   1.00
         I                              I                     I                     I                              I
         I                              I                     I                     I                              I
         I                              I                     I                     I                              I
     .00 +                              I                     I                     I                              +    .00
         .+----+----+----+----+----+----+----+----+----+----+----+----+----+----+----+----+----+----+----+----+----+----.
          18.00      21.30      24.60      27.90      31.20      34.50      37.80      41.10      44.40      47.70      51.00
PLOTTED VALUES -         77              EXCLUDED VALUES-        1              MISSING VALUES -        0
```

	AGE	ATTITUDE
AGE	1.0000 (0) P=*****	-.3474 (78) P= .001
ATTITUDE	-.3474 (78) P= .001	1.0000 (0) P=*****

(COEFFICIENT / (CASES) / SIGNIFICANCE)   (A VALUE OF 99.0000 IS PRINTED IF A COEFFICIENT CANNOT BE COMPUTED)

Using the NEW REGRESSION Procedure Statement

The statistical procedure regression is a powerful statistical tool and perhaps the single most commonly used statistic among social researchers. Regression procedures allow the researcher to use one variable (traditionally labeled the X variable) to predict another (traditionally labeled the Y variable). Regression requires interval or ratio level data, although it is possible to transform nominal level data into a form acceptable to the regression procedure. Like the *t*-test and the oneway analysis of variance, it must be assumed that there is a normal distribution of Y's across all categories of X, that these Y's have homogeneity of variance, and that the data represent a random sample.

Regression works on the principle of identifying the best-fitting line for a given X, Y variable combination and then using that line to predict Y values for any given value of X. Theoretically, every possible point on the X continuum can be thought of as a category. For every X value (or category) there is a normal distribution of Y's, each of the Y distributions having its own mean. Thus, once we identify the value (category) of X for which we want to make a prediction, our predicted Y becomes the mean of the distribution of Y scores for that particular value of X.

Since we cannot usually obtain access to the entire population of Y scores for a given value of X, we find the Y score for a value of X using the formula for a straight line:

$$Y' = a + bX$$

where
$Y' =$ the predicted Y
$a =$ the Y intercept—the point where the line crosses the Y axis (the value of X is zero);
$b =$ the slope of the line (the increase in Y for a unit increase in X);
$X =$ the designated value (category) of X

Graphically, the Y is the point where the given value of X intercepts the computed line of best fit (the regression line). Each point on the regression line represents a predicted Y value for a corresponding value of X.

In actual research situations, you will have both X and Y values collected from a random sample and will compute a regression line from the data collected. The points that fall on the line will represent the predicted Y values. However, unless your correlation coefficient is either -1.00 or $+1.00$, not all of the original Y values collected from the sample will fall on that line. If you created a scattergram of your data and drew the calculated regression line onto your printout, the distance between the actual plotted points and the points on your line for the given value of X would constitute your error in prediction. Obviously, if there is very little distance between the plotted points and the points on the regression line, then there will be a small amount of error in the prediction. Likewise, a larger distance would indicate larger amounts of error in predicting. The distance between the predicted Y (a point on the regression line) and the actual Y observed from the sample is known as the error or residual. If you were to take all the calculated residuals and calculate a standard deviation on this distribution of residuals, you would obtain a statistic known as the standard error of the estimate. That is, the standard error of the estimate is really just the standard deviation of the residuals.

The correlation coefficient discussed in the last section serves as a measure of the ability of a regression line to predict accurately. The stronger the relationship between the X and Y variables (as indicated by the r coefficient), the greater the ability of the regression line to predict accurately. The scattergram, discussed in the last section, is also used in regression analysis. Scattergrams are used (1) to determine if the data are linear in form (2) to identify outliers, and (3) to analyze regression residuals.

To obtain a scattergram of the X,Y variable combination, the r coefficient, r^2, and regression statistics, the syntax is as follows.

```
NEW REGRESSION    VAR1,VAR2/
                  STATISTICS=R/
                  DEPENDENT=VAR2/
                  SCATTERPLOT=(VAR1,VAR2)/
                  STEPWISE/
```

where:
- VAR1 and VAR2 = the independent and dependent variables respectively
- STATISTICS= = the statistics to be computed, in this case correlation and r^2
- DEPENDENT= = the variable from the list of regression variables that is to be treated by SPSS as the dependent variable
- SCATTERPLOT= = the variables to be plotted on a scatterplot
- STEPWISE = the command that specifies the entry of the independent variables—in this case, only one

There are a number of statistics obtainable with NEW REGRESSION. For information on these statistics, consult the SPSS UPDATE 7-9 (1981).

Example 6: Using NEW REGRESSION in Testing Hypotheses. Many statistics courses in universities hold two concurrent sessions: a theory session and a lab session. Students schedule both the theory and lab segments but are often graded separately within each of the two seg-

FIGURE A.9
Multiple Regression

```
VARIABLE LIST NUMBER   1.  LISTWISE DELETION OF MISSING DATA.

EQUATION NUMBER  1.

DEPENDENT VARIABLE..  LAB


BEGINNING BLOCK NUMBER  1.  METHOD: ENTER       THEORY


VARIABLE(S) ENTERED ON STEP NUMBER  1..    THEORY


MULTIPLE R             .95743
R SQUARE               .91667
ADJUSTED R SQUARE      .91557
STANDARD ERROR        3.04363



FOR BLOCK NUMBER   1   ALL REQUESTED VARIABLES ENTERED.



RESIDUALS STATISTICS:

            MIN       MAX      MEAN    STD DEV   N                    MIN      MAX     MEAN   STD DEV   N
*PRED    19.4724   50.4998   38.3974  10.0289   78      *RESID    -6.6953   8.2449    .0000   3.0238   78
*ZPRED   -1.8870    1.2067    .0000    1.0000   78      *ZRESID   -2.1998   2.7089    .0000    .9935   78
*SEPRED    .3446     .7397    .4734     .1165   78      *SRESID   -2.2212   2.7369   -.0012  1.0073   78
*ADJPRED 19.3766   50.6800   38.4049  10.0232   78      *DRESID   -6.8430   8.4163   -.0075  3.1087   78
*MAHAL     .0001    3.5609    .9872    1.0078   78      *SDRESID  -2.2819   2.8636   -.0001  1.0242   78
*COOK D    .0000     .1088    .0141     .0232   78

TOTAL CASES =    78


              * * * * * * * * * * * * * * * * * * * * * * * * * * * * *

STANDARDIZED SCATTERPLOT
ACROSS - LAB      DOWN - THEORY
OUT ++-----+-----+-----+-----+-----+-----++
  3 +                                      +    SYMBOLS:
    I                                      I
    I                                      I       MAX N
  2 +                                      +
    I                                      I    .    1.
    I                  . *.                I    :    2.
  1 +                  . *                 +    *    7.
    I                . :* *.               I
    I               **** :                 I
  0 +             . ::                     +
    I                .                     I
    I            .   .. ..                 I
 -1 +              ... .                   +
    I                                      I
    I         :*:: :*                      I
 -2 +          .                           +
    I                                      I
    I                                      I
 -3 +                                      +
OUT ++-----+-----+-----+-----+-----+-----++
    -3    -2    -1     0     1     2     3 OUT
```

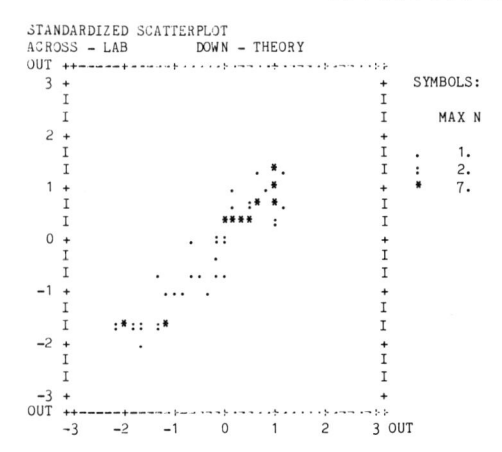

ments. One question that can arise is whether a student's mastery of the theoretical issues in statistics is a good predictor of how well he or she will perform in the lab. We will use regression to gain insight into this question.

I. STATEMENT OF STATISTICAL HYPOTHESES
1. Working hypothesis: Theory grades will be a good predictor of lab performance.

2. Null hypothesis: Theory grades will not be a good predictor of lab performance.

II. STATEMENT OF STATISTICAL TEST AND LEVEL OF SIGNIFICANCE
Linear regression and Pearson r; .05 significance level

III. STATEMENT OF IMPORTANT SAMPLE STATISTICS
Sample size = 78

IV. ASSUMING THE NULL HYPOTHESIS IS TRUE, RUN PROCEDURE REGRESSION.
Refer to Figure A.9 for SPSS output.

Looking at the first page of our output, we can see that the correlation coefficient for this bivariate relationship (found under the label MULTIPLE R) is .95743. The r^2 (we have noted before) is the proportion of variance in the dependent variable that is explained by the independent variable. In this case, r^2 represents the proportion of variance in the dependent variable LAB that is explained by the independent variable THEORY. This figure, given under the heading R SQUARED, is .91667. When translated into percentage form, this indicates that 91.667 percent of the variation in the dependent variable LAB grades can be explained by the independent variable THEORY grades. It would appear that theory grades are a good predictor of lab performance.

While these procedural commands are not exhaustive of what SPSS can do, they can be viewed as representative of what beginning researchers would use. Multivariate statistical procedures, seldom used by beginning research students, have not been discussed. Should you need multivariate analyses or procedures not mentioned here, refer to the SPSS manual.

Appendix B

Tables

TABLE 1   Random Numbers

10	09	73	25	33	76	52	01	35	86	34	67	35	48	76	80	95	90	91	17	39	29	27	49	45
37	54	20	48	05	64	89	47	42	96	24	80	52	40	37	20	63	61	04	02	00	82	29	16	65
08	42	26	89	53	19	64	50	93	03	23	20	90	25	60	15	95	33	47	64	35	08	03	36	06
99	01	90	25	29	09	37	67	07	15	38	31	13	11	65	88	67	67	43	97	04	43	62	76	59
12	80	79	99	70	80	15	73	61	47	64	03	23	66	53	98	95	11	68	77	12	17	17	68	33
66	06	57	47	17	34	07	27	68	50	36	69	73	61	70	65	81	33	98	85	11	19	92	91	70
31	06	01	08	05	45	57	18	24	06	35	30	34	26	14	86	79	90	74	39	23	40	30	97	32
85	26	97	76	02	02	05	16	56	92	68	66	57	48	18	73	05	38	52	47	18	62	38	85	79
63	57	33	21	35	05	32	54	70	48	90	55	35	75	48	28	46	82	87	09	83	49	12	56	24
73	79	64	57	53	03	52	96	47	78	35	80	83	42	82	60	93	52	03	44	35	27	38	84	35
98	52	01	77	67	14	90	56	86	07	22	10	94	05	58	60	97	09	34	33	50	50	07	39	98
11	80	50	54	31	39	80	82	77	32	50	72	56	82	48	29	40	52	42	01	52	77	56	78	51
83	45	29	96	34	06	28	89	80	83	13	74	67	00	78	18	47	54	06	10	68	71	17	78	17
88	68	54	02	00	86	50	75	84	01	36	76	66	79	51	90	36	47	64	93	29	60	91	10	62
99	59	46	73	48	87	51	76	49	69	91	82	60	89	28	93	78	56	13	68	23	47	83	41	13
65	48	11	76	74	17	46	85	09	50	58	04	77	69	74	73	03	95	71	86	40	21	81	65	44
80	12	43	56	35	17	72	70	80	15	45	31	82	23	74	21	11	57	82	53	14	38	55	37	63
74	35	09	98	17	77	40	27	72	14	43	23	60	02	10	45	52	16	42	37	96	28	60	26	55
69	91	62	68	03	66	25	22	91	48	36	93	68	72	03	76	62	11	39	90	94	40	05	64	18
09	89	32	05	05	14	22	56	85	14	46	42	75	67	88	96	29	77	88	22	54	38	21	45	98
91	49	91	45	23	68	47	92	76	86	46	16	28	35	54	94	75	08	99	23	37	08	92	00	48
80	33	69	45	98	26	94	03	68	58	70	29	73	41	35	53	14	03	33	40	42	05	08	23	41
44	10	48	19	49	85	15	74	79	54	32	97	92	65	75	57	60	04	08	81	22	22	20	64	13
12	55	07	37	42	11	10	00	20	40	12	86	07	46	97	96	64	48	94	39	28	70	72	58	15
63	60	64	93	29	16	50	53	44	84	40	21	95	25	63	43	65	17	70	82	07	20	73	17	90
61	19	69	04	46	26	45	74	77	74	51	92	43	37	29	65	39	45	95	93	42	58	26	05	27
15	47	44	52	66	95	27	07	99	53	59	36	78	38	48	82	39	61	01	18	33	21	15	94	66
94	55	72	85	73	67	89	75	43	87	54	62	24	44	31	91	19	04	25	92	92	92	74	59	73
42	48	11	62	13	97	34	40	87	21	16	86	84	87	67	03	07	11	20	59	25	70	14	66	70
23	52	37	83	17	73	20	88	98	37	68	93	59	14	16	26	25	22	96	63	05	52	28	25	62

(*continued*)

TABLE 1 Random Numbers (*Continued*)

04	49	35	24	94	75	24	63	38	24	45	86	25	10	25	61	96	27	93	35	65	33	71	24	72
00	54	99	76	54	64	05	18	81	59	96	11	96	38	96	54	69	28	23	91	23	28	72	95	29
35	96	31	53	07	26	89	80	93	54	33	35	13	54	62	77	97	45	00	24	90	10	33	93	33
59	80	80	83	91	45	42	72	68	42	83	60	94	97	00	13	02	12	48	92	78	56	52	01	06
46	05	88	52	36	01	39	09	22	86	77	28	14	40	77	93	91	08	36	47	70	61	74	29	41
32	17	90	05	97	87	37	92	52	41	05	56	70	70	07	86	74	31	71	57	85	39	41	18	38
69	23	46	14	06	20	11	74	52	04	15	95	66	00	00	18	74	39	24	23	97	11	89	63	38
19	56	54	14	30	01	75	87	53	79	40	41	92	15	85	66	67	43	68	06	84	96	28	52	07
45	15	51	49	38	19	47	60	72	46	43	66	79	45	43	59	04	79	00	33	20	82	66	95	41
94	86	43	19	94	36	16	81	08	51	34	88	88	15	53	01	54	03	54	56	05	01	45	11	76
98	08	62	48	26	45	24	02	84	04	44	99	90	88	96	39	09	47	34	07	35	44	13	18	80
33	18	51	62	32	41	94	15	09	49	89	43	54	85	81	88	69	54	19	94	37	54	87	30	43
80	95	10	04	06	96	38	27	07	74	20	15	12	33	87	25	01	62	52	98	94	62	46	11	71
79	75	24	91	40	71	96	12	82	96	69	86	10	25	91	74	85	22	05	39	00	38	75	95	79
18	63	33	25	37	98	14	50	65	71	31	01	02	46	74	05	45	56	14	27	77	93	89	19	36
74	02	94	39	02	77	55	73	22	70	97	79	01	71	19	52	52	75	80	21	80	81	45	17	48
54	17	84	56	11	80	99	33	71	43	05	33	51	29	69	56	12	71	92	55	36	04	09	03	24
11	66	44	98	83	52	07	98	48	27	59	38	17	15	39	09	97	33	34	40	88	46	12	33	56
48	32	47	79	28	31	24	96	47	10	02	29	53	68	70	32	30	75	75	46	15	02	00	99	94
69	07	49	41	38	87	63	79	19	76	35	58	40	44	01	10	51	82	16	15	01	84	87	69	38
09	18	82	00	97	32	82	53	95	27	04	22	08	63	04	83	38	98	73	74	64	27	85	80	44
90	04	58	54	97	51	98	15	06	54	94	93	88	19	97	91	87	07	61	50	68	47	66	46	59
73	18	95	02	07	47	67	72	52	69	62	29	06	44	64	27	12	46	70	18	41	36	18	27	60
75	76	87	64	90	20	97	18	17	49	90	42	91	22	72	95	37	50	58	71	93	82	34	31	78
54	01	64	40	56	66	28	13	10	03	00	68	22	73	98	20	71	45	32	95	07	70	61	78	13
08	35	86	99	10	78	54	24	27	85	13	66	15	88	73	04	61	89	75	53	31	22	30	84	20
28	30	60	32	64	81	33	31	05	91	40	51	00	78	93	32	60	46	04	75	94	11	90	18	40
53	84	08	62	33	81	59	41	36	28	51	21	59	02	90	28	46	66	87	95	77	76	22	07	91
91	75	75	37	41	61	61	36	22	69	50	26	39	02	12	55	78	17	65	14	83	48	34	70	55
89	41	59	26	94	00	39	75	83	91	12	60	71	76	46	48	94	97	23	06	94	54	13	74	08
77	51	30	38	20	86	83	42	99	01	68	41	48	27	74	51	90	81	39	80	72	89	35	55	07
19	50	23	71	74	69	97	92	02	88	55	21	02	97	73	74	28	77	52	51	65	34	46	74	15
21	81	85	93	13	93	27	88	17	57	05	68	67	31	56	07	08	28	50	46	31	85	33	84	52
51	47	46	64	99	68	10	72	36	21	94	04	99	13	45	42	83	60	91	91	08	00	74	54	49
99	55	96	83	31	62	53	52	41	70	69	77	71	28	30	74	81	97	81	42	43	86	07	28	34
33	71	34	80	07	93	58	47	28	69	51	92	66	47	21	58	30	32	98	22	93	17	49	39	72
85	27	48	68	93	11	30	32	92	70	28	83	43	41	37	73	51	59	04	00	71	14	84	36	43
84	13	38	96	40	44	03	55	21	66	73	85	27	00	91	61	22	26	05	61	62	32	71	84	23
56	73	21	62	34	17	39	59	61	31	10	12	39	16	22	85	49	65	75	60	81	60	41	88	80
65	13	85	08	06	87	64	88	52	61	34	31	36	58	61	45	87	52	10	69	85	64	44	72	77

TABLE 1 Random Numbers (*Continued*)

38	00	10	21	76	81	71	91	17	11	71	60	29	29	37	74	21	96	40	49	65	58	44	96	98
37	40	29	63	97	01	30	47	75	86	56	27	11	00	86	47	32	46	26	05	40	03	03	74	38
97	12	54	03	48	87	08	33	14	17	21	81	53	92	50	75	23	76	20	47	15	50	12	95	78
21	82	64	11	34	47	14	33	40	72	64	63	88	59	02	49	13	90	64	41	03	85	65	45	52
73	13	54	27	42	95	71	90	90	35	85	79	47	42	96	08	78	98	81	56	64	69	11	92	02
07	63	87	79	29	03	06	11	80	72	96	20	74	41	56	23	82	19	95	38	04	71	36	69	94
60	52	88	34	41	07	95	41	98	14	59	17	52	06	95	05	53	35	21	39	61	21	20	64	55
83	59	63	56	55	06	95	89	29	83	05	12	80	97	19	77	43	35	37	83	92	30	15	04	98
10	85	06	27	46	99	59	91	05	07	13	49	90	63	19	53	07	57	18	39	06	41	01	93	62
39	82	09	89	52	43	62	26	31	47	64	42	18	08	14	43	80	00	93	51	31	02	47	31	67

SOURCE: The RAND Corporation, *A Million Random Digits,* Free Press, Glencoe, Ill., 1955, pp. 1–3, with the kind permission of the publisher.

TABLE 2 Areas under the Normal Curve

Fractional parts of the total area (10,000) under the normal curve, corresponding to distances between the mean and ordinates which are Z standard-deviation units from the mean.

Z	.00	.01	.02	.03	.04	.05	.06	.07	.08	.09
0.0	0000	0040	0080	0120	0159	0199	0239	0279	0319	0359
0.1	0398	0438	0478	0517	0557	0596	0636	0675	0714	0753
0.2	0793	0832	0871	0910	0948	0987	1026	1064	1103	1141
0.3	1179	1217	1255	1293	1331	1368	1406	1443	1480	1517
0.4	1554	1591	1628	1664	1700	1736	1772	1808	1844	1879
0.5	1915	1950	1985	2019	2054	2088	2123	2157	2190	2224
0.6	2257	2291	2324	2357	2389	2422	2454	2486	2518	2549
0.7	2580	2612	2642	2673	2704	2734	2764	2794	2823	2852
0.8	2881	2910	2939	2967	2995	3023	3051	3078	3106	3133
0.9	3159	3186	3212	3238	3264	3289	3315	3340	3365	3389
1.0	3413	3438	3461	3485	3508	3531	3554	3577	3599	3621
1.1	3643	3665	3686	3718	3729	3749	3770	3790	3810	3830
1.2	3849	3869	3888	3907	3925	3944	3962	3980	3997	4015
1.3	4032	4049	4066	4083	4099	4115	4131	4147	4162	4177
1.4	4192	4207	4222	4236	4251	4265	4279	4292	4306	4319
1.5	4332	4345	4357	4370	4382	4394	4406	4418	4430	4441
1.6	4452	4463	4474	4485	4495	4505	4515	4525	4535	4545
1.7	4554	4564	4573	4582	4591	4599	4608	4616	4625	4633
1.8	4641	4649	4656	4664	4671	4678	4686	4693	4699	4706
1.9	4713	4719	4726	4732	4738	4744	4750	4758	4762	4767

(*continued*)

TABLE 2 Areas under the Normal Curve (Continued)

Fractional parts of the total area (10,000) under the normal curve, corresponding to distances between the mean and ordinates which are Z standard-deviation units from the mean.

Z	.00	.01	.02	.03	.04	.05	.06	.07	.08	.09
2.0	4773	4778	4783	4788	4793	4798	4803	4808	4812	4817
2.1	4821	4826	4830	4834	4838	4842	4846	4850	4854	4857
2.2	4861	4865	4868	4871	4875	4878	4881	4884	4887	4890
2.3	4893	4896	4898	4901	4904	4906	4909	4911	4913	4916
2.4	4918	4920	4922	4925	4927	4929	4931	4932	4934	4936
2.5	4938	4940	4941	4943	4945	4946	4948	4949	4951	4952
2.6	4953	4955	4956	4957	4959	4960	4961	4962	4963	4964
2.7	4965	4966	4967	4968	4969	4970	4971	4972	4973	4974
2.8	4974	4975	4976	4977	4977	4978	4979	4980	4980	4981
2.9	4981	4982	4983	4984	4984	4984	4985	4985	4986	4986
3.0	4986.5	4987	4987	4988	4988	4988	4989	4989	4989	4990
3.1	4990.0	4991	4991	4991	4992	4992	4992	4992	4993	4993
3.2	4993.129									
3.3	4995.166									
3.4	4996.631									
3.5	4997.674									
3.6	4998.409									
3.7	4998.922									
3.8	4999.277									
3.9	4999.519									
4.0	4999.683									
4.5	4999.966									
5.0	4999.997133									

SOURCE: Harold O. Rugg, *Statistical Methods Applied to Education,* Houghton Mifflin Company, Boston, 1917, appendix table III, pp. 389–390, with the kind permission of the publisher.

TABLE 3 Distribution of *t*

df	Level of significance for one-tailed test					
	.10	*.05*	*.025*	*.01*	*.005*	*.0005*
	Level of significance for two-tailed test					
	.20	*.10*	*.05*	*.02*	*.01*	*.001*
1	3.078	6.314	12.706	31.821	63.657	636.619
2	1.886	2.920	4.303	6.965	9.925	31.598
3	1.638	2.353	3.182	4.541	5.841	12.941
4	1.533	2.132	2.776	3.747	4.604	8.610
5	1.476	2.015	2.571	3.365	4.032	6.859
6	1.440	1.943	2.447	3.143	3.707	5.959
7	1.415	1.895	2.365	2.998	3.499	5.405
8	1.397	1.860	2.306	2.896	3.355	5.041
9	1.383	1.833	2.262	2.821	3.250	4.781
10	1.372	1.812	2.228	2.764	3.169	4.587
11	1.363	1.796	2.201	2.718	3.106	4.437
12	1.356	1.782	2.179	2.681	3.055	4.318
13	1.350	1.771	2.160	2.650	3.012	4.221
14	1.345	1.761	2.145	2.624	2.977	4.140
15	1.341	1.753	2.131	2.602	2.947	4.073
16	1.337	1.746	2.120	2.583	2.921	4.015
17	1.333	1.740	2.110	2.567	2.898	3.965
18	1.330	1.734	2.101	2.552	2.878	3.922
19	1.328	1.729	2.093	2.539	2.861	3.883
20	1.325	1.725	2.086	2.528	2.845	3.850
21	1.323	1.721	2.080	2.518	2.831	3.819
22	1.321	1.717	2.074	2.508	2.819	3.792
23	1.319	1.714	2.069	2.500	2.807	3.767
24	1.318	1.711	2.064	2.492	2.797	3.745
25	1.316	1.708	2.060	2.485	2.787	3.725
26	1.315	1.706	2.056	2.479	2.779	3.707
27	1.314	1.703	2.052	2.473	2.771	3.690
28	1.313	1.701	2.048	2.467	2.763	3.674
29	1.311	1.699	2.045	2.462	2.756	3.659
30	1.310	1.697	2.042	2.457	2.750	3.646
40	1.303	1.684	2.021	2.423	2.704	3.551
60	1.296	1.671	2.000	2.390	2.660	3.460
120	1.289	1.658	1.980	2.358	2.617	3.373
∞	1.282	1.645	1.960	2.326	2.576	3.291

SOURCE: Table 3 is abridged from Table III of R. A. Fisher and F. Yates, *Statistical Tables for Biological, Agricultural and Medical Research* (1948 ed.), published by Oliver & Boyd, Ltd., Edinburgh and London, by permission of the authors and publisher.

TABLE 4 Distribution of F

$p = .05$

n_2 \ n_1	1	2	3	4	5	6	8	12	24	∞
1	161.4	199.5	215.7	224.6	230.2	234.0	238.9	243.9	249.0	254.3
2	18.51	19.00	19.16	19.25	19.30	19.33	19.37	19.41	19.45	19.50
3	10.13	9.55	9.28	9.12	9.01	8.94	8.84	8.74	8.64	8.53
4	7.71	6.94	6.59	6.39	6.26	6.16	6.04	5.91	5.77	5.63
5	6.61	5.79	5.41	5.19	5.05	4.95	4.82	4.68	4.53	4.36
6	5.99	5.14	4.76	4.53	4.39	4.28	4.15	4.00	3.84	3.67
7	5.59	4.74	4.35	4.12	3.97	3.87	3.73	3.57	3.41	3.23
8	5.32	4.46	4.07	3.84	3.69	3.58	3.44	3.28	3.12	2.93
9	5.12	4.26	3.86	3.63	3.48	3.37	3.23	3.07	2.90	2.71
10	4.96	4.10	3.71	3.48	3.33	3.22	3.07	2.91	2.74	2.54
11	4.84	3.98	3.59	3.36	3.20	3.09	2.95	2.79	2.61	2.40
12	4.75	3.88	3.49	3.26	3.11	3.00	2.85	2.69	2.50	2.30
13	4.67	3.80	3.41	3.18	3.02	2.92	2.77	2.60	2.42	2.21
14	4.60	3.74	3.34	3.11	2.96	2.85	2.70	2.53	2.35	2.13
15	4.54	3.68	3.29	3.06	2.90	2.79	2.64	2.48	2.29	2.07
16	4.49	3.63	3.24	3.01	2.85	2.74	2.59	2.42	2.24	2.01
17	4.45	3.59	3.20	2.96	2.81	2.70	2.55	2.38	2.19	1.96
18	4.41	3.55	3.16	2.93	2.77	2.66	2.51	2.34	2.15	1.92
19	4.38	3.52	3.13	2.90	2.74	2.63	2.48	2.31	2.11	1.88
20	4.35	3.49	3.10	2.87	2.71	2.60	2.45	2.28	2.08	1.84
21	4.32	3.47	3.07	2.84	2.68	2.57	2.42	2.25	2.05	1.81
22	4.30	3.44	3.05	2.82	2.66	2.55	2.40	2.23	2.03	1.78
23	4.28	3.42	3.03	2.80	2.64	2.53	2.38	2.20	2.00	1.76
24	4.26	3.40	3.01	2.78	2.62	2.51	2.36	2.18	1.98	1.73
25	4.24	3.38	2.99	2.76	2.60	2.49	2.34	2.16	1.96	1.71
26	4.22	3.37	2.98	2.74	2.59	2.47	2.32	2.15	1.95	1.69
27	4.21	3.35	2.96	2.73	2.57	2.46	2.30	2.13	1.93	1.67
28	4.20	3.34	2.95	2.71	2.56	2.44	2.29	2.12	1.91	1.65
29	4.18	3.33	2.93	2.70	2.54	2.43	2.28	2.10	1.90	1.64
30	4.17	3.32	2.92	2.69	2.53	2.42	2.27	2.09	1.89	1.62
40	4.08	3.23	2.84	2.61	2.45	2.34	2.18	2.00	1.79	1.51
60	4.00	3.15	2.76	2.52	2.37	2.25	2.10	1.92	1.70	1.39
120	3.92	3.07	2.68	2.45	2.29	2.17	2.02	1.83	1.61	1.25
∞	3.84	2.99	2.60	2.37	2.21	2.09	1.94	1.75	1.52	1.00

Values of n_1 and n_2 represent the degrees of freedom associated with the larger and smaller estimates of variance respectively.

(continued)

TABLE 4 Distribution of *F* (Continued)

$p = .01$

n_2 \ n_1	1	2	3	4	5	6	8	12	24	∞
1	4052	4999	5403	5625	5764	5859	5981	6106	6234	6366
2	98.49	99.01	99.17	99.25	99.30	99.33	99.36	99.42	99.46	99.50
3	34.12	30.81	29.46	28.71	28.24	27.91	27.49	27.05	26.60	26.12
4	21.20	18.00	16.69	15.98	15.52	15.21	14.80	14.37	13.93	13.46
5	16.26	13.27	12.06	11.39	10.97	10.67	10.27	9.89	9.47	9.02
6	13.74	10.92	9.78	9.15	8.75	8.47	8.10	7.72	7.31	6.88
7	12.25	9.55	8.45	7.85	7.46	7.19	6.84	6.47	6.07	5.65
8	11.26	8.65	7.59	7.01	6.63	6.37	6.03	5.67	5.28	4.86
9	10.56	8.02	6.99	6.42	6.06	5.80	5.47	5.11	4.73	4.31
10	10.04	7.56	6.55	5.99	5.64	5.39	5.06	4.71	4.33	3.91
11	9.65	7.20	6.22	5.67	5.32	5.07	4.74	4.40	4.02	3.60
12	9.33	6.93	5.95	5.41	5.06	4.82	4.50	4.16	3.78	3.36
13	9.07	6.70	5.74	5.20	4.86	4.62	4.30	3.96	3.59	3.16
14	8.86	6.51	5.56	5.03	4.69	4.46	4.14	3.80	3.43	3.00
15	8.68	6.36	5.42	4.89	4.56	4.32	4.00	3.67	3.29	2.87
16	8.53	6.23	5.29	4.77	4.44	4.20	3.89	3.55	3.18	2.75
17	8.40	6.11	5.18	4.67	4.34	4.10	3.79	3.45	3.08	2.65
18	8.28	6.01	5.09	4.58	4.25	4.01	3.71	3.37	3.00	2.57
19	8.18	5.93	5.01	4.50	4.17	3.94	3.63	3.30	2.92	2.49
20	8.10	5.85	4.94	4.43	4.10	3.87	3.56	3.23	2.86	2.42
21	8.02	5.78	4.87	4.37	4.04	3.81	3.51	3.17	2.80	2.36
22	7.94	5.72	4.82	4.31	3.99	3.76	3.45	3.12	2.75	2.31
23	7.88	5.66	4.76	4.26	3.94	3.71	3.41	3.07	2.70	2.26
24	7.82	5.61	4.72	4.22	3.90	3.67	3.36	3.03	2.66	2.21
25	7.77	5.57	4.68	4.18	3.86	3.63	3.32	2.99	2.62	2.17
26	7.72	5.53	4.64	4.14	3.82	3.59	3.29	2.96	2.58	2.13
27	7.68	5.49	4.60	4.11	3.78	3.56	3.26	2.93	2.55	2.10
28	7.64	5.45	4.57	4.07	3.75	3.53	3.23	2.90	2.52	2.06
29	7.60	5.42	4.54	4.04	3.73	3.50	3.20	2.87	2.49	2.03
30	7.56	5.39	4.51	4.02	3.70	3.47	3.17	2.84	2.47	2.01
40	7.31	5.18	4.31	3.83	3.51	3.29	2.99	2.66	2.29	1.80
60	7.08	4.98	4.13	3.65	3.34	3.12	2.82	2.50	2.12	1.60
120	6.85	4.79	3.95	3.48	3.17	2.96	2.66	2.34	1.95	1.38
∞	6.64	4.60	3.78	3.32	3.02	2.80	2.51	2.18	1.79	1.00

Values of n_1 and n_2 represent the degrees of freedom associated with the larger and smaller estimates of variance respectively.

(continued)

TABLE 4 Distribution of F (Continued)

$p = .001$

$n_2 \backslash n_1$	1	2	3	4	5	6	8	12	24	∞
1	405284	500000	540379	562500	576405	585937	598144	610667	623497	636619
2	998.5	999.0	999.2	999.2	999.3	999.3	999.4	999.4	999.5	999.5
3	167.5	148.5	141.1	137.1	134.6	132.8	130.6	128.3	125.9	123.5
4	74.14	61.25	56.18	53.44	51.71	50.53	49.00	47.41	45.77	44.05
5	47.04	36.61	33.20	31.09	29.75	28.84	27.64	26.42	25.14	23.78
6	35.51	27.00	23.70	21.90	20.81	20.03	19.03	17.99	16.89	15.75
7	29.22	21.69	18.77	17.19	16.21	15.52	14.63	13.71	12.73	11.69
8	25.42	18.49	15.83	14.39	13.49	12.86	12.04	11.19	10.30	9.34
9	22.86	16.39	13.90	12.56	11.71	11.13	10.37	9.57	8.72	7.81
10	21.04	14.91	12.55	11.28	10.48	9.92	9.20	8.45	7.64	6.76
11	19.69	13.81	11.56	10.35	9.58	9.05	8.35	7.63	6.85	6.00
12	18.64	12.97	10.80	9.63	8.89	8.38	7.71	7.00	6.25	5.42
13	17.81	12.31	10.21	9.07	8.35	7.86	7.21	6.52	5.78	4.97
14	17.14	11.78	9.73	8.62	7.92	7.43	6.80	6.13	5.41	4.60
15	16.59	11.34	9.34	8.25	7.57	7.09	6.47	5.81	5.10	4.31
16	16.12	10.97	9.00	7.94	7.27	6.81	6.19	5.55	4.85	4.06
17	15.72	10.66	8.73	7.68	7.02	6.56	5.96	5.32	4.63	3.85
18	15.38	10.39	8.49	7.46	6.81	6.35	5.76	5.13	4.45	3.67
19	15.08	10.16	8.28	7.26	6.61	6.18	5.59	4.97	4.29	3.52
20	14.82	9.95	8.10	7.10	6.46	6.02	5.44	4.82	4.15	3.38
21	14.59	9.77	7.94	6.95	6.32	5.88	5.31	4.70	4.03	3.26
22	14.38	9.61	7.80	6.81	6.19	5.76	5.19	4.58	3.92	3.15
23	14.19	9.47	7.67	6.69	6.08	5.65	5.09	4.48	3.82	3.05
24	14.03	9.34	7.55	6.59	5.98	5.55	4.99	4.39	3.74	2.97
25	13.88	9.22	7.45	6.49	5.88	5.46	4.91	4.31	3.66	2.89
26	13.74	9.12	7.36	6.41	5.80	5.38	4.83	4.24	3.59	2.82
27	13.61	9.02	7.27	6.33	5.73	5.31	4.76	4.17	3.52	2.75
28	13.50	8.93	7.19	6.25	5.66	5.24	4.69	4.11	3.46	2.70
29	13.39	8.85	7.12	6.19	5.59	5.18	4.64	4.05	3.41	2.64
30	13.29	8.77	7.05	6.12	5.53	5.12	4.58	4.00	3.36	2.59
40	12.61	8.25	6.60	5.70	5.13	4.73	4.21	3.64	3.01	2.23
60	11.97	7.76	6.17	5.31	4.76	4.37	3.87	3.31	2.69	1.90
120	11.38	7.31	5.79	4.95	4.42	4.04	3.55	3.02	2.40	1.56
∞	10.83	6.91	5.42	4.62	4.10	3.74	3.27	2.74	2.13	1.00

Values of n_1 and n_2 represent the degrees of freedom associated with the larger and smaller estimates of variance respectively.

SOURCE: Table 4 is abridged from Table V of R. A. Fisher and F. Yates, *Statistical Tables for Biological, Agricultural and Medical Research* (1948 ed.), published by Oliver & Boyd, Ltd., Edinburgh and London, by permission of the authors and publishers.

TABLE 5 Distribution of x^2

Probability

df	.99	.98	.95	.90	.80	.70	.50	.30	.20	.10	.05	.02	.01	.001
1	.0³157	.0³628	.00393	.0158	.0642	.148	.455	1.074	1.642	2.706	3.841	5.412	6.635	10.827
2	.0201	.0404	.103	.211	.446	.713	1.386	2.408	3.219	4.605	5.991	7.824	9.210	13.815
3	.115	.185	.352	.584	1.005	1.424	2.366	3.665	4.642	6.251	7.815	9.837	11.341	16.268
4	.297	.429	.711	1.064	1.649	2.195	3.357	4.878	5.989	7.779	9.488	11.668	13.277	18.465
5	.554	.752	1.145	1.610	2.343	3.000	4.351	6.064	7.289	9.236	11.070	13.388	15.086	20.517
6	.872	1.134	1.635	2.204	3.070	3.828	5.348	7.231	8.558	10.645	12.592	15.033	16.812	22.457
7	1.239	1.564	2.167	2.833	3.822	4.671	6.346	8.383	9.803	12.017	14.067	16.622	18.475	24.322
8	1.646	2.032	2.733	3.490	4.594	5.527	7.344	9.524	11.030	13.362	15.507	18.168	20.090	26.125
9	2.088	2.532	3.325	4.168	5.380	6.393	8.343	10.656	12.242	14.684	16.919	19.679	21.666	27.877
10	2.558	3.059	3.940	4.865	6.179	7.267	9.342	11.781	13.442	15.987	18.307	21.161	23.209	29.588
11	3.053	3.609	4.575	5.578	6.989	8.148	10.341	12.899	14.631	17.275	19.675	22.618	24.725	31.264
12	3.571	4.178	5.226	6.304	7.807	9.034	11.340	14.011	15.812	18.549	21.026	24.054	26.217	32.909
13	4.107	4.765	5.892	7.042	8.634	9.926	12.340	15.119	16.985	19.812	22.362	25.472	27.688	34.528
14	4.660	5.368	6.571	7.790	9.467	10.821	13.339	16.222	18.151	21.064	23.685	26.873	29.141	36.123
15	5.229	5.985	7.261	8.547	10.307	11.721	14.339	17.322	19.311	22.307	24.996	28.259	30.578	37.697
16	5.812	6.614	7.962	9.312	11.152	12.624	15.338	18.418	20.465	23.542	26.296	29.633	32.000	39.252
17	6.408	7.255	8.672	10.085	12.002	13.531	16.338	19.511	21.615	24.769	27.587	30.995	33.409	40.790
18	7.015	7.906	9.390	10.865	12.857	14.440	17.338	20.601	22.760	25.989	28.869	32.346	34.805	42.312
19	7.633	8.567	10.117	11.651	13.716	15.352	18.338	21.689	23.900	27.204	30.144	33.687	36.191	43.820
20	8.260	9.237	10.851	12.443	14.578	16.266	19.337	22.775	25.038	28.412	31.410	35.020	37.566	45.315
21	8.897	9.915	11.591	13.240	15.445	17.182	20.337	23.858	26.171	29.615	32.671	36.343	38.932	46.797
22	9.542	10.600	12.338	14.041	16.314	18.101	21.337	24.939	27.301	30.813	33.924	37.659	40.289	48.268
23	10.196	11.293	13.091	14.848	17.187	19.021	22.337	26.018	28.429	32.007	35.172	38.968	41.638	49.728
24	10.856	11.992	13.848	15.659	18.062	19.943	23.337	27.096	29.553	33.196	36.415	40.270	42.980	51.179
25	11.524	12.697	14.611	16.473	18.940	20.867	24.337	28.172	30.675	34.382	37.652	41.566	44.314	52.620
26	12.198	13.409	15.379	17.292	19.820	21.792	25.336	29.246	31.795	35.563	38.885	42.856	45.642	54.052
27	12.879	14.125	16.151	18.114	20.703	22.719	26.336	30.319	32.912	36.741	40.113	44.140	46.963	55.476
28	13.565	14.847	16.928	18.939	21.588	23.647	27.336	31.391	34.027	37.916	41.337	45.419	48.278	56.893
29	14.256	15.574	17.708	19.768	22.475	24.577	28.336	32.461	35.139	39.087	42.557	46.693	49.588	58.302
30	14.953	16.306	18.493	20.599	23.364	25.508	29.336	33.530	36.250	40.256	43.773	47.962	50.892	59.703

For larger values of df, the expression $\sqrt{2x^2} - \sqrt{2df - 1}$ may be used as a normal deviate with unit variance, remembering that the probability for x^2 corresponds with that of a single tail of the normal curve. A slightly more complex transformation, which gives far better approximations for relatively small values of v, is

$$Z = [\sqrt[3]{x^2} - \sqrt[3]{v}(1 - 2/9v)]/\sqrt[3]{v}\sqrt{2/9v}$$

(See A. C. Acock and G. R. Stavig: "Normal Deviate Approximations of x^2," *Perceptual and Motor Skills,* vol. 42, p. 220, 1976.)

SOURCE: Table 5 is reprinted from Table IV of R. A. Fisher and F. Yates, *Statistical Tables for Biological, Agricultural and Medical Research* (1948 ed.), published by Oliver & Boyd Ltd., Edinburgh and London, by permission of the authors and publishers.

Glossary

Abstract A short summary of the method, data and primary findings reported in a book or journal article, together with full bibliographic identification of the source.

Anonymity Maintaining a condition among participants in research in which the identity of individuals is not known.

Behaviorist paradigm The patterning of theory definition and research questions on the assumption that social behavior and social relations result from conditioning stimuli that are either rewarding or nonrewarding outcomes for individuals.

Bibliographic reference A listing of author(s), title, date, and place of issue of a book or periodical, sufficiently complete that any reader could correctly identify it in a research library.

Closed-end question A question in which a series of response alternatives are provided; also a forced choice question.

Cluster sample Cluster units such as cities, neighborhoods, or census tracts are randomly selected for a sample. Cannot be truly random, since large parts of the population are excluded.

Coder reliability The degree to which different coders code the same data with similar results.

Coding The assignment of numbers or category names to data determined either arbitrarily or by research design.

Cohort analysis The study of population characteristics by a uniform series of temporal strata such as single years, five-year strata, or ten-year strata.

Colinearity Refers to correlations among explanatory or independent variables in multiple correlation analysis. So far as these variables are uncorrelated or weakly correlated among themselves, the multiple correlation coefficient is meaningful. If they are correlated, the multiple correlation coefficient very well may be spurious.

Computer publication search A library service to scan a large registry of subjects, titles, and authors by accessing a central computer library, usually for a service charge.

Concept An understanding or idea or mental image; it includes a way of viewing and categorizing objects, processes, relations, and events.

Confidence interval The cases of a population distribution, typically 95 percent included between the limits of tolerable error, typically 5 percent.

Conflict paradigm A patterning of theory, definition, and research questions on the assumption that competition and conflict over shares of scarce resources dominate all social relations.

Content analysis The systematic accounting of selected aspects of written records, including prose, for purposes of comparison and assessment.

Contingency data cleaning Elimination of inappropriately coded responses that depend on responses assigned to another variable.

Contingency question A question that depends on the response to a previous question.

Continuous data Data that can be indefinitely subdivided and normally arise from ratio scale of measurement. Examples include grade-point ratios and unemployment rates.

Control The researcher's ability to manipulate an independent variable to test for predicted effects on a dependent variable.

Control group The set of persons or social objects randomly taken from the same population as the experimental group to test for comparative effects of the experimental treatment.

Convenience sample The selection of cases that are already grouped by some other influence, such as being students in a classroom, and readily available to the researcher.

Correlation The ratio of the covariance of two measures paired, case by case, in a sample distribution to the pooled variances of the two measures taken separately. As this ratio approaches +1.00 or −1.00, predictability from one measure to the other becomes high, as measured by the squared correlation. As the correlation approaches zero, the two measures are unrelated.

Cross-sectional research A static study that uses a sample of cases responding to a research instrument at a single point in time.

Data A collection of measurements systematically collected in strict compliance with a research design.

Data reduction The ordering and simplifying of a mass of relevant research data to reveal patterns and relations and outcomes in relatively simple, concise statements. Examples include means, standard deviation, variance, and correlation.

Deduction A conclusion about specific cases based on the assumption that they share a characteristic with an entire class of similar cases. Example: This is murder!

Definition A precise, short statement that describes and delimits a social object or relation in exact terms suitable to a research operation.

Dependent variable The variable expected to show effect resulting from manipulation of the independent or causal variable.

Descriptive research Research undertaken to increase precision of definition of knowledge in an area where basic parameters are not known.

GLOSSARY

Discrete data Data counted by integers as whole units such as age in years and number of children in the family.

Disproportionate stratified sampling Sampling in which the researcher may oversample strata that are too small to yield sufficient numbers for statistical analysis, such as severely handicapped children in the ninth grade.

Empirical Grounded in experience and fact, as observed responses, behavior, and events.

Ethics in research The requirement that data be collected and treated experimentally with careful attention to accuracy of measurement, fidelity to logic, and respect for the feelings and rights of respondents.

Evaluation research Research conducted to test for the effects of purposeful social programs, often with government support.

Evidence Factual data and integrated reasoning that are persuasive and compelling to skeptical and well-informed judges.

Experiment A research situation in which a controlled treatment is differently applied to two or more groups of research objects to determine the difference of effects.

Experimental design A pattern or system for conducting a research project, including a plan for measurement, recording, analysis, and a decision about the outcome.

Experimental group The set of persons or social objects, randomly selected from a population, to which an experimental treatment is applied.

Experimental mortality Loss of subjects through normal attrition over time when experimental design requires retesting the same subjects. Compensated by enlarging the initial sample.

Exploratory research Research undertaken to establish basic conditions in an area of inquiry where very little is already known.

External (construct) validity Correct correspondence between the terms and findings of a research operation and the real world to which it is presumed to apply.

***F* test** A statistical test to evaluate the differences among three or more sample means: ratio of larger to smaller variance.

Face validity The apparent reasonableness of the measure as in the view of the observer.

Feasibility of a research question A consideration of accessibility of data and the probable cost in time, resources, and funds in terms of the potential value of the outcome. The dedicated researcher often accepts considerable risk of expanded cost and reduced payoff.

Field experiment Application of differential treatments to experimental and control groups in social settings that the researcher does not restrict or control.

Field study Most often, an exploratory study undertaken in a natural social setting that is not controlled and only minimally influenced by the presence of the researcher.

Formulation Act of putting a research question into a precise statement in words, generally into a form that can be tested statistically.

Functional paradigm A patterning of theory, definition, and research questions on the assumption that all components of a social situation are generated and sustained by a practical need for them. Whatever is there must serve some purpose.

Generalization A universal statement concerning an entire class of objects or events based on an observation of limited number of objects or events.

Government documents Official publications and records of major government agencies such as those issued by the U.S. Government Printing Office or Her Majesty's Stationer's Office in Great Britain.

Grounded theory Theory generated from empirical data and from extensive practical experience, as opposed to abstract speculation on convoluted semantic exercises and unfounded suppositions.

Guttman scale A scale developed from a series of questions ordered so as to reflect increasing acceptance or approval of an underlying social dimension.

Heterogeneity A condition of rather wide variation and differences in kind within a population aggregate.

Homogeneity A condition of relatively similar units predominant within a population, usually characterized by relatively small variance.

Hypothesis A statement of an unknown but expected outcome in a research operation based on a theory of the relation between variables and capable of rejection.

Hypothesis cycle Each hypothesis is a segment in a series of hypotheses that raise new and more precise questions about a research objective and that, when answered, afford the basis for a modified and more precise hypothesis.

Hypothesis test Looking at all evidence, both positive and negative, as a criterion for affirming or discomfirming the hypothesis. Either outcome is valuable for quality research.

Independent variable The variable that the researcher controls or varies to test for associated variation or change in another (dependent) variable.

Induction A conclusion about a class of objects or events based on observation of a small sample taken to represent the entire class.

Instrumentation Development and application of a device or system for measuring differences in social behavior and response.

Internal validity Agreement or consistency among terms, definitions, measurements, and findings within a research report.

Interval measurement Assignment of cases to categories by a known dimension along an ordered scale made up from equal intervals. Time in years, decades, or centuries is an example.

Intuition Learning by direct awareness without conscious reasoning or inquiry.

Judgmental sample Cases selected because they manifest a property of research interest for investigation of that property, such as recidivist and nonrecidivist offenders in a limited locale.

Laboratory experiment Application of differential treatments to experimental and control groups under controlled conditions designed to exclude extraneous effects.

Likert scale A set of ranked categories, usually an odd number totaling 3 to 11, permitting a graded series of alternative responses from negative to positive, to represent the strength of a position on a question.

Literature search A scanning of books and journals for basic and up-to-date information on a research area, directed at original sources, and sufficiently thorough to minimize the chance of missing a relevant source.

Logic The rules by which relations between classes of objects must be stated.

Longitudinal research A plan applying an instrument to samples of respondents repetitively at intervals over a span of time. It is used to detect dynamic processes such as opinion change through time.

Matching A system of selecting experimental subjects so as to eliminate relevant differences except the experimental treatment.

Matrix questions A group of related items densely packed and including response alternatives in a minimal space.

Mean The authentic balance point of a distribution of values obtained by dividing the total of all scores by the number of scores. The mean is changed by a change in one score.

Measurement The assignment of numerals to objects according to rule.

Median The value that divides the ordered number of values of a distribution exactly in half.

Methodology Processes, procedures, and principles used in approaching a research project. Method is influenced by the assumptions and interests of the researcher. Also, the study and description of research methods.

Micro Reduced in scale, as a small-scale computer, or a small-scale dimension of social action, as in moment-by-moment analysis of behavior or response.

Mode The most frequent value, usually occurring near the center of a distribution.

Model A research plan or design describing the system of data collection, the presumed relations among research variables, and the statistical test on which the decision will be based.

Modest interpretation An interpretation that recognizes the need to be very conservative in making claims from a single research operation, whatever the measured analytical outcomes.

Multiple regression A measure of the change in a dependent variable associated with the combined effect of two or more independent variables. (See *Regression*.)

Multistage samples   Samples drawn at a series of points in time to identify the dynamics of a social property over time.

Naturalness   A state in which social action is unaltered and unaffected by the intrusion of research instruments and research personnel.

Nominal measurement   Assignment of cases to one of a set of named categories that are mutually exclusive and logically exhaustive of the set.

Nonparticipant observation   Nonintrusive direct observation by the researcher so as not to influence the action as it would normally occur without the observer.

Nonprobability sample   A sample drawn from a population in which the chance of inclusion is not known.

Nonreactive measures   Assessments of the physical impact of social action in the environment, such as the effect of vandalism on school buildings.

Null hypothesis   An assertion that the difference between the statistics of two comparison samples is zero and that they may be from the same population. It may be rejected if the difference is large enough to assume a small error risk.

Open-ended question   A question that calls for any words by which the respondent chooses to answer.

Operational definition   The presumption that the research outcome is defined in the way it is measured, such as the assumption that tension is whatever the tension test measures.

Ordinal measure   Assignment of cases to one of a set of rank-ordered categories based on an underlying dimension such as preferment or importance.

Panel study   A type of trend study in which the same persons making up the interview "panel" are questioned at selected times after or before a major event to identify a rate of change in public opinion.

Paradigm   A pattern of beliefs, values, techniques, and theories shared by members of a scientific community as a fundamental image of subject matter within a science. Also, an illustrative or conventional pattern, model, or arrangement of physical or mental social objects.

Participant observation   Observation in which the researcher is involved in some recognized role as a part of the social process being investigated. Being a part of the action permits more accurate appraisal and analysis.

Phenomenon   (plural: phenomena): That which appears to the senses, including events and objects that are observed.

Posttest   A reexamination of subjects after a test has been applied to measure the effect of the test.

Pragmatic validity   The utility or practicality of a research conclusion in terms of research objectives.

Predictive validity   The tendency of a research finding to support successful prediction of similar outcomes using other samples of the same population.

Pretest Pretrial of a questionnaire or other research instrument on a group of respondents similar to those of the target population. It reveals ambiguous items and flaws.

Principle A general truth or law basic to other truths; that which determines the nature or essence of a thing.

Probability The proportion of successes to total trials in drawing cases in a chance process.

Probability sample A sample in which the probability of selection from the total population is known.

Procedural error Inconsistent procedures among interviewers, and analysis and erroneous entry of digital data in the recording and analysis. Errors from careless data gathering, coding, and recording invalidate research findings.

Public records Records originated and maintained by national, state, and local agencies and usually made available for research purposes.

Publication index A voluminous listing by author, subject, and title of all materials published for a given year in a large collection of periodicals or books, and usually devoted to a specific area, such as social science, engineering, or medicine.

Qualitative research Research that depends mainly on direct observation and descriptive analysis of social interaction and outcomes in specific social settings, sometimes relying on the intuitive skills of the researcher.

Quantitative research In social science, research that depends mainly on statistical measures to evaluate differences in variance and means in a variable presumed to have been measured. Scores are often rather arbitrarily developed from cumulative intensity of response scores to groups of items.

Quasi-experiment Analytical comparison of a group that has experienced an uncontrolled event, such as a flood, with an otherwise similar group that has not, in order to assess the differential effects of the event.

Questionnaire An organized listing of relevant questions to elicit responses to one or more research variables in a social science survey.

Quota sample A nonprobability sample with a controlled number of cases drawn by research category.

Random assignment Selection of individual subjects for experimental or control treatment based on an equiprobable chance event, such as flipping a coin.

Random error Error in statistical measures which arises solely from the variability due to random selection of cases.

Random sample A drawing of sample cases in which each unit and each combination of units has the same probability of being included.

Range The range of a distribution is measured by the difference between the highest and lowest values of a distribution and indicates the scope of breadth of the distribution.

Ratio measurement Application of a scale made of ordered equal intervals originating from a mathematical zero. Financial assets are scaled positively and negatively from a mathematical zero.

Regression A measure of the change in the dependent variable of two associated measures relative to a given change in the independent variable. It is determined by the ratio of the covariance of both measures to the variance of the independent variable.

Regression effect The tendency for those scoring at the extremes to shift toward the middle or average position on a second test.

Reliability The actual or presumed characteristic of data sets drawn from the same population to manifest the same measurement properties in repeated drawings.

Replication Repetition of a previous research operation in all essentials to determine the consistency of results when using other samples from the same population as the original study.

Representativeness The appearance of nearly the same statistical properties in the sample as in the population from which it is drawn.

Research A systematic process of collecting data to represent classes of objects, together with a plan to measure properties relevant to a hypothesis.

Research design The plan of procedures to collect data and to analyze them with reference to the research hypothesis.

Research hypothesis A statement that predicts a relation between two or more variables in such form that it may be put to test in a research operation.

Research setting The social environment in which data collection is carried out.

Rhetoric Verbal communication including statements and value judgments intended to persuade recipients to an opinion or action.

Rival hypothesis A hypothesis that is a plausible alternative to the researcher's main hypothesis and that might explain the research result as well or better.

Sample A relatively small set of a few hundred cases drawn randomly from a large population so as to represent the large population in measurable characteristics and properties.

Sample distribution The ordered sequence of measures of a statistical sample ranging from least to greatest, generally with high frequencies in the middle of the range, and very low to vanishing frequencies at the extreme values.

Sample size The number of cases included in a statistical sample taken to represent a population.

Sampling error Variation in the measured statistical properties of samples drawn from the same population that results from chance variation of individuals.

Sampling theory A mathematical approach to the form of the distribution of measures for various kinds of populations. The normal curve formula is an application of sampling theory and is called a sampling distribution.

Scale A standard of measurement providing a basis for common treatment of measured properties of social elements.

Scholarly journal A periodic publication by a scientific society or institution devoted to the highest standards of objectivity, evidence, and reasoning in a research field.

Semantic differential scale Use of a series of opposed adjectives and adverbs with seven to eleven scale points between each set of extremes, such as "good-bad." An accumulation of such scale-point values permits assignment of a positional measure.

Semi-interquartile range One-half of the difference between the 25th and 75th percentile scores.

Serendipitous findings Unexpected research outcomes that lead to new insights about a social relation, fact, or social object. Such findings may reveal a widespread misconception.

Standard deviation The square root of the mean of all squared differences between each case and the distribution mean. It measures dispersion.

Stratified sampling Random selection of cases made within strata of the population proportional to the size of these strata as part of the population. In this case, randomness is permitted only within strata.

Survey A research process, usually by questionnaire or interview schedule, applied to randomly selected sample groups to determine whether the sample groups could be from the same population.

Symbolic interactionist paradigm The patterning of theory, definition, and research questions on the assumption that social relations and social events arise from individuals' use and application of symbols in interpreting and sustaining the social environment.

Systematic error A form of bias in measurement that usually distorts data and findings in one direction.

Systematic sample Selection of every nth unit, starting from a randomly selected source unit from a listing of the whole population.

t test A statistical test to evaluate the difference between two sample means measured by the pooled estimates of population variance calculated from the two sample variances.

Tabulation The art of organizing and condensing data and findings into tables.

Test–retest reliability A measure of agreement between the results of a test when it is administered a first and a second time to the same respondents.

Theory A reasoned set of propositions, derived from and supported by established evidence, which serves to explain a group of phenomena. It is at first conjectural and may or may not be supported by research data. If not supported, the theory may be discredited.

Theory–research design relation Theory guides the answer to the research question; research design guides the test to this answer.

Thurstone scale A scale of equal-appearing intervals based on average rankings placed by a large group of judges on a stated social dimension.

Treatment A controlled condition applied to an experimental group that is withheld or much reduced with a control group.

Triangulation The practice of developing more than two measures of the same phenomenon to serve as a check on accuracy in the measurement.

Unit of analysis A concrete research case relevant to the research question.

Validity The actual or presumed characteristic of a research outcome to be true and factual with regard to the class of objects treated.

Value-free research Scientific inquiry on a problem open to doubt in which the researcher freely follows the implications of the data and the hypothesis. Researchers who falsify data or the reasoning process to favor a hypothesis are invalidating the research operation.

Variable A measure of a social property or condition that varies from case to case in a sample set of cases.

Variance The mean of the squared deviations including every case in the sample distribution from the sample mean. The concept of variance also applies to the population distribution but generally is not attainable.

z score A deviation of a score from the sample mean, measured in units of the sample standard deviation.

References

Acker, S. R., and Tremens, R. K. Children's perceptions of changes in size of televised images. *Human Communication Research*, 1981, 7, 340–346.

Allen, D., and Guy, R. F. Ocular breaks and verbal output. *Sociometry*, 1977, 40, 90–96.

Aronson, E., and Carlsmith, J. M. Experimentation in social psychology. In G. Lindzey and E. Aronson (eds.), *The Handbook of Social Psychology*. Reading, Mass.: Addison-Wesley, 1968.

———, and Mills, J. The effect of severity of initiation on liking for a group. *Journal of Abnormal and Social Psychology*, 1959, 59, 177–181.

Asch, S. E. *Social Psychology*. Englewood Cliffs, N.J.: Prentice-Hall, 1952.

———. Effects of group pressure upon the modification and distortion of judgment. In T. M. Newcomb and E. L. Hartley (eds.), *Readings in Social Psychology*. New York: Holt, Rinehart and Winston, 1958.

Babbie, E. *The Practice of Social Research*. Belmont, Calif.: Wadsworth Publishing Co., 1975.

Bachrach, A. J. *Psychological Research: An Introduction*. New York: Random House, 1962.

Bailey, K. *Methods of Social Research*. New York: Free Press, 1978.

Becker, H. S. *Outsiders: Studies in the Sociology of Deviance*. New York: Free Press, 1963.

Berelson, B. *Content Analysis in Communication Research*. New York: Hafner, 1982.

Bierce, A. *The Devil's Dictionary*. Cleveland and New York: World Publishing Co., 1942.

Bierstedt, R. *The Social Order*. New York: McGraw-Hill, 1970.

Blalock, H. M. *Social Statistics*. New York: McGraw-Hill, 1973.

———. *Social Statistics*. New York: McGraw-Hill, 1981.

———, and Blalock, A. *Methodology in Social Research*. New York: McGraw-Hill, 1968.

Blumer, H. *Symbolic Interactionism: Perspective and Method*. Englewood Cliffs, N.J.: Prentice-Hall, 1969.

Bogdan, R., and Taylor, S. J. *Introduction to Qualitative Research Methods: A Phenomenological Approach to the Social Sciences*. San Francisco: Jossey-Bass, 1975.

Bogue, D. Against adjustment. *Society*, 1981, 18, 18.

Bridges, W. P. Industry, marginality, and female employment: a new appraisal. *American Sociological Review*, 1980, 45, 58–75.

Bridgman, P. W. Operational analysis. *Philosophy of Science*, 1938, 19, 114–131.

Burke, Kenneth. *A Grammar of Motives and A Rhetoric of Motives*. New York: World Publishing Co., 1962.

REFERENCES

Campbell, D. T., and Stanley, J. *Experimental and Quasi-Experimental Designs for Research*. Chicago: Rand McNally, 1963.

Cangelosi, V., Phillip, T., and Phillippe, R. *Basic Statistics*. New York: West Publishing Co., 1979.

Cicourel, A. V. *Method and Measurement in Sociology*. Glencoe, Ill.: Free Press, 1964.

Coale, A. J., and Stephan, F. F. The case of the Indians and the teen-age widows. *Journal of the American Statistical Association*, 1962, 57, 338–347.

Coleman, J. S. *Introduction to Mathematical Sociology*. New York: Holt, Rinehart and Winston, 1964.

———. *The Adolescent Society: The Social Life of the Teen-ager and Its Impact on Education*. New York: Free Press, 1961.

Cook, T. D., and Campbell, D. T. *Quasi-Experimentation Design and Analysis Issues For Field Settings*. Chicago: Rand McNally, 1979.

Darley, J. M., and Batson, C. D. From Jerusalem to Jericho: a study of situational and dispositional variables in helping behavior. *Journal of Personality and Social Psychology*, 1973, 27, 100–108.

Davies, M., and Kandel, D. B. Parental and peer influence on adolescents' educational plans: some further evidence. *American Journal of Sociology*, 1981, 87, 363–387.

Davis, K. Extreme social isolation of a child. *American Journal of Sociology*, 1940, 45, 554–565.

———. Final note on a case of extreme isolation. *American Journal of Sociology*, 1947, 52, 232–247.

Dean, D. Alienation: its meaning and measurement. *American Sociological Review*, 1961, 25, 753–758.

Denzin, N. K. *Sociological Methods: A Sourcebook*. Chicago: Aldine, 1970.

———. Symbolic interactionism and ethnomethodology. In J. Douglas (ed.), *Understanding Everyday Life*. Chicago: Aldine, 1970.

———. *The Research Act*. Chicago: Aldine, 1970.

Desmonde, W. The position of George Herbert Mead. In Stone and Farberman (eds.), *Social Psychology through Symbolic Interaction*. Boston: Ginn & Co., 1970.

Deutsch, M., and Krauss, R. *Theories in Social Psychology*. New York: Basic Books, 1965.

Dewey, J. *Human Nature and Conduct*. New York: Holt, Rinehart and Winston, 1922.

Doby, J. T. *An Introduction to Social Research*. New York: Appleton-Century-Crofts, 1967.

Duncan, O. D. *Measuring Social Change via Replication Surveys*. New York: Sage, 1975.

Durkheim, E. *Suicide*. Trans. J. A. Spaulding and G. Simpson. Ed. G. Simpson. New York: Free Press, 1964.

Eisenberg, J. M., Kitz, D. S., and Webber, R. A. Development of attitudes about sharing decision-making: a comparison of medical and surgical students. *Journal of Health and Social Behavior*, 1983, 24, 85–90.

Ellsworth, P. From abstract ideas to concrete instances: some guidelines for using natural research settings. *American Psychologist*, 1977, 32, 604–615.

Erikson, K. A comment on disguised observation in sociology. *Social Problems*, 1967, *14*, 366–373.

Evans, B. *The Natural History of Nonsense.* New York: Anchor Paperbacks, 1958.

Farnworth, M., and Horan, P. M. Separate justice—an analysis of race differences in court processes. *Social Science Research*, 1980, *9*, 381–399.

Festinger, L., and Carlsmith, J. M. Cognitive consequences of forced compliance. *Journal of Abnormal and Social Psychology*, 1959, *58*, 203–210.

Festinger, L., Reicken, H. W., and Schachter, S. *When Prophecy Fails.* Minneapolis: University of Minnesota Press, 1956.

Friedrichs, R. W. *A Sociology of Sociology.* New York: Free Press, 1970.

Gans, H. The positive functions of poverty. *American Journal of Sociology*, 1972, *78*, 278–283.

———. The uses of poverty: The poor pay all. Social Policy, July-August, 1971, 20–24.

Garfinkel, H. *Studies in Ethnomethodology.* Englewood Cliffs, N.J.: Prentice-Hall, 1967.

Gergen, K. J., Gergen, M. M., and Barton, W. H. Deviance in the dark. *Psychology Today*, 1973, *75*, 129–130.

Gibbs, J. P. Conceptions of deviance—the old and the new. *Pacific Sociological Review*, 1966, *9*, 9–14.

———. *Sociological Theory Construction.* New York: Garden Press, 1972.

Gilbert, G. M. Stereotype persistence and change among college students. *Journal of Abnormal and Social Psychology*, 1951, *46*, 245–254.

Gilbert, S. J. A study of the effects of self-disclosure on interpersonal attraction. Unpublished doctoral dissertation, University of Kansas, 1972.

———, and Horenstein, D. The communication of self-disclosure: level versus valence. *Human Communication Research*, 1975, *1*, 316–322.

Glaser, B., and Strauss, A. *The Discovery of Grounded Theory.* Chicago: Aldine, 1967.

Goffman, E. *Forms of Talk.* Philadelphia: University of Pennsylvania Press, 1981.

———. *Presentation of Self in Everyday Life.* New York: Doubleday, 1959.

Gold, R. L. Roles in sociological field observations. In G. J. McCall and J. L. Simmons, (eds.), *Issues in Participant Observation.* Reading, Mass.: Addison-Wesley, 1969.

Goldberg, P. A. A personal journal. In M. Patricia Golden (ed.), *The Research Act.* Itasca, Ill.: F. E. Peacock Publishers, 1976.

———. Misogyny and the college girl. Paper presented at the Eastern Psychological Association, Boston, 1967.

Golden, M. P. *The Research Experience.* Itasca, Ill.: F. E. Peacock Publishers, 1976.

Gross, L. *Sociological Theory: Inquiries and Paradigms.* New York: Harper and Row, 1967.

Guttman, L. The basis for scalogram analysis. In S. A. Stouffer (ed.), *Measurement and Prediction.* Princeton, N.J.: Princeton University Press, 1950.

Guy, R. F., and Allen, D. E. The effects of social class on tolerance of defeat. *Social Forces*, 1975, *54*, 160–165.

Guy, R. F., and Norvell, M. J. The neutral point on a Likert scale. *Journal of Psychology*, 1977, *95*, 199–204.

Hage, J. *Techniques and Problems of Theory Construction in Sociology.* New York: John Wiley, 1972.

Hammond, P. *Sociologists at Work.* New York: Basic Books, 1968.

Hayakawa, S. I. *Language in Action.* New York: Harcourt Brace Jovanovich, 1940.

Heilman, S. C. Jewish sociologist: native-as-stranger. *American Sociologist,* 1980, *15,* 100–108.

Henley, N. M. *Body Politics.* Englewood Cliffs, N.J.: Prentice-Hall, 1977.

Hirschi, T., and Selvin, H. C. *Delinquency Research: An Appraisal of Analytical Methods.* New York: Free Press, 1967.

———. False criteria of causality in delinquency research. In N. K. Denzin (ed.), *Sociological Methods: A Sourcebook.* Chicago: Aldine, 1970.

Hoffman, L. R., and Maier, N. R. Valence in the adoption of solutions by problem-solving groups: concept, method, and results. *Journal of Abnormal and Social Psychology,* 1964, *69,* 264–271.

Homans, G. C. *The English Villagers of the Thirteenth Century.* Cambridge: Harvard University Press, 1941.

———. *The Human Group.* New York: Harcourt Brace Jovanovich, 1950.

———. *Social Behavior: Its Elementary Forms.* New York: Harcourt Brace Jovanovich, 1961.

———. *The Nature of Social Science.* New York: Harcourt World Jovanovich, 1967.

Hoover, K. *The Elements of Social Science Thinking.* New York: St. Martin's Press, 1976.

Horowitz, I., and Rainwater, L. On journalistic moralizers. *Trans-Action,* 1970, 7.

Humphreys, L. Methods: the sociologist as voyeur. In M. P. Golden (ed.), *The Research Act.* Itasca, Ill.: F. E. Peacock Publishers, 1976.

———. *Tearoom Trade: Impersonal Sex in Public Places.* Chicago: Aldine, 1970.

Illich, I. *Medical Nemesis.* New York: Pantheon Books, 1974.

Inbar, M. *The Vulnerable Age Phenomenon.* New York: Russell Sage Foundation, 1976.

———, and Alder, C. The vulnerable age phenomenon: a serendipitous finding. *Sociology of Education,* 1976, *49,* 193–200.

Irwin, J. *Scenes.* Beverly Hills, Calif.: Sage Publications, 1977.

Jung, J. Snoopology. *Human Behavior,* October, 1975, 6–8.

Kalish, R. A. Some variables in death attitudes. *Journal of Social Psychology,* 1963, *59,* 137–145.

Kaplan, A. *Conduct of Inquiry.* San Francisco: Chandler, 1964.

Karlins, N., Coffman, T. L., and Walters, G. On the fading of social stereotypes. *Journal of Personality and Social Psychology,* 1969, *13,* 2–32.

Katz, D., and Braly, K. W. Racial stereotypes of 100 college students. *Journal of Abnormal and Social Psychology,* 1933, *28,* 175–193.

Kerlinger, F. N. *Foundations of Behavioral Research.* New York: Holt, Rinehart and Winston, 1979.

Kidder, L. H. *Sellitz, Wrightsman, and Cook's Research Methods in Social Relations.* New York: Holt, Rinehart and Winston, 1981.

Killeffer, D. H. *How Did You Think of That? An Introduction to the Scientific Method.* Garden City, N.Y.: Anchor Books, 1976.

Kinloch, G. C. *Sociological Theory: Its Development and Major Paradigms.* New York: McGraw-Hill, 1977.

Kinsey, A. C. *Sexual Behavior in the Human Female.* Philadelphia: Saunders, 1963.
Kiser, K. Male-female relationships in a changing society. Unpublished manuscript, Oklahoma State University, 1984.
Kish, L. *Survey Sampling.* New York: John Wiley, 1965.
Kuhn, T. S. *The Structure of Scientific Revolutions.* Chicago: University of Chicago Press, 1962.
Kutner, N. Use of an updated adjective check-list in research on ethnic stereotypes. *Social Science Quarterly,* 1973, 54, 639–647.
Lachenmeyer, C. *Essence of Social Research.* New York: Free Press, 1973.
Lakoff, R. *Language and Woman's Place.* New York: Harper and Row, 1975.
Lamb, T. Nonverbal and paraverbal control in dyads and triads: sex or power. *Social Psychology Quarterly,* 1981, 44, 49–53.
Land, K. C., and Spilerman, S. *Social Indicator Models: An Overview.* New York: Sage, 1975.
LeMasters, R. E. L. *Blue-Collar Aristocrats.* Madison: University of Wisconsin Press, 1975.
Lewis, G. H. *Fist Fights in the Kitchen.* Pacific Palisades, Calif.: Goodyear Publishing Co., 1975.
Liek, R. K. *Methods, Logic, and Research in Sociology.* Indianapolis: Bobbs-Merrill Company, 1972.
Likert, R. A technique for the measurement of attitudes. *Archives of Psychology,* 1932, No. 14.
Lindesmith, A., Strauss, A., and Denzin, N. *Social Psychology.* New York: Holt, Rinehart and Winston, 1975.
Lofland, J. *Analyzing Social Settings: A Guide to Qualitative Observation and Analysis.* Belmont, Calif.: Wadsworth, 1971.
———, and Lofland, L. *Analyzing Social Settings.* Belmont, Calif.: Wadsworth, 1984.
Lombroso, C. *Crime, Its Causes and Remedies.* Boston: Little, Brown, 1912.
McCall, G. J., and Simmons, J. L. *Identities and Interactions.* New York: Free Press, 1966.
McNall, S. G. *The Sociological Experience.* Boston: Little, Brown, 1969.
Madron, T. W. *Small Groups Methods.* Evanston, Ill.: Northwestern University Press, 1969.
Manheim, H. L. *Sociological Research.* Georgetown, Ont.: The Dorsey Press, 1977.
Martan, M. Comparative study of the communities of Yad Rambam in Israel. Paper presented at the World Congress of North African Jews: Jerusalem, 1972.
Maslow, A. *The Psychology of Science.* New York: Harper and Row, 1966.
Masterman, M. The nature of a paradigm. In I. Lakatos and A. Musgrave (eds.), *Criticism and the Growth of Knowledge.* Cambridge, Mass.: Harvard University Press, 1970.
Maxwell, M. A. A Quantity-Frequency Analysis of Drinking Behavior in the State of Washington. *Northwest Science,* 1958, 32, 57–67.
Matza, D. *Becoming Deviant.* Englewood Cliffs, N.J.: Prentice-Hall, 1969.
Mead, G. H. *Mind, Self, and Society from the Standpoint of a Social Behaviorist.* Chicago: University of Chicago Press, 1934.
Merton, R. K. *Social Theory and Social Structure.* New York: Free Press, 1949.
———. Patterns of Influence: A Study of Interpersonal Influence and of Commu-

nication in a Local Community. In P. F. Lazarsfeld and F. N. Stanton (eds.) *Communications Research 1948–1949*, New York: Harper and Row, 1949.

———. *Social Theory and Social Structure*. Glencoe, Ill.: Free Press, 1957.

Milgram, S. *Obedience to Authority*. New York: Harper and Row, 1974.

Miller, D. *Handbook of Research Design and Social Measurement*. New York: David McKay, 1975.

Mills, C. W. *Character and Social Structure: The Psychology of Social Institutions*. New York: Harcourt Brace Jovanovich, 1953.

Mitroff, I. Norms and counter-norms in a select group of the Apollo moon scientists: a case study of the ambivalence of scientists. *American Sociological Review*, 1974, 39, 579–595.

Myrdal, G. *An American Dilemma*. New York: Harper and Row, 1958.

Nachmias, D., and Nachmias, C. *Research Methods in the Social Sciences*. New York: St. Martin's Press, 1976.

Neyman, J., and Pearson, E. S. *Joint Statistical Papers*. Berkeley: University of California Press, 1967.

Norvell, M. J., and Guy, R. F. A comparison of self-concept in adopted and non-adopted adolescents. *Adolescence*, 1977, 12, 443–448.

Nunnally, J. C., and Wilson, W. H. *Method and Theory for Developing Measures in Evaluation Research*. Beverly Hills, Calif.: Sage Publications, 1975.

Orenstein, A., and Phillips, W. R. *Understanding Social Research: An Introduction*. Boston: Allyn and Bacon, 1978.

Phillips, B. *Social Research Methods: An Introduction*. Homewood, Ill.: Dorsey Press, 1985.

Phillips, D. *Abandoning Method*. San Francisco: Jossey-Bass, 1973.

———. *Knowledge from What?* Chicago: Rand McNally, 1971.

Pomeroy, W. B. *Dr. Kinsey and the Institute for Sexual Research*. New York: Harper and Row, 1972.

Ravetz, J. *Scientific Knowledge and Its Social Problems*. New York: Oxford University Press, 1971.

Riley, M. *Sociological Research*. New York: Harcourt Brace Jovanovich, 1963.

Rist, R. *The Pornography Controversy*. New Brunswick, N.J.: Transaction Books, 1975.

Ritzer, G. *Sociology: A Multiple Paradigm Science*. Boston: Allyn and Bacon, 1975.

Robinson, J. P., and Shaver, P. R. *Measures of Social Psychological Attitudes*. Ann Arbor, Mich.: Survey Research Center—Institute for Social Research, 1973.

Roebuck, J. *Rednecks*. New York: Praeger, 1983.

Roethlisberger, F. J., and Dickson, W. J. *Management and the Worker*. New York: John Wiley, 1964.

Rogoff, N. *Recent Trends in Occupational Mobility*. Glencoe, Ill.: Free Press, 1953.

Rotter, G. Attitudinal points of agreement and disagreement. *Journal of Social Psychology*, 1972, 86, 211–218.

Rubin, H. J. *Applied Social Research*. Columbus, Ohio: Charles E. Merrill, 1983.

Rubin, L. B. *Worlds of Pain: Life in the Working-Class Family*. New York: Basic Books, 1976.

Sandhu, H., and Allen, D. E. A comparative study of delinquents and nondelinquents: family affect, religion, and personal income. *Social Forces*, 1976, 46, 263–269.

Schatzman, L., and Strauss, A. L. *Field Research: Strategies for a Natural Sociology*. Englewood Cliffs, N.J.: Prentice-Hall, 1973.

Schellenberg, J. A. *Masters of Social Psychology: Freud, Mead, Lewin, and Skinner.* New York: Oxford University Press, 1978.

Selltiz, C., Wrightsman, L. S., and Cook, S. *Research Methods in Social Relations.* New York: Holt, Rinehart and Winston, 1976.

Senn, P. *Social Science and Its Methods.* Boston: Holbrook Press, 1971.

Shafer, R., and Keith, P. Equity and depression among married couples. *Social Psychology,* 1980, *43,* 430–435.

Sherif, M. *The Psychology of Social Norms.* New York: Harper and Row, 1948.

Simon, J. L. *Basic Research Methods in Social Sciences.* New York: Random House, 1978.

Sjoberg, G., and Nett, R. *A Methodology for Social Research.* New York: Harper and Row, 1968.

Smith, H. W. *Strategies of Social Research: The Methodological Imagination.* Englewood Cliffs, N.J.: Prentice-Hall, 1981.

Smith, J. P., and Ward, M. P. Asset accumulation and family demography. *Demography,* 1980, *17,* 243–260.

Snider, J. G., and Osgood, C. E. *Semantic Differential Technique: A Source Book.* Chicago: Aldine, 1969.

Spiegelman, M. *Introduction to Demography.* Cambridge: Harvard University Press, 1968.

Stephens, W. N. *Hypotheses and Evidence.* New York: Thomas Y. Crowell, 1968.

Stevens, S. S. On the theory of scales of measurement. *Science,* 1946, *684,* 677–680.

Stinchcombe, A. L. *Constructing Social Theory.* New York: Harcourt Brace Jovanovich, 1968.

———, and Wendt, J. Theoretical domains and measurement in social indicator analysis. In K. Land and S. Spilerman (eds.), *Social Indicator Models.* New York: Sage, 1975.

Stouffer, S. Sociology and sampling. In L. L. Bernard (ed.), *The Fields and Methods of Sociology.* New York: Long and Smith, 1934.

Survey Research Center. *General Social Science Survey Codebook.* Ann Arbor: Institute for Social Research—University of Michigan, 1973.

Thiabaut, J. W., and Kelley, H. H. *The Social Psychology of Groups.* New York: John Wiley, 1959.

Thomas, W. I. The relation of research to the social process. In W. I. Thomas (ed.), *Essays on Research in the Social Sciences.* Washington, D.C.: Brookings Institute, 1931.

———, and Znaniecki, F. *The Polish Peasant in Europe and America.* Chicago: University of Chicago Press, 1918.

Thorne, B. Political activists as participant observers: conflicts of commitment in a study of the draft resistance movement of the 1960's. *Symbolic Interactionist,* 1979, *2,* 73–88.

Thurstone, L. L. Attitudes can be measured. *American Journal of Sociology,* 1929, *33,* 529–554.

———. *The Measurement of Values.* Chicago: University of Chicago, 1959.

———. *The Measurement of Attitude.* Chicago: University of Chicago Press, 1929.

Torgerson, W. S. *The Theory and Methods of Scaling.* New York: John Wiley, 1958.

Veevers, J. E. Drinking attitude and drinking behavior: an exploratory study. *Journal of Social Psychology,* 1971, *85,* 103–109.

Von Hoffman, N. Sociological snoopers. *Washington Post,* January 30, 1970.

Walizer, M., and Weiner, P. *Research Methods and Analysis: Searching for Relationships.* New York: Harper and Row, 1978.

Wallin, P. A Guttman scale for measuring women's neighborliness. *American Journal of Sociology,* 1953, 59, 243-246.

Wallis, W. A., and Roberts, H. V. *The Nature of Statistics.* New York: Free Press, 1962.

Warner, W. L., and Lunt, P. S. *The Social Life of a Modern Community.* New Haven, Conn.: Yale University Press, 1941.

Warwick, D. Social scientists ought to stop lying. *Psychiatry Today,* February 1975, 249-260.

———, and Oshersen, S. *Comparative Research Methods.* Englewood Cliffs, N.J.: Prentice-Hall, 1973.

Watson, J. D. *The Double Helix: A Personal Account of the Discovery of the Structure of DNA.* New York: Atheneum, 1968.

Webb, E., Campbell, D., Schwartz, R., Sechrest, L., and Grove, J. *Non-Reactive Measures in the Social Sciences.* Boston: Houghton Mifflin, 1981.

Weber, M. *The Protestant Ethic and the Spirit of Capitalism.* New York: Scribner's, 1958.

Weisberg, H., and Bowen, B. *An Introduction to Survey Research and Data Analysis.* San Francisco: W. H. Freeman, 1977.

Willer, D. *Scientific Sociology: Theory and Method.* Englewood Cliffs, N.J.: Prentice-Hall, 1967.

Williams, C. T., and Wolfe, G. K. *Elements of Research: A Guide for Writers.* Sherman Oaks, Calif.: Alfred Publishing Co., 1979.

Williamson, J. B., Karp, D. A., and Dalphin, J. R. *The Research Craft: An Introduction to Research Methods.* Boston: Little, Brown, 1977.

Wilson, J. Q. Violence, pornography, and social science. *Journal of the Public Interest,* 1975, 22, 45-61.

Women on Words and Images. *Dick and Jane as Victims: Sex Stereotyping in Children's Readers.* Princeton, N.J., 1972.

Yankelovitch, D. *New Rules.* New York: Random House, 1981.

Zetterberg, H. *On Theory and Verification in Sociology.* Totowa, N.J.: Bedminster Press, 1965.

Ziller, R., Hagey, J., Smith, M., and Long, B. Self-esteem: a self-social construct. *Journal of Consulting and Clinical Psychology,* 1969, 33, 84-95.

Zito, G. *Methodologies and Meaning.* New York: Praeger, 1975.

Index

Abstract(s), 42–45
　figure, 46–48
　writing, 388–389
Abstraction, 15–16
Act, in symbolic interactionist paradigm, 86
Adequacy of the fit
　multiple regression, 355–360
　simple regression, 348–352
Alphabet-number system of identifying references, 401
Appendix, in research report, 404
Appreciation, 257–258
Associationism, 81
Authority, as a source of knowledge, 8
Autocorrelation, 358

Babbie, E., 30–31
Bar graph, 313
Behaviorist paradigm, 80–81
Blumer, Herbert, 82, 85–88
Bogdan, R., 256
Books, in search of literature, 40–42
Bridgeman, Percy, 21
Burke, Kenneth, 270

Campbell, D. T., 213
Causality, criteria for, 206–207
Central tendency, measures of, 320–322
Chart, pie, 314
Citation indexing, 45
Classical theory, hypotheses constructed from, 117–118
Closed-ended questions, 230
Cluster samples, 188
Codebook
　developing, 292–294

for short questionnaire, *figure*, 298
Coding data, 291–295
Coefficient of reproducibility, 156
Cognitive dissonance theory, 51–52
Cohort analysis, 228
Colinear data, 358–360
Common sense, as source of knowledge, 5–7
Comparative rating scales, 147
Computer(s)
　card, 295–298
　formatting data for input, 295–298
　introduction to, 289–291
　preparing data for input, 291–295
　role in data reduction, 287–288
　search, for literature, 49–50
Concurrent validity, 168–169
Confidence interval estimates, 192–194
Conflict paradigm, 79–80
Consequences of research, 375–378
Construct validity, 23, 169
Content validity, 168
Contingency cleaning, of data, 303–304
Continuous data, 310
Continuous frequency distributions, 316–319
　graphing, 318–319
Contrast error, 148
Control in evaluation research, 212–213
Convenience samples, 189
Correction, 257–258
Correlation, 345–364

auto-, 358
coefficient
　multiple regression, 356
　simple regression, 349–350
　squared, 350
multiple
　analysis, 352–364
　composite example, 360–364
simple, 345–356
　composite example, 350–352
Cronbach's alpha, 170–171
Cross-sectional studies, 98, 226

Darwin, Charles, 82, 83
Data
　analyzing
　　descriptive statistics, 307–329
　　inferential statistics, 331–364
　codebook, developing, 292–294
　coding, 291–295
　colinear, 358–360
　collection, and research design, 112–113
　continuous, 310
　descriptive summary measures, 319–329
　discrete, 310
　　grouping, 314–316
　editing for errors, 302–304
　formatting for computer input, 295–298
　interpretation
　　and consequences of, 367–381
　　ethical nature of, 371–375
　　inductive and deductive, 378–380
　　logic of, 378–379

465

Data (cont.)
  modest versus immodest, 370–371
  role of theory in, 368–370
keypunching, 299–302
meaning of, 284–285
missing, handling, 312
preparing for computer input, 291–295
qualitative, analysis of, 278–280
reduction
  computer in, 287–289
  and organization, 283–305
sources, effect of, on evidence, 128–129
storing, 304–305
Datum, meaning of, 284–285 (see also Data)
de Moivré, Abraham, 333
Deception of experiment subjects, 26–28
Deduction, 14–15, 71–72
Deductive interpretations of data, 378–380
Deductive theory construction, 73–75
Definitions, 70
Denzin, Norman, 269
Description, as a research purpose, 102–103
Descriptive statistics, 307–329
Design
  choosing, 91–113
    factors to consider in, 95–106
  and data collection, 112–113
  defined, 92–93
  effect of, on evidence, 129–130
  experiment, 106–108
    flowchart of decision-making process, *figure*, 107
  field study, 108–111
    flowchart of decision-making process, *figure*, 110
    general considerations, 111–112
  importance of, 94–95
  judging adequacy of, 104–106
  relation of theory to, 93–94
  survey, 108
    flowchart of decision-making process, *figure*, 109

Direct keyboard entry, 301–302
Discrete data, 310
  grouping, 314–316
Discrete frequency distributions, 311–316
  graphing, 313–314
Discriminant validity, 169
Discussion section of research report, 397–400
Distribution of F, *table*, 442–444
Distribution of t, *table*, 441
Distribution of x^2, *table*, 445
Doby, J. T., 106
Double Helix, The, 19–20
Durbin-Watson statistic d, 358

Edge coding, 300
Ellsworth, P., 99
Erikson, K., 32, 282
Ethics
  in data interpretation, 371–375
  in field research, 282
  of research questions, 61
  of social research, 25–32
Ethnomethodological paradigm, 88–90
Evaluation research, control in, 212–213
Evans, Bergen, 6
Evidence
  effect of data sources on, 128–129
  effect of research design on, 129–130
  hypotheses and, 115–134
  in hypotheses testing, 127–131
Exchange theory, 81
Experiment(s), 199–218
  ex-post-facto, 217–218
  field (*see* Field, experiment)
  laboratory versus field, 209–210
  quasi-, 217–218
  research design, 106–108
    flowchart of decision-making process, *figure*, 107
  true, versus quasi-experiment, 217
Experimental and Quasi-Experimental Designs for Research, 213
Experimental design, 207–209

Experimental mortality, 215–216
Explanation, as a research purpose, 101–102
Exploration, as a research purpose, 103–104
Ex-post-facto experiments, 217–218
External validity, 23, 216–217

F, distribution of, *table*, 442–444
F test, 342–345
Face validity, 168
Field
  concept of, 255–256
  experiment, 210–213
    control in, 211–212
    laboratory versus, 209–210
  research, 253–282
    ethical issues in, 282
    major research strategies in, 259–273
    nature of, 254–259
    paradigms consistent with, 258–259
    recording and analyzing, 274–282
    sample strategies in, 267–269
    starting, 263–267
  study
    research design, 108–111
    research design, flowchart of decision-making process, *figure*, 110
Files, 277–278
Flowchart of decision-making process
  for experimental design, *figure*, 107
  for field study design, *figure*, 110
  for survey design, *figure*, 109
Frequency distribution
  continuous, 316–319
  discrete, 311–316
    graphing, 313–314
Functionalist paradigm, 75–79

Garfinkel, Harold, 88–90
Generosity error, 148
Glaser, B., 73
Gold, R. L., 261
Government documents, 49

INDEX

Government-financed studies, 212–213
Graph, bar, 313
Graphic rating scales, 145
 figure, 146
Graphing
 continuous distribution, 318–319
 discrete frequency distributions, 313–314
Grounded theory, 73, 264
 hypotheses, constructed from, 118–120
Groups, creating equal, 202–204
Guttman scales, 155–158
 figure, 157

Halo effect, 147–148
Hammond, Phillip, 20
Harvard system of identifying references, 401
Hayakawa, S. I., 15
Histogram, 318–319
History, 213–214
Hoover, K., 103–104
Humphreys, Laud, 27–28
Husserl, Edmund, 88
Hypotheses, 70–71
 characteristics of, 121–125
 constructed from classical theory, 117–118
 constructed from grounded theory, 118–120
 construction as it relates to theory, 117–120
 cycle, 131–134
 defined, 116–117
 and evidence, 115–134
 null, 120–121
 research, 120
 rival, 100–101, 206–207
 testing, 125–126
  typology, 120–121
 use of evidence in, 127–131
Hypothetical relationship, 131–134

Independent variable
 manipulating, 205
 technical considerations concerning, 204–207
Indexes, 45–49
 figure, 46–49
Indexing

 citation, 45
 permuterm, 45
Induction, 14–15, 71–72
Inductive interpretations of data, 378–380
Inferential statistics, 331–364
Instrumentation, 215
Internal consistency, 170–171
Internal level of measurement, 142–143
Internal validity, 23, 213–216
 figure, 216
Interpenetration of data and analysis, 379
Interviewer characteristics, effects of, 246
Interviewing, tips for, 246–248
Interviews
 face-to-face, 244–248
 telephone, 248
 using secondary data to supplement, 250–252
 versus the self-administered questionnaire, 249
Introduction, writing, 389–392
Itemized rating scales, 145–147

Joint action, in symbolic interactionist paradigm, 88
Journals, scholarly, 42–49
Judgmental samples, 190

Kinloch, G. C., 73–74
Knowledge, everyday sources of, 5–8
Kuhn, Thomas, 9–10

Laboratory versus field experiment, 209–210
Likert scales, 150–155
 figure, 153–154
Listening, 269–273
Literature
 reviewing, 50–58
 search of, 39–50
Lofland, John, 270, 379
Lofland, Lyn, 379
Longitudinal studies, 98, 226
Lundberg, George, 21

Manipulation, of subjects, 28–29
Marketing surveys, 223–224
Maslow, Abraham, 20

Maturation, 214
Matza, David, 257
McCall, G. J., 268
Mead, George Herbert, 82–87, 271
Mean, 320–322
Measure(s)
 evaluating the adequacy of, 167–171
 nonreactive, 159–161
 reliability, 169–171
 scales as, 145–158
 single indicators as, 143–145
 validity, 167–169
 and reliability, relationship between, 171
Measurement
 definition, 138–139
 errors, sources of, 164–167
 errors, types of, 162–163
 levels of, 140–143
 process of, 137–171
 theory of, 161–162
 uses of, 139–140
Median, 320–322
Method, theory and, relationship between, 64–67
Methodology, 12
Methods, writing about in research report, 392–395
Miller, Delbert, 106, 145
Mills, C. Wright, 64–65
Mitroff, Ian, 16–18
Mode, 320–322
Mortality, experimental, 215–216
Multistage sampling, 188–189

Natural History of Nonsense, The, 6
Nett, R., 29–30
Neymen, J., 121
Nominal level of measurement, 140–141
Nonprobability samples, 185, 189–190
Nonreactive measures, 159–161
Normal curve, 333–334
 areas under, *table*, 439–440
 figure, 193, 334
 standard, 334–335
 as a probability distribution, 335–340
Notes, types of, 276–277

Null hypotheses, 120–121

Objects, in symbolic interactionist paradigm, 87–88
Open-ended questions, 230
Operational definitions, 20–22
Optical scanning sheets, 300–301
Ordinal level of measurement, 141–142
Orenstein, A., 212–213

Panel studies, 227–228
Paradigm(s), 74–75
  behaviorist, 80–81
  conflict, 79–80
  consistent with field research, 258–259
  in data interpretations, 368–375
  defined, 9–10
  ethnomethodological, 88–90
  functionalist, 75–79
  as puzzles and solutions, 10–11
  symbolic interactionist, 81–88
Park, Robert, 259–260
Participant observation, 259–263
  definitions, 260–261
Pearson, E. S., 121
Permuterm indexing, 45
Personal consequences of research, 375–376
Phillips, W. R., 212–213
Pie chart, 314
Point estimate, 192–193
Polygon, 319
Population distribution, 179–181
  figure, 180
Possible punch cleaning, of data, 302–303
Posttest-only control group design, 208–209
Pragmatic validity, 22
Pragmatism, 82
Predictive validity, 22–23, 168–169
Pretest/posttest control group design, 207–208
Probability distribution, 332–333, 335–340
Probability samples, 184, 185–189

Project selection, 29–30
Psychological Abstracts, 43–45
  table, 44
Psychology of Science, The, 20
Public opinion polling, 222–223
Public opinion surveys, 177–179
Purposive samples, 190

Qualitative analysis, 278–280, 308
Qualitative research, 256–257
Qualitative researcher, attitude of, 257–258
Quantitative analysis, 308–309
Quantitative research, 256–257
Quasi-experiment, 217–218
  true experiment versus, 217
Questionnaire (*see also* Survey(s))
  -based scales, 148–158
  composite illustration of, 236–242
  constructing, 229–242
  content, 231–232
  cover letter and introduction, 235
  first draft, 231–234
  mailed, 243–244
  pretest, 235–236
  self-administered, 243
    interview versus, 249
Questions
  closed-ended, 230
  contingency, 233
  format, 232–234
  matrix, 234
    figure, 234
  open-ended, 230
  types of, 229–230
Quota samples, 190

Random error, 163
Random numbers, *table*, 437–439
Random samples, simple, 185–186
Range, 323
  semi-interquartile, 323
Rating scales, 145–148
  precautions, 147–148
Ratio level of measurement, 143
Real group, 97
Reference, evaluation, 40–41

References, in research report, 400–402
Regression, 345–364
  analysis, multiple, 352–364
    plotting the residuals, 356–358
  effect, 215
  multiple, composite example, 360–364
  simple, 345–356
    composite example, 350–352
Reliability, 22–24
  of measures, 169–171
Replication, 55–56
Representative sample, 176
Research
  challenging prior, 53
  consequences of, 375–378
  design (*see* Design)
  field (*see* Field research)
  as human activity, 4–5
  hypotheses, 120
  impetus, identifying, 50–58
  objectives, defining, 224–225
  process
    nature of, 4–12
    role of statistical methods in, 309–310
    role of theory, 63–90
  purpose, 101–104
  qualitative, 256–257
  quantitative, 256–257
  question
    choosing and formulating a, 33–61
    defined, 34–35
    ethics, 61
    evaluating, 58–61
    factors influencing choice of, 36–39
    feasibility, 59–61
    formulating, 39–58
    role of values in choosing and formulating, 35–36
    using theory to understand, 52–53
  replication in, 130–131
  report, rewriting, 405
  report, writing, 383–405
    abstract, 388
    appendix, 404
    characteristics of, 385–387
    discussion section, 397–400
    factors to consider, 385

introduction, 389–392
methods, 392–395
organization of, 387–405
presentation of results, 395–397
reasons for writing, 384
references, 400–402
tables, 402–404
setting, 98–101
theory and, 11
time frame, 98, 226–228
Ritzer, George, 10, 369
Rival hypotheses, 100–101, 206–207
Role-taking, 271
Rotter, G., 154–155
Rubin, Lillian, 255

Sample(s)
cluster, 188
convenience, 189
distribution, 181–182
figure, 181, 182
of sample means, 182–184
of sample means, *figure*, 183
judgmental, 190
means, sample distribution of, 182–184
figure, 183
nonprobability, 185, 189–190
probability, 184, 185–189
purposive, 190
quota, 190
representativeness of, 176–179
simple random, 185–186
size, 191–197
determining, 194–197
determining, *figure*, 194
snowball, 190
stratified, 186–188
systematic, 186
Sampling, 173–197
definition, 174
multistage, 188–189
plans, 184–191
reasons for, 174–176
techniques, combining probability and nonprobability, 190–191
theory, 179–184
Scale(s)

Guttman, 155–158
figure, 157
Likert, 150–155
figure, 153–154
as measures, 145–158
questionnaire-based, 148–158
rating, 145–148
precautions, 147–148
semantic-differential, 158
Thurstone, 149–150, 152
figure, 150–151
Scaling techniques, comparison of, 158–159
Schatzman, L., 265, 272, 276–277, 279
Scholarly journals, 42–49
Schutz, Alfred, 88
Science
language and rhetoric of, 20–24
practice of, 16–24
promise and limitations of, 24–25
in the real world, 18–20
traditional models of, 12–16
Scientific attitude, myths and realities, 12–25
Self, in symbolic interactionist paradigm, 85–86
Semantic-differential scales, 158
Semi-interquartile range, 323
Serendipitous findings, 54–55, 133–134
Serial method of identifying references, 401
Simmons, J. L., 268
Simon, Julian L., 20–21, 72, 217
Single indicators, as measures, 143–145
Sjoberg, G., 29–30
Skinner, B. F., 80
Snowball samples, 190
Social behaviorism, 82
Social interaction, in symbolic interactionist paradigm, 86–87
Social objects, in symbolic interactionist paradigm, 87–88
Social Science Citation Index, 45–49
figure, 49
Social Science Index, 45
figure, 48–49

Sociological Abstracts, 42–43
classifications for, *table*, 44
figure, 46–48
Sociologists at Work, 20
Split-half reliability, 170
SPSS: Statistical Package for the Social Sciences, 407–436
about, 407
data definition commands, 408–413
getting started, 408
procedural commands, 414–436
task commands, 413–414
Squared correlation coefficient, 350
Standard deviation
applying, 328–329
defining, 323–325, 327–328
Standard error of the estimate
multiple regression, 355
simple regression, 349
Standard normal curve, 334–335 (*see also* Normal curve)
as a probability distribution, 335–340
Stanley, J., 213
Statistical group, 97–98
Statistical inference, 179
Statistical methods, role of, in the research process, 309–310
Statistical Package for the Social Sciences (*see* SPSS: Statistical Package for the Social Sciences)
Statistics
descriptive, 307–329
inferential, 331–364
Stephens, William, 116–117
Stevens, S. S., 138
Stratified samples, 186–188
Strauss, A. L., 73, 265, 272, 276–277, 279
Structure of Scientific Revolutions, The, 9
Survey(s), 219–252 (*see also* Questionnaire)
defined, 220–224
design, planning, 224–228
marketing, 223–224
public opinion, 177–179

Survey(s) (cont.)
  research
    design, 108
    design, flowchart of decision-making process, *figure*, 109
    objectives, 224
    strengths and weaknesses, 249–250
Symbolic interactionist paradigm, 81–88
Systematic error, 163
Systematic samples, 186

t, distribution of, *table*, 441
t test, 340–341
Tables, in research report, 402–404
Tape recorders, using, 275–276
Taylor, S. J., 256
Test-retest reliability, 170
Testing, 214
Theoretical distribution, 333
Theory, 63–90 (*see also* specific theories)
  construction, 73–75
  defined, 68–69
  in everyday life, status of, 65–66
  hypotheses construction as it relates to, 117–120
  of measurement, 161–162
  and method, relationship between, 64–67
  nature of, 68–90
  relation to research design, 93–94
  and research, 66–67
  role of, in data interpretation, 368–370
  testing, 51–52
  using to understand a research question, 52–53
Thesis statement, 224
Thurstone scales, 149–150, 152
  figure, 150–151
Time order, of variables, 206
Tradition, as a source of knowledge, 7–8
Transfer sheet, 300
  figure, 301
Treatment group, 97
Trend studies, 226–227
Triangulation, 112–113, 126–127

Unit of analysis, 95–98
United States Census, 221–222

Validity, 22–24
  external, 216–217
  internal, 213–216
    figure, 216
  of measures, 167–169
Variability, measures of, 322–329
Variables, relationship between, 206
Variance
  applying, 328–329
  defining, 323–327
Veevers, J. E., 158–159

Watching, 269–273
Watson, James, 19–20
Watson, John, 81
Weber, Max, 35–36
Williams, Carol, 41
Wolfe, Gary, 41
Writing, strategies for, 281–282

X^2, distribution of, *table*, 445

Z score, 334–335
  transformation, 192
Ziller, R., 147